INTERNATIONAL MACROECONOMICS: RECENT DEVELOPMENTS

INTERNATIONAL MACROECONOMICS: RECENT DEVELOPMENTS

AMALIA MORALES ZUMAQUERO
EDITOR

Nova Science Publishers, Inc.
New York

For permission to use material from this book please contact us:
Telephone 631-231-7269; Fax 631-231-8175
Web Site: http://www.novapublishers.com

NOTICE TO THE READER

The Publisher has taken reasonable care in the preparation of this book, but makes no expressed or implied warranty of any kind and assumes no responsibility for any errors or omissions. No liability is assumed for incidental or consequential damages in connection with or arising out of information contained in this book. The Publisher shall not be liable for any special, consequential, or exemplary damages resulting, in whole or in part, from the readers' use of, or reliance upon, this material.

This publication is designed to provide accurate and authoritative information with regard to the subject matter covered herein. It is sold with the clear understanding that the Publisher is not engaged in rendering legal or any other professional services. If legal or any other expert assistance is required, the services of a competent person should be sought. FROM A DECLARATION OF PARTICIPANTS JOINTLY ADOPTED BY A COMMITTEE OF THE AMERICAN BAR ASSOCIATION AND A COMMITTEE OF PUBLISHERS.

LIBRARY OF CONGRESS CATALOGING-IN-PUBLICATION DATA
International macroeconomics : recent developments / Amalia Morales Zumaquero, editor.
    p. cm.
Includes index.
ISBN 1-59454-901-X
1. Foreign exchange rates. 2. Financial crises. 3. Macroeconomics. I. Morales Zumaquero, Amalia.
HG3851.I52   2006
339--dc22   2005036599

Published by Nova Science Publishers, Inc. ✦ New York

To my parents who gave me the life
To Cristóbal who gives me life everyday
To Rodrigo Peruga who lost his life but lives in my memory

CONTENTS

PREFACE

The international macroeconomics area has experienced a substantial growth over the past decade. The goal of this volume is to present the most important developments in the international macroeconomics field in recent years. The literature in this area has evolved mainly in four directions that constitute the four parts of this book. In particular, Part I focuses on the purchasing power parity (PPP) puzzle; Part II presents papers that try to explain the behavior of nominal and real exchange rates; Part III covers the financial crises, currency crises and contagion recent literature and, finally, the behavior of exchange rates, inflation and output convergence in Central and Eastern European transition economies are considered in Part IV.

The choice of these four parts are motivated by the attempt to unify in a volume the central contributions and advances, overall from an empirical point of view, that international macroeconomics has recently experienced. We have placed emphasis on works that uses new econometric techniques and modern analytical tools in this field. It is difficult to cover all research topics and, of course, omissions are presented.

PART I. THE PURCHASING POWER PARITY PUZZLE

Although the purchasing power parity doctrine appears quite simple it constitutes a persistent puzzle in the international macroeconomics field. The very large and fruitful recent literature on testing for purchasing power parity has tried to give some light on this puzzle using new econometrics techniques and new data sets, such as longer and more disaggregate series. Part I tries to offer an overview about recent research on purchasing power parity starting with a survey and other three chapters that attempt to explain this puzzle.

Chapter 1 presents a selective survey by Simón Sosvilla-Rivero and Emma García on the econometric methodology used in the empirical evaluation of the purchasing power parity hypothesis, and examines recent empirical attempts to test this hypothesis. The central message from this work is that the empirical testing of the validity of PPP has continuously changed as econometric technical innovations have appeared together with the increasing availability of data sets.

David Papell and Sarah Culver present in Chapter 2 panel evidence of PPP using intranational and international data for Canada and United States cities and European countries. Their main result suggests less evidence of PPP with relative prices between cities within the same nation than with real exchange between European countries.

Chapter 3 by Mohsen Bahmani-Oskooee and Taggert J. Brooks offers another attempt in testing the PPP for twenty developing countries by incorporating structural breaks into the testing procedure. They find, in many cases, periods of stationary exchange rate fluctuations for the effective exchange rate. Their results suggest evidence, in favor of the, so-called, Quasi-PPP.

The analysis done in Chapter 4 by Raj Aggarwal, Antonio Montañés and Montserrat Ponz tries to explain the mixed results regarding the validity of PPP for the Japanese Yen. These authors, using new statistical procedures that account for outliers and allow for structural breaks in unit root tests, analyze the PPP hypothesis between the Japanese Yen and other Asian and major world currencies. Results suggest strong evidence in favor of the PPP.

PART II. THE BEHAVIOR OF NOMINAL AND REAL EXCHANGE RATES

Exchange rates play a central role in any open economy. A set of five chapters that try to explain exchange rates behavior are developed in this Part. Chapter 5 could be considered as a bridge between Part I and Part II because it mainly concentrates on international parity relationships and the persistence of real exchange rates. The next two chapters attempt to explain the behavior of real exchange rates. Chapter 6 is based on the nontradable approach to real exchange rate determination. On the other hand, Chapter 7 presents one of the most recent approaches to explain the behavior of real exchange rate, i.e., testing for non-linearities in it. Chapter 8 and 9 are mainly theoretical works. Chapter 8 discusses the extent to which an exchange rate regime contributes to real adjustment in the face of supply and demand disturbances in emerging countries. Chapter 9 develops a new approach to modeling rational expectations, that embedded in a modified monetary model, can explain the swings in the exchange rate away from PPP.

Katarina Juselius and Ronald MacDonald in Chapter 5 examine the interrelations between the purchasing power parity, term structure of interest rates and the Fischer real interest parity condition using cointegration techniques, for Germany against the United States in the post Bretton Woods period. They try to shed light on the interaction of these parity conditions and to address a number of unresolved issues: the persistence in real exchange rates, the extent to which German or United States variables are the driven variables in the system, and to analyze whether the Fischer condition and real interest rate parity hold over the period 1975 to 1998. In general, results suggest that the transmission mechanisms over the post Bretton Woods period have been signicantly different from standard theoretical assumptions.

Stephen Y.L. Cheung and Vikas Kakkar examine in Chapter 6 whether permanent changes in the relative price of nontradables can explain permanent changes in the real exchange rates, in five East Asian economies vis-à-vis the United States dollar. If it is so, they use these long run comovements to construct an alternative measure of real exchange rate misalignment. For all four countries, that alternative measure yields protracted and economically significant overevaluations prior to the crises.

Mark J. Holmes tests for non-linearities in the real exchange rate in Chapter 7. He concentrates on non-linear behavior of thirty less-developed countries' real exchange rates, using the logistic and exponential smooth transition regression models. Results suggest that there is evidence in favor of non-linearity in sixteen cases and a considerable variation in the smoothness of adjustment from one regime to another.

The main purpose of Chapter 8 by José García-Solanes is to provide theoretical and empirical evidence supporting the virtues of a managed floating regimen to contribute real adjustments in the face of real external disturbances in emerging market economies. Results from the theoretical part of this work suggest that even when the analysis is restricted to the financial framework, which seems appropriate when output has achieved its long run level, some institutional arrangements could be engineered to reduce the destabilizing effects of controlled floating. Moreover, the advantages of managing floating increase with the frequency of asymmetric real shocks and the presence of nominal rigidities. In addition, optimal policy reactions, in the face of real external shocks, as opposed to "fear floating", may explain why nominal exchange rates have exhibited lower variability than nominal interest rates. Results from the empirical part of this chapter suggest evidence in favor of the Balassa-Samuelson hypothesis in eleven managed exchange rate regimen Latin American countries.

Chapter 9 closes this Part with the contribution of Roman Fryman and Michael Goldberg. These authors develop a new framework for modeling exchange rates expectations that recognize the importance of imperfect knowledge and yet is consistent with the postulate of individual rationality. They show how this alternative approach, when embedded into a modified monetary model, can produce movements of exchange rate away from PPP. This new approach sheds light on the exchange rate disconnect puzzle too.

PART III. FINANCIAL CRISES, CURRENCY CRISES AND CONTAGION

Literature on financial crises, currency crises and contagion has grown substantially over the last years. It has been one of the directions in which the international macroeconomics literature has extremely evolved. Part III focuses on this area reviewing the literature on crises and contagion and providing an assessment on the past, present and future of the European Monetary System (EMS).

Sergio L. Schmukler, Pablo Zoido and Marina Halac, in Chapter 10, after discussing the sources of an increasing financial globalization, reviews the channels through which financial globalization can be related with crises and how financial globalization can also lead to financial crises through contagion. Their results suggest that, in the long run, the net effect of financial globalization are still positive. Crises and contagion seem to be the price that some countries have to pay to integrate with the international financial system.

Chapter 11 by Roberto Rigobon, presents a survey on new empirical methods that has been used to measure the channels of contagion. He discusses three approaches to study contagion that use either firm level data, estimate the contagion using spatial models (due to their simplicity and their capacity to capture the contagion regional features), or concentrate on the importance of financial linkages by analyzing hedge/mutual funds positions. Finally, this author describes two approaches that try to disentangle the importance of each channel of contagion (traded versus financial linkages).

In Chapter 12 Simón Sosvilla-Rivero and Francisco Pérez-Bermejo focuses on the European Monetary System, credibility and currency crises. They review the structure and operation of the EMS as well as the theoretical framework to explain exchange rate movements inside official fluctuations bands. Moreover, they briefly survey the currency crises literature from a theoretical and empirical point of view, presenting the most important results from the empirical evidence on the relevance of the currency crises literature in the case of the EMS.

PART IV. CENTRAL AND EASTERN EUROPEAN TRANSITION ECONOMIES: EXCHANGE RATES, INFLATION AND OUTPUT CONVERGENCE

Recently, researchers have focused on analyzing the process of accession of a set of Central and Eastern European transition economies to the European Union (EU). This Part is concentrated in the analysis of a set of central key issues in these economies: the behavior of nominal and real exchange rates, the moderation of inflation in transition economies and, finally, the output convergence in the these economies by comparison with output convergence in current members.

Chapter 13 reviews the behavior of real and nominal exchange rates in the countries that are candidates to access in the EU since the start of the transition. Fabrizio Coricelli, Boštjan Jazbec and Igor Masten discuss the choice of the exchange rate regime in those transition economies. Firstly, they attempt to evaluate whether the heterogeneity in exchange rates regimens could be justified by structural heterogeneity and different policy goals between countries. Secondly, they try to analyze the working of different policy rules. Thirdly, they identify the main channels through the exchange rate which affects the economy, i.e., the relationship between exchange rates and inflation, the pass-through issue. This work concludes that the accession countries are very small and very open economies: they have achieved a high degree of real and financial integration with the European Union.

Chapter 14 by Balázs Égert and Kirsten Lommatzsch focuses on explaining the sources of appreciation of the real exchange rate in transition economies during the transition period. This paper considers, besides the traditional Balassa-Samuelson effect, the role of regulated prices, the nontradable component of tradable goods and the change in supply capacities as potential sources of that appreciation. They obtain strong empirical support in favor of the tradable price channel and show that the Balassa-Samuelson effect and regulated prices may also determine the long-run real exchange rate fluctuations, although to a much lesser extent than that assumed in the literature.

Zorica Mladenovic analyzes the behavior of the real exchange rate in the case of Serbia in Chapter 15. In particular, she concentrates on the relative importance of nominal and real shocks in the Serbian real exchange rate, examines the main determinants of it in the long-run and the short-run dynamics is considered too. She finds that real shocks has had a larger influence than nominal shocks in explaining the real exchange rate fluctuations. Moreover, results suggest that the real exchange rate is determined in the long-run by real gross domestic product and part of the dynamics in the real exchange rate is corrected each moth towards equilibrium term.

Chapter 16 discusses the moderation of inflation in three transition economies, the Czech Republic, Hungary and Poland at the end of the 1990s. Josef C. Brada and Ali M. Kutan find that foreign prices and the persistence of inflation have been the central determinants of inflation in these economies. Thus, the moderation of inflation in these economies was due largely to the decline in import prices from 1997 on, and it is likely to be a temporary phenomenon.

Arielle Beyaert in Chapter 17 examines output convergence in both existing and future member countries of the EU. Results suggest that the richer economies of the European Union have been in absolute convergence since 1970. However, the poorer economies of the EU have only conditionally converged to their European partners at the time of their entrance. Moreover, the transition economies of Poland, Hungary and Czech Republic were diverging until 1990 but they are now in a situation of conditional convergence with respect to each other as well as with respect to the EU current members.

ACKNOWLEDGMENTS

I owe a debt of gratitude to a large number of individuals who have made this volume possible.

First of all, thank you very much to Frank Columbus, president of Nova Science Publishers, to have confidence in me and give me the opportunity to carry out this project. It has been a dream for me and I think my best present in Christmas of 2003.

Thank you very much to the chapter authors Raj Aggarwal, Mohsen Bahmani-Oskooee, Arielle Beyaert, Josef C. Brada, Taggert J. Brooks, Stephen Y.L. Cheung, Fabrizio Coricelli, Sarah Culver, Balázs Égert, Roman Fryman, Emma García, José García-Solanes, Michael Goldberg, Marina Halac, Mark J. Holmes, Boštjan Jazbec, Katarina Juselius, Vikas Kakkar, Ali M. Kutan, Kirsten Lommatzsch, Ronald MacDonald, Igor Masten, Zorica Mladenovic, Antonio Montañés, David Papell, Francisco Pérez-Bermejo, Montserrat Ponz, Roberto Rigobon, Sergio L. Schmukler, Simón Sosvilla-Rivero and Pablo Zoido. These researchers (or I think I could call them "friends") have worked hard to send me the papers on time and they have been delighted with this project. I hope they like the book!

Finally, thank you very much to my family, friends and, most importantly, to Cristóbal for providing me his love and moral support.

Amalia Morales-Zumaquero
December 2003

In: International Macroeconomics: Recent Developments   ISBN: 1-59454-901-X
Editor: Amalia Morales Zumaquero, pp. 1-37   © 2006 Nova Science Publishers, Inc.

Chapter 1

PURCHASING POWER PARITY REVISITED

Simón Sosvilla-Rivero[1] and Emma García[2]

[1]Univ. Complutense de Madrid and Foundation
for Applied Economic Research, FEDEA
[2]Foundation for Applied Economic Research, FEDEA

Abstract

This paper presents a selective survey on some recent empirical attempts to test the validity of Purchasing Power Parity (PPP) to explain exchange-rate movements in the main currencies, as well as a review of the econometric methodology used in such tests. Finally, we offer some encouraging results regarding the forecastability of exchange rate using PPP.

1   Introduction

> "I go to seek a Great Perhaps"
> *François Rabelais*

The concept of purchasing power parity (PPP) has long played a prominent role in theoretical and empirical research. The originators of the PPP hypothesis were Spanish scholars of the sixteenth century who taught at the University of Salamanca [see, e.g., Grice-Hutchinson (1952, 1978) and Oficer (1982)]. These theologians and jurists, interested also in international commercial activity, proposed the quantity theory of money that, combined with the medieval analysis of foreign exchange rate that ease (scarcity) of money gave it a low (high) value against foreign exchange, led to the formulation of the PPP hypothesis in a context of radical changes in economic conditions, due to the streams of gold and silver from the New World. Later, Sweden and France in the second part of the eighteen century, and England in the early nineteenth century, moved from a fixed-rate metallic standard to a floating-rate regime, arising controversy over the cause of the falling external value of the domestic currency, defending the so-called bullonists PPP point of view. Following the bullonist period, the PPP hypothesis remained dormant in literature until World War I, where severe episodes of hyperinflation and dislocated exchange rates in the belligerent countries stimulated once more the renewed interest in the PPP. Cassel (1922) named this hypothesis, being largely responsible for the popularity enjoyed by the PPP in the 1920s. At the end of World War II, a new wave of interest in the PPP hypothesis emerged, when once again attempts were made to determine exchange rates following the wartime suspension of trade and convertibility, leading the move to flexible exchange rates in the early 1970s to yet another intellectual upturn to the PPP hypothesis.

In the last decade or so, important developments in econometrics and the increasing availability of data sets have stimulated the empirical work on PPP. The aim of this paper is to provide a selective survey on some recent empirical attempts to test the validity of PPP to explain exchange-rate movements in the main currencies, as well as the econometric methodology used in such tests.

The paper is organised as follows. Section 2 discusses the basic concepts of the PPP hypothesis, not only examining the absolute and relative PPP versions and the interpretations of PPP, but also considering the choice of the appropriate price index in a PPP calculation and the factors responsible for deviations of actual exchange rates from PPP rates. In Section 3, we focus on the econometric methodology used in the empirical evaluation of the PPP, providing an up-to-date survey of the burgeoning literature on testing, estimation and model specification in the presence of integrated variables. Section 4 examines some of the empirical evidence which tests the validity of PPP. In Section 5, we offer some encouraging results regarding the forecastability of exchange rate using PPP. Finally, Section 6 provides some concluding remarks.

2   The Purchasing Power Parity Hypothesis

"Under the skin of any international economist lies a deep-seated belief in some variant of the PPP theory of exchange rate"

Dornbusch and Krugman (1976, 540)

2.1   The Absolute and Relative PPP Versions

In its absolute version, the PPP theory establishes a relationship between the exchange rate, S, (expressed as the home currency price of a unit of foreign exchange), and the ratio of domestic and foreign prices (P and P^*, respectively), so that

$$S_t = P_t / P_t^*$$ (1)

Its implication is that the higher the domestic price level relative to the foreign price level, the higher the exchange rate must be in order to retain purchasing power parity between domestic and foreign currencies.

Factors such as costs of gathering and processing information, transport costs and other obstacles to trade (in particular tariffs and quotas), and market imperfections can limit spatial arbitrage and therefore account for deviations from absolute PPP. Furthermore, it is more than likely that the weights used in the computation of a price level could differ across countries.

For these reasons, a less restrictive relationship between prices and exchange rates is considered. This is the relative PPP, which asserts that the percentage rate of change of the exchange rate will equal the differential between the percentage rates for change of price levels at home and abroad. That is

$$\Delta s_t = \Delta p_t - \Delta p_t^*$$ (2)

where Δ denotes first difference and lower-case letters denotes logarithms. Therefore, $100\,\Delta\,s_t$ is the percentage change in S_t since $\Delta\,s_t=\log(S_t/S_{t-1})=\log(1+\Delta\,S_t/S_{t-1}) \approx \Delta\,S_t/S_{t-1}$.

We usually refer to the percentage changes in the price level (Δp_t) as the rate of inflation. Hence, from equation (1), if the domestic inflation rate exceeds the foreign inflation rate, a domestic currency depreciation (i.e., an increase in Δs_t) is required to sustain purchasing power parity between domestic and foreign currencies. Similarly, if the foreign inflation rate exceeds the domestic inflation rate, this will be associated with a domestic currency appreciation (i.e., a reduction in Δs_t). In summary, equation (2) is less strict than equation (1) in allowing domestic and foreign prices (expressed in domestic currency) to differ from each other, but still sustains the assumption that these deviations allowing domestic and foreign prices (expressed in domestic currency) will not grow or diminish persistently over time. The relative purchasing power of domestic money *vis-à-vis* foreign money will therefore be fixed over time, with exchange rate changes Δs_t assuring such parity.

The relative version of PPP has a further advantage over absolute PPP in that, as long as the weights used to define the domestic and foreign price indices remain constant over time, then, the two weighting schemes do not need to be the same.

It should be noted that, if absolute PPP holds, then relative PPP will also hold. But if absolute PPP does not hold, then relative PPP may still hold. This is because the level S may not equal P/P*, but the change in S could still equal the inflation differential, $(\Delta p - \Delta p^*)$

2.2   Interpretations of PPP

There are three major approaches to PPP: the arbitrage, the expectations, and the monetary approach.

The arbitrage version of PPP was the first well-developed theory of the determination of exchange rates. The basic idea is that exchange rates tend to settle at the level where the purchasing power of a given currency is the same, or at parity, in all countries.

Consider a homogeneous commodity i produced both at home and abroad. Let P_i and P_i^* represent the price of that commodity at home an abroad, stated in home and foreign currency, respectively, and S the exchange rate. Then ignoring information and transaction costs and assuming integrated competitive markets with effective arbitrage, the price of commodity i should be the same in all locations when quoted in the same currency, say the home currency, i.e.:

$$P_i = P_i^* S \tag{3}$$

This is commonly referred to as the "law of one price".

If equation (3) does not hold, it would be profitable for the arbitrageurs of commodities to buy the commodity in the country in which it is cheaper and sell it in the country would eventually eliminate the discrepancy between the two sides of equation (3), restoring the equality.

Assume now that the domestic and foreign economies produce a range of η commodities and that the law of one price holds for each of the η commodities. Let P and P^* be a price level at home and abroad quoted in the respective currencies, where $P = g(P_1, P_2, \dots P_i, \dots P_\eta)$ and $P^* = g^*(P_1^*, P_2^*, \dots P_i^*, \dots P_\eta^*)$. Then by using identical weights in constructing each country's price level (i.e., assuming that the homogeneous-of-degree-one g(.) and g^*(.) functions are the same, we obtain

$$P = SP^* \tag{4}$$

and on rearranging the terms of the exchange rate, we get equation (1). Hence when the price indices in both countries are identical, the law of one price justifies absolute PPP.

The arbitrage approach can also be used to argue that competitive trade will tend to ensure that movements in exchange rate will be such as to compensate for differences in national inflation rates (i.e., relative PPP).

Whereas the arbitrage approach to PPP concentrates solely on trade in commodities, the expectations approach integrates parity conditions in the commodity and financial (bond) markets. This approach which is also known as the "efficient market approach" (see Roll, 1979), is based on the Fisher hypothesis and on the assumption of uncovered interest parity.

The Fisher hypothesis postulates that a country's nominal interest rate should equal its real interest rate plus the expected rate of inflation. Thus,

$$i = r + \Delta p^e \tag{5a}$$

$$i^* = r^* + \Delta p^{*e} \tag{5b}$$

where i is the nominal interest rate, r is the real interest rate, Δp^e is the expected change in the natural logarithm of the price level ($\Delta p^e = \log P_{t+1}^e - \log P_t = p_{t+1}^e - p_t$), and an asterisk (*) denotes a foreign variable.

Uncovered interest parity requires that the nominal interest differential between a domestic currency investment and a foreign currency investment is equal to the expected change in the logarithm of the exchange rate ($\Delta s^e = \log S_{t+1}^e - \log S_t = s_{t+1}^e - s_t$).

$$\Delta s^e = i - i^* \tag{6}$$

But international investors are concerned with real, not nominal, returns on their assets. In attempting to maximise the real return on their assets, they transfer capital from a country with a lower interest rate to one with a higher real rate. Therefore, abstracting from transaction costs, riskiness of returns, and taxation, this arbitrage process results in the equalisation of real interest rates across countries:

$$r = r^*$$ (7)

By subtracting (5b) from (5a), using (7) and (6), and rearranging, we obtain

$$\Delta s^e = \Delta p^e - \Delta p^{*e}$$ (8)

Equation (8) provides a relative PPP theory in which all variables take on their expected value rather than the current value.

If we assume certainty about the future (ie., $p_{t+1}^e = P_{t+1}, P_{t+1}^{*e} = p_{t+1}^*$ and $s_{t+1}^e = s_{t+1}$), then

$$\Delta s = \Delta p - \Delta p^*$$ (9)

which is an expression of relative PPP.

Equation (9) can be rewritten as follows,

$$s_{t+1} - p_{t+1} + p_{t+1}^* = s_t - p_t + p_t^*$$ (10)

In the terminology of the efficient market literature, equation (10) means that all the information relevant for determining the real exchange rate next period is already fully reflected in the current real exchange rate.

When the future is uncertain, if we assume that expected values in equation (8) are formed rationally, we obtain

$$\Delta s = \Delta p - \Delta p^* + \varepsilon$$ (11)

or

$$\Delta s - \Delta p + \Delta p^* = \varepsilon$$ (12)

where ε is a composite white-noise error from rational expectations. From equation (12) we see that deviations from PPP (i.e., the real exchange rate) may be characterised as a martingale process or, more particularly, as a random walk (see Roll, 1979).

The monetary approach to PPP emphasises relative money conditions. This approach assumes some sort of neutrality of money to hold at least in the long run. That is, a change in the money supply in one country, with no change in the other country, induces proportional changes in the nominal variables of that country, including the exchange rate. PPP can be viewed from this perspective as an implication of this neutrality proposition

2.3   The Price Index Issue

The formulation of the PPP theory in equations (1) and (2) does not specify which price measurement should be used in the computation. Since most published measures of price are in the form of indices, the controversy about the choice of the adequate measures in the literature on PPP is conducted mainly in terms of price indices, rather than in terms of price levels.

The various interpretations of PPP are relevant for the selection of appropriate price indices. For those who consider arbitrage as the motivating force behind the PPP relationship, the logical choice is the price index of traded goods: In contrast, the monetary approach to PPP requires the use of a broad price index, encompassing a very large number of goods, both traded and non-traded.

Regarding this point, Cassel (1928, p 37) states the need to use "a general index figure representing as far as possible the whole mass of commodities marketed in the country", and Keynes argued that if the price levels taken into account were only those of commodities entering into international trade, then the theory was "little more than a truism" (Keynes, 1923, 1971, p. 75).

Four alternative price indices have traditionally been used as possible candidates for the comparison of the PPP equations (1) and (2): consumer price indices (CPIs), gross domestic product (GDP) deflators, wage rate indices (WRIs), and wholesale price indices (WPIs). The first three include a broad group of goods and services, while the last one represents a sort of compromise with the arbitrage interpretation of PPP due to the large share of tradeable goods.

The most commonly used price indices for PPP calculations are CPIs. The periodic publication of data on CPI behaviour for almost every country is an advantage of this index. However, it can be subjected to direct distortions stemming from price controls. The GDP deflator is not subject to such distortions and is thought to provide a good indicator of changes in competitiveness in production (see Officer, 1982 and Barro, 1983). Some authors (see, e.g., Artus, 1978 and Artus and Knight, 1984) prefer to use unit labour costs, since it is argued that relative labour costs are more stable than relative goods price (Artus, 1978; Officer, 1982). Nevertheless, the WRIs also have some drawbacks (they are highly one factor of production, and they are only available for some time frequency-generally on a yearly basis). The WPIs are also subject to criticism. In addition to Keynes's criticism that relative price parities calculated from these indices come close to the actual exchange rate (due to the inclusion of highly homogeneous traded goods whose prices tend to be equated across countries when expressed in a common currency), resulting in a spurious verification of the theory, the use of only tradeable goods raises other problems. First, prices of tradeable goods may be set in the short run to maintain competitiveness in world markets, regardless of overall domestic prices and cost levels. Second, computations of PPP based on WPIs (as well as other indices) may be distorted by the use of different weights across countries. Third, practically all tradeable goods can be considered to be differentiated by country of production, if only because of differences in quality, delivery terms, etc. There is no reason to expect the law of one price to apply to them even in the long run.

2.4   Deviations from PPP

From the statistical point of view, the fact that actual price indices are calculated from individual prices of only a sample of commodities rather than all commodities in the economy (Pigou, 1922, pp. 67-68), and the possibility of different weighting schemes in different countries arising from differences in tastes, economic structures and accounting practices (Katseli-Papaefstratiou, 1979. p. 5) can restrict the validity of the PPP theory.

Regarding the economic reasons for deviation from PPP, we can distinguish between the short run and the long run. In the short run, the existence of transportation and information costs can make arbitrage difficult or even impossible. More fundamentally, exchange rates and commodity prices are determined in different kinds of markets. The prices are not as flexible as financial asset prices (the exchange rate is the price of two moneys). This different speed of adjustment between exchange rates and prices can explain short-run deviation from PPP. However, the fact that expectations play a much smaller role in goods and services markets (apart from primary commodities) than in the foreign exchange market implies that "… in periods during which there is ample "news" [i.e., unanticipated changes] which causes large fluctuations in exchange rates there will also be large deviations from purchasing power parities" (Frenkel, 1983, p. 27). The nature of adjustment back to the norm will depend on the degree to which news is seen as indicating permanent or transitory change (see Booth *et al.*, 1985).

In the long run, problems such as the productivity bias can be important: Balassa (1964) and Samuelson (1964) argue that different sectoral rates of productivity growth change real costs and relative prices, and therefore bring about divergences in PPP. The relative price level is high in high productivity (high income) countries compared with low productivity (low income) countries, and it rises rapidly in fast-growing countries compared with slow-growing countries. Although cross-section evidence in favour of this productivity-bias hypothesis is strong (see Balassa, 1964, and Officer, 1976), Hsieh (1982) shows that it is confirmed by time series tests[1.]

Factors such as the existence of price contracts and/or rationing, changes in the structure of relative prices in the domestic and foreign economies, monopolistic and oligopolistic forces, product differentiation, trading restrictions (e.g., tariffs and quotas on imports), changes in consumers' preferences away from the home country's goods towards the foreign country's goods, and a natural resource discovery can also account for persistent deviations from PPP.

---

[1] Hsieh (1982) suggests that this occurs because country-specific factors such as taste vary relatively little over time.

3   Econometric Issues

"At the present stage of development in Economics it is probably an advantage to have different groups looking at the same problem from different viewpoints, so that their conclusions can be compared and possibly then form the basis for a new compressive model"

Granger (1990, 1)

3.1   Time Series Econometrics

Economic theory generally deals with equilibrium relationships. Most empirical econometric studies are an attempt to evaluate such relationships by summarising economic time series using statistical analysis.

To apply standard inference procedures in a dynamic time series model we need the various variables to be stationary, since the majority of econometric theory is built upon the assumption of stationarity, meaning a process whose means and variances are constant over time. However, in applied research we usually find integrated variables, which are a specific class of non-stationary variables with important economic and statistical properties: the variance increases over time and successive observations are highly interdependent. These are derived from the presence of unit roots which give rise to stochastic trends, as opposed to pure deterministic trends, with innovations to an integrated process being permanent instead of transient.

Statisticians have been aware for many years of the existence of integrated series and, in fact, Box and Jenkins (1970) argue that a non-stationary series can be transformed into a stationary one by successive differencing of the series. Therefore, from their point of view, the differencing operation seemed to be a prerequisite for econometric modelling both from an univariate and a multivariate perspective.

After the seminal paper by Engle and Granger (1987), cointegration techniques have been a dominant force in applied macroeconomics (see, e.g., McKenzie, 1997). The key motivation for using the cointegration analysis is to avoid spurious regression results. In addition, cointegration techniques play a useful role in identifying meaningful long-run economic relationships among non-stationary variables.

The literature on cointegration and unit roots is surveyed in Dolado, Jenkinson and Sosvilla-Rivero (1990) or Hendry and Juselius (2000, 2001).

As it is well known, a previous step in cointegration analysis consists of testing the order of integration of the variables. Therefore, we start by reviewing in subsection 3.1.1 several alternative tests for the existence of unit roots. Subsection 3.1.2 introduces the concept of cointegration and surveys several tests to determine the existence of long-run equilibrium relationships.

3.1.1   Unit Root Tests

Several statistical tests for unit roots have been developed to test for stationarity in time series. The most commonly used to test that a pure AR(1) process (with or without drift) has a unit root are the Dickey-Fuller (DF) statistics. These test statistics were proposed by Dickey and Fuller (1979).

They consider the three following alternative data generating processes (DGP) of a time series:

$$y_t = \rho_n y_{t-1} + \varepsilon_t \tag{13}$$

$$y_t = \mu_c + \rho_c y_{t-1} + \varepsilon_t \tag{14}$$

$$y_t = \mu_{c\tau} + \gamma_\tau + \rho_{c\tau} y_{t-1} + \varepsilon_t \tag{15}$$

where $\varepsilon_t \sim iid(0, \sigma_\varepsilon^2)$, t is a time trend and the initial condition, y_0 is assumed to be a known constant (zero, without loss of generality). For equation (13), if $\rho_n < 1$, then the DGP is a stationary zero-mean AR(1) process and if $\rho_n = 1$, then the GDP is a pure random walk. For equation (14), if $\rho_c < 1$, then the DGP is a stationary AR(1) process with mean $\mu_c / (1 - \rho_c)$ and if $\rho_n = 1$, then the GDP is a random walk with a drift μ_n. Finally, for equation (15), if $\rho_{c\tau} < 1$, then the DGP is a trend-stationary AR(1) process with mean $\frac{\mu_{c\tau}}{1 - \rho_{c\tau}} + \gamma_{c\tau} \sum_{j=0}^{t} [\rho_{c\tau}^j (t - j)]$ and if $\rho_{c\tau} = 1$, then the GDP is a random walk with a drift changing over time.

The tests are carried out by estimating the following equations:

$$\Delta y_t = (\rho_n - 1) y_{t-1} + \varepsilon_t \tag{13'}$$

$$\Delta y_t = \beta_{0c} + (\rho_c - 1) y_{t-1} + \varepsilon_t \tag{14'}$$

$$\Delta y_t = \beta_{0c\tau} + \beta_{1c\tau} t + (\rho_{c\tau} - 1) y_{t-1} + \varepsilon_t \tag{15'}$$

The tests are implemented though the usual t-statistic on the estimated $(\rho\text{-}1)$. They are denoted τ, τ_μ and τ_τ, respectively. Given that under the null hypothesis this test statistic does not have the standard t distribution, Dickey and Fuller (1979) simulated critical values for selected sample sizes. More extensive critical values are reported by MacKinnon (1991, 1994).

Hitherto, we have assumed that the DGP is a pure AR(1) process. If the series is correlated at higher order lag, the assumption of white noise disturbance is violated. Dickey and Fuller (1979) have shown that we can augment the basic regression models (13')-(15') with p lags of Δy_t:

$$\Delta y_t = (\rho_n - 1) y_{t-1} + \sum_{i=1}^{p} \alpha_i \Delta y_{t-i} + \varepsilon_t \tag{13''}$$

$$\Delta y_t = \beta_{0c} + (\rho_c - 1)y_{t-1} + \sum_{i=1}^{p} \alpha_i \Delta y_{t-i} + \varepsilon_t \qquad (14'')$$

$$\Delta y_t = \beta_{0c\tau} t + \beta_{1c\tau} t + (\rho_{c\tau} - 1)y_{t-1} + \sum_{i=1}^{p} \alpha_i \Delta y_{t-i} + \varepsilon_t \qquad (15'')$$

The tests are based on the t-ratio on $(\hat{\rho} - 1)$ and are known as "Augmented Dickey Fuller" (ADF) statistics. The critical values are the same as those discussed for the DF statistics, since the asymptotic distributions of the t-statistics on $(\hat{\rho} - 1)$ is independent of the number of lagged first differences included in the ADF regression. Regarding the lag length selection, p should be sufficiently large to remove serial correlation in the residuals. Here we can make use the Akaike information criterion (AIC) or the Schward Bayesian information criterion (BIC). Alternatively, we can follow Hall (1994) general to specific sequential rule, starting with a large value of p (p_{max}), testing the significance of the last coefficient and reducing p iteratively until a significant statistic is encountered.

An alternative approach to dealing with autocorrelation has been presented by Phillips (1987) and Phillips and Perron (1988). Rather than including extra lags of Δy_t (as in the Augmented Dickey Fuller test), they suggest amending these statistics to allow weak dependence and heterogenity in ε_t. Under such general conditions, a wide class of DGP's for ε_t such as most finite order ARIMA(p,0,q) models, can be allowed. The procedure consists of computing the DF statistics and using some non-parametric adjustment of τ, τ_μ and τ_τ in order to eliminate the dependence of their limiting distributions on additional nuisance parameters stemming from the ARIMA process followed by the error terms. Their adjusted counterparts are denoted $Z(\tau)$, $Z(\tau_\mu)$ and $Z(\tau_\tau)$ respectively.

For regression model (13'), Phillips and Perron (PP) define

$$Z(\tau) = \left(\hat{V}/\hat{V}_{Tm}\right)\tau - 0.5\left(\hat{V}_{Tm}^2/\hat{V}^2\right)\left\{\hat{V}_{Tm}^2\left(T^{-2}\sum_{i=2}^{T}\left(y_{t-1}^2\right)\right)\right\}^{-1/2}$$

where T is the sample size and m is the number of estimated autocorrelations; $\hat{V}$ and τ are, respectively, the sample variance of the residuals and the t-statistic associated with $(\rho_c - 1)$ from the regression (13'); and $\hat{V}_{Tm}^2$ is the long-run variance estimated as

$$\hat{V}_{Tm}^2 = T^{-1}\sum_{t=1}^{T}\varepsilon_t^2 + 2T^{-1}\sum_{s=1}^{l}w_{sm}\sum_{t=s+1}^{T}\hat{\varepsilon}_t\hat{\varepsilon}_{t-s}$$

where $\hat{\varepsilon}$ are the residuals from the regression (13') and where the triangular kernel

$$w_{lm} = \left[1 - s\left(m+1\right)\right], l = 1, ..., m$$

is used to ensure that the estimate of the variance $\hat{V}_{Tm}^2$ is positive (see Newey and West, 1987).

For regression model (14'), the corresponding statistic is

$$Z\left(\tau_\mu\right) = \left(\hat{V} / \hat{V}_{Tm}\right)\tau_\mu - 0.5\left(\hat{V}_{Tm}^2 / \hat{V}^2\right)T\left\{\hat{V}_{Tm}^2 \sum_2^T \left(y_t - \bar{y}_{-1}\right)^2\right\}^{-1/2}$$

where $\hat{V}$ and $\hat{V}_{Tm}^2$ are defined as above, but with residuals from equation (14'); $\bar{y}_{-1} = (T-1)^{-1}\sum_2^T y_{t-1}$, and τ_μ is the t-statistic associated with $(\rho_n - 1)$ from the regression (14').

Finally, for regression model (15') we have

$$Z\left(\tau_\tau\right) = \left(\hat{V} / \hat{V}_{Tm}\right)\tau_\tau - \left(\hat{V}_{Tm}^2 - \hat{V}^2\right)T^3\left\{4\hat{V}_{Tm}\left[D_{xx}\right]^{1/2}\right\}^{-1}$$

where $\hat{V}$ $\hat{S}$ and $\hat{V}_{Tm}^2$ are defined as above, but with the residual obtained from the estimation of (3'). τ_τ is the t-statistic associated with $(\rho_{c\tau} - 1)$ from the regression (15'). D_{xx} is the determinant of the regressor cross product matrix, given by

$$D_{xx} = \left[T^2(T^2 - 1)/12\right]\sum y_{t-1}^2 - T\left(\sum ty_{t-1}\right)^2 +$$
$$+ T(T+1)\sum ty_{t-1}\sum y_{t-1} - \left[T(T+1)(2T+1)/6\right]\left(\sum y_{t-1}\right)^2$$

The Phillips and Perron statistics have the same limiting distributions as the corresponding DF and ADF statistics, provided that $m \to \infty$ as $T \to \infty$, such that $m/T^{1/4} \to 0$.

Both, the ADF and PP tests, take a unit root as the null hypothesis. Kwiatkowski, Phillips, Schmidt and Shin (1992) provide an alternative test (known as the KPSS test) for testing the null of stationarity against the alternative of a unit root. This method considers models with constant terms, and either with or without a deterministic trend (their v_τ and v_μ statistics, respectively).

Formally, the KPSS test is given by:

$$LM = \frac{\sum_{t=1}^T \Phi_t^2}{\hat{\sigma}_e^2} \tag{16}$$

where $\Phi_t^2 = \sum_{i=1}^{T} e_i$ is the running partial sum of the residuals and $\hat{\sigma}_\varepsilon^2$ is the estimated residual variance from the regression:

$$y_t = \alpha + \varepsilon_t \tag{17}$$

for the model without trend, or

$$y_t = \alpha + \beta t + \varepsilon_t \tag{18}$$

for the model with trend.

The critical values for the KPSS tests are given in Kwiatkowski, Phillips, Schmidt and Shin (1992). Recently, it has been argued that confirmatory analysis (i.e., applying ADF or PP unit rot tests in conjunction with KPSS stationarity tests) may in some cases lead to a better description of the series, improving upon the separate use of each type of test (see, e.g., Maddala and Kim, 1998). If the ADF/PP tests reject the null while the KPSS test fails to do so, the results of both tests are consistent, suggesting that a given series is stationary. Alternatively, if the ADF/PP tests fail to reject the null while the KPSS test does reject it, both approaches give consistent results, and one may conclude in this case that the series is not stationary. Finally, both ADF/PP and KPSS tests fail to reject the respective nulls or both reject their nulls, the results are inconclusive.

Finally, given that conclusions drawn from unit root tests may well be sensitive to structural breaks in the underlying stochastic process, a number of tests have been proposed for unit roots under structural change (see, e.g. Maddala and Kim, 1998). Following Perron (1989, 1997), we can allow for the possibility of a one-time structural change in the trend function occurring at time T_b. Three situations are considered: a change in the intercept, a change in both the intercept and the slope, and a change in the slope. Regarding the transition to the new trend path, and following Perron (1989), two models are evaluated: the "additive outlier model" (AOM) and the "innovational outlier model" (IOM). While the AOM specifies that the change to the new trend function occurs instantaneously (with no further effect on future observations), in the IOM that change takes place gradually (feeding back into the process dynamics).

In the case of the IOM, the unit-root test is performed using the t-statistic for testing $\alpha = 1$ in the following regressions:

$$\text{IOM-1: } y_t = \mu + \beta t + \theta DU_t + \delta D(T_b)_t + \alpha y_{t-1} + \sum_{i=1}^{p} c_i \Delta y_{t-i} + \varepsilon_t \tag{19}$$

$$\text{IOM-2: } y_t = \mu + \beta t + \theta DU_t + \gamma T_t + \delta D(T_b) + \alpha y_{t-1} + \sum_{i=1}^{p} c_i \Delta y_{t-i} + \varepsilon_t \tag{20}$$

$$\text{IOM-3: } y_t = \mu + \beta t + \gamma DT_t + \alpha y_{t-1} + \sum_{i=1}^{p} c_i \Delta y_{t-i} + \varepsilon_t \tag{21}$$

where $D(T_b)_t = 1$ if $t = T_b + 1$ (0 otherwise); $DU_t = 1$ if $t > T_b$ (0 otherwise); and $DT_t = (t - T_b)$ if $t > T_b$ (0 otherwise). In equation (19) we allow for a one-time change in the intercept of the trend function, while in equation (20) we allow for both a change in the intercept and in the slope of the trend function, whereas in equation (21) there is a change in the slope of the trend function.

Regarding the AOM, the following two-step procedure is used. First, the series is detrended using the following regressions:

$$\text{AOM-1: } y_t = \mu + \beta t + \theta DU_t + \tilde{y}_t \tag{22}$$

$$\text{AOM-2: } y_t = \mu + \beta t + \theta DU_t + \gamma DT_t + \tilde{y}_t \tag{23}$$

$$\text{AOM-3: } y_t = \mu + \beta t + \gamma DT_t + \tilde{y}_t \tag{24}$$

where $\tilde{y}_t$ is accordingly defined as the detrended series. As can be seen, in equation (22) we allow for a one-time change in the intercept of the trend function, in equation (23) we allow for both the change in the intercept and the slope of the trend function to take place simultaneously, and in equation (24) we allow for a change only in the slope of the trend function.

For models IOM-1 and IOM-2, the test is then performed using the t-statistic for testing $\alpha = 1$ in the regression:

$$\tilde{y}_t = \alpha \tilde{y}_{t-1} + \sum_{j=0}^{p} d_j D(T_b)_{t-j} + \sum_{i=1}^{p} c_i \Delta \tilde{y}_{t-i} + \varepsilon_t \tag{25}$$

while for model IOM-3, the second step is of the form:

$$\tilde{y}_t = \alpha \tilde{y}_{t-1} + \sum_{i=1}^{p} c_i \Delta \tilde{y}_{t-i} + \varepsilon_t \tag{26}$$

Note that in regressions (19) to (26), the break date (T_b) and the truncation lag (p) are treated as unknowns. Therefore, to carry out the test procedure, one needs to consider a method to choose T_b and k. In order to select the break date endogenously, we can consider the procedure whereby T_b is selected as the value, for all possible break points, which minimises the test statistic for testing $\alpha = 1$ in the appropriate autocorrelation specification (see Zivot and Andrews, 1992). Regarding the truncation lag parameter (p), we use a general-to-specific recursive approach based on the value of the t-statistic on the coefficient associated with the last lag in the estimated autocorrelation (see Perron, 1989).

3.1.2   Cointegration

Consider two time series y_t and x_t which are both $I(d)$ (i.e., they have comparable long-run properties). In general, any linear combination of y_t and x_t will be also $I(d)$. If, however, there exists a vector $(1, -\beta)'$, such that the combination

$$z_t = y_t - \alpha - \beta x_t \qquad (27)$$

is $I(d-b)$, $b>0$, then Engel and Granger (1987) define y_t and x_t as cointegrated of order $(d-b)$ [or $(y_t, x_t)' \sim CI(d,b)$] with $(1, -\beta)'$ called the cointegrating vector. Notice that a constant term has been included in (19) in order to allow for the possibility that z_t may have a non-zero mean.

The concept of cointegration tries to mimic the existence of a long-run equilibrium to which an economic system converges over time. In the case of PPP, from equation (1) we have:

$$s_t = \alpha + \beta(p - p^*)_t + \varepsilon_t \qquad (28)$$

where s_t is the logarithm of the spot exchange rate at time t and p_t (p_t^*) is the logarithm of the domestic (foreign) price level. Therefore, $z_t = s_t - \alpha - \beta(p - p^*)_t$ can be interpreted as the equilibrium error (i.e., the distance that the exchange rate is away from equilibrium at any point of time).

Engle and Granger also show that if s_t and $(p - p^*)_t$ are cointegrated $CI(1,1)$, then there must exist an error correction model (ECM) representation of the following form:

$$\Delta s_t = \mu + \sum_{i=0}^{p} \phi_i \Delta s_{t-i} + \sum_{j=1}^{q} \gamma_j \Delta(p - p^*)_{t-j} + \theta z_{t-1} + \xi_t \qquad (29)$$

where ξ_t is a sequence of independent and identically distributed random variables with mean zero and variance σ_ξ^2. Furthermore, they prove the converse result that an ECM generates cointegrated series.

Note that the term z_{t-1} in equation (21) represents the extent of disequilibrium between levels of s and $(p - p^*)$ in the previous period. The ECM states that changes in s_t depend not only on changes in $(p - p^*)_t$, but also on the extent of disequilibrium between levels of s and $(p - p^*)$. Therefore, the ECM could be seen as capturing the dynamics of the system whilst incorporating the equilibrium suggested by economic theory (see Hendry, 1995).

Based upon the concept of cointegration and on its closely related concept of ECM representation, Engle and Granger (1987) suggest a two-step estimation procedure for dynamic modelling which has become very popular in applied research. In the cases of PPP, if s_t and $(p - p^*)_t$ are both $I(1)$, then the procedure goes as follows:

i)   First, in order to test whether the series are cointegrated, the cointegrating regression (28) is estimated by ordinary least squares (OLS) and it is tested whether the cointegrating residuals' $\hat{z}_t = s_t - \hat{\alpha} - \hat{\beta}(p-p^*)_t$ are $I(0)$.

ii)   Finally, the residuals $\hat{z}_t$ are entered into the ECM (29), where now all the variables are $I(0)$ and conventional modelling strategies can be applied.

Regarding the first step, Engle and Granger (1987) suggest seven alternative tests for determining if z_t is stationary. The two most widely used are the Durwin-Watson statistic for the cointegrating regression (CRDW) and the ADF stastistic for the cointegrating residuals (CRADF).

The DW statistic for equation (20) will approach zero if the cointegrating residuals contain an autoregressive unit root, and thus the test rejects the null hypothesis of non-cointegation if the CRDW is significantly greater than zero.

The CRADF statistic is based upon the OLS estimation of

$$\Delta\hat{z}_t = \eta_1\hat{z}_{t-1} + \sum_{i=1}^{p}\eta_{2i}\Delta\hat{z}_{t-i} + \varepsilon_t \tag{30}$$

where again p is selected on the basis of being sufficiently large to ensure that ε_t is a close approximation to white noise. The t-ratio statistic on $\hat{\eta}_1$ is the CRADF statistic.

Engle and Granger (1987, p. 269) present the critical values for the CRDW and the CRADF statistics generated from Monte Carlo simulations of 100 simulations for a bivariate case as PPP in equation (28) (i.e., for one dependent variable and one independent variable in the cointegrating regression). Engle and Yoo (1987) produce expanded critical values for CRDW and CRADF ststistics for 50, 100 and 200 observations, and for systems of up to five variables. Finally, MacKinnon (1991) provides an approximation formula for computing critical values for all small samples, while MacKinnon (1994) expands his methodology to calculate both asymptotic and finite sample critical values.

As can be seen, both CRDW and CRADF statistics test the null of no-cointergration against the alternative of cointegration. It has been often argued that cointegration would be a more natural choice, but there are only a few tests for the null of cointegration. Shin (1994), for example, proposes a test based on the cointegrating residuals which is an extension of the LM test of KPSS univariate stationarity. The procedure consists of introducing past and future values of $\Delta(p-p^*)_t$ in equation (28), so that the cointegrating regression becomes

$$s_t = \alpha + \beta(p-p^*)_t + \sum_{i=-n}^{n}\varphi_i\Delta\hat{z}_{t-i} + \varepsilon_t \tag{31}$$

Applying OLS to the modified regression (31) will yield efficient estimates (see Saikkonen, 1991). A version of (16) may be constructed with the residuals $\hat{\varepsilon}_t$ from (31).

A test for absolute PPP consists in testing the joint hypothesis H_0: $(\alpha,\beta)=(0,1)$ in equation (28). Stock (1987) has shown that if two I(1) series are cointegrated, then the OLS estimates from equation (28) provide "super-consistent" estimates of the cointegrating vector (α,β). Nevertheless, the joint dependence of most aggregate time series and their non-stationarity invalidates the routine application of many standard statistical procedures in equation (28). Phillips and Hansen (1990) present a class of Wald tests which are modified by semiparametric corrections for serial correlation and for endogeneity. The resulting test statistics (termed fully-modified Wald tests) have limiting χ^2 distributions and therefore allows inference to proceed conventionally (for an explanation see, e.g., Ngama and Sosvilla-Rivero, 1991). Notice that in equation (28) we are imposing that p_t and p_t^* have the same coefficient (β), allowing us to combine the domestic and the foreign price levels forming a differential in prices. Alternatively, we would have assumed that the coefficients are different, so testing PPP should be based on estimates of the following equation :

$$s_t = \alpha + \beta p_t + \beta^* p^*_t + \varepsilon_t \tag{28'}$$

In this case, a test for absolute PPP consists in testing the joint hypothesis H_0: $(\alpha,\beta,\beta^*)=(0,1,-1)$ in equation (28'). However, a distinction is often made between the test that β and β^* are equal and of opposite sign (the so-called "symmetric condition") and the test that they are equal to unity and minus unity, respectively (the so-called "proportionality condition").

As an alternative two-step Engle-Granger procedure, Banerjee *et al.* (1986) propose a single-step dynamic model approach, based upon the t-ratio of the coefficient on the error-correction term θ in the following ECM for the PPP hypothesis:

$$\Delta s_t = \mu + \sum_{i=0}^{p}\phi_i\Delta s_{t-i} + \sum_{j=1}^{q}\gamma_j\Delta(p-p^*)_{t-j} + \theta[s_{t-1}-\alpha-\beta(p-p^*)_{t-1}] + \xi_t \tag{32}$$

The t-ratio is denoted the ECM statistic. Kremers, Ericsson and Dolado (1992) find that the ECM statistic can generate more powerful tests than those based upon the DF statistic applied to the residuals of a static cointegrating relationship such as (28). More generally, if we think that $(p-p^*)_t$ may be only weakly exogenous to the parameters of interests, Banerjee, Dolado and Mestre (1998) recommend estimating the following (unrestricted) ECM regression by OLS:

$$\Delta s_t = \mu + \sum_{i=0}^{p}\phi_i\Delta s_{t-i} + \sum_{j=1}^{q}\gamma_j\Delta(p-p^*)_{t-j} + \theta_1 s_{t-1} + \theta_2(p-p^*)_{t-1} + \xi_t \tag{33}$$

When θ_1 exceeds the critical values (provided in Banerjee, Dolado and Mestre, 1998), the null hypothesis of non-cointegration is rejected.

The parameters in the cointegrating regression (28) may not be constant through time. Gregory and Hansen (1996) generalised the usual residual based cointegration tests, allowing for a broader view of cointegration when they consider an alternative hypothesis in which the cointegration vector suffers shift at an unknown time. The new regression model is:

$$s_t = \alpha_1 + \alpha_2 D(t_0) + \beta_1 (p - p^*)_t + \beta_2 (p - p^*)_t D(t_0) + \varepsilon_t \tag{34}$$

where $D(t_0)$ is a dummy variable such that $D(t_0) = 0$ if $0 < t \leq t_0$ and $D(t_0) = 1$ if $t_0 < t \leq T$. The test for cointegration is conducted by testing for unit roots (for instance, with an ADF test) on the residuals $\hat{z}_t = s_t - \hat{\alpha}_1 - \hat{\alpha}_2 D(t_0) - \hat{\beta}_1 (p - p^*)_t - \hat{\beta}_2 (p - p^*)_t D(t_0)$ for each t_0. Gregory and Hansen (1996) propose and tabulate the critical values of the test statistic $ADF^* = \inf_{1 < t_0 < T} \{ADF(t_0)\}$. The null hypothesis of no cointegration and no structural break is rejected if the statistic ADF^* is smaller than the corresponding critical value. In this case, the structural break can be located at time t^* where the *inf* of the ADF test is obtained.

Johansen (1988) and Johansen and Juselius (1990) develop a maximum likelihood estimation procedure that has several advantages on the two-step regression procedure suggested by Engle and Granger. It relaxes the assumption that the cointegrating vector is unique and it takes into account the error structure of the underlying process.

Johansen considers the ρ-th order autoregressive representation of X_t

$$X_t = \Pi_1 X_{t-1} + \Pi_2 X_{t-2} + ... + \Pi_\rho X_{t-\rho} + \varepsilon_t \tag{35}$$

which, following a similar procedure to the ADF test, can be re-parameterised as

$$\Delta X_t = \tilde{\Pi}'_t \Delta X_{t-1} + ... + \tilde{\Pi}'_{\rho+1} \Delta X_{t-\rho+1} + \tilde{\Pi}_\rho X_{t-\rho} + \varepsilon_t \tag{36}$$

where $\Pi'_\rho = -\Pi(1) \; \left(= -(\Pi_1 + ... + \Pi_\rho) \right)$. To estimate $\tilde{\Pi}'_\rho$ by maximum-likelihood, we estimate by OLS the following regressions

$$\Delta X_t = \Gamma_{01} \Delta X_{t-1} + ... + \Gamma_{0k-1} \Delta X_{t-k+1} + e_{0t} \tag{37}$$

and

$$\Delta X_{t-\rho} = \Gamma_{11} \Delta X_{t-1} + ... + \Gamma_{1k-1} \Delta X_{t-k+1} + e_{1t} \tag{38}$$

and compute the product moment matrices of the residuals

$$\hat{M}_{ij} = T^{-1} \sum_{t=1}^{T} \hat{e}_{it} \hat{e}'_{jt}; i, j = 0, 1 \tag{39}$$

To test of the null hypothesis $H_0 : \prod_\rho = B\Gamma'$, i.e. there are at most r cointegrating vectors, can be conducted using either of the following two test statistics

$$\lambda_{ir}(r) = -T \sum_{i=r+1}^{\rho} \ln(1 - \hat{\lambda}_i) \tag{40}$$

$$\lambda_{\max}(r, r+1) = -T \ln(1 - \hat{\lambda}_{r+1}) \tag{41}$$

where $\hat{\lambda}_{r+1}, ..., \hat{\lambda}_\rho$ are the ρ-r smallest eigenvalues of $\hat{M}_{10}\hat{M}_{00}\hat{M}_{01}$ with respect to $S_{11}M_{11}$, obtained from the determinant

$$\left| \hat{\lambda}\hat{M}_{11} - \hat{M}_{10}\hat{M}_{00}\hat{M}_{01} \right| = 0 \tag{42}$$

The statistic in (40), known as the trace statistic, tests the null hypothesis that the number of cointegrating vectors is less than or equal to r against a general alternative. On the other hand, the statistic in (41), known as the maximum eigenvalue statistic, test a null of r cointegrating vectors againts the specific alternative of $r+1$. Osterwald-Lenum (1992) offers critical values for both tests using Monte Carlo simulations.

Finally, an alternative approach, which has certain advantages over both the OLS and the maximum likelihood procedures, has been proposed by Stock and Watson (1993). Their dynamic ordinary least squares (DOLS) improves on OLS by coping with small sample and dynamic sources of bias. The Johansen method, being a full information technique, is exposed to the problem that parameter estimates in one equation are affected by any misspecification in other equations. The Stock Watson method is, by contrast, a robust single equation approach which corrects for regressor endogeneity by the inclusion of leads and lags of first differences of the regressors. In addition, it has the same asymptotic optimality properties as the Johansen distribution. For the PPP hypothesis the DOLS regression would be as follows:

$$s_t = \alpha + \beta(p - p^*)_t + \sum_{j=-q_1}^{q_2} \varphi_j \Delta(p - p^*)_{t-j} + \varepsilon_t \tag{28''}$$

where q_1 and q_2 are selected to increase at an appropriate rate with T.

Stock and Watson (1993) suggest correcting for serial correlation in (28'') by using generalised least squares GLS (the so-called dynamic GLS: DGLS).

3.2   Panel Estimation with Non-stationary Data

Standard cross-section analysis focuses on long-run average relationships and ignores the time-series variation in the data. But the variation of variables over time contain additional information, which may be particularly valuable in situations where the cross-section variation in the data is relatively limited.

The panel cointegration approach exploits both cross-section as well as time series variation in the data. Compared to individual time series tests, these panel cointegration tests have higher power. In subsection 3.2.1 we review some tests that have been proposed to deal with the existence of unit roots in panel data, while the next subsection 3.2.2 surveys several alternative tests to analyse the theory of panel cointegration.

3.2.1   Panel Unit Root Tests

Before testing for cointegration, we need to confirm whether the variables are actually non-stationary. A variety of procedures for the analysis of unit roots in panel. One of the first tests was the Levin-Lin (LL) test [Levin and Lin (1993) and Levin, Lin and Chu (2002)]. Their test is based on analysis of the following equation

$$\Delta y_{i,t} = \alpha_i + \delta t + \rho y_{i,t-1} + \sum_{j=1}^{p} \phi_j \Delta y_{i,t-j} + \varepsilon_{i,t} \tag{43}$$

where $i=1, 2,..., N$ indexes cross-section units (e.g., countries) and $t=1, 2, .., T$ indexes time periods (e.g., years). Corresponding to the maintained hypothesis of common dynamics, the null hypothesis and alternative hypothesis are given by $H_0 : \rho = 0, H_A : \rho < 0$.

Equation (43) can be estimated using the within estimator and the LL test statistic is based on the usual t-statistic:

$$t_\rho = \frac{\hat{\rho}}{\hat{\sigma}_\rho}. \tag{44}$$

Levin and Lin (1993) propose two transformations of the t-statistic t_ρ that are asymptotically normally distributed as N and $T \to \infty$:

$$LL_1 = \sqrt{1.25}t_{\hat{\beta}} + \sqrt{1.55}N \Rightarrow N(0,1)(as\sqrt{N}/T \to \infty)$$

$$LL_2 = \sqrt{1.25}[t_{\hat{\beta}} - (\sqrt{N}\mu_{1T}/\sqrt{\mu_{2T}}) \Rightarrow N(0,1)$$

with $\mu_{1T} = -\frac{1}{2} - \frac{1}{2}T^{-1}$ and $\mu_{2T} = \frac{1}{6} + \frac{5}{6}T^{-2}$. The two tests LL_1 and LL_2 coincide asymptotically, but in finite samples they will differ.

Im, Pesaran and Shin (1997, 2003) (IPS hereafter) extend the LL test to allow for heterogeneity in the value of ρ_i among observations under the alternative hypothesis. The relevant equation is the following:

$$\Delta y_{i,t} = \alpha_i + \delta_i t + \rho_i y_{i,t-1} + \sum_{j=1}^{p} \phi_j \Delta y_{i,t-j} + \varepsilon_{i,t} \qquad (43')$$

The null and alternative hypotheses are defined as $H_0 : \rho_i = 0, \forall i; H_A : \rho_i < 0, i = 1, 2, ..., N_1, \rho_i = 0, i = N_1 + 1 N_1 + 2, ..., N$. Due to the heterogeneity, equation (43') is estimated separately buy OLS for each cross-section unit based on T observation. Let t_i ($i = 1, 2,.., N$) denote the individual t-statistics for testing unit roots. Then, to test the null of a unit root across all individuals, merely take the average of these t-statistics to obtain the IPS t-bar statistic:

$$\bar{t} = \frac{1}{N} \sum_{i=1}^{N} t_i \qquad (45)$$

Assuming that the cross-section units are independent, IPS propose the use of the standardised t-bar statistic:

$$\Gamma_{\bar{t}} = \frac{\sqrt{N}\left[\bar{t} - E(t_i / \rho_i = 0)\right]}{\sqrt{Var(t_i / \rho_i = 0)}} \qquad (46)$$

The means $E(t_i / \rho_i = 0)$ and the variance $Var(t_i / \rho_i = 0)$ are obtained from Monte Carlo methods.

IPS also propose an LM-bar test statistic where they compute an average Lagrange multiplier test of the null that the lagged level has no explanatory power ($\rho_i=0$, for all i) across all individuals. The Monte Carlo results indicate that the t-bar test is somewhat more powerful.

3.2.2 Panel Cointegration Tests

Consider the following system of cointegrated regressions to test PPP as a long-run equilibrium:

$$s_{i,t} = \alpha_i + \beta(p - p^*)_{i,t} + \varepsilon_{i,t} \qquad (47.1)$$

$$(p - p^*)_{i,t} = (p - p^*)_{i,t-1} + \xi_{i,t} \qquad (47.2)$$

where as before $i=1, 2,..., N$ indexes cross-section units (e.g., countries) and $t=1, 2, .., T$ indexes time periods (e.g., years), and where $s_{i,t}$ and $(p - p^*)_{i,t}$ are integrated processes of order one for all i.

The zero mean innovation vector $\zeta_{i,t} = (\varepsilon_{i,t}, \xi_{i,t})'$ satisfies

$$\frac{1}{\sqrt{T}} \sum_{t=1}^{Tr} \varsigma_{i,t} \Rightarrow B_i(\Omega), \text{ for all } i \text{ as } T \to \infty \tag{48}$$

where $B_i(\Omega)$ is a vector Brownian motion with asymptotic covariance Ω.

Kao (1999) derives two types of panel cointegration tests. The first is a DF type test and the second is an ADF type test. Both tests can be calculated from[2]:

$$\Delta \hat{z}_{i,t} = \rho \hat{z}_{i,t-1} + \sum_{i=1}^{p} \psi_i \Delta \hat{z}_{i,t-i} + \varepsilon_{i,t} \tag{49}$$

where the residuals $\hat{z}_{i,t} = s_{i,t} - \hat{\alpha}_i - \hat{\beta}(p - p^*)_{i,t}$ are based on the OLS estimation of equation (48). The null and alternative hypotheses are defined as $H_0 : \rho = 1, H_A : \rho < 1$. Kao (1999) propose four DF-type statistics. The first two DF statistics are based on assuming strict exogeneity of the regressors, while the remaining two allow for endogeneity of the regressors. In addition, Kao (1999, pp. 6-11) proposes an ADF test statistic. Finally, the DF statistics, which allow for endogeneity, and the ADF statistic involve deriving some nuisance parameters from the long-run conditional variances Ω. The asymptotic distributions of all tests converge to a standard normal distribution N(0.,1) as $T \to \infty$ and $N \to \infty$.

Using system (47) and allowing for heterogeneity of the long-run variance matrix Ω_i for each i and heterogeneity of the slope parameters across all cross-section units i, Pedroni (1999) presents a total of seven tests of the null of no cointegration, of which four involve pooling on the within dimension and three on the between dimension. The first category of tests uses the following specification for the null and alternative hypotheses; $H_0 : \rho = 1, H_A : \rho < 1$, while the second category uses $H_0 : \rho_i = 1, H_A : \rho_i < 1$ for all i, therefore requiring to compute N autoregressive coefficients ρ_i by using equation (48) for each ith cross-section unit. Pedroni's ststistics also require estimating some nuisance parameters from the long-run conditional variances Ω_i. Each of the seven test statistics can be rescaled so that it is distributed as a normal distribution. The appropriate factors for these tests are given in Pedroni (1999).

McCoskey and Kao (1998) also develop a residual-based panel test, but in contrast to Kao´s tests and Pedroni´s tests, takes cointegration as the null hypothesis. The test is given by

$$LM = \frac{1}{N} \sum_{n=1}^{N} \left\{ \frac{\frac{1}{T^2} \sum_{t=1}^{T} \Phi_{it}^2}{\sigma_z^2} \right\} \tag{50}$$

---

[2] In the case of DF tests all $\psi_i = 0$.

where $\Phi_{it} = \sum_{j=1}^{t} \hat{z}_{ij}$ is the running partial sum of the residuals and

$\sigma_z^2 = \frac{1}{NT} \sum_{i=1}^{N} \sum_{j=1}^{T} \hat{z}_{ij}^2$. The residuals $\hat{z}_{i,t} = s_{i,t} - \hat{\alpha}_i - \hat{\beta}(p - p^*)_{i,t}$ can be estimated using either the dynamics OLS [DOLS, built upon the work of Saikkonen (1991) and Stock and Watson (1993)] or the fully modified OLS [FMOLS, based upon Phillips and Hansen (1990)] estimator, both of which correct for serial correlation and endogeneity of regressors. McCoskey and Kao (1998) show that a standardised version of the statistic converges to a normally distributed random variable under the null hypothesis of cointegration.

4 Empirical Evidence on PPP

"I have no data yet. It is a capital mistake to theorise before one has data. Insensibly one begins to twist facts to suit theories, instead of theories to suit facts"

From a dialogue between Sherlock Holmes and Dr. Watson in A Scandal in Bohemia, by Sir Arthur Conan Doyle

4.1 Reviewing the Literature on Empirical Evidence on PPP

In this section we provide a review of the vast empirical literature testing the validity of the PPP hypothesis. This area has proven fruitful ground for applying different estimation methods to different periods and countries. Therefore, we have selected the most relevant contributions classifying them from the point of view of the econometric methods used in the empirical application.

Firstly, we have considered some representative studies from the seventies, when the econometric methodologies applied in these papers (OLS, Instrumental Variables) did not take into account the statistical properties of the time series. Secondly, we examine the contributions of some of the authors who applied modern methods for dealing with nonstationary time series, using the concept of cointegration. Finally, there are relatively fewer papers that test the PPP hypothesis using the newest econometric methodology: panel cointegration.

Table 1 contains the name and abbreviations of the currencies and countries analysed in the empirical papers, while Table 2 shows the different econometric tests and methodologies used in such papers.

In Table 3 we report the empirical application under study, giving very summarised information regarding its relevant features. The first column gives the reference of a particular paper. The second contains the currencies examined. The third specifies the period (or subperiods) under investigation, as well as the characteristics of the sample (monthly, annual or quarterly), and span. The fourth column shows the variables that are used: "NER"[3] stands

---

[3] In many works, there is also information about Real Exchange Rates (RER). As our aim is to provide information of studies that analyse the equations related to the Nominal Exchange Rates, rather than summarizing those that study stationarity properties of RER, and in order to maintain the concreteness of the table, its presence is not always notified.

for "nominal exhange rate", "CPI" means "consumer price index", "WPI" is the "wholesale price index", "GDPD" is the "deflactor of the GDP", "MPI" stands for "manufacturing price index", "IPI" is the "industrial price index", and "TPI" represents the "price index of traded goods". In the fifth column we report the econometric methodology used in the empirical evaluation. After a short comment on each paper, we provide the results of the analysis regarding the validity of the PPP hypothesis (i.e., if the empirical evidence found is favourable or not to this hypothesis) .

Table 1: Currency Abbreviations

Country	Currency	Abbr.	Country	Currency	Abbr.	Country	Currency	Abbr.	COUNTRY	Currency	Abbr.
Algeria	Dinar	DZD	Ethiopia	Birr	ETB	Malaysia	Ringgit	MYR	Singapore	Dollar	SGD
Argentina	Peso	ARS	Europe	Ecu	ECU	Mexico	Peso	MXN	Slovakia	Koruna	SKK
Belgium	Franc	BEF	France	Franc	FRF	Nepal	Rupee	NPR	South Korea	Won	KRW
Bolivia	Boliviano	BOB	Germany	Marc	DEM	Netherlands	Guilder	NLG	Spain	Peseta	ESP
Brazil	Real	BRL	Ghana	New cedi	GHC	New Zealand	Dollar	NZD	Sweden	Krona	SEK
Bulgaria	Leva	BGL	Greece	Drachma	GRD	North Korea	Won	KPW	Sri Lanka	Rupee	LKR
Canada	Dollar	CAD	Hungary	Forint	HUF	Norway	Krone	NOK	Switzerland	Franc	CHF
Chile	Peso	CLP	India	Rupee	INR	Pakistan	Rupee	PKR	Thayland	Baht	THB
Colombia	Peso	COP	Indonesia	Rupiah	IDR	Peru	New Sol	PEN	Turkey	Lira	TRL
Czech Republic	Koruna	CZK	Israel	New Shekel	ILS	Philippines	Peso	PHP	United Kingdom	Pound	GBP
Denmark	Krone	DKK	Italy	Lira	ITL	Poland	Zloty	PLN	United States	Dollar	USD
Dominican.Rep.	Peso	DOP	Japan	Yen	JPY	Portugal	Escudo	PTE	Uruguay	Peso	UYU
Egypt	Pound	EGP	Kenya	Shilling	KES	Romania	Leu	ROL	Venezuela	Bolivar	VEB

Table 2: Econometric Methodologies and Tests Abbreviations

Abbr.	Econometric Method/Test
ADF	Augmented Dickey Fuller
CRADF	Augmented Dickey Fuller test for Cointegration
CRDF	Dickey Fuller test for Cointegration
CRDW	Durbin Watson test for Cointegration
CRPP	Phillips Perron test for Cointegration
DF	Dickey Fuller
DGLS	Dynamic Generalised Least Squares
DOLS	Dynamic Ordinary Least Squares
ECM	Error Correction Model
FDOLS	Fully Modified Ordinary Least Squares
GLS	Generalised Least Squares
IPS	Im, Pesaran and Shin
IV	Instrumental Variables
KPSS	Kwiatkowski, Phillips, Schmidt and Shin
LL	Levin-Lin
(M)SB	(Modified) Sargan-Bhargava
2S-OLS	Two Stages Ordinary Least Squares
OLS	Ordinary Least Squares
PP	Phillips Perron
SBC	Schwarz's Bayesian Critetion

Table 3: Empirical Evidence on Purchasing Power Parity

AUTHOR	CURRENCIES	PERIOD	VARIABLES	ECONOMETRIC METHOD	CHARACTERISTICS	RESULT
Krugman (1978)	DEM, CHF, FRF, ITL, GBP and USD	Monthly: 1921-1925 1973-1976	NER, WPI	OLS IV	Studies the autocorrelation and suggests that movements on the exchange rates are due to omited variables	Not Fav. Fav.
Frenkel (1981)	USD, DEM, FRF, GBP	Monthly: 1921-1925 1973-1979	NER, CPI, MPI, WPI	2S-OLS, IV	Studies both absolute and relative PPP	Fav. (first period andlast period for EU). Not fav (during the last period for USD)
Miller (1984)	FRF, GBP, DEM, USD	Quarterly 1973-1980	NER, Indices Divisia?	GLS	Finds that deviations in prices are persistent	Fav (within EU)
Edison and Klovland (1987)	NOK and GBP	Annual 1974-1971	NER, GDPD at market prices	Cointegration (CRADF, CRDW)	Focus on l.r.structural factors such as productivity and therms of trade that could cause the simple PPP to fail and s.r cyclical factors that cause temporary deviations from PPP, and suggest an expanded model	Fav. (PPP holds only in the l.r after having taken into account the effects of changes in real, structural favors like the relative levels of productivity and the terms of trade)
Taylor (1988)	GBP, DEM, FRF, CAD, JPY against USD	Monthly 1973:06-1985:12	NER, MPI	Unit Root (DF, ADF) Cointegration (DF, ADF, DW)	Allowance for measurement error and/or transportation costs	Not Fav.
Taylor and McMahon (1988)	DEM, FRF, USD against GBP	Monthly 1921:01-1925:05 Data for Germany: 1921:02-1923:08	NER, WPI	Unit Root (ADF) Cointegration (CRDW, CRADF)	Results are largely invariant to the choice of normalising variable. The failure is attributable to non-stationary and non-fundamental factors during the last year before Britain's return to the Gold Standard	Fav. Except for USD-GBP
Mikkelsen (1989)	ARS,CLP, MXN, BRL, UYU, and PEN	Quarterly 1948-1988	NER Relative WPI	Unit Root (DF, ADF) Cointegration (CRADF)	e and p in Brazil are I(2) In Peru, e is I(1) while p is I(2)	Fav.for ARS, CLP, MXN, UYU
McNown and Wallace (1989)	CLP, ARS, BRL, ILS against USD	Monthly: Different periods (from 1972 to 1986)	NER, CPI and WPI	Cointegration (CRDF, CRADF, CRDW)	Cointegration when WPI is used, not for CPI. Uses the ECM model to describe the mechanics of adjustment to the l.r.equilibrium	Fav.for CLP, ARS and BRL
Taylor (1990)	GBP, USD	Monthly 1921:01-1925:05	NER, WPI	Unit Root (PP, ADF, Johansen) Cointegration (CRADF, Johansen)	Includes ECM method. By mid 1926, GBP was undervalued against USD by some 2% Some form of PPP held for the whole of the 1920s float between GBP and USD.	Fav.

AUTHOR	CURRENCIES	PERIOD	VARIABLES	ECONOMETRIC METHOD	CHARACTERISTICS	RESULT
Ahking (1990)	USD against GBP	Monthly 1921:01-1925:05	NER, WPI	Unit Root (ADF) Cointegration (Engle and Yoo,1987)	Tests that the variables contain no deterministic components	Not Fav.
McNown and Wallace (1990)	GBP, CAD, JPY against USD	Monthly Different periods from 1957:03-1986:06	NER, CPI and WPI	Unit Root (DF, ADF) Cointegration (CRDF, CRADF)	Period encomprises fixed and flexible exchange rate regimes. The strongest support for cointegrationn comes from the fixed rate subperiod. Except for Canada (WPI), cointegration is rejected for the last period of flexible exchange rates	Fav. for fixed periods, not for flexible. Not fav.for GBP
Canarella, Pollard and Lai (1990)	CAD, DEM, JPY, GBP against USD	Monthly 1974:01-1987:12	NER, WPI	Cointegration (CRDF, CRADF, CRDW) Kalman Filter	Introduction of the time-varying parameter Failure on monetary exchange rate models can come from the presence of structural changes	Fav.
Nachane and Chissanthaki (1991)	FRF, BEF, GLR, ITL, BS, JPY, CAD against USA and DEM	Monthly 1973-1985/6 and 1979-1985/6	NER, WPI	Band-spectral analysis Cointegration (CRDF, CRADF, SB)	Using the Wu-Hausman test, verifies if omitted variables or endogeneity of relative inflation differentials cause misspecification in the model. PPP was likely to fare better with the DEM as a base.Formation of the MSE seems to have contributed to exchange rates stability for its members	Half of the cases
Ngama and Sosvilla-Rivero (1991)	ESP against USD and DEM	Monthly, Quarterly: 1977:01/I-1988:12/IV	NER, CPI, WPI	Unit Root (PP) Cointegration (CRADF) FMOLS	Includes Unrestricted ECM and an analysis of Granger-causality	Only Fav. For ESP/DM with WPI
Phylaktis (1992)	GBP, FRF, USD against GRD	Monthly 1923:01-1925:12	NER, Relative Prices	Unit Root (DF, ADF, Johansen) Cointegration (Johansen)	Speed at which long run PPP was reached following a shock was 50% per month	Fav.
Bleaney (1992)	CHF, GBP, ITL, CAD, FRF, JPY against USD	1900-1972 / 1973-1988	NER, Relative Prices	Cointegration (CRDF, CRADF) ECM Structural Breaks	Also considers RER, studying for unit roots and structural breaks due to regime changes If a heteroscedasticity correction is applied, the results are less favourable to PPP	Fav.: FRF,ITL, GBP, JPY (Not Fav: CHF, CAD) Not Fav.(except for FRF) Not Fav.
Taylor (1992)	USD against GBP	Monthly 1921:01-1925:05	NER, WPI	Unit Root (PP, ADF, Johansen)) Cointegration (CRADF, Johansen)	Includes ECM estimation UK prices are I(0), there is a deterministic trehnd in this serie. Overvaluation of GBP when fixed	Fav.
Bleaney (1993)	FRF, DEM, GBP and USD against CHF	Monthly: 1921:02-1924:11 (1923:08 for Germany)	NER, WPI, Cost-of-living Index	Unit root (ADF) Cointegration (CRADF) ECM	Performes two more tests than other studies. ECM turns PPP for GBP to hold	Fav: FRF, DEM Not fav: GBP, USD

AUTHOR	*CURRENCIES*	*PERIOD*	*VARIABLES*	*ECONOMETRIC METHOD*	*CHARACTERISTICS*	*RESULT*
Kugler and Lenz (1993)	15 currencies against DEM	Monthly 1973:01-1990:11	NER, CPI	Unit Root (DF, PP) Multivariate Cointegration (Johansen)	Empirical evidence for PPP is as strong within the EMS than for the european countries outside this system. For the rejection of PPP in the case of the USD we could argue that shocks (fiscal policy shocks) could explain permanent changes of the relative prices	Fav.: GBP, ITL, NWK, ATS, PTE, ESP. Not Fav.: USD, CAD, BEF, DKK Mixed: CHF, FRF, JPY, NLG, SEK
Steigerwald (1996)	CAD, FRF, DEM, GBP, ITL, USD (15 pairs)	Annual 1927-1990	NER, CPI	Unit Root (ADF, PP) Cointegration (Johansen, DOLS)	Specifies a general dynamic structure, which provides evidence of PPP for the 14 of 15, instead of 8 of 15 (result obtained with unit-root tests)	Fav.
Maeso (1997)	19 countries against USD	Quaterly 1974:I-1994:III	NER, IPI, CPI	Unit Root (ADF, PP) Cointegration (Johansen)	Less favourable results when IPIs are used. Suggests that PPP should be studied taking into account that causality can come from both directions (NER⇔Prices)	Fav.
Papell (1997)	20 developed countries (relative to DEM and USD)	Monthly, Quarterly: 1973:01/I-1994:09/III	NER, CPI	ADF and Panel Unit Root	Stronger conclusions can be made when panel is larger, for DEM (monthly) rather than USD (quarterly) data.	Fav
Telatan and Kazdagli (1998)	TRL against DEM, FRF, GBP and USA	Monthly 1980:10-1993:10	NER, CPI	Unit Root (ADF and PP) Cointegration (CRADF, CRPP)	Unique economic features of high inflation, structural changes, changes in taste and technology in Turkey	Not Fav.
Jacobson and Nessén (1998)	DEM, GBP, USD, JPY	Annual 1936-96	NER, WPI	Multivariate Cointegration (Johansen)	Use the ECM. Find three long-run, cointegrating relations but none can be interpreted in terms of PPP	Fav.to a weak form of PPP. Reject PPP
Salehizadeh and Taylor (1999)	27 countries (semi-advanced countries, emerging economies and developing nations)	Monthly 1975:01-1997:09	NER, CPI	Unit Root (ADF) Cointegration (Johansen, CRADF)	Simmetry and proporcionality conditions are rejected (all but one)	Fav. (14 of 27)
Christev and Noorbakhsh (2000)	BGL, CZK, HUF, PLN, ROL, SKK, USD, DEM and ECU	Monthly 1990:01-1998:11	NER, CPI	Unit Root (ADF, PP) Cointegration (Johansen, DOLS)	Use ECM Provide an explanation for such behaviour that is consistent with the literature on transition and foreign exchange markets	Weak evidence to support long-run equilibria
Wang (2000)	PHP, THB, IDR SID, MYR, JPY KRW against USD	Monthly 1979:01-1996:12 1973-01-1996:12 1980:01-1996:12	NER, CPI	Unit Root (ADF) Multivariate Cointegration (Johansen)	PPP vector does not exist in the cointegration space (conditions of symmetry and proportionality are rejected) Flexible exchange rate period	Fav.
Bai and Ng (2001)	21 countries (against USD)	Quarterly: 1974:I-1997:IV	RER, NER, CPI	Panel Unit Root (KPSS, MSB)	Model strong cross-section correlation via a factor model	Not Fav.

AUTHOR	CURRENCIES	PERIOD	VARIABLES	ECONOMETRIC METHOD	CHARACTERISTICS	RESULT
Pedroni(2001)	GBP. BEF, DKK, FRF, ITL, DEM, NLG, SEK, CHF, CAD, JPY, GRD, PTE, ESP, TRL, NZD, CLP, MXN, INR, KRW against USD	Monthly: 1973:06 1993:11	NER, CPI	Panel cointegration (within-dimension and between-dimension panel FMOLS and DOLS tests)	The approach allows to pose the null hypothesis so that he can test if strong PPP holds consistently for all countries in the panel or not.	Not Fav.
Nagayasu (2002)	17 African countries against USD	Annual: 1980-1994	NER, Relative Prices	Unit Root (infivual: ADF and Panel: IPS) Panel Cointegration (FMOLS)	Uses parallel market rather than official exchange rates (the last are fixed against a single currency or a basquet of other currencies) Any significant discrepancy between official and parallel exchange rates may serve as a warning sing that official rates are misaligned	Fav. (weak form)
Xu (2003)	CAD, FRF, DEM, ITL, JPY, KRW, NGL, GBP, USD	Quarterly: 1974:I-1997:IV	NER, RER, WPI, CPI, TPI	Unit root (ADF, SBC)	Cointegration for RER Prediction of NER, using PPP relationship. The l.r.PPP is rejected with the restrictions (symmetry and proporcionality) imposed a priori on the exchanche rate and price data, but unequivocally supported in their absence.	Mixed
Cerrato and Sarantis (2003)	20 developing countries against the USD	Monthly: 1973:01 1993:12	NER, CPI	Panel unit root (Individual:ADF, panel: IPS) Panel cointegration (DOLS, DGLS, McCoskey and Kao, Larsson)	Results imply the absence of persistently over-valued or under-valued black market exchange rates (if this were not the case, it would cause some damaging effects on economic growth and the allocation of resources)	Fav.
Basher and Mohsin (2003)	10 Asian developing countries against the USD (INR, IDR, KRW, MYR, NPR, PKR, PHP, SGD, LKR, THB)	Monthly, Quarterly: 1980:01/I-1999:12/IV	NER, CPI	Unit Root (individual: ADF; panel: LL and IPS) Cointegration (individual: Johansen-Juselius; panel: FMOLS, DOLS)	The between-dimension estimators consistently produce larger estimates than the within-dimension estimators. Analysis of individual countries indicate that the failure of the PPP is not driven by the data from only a few countries. Empirical findings do not support neither the relative nor the absolute versions of PPP.	Not Fav.

4.2 Reviewing the Empirical Evidence on PPP

It is important to note that most papers attempt to test the relative version of PPP [equation (2)] following two different paths: some authors [Frenkel (1981), Jacobson and Nessen (1998) or Basher and Mohsin (2003)] test both the absolute (or strong) version of PPP [equation (1)] and the relative version [equation 2]. Some other papers directly test the relative version of PPP. From a theoretical point of view, both versions are suitable for being tested, but traditional literature has pointed out that almost always it is not possible to accept the accomplishment of the strong version. Therefore, the wide majority of papers only consider the relative version of PPP.

While there is a large coincidence on the fact that absolute PPP is almost always rejected, the evidence on relative PPP is mixed. In order to make clear what this inconclusive result means, it is necessary to refer to specific countries, periods and econometric methodologies and proceedings.

Pre-cointegration methodologies [Krugman (1978), Frenkel (1981)] tend to support PPP when instrumental variables are used and USD is excluded of the analysis, which would suggest an effect of the economic trading environment on the convergence of relative prices.

Time-series cointegration includes the largest part of reviewed papers. Indeed, PPP testing would seem to provide the perfect context for applying cointegration methods. There are some studies in which the area of interest is Europe [Edison and Klovland (1987)], but in most of them the base currency is the US Dollar [Ngama and Sosvilla-Rivero (1991), Taylor and McMahon (1988) Taylor (1990), among others], or the US Dollar, the Canadian Dollar or the Japan Yen [see, e.g., McNown (1990), Canarella (1990), Taylor (1988), Steigerwald (1996) or Phylatkis (1992)]. Both the pre-cointegration and the time-series cointegration stages of testing PPP combine different price indices (CPI, WPI, MPI, etc.). The authors have also tried to explore if there is a positive relation between the acceptance (rejection) of PPP and the selected price index. This would be in line with the theoretical framework that suggests a higher probability of rejection in the presence of important differences in the basket of goods included in the CPI, as well as the presence of non tradable goods in them. It would seem that the use of WPI would help to correct this problem, and in general, the papers have made an extensive use of the WPI as a measure of prices in the different countries. When GB Pound is considered, specially when using data of the twenties, the results indicate inconclusive evidence, but in general, there is a supportive evidence on the accomplishment of PPP. Mikkelsen (1989) and McNown et al. (1989) extend the area of study to Latin America using recent time series data and obtaining evidence in favour of the PPP hypothesis.

Panel cointegration is the newest econometric technique in testing PPP. Basher and Mohsin (2003), Cerrato (2003) or Xu (2003) have made use of this technique in order to overcome some of the limitations of time-series cointegration. The wider possibilities of the new methodology and the long tradition in testing PPP, encouraged the economists[4] to increase the areas of analysis, and therefore they provide some evidence for Africa [Nagayasu (2002)], Asia [Wang (2000) or Basher et al. (2003)] or Oceania [Pedroni (2001)]. This last paper only provides evidence for the validity of a strong version of PPP, and the author concludes by rejecting the absolute version of PPP in countries of Europe, Asia, Oceania and America (using data from 1973 to 1993). Bai and Ng (2001), using approximately the same period and test PPP for twenty-one countries, find evidence against PPP. Basher and Mohsin (2003) extend their analysis from 1980 to 1999, considering some Asian countries, and obtain the same result as Pedroni (2001). The other papers tend to find a more supportive evidence

---

[4] They coincide in using the Consumer Price Index in their analysis.

on the empirical accomplishment of PPP, which is at least, mixed in favour of PPP[5], or unqualifiedly favourable to PPP.

5   Forecasting with PPP

> "Prediction is very difficult, especially about the future"
> ***Niels Bohr***

Despite the paramount modelling effort registered in the last two decades, it is widely recognised that exchange rates are extremely difficult to forecast.

The pessimism about the forecasting ability of exchange rate models has been generally accepted after the publication of the influential paper by Messe and Rogoff (1983). These authors performed a large number of statistical tests, indicating the superiority of the linear out-of-sample forecast of exchange obtained through a simple random walk model compared with the forecast based exchange-rate determination models that used a wider set of economic variables as regressors. This superiority is also clear when the forecast is determined *ex post* (i.e., using real historical values of the explicative variables in the regression). Recently, Cheung, Chinn and García-Pascual (2002) have evaluated the predictability of a wide variety of models that have been proposed over the past decade, and they conclude that these models are still unable to improve a random walk forecast.

Several explanations for the failure of structural models have been suggested, including misspecification of the models and poor modelling of expectations [Frankel and Rose (1995) for a survey]. Recently, interest has been shown in the possibility that non-linearities account for the apparent unpredictability of exchange rates, and some papers have highlighted the importance of non-linear adjustment of the exchange rate to the value implied by fundamentals, including Taylor and Peel (2000) and Clarida *et al.* (2003).

Based on these non-linearities some authors have explored the non-parametric, nearest neighbour forecasting technique (see Fernández-Rodríguez *et al.*, 2003 for a survey). The basic idea behind these predictors, inspired in the literature on forecasting in non-linear dynamical systems, is that pieces of time series sometime in the past might have a resemblance to pieces in the future. In order to generate predictions, similar patterns of behaviour are located in terms of nearest neighbours. The time evolution of these nearest neighbours is exploited to yield the desired prediction. Therefore, the procedure only uses information local to the points to be predicted and does not try to fit a function to the whole time series at once [see, e.g. Fernández-Rodríguez, Sosvilla-Rivero and Andrada-Félix (1999)].

Regarding PPP, Cochran and Defina (1995) examine the usefulness of PPP as a guide to future exchange rate movements. To that end, they use duration analysis to investigate whether deviations from PPP exhibit positive dependence (i.e., as time passes the probability that an exchange rate will return to its PPP level after a deviation occurs). They use monthly data covering January 1974 to December 1992 to compute PPP series for eighteen currencies (all *vis-à-vis* the US dollar). Their results suggest that PPP can not help in forecasting future exchange rate changes, a result consistent with market efficiency.

---

[5] For example, Xu (2003) rejects long run PPP when symmetry and proportionality restrictions are imposed, but supports PPP when these restrictions are absent a priori.

From 1986, *The Economist* published the Big Mac index, based upon the PPP hypothesis. Their "basket" is a McDonald's Big Mac, produced locally to roughly the same recipe in 120 countries. The Big Mac PPP is the exchange rate that would leave hamburgers costing the same in America as abroad. Comparing actual rates with PPPs signals whether a currency is under- or overvalued. Although the Big Mac index is not a perfect measure of PPP (since hamburgers cannot be traded across borders, prices may be distorted by taxes, different profit margins or differences in the cost of non-tradable goods and services, such as rents), several studies have found that the Big Mac PPP is a useful predictor of future movements. In this sense, when Europe's new currency was launched in January 1999, the Big Mac index suggested that the euro was already overvalued at its launch, when virtually everybody predicted that it would rise against the dollar. Moreover, Ong (2003) finds that the Big Mac index has been surprisingly accurate in tracking exchange rates in the long term, although there are some persistent deviations from PPP (in particular emerging-market currencies are consistently undervalued).

On the other hand, Kilian and Taylor (2003) explore whether a nonlinear, exponential smooth transition autoregressive (ESTAR) model based on PPPP may help in beating the random walk forecast of exchange rates. They develop a bootstrap test of the random walk hypothesis of the nominal exchange rate, given ESTAR real exchange rate dynamics. Using quarterly data for seven OECD countries covering the 1973.I-1998.IV period, they do find strong evidence of predictability at horizons two to three years, but not at shorter horizons.

Finally, Sosvilla-Rivero and García (2005) assess the empirical relevance of an expectations version of PPP in forecasting the Dollar/Euro exchange rate, based on the differential of inflation expectations derived from inflation-indexed bonds for the Euro area and the USA. To that end, they use daily data covering the 16 September 1998-31 December period for the Dollar/Euro exchange rate and for the inflation expectations. Regarding the inflation expectations, both for the Euro area and for the United States, they were calculated as the break-even inflation rates using the information provided by ten-year public bond yields, therefore allowing instantaneous processing of all of the information that exchange-ratethese operators receive concerning the behaviour of prices in the economies under study. The results in Sosvilla-Rivero and García (2005) suggest that, with few exceptions, the PPP-based predictors behave significantly better than a random walk in forecasts up to five days, both in terms of prediction errors and in directional forecast.

6   Concluding Remarks

> "I´ll give you a definitive maybe"
> **Samuel Goldwyn**

The main feature of the PPP hypothesis is that, in the long run, the exchange rate between two currencies should move towards the rate that would equalise the prices of an identical basket of goods and services in each country. This hypothesis is one of the oldest and controversial one in economics. As Officer (1982) has pointed out, over the centuries, the PPP hypothesis has been discovered, fallen into disuse, and been rediscovered (this pattern repeated several times). As stated by Samuelson (1964, p. 149), it seems that "each generation must rekill its phoenixes". Each episode of support for the hypothesis has been associated with a traumatic development: inflation following price stability and/or a change from a fixed-exchange rate regime to a flexible-exchange rate one. Empirical research on PPP enjoyed a rebirth after the move to flexible exchange rates in the early 1970s, although this re-emergence does not seem to have led to any consensus as to its general empirical validity.

We have reviewed a selection of empirical papers in order to explore the ongoing discussion on PPP. Given the close relation between successive developments in econometric techniques and the evolution of such empirical research, we have also surveyed the econometric methodology used in testing the validity of PPP during the last decades.

Even though we have seen that there are good reasons why PPP should not be expected to hold (the existence of transportation costs, tariffs and other legal barriers to commerce, non tradable goods, different productivity shocks and preferences for goods in different countries and differences in price indices), PPP remains an essential element of open economic macroeconomics. Its simplicity and intuitive appeal, its concreteness (the ingredient of the hypothesis are minimal and basic), and its usefulness (whether to know to what extent it is valid or used to measure deviations from PPP) lead us to conclude with Houthakker (1978, p. 71) that "the complete rejection of PPP is as mistaken as its complete acceptance". Indeed, the results from the empirical evidence revised in this paper are not conclusive, although many economists would recognise PPP as an important empirical possibility in the long run as Keynes (1923, p. 79).

What can we learn from the precedent lines? Are we ready for giving a definitive answer to the question about if PPP is true or false? We are not. But we are not ready because this was not at all our aim while we were writing this chapter. In fact, we certainly believe in the words of Dornsbuch and Krugman (1976), when they claimed that "under the skin of any international economist lies a deep-seated belief in some variant of the PPP theory of exchange rate". Therefore, the certainty of PPP is something we have no doubts about. What we then were looking for was the degree of empirical evidence that supports this undoubtable theory, and the results are not conclusive. Some well-known facts seem to affect the validity of PPP, at least in its strong version. The existence of transportation costs, tariffs and other legal barriers to commerce, non tradable goods, different productivity shocks and preferences for goods in different countries and differences in price indices may justify that the strong or absolute version of PPP is not empirically supported.

The most interesting feature in the empirical effort to test the validity of PPP is that this paramount endeavour to test the empirical reality of one of the simplest and main pillars of the economy has contributed to a great development of many econometric techniques. Indeed, empirical testing validity of PPP has been continuously changing as at the time that these technical innovations were appearing to that extent, and we can point out a clear causality in this area: PPP testing as a main stimulating factor behind the growth of time series econometrics, which were born to overpass the limitations (and wrong proceedings) of traditional ordinary least square estimation. In a second stage, panel cointegration has appeared to overcome the power problems that had the recent Nobel Price winners, Engle and Granger procedures.

In another way, statistical registration of data has improved long periods for the main currencies and has played a major mitigating role, too. Most of the inconsistent results we have summarized are related to the problems associated with small samples. In this sense, the panel cointegration approach, exploiting both cross-section as well as time series variation in the data is called to become an important tool in PPP to be tested in the years to come as the development of new data sets will allow researchers to investigate both longer and more disaggregated time series. In view of the mildly encouraging results from this latter approach, some optimism about the benefits from implementing new extensions in this area seems justified.

Finally, recent investigations have indicated some evidence of predictability using PPP both at long (two to three years) and short horizons (up to five days), opening new avenues that seem worthy of further research.

References

[1]   Ahking, F.W. (1990): "Further Results on Long-run Purchasing Power Parity in the 1920's", *European Economic Review*, Vol.34, pp. 913-919.

[2]   Artus J.R. (1978): "Methods of Assessing the Long-Run Equilibrium Value of an Exchange Rate". *Journal of International Economics*, Vol. 8, pp. 277-299.

[3]   Artus, J. R. and Knight, M. D. (1984): "Issues in the Assessment of the Exchange Rates of Industrial Countries", *IMF Occasional Paper* No. **29**. International Monetary Fund).

[4]   Bai, J. and Ng, S. (2001): "A New Look at Panel Testing of Stationarity and the PPP Hypothesis", *Working Paper in Economics* **518**, Boston College.

[5]   Balassa, B. (1964): "The Purchasing Power Parity Doctrine: A Reappraisal". *Journal of Political Economy*, Vol. 72, pp. 584-596.

[6]   Banerjee, A., Dolado, J. J. and Mestre, R. (1998): "Error-Correction mechanism tests in a single-equation framework", *Journal of Time Series Analysis*, Vol. 19, pp. 267-285.

[7]   Banerjee, A., Dolado, J. J., Hendry, D. F. and Smith, G. W. (1986): "Exploring equilibrium relationships in Econometrics through static models: Some Monte-Carlo evidence". *Oxford Bulletin of Economics and Statistics*, Vol. 48, pp 253-277.

[8]   Barro, R. (1983): Inflationary Finance Under Discretion and Rules", *Canadian Journal of Economics*, Vol. 16, pp. 1-25.

[9]   Basher, S.A., and Mohsin, M. (2003): "Purchasing Power Parity Tests in Cointegrated Panels: Evidence from Asian Developing Countries", forthcoming *Applied Economics Letters*.

[10] Bleaney, M. (1992): "A test of long-run Purchasing Power Parity Using Annual Data for Seven Countries, 1900-88", *Economia Internazionale*, Vol. 45, pp. 180-196.

[11] Bleaney, M. (1993): "Purchasing Power Parity in the 1920's: Some Further Tests", Discussion Paper in Economics 93/10, University of Nottingham.

[12] Booth, G., Duggan. J., and Koveos, P. (1985): "Deviations from purchasing Power Parity, Relative Inflation, and Exchange Rates: The Recent Experience", *Financial Review*, Vol. 20, pp. 195-218.

[13] Box, G. E. P. and Jenkins ,G. M. (1976): *Time Series Analysis: Forecasting and Control*, Revised Edition (San Francisco: Holden-Day).

[14] Canarella, G., Pollard, S.K., and Lai, K.S. (1990):"Cointegration between Exchange Rates and Relative Prices: Another View", *European Economic Review*, Vol.34, pp. 1303-1322.

[15] Cassel G. (1928): "The International Movements of Capital". In *Foreign Investments* (Chicago: Chicago University Press), pp. 1-93.

[16]   Cassel, G. (1916): "The Present Situation of the Foreign Exchanges", *Economic Journal*, Vol. 26, pp. 62-65.

[17]   Cerrato, M.and Sarantis, N. (2003): "Does the Purchasing Power Parity Hold in Developing Countries? Evidence from a Panel of Black Market Exchange Rates", Department of Economics, Finance and International Business, London Metropolitan University.

[18]   Cheung, Y-W, Chinn, M. D. and García-Pascual, A. (2002): "Empirical Exchange Rate Models for the Nineties: Do Are Any Fit to Survive?", *NBER Working Paper* **9393**, National Bureau of Economic Research .

[19]   Christev, A. and Noorbakhsh, A. (2000): "Long-run Purchasing Power Parity, Prices and Exchange Rates in Transition. The Case of Six Central and East European Countries". *Global Finance Journal*, Vol. 11, pp. 87-108.

[20]   Clarida, R. H., Sarno, L., Taylor, M. P. and Valente, G. (2003): "The Out-of-sample Sucess of Term Structure Models as Exchange Rate Predictors: A Step Beyond", *Journal of International Economics*, Vol. 60, pp. 61-83.

[21]   Cochran, S. J. and Defina, R. H. (1995): "Can Purchasing Power Parity Help Forecast the Dollar?", *Journal of Forecasting*, Vol. 14, pp. 523-32.

[22]   Dickey, D. A. and W. A. Fuller (1979): "Distribution of the Estimators for Autoregressive Time Series with a Unit Root", *Journal of the American Statistical Association*, Vol. 74, pp. 427-431.

[23]   Dolado, J. J., Jenkinson, T. and Sosvilla-Rivero, S. (1990): "Cointegration and Unit Roots", *Journal of Economic Surveys*, Vol. 4, pp. 249-273.

[24] Edison, H.J. and Klovland, J.T. (1987): "A Quantitative Reassessment of the Purchasing Power Parity Hypotheses: Evidence from Norway and the United Kingdom", *Journal of Applied Econometrics*, Vol. 2, pp. 309-333.

[25]   Engle, R. and Granger, G. (1987): "Cointegration and Error Correction: Representation, Estimation and Testing", *Econometrica*, Vol. 55, pp. 251-276.

[26]   Engle, R. and Yoo, S. (1987): "Forecasting and testing in cointegrating systems", *Journal of Econometrics*, Vol. 35, pp. 143-159.

[27]   Fernández-Rodríguez, F., Sosvilla-Rivero, S. and Andrada-Félix, J. (1999): "Exchange-rate Forecasts with Simultaneous Nearest-neighbour Methods: Evidence from the EMS", *International Journal of Forecasting*, Vol. 15, pp. 383-392.

[28]   Fernández-Rodríguez, F., Sosvilla-Rivero, S. and Andrada-Félix, J. (2003): "Nearest-Neighbour Predictions in Foreign Exchange Markets", in S.-H. Chen and P. Wang (eds): *Computational Intelligence in Economics and Finance* (Berlin: Physica Verlag), pp. 297-325.

[29]   Frankel, J. A. and Rose, A. K. (1995): "Empirical Research on Nominal Exchange Rates", in G. M. Grossman and K. Rogoff (eds.): *Handbook of International Economics*, Vol. III (Amsterdam: North-Holland), pp. 1689-1729.

[30]   Frenkel J. A. (1983): "Flexible Exchange Rates, Prices and the Role of News: Lessons from the 1970's". In Bhanderi, J. S. And Putman B.H., eds., *Economic Interdependence and Flexible Exchange Rates* (Cambridge, Mass.: The MIT Press), pp. 3-41.

[31]   Frenkel, J.A. (1981): "The Collapse of Purchasing Power Parities during the 1970's", *European Economic Review*,Vol. 16, pp. 145-165.

[32]   Granger, C. W. J. (1990): "Where Are the Controversies in Econometric Methodology?". General Introduction to Granger, C. W. J. (ed.) *Modelling Economic*

Time Series: Reading in Econometric Methodology (Oxford: Oxford University Press), pp. 1-23.

[33] Gregory, A. W. and Hansen, B. E. (1996): "Residual-based Test for Cointegration in Models with Regime Shifts", *Journal of Econometrics*, Vol. 70, pp. 99-126.

[34] Grice-Hutchinson, M. (1952): *The School of Salamanca* (Oxford: The Clarendon Press).

[35] Grice-Hutchinson, M. (1978): *Early Economic Thought in Spain* **1177**-1740 (London: George Allen and Unwin).

[36] Hall, A. (1994): "Testing for a Unit Root in Time Series with Pretest Data-Based Model Selection", *Journal of Business and Economic Statistics*, Vol. 12, pp. 461-470.

[37] Hendry, D. (1995): *Dynamic Econometrics* (Oxford: Oxford University Press).

[38] Hendry, D.F. and Juselius, K. (2000): "Explaining Cointegration Analysis: Part I", *Energy Journal*, Vol. 21, pp. 1-42.

[39] Hendry, D.F. and Juselius. K. (2001): "Explaining Cointegration Analysis: Part II", *Energy Journal*, Vol. 22, pp. 75-120.

[40] Houthakker, H. S. (1978): "Purchasing Power Parity as an Approximation to the Equilibrium Exchange Rate", *Economics Letters*, Vol. 1, pp. 71-75.

[41] Hsieh, D. A. (1982): "The Determination of the Real Exchange Rate. The Productivity Approach", *Journal of International Economics*, Vol. 12, pp. 355-362.

[42] Im, K. S., Pesaran, M. H. and Shin, Y. (2003): "Testing for Unit Roots in Heterogeneous Panels", *Journal of Econometrics*, Vol. 115, pp. 53-74.

[43] Im, K.S., M.H. Pesaran, and R. Smith (1997): "Testing for Unit Roots in Heterogeneous Panels", Mimeo, Department of Applied Economics, University of Cambridge.

[44] Jacobson, T. and Nessén, M. (1998): "World-Wide Purchasing Power Parity", Forthcoming in *Empirical Economics.*

[45] Johansen, S. (1988): "Statistical Analysis of Cointegration Vector", *Journal of Economic Dynamics and Control*, Vol. 12, pp. 231-254.

[46] Johansen, S. (1995): *Likelihood-Based Inference in Cointegrated Vector Autoregressive Models* (Oxford: Oxford University Press).

[47] Johansen, S. and Juselius, K. (1990): "Maximum Likelihood Estimation and Inference on Cointegration - With Applications to the Demand for Money", *Oxford Bulletin of Economics and Statistics*, Vol. 52, pp. 169-210.

[48] Kao, C. (1999): "Spurious Regression and Residual-Based Tests for Cointegration in Panel Data", *Journal of Econometrics*, Vol. 90, pp. 1-44.

[49] Katseli-Papaefstratiou L. T. (1979): "The Re-emergence of Purchasing Power Parity Doctrine in the 1970x". Special Papers in International Economics No. 13. International Finance Section, Princeton University.

[50] Keynes, J. M. (1923, 1971): "A Trade on Monetary Reform". First edition 1923, Vol. IV in *The Collected Writings of J. M. Keynes* (London: Macmillan, 1971).

[51] Kilian, L. And Taylor, M. P. (2003): "Why Is It So Difficult to Beat the Random Walk Forecast of Exchange Rates?", *Journal of International Economics*, Vol. 60, pp. 85-107.

[52] Kremers, J. J., Reicsson, N. R. and Dolado, J. J. (1992): "The power of cointegration tests", *Oxford Bulletin of Economics and Statistics*, Vol. 54, pp. 325-348.

[53] Krugman, P. (1978): "Purchasing Power Parity and Exchange Rates. Another look at the Evidence", *Journal of International Economics*, Vol. 8, pp. 397-407.

[54] Kugler, P. and Lenz, C. (1993): "Multivariate Cointegration Analysis and the Long-run Validity of Purchasing Power Parity", *The Review of Economics and Statistics*, Vol. 75, pp. 180-184.

[55] Kwiatkowski, D., Phillips, P. C. B., Schmidt, P. and Shin, Y. (1992): "Testing the Null Hypothesis of Stationarity against the Alternative of a Unit Root", *Journal of Econometrics*, Vol. 54, pp. 59-178.

[56] Levin, A. and Lin, C.-F. (1993): Unit Root Tests in Panel Data: Asymptotic and Finite-Sample Properties, University of California San Diego, Unpublished Working Paper.

[57] Levin, A., Lin, C. F. and Chu, C. S. (2002): "Unit Root Tests in Panel Data: Asymptotic and Finite-sample Properties", *Journal of Econometrics*, Vol. 108, pp.1-24.

[58] MacKinnon, J. G. (1991): "Critical Values for Cointegration Tests ". In R. F. Engle and C. W. J. Granger (eds.), *Long-run Economic Relationships: Readings in Cointegration* (Oxford: Oxford University Press), pp. 267-276.

[59] MacKinnon, J. G. (1994): "Approximate Asymptotic Distribution Functions for Unit-root and Cointegration Tests", *Journal of Business and Economic Statistics*, Vol. 12, pp. 167-176

[60] Maddala, G. S. and Kim, I.-M. (1998): *Unit Roots, Cointegration, and Structural Change* (Cambridge: Cambridge University Press).

[61] Maeso, F. (1997): "Análisis Multivariante de la Paridad del Poder Adquisitivo", *Revista de Economía Aplicada*, N.**15**, pp. 49-69.

[62] McCoskey, S., and Kao, C. (1998): "A Residual-Based Test of the Null of Cointegration in Panel Data", *Econometric Reviews*, Vol. 17, pp. 57-84.

[63] McKenzie, C. (1997): "Unit Roots and Cointegration Analysis: The Impact on Empirical Analysis in Economics", *Japanese Economic Review*, Vol. 48, pp. 18-28.

[64] McNown, R. and Wallace, M.S. (1989): "National Price Levels, Purchasing Power Parity and Cointegration: a Test of Four High Inflation Economies", *Journal of International Money and Finance*, Vol. 8, pp. 533-545.

[65] McNown, R. and Wallace, M.S. (1990): "Cointegration tests of Purchasing Power Parity among Four Industrial Countries: Results for Fixed and Flexible Rates", *Applied Economics*, Vol. 22, pp. 1729-1737.

[66] Meese, R. A. and Rogoff, K. (1983): "Empirical Exchange Rate Models of the Seventies: Do They Fit Out of Sample?", *Journal of International Economics*, Vol. 14, pp. 3-24.

[67] Mikkelsen, J.G. (1989): "Long run Purchasing Power Parity in Latin America", Danmarks Nationalbank.

[68] Miller, S. (1984): "Purchasing Power Parity and Relative Pirce Variability. Evidence from the 1970's", *European Economic Review*, Vol. 26, pp. 353-367.

[69] Nachane, D.M, and Chissanthaki, A. (1991): "Purchasing Power Parity in the Short and Long-run: a Reappraisal of the Post-1973 Evidence", *Applied Economics*, Vol. 23, pp. 1257-1268.

[70] Nagayasu, J. (2002): "Does the Long-Run Purchasing Power Parity Hypothesis Hold for Africa? Evidence from a Panel Cointegration Study" *Bulletin of Economic Research*, Vol. 54, pp. 181-187.

[71] Newey, W. K. y West, K. D. (1987): "A Simple, Positive Semi-definite, Heteroscedasticity and Autocorrelation Consistent Covariance Matrix", *Econometrica*, Vol. 55, pp. 703-708.

[72] Ngama Y.L. and Sosvilla-Rivero, S. (1991): "An Empirical Examination of Absolute Purchasing Power Parity: Spain 1977-1988", *Revista Española de Economía*, Vol. 8, pp. 285-311.

[73] Officer, L. H. (1976): "The Purchasing Power Theory of Exchange Rates: A Review Article". *IMF Staff Papers*, Vol. 23, pp. 1-61.

[74] Officer, L. H. (1982): *Purchasing Power Party and Exchange Rates: Theory, Evidence and Relevance* (Greenwich, Conn.: JAI Press).

[75] Osterwald-Lenum, M. (1992): "A Note Wwth Quantiles of the Asymptotic Distribution of the Maximum Likelihood Cointegration Rank Test Statistics", *Oxford Bulletin of Economics and Statistics*, Vol. 54, pp. 461-471.

[76] Papell, D.H. (1997): "Searching for Stationarity: Purchasing Power Parity under the Current Float", *Journal of International Economics*, Vol. 43, pp. 313-332.

[77] Pedroni, P. (1995): "Panel Cointegration; Asymptotic and Finite Sample Properties of Pooled Time Series Tests with an Application to the PPP Hypothesis", Working Paper in Economics No. 95-013, Indiana University.

[78] Pedroni, P. (1999): "Critical Values for Cointegration Tests in Heterogeneous Panels with Multiple Regressors", *Oxford Bulletin of Economics and Statistics*, Special Issue, pp. 652-670.

[79] Pedroni, P. (2001): "Purchasing Power Parity Tests in Cointegrated Panels", *The Review of Economics and Statistics*, Vol. 83, pp. 727-731.

[80] Perron, P. (1989): "The Great Crash, the Oil Price Shock and the Unit Root Hypothesis", *Econometrica*, Vol. 57, pp. 1361-1401.

[81] Perron, P. (1997): "Further Evidence on Breaking Trend Functions in Macroeconomic Variables", *Journal of Econometrics*, Vol. 80, pp. 355-385.

[82] Phillips, P. C. B. (1987): "Time Series Regression with a Unit Root", *Econometrica*, Vol. 55, pp. 277-301.

[83] Phillips, P. C. B. and P. Perron (1988): "Testing for a Unit Root in Time Series Regression", *Biometrika* Vol. 75, pp. 335-346.

[84] Phylakis, K. (1992): "Purchsing Power Parity and Cointegration: the Greek Evidence from the 1920s", *Journal of International Money and Finance*, Vol. 11, pp. 502-513.

[85] Pigou, A. C. (1922): "The Foreign Exchanges", *Quarterly Journal of Economics*, Vol. 37, pp. 52-74.

[86] Rogoff, K. (1996): "The Purchasing Power Parity Puzzle", *Journal of Economic Literature*, Vol. 34, pp. 647-668.

[87] Roll R. (1979): "Violations of Purchasing Power Parity and Their Implications for Efficient International Commodity Markets". In Sarnat, M. and Szego, G. P., eds., *International Finance and Trade* (Cambridge, Mass.: Ballinger), Vol. 1, pp. 133-176.

[88] Saikkonen, P. (1991): "Asymptotically Efficient Estimation of Cointegration Regressions", *Econometric Theory*, Vol. 7, pp. 1-21.

[89] Salehizadeh, M and Taylor, R. (1999) : "A Test of Purchasing Power Parity for Emerging Economies". *Journal of International Financial Markets, Institutions and Money*, Vol. 9, pp. 183-193.

[90] Samuelson, P. A. (1964): "Theoretical Notes on Trade Problems", *Review of Economics and Statistics*, Vol. 46, pp. 145 -154.

[91] Shin, Y. (1994): "A Residual-based Test of the Null of Cointegration Against the Alternative of No Cointegration", *Econometric Theory*, Vol. 10, pp. 95-115

[92] Sosvilla-Rivero, S. and García, E. (2005): "Forecasting the Dollar/Euro Exchange Rate: Can International Parities Help?", Journal of Forecasting, Vol. 24, pp. 369-377.

[93] Steigerwald, D.G. (1996): "Purchasing Power Parity, Unit Roots and Dynamic Structure", *Journal of Empirical Finance*, Vol. 2, pp. 343-357

[94] Stock, J. (1987): "Asymptotic Properties of Least Squares Estimators of Cointegrating Vectors", *Econometrica*, Vol. 55, pp. 381-386

[95] Stock, J. and Watson, M. W. (1993): "A Simple Estimator of Cointegrating Vectors in Higher Order Integrated Systems", *Econometrica* , Vol. 61, pp. 783-820.

[96] Taylor, M. P. and Peel, D. A. (2001): "The Behaviour of Real Exchange Rates During the Post Bretton Woods Period", *Journal of International Money and Finance*, Vol. 19, pp. 33-53.

[97] Taylor, M.P. (1988): "An Empirical Examination of Long-run Purchasing Power Parity Using Cointegration Techniques", *Applied Economics*, Vol.20, pp. 1369-1381.

[98] Taylor, M.P. (1990): "Long run Purchasing Power Parity and the Dollar-Sterling Exchange Rate in the 1920's", *IMF Working paper* **90**/118. International Monetary Fund.

[99] Taylor, M.P. (1992): "Dollar-Sterling Exchange Rte in the 1920's: Purchasing Power Parity and the Norman Conquest of $4.86", *Applied Economics*, Vol.24, pp. 803-811.

[100] Taylor, M.P., and McMahon, P.G, (1988): "Long run Purchasing Power Parity in the 1920's", *European Economic Review*, Vol. 32, pp. 179-97.

[101] Telatar, E. and Kazdagli, H. (1998): "Re-examine the Long-run Purchasing Power Parity Hypothesis for a High Inflation Country: the Case of Turkey 1980-1993", *Applied Economic Letters*, Vol 5, pp. 51-53.

[102] Wang, P. (2000): "Testing PPP for Asian Economies During the Recent Floating Period", *Applied Economics Letters*, Vol. 7, pp. 545-548.

[103] Xu, Z. (2003): "Purchasing Power Parity, Price Indices and Exchange Rate Forecasts", *Journal of International Money and Finance*, Vol.22, pp. 105-130.

[104] Zivot, E. and Andrews, D. W. K. (1992): "Further Evidence on Great Crash, the Oil Price Shock and the Unit Root Hypothesis", *Journal of Business and Economic Statistics*, Vol. 10, pp. 251-270.

In: International Macroeconomics: Recent Developments   ISBN: 1-59454-901-X
Editor: Amalia Morales Zumaquero, pp. 39-51   © 2006 Nova Science Publishers, Inc.

Chapter 2

PANEL EVIDENCE OF PURCHASING POWER PARITY USING INTRANATIONAL AND INTERNATIONAL DATA[1]

Sarah E. Culver[1] and David H. Papell[2]***

[1]Department of Finance, Economics, and Quantitative Methods
University of Alabama at Birmingham, Birmingham, AL 35294-4460
[2]Department of Economics, University of Houston, Houston, TX 77204-5882

Abstract

We investigate purchasing power parity (PPP) with CPI data for Canadian and United States cities, as well as for European countries. Using panel methods to test for the presence of a unit root, we find much less evidence of PPP with relative prices between cities within the same nation than with real exchange rates between European countries. The rates of price convergence are slower for United States cities than for Canadian cities or for European countries. We conduct a power analysis of the tests, and show that the results are consistent with differences in panel sizes and speeds of adjustment.

I Introduction

Purchasing power parity (PPP) remains an important research topic not only because it forms the basis of many international macroeconomic models but also because researchers have had a difficult time convincingly proving its existence and, when applicable, explaining the slower than expected rates of convergence. This is especially true for the post-Bretton-Woods era of flexible nominal exchange rates. After the first few years of generalized floating, it was obvious that PPP did not hold in the short-run. Price levels do not quickly counteract nominal exchange rate movements. However, whether *long-run* parity holds remains an actively researched topic.[1]

---

[1] We are grateful to John Rogers for providing us with the Canadian data.
* E-mail address: sculver@uab.edu; (205) 934-8879
** E-mail address: dpapell@uh.edu; (713) 743-3807
[1] Surveys of the PPP literature include Froot and Rogoff (1995) and Rogoff (1996).

Econometric analysis of long-run PPP typically involves conducting unit root tests for the real exchange rate. If the unit root null hypothesis is rejected, then the real exchange rate is mean stationary and any deviations from parity should diminish (even if slowly) over time.[2] Early investigations of PPP involved conducting Augmented-Dickey-Fuller (ADF) tests on univariate real exchange rates for industrialized countries. When these tests rarely rejected the unit root null, the validity of PPP was brought into question; today, however, those results are attributed mainly to the low power of the ADF tests with short time spans of data.[3]

One response to these findings is that to better test long-run reversion, longer spans of lower frequency data are needed.[4] However, those long time series encompass periods in which nominal exchange rate regimes shifted from floating to fixed and back again. Since real exchange rate behavior varies over exchange rate regimes, these studies cannot answer the question of whether the unit root null would be rejected with a century of flexible exchange rate data. Further, Engel (1999) shows that with longer spans of data, unit root (and cointegration) tests suffer from a serious size bias, whereby a large and economically significant unit root component in the real exchange rate can go undetected. Hegwood and Papell (1998), by demonstrating the importance of testing for possible structural breaks with longer spans of data, also caution against inferring that rejections of the unit root null constitute evidence of long-run PPP.[5]

An alternative approach has been to pool real exchange rates across countries and use panel econometric procedures. Inspired by Levin, Lin, and Chu (2002) and Im, Pesaran and Shin (2003), the advantage here is that in situations like the recent float, where there is not enough time series variation to produce good power in univariate unit root tests, a relatively small amount of cross-section variation can substantially improve power. Levin, Lin, and Chu (2002) and Bowman (1999) both report very high size adjusted power for panels of the size, time span and half-lives of the post-1973 period.

Despite the improved power, empirical studies of the current float have not provided persuasive evidence of long-run PPP with the U.S. dollar as the numeraire currency. Papell (2002) and Papell and Theodoridis (1998), with a panel of quarterly data for 21 industrialized countries, cannot reject the unit root null at even the ten percent level of significance. These results are sensitive to the choice of numeraire. Jorion and Sweeney (1996), Papell (2002), and Papell and Theodoridis (1998), using CPIs, and Wei and Parsley (1995) and Canzoneri, Cumby, and Diba (1999), using tradable goods prices, all report stronger rejections of unit roots in real exchange rates with the German mark, instead of the U.S. dollar, as the

---

[2] Alternatively, researchers have tested for cointegration between the nominal exchange rate, the domestic price level and the foreign price level. However, rejection of the no cointegration null provides necessary but not sufficient evidence of PPP; symmetry between the respected price levels and proportionality between relative prices and the nominal exchange rate must also hold. Otherwise, cointegration results offer evidence of "weak" PPP.

[3] Cheung and Lai (2000) use the DF-GLS test of Elliot, Rothenberg, and Stock (1996) on post-73 real exchange rates for industrialized countries to provide some additional rejections of the unit root null hypothesis. Culver and Papell (1999), using tests where the null hypothesis is stationarity, also provide some additional evidence of PPP.

[4] Frankel (1986), using 116 years of dollar/pound exchange rate data, was among the first to do this. More recent studies include Lothian and Taylor (1996). Froot and Rogoff (1995) show that, using a 5% Dickey Fuller critical value, 72 years of data would be needed to reject the unit root null hypothesis for a stationary AR(1) process with a PPP deviation half life of 3 years. Lothian and Taylor (1997) conclude from simulation studies that close to 200 years of real exchange rate data is needed to reject the unit root hypothesis for the dollar/pound exchange rate.

[5] In addition, Hegwood and Papell (1998) report much faster rates of convergence when structural change is taken into account. Reported half lives range between 0.44 and 2.32 years.

numeraire currency. Papell and Theodoridis (2001) extend the analysis of the numeraire to European versus non-European currencies.

Perhaps another reason for the lack of conclusive evidence relates to international price level data limitations and real-world factors that interfere with relative price convergence. To rule out this possibility, many focus on their attention on disaggregated and/or *intra*national price data. Disaggregated data avoids potential price stickiness problems that nontradable goods in the price index pose, while intranational price data avoids factors such as trade barriers, differences in market baskets, and other frictions that obstruct goods market arbitrage across borders.[6] Within country comparisons also have better integrated markets, identical monetary policies, and, by definition, a fixed nominal exchange rate. Therefore, if PPP is a good model of long run international price movements, then it should certainly hold within countries and maintain faster rates of convergence.

Although the above framework for answering the PPP question is appealing, studies using these types of data have not been able to provide strong evidence of PPP. The following studies, all using annual (roughly 1918-1996) U.S. city CPI data from the Bureau of Labor Statistics (BLS), report some interesting results. Chen and Devereux (2003), using ADF and cointegration tests, find little evidence for PPP or weak PPP. Their univariate results are particularly sensitive to the choice of numeraire city. For example, with Atlanta as the base city, they report the greatest number (13 out of 18) of unit root null rejections at the 5% level of significance. At the other extreme is San Francisco as the base city, which never rejects the unit root null at the 5% level. Their reported convergence rates (for those city pairs that reject the unit root null) are similar to international comparisons.[7] Sonora (1997) and Cecchetti, Mark and Sonora (2000), using Chicago as the numeraire, are able to reject the unit root null with panel methods, but report rates of convergence slower than those found across countries.[8]

We also employ panel econometric methods on intranational price data, but our study differs from those mentioned above in several ways. First, our period of interest is the post-1973 float. As such we use monthly data over the post-Bretton-Woods period to examine long-run PPP. Second, not only do we make use of U. S. city CPI data collected by the Bureau of Labor Statistics (BLS) but also Canadian city CPI data collected by Statistics Canada. As a benchmark we also use European Union real exchange rate data. Since trade barriers between European Union countries have mostly been eliminated and, through the EMS, currency fluctuations reduced for a subset of the countries, it provides an international data set that is as similar as possible to the intranational data sets. We construct two sets of intranational panels, U.S. and Canada, and compare these results against one another and against an international panel for the European Union.

---

[6] The extreme case is testing the law of one price (LOOP) either across borders, such as Engel and Rogers (1996), or with-in borders, such as Parsley and Wei (1996) and O'Connell and Wei (1997). CPI analysis, though, is useful because of its role in formulating expectations and in calculating cost of living adjustments, inflation, and real output.

[7] For those city pairs that reject the unit root null at the 5%, the half life is 3.91 years; at the 10%, the half life is 3.37 years. As a basis for comparison, studies using longer spans of data report very slow convergence rates back to PPP, with half lives of between 3-5 years. Panel studies using the current float report somewhat shorter half lives.

[8] For example, half lives tabulated using Levin-Lin panel tests on the full sample range between 7.141-8.153 years for Sonora (1997) and 8.9 years for Cecchetti, Mark and Sonora (2000).

We find much stronger evidence of PPP for the European Union panel than for the U.S. and Canada panels. These results are striking because, *a priori*, we expected to find more evidence of stationarity with intranational than with international data. The U.S. results are not sensitive to the numeraire choice: we are unable to reject the unit root null at even the 10% level for all panels but one, that panel with Detroit as the numeraire city. Choice of the numeraire matters more for the Canadian and European Union panels. We reject the unit root null for three out of nine panels at the 10% level only for the Canadian cities and for eight out of fifteen at the 5% level for the European panel of 14 countries.

Finally, we compare the rates of price convergence in the U.S. relative to Canada and the European Union. We find rates of price convergence for U.S. intranational city pairs to be slower than for Canada and the European Union. The comparison between the U.S. and Europe accords with the evidence from the unit root tests: the stronger rejections of the unit root null for the European Union countries are associated with faster convergence towards PPP. The evidence for Canada is puzzling. While the strength of the unit root rejections is comparable to the U.S., the speed of convergence towards PPP is comparable (and even slightly faster) than within the European Union. We provide some simulation evidence that the different results for Canada and Europe can be explained by the different size of the panels.

II Data Description

This paper sets out to test the purchasing power parity hypothesis over the post-Bretton-Woods flexible exchange rate period by exploiting the differences between international and intranational data. We use three data sets in this paper. The first is United States city CPI data from the BLS. It contains monthly seasonally unadjusted all-items CPI observations for fourteen metropolitan areas, spanning from 1978:04 to 1997:04.[9] The BLS reports monthly price data for four "core" metropolitan areas (Chicago, Los Angeles, New York City, and Philadelphia) and bimonthly data for ten others.[10] Of these ten metropolitan areas, five report data on an odd-month basis (Baltimore, Boston, Miami, St. Louis, and Washington D.C.) and five report data on an even-month basis (Dallas/Ft. Worth, Detroit, Houston, Pittsburgh, and San Francisco).[11] The even-month series span from 1978:04 to 1997:04, and the odd-month series span from 1978:05 to 1997:05. Because we have monthly data for only four U.S. metropolitan areas, we construct monthly data from the bimonthly series.[12] This provides us with monthly observations for fourteen U.S. cities.

The second data set is monthly seasonally unadjusted all-items CPI observations for nine Canadian metropolitan areas. Obtained from Statistics Canada, the cities are Calgary, Edmonton, Montreal, Ontario, Quebec City, Regina, Toronto, Vancouver, and Winnipeg. To

---

[9] Only seasonally unadjusted data is available on a monthly basis for the city price data.

[10] They also report bimonthly data for an eleventh city, Cleveland, but we delete this from our analysis because it switched in 12:86 from odd-month reporting to even-month reporting.

[11] Although monthly data is available for part of the Detroit and San Francisco series, we treat both cities in the even-month series. In 12:86 Detroit changed from monthly to bi-monthly reporting and San Francisco changed from bimonthly to monthly reporting.

[12] We use an interpolate source program available in RATS.

make the Canadian data comparable to the U.S. data, we restrict the data set to span from 1978:09 to 1997:06.

Although we would like to construct a comparable panel of European Union city pairs, the only city consumer price data available (that we are able to access) are Paris and Istanbul. When we calculate correlation coefficients between these cities and their respective national CPI, the values are 0.996 and 0.998, respectively. Given that the city CPI series are highly correlated with the respective country CPI series, we use European Union country data as a proxy for EU city CPI data. Obtained from *International Financial Statistics,* the European data set also includes seasonally adjusted monthly exchange rate data for fifteen countries, spanning from 1978:01 to 1997:02. We restrict the time span to correspond with the U.S. and Canadian city data sets.[13]

III Unit Root Tests

Let the relative price level (or real exchange rate) between cities (or countries) be calculated as

$$q = e + p^* - p \tag{1}$$

where q is the logarithm of the real exchange rate, e is the logarithm of the nominal (numeraire) exchange rate, p is the logarithm of the domestic Consumer Price Index, and p^* is the logarithm of the Consumer Price Index of the city (or country) whose currency we use as the numeraire currency. Note that because the within-country exchange rate is 1, e drops out of the equation so that the real exchange rate is just the relative price level, $p^* - p$. Also, because the IFS reports bilateral dollar exchange rates, for the European panels e is the difference between the logarithm of the nominal (dollar) exchange rate of the domestic country and the logarithm of the nominal (dollar) exchange rate of the country whose currency we use as the numeraire currency.

Univariate ADF tests regress the first difference of a variable (in this case the logarithm of the real exchange rate) on a constant, its lagged level and k lagged first differences using the following equation:

$$\Delta q_t = \mu + \alpha q_{t-1} + \sum_{i=1}^{k} c_i \Delta q_{t-i} + \varepsilon_t \tag{2}$$

We omit a time trend in equation (2) to be theoretically consistent with long-run PPP. The null hypothesis of a unit root is rejected in favor of the alternative of level stationarity if α is significantly different from zero.

---

[13] The countries include Austria, Belgium, Denmark, Finland, France, Germany, Greece, Italy, Netherlands, Norway, Portugal, Spain, Sweden, Switzerland, and the United Kingdom. Ireland is excluded because it does not have monthly CPI data. Luxembourg is excluded because it has a currency union with Belgium.

We use a recursive t-statistic procedure to select the value of k. We first set $k_{max} = 36$ (months), which is the upper bound on k, and estimate the model with all lags.[14] If the last included lag is significant then $k = k_{max}$. If the last included lag is not significant, then we reduce k by one until the last lag becomes significant. If no lags are significant, then k = 0. We use the ten percent value of the asymptotic normal distribution, 1.645, to determine significance. Campbell and Perron (1991) and Ng and Perron (1995) show that this recursive t-statistic procedure has better size and power properties than alternative procedures, such as selecting k based on AIC or BIC methods.

Very rarely do the ADF tests reject the unit root null for the within country relative price levels or for the international real exchange rates, and then only at the ten percent level of significance. ADF tests provide little if any evidence of long-run PPP for the post-73 float.[15] This is not surprising, however, given the unit root test's low power against a highly persistent alternative.

Panel unit root tests, by exploiting both cross section and time series variation, have power and size advantages over univariate unit root tests in small spans of data like the recent float. Among those to apply panel test procedures to PPP during the recent float include Abuaf and Jorion (1990), Frankel and Rose (1996), Jorion and Sweeney (1996), O'Connell (1998), Papell (2002), and Papell and Theodoridis (1998, 2001).

The ADF test in Equation (2) can be extended to a panel by estimating the following equations:

$$\Delta q_{jt} = \mu_j + \alpha q_{jt-1} + \sum_{i=1}^{k} c_{ij} \Delta q_{jt-i} + \varepsilon_{jt} \qquad (3)$$

where the subscript j indexes the cities (or countries) and μ_j denotes the heterogeneous intercept. We estimate Equation (3) by feasible GLS to account for contemporaneous correlation, with the coefficient α equated across cities and the values for k taken from the results of a univariate Augmented Dickey-Fuller test.[16] As in the univariate tests, these tests omit a time trend for theoretical consistency with PPP. The test statistic is the t-statistic on the coefficient α where, like the ADF test, the null hypothesis of a unit root is rejected in favor of the level stationarity alternative if α is significantly different from zero.[17]

With fourteen cities in the United States data set, we construct fourteen different panels (each with a different city as the numeraire city) of thirteen relative price levels each. For the Canadian data set we construct nine different panels of eight relative price levels each.[18] For the European Union data we construct fifteen panels of fourteen real exchange rates each.

---

[14] $K_{max} = 24$ months was insufficient to account for serially correlation in the data.

[15] These results are available upon request.

[16] O'Connell (1998) has shown that, if the lag length k and the value of the c's are equated across countries, panel tests of PPP using GLS are invariant to the choice of numeraire. Since we do not impose these restrictions, numeraire invariance is not imposed by our methods.

[17] These tests follow Levin, Lin, and Chu (2002) by restricting α to be equal across countries. Im, Peseran, and Shin (2003) develop tests where α can vary across countries. Based on the results of univariate ADF tests, this does not appear to be important for the real exchange rates or relative price levels investigated here. Bowman (1999) shows that, since the alternative hypothesis is that one element of the panel is stationary, the LLC tests are more conservative than the IPS tests.

[18] Nine Canadian cities was the most available. Fourteen would have made a better cross panel comparison.

Table 1. United States City Relative CPI Indexes

Numeraire City	α	t_α	p-values
Baltimore	-0.015	-5.397	.273
Boston	-0.013	-4.963	.425
Chicago	-0.018	-5.125	.363
Dallas/Ft. Worth	-0.015	-5.532	.225
Detroit	-0.019	-6.176*	.086
Houston	-0.012	-4.230	.691
Los Angeles	-0.015	-4.474	.609
Miami	-0.013	-4.727	.514
New York City	-0.013	-5.078	.380
Philadelphia	-0.018	-5.413	.267
Pittsburgh	-0.014	-5.199	.338
San Francisco	-0.017	-5.454	.255
St. Louis	-0.014	-5.117	.366
Washington D.C.	-0.014	-5.248	.323
Average	-0.015	-5.152	.365

Note: Kmax = 36 months. Each panel consists of 13 relative CPI series. Number of observations = 228, which span from 1978:05 to 1997:04. We restrict α to be the same across equations. The critical values for t_α are -7.19, -6.48, -6.10 for the 1%, 5%, and 10% level of significance, respectively.

We calculate critical values using Monte Carlo methods with randomly generated data. First we fit autoregressive (AR) models to the first differences of each series, using the Schwartz criterion to choose the optimal AR model. Then we use the optimal AR model in order to generate the errors for each series. For each panel of n relative price levels (or real exchange rates) we use the optimal AR model with iid N $(0, \sigma^2)$ innovations to construct pseudo samples of size equal to the actual size of the n series (228 for U.S. monthly series, 226 for the Canadian series, and 230 for the European series). The critical values for the finite sample distributions are taken from the sorted vector of 5000 replicated statistics and reported along with the panel tests results. Our critical values are greater, in absolute value, than those in Levin, Lin, and Chu (2002) because we are accounting for serial correlation.[19]

We begin by conducting panel tests on the U.S. city relative price level series. Table 1 reports the results of the panel tests of the monthly city pairs for the United States. The panel tests fail to reject the unit root null hypothesis. Only one numeraire, Detroit, rejects the unit root null, and even then only at the ten percent level. This is much less evidence of PPP than is found using post-1973 monthly data with the U.S. dollar as numeraire. Papell (2002), testing all combinations of 13 (the size of the intranational panel of U.S. cities) out of 17 (the size of his international monthly data set) real exchange rates, rejects the unit root null at the 10% level in about 70% of the cases.

---

[19] We do not incorporate contemporaneous correlation in the data generating process because, as shown by O'Connell (1998), the distribution of the FGLS estimate of α is invariant to the degree of correlation between real exchange rate innovations.

A common method for measuring persistence is to calculate the half lives of PPP deviations, the amount of time that it takes a shock to the series to revert halfway back to its mean value, with the formula defined as ln (.5)/ln (1+α).[20] The average half-life for U.S. city panels is 45.86 months, or 3.82 years. While this result is consistent with Rogoff's (1996) characterization of 3 - 5 year half-lives for PPP deviations, it represents a speed of reversion which is considerably slower than the 2.5 year half-life found in Papell (2002) for a panel of industrialized countries with the U.S. dollar as the numeraire currency. Even for the panel with Detroit as numeraire, which is the only panel that reports any evidence of stationarity, the calculated half-life is 36.13 months or 3.01 years.

We next examine how the U.S. within country findings compare with the Canadian relative price panels. Table 2 reports the findings from panel tests conducted on Canadian price level city pairs. For three out of the nine panels, the unit root hypothesis is rejected at the ten percent level. Although the Canadian panels are smaller (with 8 relative price levels) than the U.S. monthly panels (which have 13 relative price levels), with consequent reduction in power of the panel unit root tests, Canadian panels give more evidence against the unit root null. Using another metric, the average p-value for the Canadian panels is .166. This indicates much stronger evidence against the unit root null than the average p-value, .365, for the U.S. panels.

There are considerable differences in convergence rates between the U.S. panels and the Canadian panels. The average half-life for Canadian city panels is 22 months or 1.83 years. This speed of convergence is not only much faster than we found for U.S. cities; it is faster than the convergence speeds that are found for industrialized countries. For those Canadian numeraire cities where relative price levels are stationary, Quebec City, Toronto, and Winnipeg, the calculated half-lives are between 1.67 and 1.83 years.[21]

Table 2. Canadian City Relative CPI Indexes

Numeraire City	α	t_α	p-values
Calgary	-0.028	-4.495	.245
Edmonton	-0.028	-4.406	.273
Montreal	-0.033	-4.980	.122
Ottawa	-0.030	-4.774	.167
Quebec City	-0.035	-5.341*	.059
Regina	-0.029	-4.567	.226
Toronto	-0.031	-5.181*	.083
Vancouver	-0.029	-4.507	.241
Winnipeg	-0.034	-5.210*	.077
Average	-0.031	-4.622	0.166

Note: Kmax = 36 months. Each panel consists of 8 relative price level series. Number of observations = 226, which span from 1978:09 to 1997:06. We restrict α to be the same across equations. The critical values for t_α are -6.08, -5.42, -5.09 for the 1%, 5%, and 10% level of significance, respectively.

---

[20] Andrews and Chen (1994) show that the half-life is a good scalar measure of persistence.

[21] Engel and Rogers (1996) report that average price volatility is higher between U.S. city pairs than between Canadian city pairs, and postulate that this might be because the U.S. is a more heterogeneous country.

As a benchmark for comparison, we use European Union country real exchange rates as a proxy for European Union city pairs.[22] These results are reported in Table 3. Like other international PPP studies using European data, we find strong rejections of the unit root null over the current floating exchange rate period. Out of fifteen panels, we are able to reject the unit root null hypothesis for 10 panels at the 10% level, 7 panels at the 5%, and 1 at the 1% level of significance. The average half-life for the European panels is 26.31 months or 2.19 years. This is very similar to the half-lives reported in Papell (2002) with the German mark as the numeraire currency. The calculated half-lives for the European real exchange rates that exhibit stationarity range between 1.83 to 2.28 years, slightly greater than those for Canada but less than those for the United States.

The comparison of results between the United States and the European Union panels are consistent with the findings in Sonora (1997) and Cecchetti, Mark, and Sonora (2000). Using long-term annual U.S. CPI data, they report half-lives which are considerable longer than are found in studies using comparable length international real exchange rate data. They are not, however, consistent with the results of Parsley and Wei (1996), who find that, using disaggregated data, the speed of convergence to the law of one price is substantially higher for intranational data than is found in cross-country data.

Table 3. European Country Real Exchange Rates

Numeraire Country	α	t_{α}	p-values
Austria	-0.028	-7.378***	.007
Belgium	-0.029	-7.225**	.011
Denmark	-0.025	-6.583*	.052
Finland	-0.023	-5.721	.235
France	-0.025	-6.336*	.087
Germany	-0.025	-6.838**	.029
Greece	-0.024	-5.798	.213
Italy	-0.031	-6.673**	.042
Netherlands	-0.025	-6.902**	.025
Norway	-0.029	-7.025**	.018
Portugal	-0.024	-5.776	.221
Spain	-0.025	-5.963	.169
Sweden	-0.028	-6.630**	.046
Switzerland	-0.028	-6.781**	.033
United Kingdom	-0.024	-5.605	.271
Average	-0.026	-5.773	.097

Note: Kmax = 36 months. Each panel consists of 14 real exchange rates. Number of observations = 230, which span from 1978:01 to 1997:02. We restrict α to be the same across equations. The critical values for t_{α} are -7.27, -6.60, -6.26 for the 1%, 5%, and 10% level of significance, respectively.

---

[22] We were only able to access two European city CPIs, those of Paris and Istanbul. Because two series makes for a small panel and because the city data was highly correlated with the corresponding country data, we use country CPI data as a proxy.

The findings for Canada are puzzling. Although the speed of convergence towards PPP is comparable (and even slightly faster) than within the European Union, there is little evidence against unit roots. An obvious difference is that the cross-section dimension is 8 for the Canadian panels versus 14 for the European panels. While the size of the panels of U.S. cities, 13, is similar to the European panels, the speed of convergence is much slower for U.S. cities. In order to explore both the hypothesis that the non-rejections of unit roots for the Canadian panels can be explained by the smaller size of the panels and the hypothesis that the non-rejections of unit roots for the U.S. panels can be explained by the slower speeds of convergence, we conduct a power analysis of the tests.

The results of the power analysis are presented in Table 4. Using Monte Carlo methods similar to those described above for the calculation of critical values, we generate panels of 8, 13, and 14 series. Each series is an AR (1), with the autoregressive coefficient, $1-\alpha$, calculated from the average value of α in the Canadian, U.S., and European panels, respectively.[23] These series are stationary by construction. The panel unit root tests are then conducted 5000 times. The entries in Table 4 describe the fraction of times that the unit root null can be rejected at the 1%, 5%, and 10% levels.

Table 4. Power Analysis of the Unit Root Tests

Panel	N	T	$1-\alpha$	1%	5%	10%
United States Cities	13	228	.985	.170	.425	.596
Canadian Cities	8	226	.969	.225	.522	.666
European Countries	14	230	.974	.362	.661	.793

Note: N is the number of elements in each panel and T is the number of observations. $1-\alpha$ is calculated from the average value of α in Tables 1-3. Kmax = 36 months. α is restricted to be the same across equations.

The power of the unit root tests is considerably lower for the panel replicating the characteristics of 8 Canadian cities than for the panel of 14 European countries, even though the speed of convergence is faster ($1-\alpha$ is smaller) for the Canadian panel. This can explain why the rejections of unit roots are so much stronger for the European countries than for the Canadian cities. The power of the tests is even lower for the panel replicating the U.S. cities. Since the number of elements is almost the same between the U.S. and the European panels, the fall in power is clearly due to the much slower speed of convergence for the U.S. cities. This can explain the almost total inability to reject the unit root null for the U.S. panels.

For all three panels, the power analysis predicts more rejections of the unit root null than occur with the actual data. This can be explained by contemporaneous correlation. For the power simulations, the disturbances are independent. With the actual data, because shocks to the "domestic" price level and, for the European panels, the nominal exchange rate are common across elements, there is considerable contemporaneous correlation. Since correlated disturbances reduce the additional information gained from increasing the size of the panels, the number of rejections of the unit root null with actual data would not be expected to match the power results with simulated data.

---

[23] The number of observations also match the actual series.

V Conclusions

This paper sets out to provide evidence on the purchasing power parity hypothesis over the post-Bretton-Woods period by exploiting the differences between international and intranational data. Since intranational data avoids problems such as trade barriers, exchange rate volatility, differential monetary policies, nonintegrated markets, and other factors that restrict goods market arbitrage, we expected to find that the evidence of PPP was stronger among cities in Canada and the United States than across countries in Europe. However, we find just the opposite. Compared to the European Union panels, our results from the within country panels find at best weak evidence of PPP, and then only for the Canadian panels.

We calculate the half lives of PPP deviations as a metric to calibrate the rate of mean reversion. Here we find that the rate of price convergence is slower for U.S. cities than for either Canadian cities or for European countries. While this explains the stronger rejections of unit roots in real exchange rates for the European Union countries compared with the U.S. cities, the Canadian results are puzzling. While the speed of mean reversion is actually faster for Canadian cities than for European countries, the evidence of PPP is much weaker. We conduct a power analysis of the panel unit root tests, and show that the results can be explained by the different sizes of the panels.

Intranational data for U.S. cities has been used by Parsley and Wei (1996) to provide an upper bound of the rate of convergence to purchasing power parity. With the end of nominal exchange rate fluctuations among those European Union countries that have adopted the Euro, Cecchetti, Mark, and Sonora (2000) use evidence of price level convergence among U.S. cities to provide lessons for the European Central Bank. These studies reflect a presumption that the evidence of PPP should be stronger with intranational than with international data. Our major result, that the rejections of unit roots in relative prices are much stronger among European countries than among either U.S. or Canadian cities, is not in accord with that presumption. Further investigation of the power of the tests, however, shows that our results are in accord with what would be expected considering the differences in panel sizes and speeds of adjustment to PPP among the panels.

References

[1] Abuaf, N. and P. Jorion (1990), "Purchasing Power Parity in the Long Run," *Journal of Finance*, **45**, 157-174.

[2] Andrews, D., and H.-Y. Chen, (1994), "Approximately Median-Unbiased Estimation of Autoregressive Models," *Journal of Business and Economic Statistics* **12**, 187-204.

[3] Bowman, D., (1999), "Efficient Tests for Autoregressive Unit Roots in Panel Data," *International Finance Discussion Papers, Federal Reserve Board*, No. **646**.

[4] Campbell, J. and P. Perron (1991), "Pitfalls and Opportunities: What Macroeconomists Should Know About Unit Roots," *NBER Macroeconomics Annual*, **141**-201.

[5] Canzoneri, M., Cumby, R., and B. Diba, (1999), "Relative Labor Productivity and the Real Exchange Rate in the Long Run: Evidence for a Panel of OECD Countries," *Journal of International Economics*, **47**, 245-266.

[6]   Cecchetti, S., Mark, N., and R. Sonora, (2000), "Price level Convergence Among United States Cities: Lessons for the European Central Bank," *NBER Working Paper*: **7681**, May 2000.

[7]   Chen, L.L. and J. Devereux (2003), "What Can US City Price Data Tell Us about Purchasing Power Parity?" *Journal of International Money and Finance*, **22**,213-22.

[8]   Cheung, Y.-W. and K. Lai, (2000), "On Cross-Country Differences in the Persistence of Real Exchange Rates, *Journal of International Economics*, **50**, 375-97.

[9]   Culver, S. and D. Papell (1999), "Long-Run Purchasing Power Parity with Short-Run Data: Evidence with a Null Hypothesis of Stationarity," forthcoming, *Journal of International Money and Finance*.

[10] Elliot, Rothenberg, and Stock (1996), "Efficient Tests for an Autoregressive Unit Root," *Econometrica*, **64**, 813-836.

[11] Engel, C., (1999), "Long-Run PPP May Not Hold After All," forthcoming, *Journal of International Economics*.

[12] Engel, C. and J.H. Rogers, (1996) "How Wide Is the Border?," *American Economic Review*, **86**, No.5, 1113-1125.

[13] Frankel, J. (1986), "International Capital Mobility and Crowding Out in the U.S. Economy: Imperfect Integration of Financial Markets or of Goods Markets?" in *How Open is the U.S. Economy?*, R. Hafer, ed., Lexington Books.

[14] Frankel, J. and A. Rose (1996), "A Panel Project on Purchasing Power Parity: Mean Reversion Within and Between Countries," *Journal of International Economics*, **40**, 209-224.

[15] Froot, K. and K. Rogoff (1995), "Perspectives on PPP and Long-Run Real Exchange Rates" in *Handbook of International Economics*, G. Grossman and K. Rogoff, eds., North-Holland, Amsterdam.

[16] Hegwood, N. and D. Papell (1998), "Quasi Purchasing Power Parity," *International Journal of Finance and Economics*, **3**, 279-289.

[17] Im, S., Pesaran, H. and Y. Shin (2003), "Testing for Unit Roots in Heterogeneous Panels," *Journal of Econometrics*, **115**, 53-74.

[18] Jorion, P. and R. Sweeney (1996), "Mean Reversion in Real Exchange Rates: Evidence and Implications for Forecasting," *Journal of International Money and Finance*, **15**, 535-550.

[19] Levin, A., Lin, C. F. and J. Chu, (2002), "Unit Root Tests in Panel Data: Asymptotic and Finite-Sample Properties," *Journal of Econometrics*, **108**, 1-24. 6, 19-35.

[20] Lothian, J. and M. Taylor (1996), "Real Exchange Rate Behavior: The Recent Float From the Perspective of the Past Two Centuries, "*Journal of Political Economy*, **104**, 488-509.

[21] Lothian, J. and M. Taylor (1997), "Real Exchange Rate Behavior," *Journal of International Money and Finance*, **16**, 945-954.

[22] Ng, S. and P. Perron (1995), "Unit Root Tests in ARMA Models with Data Dependent Methods for the Selection of the Truncation Lag," *Journal of the American Statistical Association*, **90**, 268-281.

[23] O'Connell, P. (1998), "The Overvaluation of Purchasing Power Parity," *Journal of International Economics*, **44**, 1-19.

[24] O'Connell, P. and S.J. Wei (1997), "The Bigger They Are, The Harder They Fall: How Price Differences between U.S. Cities are Arbitraged," *NBER Working Paper*: **6089**, July 1997.

[25] Papell, D. (1997), "Searching for Stationarity: Purchasing Power Parity Under the Current Float," *Journal of International Economics,* **43**, 313-332.

[26] Papell, D. (2002), "The Great Appreciation, the Great Depreciation, and the Purchasing Power Parity Hypothesis," Journal of International Economics, **57**, 51-82.

[27] Papell, D. and H. Theodoridis (1998), "Increasing Evidence of Purchasing Power Parity over the Current Float," *Journal of International Money and Finance*, **17**, 41-50.

[28] Papell, D. and H. Theodoridis (2001), "The Choice of Numeraire Currency in Panel Tests of Purchasing Power Parity," *Journal of Money, Credit and Banking*, **33**, 790-803.

[29] Parsley, D. and S.-J. Wei (1996), "Convergence to the law of One Price without Trade Barriers or Currency Fluctuations," *Quarterly Journal of Economics*, **111**, 1211-1236.

[30] Rogoff, K. (1996), "The Purchasing Power Parity Puzzle," *Journal of Economic Literature* **34**, 647-668.

[31] Sonora, R. (1997), "Relative Price Level Convergence in the United States," manuscript, The Ohio State University.

[32] Wei, S.J. and D. Parsley (1995), "Purchasing Power Disparity During the Floating Rate Period: Exchange Rate Volatility, Trade Barriers and Other Culprits," *NBER Working Paper*: **5032**, February, 1995.

In: International Macroeconomics: Recent Developments
Editor: Amalia Morales Zumaquero, pp. 53-61

ISBN: 1-59454-901-X
© 2006 Nova Science Publishers, Inc.

Chapter 3

THE PURCHASING POWER PARITY PUZZLE IN DEVELOPING COUNTRIES

Mohsen Bahmani-Oskooee[1] and Taggert J. Brooks[2]

[1]Wilmeth Professor of Economics, The Center for Research on International Economics
and
The Department of Economics, University of Wisconsin-Milwaukee
[2]Assistant Professor of Economics, Department of Economics
University of Wisconsin-La Crosse

Abstract

Purchasing power parity (PPP) is one of the oldest theories of exchange rate determination that has received great deal of attention in the literature. The attention has grown even faster in more recent years due to advances in time series econometrics. Whether an old or a new method is applied in testing the PPP, its validity is not yet settled among researchers. In this chapter we make another attempt in testing the PPP for 20 developing countries by incorporating structural breaks into the testing procedure. We find support for the PPP in nine countries.

I Introduction

Attempts to establish the validity of Purchasing Power Parity (PPP) as a theory of exchange rate determination have a long history which continues to puzzle researchers. Neither time nor an abundance of empirical papers have been able to satisfactorily resolve the conflicting results reported in the literature. In this chapter we investigate two sources for the persistence of the puzzle. The first considers the empirical methods used and the second considers the measure of the real exchange rate used.

We employ Perron's (1997) test for a unit root that allows for a structural break in the data. The test is applied to the real effective exchange rate for 20 developing countries constructed and published by Bahmani-Oskooee and Mirzai (2000). Perron's technique represents an improvement over previous econometric techniques used to determine the validity of PPP. It offers a resolution to some of the contradictory evidence by allowing for the endogenous identification of departures from PPP by distinguishing between permanent departures (unit roots, mean shifts) and temporary departures. In addition, it will differentiate between permanent shifts in the underlying process from mere shifts in the trend.

The second source of difficulty when verifying the validity of PPP concerns the exchange rate used. We provide a discussion of the challenges and potential problems with using a constructed real exchange rate index. In particular we discuss the importance of selecting the base year when constructing the effective exchange rate indices. The rest of the chapter is organized as follows. In section II we discuss the PPP puzzle. Section III discusses the testing procedures for PPP with the importance of structural break identified in Section IV. The empirical results for developing countries are reported and discussed in Section V with index number problems in Section VI. Finally Section VII concludes.

II The PPP Puzzle

The search for verification of the Purchasing Power Parity (PPP) theory continues to puzzle researchers. While the first empirical investigation was done by Gustav Cassel in 1916[1] and repeated by many researchers after 1916, recent advances in time series methods cast doubt on the appropriateness and results of the older research. Armed with more appropriate time series techniques legions of researchers have taken up the challenge presented by this problem. Unfortunately, even with the recent resurgence in empirical work, little consensus has been established on the existence of PPP. In this chapter we investigate two related reasons for the persistence of the puzzle. The first considers the empirical methods used and the second considers the form of the real exchange rate used in the analysis.

Purchasing power parity's appeal as a theory of exchange rates can be explained by its' simple elegance. Derived from the law of one price and applied to a basket of goods it gives us a prediction for the nominal exchange rate which, if arbitrage is complete, should result in the exchange rate equaling the ratio of prices between countries. The real exchange rate should then be equal to 1 if PPP is to hold, which is often called absolute or strict PPP. A relaxed version of PPP, called weak or relative PPP doesn't require the real exchange rate to be one, but rather requires any changes in the relative price levels be proportional to changes in the nominal exchange rate. Therefore the real exchange rate will be constant, but not necessarily equal to one.

III Testing for PPP

Empirical tests of PPP have largely focused on the weaker version by testing the real exchange rate's deviations from its' mean, where permanent deviations from the mean are evidence that the exchange rate follows a unit root process and thus relative PPP fails to hold. The rapid innovation in time series methods which test for the existence of a unit root, (for a primer see Phillips & Xiao, 1998), is responsible for an explosion in research. However, the application of unit root tests to the PPP puzzle have so far failed to yield conclusive results,

---

[1] See (Rogoff, 1996)

although the picture is becoming clearer. The initial modern attempts to test the theory of PPP relied on a unit root test proposed by Dickey and Fuller (1979; 1981) where the null hypothesis is that the series contains a unit root. Unfortunately, it has been shown to have low power against the alternative, particularly in small samples; see for example Phillips and Perron (1988), Faust (1996), and Campbell and Perron (1991). Using the augmented Dickey Fuller (ADF) test several authors fail to reject the null and find little evidence in favor of PPP. This led Bahmani-Oskooee (1998), and Bahmani-Oskooee and Mirzai (2000), among others, to use an additional test suggested by Kwiatkowski, Phillips, Schmidt, and Shin (1992) known as KPSS which switches the null and alternative hypotheses of the ADF test. The results of these studies have perpetuated the puzzle, as the KPSS test suffers from its own power problems, often leading to conflicting results.

Overcoming the problems of low power resulted in attempts to increase the sample size, either through adding to the cross sectional dimension in a panel model or through increasing the time span of data. The increased number of observations along the time dimension helped overcome the low power problems, largely finding support for the PPP in the long run, thus overturning the results from smaller samples (see for example Abuaf & Jorion, 1990; Lothian & Taylor, 1996). Still other studies (Lothian, 1997; MacDonald, 1996; Oh, 1996) overcame the power problem by increasing the sample along the cross sectional dimension and employing panel unit root techniques. Here the initial results again supported PPP in the long run, but recent challenges have emerged due to the difficulty of handling the cross sectional dependence in panel models (O'Connell 1998).

Rogoff (1996) reviews the recent advances, but as evidence for PPP, he finds them lacking. He believes that the convergence to PPP takes too long to be considered a verification of the theory. Even after allowing for potential nominal frictions, as in the exchange rate overshooting model proposed by Dornbusch (1976), convergence to PPP takes more than twice as long as expected. Hegwood and Papell (1998) propose a solution to this puzzle by demonstrating the exchange rate process may be typified by structural breaks. After accounting for potential structure breaks they find convergence to PPP occurs at a rate consistent with Dornbusch's model.

IV PPP and Structural Breaks

Perron (1989) recognized that stationary series can masquerade as non-stationary if they experience a structural break. Perron (1989) alters the traditional ADF test to allow for a structural break(s) through the inclusion of time specific dummy variables selected by the researcher. Applying Perron's method to the Australian real effective exchange rate Corbae and Ouliaris (1991) fail to support PPP, even after allowing for structural breaks in 1922 and 1973. However, they find support for PPP when they use a bilateral exchange rate between Australia and the UK, using the same break dates. Still other authors using various methods to identify structural breaks in the exchange rate generally find support in favor of PPP (see for example Clemente, Montañés, & Ponz, 1999; Hegwood & Papell, 1998; Wu, 1997).

Unfortunately Perron's method gives little guidance on selecting the number and location of the break points. Dating them becomes arbitrary and dependant upon the particular researcher. In fact several authors (see for example Christiano, 1992; Zivot & Andrews, 1992) argued that Perron's method of exogenously determining the break point through data inspection, generates biased results, as it is invariably correlated with the data. Perron (1997), Christiano (1992), and Bai and Perron (1998) answered this problem with alternative methods of endogenously determining the break point.

Hegwood and Papell (1998), using the alternative method of Bai and Perron (1998) found many of the bilateral rates can be classified as stationary around one or more structural breaks. Using real bilateral exchange rates for the US against the rest of the G-7 they considered their findings a refutation of the PPP hypothesis even though the series is stationary. Since it is stationary around a mean which changes over time, they refer to it as Quasi Purchasing Power Parity (QPPP).

V PPP and Developing Countries

In most of the work done on PPP relatively little attention is given to developing countries (some notable exceptions Bahmani-Oskooee, 1993; Bahmani-Oskooee & Mirzai, 2000). In this section we apply a recent technique, proposed by Perron (1997), to the real effective exchange rate indices of 20 developing countries[2]. The data for the real effective exchange rates come from Table 1 in Bahmani-Oskooee and Mirzai (2000). They construct quarterly real effective exchange rate indices from 1973:1 to 1997:3[3] The real effective exchange rate for home country j is constructed according to equation 1.

$$\sum_{i=1}^{n} \alpha_{ji} \left(\frac{(P_j R_{ji}/P_i)_t}{(P_j R_{ji}/P_i)_{95}} \times 100 \right)$$

(1)

Where n is the number of trading partners and P_j is the price level in home country j and P_i is the price level in trading partner i. The nominal exchange rate, R, is defined as the number of units of i's currency per unit of j's currency. Therefore an increase in the index indicates a real appreciation of country j's currency. The trade shares, α_{ji}, are based upon the 1995 import shares from trade between country j, and countries i, where i represents: Australia, Austria, Belgium, Canada, Denmark, Finland, France, Germany, Ireland, Italy, Japan, Netherlands, New Zealand, Norway Spain, Sweden, Switzerland, UK and the US.

Following Bahmani-Oskooee and Mirzai (2000) we first test each series for unit root using the KPSS test. Table 1 reports the results for the ε_τ test where the null is trend stationary[4].

---

[2]The countries included were: Colombia, Costa Rica, Ecuador, Egypt, Greece, India, Indonesia, Korea, Malaysia, Mexico, Pakistan, Philippines, Portugal, Singapore, South Africa, Srilanka, Thailand, Tunisia, Turkey, Ethiopia

[3] Except Ethiopia which ends with 1996:3

[4] Results for the ε_μ test for mean stationarity are available from the authors upon request.

Table 1: KPSS Test ε_τ

Colombia	0.247*
Costa Rica	0.346*
Ecuador	0.290*
Egypt	0.495*
Greece	0.349*
India	0.170*
Indonesia	0.210*
Korea	0.094
Malaysia	0.119
Mexico	0.266*
Pakistan	0.073
Philippines	0.167*
Portugal	0.366*
Singapore	0.128
South Africa	0.094
Srilanka	0.402*
Thailand	0.112
Tunisia	0.264*
Turkey	0.239*
Ethiopia	0.357*

Notes: Source: Author's calculations using the KPSS test with 4 lags
Data: (Bahmani-Oskooee & Mirzai, 2000) 1973:1-1997:3
Critical Values: 1% 0.216; 5% 0.146; 10% 0.119

It is clear from Table 1 that most of the series can not be considered stationary around a linear trend. There are 6 cases, including Korea, Malaysia, Pakistan, Singapore, South Africa, and Thailand where we can not reject the null hypothesis of stationarity around a linear trend. Combining these results with those of the ADF test in Bahmani-Oskooee and Mirzaie (2000), we have good evidence of stationarity for Korea, Pakistan, and Singapore, leaving us to puzzle over Malaysia, South Africa, and Thailand.

Returning to the results of the KPSS test, in 14 of the cases, using 4 as the lag truncation parameter, we can reject the null hypothesis of trend stationarity. However, as we previously noted, this is not necessarily evidence in favor of the unit root hypothesis as the series may contain a structural break. In order to test for this possibility we turn to the method proposed by Perron (1997). It is similar to the Dickey -Fuller test and involves estimating:

$$y_t = \alpha y_{t-1} + \mu + \theta DU_t + \beta t + \delta D(T_b)_t + \sum_{i=1}^{k} c_i \Delta y_{t-i} + e_t$$

(2)

Where y is the series of interest and T_b is the date of the structural break. Perron (1997) provides three methods for selecting the break date. We use the method which involves maximizing the t-statistic used to test $\alpha = 1$. The other methods focus on choosing the break point that maximizes the t-statistic on the intercept break point or the slope break point. Since we choose a model where both the slope and intercept are allowed to change, neither of the alternative methods provide us with an obvious choice between testing the intercept or testing the slope. Once the break date is selected, the test reduces to the traditional ADF test, where a rejection of the null hypothesis suggests that the series is stationary around a structural break. The results of this step are reported in Table 2.

Table 2: Perron's Test

Country	t alpha (k)
Colombia	-3.97 (6)
Costa Rica	-10.92(9)*
Ecuador	-6.76(1)*
Egypt	-6.00(7)*
Greece	-5.80(4)*
India	-3.84(12)
Indonesia	-6.88(11)*
Korea	-6.29(7)*
Malaysia	-5.02(12)
Mexico	-5.84(0)*
Pakistan	-3.99(9)
Philippines	-5.14(2)
Portugal	-4.77(7)
Singapore	-4.92(4)
South Africa	-4.46(3)
Srilanka	-6.78(12)*
Thailand	-4.41(2)
Tunisia	-6.03(4)*
Turkey	-4.10(0)
Ethiopia	-4.57(11)

Source: Author's calculations using 12 as the maximum lags
Data: Bahmani-Oskooee and Mirzai (2000) 1973:1-1997:3
Critical values for 100 observations at 5% -5.55
* Reject the unit root null at 5%

From Table 2 we gather that in nine of the cases, including: Costa Rica, Ecuador, Egypt, Greece, Indonesia, Korea, Mexico, Srilanka, and Tunisia where the KPSS test provided good evidence against stationarity, we can reject the hypothesis of a unit root, after we allow for a structural break. Following Hegwood and Papell (1998) we refer to this as Quasi Purchasing Power Parity. In fact, since we include a linear trend in our test this is even further from the traditional concept of relative PPP than their work. In their case the exchange rate reverts to a shifting mean, whereas in our case both the mean and slope are changing. Including a shifting mean and trend may help to account for the impact that productivity differentials have on the exchange rate as noted by Balassa (1964).[5] The trend may capture the difference in productivity growth rates between the developing countries and their developed trading partners.

Looking at the break dates selected by Perron's test 11 of them lie between the fourth quarter of 1984 and the third quarter of 1985. As Hegwood and Papell (1998) noted this roughly coincides with the Plaza Accord, a time when the real value of the US dollar was quite high relative to its' recent value. There are many other reasons that may explain the structural breaks, such as a change in trade barriers, or a shift in transportation costs. Another reason could be the exchange rate that we use. As Corbae and Ouliaris (1991) note, a non-stationary effective exchange rate index can disguise a stationary bilateral exchange rate.

VI Index Number Problems

The index number problem is not new, and not particular to tests of PPP, but it is worth noting. The real exchange rate consists of two price indices which represent both domestic and foreign prices. It is clear that these indices likely do not contain the same goods or the same relative weights, and they often include non-tradables. Rogoff (1996) discusses the difficulty with testing PPP using these measures, and the attempts to overcome the problem. The problem is potentially more serious when using effective exchange rates as it creates still another index.

While employing effective exchange rate indices can be extremely useful in capturing international relative prices, care must be used. In Bahmani-Oskooee and Mirzai (2000) they choose the trade shares in 1995. Fixing the trade shares, as with any Laspeyres index, results in a substitution bias. If the US dollar rapidly appreciates against the Indian rupee, the share of India's imports from the US is likely to fall, however the exchange rate index will not capture this. This phenomenon may be exactly what the structural break tests detect. Since 1995 saw the dollar at historically low values against other currencies, and 1984 historically high, the break may not have been a break at all. It may simply be a failure to measure the obvious substitution that must have occurred.

There are several studies, (see for example Bahmani-Oskooee, 1993; Bahmani-Oskooee, 1998; Bahmani-Oskooee & Mirzai, 2000) that utilize real effective exchange rates to test PPP and several others also account for potential structural breaks (Clemente et al., 1999; Corbae & Ouliaris, 1991; Wu, 1997).

VII Conclusions

In this chapter we highlighted the progress made in the empirical methods applied to the PPP puzzle. Newer techniques allow us, in many cases, to find periods of stationary exchange rate fluctuations for the effective exchange rate. This predictability leads us to reject PPP in favor of a new variant called Quasi-PPP.

---

[5] For more on PPP and productivity differentials see Bahmani-Oskooee (1992) and Bahmani-Oskooee and Nasir (2001, 2002).

The failure to find conclusive empirical results in favor of traditional PPP isn't such a puzzle. Exchange rates shocks have a long memory, too long to be explained by nominal rigidities. However, allowing for structural breaks reduces the length of time the remaining shocks persist, resulting in something more accordant with Dornbusch's (1976) overshooting hypothesis. The structural breaks are most likely the result of large real shocks which frequently buffet the economy. This includes changes in trade policies, acceleration or deceleration of productivity growth rates, all of which have consequences for exchange rate. These factors conspire against finding consistent evidence in favor of PPP.

References

[1] Abuaf, N., & Jorion, P. (1990). Purchasing Power Parity in the Long Run. *Journal of Finance,* **45**(1), 157-174.

[2] Bahmani-Oskooee, M. (1992). A Time-Series Approach to Test the Productivity Bias Hypothesis in Purchasing Power Parity. *Kyklos,* **45**(2), 227-236.

[3] Bahmani-Oskooee, M. (1993). Purchasing Power Parity Based on Effective Exchange Rate and Cointegration: 25 LDCs' Experience with its Absolute Formulation. *World Development,* **21**(6), 1023-1031.

[4] Bahmani-Oskooee, M. (1998). Do Exchange Rates Follow a Random Walk Process in Middle Eastern Countries? *Economics Letters,* **58**(3), 339-344.

[5] Bahmani-Oskooee, M., & Mirzai, A. (2000). Real and Nominal Effective Exchange Rates for Developing Countries: 1973:1-1997:3. *Applied Economics,* **32**(4), 411-428.

[6] Bahmani-Oskooee, M., & Nasir, A. (2001). Panel Data and Productivity Bias Hypothesis. *Economic Development and Cultural Change,* **49**(2), 395-402.

[7] Bahmani-Oskooee, M., & Nasir, A. (2002). Corruption, Law and Order, Bureaucracy and Real Exchange Rate. *Economic Development and Cultural Change,* **50**(4), 1021-1028.

[8] Bai, J., & Perron, P. (1998). Estimating and Testing Linear Models with Multiple Structural Changes. *Econometrica,* **66**(1), 47-78.

[9] Balassa, Bela (1964). The Purchasing-Power Parity Doctrine: A Reappraisal. *Journal of Political Economy,* **72**(6), 584-96.

[10] Campbell, J. Y., & Perron, P. (1991). Pitfalls and Opportunities: What Macroeconomists Should Know about Unit Roots. In O. J. Blanchard & S. e. Fischer (Eds.), *NBER macroeconomics annual* **1991**.

[11] Christiano, L. J. (1992). Searching for a Break in GNP. *Journal of Business and Economic Statistics,* **10**(3), 237-250.

[12] Clemente, J., Montanes, A., & Ponz, M. (1999). Are Real Effective Exchange Rates Stationary? Evidence for OECD Countries. *Konjunkturpolitik,* **45**(3), 258-271.

[13] Corbae, D., & Ouliaris, S. (1991). A Test of Long-Run Purchasing Power Parity Allowing for Structural Breaks. *Economic Record,* **67**(196), 26-33.

[14] Dickey, D. A., & Fuller, W. (1979). Distribution of the Estimators for Autoregressive Time Series with a Unit Root. *Journal of the American Statistical Association,* **74**(366), 427-431.

[15] Dickey, D. A., & Fuller, W. A. (1981). Likelihood Ratio Statistics for Autoregressive Time Series with a Unit Root. *Econometrica,* **49**(4), 1057-1072.

[16] Dornbusch, R. (1976). Expectations and Exchange Rate Dynamics. *Journal of Political Economy,* **84**(6), 1161-1176.

[17] Faust, J. (1996). Near Observational Equivalence and Theoretical Size Problems with Unit Root Tests. *Econometric Theory,* **12**(4), 724-731.

[18] Hegwood, N. D., & Papell, D. H. (1998). Quasi Purchasing Power Parity. *International Journal of Finance and Economics,* **3**(4), 279-289.

[19] Kwiatkowski, D., Phillips, P. C. B., Schmidt, P., & Shin, Y. (1992). Testing the Null Hypothesis of Stationarity against the Alternative of a Unit Root: How Sure Are We That Economic Time Series Have a Unit Root? *Journal of Econometrics,* **54**(1-3), 159-178.

[20] Lothian, J. R. (1997). Multi-country Evidence on the Behavior of Purchasing Power Parity under the Current Float. *Journal of International Money and Finance,* **16**(1), 19-35.

[21] Lothian, J. R., & Taylor, M. P. (1996). Real Exchange Rate Behavior: The Recent Float from the Perspective of the Past Two Centuries. *Journal of Political Economy,* **104**(3), 488-509.

[22] MacDonald, R. (1996). Panel Unit Root Tests and Real Exchange Rates. *Economics Letters,* **50**(1), 7-11.

[23] O'Connell, P. G. J. (1998). The Overvaluation of Purchasing Power Parity. *Journal of International Economics,* **44**(1), 1-19.

[24] Oh, K.-Y. (1996). Purchasing Power Parity and Unit Root Tests Using Panel Data. *Journal of International Money and Finance,* **15**(3), 405-418.

[25] Perron, P. (1989). The Great Crash, the Oil Price Shock, and the Unit Root Hypothesis. *Econometrica,* **57**(6), 1361-1401.

[26] Perron, P. (1997). Further Evidence on Breaking Trend Functions in Macroeconomic Variables. *Journal of Econometrics,* **80**(2), 355-385.

[27] Phillips, P. C. B., & Perron, P. (1988). Testing for a Unit Root in Time Series Regression. *Biometrika,* **75**, 335-346.

[28] Phillips, P. C. B., & Xiao, Z. (1998). A Primer on Unit Root Testing. *Journal of Economic Surveys,* **12**(5), 423-469.

[29] Rogoff, K. (1996). The Purchasing Power Parity Puzzle. *Journal of Economic Literature,* **34**(2), 647-668.

[30] Wu, Y. (1997). The Trend Behavior of Real Exchange Rates: Evidence from OECD Countries. *Weltwirtschaftliches Archiv,* **133**(2), 282-296.

[31] Zivot, E., & Andrews, D. W. K. (1992). Further Evidence on the Great Crash, the Oil-Price Shock, and the Unit-Root Hypothesis. *Journal of Business and Economic Statistics,* **10**(3), 251-270.

In: International Macroeconomics: Recent Developments
Editor: Amalia Morales Zumaquero, pp. 63-78

ISBN: 1-59454-901-X
© 2006 Nova Science Publishers, Inc.

Chapter 4

LONG-RUN PURCHASING POWER PARITY FOR THE JAPANESE YEN: NEW STATIONARITY TESTS WITH BREAKS FOR REAL ASIAN AND MAJOR CURRENCIES

Raj Aggarwal[1], Antonio Montañés[2] and Monserrat Ponz[2+]*
[1] Firestone Professor, BSA 434, Kent State University, Kent, OH 44242
[2] Department of Economic Analysis, University of Zaragoza (Spain)

Abstract

Recent literature has found conflicting results regarding the validity of PPP for the Japanese Yen. This paper uses more recent data and improved statistical procedures that account for outliers and allow for structural breaks in unit root tests to assess if PPP holds between the Japanese Yen and other Asian and major world currencies. In contrast to some prior literature, our tests for the period 1974-2000 find strong support for PPP between the Japanese Yen and other Asian and world currencies.

I   Introduction

In a recent paper, Aggarwal, Montañés and Ponz (2000) (AMP hereafter) have offered evidence in favour of the Purchasing Power Parity (PPP hereafter) hypothesis analysed for the Japanese Yen and a group of South-east Asian currencies. These authors show that the unit root null hypothesis is not supported empirically by the data for these currencies. This result is important in that it can also be interpreted as additional evidence for the existence of a 'Yen bloc', as suggested in Aggarwal and Mougoué (1997, 1998) and in Tse and Ng (1996). AMP reject the unit root null hypothesis for the Japanese Yen real exchange rates for the currencies

---

[*] E-mail address: amontane@posta.unizar.es, Phone: +34 +976 76 22 21, fax: +34 +976 76 19 96. Corresponding Address: Departamento de Análisis Económico. Facultad de Ciencias Económicas y Empresariales, Gran Vía, 2. 50005 Zaragoza (Spain).
[+] The authors are thankful to their colleagues for useful comments but remain solely responsible for the contents.

of the following South-East Asian countries: Indonesia, Malaysia, Philippines, Singapore, Sri Lanka and Thailand. The results for another very important Southeast Asian economy, Korea, are not so conclusive. Finally, the AMP evidence for the major non-Asian currencies, the USA dollar and the German Mark mainly, does not support the PPP hypothesis. According to these AMP results, the existence of a, so-called, Yen bloc with the South-east Asian currencies seems to be well supported by the data whilst, by contrast, there is not much evidence in favour of a linkage between these currencies and those of the major economies, USA and European countries.

The aim of this paper is to offer further evidence on the behaviour of the Japanese real exchange rate, focusing the analysis on the verification of the PPP hypothesis. There exist several reasons for this study. First, the sample used in AMP ends in 1998. Thus, AMP and many other prior studies do not take into account the events that have continued to shake and impact the South-east Asian and global financial markets after this date; such as the global impact of the currency crises in Russia and Latin America in the late 1990s or the major restructurings, devaluations, and other IMF programs in the aftermath of the 1997 economic and political crises in Southeast Asia (e.g., Bank for International Settlements Annual Report, 2000). Furthermore, recent studies have shown that most of the Asian countries have changed their exchange rate policies during and after these late 1990s crises, abandoning the *de facto* dollar peg and embracing a deeper relationship with the Japanese Yen[1]. Taking into account all these changes, it seems advisable and useful to extend the period of study by including new and more recent observations in order to verify if these movements have caused a failure in the PPP hypothesis or, by contrast, if they have increased the evidence on its favour.

A second reason for new research in this area is the development of new and improved statistical procedures for testing the unit root null hypothesis that offer significant advances on the statistical procedures used in AMP and other prior studies of this topic. For example, Ng and Perron (2001) have recently proposed useful modifications to some unit root tests, which lead to a notable gain in efficiency and power and allow for structural breaks in the data. Furthermore, Cati et al. (1999) show that some of these statistics perform well in circumstances where the variable being studied is affected by the presence of outliers. As noted elsewhere and confirmed by the analysis of outliers in this paper, the post 1997 period was characterized by significantly increased exchange rate volatility in the Southeast Asia region.

Finally, it is now being contended that the East Asian currencies were overvalued before the 1997 crises (Chinn, 2000), and that for the period 1973-98, PPP does not hold for Asian and less developed country currencies (Holmes, 2001). In contrast, other recent research using quarterly data from 1977-97 contends that PPP does hold between the Japanese and other Asian currencies (Azali et al, 2001). Thus, in view of these mixed and conflicting results, it seems appropriate to use recent data and these new and improved statistical procedures to determine if PPP holds for the Japanese Yen relative to other Asian and global currencies.

Using more recent data (for 1974-2000) for an expanded set of currencies and improved statistical procedures, this paper helps resolve this controversy in the literature as it documents that PPP does hold between the Japanese Yen and other Asian and world

---

[1] In this regard, see Fukuda (2002) or Kawai and Akiyama (2000) who study the movements of the Asian exchange rates during the crisis.

currencies. In this paper, the real Japanese Yen is assessed with respect to the regional currencies, the Australian and New Zealand Dollars, Indian and Sri Lanka Rupees, Indonesian Rupiah, Korean Won, Malaysian Ringgit, Philippines Peso, Singapore Dollar, and the Thailand Bhat; and the major global currencies, the US Dollar and the German Mark.

The rest of the paper is organised as follows. The next section briefly reviews empirical evidence for PPP. Section 3 presents the unit root tests that we have used in the empirical section including the improved statistical procedures based on Generalized Least Squares (GLS) estimation that provide significant improvements over the traditional unit roots tests (Ng and Perron, 2001). Section 4 presents the results of the application of these statistics to the analysis of the integration order of the Japanese Yen real exchange rate versus a group of Asian and non-Asian currencies. Finally, some conclusions end the paper in Section 5.

2   Empirical Evidence on Purchasing Power Parity

Prior literature indicates that there seems to be fairly clear evidence that real exchange rates, i.e., exchange rates adjusted for international differences in inflation rates, tend towards purchasing power parity in the very long run. However, the speed of adjustment seems to be low and there are significant short and medium term deviations from purchasing power parity. Indeed, short-term deviations from PPP are large and volatile with one-month conditional volatility of real exchange rates being of the same order of magnitude as the volatility of nominal exchange rates (e.g., Rogoff, 1996). Most explanations of this short-term volatility of real exchange rates point to monetary and asset price shocks with sticky wages and prices. Mussa (1986) shows that real exchange rates should be much less volatile under floating exchange rates, but recent studies document that the real exchange rate seems to be more volatile under floating exchange rates than under fixed exchange rates. Thus, much empirical work on real exchange rates, including unit root and cointegration tests, has failed to reject the random walk in real exchange rates, i.e., it was difficult to prove any convergence towards PPP (for details see, for example, Rogoff 1996). This failure to find support for the PPP has been inconsistent with most theory and particularly embarrassing for the periods when exchange rates were floating.

Using data from 1869-1984 covering both fixed and floating exchange rate periods, Frankel (1990) was able to reject the random walk hypothesis for real exchange rates using standard Dickey-Fuller tests of unit roots. These results in favour of the PPP have been confirmed for other time periods and for larger groups of countries by others such as Abuaf and Jorion (1990), Lothian (1997), and Cheung and Lai (1998).

Most prior studies of PPP have examined US dollar exchange rates for large groups of countries that have included the major economies. In contrast, this paper focuses on Japanese Yen exchange rates.[2] As indicated above, there seems to be some controversy in prior literature regarding PPP for the Japanese Yen. For example, using data for the period 1973-98 Holmes (2001) finds that PPP does not hold for Asian and less developed country currencies. In contrast, other recent research using quarterly data from 1977-97 contends that PPP does hold between the Japanese and other Asian currencies (Azali et al, 2001). AMP (2000) using

---

[2] Such studies also have implications for regional currency blocs in Asia (e.g., Bayoumi and Mauro, 2001).

real exchange rate data for 1974-1998 for Asian currencies with strong economic ties to Japan also find support for PPP for the Japanese Yen.

However, these prior studies of the Japanese Yen do not use recent data and, as indicated above, there have been many important developments in the late 1990s affecting Asian currencies. For example, there have been a number of changes in Asian exchange rate regimes following the Asian currency and economic crises in the late 1990s - the crises started in July 1997 with major drops in successive Asian currencies and economic growth rates (Hunter, Kaufman and Krueger, 1999). The subsequent recoveries are still in process in 2003. These crises in Asia were followed by other crises in Latin America and Russia in the late 1990s that had global impacts (e.g., Bank for International Settlements Annual Report, 2000). Furthermore, recent studies have shown that most of the Asian countries have changed their exchange rate policies during and after these late 1990s crises, abandoning the de facto dollar peg and embracing a deeper relationship with the Japanese Yen (e.g., Fukuda 2002, Kawai and Akiyama 2000). Thus, it seems to be appropriate to use more recent data and new and improved statistical procedures to determine if PPP holds for the Japanese Yen.

3   Unit Roots Tests, Temporary Changes and Level Shifts

In order to determine the integration order of the Japanese Yen real exchange rate we can use a great number of statistics. The most common way to carry out this analysis is by way of testing the unit root null hypothesis for the real exchange rate. If we cannot reject the unit root null hypothesis, we should interpret this as evidence against the PPP hypothesis. By contrast, if we cannot accept the unit root hypothesis, this claim would be in favour of the PPP hypothesis.

We note here that there exists a wide range of statistics for testing the unit root hypothesis available to us. A first approach would be the use of the Dickey-Fuller family of tests, Dickey and Fuller (1979), Said and Dickey (1984). These statistics are obtained from the estimation of the following model:

$$\Delta y_t = d_t + \beta_o\, y_{t-1} + \sum_{i=1}^{k} \beta_i\, \Delta y_{t-i} + \varepsilon_t$$

$$(1)$$

where d_t reflects the deterministic elements considered[3]. Later, we should calculate the pseudo t-ratio for testing whether the autoregressive parameter is 1, which is equivalent to test for the single significance of β_o in [1].

A second approach is originally proposed in Phillips and Perron (1988), but Ng and Perron (1996) have recently proposed useful modifications of these statistics. These can be defined, for the no deterministic element case, as follows:

$$MZ_{\square} = \left(T^{-1} y_T^2 - s_{AR}^2 \right) \left(2 T^{-2} \sum_{t=1}^{T} y_{t-1}^2 \right)^{-1}$$

---

[3] In the empirical application, we will always consider a specification that includes an intercept but not a deterministic trend.

$$MSB = \sqrt{\frac{T^{-2} \sum\limits_{t=1}^{T} y_{t-1}^2}{s_{AR}^2}}$$

and $MZ_t = MZ_\square MSB$. These three statistics, which are modifications of those proposed in Phillips and Perron (1988) and Sargan and Bhargava (1983), respectively, are based on the use of the autoregressive estimate of the spectral density at the frequency zero, which is defined as follows:

$$s_{AR}^2 = \frac{\hat{\sigma}_k^2}{\left[1 - \hat{\beta}(1)\right]^2}$$

with $\hat{\sigma}_k^2 = (T-k)^{-1} \sum_{t=k+1}^{T} \hat{e}_{tk}$ and $\hat{\beta}(1) = \sum_{i=1}^{k} \hat{\beta}_i$ where both of them obtained from the estimation of (1). Ng and Perron (1995, 2001) show that the selection of an adequate value of the parameter k is essential in order to improve the properties of the tests.

Elliot, Rothenberg and Stock (1996) derived the feasible point optimal PP tests. This statistic is based on the GLS de-trending of the variable being studied and the Monte Carlo simulations show that this test exhibits a great gain in power versus those based on OLS de-trending methods.

As we can see, the keys for improving the properties of the tests are an appropriate method for removing the deterministic elements, as well as an adequate selection of the value of k. Ng and Perron (2001) have combined the GLS de-trending method with a new information criterion, mic, in order to obtain statistics with desirable power and properties (we will use these statistics in our empirical estimates).

The use of these unit root tests will be complemented by the use of the tests employed in AMP (2000). These statistics improve the unit root tests considered up to this point as they allow for the presence of some structural breaks. Following Perron (1989, 1990), these tests can be obtained from the estimation of the following equation

$$y_t = \mu + \sum_{i=1}^{n} d_i DTB_{it} + \sum_{i=1}^{n} \delta_i DU_{it} + \rho y_{t-1} + \sum_{i=1}^{k} c_i \Delta y_{t-i} + \varepsilon_t \tag{2}$$

where $DU_{it} = 1$ if $t > TB_i$ and $DTB_{it} = 1$ if $t = TB_i$ and 0 otherwise. With $i=1,2,...n$, TB_i is the parameter that controls the period where the break appears. Once we have estimated this equation we have two different ways to test for the existence of a unit root in the variable y_t. First, it is possible to test the single null hypothesis H_o: $\rho=1$ by constructing a simple pseudo t-ratio, with the distribution of this statistic derived and tabulated in Perron and Vogelsang (1992) and Clemente et al. (1998), for respectively, $n=1$ and $n=2$. It is also possible to test for the joint null hypothesis H_o: $\rho=1$; $\delta_1=\delta_2=...=\delta_n=0$ by way of a pseudo F-ratio, hereafter referred to as max Φ_n, where the sub-index n indicates the number of breaks included in the empirical model. As AMP offers further discussion on the use of these tests, such discussion is omitted here[4].

4 Empirical Results

In this Section, we present the results of tests for the integration order of the real exchange rate between the Japanese currency and the currencies of the following Southeast Asian countries: Indonesia, Korea, Malaysia, Philippines, Singapore, Sri Lanka and Thailand. We also include the U.S. Dollar and the German Mark as representatives of the most important western economies and the Indian Rupee, Australian Dollar, and New Zealand Dollar as other major currencies in the region. The Consumer Price Index (CPI) and the Produced Price Index (PPI) have both (when available) been used as measures of inflation in this analysis. We have used quarterly data from the International Financial Statistics. The data cover the period 1974:1-2000:4[5] for most of the countries. However, we should note that for India, Indonesia, Malaysia and Sri Lanka the sample ends in 2000:3 when prices are measured by the CPI.

First, we think that it is advisable to begin this study by carrying out an analysis of outliers. This would help us assess if changes in the evolution of the various real exchange rates is a reasonable hypothesis. Another reason to do this analysis is that it is very well known in the time series literature that the omission of these changes may distort the results obtained when testing for unit roots. We have carried out this analysis using the SEATS/TRAMO programme[6], which allows for an automatic determination of both the most appropriate ARIMA model and the number and type of outliers. This programme considers three different types of outliers: additive outlier (AO), level shifts (LS) and temporary change (TC). The main difference between them has to do with the duration of their effect. An additive outlier has an influence limited to a single period. A level shift shows a permanent effect on the evolution of the variable being studied; and finally, a temporary change exhibits a hybrid performance, in the sense that it does not have a permanent effect, but its effect lasts more than a single period. The results that we have obtained are reported in Table 1.

Table 1. Analysis of outliers

Country	ARIMA model	Outliers detected		ARIMA model	Outliers detected	
	Prices measured by CPI			Prices measured by PPI		
AUSTRALIA	(0,1,1)(0,0,0)	TC	1986:3	(0,1,1)(0,0,0)	AO	1986:3
		TC	1995:2		TC	1995:2
GERMANY	(1,1,0)(0,0,0)	AO	1993:1	(1,1,0)(0,0,0)	AO	1993:1
		TC	1995:2			
INDIA	(0,1,1)(0,0,0)	LS	1991:3	(0,1,1)(0,0,0)	LS	1991:3
		LS	1993:2		TC	1993:2
		AO	1995:2		AO	1995:2
		AO	1998:3		LS	1998:4

---

[4] In this regard, see also Gadea et al. (2002).
[5] For reasons of data availability, the PPI for Indonesia and Sri Lanka covers the sample 1980:1-1997:4
[6] For further information on this programme, readers are referred to Gómez and Maravall (1992).

Country	ARIMA model	Outliers detected	ARIMA model	Outliers detected
INDONESIA	(0,1,1)(0,1,1)	LS 1983:1 TC 1998:1 AO 1998:4		
KOREA	(0,1,1)(0,0,0)	AO 1998:1	(0,1,1)(0,0,0)	LS 1997:4 AO 1998:1
PHILLIPINES	(0,1,1)(0,0,0)	AO 1983:4 TC 1990:4 AO 1995:2	(0,1,1)(0,0,0)	AO 1983:4 TC 1995:2 TC 1998:2
MALAYSIA	(0,1,1)(0,0,0)	AO 1988:3 AO 1994:1 AO 1995:2 TC 1997:1 TC 1998:2 AO 1999:4		
NEW ZEALAND	(0,1,1)(0,0,0)	AO 1986:3 AO 1995:2 LS 1998:4	(0,1,0)(0,1,1)	TC 1986:3 TC 1984:3 AO 1995:2 TC 1986:1
SINGAPOUR	(0,1,1)(0,0,0)	AO 1983:4 TC 1990:4 AO 1995:2	(0,1,1)(0,0,0)	TC 1988:4 AO 1987:3 AO 1993:1 TC 1995:2 AO 1998:1
SRI LANKA	(0,1,1)(0,0,0)	LS 1977:4 TC 1995:2	(0,1,1)(0,0,0)	LS 1980:4 TC 1998:2
THAILAND	(0,1,1)(0,0,0)	AO 1984:3 AO 1987:2 AO 1988:3 AO 1995:2 LS 1997:3 LS 1998:2 LS 1999:3 AO 1999:4	(0,1,1)(0,0,0)	AO 1995:2 LS 1997:3 LS 1998:2 TC 2000:1
USA	(0,1,1)(0,0,0)	TC 1995:2 LS 1998:4	(0,1,1)(0,0,0)	TC 1995:2

This Table reflects the outliers found when the SEATS/TRAMO methodology is employed. The ARIMA model column presents the ARIMA model automatically selected by this methodology, whilst the column Outliers detected reports the outlier type and the period when they are found. LS, AO and TC means Level Shifts, Additive Outlier and Temporary Change, respectively.

From this Table we can see that all of the real exchange rates examined here exhibit the presence of al least one outlier. We have 39 outliers for the CPI-based real exchange rates, whilst only 27 outliers are detected when prices are measured by PPI (although we should note that we do not have available information on the PPI in Malaysia and Indonesia). We can also see that most of these outliers do not show a permanent effect: we have only found 9 level shifts for the CPI case and 6 for the PPI. Furthermore, nearly a quarter of the outliers are associated with the post-1997 period but most of them are additive outliers. Thus, an important insight that emerges from the analysis of this Table is that the recent crisis has not implied a structural change in the PPP equilibrium, in the sense that it has only caused transitory movements in the real exchange rates of the Asian currencies versus the Japanese Yen.

Finally, we should note that all the ARIMA models automatically selected imply the need of taking first differences of the variables. This should be considered as preliminary evidence against the PPP hypothesis, in that the real exchanges rates are being characterised as non-stationary variables. However, we should also note that the presence of these outliers may distort the results. Moreover, we can also see that most of the ARIMA models that have been selected are ARIMA(0,1,1). Thus, it is quite possible that the selection of this type of model has been caused by an over-differentiation of the variables. In order to verify the correct integration order of these variables, we should use the new statistics presented in Section 2 and test for the unit root null hypothesis, given that these statistics show good properties under the presence of negative moving average roots.

Table 2. Testing for unit roots. No breaks allowed

	MZ_α	MZ_τ	MSB	M PT	DF^{GLS}	ADF
Panel A. Prices measured by CPI						
AUSTRALIA	-0.18	-0.09	0.51	19.23	0.01	-1.22
GERMANY	-0.13	-0.06	0.45	16.31	-0.10	-1.45
NEW ZEALAND	0.35	0.17	0.48	19.13	0.17	-1.55
USA	-2.34	-0.96	0.41	9.75	-0.96	-1.80
INDIA	0.31	0.22	0.73	35.41	0.07	-1.54
INDONESIA	0.61	0.40	0.65	31.15	0.33	-0.74
KOREA	-2.63	-0.92	0.35	8.48	-0.83	-1.51
MALAYSIA	0.49	0.33	0.68	32.70	0.27	-1.13
PHILIPPINES	-0.12	-0.07	0.55	21.47	-0.16	-1.47
SINGAPORE	-0.61	-0.34	0.55	19.08	-0.36	-1.94
SRI LANKA	-0.23	-0.16	0.70	29.20	-0.22	-2.58
THAILAND	0.63	0.38	0.61	28.40	0.30	-1.11
Panel B. Prices measured by PPI						
AUSTRALIA	-6.77^c	-1.60	0.24^c	4.43	-1.12	-1.37
GERMANY	-6.52^c	-1.45	0.22^b	4.89	-1.50	-1.64
NEW ZEALAND	-8.13^b	-1.72^c	0.21^b	4.10^c	-1.80^c	-2.10
USA	-9.29^b	-2.14^b	0.23^b	2.69^b	-2.07^b	-2.27
INDIA	0.01	-0.72	0.63	26.12	0.16	-1.25
KOREA	-2.60	0.95	0.37	8.67	0.96	-1.13
PHILIPPINES	-8.75^b	-1.77^c	0.20^b	3.98^c	-1.86^c	-1.98
SINGAPORE	-1.92	0.78	0.41	10.63	0.79	-1.55
SRI LANKA	-2.06	-0.85	0.41	10.39	-1.01	-4.69
THAILAND	0.06	0.03	0.47	17.74	0.10	-1.20

[a], [b] and [c] mean rejection of the unit root null hypothesis at the 10%, 5% and 1% significance level, respectively

Table 2 reports the results for the case that does not include a break in the model specification. We present the statistics discussed in Section 2, as well as the traditional Said-Dickey statistic. The analysis of the results presented in this table leads us to some very rich insights. First, we can see that the unit root null hypothesis has a great amount of support when prices are measured by CPI. This generally does not occur for PPI-based real exchange rates (we do observe only mild evidence against the non-PPP hypothesis for Australia and Sri Lanka but the evidence is much more robust for the German mark, New Zealander dollar, Philippine peso and the USA dollar). The result for the USA dollar is extremely important in that we have found strong evidence on the interconnection between the American and the Japanese exchange rates, a result that could receive only mild support in AMP (2000). For the rest of the cases, there is no evidence against the non-PPP hypothesis. Moreover, it is surprising that MZ_α^{GLS}, MZ_t^{GLS} and DF^{GLS} statistics take positive values for some currencies. This result should be interpreted by considering that the autoregressive parameter is greater than 1 in these cases, which would imply that these real exchange rates show explosive behaviour. We doubt that this kind of behaviour is possible for these currencies and it is more likely that this result is caused by a misspecification problem. If we account for the results of our outlier analysis, we can conclude that the omission of changes such as structural breaks is inflating the value of the estimated autoregressive parameter. Thus, in order to solve these problems, we should test the unit root null hypothesis allowing for the presence of some breaks in the evolution of the real exchange rates.

Table 3. Testing for unit roots under the presence of a single structural break

| | Panel A. H_o: $\rho=1$ | | Panel B. H_o: $\rho=1$, $d_1=0$ | |
	min t_ρ	TB_1	max Φ_1	TB_1
Panel A. Prices measured by CPI				
AUSTRALIA	-3.74	84:3	7.09	84:3
GERMANY	-2.98	79:4	5.37	98:2
NEW ZEALAND	-2.90	89:4	5.65	98:2
USA	-4.19[b]	84:4	8.99	84:4
INDIA	-3.84[c]	85:2	7.41	85:2
INDONESIA	-3.00	85:2	4.72	85:2
KOREA	-4.28[b]	84:4	9.33	84:4
MALAYSIA	-4.30[b]	85:2	9.52	85:2
PHILLIPINES	-5.48[a]	85:2	15.16[a]	85:2
SINGAPOUR	-4.82[b]	85:2	11.63[c]	85:2
SRI LANKA	-4.41[b]	77:1	10.06[c]	77:1
THAILAND	-3.86[c]	85:2	7.55	85:2
Panel B. Prices measured by PPI				
AUSTRALIA	-4.26[b]	84:3	9.24	84:3
GERMANY	-4.09[c]	79:4	8.76	79:4
NEW ZEALAND	-3.22	86:2	7.27	99:1
USA	-4.17[c]	84:4	8.95	84:4
INDIA	-3.71	85:2	7.14	85:2
KOREA	-4.12[c]	84:4	8.91	84:4
PHILLIPINES	-4.44[b]	84:4	10.36[c]	84:4
SINGAPOUR	-5.29[a]	85:2	14.22[a]	85:2
SRI LANKA	-4.34[b]	81:4	10.48[c]	81:4
THAILAND	-4.05[c]	84:2	8.41	84:2

[a], [b] and [c] mean rejection of the unit root null hypothesis at the 10%, 5% and 1% significance level, respectively

Table 3 reports the results obtained from the application of the different unit root tests that allow for the presence of a single level shift in the model specification. Panel A presents the results obtained from testing the single unit root hypothesis H_o: $\rho=1$, whilst Panel B those from testing the joint null hypothesis H_o: $\rho=1$, $\delta_1=0$. We can see that, if we introduce the 'a priori' mild hypothesis that the sign of the break is positive, the results of Panel A allows us to reject the unit root null hypothesis for 8 currencies for both price indexes. When this restriction is not included, the number of rejections is clearly lower, although slightly greater than the number of rejections obtained from the use of the max $\square_1$ statistic. We should note that the unit root null hypothesis is clearly rejected for the currencies of Philippines, Singapore and Sri Lanka, whichever statistic is used and, in general, the evidence against the unit root null hypothesis seems to be robust for the Asian currencies. The results presented in this table also confirm the rejection of the unit root null hypothesis for the US Dollar, increasing the evidence on the linkage between the two currencies. It is also remarkable that we can now reject the unit root null hypothesis for the Korean currency. This is another important result, given the increasing importance of this Asian economy. We note that the evidence against the non-PPP hypothesis is limited for the Australian Dollar and the German Mark, and non-existent for the New Zealander Dollar.

Table 4. Testing for unit roots under the presence of two changes in the mean

	H_o: $\rho=1$			H_o: $\rho=1$, $d_1=d_2=0$		
	Min t_ρ	TB$_1$	TB$_2$	Max Φ_2	TB$_1$	TB$_2$
Panel A. Prices measured by CPI						
AUSTRALIA	-4.76	84:3	92:1	7.62	84:3	92:1
GERMANY	-4.36	82:3	92:2	7.98	79:4	98:2
NEW ZEALAND	-3.72	82:3	91:2	6.44	95:1	97:1
USA	-4.79	80:4	85:2	8.81	85:2	95:1
INDIA	-5.54[b]	85:2	90:2	10.37	85:2	90:2
INDONESIA	-5.10	85:2	97:1	10.81[c]	97:1	98:1
KOREA	-5.43[c]	84:4	97:2	10.03	84:4	97:2
MALAYSIA	-5.55[b]	85:2	96:4	11.04[c]	85:2	96:4
PHILLIPINES	-6.02[a]	85:2	95:1	12.29[b]	85:2	95:1
SINGAPOUR	-5.55[b]	80:3	85:2	11.22[c]	78:2	85:2
SRI LANKA	-7.41[a]	77:2	85:2	18.5[a]	77:2	85:4
THAILAND	-5.10	85:2	96:4	9.41	85:2	96:4
Panel B. Prices measured by PPI						
AUSTRALIA	-5.02	84:3	95:1	8.62	84:3	95:1
GERMANY	-4.91	79:3	99:1	9.52	79:3	98:2
NEW ZEALAND	-3.90	95:1	99:1	7.78	85:2	86:3
USA	-4.77	85:2	95:1	9.61	84:4	95:1
INDIA	-5.51[b]	85:2	90:2	10.43	85:2	90:2
KOREA	-5.45[c]	85:2	92:4	10.11	85:2	92:4
PHILLIPINES	-5.02	84:4	99:1	9.78	84:4	99:1
SINGAPOUR	-5.95[b]	78:2	85:2	12.65[b]	78:2	85:2
SRI LANKA	-5.19	81:4	92:1	10.09	81:4	92:1
THAILAND	-4.95	84:2	96:4	9.09	84:2	96:4

[a], [b] and [c] mean rejection of the unit root null hypothesis at the 10%, 5% and 1% significance level, respectively

Finally, we have considered the presence of a second level shift, reporting in Table 4 the results of testing the unit root null hypothesis under the presence of two breaks. Once again, Panel A considers the minimisation of the pseudo t-ratio for testing whether the autoregressive parameter is 1, while Panel B contains the results related to the maximisation of the max Φ_2 statistic. As we can see, the evidence against this null hypothesis is lower than in the previous case. In spite of this fact, the use of these statistics allows us to reject this hypothesis for Indonesia, when CPI is used to measure the price differential.

It is also notable to see that the results presented in Tables 2, 3, and 4 lead us to conclude in favour of the PPP hypothesis not only for the Southeast Asian currencies, but also for the US Dollar and in a weaker sense for the German Mark. This evidence could be interpreted as evidence in favour of the global integration of these economies. This result was intuited in AMP, but the evidence provided in that paper was not as robust as that presented here.

Another important source of interesting insights is the analysis of the period where the different breaks appear. We can observe that they reflect two periods of time of particular interest, namely mid 1980's and mid-to-late 1990's. The first break reflects the effects of the decline of the U.S. dollar following the Plaza Accord and this break has a positive sign for all Southeast Asian currencies implying their depreciation versus the Japanese Yen. The second break reflects the financial crisis in Southeast Asian economies and the associated outflows of capital.

It seems that the inclusion of the post crisis period has strengthened and not altered the basic conclusions presented in AMP. Indeed, while we note some transitory changes in the late 1990s, we can conclude that in contrast to the events of the late 1980s, the 1997 Asian crises have not changed the PPP equilibrium level for the Japanese Yen versus the currencies considered.

4.1   Robustness Checks for Structural Breaks

We should note that the above conclusions might be limited by the fact that we have only considered up to two breaks in the previous unit root tests. It is possible that the consideration of a higher number of breaks could lead us to observe a break related to the 1997 crisis, which would invalidate our preliminary conclusions. In this regard, we should first note that we have also considered the case of 3 and 4 breaks, obtaining the statistics max Φ_3 and max Φ_4. None of them offered any improvement with respect to the results presented in Tables 3 and 4. Thus, from this point of view, the selection of 1 or 2 breaks in order to capture the evolution of these real exchange rates would seem appropriate.[7]

Further, we should also recognise that the procedures used above perhaps are not the most accurate method for determining the number of breaks. For example, we could use the procedure recently proposed in Bai and Perron (1998, 2003), where these authors develop a more powerful method to detect and estimate multiple structural breaks (BP hereafter). Thus, the BP method may be more appropriated to verify whether the 1997 crisis has implied a

---

[7] Finally, we should note that we have considered a maximum number of breaks of 5 and that we have used the quadratic spectral kernel in order to take into account the presence of possible autocorrelation and heterogeneity in the residuals, combined with. the Andrews (1991) automatic bandwidth selection with AR(1) approximation.

structural change in the PPP equilibrium. This method is based on the estimation of the following linear model with m breaks:

$$y_t = \mu_j + u_t, \qquad t = TB_{j-1}, \ldots, TB_j \qquad j = 1, 2, \ldots m+1 \qquad (3)$$

where TB_j has been also used in equation [2]. Then, the Bai-Perron procedure implies the estimation of the above equation considering that the break may appears in any period of the sample size. A Chow type tests is then defined in order to determine the existence of a first break, which coincides with the period where this Chow type statistic attains its maximum value. Then, the existence of multiple breaks is analysed applying this procedure sequentially combining with the repartition method described in Bai (1997). In order to determine the existence of breaks, we can use the UD_{max} and WD_{max} statistics, which test the null hypothesis of no structural breaks versus the presence of an unknown number of breaks. We can also use some information criteria, such as BIC or LWZ. However, the use of the UD_{MAX} or WD_{MAX} statistics is recommended in the light of the results obtained from some Monte Carlo simulations reported in Bai and Perron (1998, 2003). Given that this method only works properly once regime-wise stationarity is proved, we can only apply it to those cases where the unit root null hypothesis has been previously rejected. The results that have obtained from the application of this method are presented in Table 5.

Table 5. Bai-Perron estimation of the breaks periods

	UD_{max}	WD_{max}	x_1	x_2	x_3	x_4
Panel A. Prices measured by CPI						
USA	14.78[a]	24.90[b]	-5.24	-4.86 _86:1_		
INDIA*	22.34[a]	42.75[b]	-2.92	-2.65 _77:4_	-2.14 _86:1_	-1.66 _91:2_
KOREA	31.16[a]	40.97[b]	1.39	1.80 _85:3_		
MALAYSIA	35.71[a]	75.53[b]	-4.59	-3.87 _86:1_		
PHILLIPINES	35.05[a]	35.05[b]	-2.26	-1.76 _85:4_		
SINGAPOUR	13.59[a]	13.59[b]	-4.72	-4.30 _85:4_		
SRI LANKA*	14.71[a]	32.30[b]	-2.47	-1.62 _77:4_	-1.22 _86:1_	
THAILAND	18.81[a]	18.81[b]	-2.17	-1.59 _85:4_		

		Panel B. Prices measured by PPI			
AUSTRALIA	8.73^c	8.73^c	-4.81	-4.54 *85:3*	
GERMANY	10.32^b	17.08^b	-4.52	-4.33 *80:3*	
USA	49.11^a	86.80^b	-5.14	-4.87 *86:2*	
INDIA*	34.27^a	69.82^b	-2.53	-2.13 *86:2*	-1.76 *91:2*
KOREA	44.44^a	57.83^b	1.42	1.78 *85:3*	
SINGAPOUR	38.48^a	38.48^b	-4.67	-4.23 *85:4*	
SRI LANKA	8.62	15.84^b	-1.55	-1.23 *82:3*	
THAILAND	22.77^a	22.77^b	-2.01	-1.63 *85:3*	

x_1-x_4 represent the estimation of the mean of the real exchange rate (in logs) for each of the currencies considered. The estimation of the period where the mean beaks appear in italics. We have not found evidence in favour of the presence of changes in the mean for New Zealander Dollar and the Philippine Peso (prices measured by PPI) and, therefore, we have not included the results for these currencies

* For these currencies, we have estimated the number of breaks by way of the use of the LWZ criteria.

[a], [b] and [c] mean rejection of the unit root null hypothesis at the 10%, 5% and 1% significance level, respectively.

The results of Table 5 do confirm the presence of some structural breaks in the real exchange rates that we have analysed, verifying the need for testing the unit root null hypothesis using statistics that allow for the presence of structural breaks. We also observe that the highest number of breaks selected is 3, for India; while for the rest of the currencies only 1 break seems to be enough to capture the evolution of the real exchange rates. The estimation of the period where this break appears lead us to conclude that mid-1980's is a very important period in order to explain the evolution of the real exchange rates in Asia. Related to this result, we should note that the Japanese Yen-US dollar rate appreciated a near 40%, when measured by CPI, or some 27%, when measured by PPI. Both values are concordant with the results presented in Gadea, Montañés and Reyes (2002) for the analysis of the real exchange rate between major European currencies versus the US dollar. When analysing Asian currencies, we see that the appreciation of this rate is also some 40% with the exception of the Malaysia Ringgit, the Indian Rupee, and the Philippine Peso, where this appreciation is greater than 50% and in the case of the Malaysian ringgit where this appreciation reaches some 72%.

Finally, we should note the especially remarkable result that there is no evidence for structural breaks in real exchange rates related to the 1997 crisis for any of the currencies under analysis. The results of our outlier analysis indicate that this episode has only had some transitory effects on real exchange rates without affecting the PPP equilibrium level. The importance of this result is especially remarkable if we take into account the large nominal movements in the exchange rates and changes in macro-economic policies in the region in the second half of the 1990s indicating that far from being abandoned, PPP was reinforced.

However, our analysis should be considered preliminary and further research on this topic would be useful especially as we accumulate data over a longer post-crises period.

5 Conclusions

There seems to be some controversy in the literature regarding the validity of PPP for the Japanese Yen. This paper uses more recent data and improved statistical procedures that allow for multiple breaks in the data to test if PPP holds between the Japanese Yen and an expanded set of other Asian and major world currencies. Allowing for structural breaks, our unit root tests of real exchange rate series for the period 1974-2000 find strong support for PPP between the Japanese Yen and other Asian and world currencies.

In addition, the results presented in this paper allow us to confirm the results of AMP in the sense that we have further, and even stronger, evidence for the presence of a high degree of linkage between the Southeast Asian currencies and the Japanese Yen. This could lead to a conclusion in favour of the existence of a Yen bloc for these currencies. In addition, in contrast to AMP, we now offer more robust evidence in favour of a high degree of relationship between the Japanese Yen and the USA dollar and for similar but somewhat weaker relationships also between the Japanese Yen and other non-Asian currencies like Australian dollar, New Zealander dollar or German Mark. These results are consistent with the increasing degree of international linkages between currencies and economies.

References

[1]   Abuaf, N. and P. Jorion, 1990, Purchasing Power Parity in the Long Run, *Journal of Finance* **45**, 157-174.

[2]   Aggarwal, R., A. Montañés and M. Ponz, 2000, Evidence of Long-Run Purchasing Power Parity: Analysis of Real Asian Exchange Rates in terms of the Japanese Yen, *Japan and the World Economy* **12**, 351-361.

[3]   Aggarwal, R. and M. Mougoué, 1997, Cointegration Among Asian Currencies: Evidence of the Increasing Influence of the Japanese Yen, *Japan and the World Economy* **8**, 291-308.

[4]   Aggarwal, R. and M. Mougoué, 1998, Common Stochastic Trends Among Asian Currencies: Evidence for Japan, Aseans and Asian Tigers, *Review of Quantitative Finance and Accounting* **10**, 193-206.

[5]   Andrews, D.W., 1991, Heteroskedasticity and Autocorrelation Consistent Covariance Matrix Estimation, *Econometrica* **59**, 817-858.

[6]   Azali, M., M.S. Habibullah and A.Z. Baharumshah, 2001, Does PPP Hold Between Asian and Japanese Economies?: Evidence Using Panel Unit Root and Panel Cointegration, *Japan and the World Economy* **13**, 35-50.

[7]   Bai, J., 1997, Estimating Multiple Breaks One at Time, *Econometric Theory* **13**,315-352

[8]   Bai, J and P. Perron, 1998, Estimating and Testing Linear Models with Multiple Changes, *Econometrica* **66**, 47-78.

[9]   Bai, J and P. Perron, 2003, Computation and Analysis of Multiple Structural Change Models, *Journal of Applied Econometrics*, **18**, 1-22.

[10] Bayoumi, T. and P. Mauro, 2001, The Suitability of ASEAN for a Regional Currency Arrangement, *World Economy* **24** (No. 7, July), 933-954.

[11] Cati. R., Garcia, M.G. P. and P. Perron, 1999, Unit Roots in the Presence of Abrupt Governmental Interventions with an Application to Brazilian Data, *Journal of Applied Econometrics* **14**, 27-56

[12] Cheung, Y. W. and K. S. Lai, 1998, Economic Growth and Stationarity of Real Exchange Rates: Evidence from Some Fast-Growing Asian Countries, *Pacific-Basin Finance Journal* **6**, 61-76.

[13] Chinn, M.D., 2000, Before the Fall Were East Asian Currencies Overvalued? *Emerging Markets Review* 1, 101-126.

[14] Clemente, J., A. Montañés and M. Reyes, 1998, Testing for a Unit Root in Variable with Two Changes in the Mean, *Economic Letters* **59**, 175-182.

[15] Dickey, D. and W. Fuller, 1979, Distribution of the Estimators for Autoregressive Time Series With a Unit Root, *Journal of the American Statistical Association* **74**, 427-431.

[16] Dropsy, V., 1996, Real Exchange Rates and Structural Breaks, *Applied Economics* **28**, 209-19.

[17] Elliott, G., Rothenberg, T. J. and J. H. Stock, 1996, Efficient Tests for an Autoregressive Unit Root, *Econometrica* **64**, 813–836.

[18] Frankel, J. A., 1990, Zen and the Art of Macroeconomics: A Commentary, in: W. S. Haraf and T. D. Willett (Eds.), *Monetary Policy for a Volatile World*, Washington, DC: American Enterprise Institute, 117-123.

[19] Fukuda, S., 2002, Post-crisis Exchange Rates in East Asia, Mimeo, University of Tokyo.

[20] Gadea, M.D., A. Montañés and M. Reyes, 2002, The European Union Currencies and the US Dollar: From post-Bretton-Woods to the Euro, University of Zaragoza, Mimeo.

[21] Gómez, V. and Maravall, A., 1992, Time series regression with ARIMA noise and missing observations. Program TRAM. European University Institute, Working Paper ECO 92/81.

[22] Holmes, M.J., 2001, New Evidence on Real Exchange Rate Stationarity and Purchasing Power Parity in Less Developed Countries, *Journal of Macroeconomics* **23**, 601-614.

[23] Hunter, W. C., G. G. Kaufman and T. H. Krueger, (Eds.), *The Asian Financial Crises: Origins, Implications, and Solutions*, Kluwer Academic Publishers, Boston.

[24] Kawai, M. and S. Akiyama, 2000, Implications of the Currency Crisis for Exchange Rate Arrangements in Emerging East Asia, *World Bank Working Paper* **2502**.

[25] Lothian, J. R., 1997, Multi-Country Evidence on the Behaviour of Purchasing Power Parity Under the Current Float, *Journal of International Money and Finance* **16**, pp. 19-36.

[26] Mussa, M., 1986, Nominal Exchange Rate Regimes and the Behaviour of Real Exchange Rates *Carnegie-Rochester Series in Public Policy* **25**, 117-213.

[27] Ng, S. and P. Perron, 1995, Unit Root Tests- ARIMA Models with Data-Dependent Method for Selection of the Truncation Lag, *Journal of American Statistical Association* **90**, 268-281.

[28] Ng, S. and P. Perron, 1996, Useful Modifications to Some Unit Root Tests with Dependent Errors and Their Local Asymptotic Properties, *Review of Economic Studies* **63**, 435-463.

[29] Ng, S. and P. Perron, 2001, Lag Length Selection and the Construction of Unit Root Tests With Good Size and Power, *Econometrica* **69**, 1519-1554.

[30] Perron, P., 1989, The Great Crash, the Oil Shock and the Unit Root Hypothesis, *Econometrica* **57**, 1361-402.

[31] Perron, P., 1990, Testing for a Unit Root in Time Series With a Changing Mean, *Journal of Business and Economic Statistics* **8**, 153-162.

[32] Perron, P. and T. Vogelsang, 1992, Nonstationarity and Level Shifts With an Application to Purchasing Power Parity, *Journal of Business and Economic Statistics* **10**, 301-320.

[33] Phillips, P. C. B. and P. Perron, 1988, Testing for a Unit Root in Time Series Regression, *Biometrika* **75**, 335–346.

[34] Rogoff, K., 1996, The Purchasing Power Parity Puzzle, *Journal of Economic Literature* **34**, 647-668.

[35] Sargan, J. D. and A. Bhargava, 1983, Testing Residuals from Least Squares Regression for Being Generated by the Gaussian Random Walk, *Econometrica*, **51**, 153-74.

[36] Tse, Y.K. and L.K. Ng, 1997, The Cointegration of Asian Currencies Revisited, *Japan and the World Economy* **9**,109-114

In: International Macroeconomics: Recent Developments   ISBN 1-59454-901-X
Editor: Amalia Morales Zumaquero pp. 79-103   © 2006 Nova Science Publishers, Inc.

Chapter 5

INTERNATIONAL PARITY RELATIONSHIPS AND A NONSTATIONARY REAL EXCHANGE RATE. GERMANY VERSUS THE US IN THE POST BRETTON WOODS PERIOD

Katarina Juselius[1] *and Ronald MacDonald*[2]
[1]Institute of Economics, University of Copenhagen
[2]Department of Economics, University of Glasgow

Abstract

This paper examines the interrelations between purchasing power parity, uncovered interest parity, the term structure of interest rates and the Fisher real interest rate parity condition using cointegration analysis. Dynamic adjustment and feed-back effects are estimated jointly in a full system of equations. An important finding is that the very slow, though significant, price adjustment towards sustainable levels of real exchange rates, has been compensated by corresponding changes in the spread of long-term bond rates. Related to this is the strong empirical support for the weak exogeneity of long-term bond rates, signifying the importance of the large US trade deficits (i.e. the low levels of US savings) and, hence, their linkage to international finance. Altogether, the results suggest that the transmission mechanisms over the post Bretton Woods period have been significantly different from standard theoretical assumptions.

JEL Classifications: E31, E43, F31, F32.

Keywords: PPP, UIP, Fisher parity, Term structure, Cointegrated VAR.

1 Introduction[1]

Parity conditions are central to international finance and, more specifically, to many open economy macro-models, such as the celebrated Dornbusch (1976) overshooting model. Al-

---

[1]A special thank goes to Charles Lai Tong who found some mistakes in a previous version of this paper. In addition the paper has benefitted from valuable comments from, Frederique Bec, David Hendry, Hans Christian Kongsted, Grayham Mizon, Adrian Pagan, Hans-Martin Krolzig, and Søren Johansen. Financial support from the Danish Social Sciences Research Council is gratefully acknowledged.

though international parity conditions, such as purchasing power parity (PPP) and uncovered interest rate parity (UIP), have received considerable empirical scrutiny, very little empirical research has focussed on modelling such conditions jointly (exceptions are Johansen and Juselius (1992), Juselius (1991,1995) and MacDonald and Marsh (1997,1999)). This perhaps seems surprising since such parity conditions can be shown to be closely linked through interest rates and expected inflation. By modelling international parity conditions jointly, extra information may brought to bear on each individual parity condition, thereby increasing the likelihood of establishing well-defined results. In this paper we attempt to push this nascent literature further by jointly modelling PPP and UIP with the term spread (TS), or yield gap, for Germany against the United States, over the period 1975 to 1998. In addition to shedding light on the interaction of these parity conditions, we hope to address a number of unresolved issues.

One important issue concerns the persistence in real exchange rates. For example, a number of studies have demonstrated that for the recent floating experience real exchange rates are $I(1)$ processes (see Froot and Rogoff (1995) and MacDonald (1995) for surveys). The modelling approach adopted in this paper shows that although this non-stationarity may be removed using inflation and interest differentials, it, in turn, is an important determinant of interest differentials and inflation. A second issue, which is essentially a corollary of the first, concerns the extent to which German (European) or US variables are the driving variables in the system. For much of the post-war period, particularly during the Bretton Woods period, the US has been seen as the 'locomotive' economy. But with increased integration and convergence in Europe it may be expected that European variables, represented here by Germany, will be as important in international financial linkages as US variables. A third issue we seek to address is the extent to which 'implicit' parity conditions - namely the Fisher conditions and real interest rate parity - hold for our sample period. Thus although the linkage between nominal interest rates, as in UIP, describes capital mobility between financial centres, it is the lock between real interest rates which governs the efficiency with which savings and investment are allocated internationally. To what extent does the joint modelling of UIP, PPP and the TS shed light on this issue?

The outline of the remainder of this paper is as follows. In the next section we provide a motivational discussion of a number of parity conditions used in this paper. In Section 3 a visual interpretation of the parities is presented, while in Section 4 our model specification is detailed. Section 5 contains the cointegration and weak exogeneity properties of our system. A fully identified long-run structure is detailed in Section 6, while the short-run adjustment structure is contained in Section 7. The estimated long-run impacts of shocks to the system are reported in section 8. The final section of the paper contains summary results and conclusions.

2   International Parity Conditions.

Purchasing power parity (PPP), one of the most important parity conditions in international finance, is defined as:

$$p = p^* + e, \tag{1}$$

where p is the log of the domestic price level, p^* is the log of the foreign price level, and e denotes the log of the spot exchange rate (home currency price of a unit of foreign currency). Thus, the departure at time t from (1) is given by:

$$ppp_t = p_t - p_t^* - e_t. \tag{2}$$

The strong form of PPP requires $ppp_t{}^2$ to be stationary.

The nature of the empirical support for PPP is very dependent on the sample period chosen in the following sense: if the time it takes for ppp to return to its steady-state value is very long, say ten years, then we need a long sample to get statistically significant mean reversion effects[3]. Over century long historical data spans, there is mounting evidence that a version of the strong-form PPP is valid, but with a very small adjustment coefficient (see, for example, Froot and Rogoff (1995) and MacDonald (1995)). For the recent floating experience the sample period is too short for such a small adjustment coefficient to be statistically significant and, thus, econometrically ppp_t behaves as an $I(1)$ process.

Though there are many potential reasons why the adjustment to strong-form PPP is so slow we will here primarily pursue the idea that the persistence in ppp_t is due to the existence of important real factors working through the current account, such as productivity differences, net foreign asset positions and fiscal imbalances. This hypothesis has received some empirical support by researchers who have explicitly modelled the real determinants of real exchange rates (see the papers contained in MacDonald and Stein (1999)).

However, through the balance of payments constraint we know that any current account imbalance generated by such movements has to be financed through the capital account. The implication of this is that the PPP condition is likely to be strongly related with another parity condition, namely uncovered interest rate parity (UIP) (see Johansen and Juselius (1992), Juselius (1991,1995) and MacDonald and Marsh (1997,1999)). Therefore, by combining the two parity conditions we may pick up the influence of the real factors on PPP indirectly.

The condition of UIP may be stated as:

$$E_t^e(\Delta_m e_{t+m})/m - (i_t^m + i_t^{m*}) = 0, \tag{3}$$

where i_t^m denotes a bond yield with maturity $t + m$, $m = l, s$ where l and s denote a long and short maturity, respectively, and E_t^e denotes an economic expectation on the basis of time t information. A number of researchers (see, for example, Cumby and Obstfeld (1981)) have tested this version of UIP and essentially find that ε_t is non-stationary. However, when the UIP condition is modelled jointly with PPP more satisfactory results have been obtained in the sense that deviations from the conditions are stationary and the sign of the coefficients conform with priors. Nevertheless, the empirical evidence strongly suggests that the assumption of market clearing underlying (3) would have to be replaced by an assumption of price adjustment.

---

[2]Note that the ppp term is also the (logarithm) of the real exchange rate. We prefer to use the label ppp in this paper because we are adopting a parity perspective and also because we do not model the real exchange rate in terms of so-called real fundamentals.

[3]See Juselius (1999) for a discussion of the statistical versus economic interpretation of unit root econometrics.

This takes us to two further parity conditions, related to PPP and UIP, which are needed for a full understanding of some of the puzzles noted in the introduction. The first relates interest rates of different maturities, based on the expectations model of the term structure. In this model it is assumed that a long rate is a weighted average of current and expected rates of shorter interest rates, and short rates are predicted to 'drive' long rates. An implication of the standard expectations model of the term structure is that the term spread (TS) should be stationary (Campbell and Shiller, 1987). The TS is defined as:

$$i_t^l - i_t^s = v_t, \tag{4}$$

where i_t^s denotes the yield on a short maturity bond, i_t^l on a long maturity, and v_t denotes a generic random error term which, under the expectations hypothesis, should be stationary. However, based on a variety of empirical tests (see Campbell, 1995) v_t has often been found to be non-stationary.

It is conventional to think of nominal interest rates being decomposed into real and expected inflation components using the Fisher decomposition:

$$i_t^m = r_t^m + E_t^e(\Delta_m p_{t+m})/m, \tag{5}$$

where r denotes the real interest rate. Combining (4) and (5) gives:

$$i_t^l - i_t^s = r_t^l - r_t^s + E_t^e\{(\Delta_{l-s} p_{t+l})/(l - s)\} + v_t,$$

showing that a nonstationary interest rate spread is logically consistent with expected inflation rate being a nonstationary variable. Since actual inflation is frequently found to be a nonstationary variable this seems to be a plausible explanation to the finding that interest rate spreads are nonstationary.

The final parity condition to consider here is that of real interest rate parity (RIP):

$$r_t^m - r_t^{m*} = (i_t^m - i_t^{m*}) - (E_t(\Delta_m p_m - \Delta_m p_m^*)/m) \quad = \quad v_t \tag{6}$$

where m is the maturity of the underlying asset. The empirical literature on RIP usually focuses on testing if the restrictions necessary to move from (3) and (5) to (6) actually hold in the data. The majority of such studies find that RIP is strongly rejected for most country pairings (see, for example, the overview in Hallwood and MacDonald (1999)). By combining (3), (5) and (4) we get:

$$\begin{aligned} (i_t^l - i_t^{l*}) - (i_t^s - i_t^{s*}) &= E_t(\Delta_l e_{t+l} - \Delta_s e_{t+s})/(l - s) \\ &= E_t(\Delta_{l-s} p_{t+l} - \Delta_{l-s} p_{t+l}^*)/(l - s) \end{aligned} \tag{7}$$

which shows that if the spread between expected domestic and foreign inflation from $t + s$ to $t + l$ is nonstationarity, then the spread between the domestic and foreign yield gap would also have to be nonstationary. Since inflation is found to be nonstationary in itself this seems very plausible. In this view (4), (5) and (7) are likely to be non-stationary, or $I(1)$.

We now draw out the implications for the modelling of PPP, UIP and TS under the assumption that the simple parity conditions are nonstationary and that the very slow adjustment to sustainable real exchange rates is the basic reason for this nonstationarity. We formulate the following hypothetical relation for the expected exchange rate:

$$E_t^e \Delta_l e_{t+l} = \omega_1 E_t^e \Delta_l (p_{t+l} - p_{t+l}^*) + \omega_2 E_t^e ppp_{t+l} + v_t, \tag{8}$$

where the expected depreciation can be related to the expected inflation differential and to the expected real depreciation rate, with the weights ω_1 and ω_2. If the expected exchange rate in (3) is formed using (8) we can derive a relationship by combining the PPP and the UIP conditions:

$$(i_t^l - i_t^{l*}) - (i_t^s - i_t^{s*})_t = \omega_1 E_t((\Delta_{l-s}p - \Delta_{l-s}p^*)/l - s)_{t+l} + \omega_2 E_t^e ppp_{t+l} + v_t. \tag{9}$$

Even if expectations are generally not observable the cointegration results will be unaffected when replacing expectations with actual values under the following two conditions: (i) the difference between $E_t(x_{t+l})$ and x_{t+l} is stationary or, preferably, white noise (i.e. agents do not make systematic forecast errors), (ii) the differenced process $(x_{t+l} - x_t)$ is stationary. Under these two assumptions we can derive an empirical relationship between the interest rate spreads, the inflation spread and the real exchange rate:

$$i_t^l - i_t^{l*} = \omega_1 (\Delta p - \Delta p^*)_t + \omega_2 (i_s - i_s^*)_t + \omega_3 ppp_t + v_t. \tag{10}$$

Thus, we note that implicit in (10) is all of the parity relationships discussed above: the two Fisher conditions, international real interest rate parity condition, the ppp condition, and the term structure relationship. For example, (10) becomes the real long-term interest parity relationship for $\omega_1 = 1$ and $(\omega_2 = 0, \omega_3 = 0)$. By modelling these relationships jointly we can test the stationarity of the simple parity conditions as special cases of (10). If these are rejected we can test whether combinations of the parity relationships become stationary.

3   An Ocular Analysis of the Parities

In this section we offer a first pass at how closely the various parity conditions considered above hold. We also introduce some of the relevant institutional background which will have a bearing on our econometric results.

The salient feature of the graphs in Figures 1, 2, and 3[4] is the slow adjustment back to the parities. Figure 1, upper panel, shows clearly that the spot exchange rate does not closely mirror the price differential between Germany and the USA, although there seems to be a tendency for it to follow the same (very) long-run movements. The much greater variation in the spot exchange rate as compared to the price differential is quite striking[5]. In particular, the period between 1980 and 1985 (showing up here as a depreciation of the mark) is notable. Lothian (1997), for example, has argued that the behavior of the dollar in this period is likely to confound any test of PPP for the recent floating period when the US dollar is used as the numeraire currency. Given the importance of this episode for the kinds of tests conducted in this paper, we believe it merits a brief discussion here.

---

[4]The measurements of the variables discussed in this section are defined in Section 5.

[5]See for example Krugman (1993) for an economic explanation.

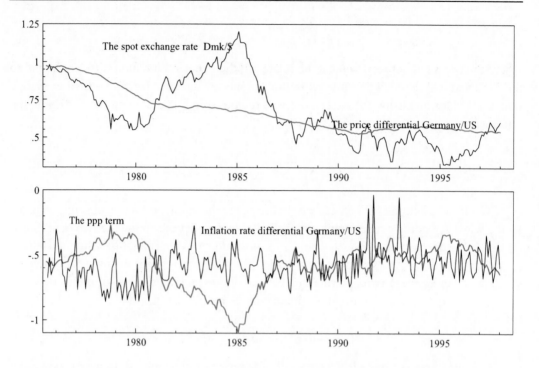

Figure 1: The monthly price differential and the spot exchange rate (upper panel) and the ppp term and the inflation rate differential (lower panel) between Germany and USA .

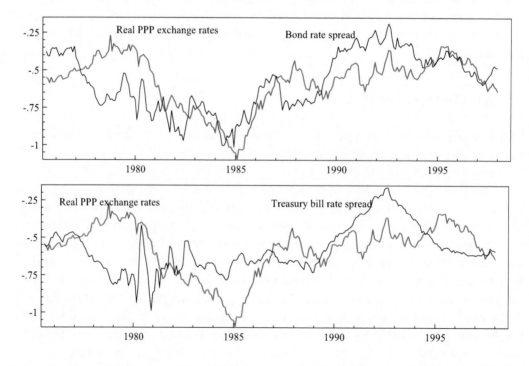

Figure 2: The ppp term relative to the bond rate spread (upper panel) and to the Treasury bill rate spread (lower panel).

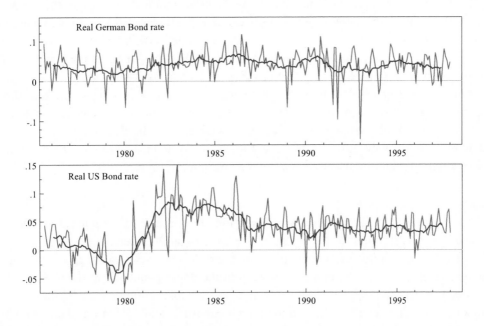

Figure 3: Real yearly bond rates (in 0.01%) for Germany (upper panel) and USA (lower panel) together with ±6 months moving averages

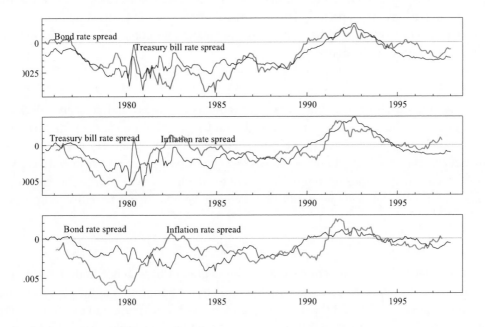

Figure 4: The monthly bond rate spread and Treasury bill rate spread (upper panel), the inflation rate spread relative to the treasury bill rate spread (middel panel) and to the bond rate spread (lower panel).

The dollar appreciation was kick-started by the effects on interest rates of the so-called 'Reagan Experiment' of increasing the US fiscal deficit. However, the prolonged nature of the appreciation would seem to be unwarranted solely in terms of a real interest differential or, indeed, other fundamentals which were extant at the time, such as portfolio balance or 'safe-haven' effects (see MacDonald (1988)). The consensus view seems to be that in large part it was a speculative bubble, unrelated to economic fundamentals, which drove the currency to such stratospheric levels. However, whatever the actual cause of the dollar's rise we believe that ultimately it could not have behaved as it did if it was not accepted as the key reserve currency in the international monetary system. The role of the dollar as a reserve currency is an important element in how we interpret our results.

The lower panel of Figure 1, shows that the long movements of the *ppp* cannot directly be related to an adjustment of the inflation rates; the inflation spread appears too small to facilitate a long-run adjustment towards a stationary level of real exchange rates. Figure 2 relates the ppp_t term to the bond rate spread in the upper panel and to the Treasury bill rate spread in the lower panel. There is a quite remarkable co-movement in the long-run behavior of the real exchange rate and the long bond differential. However, there is not the same close correspondence with respect to the short-term Treasury bill rates. This in large measure reflects the nature of these two yields. The latter are driven by short term policy considerations, whereas the former are market determined and have a term to maturity which more closely matches the long persistence in the real exchange rate (we discuss the importance of relative interest rates further below). Figure 3 demonstrates the large variation in real bond rates over this period. This is particularly so for the US real bond rate, which has varied between -7% and +15%. These are huge variations considering that theoretically it is usually assumed to be constant!

Finally, Figure 4 compares the spread of the bond rates and of the Treasury bill rates in the upper panel, and the inflation rate spread with treasury bill rate spread (middle panel) and the bond rate spread (lower panel), respectively. There are clearly periods in which both spreads mirror relative inflation quite closely and periods in which they diverge and the real interest rate spreads open up. The extent to which such real interest rate spreads are consistent with real interest rate parity is something we investigate formally in Sections 6 and 7.

The graphical inspection demonstrated a fair degree of persistence both in the spreads and the parities which is inconsistent with the stationarity assumption of the simple parities. Econometrically, we will treat these persistencies as stochastic trends and use cointegration analysis to find out how they are related. This is based on the simple idea that a persistent imbalance in one place should create a corresponding imbalance in another. The purpose is to use the econometric analysis to suggest reasons why these simple parity relationships are inadequate on their own and how they could be modified to describe the variation in the data.

4   Model Specification

All test and estimation results are based on the VAR model with a constant term, μ, seasonal dummies, S_t, and intervention dummies, D_t, given by:

$$\Delta x_t = \Gamma_1 \Delta x_{t-1} + \Gamma \Delta x_{t-1} + \Pi x_{t-2} + \mu + \Phi_1 S_t + \Phi_2 D_t + \varepsilon_t,$$
$$\varepsilon_t \sim N_p(0, \Sigma \,), \, t = 1, ..., T$$
(11)

where x_t is a vector of the following monthly variables:

$$[ppp, \Delta p_t, \Delta p_t^*, i_t^l, i_t^{l*}, i_t^s, i_t^{s*}] \sim I(1)$$
(12)

observed for $t = 1975:7\text{-}1998:1$. The set of variables is defined by

$ppp_t = p_t - p_t^* - e_t$, where

p_t = the German, or 'home', price index,

p_t^* = the US, or 'foreign', price index,

e_t = the spot exchange rate, defined as DM/\$,

i_t^l = the German long bond yield,

$i_t^{l,*}$ = the US long bond yield,

i_t^s = the German 3 month Treasury bill rate,

$i_t^{s,*}$ = the US 3 month Treasury bill rate.

The deviations from constant ppp are very large in absolute terms compared to the remaining variables in (12). Therefore, the ppp term has been divided by 100 to avoid getting very small coefficients in absolute magnitude. Nevertheless, the interpretation of the results are for the original ppp term. All of the data used in this study have been extracted from the International Monetary Funds CD-Rom disc (December 1998). Both price series are Consumer Price Indices (line 64), the long interest rates are 10 year bond yields (line 61), the short rates are Treasury bill rates (60c), and the exchange rate is the end of period rate (line ae). All variables, apart from the interest rates (which appear as fractions), are in natural logarithms.

The graphs of the differenced variables in Appendix II show that the multivariate normality assumption underlying (11) is not likely to be satisfied. Many of the marginal processes exhibit extraordinarily large observations inconsistent with the normality assumption. This is particularly so for the short-term treasury bill rates, signifying the high volatility of short-term interest rates in 1980-1983, the period of M3 targeting. To secure valid statistical inference we need to control for the largest of these observations by dummy variables or leave out the most volatile years from our sample. Since the volatile years could potentially be informative about agents' behavior we choose the former alternative and use a dummy when a residual is larger than $|3.5\sigma_\varepsilon|$. The implications of this criteria is that most observations in 1979-1982 were classified as 'too large' and dummied out. Thus, the impact of this period is more or less annihilated in the results. This is consistent with the findings in Hansen and Johansen (1999) that this period defines a structurally different regime.

The following dummy variables where used in the analysis:

$D_t' = [D78.09, Di78.10, D79.12, D79.11, Di80.02, Di80.03, D80.05, D80.07,$
$\qquad D80.11, D81.01, D81.02, D81.03, D81.05, D81.10, D81.11, Di82.01, D82.08,$
$\qquad D82.10, Di84.12, D88.08, D89.02, D91, Ds91.03, \Delta Ds91.03,]_t,$

where, $Dxx.yy_t$ is 1 at 19xx:yy, 0 otherwise, $Dixx.yy_t$ is 1 at 19xx:yy, -1 at 19xx:yy+1,

Table 1: Misspecification tests and cointegration rank

Multivariate tests:							
Residual autocorr. LM_1	$\chi^2(49)$	=	72.2	p-val.	=	0.02	
Residual autocorr. LM_4	$\chi^2(49)$	=	63.8	p-val.	=	0.08	
Normality: LM	$\chi^2(14)$	=	**120.0**	p-val.	=	0.00	
Univariate tests:	Δp_t	Δp_t^*	Δi_t^l	Δi_t^{l*}	Δi_t^s	Δi_t^{s*}	Δppp_t
ARCH(2)	0.01	2.28	**9.11**	2.06	2.42	**8.34**	4.85
Jarq.Bera(2)	**12.3**	**8.12**	5.05	**6.72**	**7.36**	**48.26**	2.90
Skewness	0.26	0.01	0.22	0.18	0.24	-0.09	0.06
Ex. Kurtosis	4.07	3.79	3.54	3.69	3.73	5.52	3.40
$\hat{\sigma}_\varepsilon \times 0.01$	0.18	0.15	0.01	0.02	0.01	0.02	0.02
The trace test and the characteristic roots of the process:							
$p-r$		7	6	5	4	3	2	1
Q_{95}		132	102	76	53	35	20	9
λ		0.41	0.31	0.14	0.08	0.05	0.02	0.01
Trace test		327	183	85	**43**	22	8	4
Modulus of 7 largest roots								
$r=4$		1.0	1.0	1.0	**0.96**	0.87	0.54	0.35
$r=3$		1.0	1.0	1.0	1.0	**0.78**	0.61	0.39

and 0 otherwise, $D91$ is a variable measuring the effect on German prices of various excise taxes to pay for the German reunification, and $Ds91.03_t$ is 0 for t = 1975:7 - 1991:03 and 1 otherwise. $Ds91.03$ is restricted to lie in the cointegration relations to aviod a broken linear trend effect in the model. By controlling for these extraordinary shocks the residuals of the VAR model became reasonably well-behaved as seen from Table 1, where a significant test statistic is given in bold face. The multivariate LM test for first order residual autocorrelations is borderline significant, whereas multivariate normality is clearly rejected due to excess kurtosis. Furthermore, the $ARCH(2)$ tests for second order autoregressive heteroscedastisity is rejected for the German bond rate and the US treasury bill rate. Since cointegration results have been found quite robust to ARCH and excess kurtosis (Gonzalo, 1994) we regard the present model specification to be acceptable.

In the lower part of Table 1 we report the estimated eigenvalues and trace statistics associated with this system. The trace test suggests four common stochastic trends and, consequently, three cointegration relations. However, the trace statistic for $p - r = 4$ is quite close to the 95% quantile, which suggests that $p - r = 3$ might be borderline acceptable. To check the sensitivity of the model to the choice of r we have also calculated the roots of the characteristic polynomial. There are approximately four 'near unit roots' in the unrestricted system, the choice of $r = 3$ removes all large roots, whereas $r = 4$ leaves a near unit root in the model. We conclude that $r = 3$ is the appropriate choice.

5 Cointegration Properties and Weak Exogeneity

The hypotheses reported in Table 2 have the form $\mathcal{H}_i : \beta_i = \{H_i\phi_i, \psi_i\}$, that is they test whether a single restricted relation is in $sp(\beta)$ leaving the other two relations unrestricted. Only the restricted vectors $H_i\phi_i$, $i = 1, ..., 25$, are reported in the table. If the hypothetical relations exist empirically, then this procedure will maximize the chance of finding them. For a technical derivation of the test procedures, see Johansen and Juselius (1992).

Table 2: Cointegration properties and weak exogeneity

	Δp	Δp^*	i^l	i^{l*}	i^s	i^{s*}	$ppp^{1)}$	$\chi^2(v)$	p.val.
$\mathcal{H}_1$	1	-1	0	0	0	0	0	25.9 (3)	0.00
$\mathcal{H}_2$	0	0	1	-1	0	0	0	30.3(4)	0.00
$\mathcal{H}_3$	0	0	0	0	1	-1	0	28.4(4)	0.00
$\mathcal{H}_4$	1	0	-1	0	0	0	0	7.5(4)	**0.11**
$\mathcal{H}_5$	0	1	0	-1	0	0	0	24.8(4)	0.00
$\mathcal{H}_6$	1	0	0	0	-1	0	0	28.6(4)	0.00
$\mathcal{H}_7$	0	1	0	0	0	-1	0	23.3(4)	0.00
$\mathcal{H}_8$	0	0	1	0	-1	0	0	35.1(4)	0.00
$\mathcal{H}_9$	0	0	0	1	0	-1	0	20.22(4)	0.00
$\mathcal{H}_{10}$	1	-1	0.51	-0.51	0	0	0	10.0(3)	0.00
$\mathcal{H}_{11}$	1	-1	0	0	-0.09	0.09	0	12.67(3)	0.01
$\mathcal{H}_{12}$	1	-0.21	-1	0.21	0	0	0	2.7(3)	**0.44**
$\mathcal{H}_{13}$	0.14	1	0	0	-0.14	-1	0	23.3(3)	0.00
$\mathcal{H}_{14}$	0	0	1	-1	-0.68	0.68	0	21.1(3)	0.00
$\mathcal{H}_{15}$	1	-1	0	0	0	0	0.42	6.2(3)	0.08
$\mathcal{H}_{16}$	0	0	-1	1	0	0	-0.56	16.7(3)	0.00
$\mathcal{H}_{17}$	0	0	0	0	1	-1	-0.64	25.2(3)	0.00
$\mathcal{H}_{18}$	1	0	-1	0	0	0	-0.24	2.8(3)	**0.43**
$\mathcal{H}_{19}$	0	1	0	-1	0	0	-1.16	2.9(3)	**0.41**
$\mathcal{H}_{20}$	1	0	0	0	-1	0	-0.24	27.7(3)	0.00
$\mathcal{H}_{21}$	0	1	0	0	0	-1	-0.99	4.6(3)	**0.21**
$\mathcal{H}_{22}$	1	-1	-1	1	0	0	0.92	2.61(3)	**0.46**
$\mathcal{H}_{23}$	0	0	1	-1	-0.41	0.41	-0.37	0.29(2)	**0.90**
$\mathcal{H}_{24}$	1	-1	1.58	-1.58	-1	1	0	0.8(3)	**0.84**
$\mathcal{H}_{25}$	1	-0.34	-0.66	0	0	0	0	0.15(3)	**0.87**
W.E.	110	55	0.2	3.2	16.6	21.9	9.5		
	(.00)	(.00)	(.98)	(.36)	(.00)	(.00)	(.02)		

Note 1: The ppp term has been divided by 100

Note 2: All relations are estimated with a constant and the 1991 shift dummy

$\mathcal{H}_1$ to $\mathcal{H}_7$ are hypotheses tests on pairs of variables, such as relative inflation ($\mathcal{H}_1$), relative nominal interest rates ($\mathcal{H}_2$ and $\mathcal{H}_3$), Fisher parity conditions for long and short interest rates ($\mathcal{H}_4$ to $\mathcal{H}_7$) and yield gap relationships ($\mathcal{H}_8$ and $\mathcal{H}_9$). These tests therefore seek to determine if some of the key parity conditions introduced in Section 2 are empirically verifiable on their own. Since all, apart from one, of the p-values are less than the 5% critical value, these tests offer little support for the parity conditions on their own. The remaining hypotheses tests in Table 3 involve combining parity conditions without the ppp term ($\mathcal{H}_{10}$ to $\mathcal{H}_{14}$ and $\mathcal{H}_{24}$ and $\mathcal{H}_{25}$), and combining parity conditions with the ppp term ($\mathcal{H}_{15}$ to $\mathcal{H}_{23}$).

$\mathcal{H}_{10}$ to $\mathcal{H}_{13}$ are tests of variants of real interest rate parity in which full proportionality has not been imposed. Restricting the two inflation rates to have unitary coefficients and the nominal interest rates to have equal and opposite signs ($\mathcal{H}_{10}$ and $\mathcal{H}_{11}$) is rejected. Relating the *ex post* German real long-term interest rate with *ex post* US real long-term interest rate ($\mathcal{H}_{12}$) gives a stationary relation with a p-value of 0.44, but with a very small coefficient on the US rate. A similar test for the *ex post* real short-term interest rates is rejected ($\mathcal{H}_{13}$). Testing a form of the relative term structure relationship ($\mathcal{H}_{14}$) is clearly rejected. Therefore, combinations of parity conditions which do not include the ppp term are not very successful.

Hypothesis tests $\mathcal{H}_{15}$ to $\mathcal{H}_{23}$ involve joint tests of parity conditions which include the ppp term. With these tests there is now a high strike record of the joint parity conditions producing stationary relationships. For example, in $\mathcal{H}_{18}$ and $\mathcal{H}_{19}$ we note that the strong form of the Fisher condition (that is with proportionality imposed) goes through for long rates when the ppp term is in the conditioning information set. The usefulness of including the ppp term in these kind of tests is underscored in $\mathcal{H}_{22}$ in which *ex post* real interest rates are equalized across countries, for long maturity yields. This result, which does not receive much support in the extant empirical literature, implies that a strict form of real interest rate parity is likely to be found in periods of a stationary ppp exchange rate. It is also interesting to note that the long interest differential seems to play a similar role to the ppp term since its inclusion with the short rates and inflation rates produces a strong form of real interest parity for the short rates ($\mathcal{H}_{24}$). Including the ppp term in the relative interest rate relationships does not, however, produce stationary relationships ($\mathcal{H}_{16}$ and $\mathcal{H}_{17}$, respectively) and only weak support for stationarity for ppp and relative inflation rates ($\mathcal{H}_{15}$). Finally, $\mathcal{H}_{25}$ describes a homogeneous relationship (i.e., the coefficients sum to zero) between German inflation, US inflation, and the German bond rate.

The test of long-run weak exogeneity (Johansen and Juselius, 1990) investigates the absence of long-run levels feed-back and is formulated as a zero row of α, i.e. $H_\alpha^i : \alpha_{ij} = 0$, $j = 1, ..., r$, where H_α^i is a hypothesis that the variable x_i, $i = 1, ..., p$, does not adjust to the equilibrium errors $\beta_i' x_t$, $i = 1, ..., r$. If accepted, the variable in question can be considered a driving variable in the system: it 'pushes' the system, but is not being 'pushed' by it.

The last row of Table 2 reports the LR test results of weak exogeneity. Both of the long-term bond rates were found to be weakly exogenous. The joint test of weak exogeneity was accepted with a p-value of 0.70. This result, together with the rejection of weak exogeneity of the short-term interest rates, suggests that it is the shocks to long-term interests rates, rather than to the short-term interest rates which are driving the variables of this system. The rejection of weak exogeneity for the inflation rates, (similarly rejected in Juselius and MacDonald (2003)) suggests that prices have adjusted to deviations from the parity conditions. This is a surprising result as the theoretical prediction of a floating DM/USD rate and price stickiness would suggest the opposite. However, this finding seems to be consistent with the result in Frydman and Goldberg (2003) which shows that with imperfect infor-

Table 3: A structural representation of the cointegrating space.

	$Eigenvectors\ \beta$ (appr. t−values in brackets)				$Weights\ \alpha$ (t−values in brackets)		
Var	$\hat{\beta}_1$	$\hat{\beta}_2$	$\hat{\beta}_3$	Eq.	$\hat{\alpha}_1$	$\hat{\alpha}_2$	$\hat{\alpha}_3$
Δp_t	**1.0**	**−1.0**	1.0	$\Delta^2 p_t$	**−1.02** (-9.4)	−0.11 (-1.0)	0.04 (0.5)
Δp_t^*	**−0.30** (7.6)	**1.0**	**-1.0**	$\Delta^2 p_t^*$	**−0.56** (-6.08)	**- 0.56** (-6.32)	**0.16** (2.2)
i_t^l	**−0.70** (17.3)	**1.0**	**1.55** (8.15)	Δi_t	0.01 (0)	0.00 (0)	0.00 (0)
i_t^{l*}	0	**−1.0**	**−1.55**	Δi_t^*	0.00 (0)	0.00 (0.0)	0.00 (0)
i_t^s	0	0	**−1.0**	Δi_t^s	0.01 (1.3)	**0.04** (4.45)	**0.03** (−3.7)
i_t^{s*}	0	0	**1.0**	Δi_t^{s*}	−0.01 (−1.1)	**−0.05** (−2.3)	**−0.04** (−4.1)
$ppp_t^{1)}$	0	**-0.94** (13.4)	0	Δppp_t	**0.03** (1.9)	**0.05** (4.2)	**0.02** (1.77)
$Ds91.03$	-0.001	0.002	-0.002				
$const.$	0.003	-0.003	0.003				

[1)] The ppp term has been divided by 100

mation expectations, traders' behavior is likely to push exchange rates away from the PPP benchmark level, even if expectations are based on macroeconomic fundamentals. Thus, it seems hard to interpret the large fluctuations in real (and nominal) exchange rates as being caused by rigidities in the goods markets. Instead, it seems more likely that they have been generated by traders' behavior in the foreign exchange market.

6   A Fully Identified Long-Run Structure

Relying on the test results reported in Table 2 we tested the following joint hypothesis on the full cointegration structure:

$$\mathcal{H}_{26}: \quad \beta = \{H_1\varphi_1, H_2\varphi_2, H_3\varphi_3\}, \tag{13}$$

where H_1 corresponds to a homogeneous relation between German price inflation, US price inflation and German bond rate ($\mathcal{H}_{25}$), H_2 to a real interest rate parity relation between Germany and USA and the ppp term ($\mathcal{H}_{22}$), and H_3 to a relation between the real German and US tbill spread and the ppp term ($\mathcal{H}_{24}$). The nine overidentifying restrictions were tested with the LR test procedure in Johansen and Juselius (1994) and accepted with a p-value of 0.85. The joint test of the structure (13) together with the weak exogeneity of the two bond rates (six zero coefficients) produced the same p-value of 0.85. Table 3 reports the estimated results based on the latter case. All β coefficients are strongly significant, implying that the estimated structure is both formally and empirically identified. Figure 5 shows the graphs of the three equilibrium error correction mechanisms, $\beta_i' x_t$, $i = 1, 2, 3$, all of which appear very stationary.

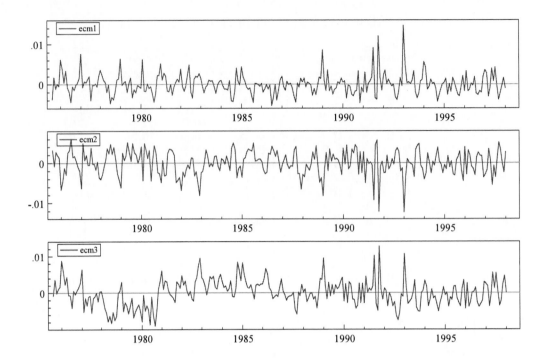

Figure 5: The graphs of the three equilibrium error correction mechanisms

The first vector represents a German inflation relation and is given by:

$$\Delta p_t = 0.30\Delta p_t^* + 0.70 i_t^l + 0.001 D91.3_t - 0.003 + stat.error. \qquad (14)$$

The interpretation is that German inflation is related both to the US inflation rate (an imported inflation effect) and to the domestic long-term bond rate. The shift dummy is consistent with a small increase in German inflation after the reunification, and the constant term shows that German inflation, on average, is lower than the implied value as given by the determinants. As reported in Table 3, the short-run adjustment to (14) occurs primarily through changes in the German inflation rate, signifying its importance as a German relationship. However, the US inflation has reacted similarly, i.e. negatively, though less strongly so, to positive deviations from this relation.

The second cointegrating relationship, representing international real interest rate parity, is given by:

$$(i_t^{l*} - \Delta p_t^*) = (i_t^l - \Delta p_t) - 0.01 ppp_t + 0.002 D91.3_t - 0.003 + stat.error. \qquad (15)$$

The short-run adjustment to (15), reported in Table 3, occurs primarily through changes in US inflation rate, signifying its importance for the US economy. The interpretation is that the US real interest rate increases relative to the German rate when the ppp term is negative; i.e. when US prices are above German prices measured in the same currency. However, the US real interest rate is on average lower (0.003) than the German real interest rate given the *ppp* effect (we interpret this as a safe haven effect). Considering the large variations in real bond rates over this period, illustrated by the graphs of Figure 3, the fact that we have been able to recover a strong-form version of real interest rate parity seems quite remarkable.

The third vector is a function of real short-term interest rates and the bond spread and can be written as:

$$i_t^{s*} - \Delta p_t^* = (i_t^s - \Delta p_t) + 1.55(i_t^l - i_t^{l*}) + 0.002D91.3 + 0.003.$$

This relationship is interesting since it suggests that short-term real interest rate parity would be satisfied as a stationary relation if the long-term bond spread would become stationary. However, the nonstationarity of the bond spread is likely to be related to the nonstationary deviations from the steady-state value of the *ppp* rate. *Empirically, this means that only in periods when the ppp rate has returned to its steady-state path and the bond yield differential has become stationary is it possible to find evidence of real interest rate parities, as the stationary relations theory would predict.*

Thus our analysis suggests that empirical support for the theoretical parities might very well be found in the data, but as long as the economies stay away from their fundamental steady-state positions, direct evidence is unlikely to be found. In that sense the cointegrating relationships which we have established could be said to contain the 'theoretical' parities as a special case. For example, in the hypothetical situation where real exchange rates have returned to their steady-state path, the *ppp* term should be stationary and so the current account should also be balanced. With no need to finance the current account, the spread between bond yields should be stationary and the other parities would also be individually stationary.

It is noteworthy that the long-term bond rates show no evidence of adjusting to any of the long-run relations, whereas the two treasury bill rates are strongly adjusting to the last two steady-state relations. This seems to be against the expectation's hypothesis which predicts that short-term interest rates should act as exogenous variables and, hence, drive long-term rates. The significant adjustment of the US short rate to the cointegrating vectors reflects its role as a money market determined interest rate, but the lack of adjustment in the long-term bond rates seems to suggest that the transmission of the money market effects to the long-rates is not there, or only weakly so. This will be further investigated in the next section.

The ppp_t is adjusting to all three cointegrating relations although very slowly so. Therefore the finding in Table 2 that the ppp_t term is quite close to being weakly exogenous does not imply that future real exchange rates can drift away without any bounds, but only that there is a lot of inertia in the movements back to its fundamental value. Although the predictive value of ppp_t for one-step-ahead predictions may not be very high, when it comes to predictions over longer periods it is likely to increase substantially. This interpretation is strongly supported by the results of the long-run impact analysis in Section 8.

Table 4: A multivariate equilibrium-correction model

Eq.	$\Delta^2 p_t$	$\Delta^2 p_t^*$	Δi_t^l	Δi_t^s	Δi_t^{s*}	Δppp_t
Δi_t^{l*}	1.11 (2.7)	1.29 (3.5)	0.26 (8.2)	−0.22 (3.8)	0.52 (10.1)	−0.20 (3.0)
Δi_{t-1}^{l*}	-	-	-	1.16 (7.3)	-	0.14 (2.2)
Δi_{t-1}^{l}	-	-	0.34 (6.6)	-	−	−
Δi_{t-1}^{s}	-	1.57 (3.2)	−	0.11 (2.4)	-	-
Δi_{t-1}^{s*}	-	−	0.03 (2.0)	-	0.34 (13.0)	-
$ecm1_{t-1}$	−1.06 (11.2)	−0.51 (6.0)	0.01 (3.0)	-	-	-
$ecm2_{t-1}$	−0.20 (2.5)	−0.67 (9.4)	−	0.02 (4.1)	−0.02 (2.7)	0.03 (2.8)
$ecm3_{t-1}$	-	−	-	0.01 (2.1)	−0.02 (2.9)	0.02 (2.0)

The standardized residual covariance matrix (standard errors in diag)

$\Delta^2 p_t$	(0.00193)					
$\Delta^2 p_t^*$	0.25	(0.00169)				
Δi_t^l	0.04	0.12	(0.00014)			
Δi_t^s	−0.12	−0.05	−0.51	(0.00018)		
Δi_t^{s*}	−0.10	−0.08	0.01	−0.01	(0.00020)	
Δppp_t	−0.01	−0.02	0.03	−0.02	−0.09	(0.00030)

7　A Short-Run Adjustment Structure

Using the identified cointegration relations reported in Table 3 we first estimated a multi-variate dynamic equilibrium error correction model for the system.[6] Because the US bond rate was found to be strongly exogenous we re-estimated the system conditional on the marginal model for this rate. By first removing insignificant lagged variables from the system, based on an F-test, and then removing insignificant coefficients from the equations, based on a Likelihood Ratio test, we arrived at the parsimonious model presented in Table 4. The column heading in the top half of the table indicates the dependent variable in each of the model equations, while the row headings indicate the conditioning variables.

Except for a negative correlation between the shocks to the German interest rates (-0.51) the residual cross correlations are essentially zero. Note that the standard deviation of the residuals from the monthly changes in CPI inflation rates is approximately 0.2%. The estimated coefficients of the included dummy variables are presented in Appendix I. The LR test of overidentifying restrictions, distributed as $\chi^2(136)$, was 156.7 and the restrictions were accepted with a p-value of 0.11. Of the 136 exclusion restrictions only 12 are related to the system variables. The latter were accepted with a p-value of 0.71. The remaining restrictions are associated with the many intervention dummies needed to account for the turbulent movements in US treasury bill rate during the period of monetary targeting in

---

[6] All calculations have been performed in PcFiml (see Doornick and Hendry (1998)).

the beginning of the eighties. In addition, the monthly seasonal dummy variables are only included in the US and German inflation rate equations.

In terms of the contemporaneous effects, we note that the weakly exogenous US bond rate is the only significant one and it has a pervasive effect, appearing in all equations, whereas a change in the German bond rate only has an immediate effect on the German treasury bill rate. The effect of lagged changes to the system variables can be seen to be very modest.

The significant adjustment effects of the error correction terms are notable. Both inflation rates are strongly adjusting to $ecm1$, the German inflation relation, and $ecm2$, the long-term real interest parity relation, but German inflation adjusts much more strongly to $ecm1$ and US inflation more strongly to $ecm2$. The adjustment coefficients to the two ecm terms are negative, both in the German and US inflation equations which seems surprising. To be able to interpret this result we have calculated the underlying steady-state relation, being a combination of the significant ecm's weighted by the adjustment coefficients, for each of the two inflation rates.

For the German inflation rate the combined effects became:

$$\Delta p = 0.18\Delta p^* + 0.59i^l + 0.23i^{l*} + 0.003ppp,$$

and for the US inflation:

$$\Delta p^* = 0.32\Delta p + 0.68i^{l*} + 0.65(i^{l*} - i^l) + 0.010ppp.$$

It appears that German inflation has adjusted homogeneously to German and US bond rates and to US inflation. US inflation has similarly adjusted homogeneously to the German inflation rate and the US bond rate, and, additionally, also to the bond rate spread. Altogether, the results seem to indicate the long-term interest rates play a very fundamental role for the determination of inflation rates *implying that the cost of long-term financing has an important effect on prices.* Furthermore, US inflation is equilibrium error correcting to the ppp term (though not sufficiently fast to restore fundamental equilibrium exchange rates), whereas the ppp effect on German inflation is neglible.

The German bond rate is only very weakly reacting to $ecm1$, i.e. to 'excess' German inflation, consistent with the previous finding that it is essentially weakly exogenous. The two treasury bill rates and the ppp term adjust similarly to $ecm2$ and $ecm3$, i.e. to deviations from the long-term and short-term real interest rate parity conditions. To facilitate interpretation of these relationships we also derive the combined steady state relations for these variables. The combined steady-state relation for the German treasury bill rate became:

$$i^s - i^{s*} = 3.5(i^l - i^{l*}) + (\Delta p^* - \Delta p) - 0.02ppp,$$

and for US treasury bill rate:

$$i^{s*} - i^s = 2.5(i^{l*} - i^l) + 0.01ppp.$$

and, finally, for the ppp term:

$$ppp = 0.35(\Delta p^* - \Delta p) - 2(i^{l*} - i^l) + 0.65(i^{s*} - i^s).$$

Thus, the treasury bill rates adjust strongly to the long-term bond spread, but also to the deviation from the *ppp* term and in the case of German rate the inflation rate differential.

The *ppp* term adjusts homogeneously to the inflation spread and the short-term interest spread and shows a strong negative effect from the US-German long-term bond spread. The results confirm the crucial role of the long-term interest rate, but also the short-term interest rates for the development of the real exchange rates in this period. It is quite interesting that an increase in the spread between US and German bond rates is associated with an appreciation of the dollar, whereas the opposite is the case with an increase in the short spread and the inflation rate differential.

Altogether the results seem to suggest that the reserve currency (safe haven) effect of the dollar has indeed prevented the adjustment towards equilibrium exchange rates and resulted in the overvalued dollar. The need to finance the low US savings rate drives up the US bond rate relative to the German rate and the increase in the bond yield results in the US\$ appreciating, making the adjustment towards stationary real exchange rates very slow.

8 The Long-Run Impact of Shocks

We noted above that the German and US long bond yields are weakly exogenous for the long-run parameters, β, implying that they act as driving variables (a common stochastic trend) in the system. By inverting the VAR subject to the reduced rank restriction $\Pi = \alpha\beta'$ we get the so called moving average representation:

$$x_t = C \sum_1^t \varepsilon_i + C\Phi_1 \sum_1^t D_i + C\Phi_2 \sum_1^t S_i + C^*(L)(\varepsilon_t + \mu + \Phi_1 S_t + \Phi_2 D_t) + Z_0 \quad (16)$$

where $C = \beta_\perp(\alpha'_\perp \Gamma \beta_\perp)^{-1}\alpha'_\perp$, $C^*(L)$ is an infinite polynomial in the lag operator L, and Z_0 is a function of the initial values. Based on (16) it is possible to calculate the impulse responses of a shock to one variable and how it is transmitted over time within the system. Instead of reporting the impulse response functions for a unitary change of $\hat{\varepsilon}_{it}$, we report only the final impact matrix, C in Table 5.

The estimates of the columns of the C matrix in Table 5 measures the total impact of permanent shocks to each of the variables on all other variables of the system. A row of the C matrix gives an indication of which shocks have been particularly important for the stochastic trend behavior of the variable in that specific row. The t-ratios in parenthesis are based on the asymptotic standard errors suggested by Paruolo (1997).

These results reinforce our previous findings from the analysis of the long-run relations. We note that cumulative shocks to the inflation rates have no significant long-run impact on any of the variables, accentuating our previous findings that inflation rates are solely adjusting in this system, but not pushing. We also note that the two long term bond yields have significant cumulative impacts on the US short term interest rate yield (the German long bond yield also has a significant impact on the German short rate), the *ppp* term and to some extent also on inflation rates, whereas shocks to the short-term interest rates have no long-run impact on the bond rates. The latter result is again in conflict with the basic premise of the expectations hypothesis of the term structure. Furthermore, permanent

Table 5: The estimates of the long-run impact matrix C

	$\Sigma\varepsilon_{\Delta p}$	$\Sigma\varepsilon_{\Delta p*}$	$\Sigma\varepsilon_{i^b}$	$\Sigma\varepsilon_{i^{b*}}$	$\Sigma_{\varepsilon i^s}$	$\Sigma\varepsilon_{i^{s*}}$	$\Sigma\varepsilon_{ppp}$
Δp_t	0.00 (0.3)	0.01 (0.6)	**0.68** (3.7)	0.17 (1.2)	0.10 (1.1)	**0.25** (2.6)	**0.29** (5.3)
Δp_t^*	0.01 (0.5)	0.02 (1.1)	-0.29 (-0.8)	0.28 (1.1)	0.15 (0.9)	**0.73** (4.1)	**0.97** (9.4)
i_t^l	0.00 (0.0)	0.00 (0.0)	**1.33** (5.6)	0.26 (1.4)	0.00 (0.2)	0.02 (0.2)	0.03 (0.4)
i_t^{l*}	-0.00 (-0.0)	- 0.00 (−0.0)	0.08 (0.3)	**1.21** (5.4)	0.00 (0.0)	−0.00 (-0.0)	−0.01 (−0.1)
i_t^s	-0.00 (-0.2)	0.00 (0.1)	**1.22** (3.9)	-0.33 (-1.4)	**0.91** (6.6)	**0.41** (2.5)	-0.26 (-2.8)
i_t^{s*}	0.00 (0.2)	0.01 (0.6)	**-1.27** (-2.9)	**1.49** (4.5)	**0.53** (2.8)	**0.61** (2.7)	**0.42** (3.3)
ppp_t	0.01 (0.5)	0.02 (0.8)	**0.44** (1.5)	**-0.70** (-3.1)	−0.29 (-2.3)	**0.35** (2.2)	**0.82** (9.1)

shocks to the short-term US treasury bill rate have a permanent positive impact on inflation rates. Thus, increases in the US short-term interest rate tend to increase inflation and not the other way around, as a standard macro model would predict. Permanent shocks to the *ppp* term are also important as they have a significant long-run impact on inflation rates and short term bill yields.

Therefore, the results strongly suggest that developments in 'world' financial markets, as measured by the dominant rate yields - the US and German long rates and the treasury bill rates - are driving this system and inflation rates are essentially adjusting. This latter finding reinforces the point made earlier that the Fisher conditions do not seem to work in the predicted manner.

9 The Role of Short-Term Interest Rates

To gain further perspective on the role of short-term interest rates relative to long-term interest rates we report, in Table 6, a comparative analysis of the combined effects, as measured by $\hat{\alpha}_r\hat{\beta}_r' = \hat{\Pi}_r$, where the subscript r stands for the restricted estimates as reported in Table 3, for the full system, including both long and short interest rates and for a smaller system without short rates (as reported in Juselius and MacDonald (2000)).

¿From these results it appears that German inflation is essentially unaffected by the inclusion of the treasury bill rates into the analysis. It is, as in the small system, determined by the long bond rate and US inflation. The results for US inflation show that the US short-term treasury bill rate has now replaced the long-term bond rates in the small system. However, the results for the US treasury bill rate show significant reaction from the bond yield spread.

Our analysis suggests it seems likely that the short-run effects go from bond rates influencing treasury bill rates, influencing inflation rates. Indeed, the results in Table 5 showed that the long-run impact on US inflation derives from permanent shocks to the short-term

Table 6: The combined long-run effects

Eq.	Δp_t	Δp_t^*	i_t^l	i_t^{l*}	ppp_t		
	The combined effects $\Pi = \alpha\beta'$						
$\Delta^2 p_t$	**-0.88** (-12.8)	**0.19** (2.9)	**0.58** (12.0)	-0.12 (-1.5)	0.15 (1.8)		
$\Delta^2 p_t^*$	0.08 (1.3)	**-0.47** (-7.3)	**-0.13** (-2.6)	**0.44** (7.5)	**0.58** (7.5)		
Δi_t^l	0.01 (0.8)	-0.00 (-0.3)	-0.00 (-0.8)	0.00 (0.0)	0.00 (0.0)		
Δi_t^{l*}	-0.01 (-1.6)	0.01 (0.7)	0.01 (1.5)	-0.02 (-0.2)	-0.00 (-0.2)		
Δppp_t	0.006 (0.5)	0.012 (1.1)	-0.002 (-0.2)	-0.014 (-1.5)	-0.02 (1.5)		
	Δp_t	Δp_t^*	i_t^l	i_t^{l*}	ppp_t	i_t^s	i_t^{s*}
$\Delta^2 p_t$	**-0.88** (-12.4)	**0.15** (2.1)	**0.46** (2.4)	-0.01 (-0.0)	0.11 (1.2)	0.07 (0.9)	0.05 (0.6)
$\Delta^2 p_t^*$	**0.13** (2.2)	**-0.56** (-9.0)	-0.19 (-1.2)	0.21 (1.2)	**0.52** (6.3)	0.08 (1.24)	**0.23** (3.0)
Δi_t^l	-0.00 (-0.0)	0.00 (0.4)	-0.00 (-0.2)	0.00 (0.2)	-0.00 (-0.1)	0.00 (0.2)	-0.00 (-0.4)
Δi_t^{l*}	-0.01 (-1.7)	0.01 (1.1)	-0.01 (-1.0)	0.02 (1.3)	0.01 (0.6)	0.01 (1.1)	-0.01 (-1.0)
Δppp_t	0.008 (0.7)	0.01 (1.3)	**0.08** (2.6)	**-0.09** (-2.8)	**-0.05** (-3.2)	**-0.03** (-2.8)	0.02 (1.8)
Δi_t^s	0.00 (0.3)	0.01 (1.46)	**0.07** (4.4)	**-0.08** (-4.5)	**-0.04** (-4.7)	**-0.03** (-4.6)	**0.02** (3.3)
Δi_t^{s*}	-0.01 (-1.3)	-0.00 (-0.2)	**-0.12** (-5.1)	**0.13** (5.3)	**0.05** (4.7)	**0.05** (5.4)	**-0.05** (-4.6)

treasury bill rates, and the effect is positive rather than the negative sign [7] that would be expected form conventional theory.

Consistent with the weak exogeneity results of Table 2, the equations for the German and US bond rate exhibit hardly any significant effects. The ppp term is significantly affected by the bond and the short-term spread, such that the US\$ appreciates with an increasing bond spread and depreciates with an increasing treasury bill spread.

The results for the short-term treasury bill equations show strong adjustment to essentially all determinants except for inflation rates! The lack of significant inflationary effects in all four interest rate equations is very pronounced. This is to be contrasted with the significant interest rate effects in the inflation rate equations. Similar results have also been found in Danish, Spanish, and Italian data (Juselius, 1991, Juselius and Toro, 2004, Juselius, 2001).

10 Summary and Conclusions

This paper has empirically examined the joint determination of a number of key parity conditions for Germany and the US using monthly data from the recent experience with floating exchange rates. The vector of variables considered in this paper, consisted of the German

---

[7]This is a frequent empirical finding, the so called "price puzzle".

Mark-US dollar exchange rate, prices, short term interest rates and long term interest rates. We used the cointegrated VAR model to define long-run stationary relationships as well as common stochastic trends, and a general-to-specific approach to produce parsimonious dynamic short-run equations. We now summarize our main findings.

Our results strongly rejected the stationarity hypothesis of the 'pure' parity conditions. However, by allowing them to be interdependent, stationarity was recovered. The important finding was that the nonstationarity of the 'simple' parity relationships was primarily related to the nonstationarity of the ppp exchange rate and the long-term bond rate differential. An obvious interpretation of the results was that the lack of empirical support for the simple parity conditions was due to the lack of (or very, very slow) adjustment to a stationary ppp steady state and increasing long-term bond spreads as a plausible consequence of the latter. Thus, the theoretical assumption of stationary parity conditions appeared to be a special case of a more general formulation allowing for persistent deviations from steady-state and, hence, market failure in a simple model framework.

Our cointegration analysis indicated the existence of four common trends (three cointegrating relationships) and we propose interpreting these as: (1) a nominal price trend driving the goods market, (2) a trend describing relative national savings behavior, (3) a 'safe haven' trend capturing the role of the dollar as a world reserve currency, and (4) a short-term capital market trend describing central bank policy behavior.

Not surprisingly, the empirical modification of the original parity conditions as a result of the above 'market failure' trends, produced a number of new results related to the dynamics of the international transmission mechanism. Some of the major (empirically strong) findings were the following:

1. In our system of inflation rates, ppp exchange rates, 10 year bond rates and 3 months treasury bill rates, US and German long-term bond rates proved to be the main driving forces and not the short-term interest rates.

2. US and German inflation rates were strongly adjusting to the other variables of the system, primarily to the bond rates and the ppp term, but they were not affecting the other variables, in particular, they did not push nominal interest rates.

3. The nonstationary movements in the bond and inflation rate differential were closely related to the nonstationary movements in the ppp exchange rate.

4. The short-term interest rates (the 3 months treasury bill rates) were important for the determination of the ppp exchange rate both in the short and the long run. They had essentially no impact on the bond rates and the inflation rates, with the caveat that the US short rate had a positive (cost push) effect on US inflation.

5. Permanent shocks to long-term, as well as to short-term, interest rates had a positive long-run impact on inflation, perhaps signifying the cost effect of interest rates on the capital stock.

The above findings were shown to be remarkably robust (empirically as well as econometrically) over a period of fundamental changes and therefore cannot be discarded as sample dependent results. Our findings seem to suggest that:

1. The role of the dollar as a reserve currency (the 'safe haven' effect) has facilitated relatively cheap financing of the large US current account deficits in this period. This might explain one of the 'market failure' puzzles: why an adequate adjustment toward purchasing power parity between the USA and Germany has not taken place.

2. The large differences between national savings rates seemed to be an important reason why the long-term bond rates were found to be so crucial in this system.

3. Though the role of central bank policy for stabilizing the short-term capital market has evidently been crucial as the turbulent years of monetary targeting in the eighties demonstrated, its role for controlling inflation seemed much more modest than is usually believed.

However, although the non-stationary of the parities will disappear with the disappearance of other disequilibria in the economy, in the presence of free capital movements we do not believe that the parity reversals in the term structure and Fisher relationships, will disappear. The latter finding would appear to have important policy implications.

Finally, by joint modelling of the parities we have managed not only to recover stationary parity conditions, but also to describe the variation of the data with a remarkable degree of precision as evidenced by the very small residual standard errors. Hence, the results should be used as a benchmark against which the results of other models, possibly with more theory content, could be evaluated.

11   Appendix I: The Data

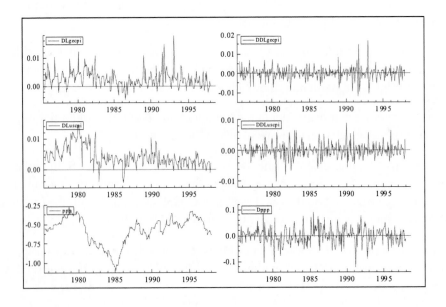

Figure 6: Figure A.1: The graphs of German and US CPI inflation and real exchange rate in levels (l.h.s. panels) and differences (r.h.s. panels).

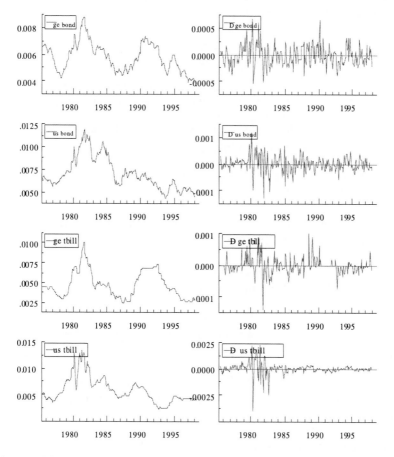

Figure 7: Figure A.2: The graphs of the German and US bond rate and 3 months tbill rates in levels (r.h.s. panels) and differences (l.h.s. panels).

References

Campbell, J.Y. (1995), 'Some lessons from the yield curve'. *Journal of Economic Perspective*s, Vol. 9, 3, pp.129-52.

Campbell, J.Y. and R. Shiller, R. (1987), 'Cointegration and tests of present value models', *Journal of Political Economy*, Vol. 95, 1062-88.

Cumby, R. and M. Obstfeld (1981), 'Exchange rate expectations and nominal interest rates: A test of the Fisher hypothesis', *Journal of Finance*, **36**, 697-703.

Doornik, J.A. and D.F. Hendry (1998), 'GiveWin. An Interface to Empirical Modelling', Timberlake Consultants.

Dornbusch, R. (1976), 'Expectations and exchange rate dynamics' *Journal of Political Economy,*pp 1161-76.

Froot, K. and K. Rogoff (1995) 'Perspectives on PPP and long-run real exchange rates', in *Handbook of International Economics*, Vol 3, (eds.), E. Grossman and K. Rogoff,

Vol. 3 Amsterdam: North Holland.

Frydman, R and M. Goldberg (2003), 'Imperfect knowledge expectations, uncertainty adjusted UIP and exchange rate dynamics' in Aghion, P., Frydman, R., Stiglitz, J. and M. Woodford (eds.), *Knowledge, Information, and Expectations in Modern Macroeconomics: In Honor of Edmund S. Phelps*, Princeton University Press.

Gonzalo, J. (1994): "Five alternative methods of estimating long-run equilibrium relationships," *Journal of Econometrics*, **60**, 203-233.

Hallwood, P. and R. MacDonald (1999), *International Money and Finance*, Third Edition, Oxford: Basil Blackwell.

Hansen, H. and S. Johansen (1999), 'Some tests for parameter constancy in the cointegrated VAR-model' *Econometrics Journal*, **2**, 306-333.

Hansen, H. and K. Juselius (1994), 'CATS in RATS, Manual to Cointegration Analysis of Time Series', Estima, Evanstone, IL.

Johansen, S. and K. Juselius (1990) 'The full information maximum likelihood procedure for inference on cointegration - with applications' *Oxford Bulletin of Statistics and Economics*, vol. 52, 2. pp 169-211.

Johansen, S. and K. Juselius (1992), 'Testing structural hypotheses in a multivariate cointegration analysis of the PPP and the UIP for UK', *Journal of Econometrics* **53**, 211-244.

Johansen, S. and K. Juselius (1994), 'Identification of the long-run and the short-run structure, An application to the ISLM model,' *Journal of Econometrics*, **63**, 7-36.

Juselius, K. (1991) 'Long-run relations in a well defined statistical model for the data generating process. Cointegration analysis of the ppp and the uip relations for Denmark and Germany.' In Gruber, J (ed.): Econometric Decision models: New Methods of Modeling and Applications. Springer Verlag.

Juselius, K. (1994), 'VAR models and Haavelmo's probability approach to macroeconomic modeling', *Empirical Economics*, **18**, 598-622.

Juselius, K. (1995), 'Do purchasing power parity and uncovered interest rate parity hold in the long run? An example of likelihood inference in a multivariate time-series model' *Journal of Econometrics*, **69**, 211-240.

Juselius, K. (1999), 'Models and relations in economics and econometrics', *Journal of Economic Methodology* **6**:2, 259-290,

Juselius, K. (2001), 'European integration and monetary transmission mechanisms: The case of Italy', *Journal of Applied Econometrics* (2001)16, 341-358.

Juselius, K. and R. MacDonald (2000), 'International parity relationships between Germany and the United States: A joint modelling approach' Institute of Economics, University of Copenhagen, *Working Paper*, **10**, http://www.econ.ku.dk/wpa/

Juselius, K. and R. MacDonald (2003), 'International parity conditions between the US and Japan' forthcoming in *Japan and the World Economy*.

Juselius, K. and J. Toro (2004)'Monetary transmission mechanisms in Spain: The effect of monetization, financial deregulation, and the EMS' forthcoming in the *Journal of International Money and Finance*.

Krugman, P. (1993), 'Exchange-Rate Instability' The MIT Press, Cambridge, Massachusetts.

Lothian, J. (1997), 'Multi-country evidence on the behaviour of purchasing power parity under the current float', *Journal of International Money and Finance*.

MacDonald, R. (1988), *Floating Exchange Rates: Theories and Evidence*, London: Allen and Unwin.

MacDonald, R. (1995), 'Long-run exchange rate modelling: a survey of the recent evidence', *International Monetary Fund Staff Papers*, **42**

MacDonald, R. and I.W. Marsh (1997) 'On Fundamentals and Exchange Rates: A Casselian Perspective', *Review of Economics and Statistics*, **78**, 655-664.

MacDonald, R. and I.W. Marsh (1999), *Exchange Rate Modelling*, Kluwer Academic Publishers.

MacDonald, R. and J. Stein (1999), *Equilibrium Exchange Rates*, Kluwer Academic Publishers.

Paruolo, P. (1997), 'Asymptotic inference on the moving average impact matrix in cointegrated $I(1)$ VAR systems'. *Econometic Theory* **13**, 79-118.

In: International Macroeconomics: Recent Developments
Editor: Amalia Morales Zumaquero, pp. 105-117

ISBN: 1-59454-901-X

Chapter 6

LONG RUN REAL EXCHANGE RATE OVERVALUATION: EVIDENCE FROM ASIA

*Stephen Y. L. Cheung[*1] and Vikas Kakkar[*2]*

Department of Economics and Finance, City University of Hong Kong
Tat Chee Avenue, Kowloon, Hong Kong, +852-2788-9707

Abstract

This paper studies the bilateral real exchange rates of 5 East Asian economies vis-à-vis the U.S. dollar and tests whether permanent changes in these real exchange rates can be explained by permanent changes in the relative prices of nontraded- to traded-goods. We find that, with the exception of the South Korean-U.S. real exchange rate, the other 4 real exchange rates are cointegrated with the relative prices of nontraded- to traded-goods. We propose a new measure of real exchange rate misalignment based on this long run relationship, and calculate estimates of misalignment prior to the Asian currency crisis. For all 4 countries, the proposed measure yields protracted and economically significant overvaluations prior to the crisis. By contrast, a PPP-based measure yields the counterintuitive result that the real exchange rates were significantly *undervalued* prior to the Asian currency crisis.

[*] The authors thank Charles Goodhart, Michael Melvin, Guy Meredith, Nicholas Sarantis, and participants at the Tenth Workshop on Asian Economic Outlook organized by the Asian Development Bank, the Joint Annual Conference of the International Economics and Finance Society-UK and the Centre for International Capital markets of the London Metropolitan University, and the Australasian Macroeconomics Workshop organized by the Hong Kong Institute for Monetary Research for helpful comments on earlier drafts. The usual disclaimer applies.

[1] E-mail address: efsteven@cityu.edu.hk

[2] E-mail address: efvikas@cityu.edu.hk

1   Introduction

The real exchange rate, defined as the relative price of domestic goods to foreign goods, is a key relative price for any open economy.[1] Economists and policy makers have long held the view that a misaligned real exchange rate significantly reduces the welfare of a country (Edwards 1988, Willet 1986). Overvalued real exchange rates, for example, are often blamed for deteriorating the trade balance of a country and making it more vulnerable to economic instability. Recent work (Kaminsky, Lizondo and Reinhart 1998) suggests that a rapid appreciation of the real exchange rate, presumably a reflection of misalignment, is among the most successful predictors of currency crises.

Identifying real exchange rate misalignments is therefore one of the most important and challenging tasks confronting students of international economics. The theory of Purchasing Power Parity (PPP) has traditionally been viewed as determining the long run equilibrium exchange rate, and is often used to assess exchange rate misalignments (Artus, 1978). However, an important drawback of the PPP-based misalignment measures is that deviations of exchange rates from their PPP*s* tend to be near permanent. Although the recent literature on PPP has documented some evidence of mean reversion, the unit-root nonstationarity of real exchange rates is virtually a stylized fact in international finance.[2]

One possible explanation for the persistent deviations from PPP that has received attention in the recent literature is the presence of nontradable goods in the general price indices used in constructing real exchange rates.[3] If PPP holds only for tradables, then any factor that permanently changes the relative price of nontradables (such as a permanent productivity shock) will cause a permanent shift in the real exchange rate. Repeated permanent shocks will therefore create long run comovements between relative prices of nontradable goods and the real exchange rate.

The main objectives of this paper are to test whether changes in the relative price of nontradables can account for the long run changes in the real exchange rates of Asian economies, and if so, to utilize these long run comovements to construct an alternative measure of real exchange rate misalignment. Although measurement of exchange rate misalignments is (justifiably) a very contentious issue, there are at least four reasons why this measure may be considered reasonable and useful.

First, it is compatible with a wide variety of economic models that use the nontradables approach to real exchange rate determination, such as the celebrated Balassa-Samuelson [Balassa (1964) and Samuelson (1964)] model. It is therefore grounded in economic theory.

Second, given that the real exchange rate is cointegrated with the relative price of nontradables, any gap between the actual real exchange rate and its estimated equilibrium

---

[1] There are several different definitions of the real exchange rate currently in use. This paper uses the "PPP-definition" of the real exchange rate. The reader is referred to Edwards (1988) for a discussion of the various definitions and their relationships.

[2] For instance, Baillie and McMahon (1989), Corbae and Ouliaris (1988), Engel (2000), Mark (1990), Meese and Rogoff (1988), O'Connell (1998), and several other researchers document evidence suggesting that real exchange rates are unit-root nonstationary, thereby implying that PPP fails to hold even in the long-run. While several recent studies (e.g. Frankel and Rose 1995, Lothian and Taylor 1996) have found evidence of mean reversion in real exchange rates, the slow rate of convergence to PPP suggests that persistent real disturbances could plausibly be playing an important role. See the surveys by Froot and Rogoff (1995) and Rogoff (1996) for further details.

[3] See, for example, Chinn (1997), De Gregorio, Giovannini and Wolf (1994), DeLoach (1997), Engel (2000) and Kakkar and Ogaki (1999).

value is not "sustainable" and will eventually be reversed. This is a natural requirement for any estimate of a "long run equilibrium value", but is not satisfied by PPP-based measures of overvaluation.

Third, this framework allows for measurement errors in the prices of tradables and nontradables. This is important because final goods can seldom be characterized as purely traded or purely nontraded. Most goods that are considered tradable, for example, have a nontraded component in the form of retailing services.

Fourth, the proposed measure is easy to compute and only utilizes data that are available over a long time period for several countries.

Our results suggest that, for four of the five Asian economies considered here, their bilateral real exchange rates vis-à-vis the U.S. dollar are indeed cointegrated with the relative prices of nontradable to tradable goods. We apply the nontradables based measure of real exchange rate misalignment to these four economies prior to the Asian currency crisis of 1997, and compare the results to a PPP-based measure of misalignment. Somewhat surprisingly, the PPP-based misalignment measure indicates that the Indonesian, Thai and Philippine currencies were *undervalued* prior to the crisis! By contrast, the proposed nontradables-based measure generally indicates persistent and economically significant overvaluations over a three-year period prior to the crisis.

In related work, Chinn (1998) has also examined the evidence for exchange rate misalignments for Asian economies prior to the crisis. In addition to the PPP-based measures, he computes a measure of misalignment based on a monetary model of exchange rate determination. He finds that the estimated misalignments do not match the prior expectations of an overvaluation very well.[4] An advantage of our framework over the monetary model is its parsimony. Since the model only requires data for three variables (the bilateral real exchange rate, the domestic relative price of nontradables and the foreign relative price of nontradables), this also enables the use of a longer span of data which is important for a reasonable performance of cointegration-based models (Pierse and Snell, 1995).[5]

Table 1. Unit Root Tests for Real Exchange Rates and Relative Prices of Nontraded-Goods

Country/ Sample	$ln(E_r)$		$ln(Q_N)$	
	Z_t^a	$J(1,5)^b$	Z_t^a	$J(1,5)^b$
Indonesia (1971-96)	-1.812	10.800	-1.533	1.967
Korea (1966-96)	-2.198	0.896	-1.108	7.971
Philippines (1949-96)	-1.466	1.883	-1.384	3.018
Singapore (1974-96)	-0.352	13.632	-1.915	3.357

[4] Chinn (1998) also augments his monetary model with the relative price of nontradables, but he does not find this variable to be significant in the case of Indonesia, Malaysia, Singapore and Thailand. Section 4 provides a comparison with his results.

[5] Chinn's sample ranges from 7 years of quarterly data for Indonesia, to 20 years of quarterly data for Singapore, with an average of about 13 years. By contrast, our sample ranges from 23 years of annual data for Singapore to 49 years of annual data for the Philippines, with an average of 35 years.

| Country/ | $ln(E_r)$ | | $ln(Q_N)$ | |
Sample	Z_t^a	$J(1,5)^b$	Z_t^a	$J(1,5)^b$
Thailand (1953-96)	-2.288	0.837	-1.937	1.365
USA (1949-96)	-----	-----	-1.491	2.897

[a] Z_t denotes the Phillips-Perron (1988) t-ratio test for the null hypothesis of a unit root against the alternative of trend stationarity. Critical values used are from MacKinnon (1991)

[b] $J(1,5)$ denotes Park's (1990) test for the null hypothesis of a unit root against the alternative of trend stationarity. The 1%, 5% and 10% critical values are 0.1228, 0.2950 and 0.4520, respectively. These are taken from Ogaki (1993).

2   Model

Consider a world economy with two countries: country H is the home country and country F is the foreign country. In each country, there are two goods: good T is tradable and good N is nontradable. Assume that the general price index of a country, measured by the GDP-deflator, can be expressed as a geometric average of prices of the traded and nontraded goods. That is:

$$P_j^{GDP} = c_j^{GDP} [P_j^N]^{\alpha_j} [P_j^T]^{(1-\alpha_j)} \quad , j = H, F, \tag{1}$$

where α_j is the share of nontradables in the price index. c_j^{GDP} is any factor that causes the geometric average of traded and nontraded goods prices to deviate from the price level, such as a measurement error. It is assumed that c_j^{GDP} is stationary.

Let E be the nominal exchange rate: E units of the domestic currency purchase one unit of the foreign currency. The relative price of nontradable goods in terms of tradable goods is denoted by

$$Q_j = \frac{P_j^N}{P_j^T} \quad , j = H, F. \tag{2}$$

The real exchange rate, E_r, is defined by the general price index:

$$E_r = (\frac{P_H^{GDP}}{EP_F^{GDP}}). \tag{3}$$

An increase in the real exchange rate increases the price of home goods relative to foreign goods, and thus corresponds to a real appreciation. Since traded goods across countries may not be identical, PPP may not hold even for the tradables in the short run. It is assumed that PPP holds for the tradables in the long run:

$$ln(P_H^T) = ln(E) + ln(P_F^T) + u \,,$$ (4)

where u is a stationary random variable with zero mean.[6] Combining equations (1) through (4), the real exchange rate may be written as

$$ln(E_r) = \theta + \alpha_H ln(Q_H) - \alpha_F ln(Q_F) + \varepsilon \,,$$ (5)

where $\varepsilon = \{ln(c_H^{GDP}) - ln(c_F^{GDP})\} - E\{ln(c_H^{GDP}) - ln(c_F^{GDP})\} + u$ is also a zero-mean stationary random variable, and $\theta = E\{ln(c_H^{GDP}) - ln(c_F^{GDP})\}$.[7]

Equation (5) implies that the real exchange rate will move together with the domestic and foreign relative prices of nontradables in the long run. In order to estimate equation (5), one needs measures for the relative price of nontradables in the home and foreign countries. However, it is difficult to measure the prices of *purely* traded and nontraded goods, as most final goods are likely to have *both* traded and nontraded components. To alleviate this measurement problem, two price indices that assign *different* weights to the traded and nontraded components are used.

The *Consumer Price Index* (*CPI*) is based on a fixed basket of goods and services consumed by the average household, and is likely to have a large share of nontraded goods in the form of retailing services, housing, transportation and other services. By contrast, the *Wholesale Price Index* (*WPI*) is generally limited to agricultural and manufacturing sector goods that are largely tradable. It also uses prices that exclude (nontraded) retailing services. Thus the *CPI* and *WPI* may be written as:

$$P_{CPI}^j = c_{CPI}^j [P_N^j]^{\beta_j} [P_T^j]^{1-\beta_j} \quad , j = H, F$$ (6a)

$$P_{WPI}^j = c_{WPI}^j [P_N^j]^{\delta_j} [P_T^j]^{1-\delta_j} \quad , j = H, F.$$ (6b)

Here $c_{CPI}^j (c_{WPI}^j)$ is any factor that causes a deviation between the geometric average of unobserved traded and nontraded goods prices and the *CPI* (*WPI*), such as a measurement error. It is assumed that $1 > \beta_j > \delta_j > 0$ so that the *CPI* has a larger share of nontradables relative to the *WPI*.

---

[6] The stationarity of u implies that a deviation from PPP for tradables is transitory, and vanishes in the long run.

[7] The stationarity of ε follows from the stationarity of c_j^{GDP} and u. It is zero-mean by construction.

As long as these shares are stable over time, the ratio of the *CPI* to the *WPI* will provide a reasonable proxy for the relative price of nontradables for the purpose of estimating a cointegrating regression. To see this, divide equation (6a) by (6b) and express the result in logs:

$$ln(P_{CPI}^{j} / P_{WPI}^{j}) = ln(c_{CPI}^{j} / c_{WPI}^{j}) + (\beta_j - \delta_j)ln(Q_j) \quad , j = H, F. \tag{7}$$

Solving for the unobservable $ln(Q_j)$ from equation (7) and substituting in equation (5) gives

$$ln(E_r) = \lambda + (\frac{\alpha_H}{\beta_H - \delta_H})ln(P_{CPI}^{H} / P_{WPI}^{H}) - (\frac{\alpha_F}{\beta_F - \delta_F})ln(P_{CPI}^{F} / P_{WPI}^{F}) + \eta \tag{8}$$

where $\lambda = \theta + E\{ln(c_{CPI}^{H}/c_{WPI}^{H}) - ln(c_{CPI}^{F}/c_{WPI}^{F})\}$ is a constant, and

$\eta = \varepsilon + \{\{ln(c_{CPI}^{H}/c_{WPI}^{H}) - ln(c_{CPI}^{F}/c_{WPI}^{F})\} - E\{ln(c_{CPI}^{H}/c_{WPI}^{H}) - ln(c_{CPI}^{F}/c_{WPI}^{F})\}$ is   a   zero-mean stationary random variable.

Equation (8) implies that the ratio of *CPI* to *WPI* can be used as a proxy for the relative price of nontradables. We can test the model by testing for cointegration, and checking for the signs and statistical significance of the estimated parameters.[8] This equation forms the basis of the empirical work.

Table 2. Tests for the Null Hypothesis of No Stochastic Cointegration between Domestic and US Relative Prices of Nontraded-Goods

Country/Sample	Z_t^a	$I(1,5)^b$
Indonesia (1971-1996)	-2.669	2.793
Korea (1967-1996)	-1.936	4.028
Philippines (1949-1996)	-2.411	1.011
Singapore (1974-1996)	-1.811	3.193
Thailand (1953-1996)	-3.135	0.304*

[a] Z_t denotes the Phillips-Ouliaris (1990) t-ratio test for the null hypothesis of no stochastic cointegration. Critical values used are from MacKinnon (1991)

[b] $I(1,5)$ denotes Park's (1990) test for the null hypothesis of no stochastic cointegration. The 1%, 5% and 10% critical values are 0.1027, 0.2506 and 0.4984, respectively. These are taken from Ogaki (1993).

* Significant at the 10% level.

---

[8] The plausibility of the magnitude of the estimated coefficients may be established as follows. Suppose that the share of nontradables in the GDP-deflator is about 0.5, about 0.7 in the *CPI*, and about 0.3 in the *WPI*. Then the coefficients of the relative price of nontradables in equation (8) should be greater than 1 in absolute value. Estimates of these coefficients significantly smaller than 1 in absolute value may be construed as evidence against the model.

3   Data and its Trend Properties

We use annual data for five Asian countries and the United States from the *IFS* CD-ROM produced by the *IMF*. The Asian countries are Indonesia, Korea, Singapore, Philippines, and Thailand.[9] Indonesia, Korea, Philippines and Thailand essentially maintained a currency peg against the U.S. dollar. During the crisis, all four countries were forced to abandon the peg, and their currencies suffered substantial depreciations. Asian countries are treated as the home country and the United States as the foreign country.

The statistical testing begins by examining the evidence for the existence of unit roots in the real exchange rate and the proxy for the relative prices of nontradables. Table 1 reports the results of the Phillips-Perron (1988) Z_t test and Park's $J(1,5)$ test for the null hypothesis of a unit root against the alternative of trend stationarity. Neither test rejects the null hypothesis at the 10% significance level for either variable for any of the countries. Thus the assumptions that, these Asian countries' bilateral real exchange rates vis-à-vis the U.S. dollar as well as the U.S. and Asian relative prices of nontradables, are unit-root nonstationary and possess stochastic trends, are supported by these results.

Prior to estimating equation (8), it is also necessary to ensure that the coefficients of home and foreign relative prices of nontradables are identified. If the relative prices of nontradables in the home (Asian) country and the U.S. share a common stochastic trend, then their coefficients cannot be identified by any econometric method. Table 2 tests whether this is the case using the Phillips-Ouliaris (1990) *t*-ratio test and Park's (1990) $I(1,5)$ test for the null hypothesis of no stochastic cointegration. The Phillips-Ouliaris test is not significant for any of the five countries at conventional significance levels, whereas the $I(1,5)$ test is significant at the 10% level only for Thailand. Thus, with the exception of Thailand, for which the evidence is mixed, for all other countries the relative price of nontradables does not appear to be cointegrated with the U.S. relative price of nontradables.

Table 3. Canonical Cointegrating Regressions between Real Exchange Rates and Relative Prices of Nontraded-Goods

Sample	β_1^a	β_2^a	$H(0,1)^b$	$H(1,2)^b$	$H(1,3)^b$
		Indonesia-US			
1971-96	0.3261	-1.3625	2.3912	5.0091	12.9424
	(0.2972)	(0.5158)	(0.1220)	(0.0252)	(0.0015)
		Philippines-US			
1949-96	2.1331	-1.5582	0.6945	0.9603	5.4244
	(0.4805)	(0.6440)	(0.4046)	(0.3271)	(0.0664)

---

[9] Malaysia was not included because its available sample size was only about 10 years.

Sample	β_1^a	β_2^a	$H(0,1)^b$	$H(1,2)^b$	$H(1,3)^b$
		Singapore-US			
1974-96	1.7261	-2.5146	4.6652	0.1604	2.0088
	(0.4218)	(0.6891)	(0.0308)	(0.6888)	(0.3663)
		Thailand-US			
1953-96	0.0931	-0.4543	0.6362	0.3059	0.8627
(Case 1)	(0.6847)	(0.4480)	(0.4251)	(0.5802)	(0.6496)
1953-96	-2.2177	-----	0.0015	2.2010	3.7247
(Case 2)	(0.7301)		(0.9691)	(0.1379)	(0.1553)
		Korea-US			
1966-96	3.7152	-3.7294	8.3310	36.4713	82.1209
	(1.3626)	(1.9722)	(0.0039)	(0.0000)	(0.0000)

[a] Standard errors are in parenthesis.

[b] $H(0,1)$ tests the null hypothesis of the deterministic cointegration restriction. $H(1,2)$ and $H(1,3)$ test the null hypothesis of stochastic cointegration. *P*-values are in parenthesis.

4   Empirical Results

Having verified that the conditions necessary for testing the existence of a long run relationship between the real exchange rate and the relative prices of nontradables are empirically supported, the next step is to estimate equation (8) via a cointegrating regression. Since the economic model implies cointegration, it is desirable to test the null hypothesis of cointegration to control the probability of rejecting a valid economic model. Park's (1992) Canonical Cointegrating Regressions (CCR) procedure is used to test the null hypothesis of stochastic cointegration and the deterministic cointegration restriction.[10] The CCR estimators are asymptotically efficient and have asymptotic distributions that can essentially be considered as normal distributions, so that their standard errors can be interpreted in the usual way.

Table 3 reports the results of the estimation of equation (8) by the CCR procedure.[11] With the exception of South Korea, the $H(1,2)$ test does not reject the null hypothesis of stochastic cointegration for any of the countries at the 1% significance level. The $H(1,3)$ test, which also maintains stochastic cointegration as the null hypothesis, is significant for Indonesia and

---

[10] See Campbell and Perron (1991) and Ogaki and Park (1997) for definitions of stochastic and the deterministic cointegration restriction. The results reported in this paper use Ogaki's (1993) Gauss CCR-package.

[11] Since the Thai relative price of nontradables may be cointegrated with its U.S. counterpart, we estimate two cointegrating regressions for Thailand, one with both relative prices, and another with only the Thai relative price.

Thailand at the 5% significance level, but not for the other countries. The $H(0,1)$ statistic tests the deterministic cointegration restriction implied by the model. With the exception of South Korea, the $H(0,1)$ statistic does not reject the deterministic cointegration restriction at conventional significance levels for any of the countries. Thus, with the exception of South Korea, both the stochastic and deterministic cointegration restrictions implied by the model are supported empirically.

The coefficients of the relative prices of nontradables have the signs predicted by the model for all the countries. For the Indonesia-U.S. regression, the coefficient of the Indonesian relative price of nontradables is not statistically significant, and for the Thailand-U.S. regression (Case 1) both coefficients are insignificant. For all other regressions, the coefficients are statistically significant at conventional levels. Their magnitudes are also plausible after taking into account the standard errors. This is further evidence in favor of the model.

The evidence in favor of cointegration between bilateral real exchange rates and relative prices of nontradables suggests that real exchange rate must eventually revert back to its "long run equilibrium value" implied by the model. Thus, given sufficient time, any disequilibrium will vanish. However, the speed with which such departures from equilibrium are eliminated may well vary across countries. It is possible to estimate the speed of reversion to equilibrium by estimating an error correction model.

Table 4. Estimated Speed of Reversion to the Long Run Equilibrium Real Exchange Rate

$$\Delta \ln(E_r)_t = \alpha_0 + \alpha_1 (ECT)_{t-1} + \sum_{i=1} \lambda_{1i} \Delta \ln(E_r)_{t-i} + \sum_{i=1} \lambda_{2i} \Delta \ln(Q_H)_{t-i} + \sum_{i=1} \lambda_{3i} \Delta \ln(Q_F)_{t-i} + \varepsilon_t$$

Country	α_1^a	Implied Half-Life Estimate[b] (Years)
Indonesia	-0.807** (0.180)	0.86
Philippines	-0.143* (0.080)	4.85
Singapore	-0.425* (0.201)	1.63
Thailand (Case 1)	-0.283** (0.129)	2.45
Thailand (Case 2)	-0.042 (0.080)	16.5

[a] α_1 is the coefficient of the error correction term, ECT, and measures the speed of adjustment to the long-run equilibrium. For e.g., α_1 = -0.283 means that, holding all else constant, 28.3% of the overvaluation in the real exchange rate relative to its long-run equilibrium level, is eliminated in one year. Standard errors are in parenthesis.

[b] The half-life refers to the duration of time required for 50% of the real exchange rate overvaluation to dissipate. It is calculated by solving the following exponential decay equation for T: $e^{\alpha_1 T} = 0.5$.

* and ** indicate statistical significance at the 10% and 5% levels of significance, respectively.

Table 4 reports the results of regressing the first difference of the real exchange rate on the lagged error correction term and lags of the first differences of the relative prices of nontradables.[12] The first column of Table 4 reports the estimated coefficient of the error correction term. The coefficient has the expected negative sign for countries and is also statistically significant with the exception of Thailand in Case 2. The second column calculates the implied half-life of a deviation from the long run equilibrium. The half-life is less than 2.5 years for Indonesia, Singapore and Thailand (Case 1), but is nearly 5 years for the Philippines. These estimates are quite reasonable given that most studies find a half-life of around 5 years for convergence to Purchasing Power Parity. Thus, relative to the constant equilibrium value of the real exchange rate implied by PPP, convergence to the equilibrium value implied by the nontradables-based model is significantly faster.

Table 5. Estimated Percentage Overvaluation of the Real Exchange Rate Prior to Crisis

Country	Average Overvaluation (1994-96)			Overvaluation (1996)		
	Nontraded Model	PPP Model	Monetary Model[*]	Nontraded Model	PPP Model	Monetary Model[*]
Indonesia	10.72	-12.12	4.67	12.68	-9.70	0.93
Philippines	19.98	-16.16	-26.45	20.09	-10.58	-24.63
Singapore	12.06	24.32	45.39	11.65	27.26	35.41
Thailand (Case 1)	6.54	-0.0505	0.0371	10.01	0.00	0.01
Thailand (Case 2)	18.10	-0.0505	0.0371	23.01	0.00	0.01

[*] These figures are based on Chinn's (1998, Table 7) estimation of a monetary model using quarterly data. The Average Overvaluation is measured for the period 1995Q2 to 1997Q1, and the Overvaluation is measured for 1997Q1.

As mentioned in the Introduction, the long run relationship between the real exchange rate and its equilibrium value implied by the model provides a natural estimate of the extent of "misalignment". We exploit this relationship to calculate the implied degree of misalignment prior to the Asian currency crises of 1997. The first column of Table 5 reports the average overvaluation during the three years preceding the currency crisis (i.e., 1994 through 1996). For all four countries, and in both cases for Thailand, the nontradables-based model suggests an overvaluation, varying from a low of about 7% (Thailand under Case 1) to a high of nearly 20% (Philippines). The fourth column of Table 5 reports the estimated overvaluation at the end of 1996, and these numbers are slightly larger than the corresponding average reported in the first column. This suggests that not only was overvaluation persistent over the 3 years preceding the crisis, it was also increasing in magnitude.

Since PPP is a widely used benchmark for calculating exchange rate overvaluation, it is useful to compare these numbers to those derived from the traditional PPP model. The second and fifth columns of Table 5 show the estimated overvaluation under the assumption that PPP

---

[12] We do not estimate an error correction model for South Korea given that the evidence does not support a long run relationship between the real exchange rate and relative prices of nontradables for this economy.

holds in the long run. The equilibrium real exchange rate is assumed to be a constant and its value is estimated by the sample mean of the real exchange rate. The PPP based estimates suggest that the Indonesian and Philippine real exchange rates were significantly *undervalued* prior to the crisis (-12 % and -16%, respectively)! The Singaporean real exchange rate appears to be significantly overvalued (25%), whereas the Thai real exchange rate is close to its equilibrium value. These results are in stark contrast to those based on the nontraded-goods model, and are also contrary to the prior expectations of most economists and financial analysts.

We also compare our results to those based on the monetary model, as reported by Chinn (1998). Chinn's estimates of overvaluation are based on the monetary model of exchange rates and are reported in the third (and sixth) column of Table 5. For the three years prior to the crisis, Chinn finds a modest overvaluation of less than 5% for Indonesia and Thailand, a significant undervaluation for the Philippines (-26%) and a huge overvaluation for Singapore (45%). On the eve of the crisis, Indonesian and Thai real exchange rates appear to be in close to equilibrium, whereas the Philippine and Singapore real exchange rates are significantly undervalued and overvalued, respectively. These estimates also do not appear to be intuitively plausible.

These results are interesting because they imply that, of the three overvaluation measures considered here, only the one based on the nontraded-goods model yields estimates that are consistent with prior expectations of an overvaluation before the Asian currency crisis.

5   Conclusions

This paper studies whether permanent changes in relative prices of nontradables can account for permanent changes in the real exchange rates of 5 East Asian economies. It is found that, with the exception of the South Korean case, all other real exchange rates are cointegrated with the relative prices of nontradable. A new measure of real exchange rate misalignment, based on the long run relationship between the real exchange rate and the relative prices of nontradables, is also considered. The proposed measure is easy to compute, and when applied to the 4 economies for which cointegration is found, yields intuitive plausible estimates of persistent overvaluation prior to the Asian currency crisis of 1997. By contrast, PPP-based measures of misalignment indicate an undervalued real exchange rate prior to the crisis.

In using the nontradables-based measure of misalignment, we implicitly allow for both supply shocks (e.g., differential productivity shocks in the tradable and nontradable goods' sectors) as well as demand shocks (e.g., changes in preferences) to affect the equilibrium real exchange rate by altering the relative price of nontraded-goods. By contrast, the PPP approach, although very popular, assumes that all shocks are necessarily temporary. This is unlikely to be true especially with regard to shocks to technology.[13]

Our approach is also consistent with recent work that views the real exchange rate as comprising both permanent and transitory components, as opposed to the conventional dichotomy that views the real exchange rate as either a purely stationary process or a random walk. Mark and Choi (1997) show that models in which the long run real equilibrium

---

[13] For instance, Kakkar (2002) documents evidence suggesting that sectoral total factor productivities are unit-root nonstationary, and are cointegrated with the relative prices of nontradables in fourteen OECD economies.

exchange rate is identified as the permanent component of the real exchange rate outperform models in which long run PPP holds in terms of out-of-sample forecasting power. Generating an artificial century long time-series of the U.S.-UK real exchange rate, Engel (2000) shows through extensive Monte Carlo simulations that the real exchange rate contains an economically significant permanent component associated with the relative price of nontraded-goods that may go undetected by standard unit root tests.

Given the importance placed on the role of real exchange rate overvaluation in currency and balance-of-payments crises, and the limited empirical support for long run PPP, it is hoped that the proposed measure will be found to be a useful and practical alternative to the existing PPP-based measures.

References

[1]   Artus, Jacques R. (1978). "Methods of Assessing the Long-Run Equilibrium Value of an Exchange Rate," *Journal of International Economics*, **8**(2), 277-299.

[2]   Baillie, Richard T. and Patric C. McMahon (1989). *The Foreign Exchange Market: Theory and Econometric Evidence*, Cambridge: Cambridge University Press.

[3]   Balassa, Bela (1964). "The Purchasing-Power Parity Doctrine: A Reappraisal," *Journal of Political Economy*, **51**, 584-596.

[4]   Campbell, John Y. and Pierre Perron (1991). "Pitfalls and Opportunities: What Macroeconomists Should Know About Unit Roots," In: O.J. Blanchard and S. Fisher, Eds., *NBER Macroeconomics Annual 1991*, Cambridge, MA, MIT Press, 141-201.

[5]   Chinn, Menzie D. (1996). "Asian Pacific Real Exchange Rates and Relative Prices," Manuscript, University of California, Santa Cruz.

[6]   Chinn, Menzie D. (1998). "Before the Fall: Were East Asian Currencies Overvalued?" *NBER Working Paper* # **6491**.

[7]   Corbae, Dean and Sam Ouliaris (1988). "Cointegration Tests of Purchasing Power Parity," *Review of Economics and Statistics*, **70** (3), 508-511.

[8] De Gregorio, Jose, Alberto Giovannini, and Holger C. Wolf (1994). "International Evidence on Tradables and Nontradables Inflation," *European Economic Review*, **38**, 1225-1244.

[9]   DeLoach, Stephen B. (1997). "Do Relative Prices of Non-Traded Goods Determine Long-Run Real Exchange Rates," *Canadian Journal of Economics*, **30**(4), 891-909.

[10] Dornbusch, Rudiger, Ilan Goldfajn, and Rodrigo Valdes (1995). "Currency Crises and Collapses", *Brookings Papers on Economic Activity*, **2**, 219-70.

[11] Dutton, Marilyn and Jack Strauss (1997). "Cointegration Tests of Purchasing Power Parity: the Impact of Non-Traded Goods," *Journal of International Money and Finance*, **16**(3), 433-444.

[12] Edwards, Sebastian (1988). "Exchange Rate Misalignment in Developing Countries," The World Bank Occasional Paper Number 2/New Series, The Johns Hopkins University Press, Baltimore and London.

[13] Engel, Charles (2000). "Long-run PPP May Not Hold After All", *Journal of International Economics*, **57**, 243-273.

[14] Frankel, Jeffrey and Andrew Rose (1996). "Panel Project on Purchasing Power Parity: Mean Reversion within and between Countries," *Journal of International Economics*, **40**(1-2), 209-24.

[15] Froot, Kenneth A. and Kenneth Rogoff (1995). "Perspectives on PPP and Long-Run Real Exchange Rates," In: Gene Grossman and Kenneth Rogoff, Eds., Handbook of International Economics, Volume 3, Elsevier, North-Holland, 1647-1688.

[16] Kakkar, Vikas and Masao Ogaki (1999). "Real Exchange Rates and Nontradables: A Relative Price Approach", *Journal of Empirical Finance*, **6**(2), 193-215.

[17] Kakkar, Vikas (2002). "The Relative Price of Nontraded-Goods and Sectoral Total Factor Productivity: An Empirical Investigation," forthcoming, *Review of Economics and Statistics*.

[18] Lothian, James R. and Mark P. Taylor (1996). "Real Exchange Rate Behavior: The Recent Float from the Perspective of the Past Two Centuries," *Journal of Political Economy*, **104**(3), 488-509.

[19] Mark, Nelson C. (1990). "Real and Nominal Exchange Rates in the Long Run: An Empirical Investigation," *Journal of International Economics*, **28**, 115-136.

[20] Mark, Nelson C. and Doo-Yull Choi (1997). "Real Exchange-Rate Prediction Over Long Horizons," *Journal of International Economics*, **43**, 29-60.

[21] Meese, R. A. and Kenneth Rogoff (1988). "Was it Real? The Exchange Rate-Interest Rate Differential Relation Over the Modern Floating-Rate Period," *Journal of Finance*, **43**, 933-948.

[22] O'Connell, Paul G. J. (1998). "The Overvaluation of Purchasing Power Parity," *Journal of International Economics*, **44**, 1-19.

[23] Ogaki, Masao (1993). "CCR: A User's Guide," Rochester Center for Economic Research *Working Paper* No. **349**: University of Rochester.

[24] Ogaki, Masao and Joon Y. Park (1997). "A Cointegration Approach to Estimating Preference Parameters," *Journal of Econometrics*, **82**, 107-34.

[25] Park, Joon Y. (1990). "Testing for Unit Roots and Cointegration," *Advances in Econometrics*, **8**, 107-33.

[26] Park, Joon Y. (1992). "Canonical Cointegrating Regressions," *Econometrica*, **60**, 119-43.

[27] Phillips, Peter C. B., Pierre Perron (1988). "Testing a Unit Root in Time Series Regression," *Biometrika*, **75**, 335-46.

[28] Phillips, P. C. B. and Sam Ouliaris (1990). "Asymptotic Properties of Residual Based Tests for Cointegration," *Econometrica*, **58**, 165-193.

[29] Pierse, R.G. and A.J. Snell (1995). "Temporal Aggregation and the Power of Tests for a Unit Root," *Journal of Econometrics*, **65**, 333-345.

[30] Rogoff, Kenneth (1996). "The Purchasing Power Parity Puzzle," *Journal of Economic Literature*, **34**(2), 647-668.

[31] Sachs, Jeffrey D., Aaron Tornell, and Andres Velasco (1996). "Financial Crises in Emerging Markets: The Lessons From 1995," *Brookings Papers on Economic Activity*, **1**, 147-98.

[32] Samuelson, Paul (1964). "Theoretical Notes on Trade Problems," *Review of Economics and Statistics*, **46**, 145-54.

[33] Willet, Thomas (1986). "Exchange Rate Volatility, International Trade and Resource Allocation," *Journal of International Money and Finance*, (Supplement), **5**, S101-112.

In: International Macroeconomics: Recent Developments   ISBN: 1-59454-901-X
Editor: Amalia Morales Zumaquero, pp. 119-132   © 2006 Nova Science Publishers, Inc.

Chapter 7

ARE THERE NON-LINEARITIES IN REAL EXCHANGE RATE BEHAVIOR? THE CASE OF LESS DEVELOPED COUNTRIES

Mark J. Holmes[*]

Department of Economics, University of Waikato, New Zealand

Abstract

This study tests for non-linearities in the real exchange rates of thirty less developed countries. For this purpose, logistic and exponential smooth transition regression models are applied to quarterly data over the sample period 1973-2001. There is evidence of non-linearities in sixteen real exchange rates where, in most of these cases, non-linearities are captured by the logistic smooth transition autoregressive model. The extent of non-linearities varies across less developed countries with India and Mauritius exhibiting the sharpest transition from one regime to another.

1   Introduction

The investigation of non-linearities and asymmetries in macroeconomic behavior constitutes an increasingly popular area of empirical research. More specifically, a number of recent studies that include Kapetanios *et al.* (2003), Iannizzotto (2001), McMillan and Speight (2001), Taylor *et al.* (2001), Serletis and Gogas (2000), Sarno (2000a, 2000b), Sarantis (1999) and Michael *et al.* (1997) examine mainly OECD real exchange rates and find that non-linearities are present in a large number of cases. On the one hand, the presence of non-linearities in real exchange rates is often attributed to the heterogeneity of participants in the foreign exchange market in terms of agents' expectations formation or investors' objectives.[1] On the other hand, there is the possibility of goods market arbitrage being limited by the

---

[*] E-mail address: holmesmj@waikato.ac.nz
[1] See Sarantis (1999) and references contained therein.

presence of transactions costs in the event of relatively moderate real exchange rate shocks.2 This purpose of this paper is to investigate whether non-linearities are present in the real exchange rate behavior of Less Developed Countries (LDCs). Using quarterly data for the period 1973Q2 to 2001Q1, thirty LDC real exchange rates are analyzed using the smooth transition autoregression (STAR) methodology advocated by Granger and Terasvirta (1993). The application of two variants of STAR modeling- logistic smooth transition autoregression (LSTAR) models and exponential smooth transition autoregression (ESTAR) models enables us to explore the possibility that non-linear adjustments are present.3

There are several important reasons of interest attached to this study. First, this study concentrates on non-linear behavior in LDC real exchange rates. While Sarno (2000b) confirms the presence of non-linearities in Turkish real exchange rates with respect to the US dollar, UK sterling, German mark and French franc, this study offers a more comprehensive examination of non-linearities involving a larger sample of LDCs. Second, the LDC economies have been subject to episodes of pronounced turbulence due to structural change, political and economic unrest and reform. This might imply a potential for complex dynamics of adjustment in the real exchange rate. A further perspective is offered by Parsley and Popper (2001) who argue that non-linear effects in real exchange rate adjustment is most striking among currencies that have at times officially pegged with respect to the US dollar. Third, evidence on purchasing power parity (PPP) for LDCs has led to mixed conclusions regarding its validity [see, *inter alia*, McNown and Wallace (1989), Liu (1992), Bahmani-Oskooee (1993), Mahdavi and Zhou (1994), Holmes (2001)]. However, the vast majority of this work is based on *linear* tests for mean-reversion in real exchange rates such as Engle-Granger and Johansen cointegration tests. It can be argued that if non-linearities are present in LDC real exchange rates then these linear tests are inappropriate. While this study does not explicitly test for PPP, the identification of non-linearities in real exchange rate behavior may nonetheless offer some explanation as to why PPP has not been confirmed in many cases. Fourth, insight into LDC real exchange rate adjustment is obtained through STAR modeling. This methodology allows for the possibility that economies do not necessarily jump suddenly from one real exchange rate regime to another, for example between increasing and decreasing competitiveness, on the basis of a single real exchange rate shock. It is more likely that the size of the real exchange rate shock will determine the extent to which the economy is in one regime or another where relatively moderate shocks provide a smoother adjustment between regimes. For policy purposes, this may assist governments in their assessment of the impact of real exchange shocks on the regime being experienced and whether some (feasible) corrective action is desirable or not.

The paper is organized as follows. The following section describes the data and methodology. The third section reports and discusses the results. From a sample of thirty LDCs there is evidence that non-linearities are present in sixteen countries where the LSTAR model is appropriate in the majority of cases. The final section concludes.

---

[2] See, *inter alia*, Obstfeld and Taylor (1997), Sercu *et al.* (1995).
[3] Other examples of studies employing the STAR methodology include Leybourne and Mizen (1997) who examine consumer prices, Mills (1995) and Ocal and Osborn (2000) who examine a range of UK macroeconomic series that includes industrial production, and Skalin and Terasvirta (1998) who examine the Swedish business cycle.

2   Methodology and Data

The above mentioned studies of exchange rates imply non-linearities with distinct characteristics associated with different real exchange rate regimes. A variety of empirical models have been developed to capture these regime-dependent properties. The main approaches to modeling non-linearities include the Markov regime-switching models, where the switch between regimes is described by a probabilistic function [see Hamilton (1989) and others], and the threshold class of models that specify the regime switch as a function of past values [see, for example, Tsay (1989), Tong (1990)]. Both these classes of model imply that the economy must be within a single regime in each time period where there is a sharp switch between regimes. Alternatively, there are the models based on a smooth transition generalization of threshold class [see, for example, Granger and Terasvirta (1993), Terasvirta (1994), Terasvirta and Anderson (1992)]. These models allow for the possibility that the real exchange rate might be in some intermediate state between regimes where the nature of adjustment varies with the extent of deviation from equilibrium. The smooth transition methodology is followed in this paper. The smoothness of adjustment between regimes is estimated and one can judge the sharpness of switching from one regime to another. Indeed, the range of possible smooth transitions encompasses sudden transitions from one regime to another. The justification for this choice of methodology is based on recent literature that considers the possibility of arbitrage being limited by the presence of transactions costs [see, *inter alia*, Obstfeld and Taylor (1997), Sercu *et al.* (1995)]. It is argued that there may be a 'band of inaction' where the marginal cost of arbitrage exceeds the marginal benefit. However, it is reasonable to argue that transactions costs will differ across markets. Moreover, there might exist a series of thresholds straddling the equilibrium value of PPP so that as one moves further away from central parity, more and more arbitrage opportunities arise. In the limit, there may be a continuum of thresholds so that the real exchange rate does not move abruptly from one regime to another but engages in a somewhat smoother adjustment. Essentially, time aggregation and non-synchronous adjustment by heterogeneous agents is likely to result in smooth regime switching.

For a given LDC, let p_t be the natural logarithm of the domestic price index where $t = 1, 2, ..., T$ observations, let p_t^* be the natural logarithm of the base country price index and let s_t be the natural logarithm of the country i nominal spot price of foreign currency. The real exchange rate r for country i is computed as

$$r_t = s_t + p_t^* - p_t \qquad (1)$$

The application and estimation of the STAR models require stationary series so the analysis proceeds using first differences $e_t = (r_t - r_{t-1})$. We are therefore examining regimes of an appreciating and depreciating real exchange rate. Earlier studies such as Michael *et al.* (1997) follow a different approach. They test for cointegration between the UK:US nominal exchange rate, US and UK prices. Using an ESTAR model, they then test whether the residuals then follow a non-linear process. As pointed out by Sarantis (1999), the problem with this approach is that if the residuals follow a non-linear process then one must surely question the validity of the earlier cointegration tests. This problem can be avoided by following the approach adopted in this paper by applying the STAR models directly to the first difference in the real exchange rate data (e). Following Granger and Terasvirta (1993), a STAR model of order k, for e_t has the following specification

$$e_t = \beta_0 + \beta_1'x_t + (\theta_0 + \theta_1'x_t)F(e_{t-d}) + w_t \qquad (2)$$

where $x_t = (e_{t-1}, e_{t-2}, ... e_{t-k})$, $\beta_1 = (\beta_1, \beta_2, ... \beta_k)^{\copyright}$, $\theta_1 = (\theta_1, \theta_2, ... \theta_k)^{\copyright}$, $w_t \sim iid(0, \sigma^2)$, $F(\cdot)$ is the continuous transition function, e_{t-d} is the switching variable, and d is the delay parameter. $F(\cdot)$ is a monotonically increasing function with $F(-\infty) = 0$ and $F(\infty) = 1$ which yields a non-linear asymmetric adjustment. Consider the following LSTAR function

$$F(e_{t-d}) = \{1 + \exp[-\gamma(e_{t-d} - c)]\}^{-1} \qquad (3)$$

where γ measures the smoothness of transition from one regime to another and c is some threshold value for e that indicates the halfway point between the two regimes. The LSTAR model assumes that different regimes may have different dynamics and that adjustment takes place in every period but the smoothness of adjustment varies with the extent of the deviation from equilibrium. The transition function of LSTAR is monotonically increasing in e_{t-d} and yields asymmetric adjustment toward equilibrium in the model. Moreover, $F(\cdot) \to 0$ as $e_{t-d} \to -\infty$ and $F(\cdot) \to 1$ as $e_{t-d} \to +\infty$ thus $F(\cdot)$ is bounded between 0 and 1 where $F(\cdot) = 0.5$ if $e_{t-d} = c$. The smaller is γ, the smoother is the transition. In the extreme, $\gamma = 0$ means that $F(\cdot)$ becomes a constant and so (2) becomes a linear model. On the other hand, as $\gamma \to \infty$ there is an ever sharper transition at $e_{t-d} = c$ where $F(\cdot)$ jumps from 0 to 1. In this latter case, (3) becomes the usual threshold transition model along the lines of Tong (1983). The LSTAR model implies the asymmetric behavior of e according to whether it is above or below its equilibrium value. The theoretical justification for the appropriateness of the LSTAR model being applied to real exchange rate adjustment is based on relative rigidities with respect to movements in s, p and p^*. For example, many LDC Governments have manipulated s while p and p^* have exhibited varying degrees of downward rigidity. Terasvirta and Anderson (1992) also define the exponential (ESTAR) function as

$$F(e_{t-d}) = 1 - \exp\{-\gamma(e_{t-d} - c)^2\} \qquad (4)$$

where, as before, γ measures the speed of transition from one regime to another and c is some threshold value for e which indicates the halfway point between the two regimes. The ESTAR function in (4) defines a transition function about c where $F(\cdot)$ is still bounded between 0 and 1. The ESTAR model yield a symmetric adjustment toward equilibrium.

The initial testing for the presence of non-linearities in e_t is based on three stages. First, a linear AR model for e is specified in order to determine the lag length k. The lag length selection is based on the Schwarz information criteria and Ljung-Box statistic for autocorrelation. The residuals are saved from the chosen AR model and denoted as v. Second, having determined k, the next stage is to test for the presence of non-linearities. This is achieved through the estimation of

$$v_t = \beta_0 + \beta_1' x_t + \beta_2' x_t e_{t-d} + \beta_3' x_t e_{t-d}^2 + \beta_4' x_t e_{t-d}^3 + w_t \tag{5}$$

where the basic linearity test is on the null $H_0 : \beta_2' = \beta_3' = \beta_4' = 0$. Equation (5) is estimated across a range of values for d where the lowest p-value attached to the linearity test determines d in the later estimation of equation (2). Economic intuition might favor setting $d = 1$. However, the sluggish adjustment of the nominal exchange rate and price levels may inhibit a prompt response of e back towards equilibrium and therefore justify a choice of $d > 1$. The third stage of the non-linearity test is to see which smooth transition model- LSTAR or ESTAR- is appropriate for the real exchange rate. For this purpose, the following null hypotheses are tested.

$$H_{04}: \beta_4' = 0 \tag{6}$$

$$H_{03}: \beta_3' = 0 / \beta_4' = 0 \tag{7}$$

$$H_{02}: \beta_2' = 0 / \beta_4' = \beta_3' = 0 \tag{8}$$

One method of choosing the appropriate STAR model is to run the following sequence of nested tests. Rejection of H_{04} implies selecting the LSTAR model. Accepting H_{04} but rejecting H_{03} implies selecting the ESTAR model. Accepting H_{04} and H_{03} but rejecting H_{02} implies selecting the LSTAR model. Having selected the form of appropriate model, this study considers the value of γ described in (3) and (4). However, Granger and Terasvirta (1993) and Terasvirta (1994) show that the strict application of this procedure can lead to the wrong conclusion. Instead, this study follows Sarantis (1999) where the p-values for each of these F tests are computed and the choice of STAR model is made on the basis of the lowest p-value. Moreover, if the rejection of H_{04} or H_{02} is accompanied by the lowest p-value then the LSTAR model is chosen. If the rejection of H_{03} is accompanied by the lowest p-value then the ESTAR model is chosen. In either case, the STAR model is estimated through non-linear least squares estimation.

The thirty LDCs included in the sample are Argentina, Barbados, Brazil, Chile, Columbia, Costa Rica, Ecuador, El Salvador, Egypt, Ghana, Guatemala, Honduras, India, Indonesia, Israel, Jamaica, Kenya, Mauritius, Mexico, Morocco, Netherlands Antilles, Nigeria, Pakistan, Philippines, Singapore, South Africa, Suriname, Thailand, Uruguay and Venezuela. All price and exchange rate data are taken from the *International Financial*

Statistics database. Real exchange rates are based on the consumer price index (line 64) and exchange rates, which are end of period spot rates with respect to the US dollar.4 All real exchange rate data are expressed in natural logarithm form. Quarterly data for the period 1973Q2-01Q1 provide a sample of size of upto 112 observations on each series for each country where the use of quarterly data is dictated by data availability across this large sample. The start of 1973 is consistent with Bahmani-Oskooee (1993), Mahdavi and Zhou (1994) and Holmes (2001) in their investigations of PPP in LDCs and can be regarded as the start of modern "floating rate" period with respect to the US dollar.

3   The Results

Table 1, reports univariate ADF unit root tests on real exchange rates for the full sample of thirty countries. In terms of lag length selection, it is well known that information criteria based on the Schwarz model has a tendency to advocate relatively few lags with the strong possibility that the null of a unit root is over-rejected. Alternatively, the Akaike information criteria (AIC) tends to advocate a longer lag length which can have negative implications for the power of the test. As a compromise, this study utilizes Said and Dickey's (1984) $T^{1/3}$ rule in determining the lag length of each ADF regression. Essentially, the lag length is set large enough to allow a good approximation for any autoregressive moving-average processes that might be present in the data thereby ensuring that the residuals are approximately white noise.5 Given the length of each time series, each lag length is therefore set at 5 quarters. The results for r_t indicate that the null of non-stationarity is accepted at the 5% significance level in all cases except Argentina and Barbados. The results for e_t confirm that first differencing the data is sufficient to achieve stationarity for all countries.6

Table 1. ADF Unit Root Tests on Real Exchange Rates

	Levels		First Differences	
	ADF (no trend)	**ADF (trend)**	**ADF (no trend)**	**ADF (trend)**
Argentina	-4.918***	-4.244***	-3.619***	-4.480***
Barbados	-3.288**	-2.727	-5.496***	-5.803***
Brazil	-1.574	-1.768	-3.491**	-3.478**
Chile	-1.025	-1.760	-6.005***	-5.979***
Columbia	-1.348	-1.792	-3.403**	-3.386*
Costa Rica	-1.956	-1.863	-5.497***	-5.529***
Ecuador	-1.091	-2.291	-4.329***	-4.246***
El Salvador	-1.416	-3.239*	-5.917***	-5.916***
Egypt	-2.323	-2.568	-3.641***	-3.620**

---

[4] Data limitations preclude the use of producer price indices across this large sample of countries.

[5] Other methods include the Phillips-Perron unit root test that is based on a non-parametric correction. Monte Carlo studies, most notably by Schwert (1989), suggest that the Phillips-Perron test has a tendency to reject the null of non-stationarity when it is true if the data generating process has moving average components. Indeed, Banerjee *et al.* (1993) favour the Said and Dickey procedure over Phillips-Perron approach.

[6] These qualitative conclusions drawn from the ADF unit root tests were unaffected by the selection of lag lengths based on the Schwarz or Akaike information criteria.

	Levels		First Differences	
	ADF (no trend)	ADF (trend)	ADF (no trend)	ADF (trend)
Ghana	-1.022	-2.452	-4.331***	-4.474***
Guatemala	-1.294	-2.078	-5.934***	-5.904***
Honduras	-1.328	-1.941	-5.846***	-5.814***
India	-1.167	-2.137	-5.964***	-5.995***
Indonesia	-0.541	-3.356*	-5.310***	-5.315***
Israel	-2.830*	-2.650	-4.079***	-4.284***
Jamaica	-1.693	-1.759	-4.895***	-4.921***
Kenya	-1.213	-2.087	-6.508***	-6.486***
Mexico	-2.678*	-2.590	-4.864***	-4.912***
Mauritius	-1.208	-1.942	-5.209***	-5.184***
Morocco	-1.586	-2.268	-3.630***	-3.625**
N' Antilles	-1.403	-2.658	-4.233***	-4.096***
Nigeria	-1.917	-2.053	-3.991***	-4.037**
Pakistan	0.721	-2.597	-4.863***	-5.100***
Philippines	-1.553	-1.877	-5.269***	-5.259***
Singapore	-0.585	-2.475	-4.421***	-4.476***
South Africa	-1.480	-2.548	-4.655***	-4.638***
Suriname	-2.300	-2.221	-5.234***	-5.238***
Thailand	-0.177	-1.693	-5.912***	-5.274***
Uruguay	-2.169	-2.355	-3.789***	-3.692**
Venezuela	-1.208	-0.669	-6.178***	-6.283***

These are Augmented Dickey Fuller (ADF) unit root tests conducted on the levels and first differences in the real exchange rate with respect to the US dollar. The full sample period is 1973Q2-2001Q1. For each test, the lag length was chosen using Said and Dickey's (1984) $T^{1/3}$ rule where T is the number of observations in each time series. ***, ** and * indicate rejection of the null of non-stationarity at the 1, 5 and 10% levels of significance respectively in the ADF tests. Relevant ADF critical values taken from Fuller (1976) are -3.51, -2.89 and -2.58, while for regressions including a trend, these are -4.04, -3.45 and -3.15 respectively.

Table 2. Tests for Non-linearities

	k	d	p-value	Q(4)
Argentina	1	3	0.726	0.854
Barbados	1	5	0.036	0.449
Brazil	2	7	0.000	0.314
Chile	6	5	0.000	0.200
Columbia	4	6	0.019	0.521
Costa Rica	6	1	0.034	0.936
Ecuador	1	3	0.000	0.219
Egypt	2	2	0.357	0.985
El Salvador	1	2	0.150	0.826
Ghana	1	1	0.128	0.918
Guatemala	1	2	0.027	0.852
Honduras	1	2	0.924	0.488
India	1	8	0.034	0.793

	k	d	*p*-value	Q(4)
Indonesia	1	1	0.432	0.350
Israel	1	2	0.000	0.061
Jamaica	1	2	0.242	0.601
Kenya	1	4	0.015	0.581
Mauritius	2	4	0.051	0.810
Mexico	1	4	0.062	0.178
Morocco	1	3	0.108	0.534
Netherlands Antilles	1	4	0.009	0.370
Nigeria	1	8	0.400	0.948
Pakistan	1	5	0.178	0.281
Philippines	2	1	0.591	0.989
Singapore	2	4	0.000	0.535
South Africa	1	5	0.009	0.554
Suriname	1	2	0.523	0.806
Thailand	1	2	0.117	0.233
Uruguay	1	7	0.138	0.931
Venezuela	1	1	0.011	0.726

These tests are based on the first difference of the natural logarithm of the real exchange rate. The null of linearity is based on equation (5). The column headed 'p-value' corresponds to the test H_0 where the null is linearity. It should be noted that the Schwarz criteria is used to determine lag length k of AR process. The residuals from AR processes were then saved. Having determined k, a range of delay parameters d (d is between 1 and $D = 8$) were employed. The value of d chosen is that which gives rise to the lowest p-value of the linearity test using the data for the residuals of the AR process. The linearity test is itself a variable-deletion F test on the restriction applied to equation (5). The column headed Q(4) refers to the p-value associated with the Ljung-Box Q statistic for serial correlation among the residuals.

Table 2 reports the tests for non-linearities in the first differenced real exchange rate series, e_t. Following the selection of the lag length k for each AR process, the delay parameter d is constrained to be $1 \leq d \leq D = 8$. Given k and the value of d that minimizes the p-value associated with H_0 in equation (5), the null of linearity is rejected at 10% significance level in sixteen cases- Barbados, Brazil, Chile, Columbia, Costa Rica, Ecuador, Guatemala, India, Israel, Kenya, Mauritius, Mexico, Netherlands Antilles, Singapore, South Africa and Venezuela. While non-linearities are confirmed for over half the sample of LDC real exchange rates, there is little evidence to suggest that economic turbulence in the form of high inflation is necessarily the driving force. Using *International Financial Statistics* data, it can be shown that the average annual inflation rate for these sixteen countries across the study period was 52.8% compared with an average of 53.4% for the full sample of thirty LDCs. Furthermore, the set of countries characterized by non-linearities has a vast range of inflationary experiences from Brazil and Israel (average annual inflation of 486% and 62%) to Singapore and Netherlands Antilles (7% and 5%).

Table 3. Specification of the Non-linear Model

	H$_{04}$	H$_{03}$	H$_{02}$	Type of Model
Barbados	0.011#	0.263	0.365	LSTAR
Brazil	0.001	0.000#	0.516	ESTAR
Chile	0.001#	0.020	0.417	LSTAR
Columbia	0.648	0.057	0.011#	LSTAR
Costa Rica	0.437	0.222	0.009#	LSTAR
Ecuador	0.002#	0.020	0.069	LSTAR
Guatemala	0.310	0.017#	0.117	ESTAR
India	0.606	0.678	0.004#	LSTAR
Israel	0.232	0.980	0.000#	LSTAR
Kenya	0.024#	0.041	0.295	LSTAR
Mauritius	0.020#	0.757	0.135	LSTAR
Mexico	0.205	0.264	0.034#	LSTAR
Netherlands Antilles	0.006#	0.887	0.049	LSTAR
Singapore	0.028	0.000#	0.025	ESTAR
South Africa	0.144	0.003#	0.640	ESTAR
Venezuela	0.006#	0.007	0.354	LSTAR

See equations (5), (6), (7) and (8). # denotes the lowest p-value associated with the variable-deletion tests and therefore the determination of the relevant STAR model. The values for k and d are reported in Table 2.

Table 3 reports the test results for the specific form of non-linearity present. Using the hypothesis tests outlined in equations (6)-(8), the results indicate that the LSTAR model is the more appropriate non-linear model in all cases except Brazil, Guatemala, Singapore and South Africa. The LSTAR model implies that regimes based on appreciating and depreciating real exchange rates have different dynamics whereas the ESTAR model implies that the two regimes have similar dynamics but the transition period can have different dynamics.

Table 4. Estimates of the STAR Models

	γ	sig	c	Q(4)	St. Err.	Type of Model
Barbados	0.083	0.000	0.106	0.517	0.021	LSTAR
Brazil	5.216	0.000	-0.048	0.943	0.131	ESTAR
Chile	0.851	0.000	-0.430	0.997	0.063	LSTAR
Columbia	3.263	0.000	-0.070	0.924	0.038	LSTAR
Costa Rica	0.353	0.000	0.081	0.237	0.079	LSTAR
Ecuador	0.664	0.639	-0.398	0.439	0.091	LSTAR
Guatemala	18.403	0.070	0.077	0.545	0.089	ESTAR
India	371.676	0.000	-0.007	0.694	0.039	LSTAR
Israel	0.312	0.072	0.085	0.000	0.191	LSTAR
Kenya	0.347	0.126	0.006	0.561	0.062	LSTAR
Mauritius	152.128	0.000	-0.063	0.934	0.048	LSTAR
Mexico	0.142	0.297	-1.175	0.230	0.112	LSTAR
Netherlands Antilles	0.032	0.057	0.001	0.658	0.008	LSTAR
Singapore	1.817	0.070	-0.003	0.746	0.081	ESTAR
South Africa	-0.047	0.66	-0.162	0.410	0.067	ESTAR
Venezuela	2.089	0.003	-0.887	0.179	0.140	LSTAR

Non-linear least squares estimation of equation (2) is by the Gauss-Newton method. The column headed *sig* refers to the *p*-value associated with a variable-deletion *F* test on the smoothness of adjustment coefficient γ, *c* is the estimated threshold value for the switching variable (see equations (3) and (4)), Q(4) refers to the *p*-value associated with the Ljung-Box *Q* statistic concerning serial correlation in the residuals, *St. err* is the standard error of the non-linear regression.

Table 4 reports estimates of the transition parameter γ. These estimates are derived from the non-linear least squares estimate of (2). In line with other studies, the LSTAR and ESTAR models are scaled by the standard deviation and variance of *e* respectively. As well as assisting convergence during estimation, this normalizes the deviations in the switching variable and facilitates interpretation of the smoothness parameter. Thus (3) and (4) may be rewritten as

$$F\!\left(e_{t-d}\right)=\left[1+\exp\left\{-\gamma\left(1/\sigma_{e}\right)\!\left(e_{t-d}-c\right)\right\}\right]^{-1} \tag{9}$$

$$F\!\left(e_{t-d}\right)=1-\exp\left\{-\gamma\left(1/\sigma_{e}^{2}\right)\!\left(e_{t-d}-c\right)^{2}\right\} \tag{10}$$

In the cases of Ecuador, Kenya, Mexico and South Africa, γ appears to be insignificant at the 10% level. While Sarantis (1999) points to the difficulty in estimating γ, Sarno (2000b) argues that the statistical significance of γ is in a sense not questionable because linearity has already been rejected in the earlier tests. Let us consider the LSTAR results first. The results suggest that countries such as Barbados and Israel are characterized by a very smooth transition from one regime to another while India and Mauritius, which feature much larger values of γ, exhibit a much sharper transition.[7] It would be useful here to comment on what the values of γ actually mean. Let us designate $F\!\left(e_{t-d}\right)=0$ and $F\!\left(e_{t-d}\right)=1$ as regimes of a pure "appreciating real exchange rate" and "depreciating real exchange rate". For example, Table 4 reports that $c=0.081$ and $\gamma=0.353$ in the case of Costa Rica. This means that a one standard deviation positive shock to e_{t-d} yields $F\!\left(e_{t-d}\right)=0.580$. The new regime is therefore a linear combination of regimes 1 and 2 with the weights [0.580,0.420]. In the case of a two standard deviation shock to e_{t-d}, we have $F\!\left(e_{t-d}\right)=0.663$ and so these weights become [0.663,0.337]. There is therefore a larger leaning towards $F\!\left(e_{t-d}\right)=1$ on account of the larger shock. In the case of India, the smoothness parameter is estimated as $\gamma=371.676$. Such a high value means that minute deviations of the switching variable from the threshold level places the real exchange rate entirely in one regime or the other. Figure 1 presents plots of the transition functions for Columbia, India and Netherlands Antilles where the stark contrast between India and Netherlands Antilles is brought out clearly.[8] In the former case, it might be interesting to

---

[7] While the residuals appear to be generally well behaved in terms of the absence of serial correlation, Israel rejects the null of zero serial correlation among its residuals.

[8] In the interests of brevity only a sample of transition functions are presented.

employ threshold models given the rapid shift between regimes. Columbia exhibits an intermediate case that lodges between very smooth and sudden adjustment.

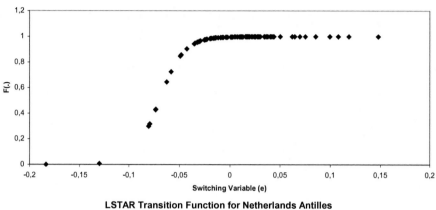

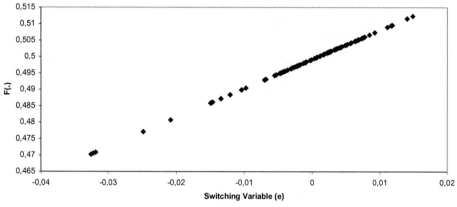

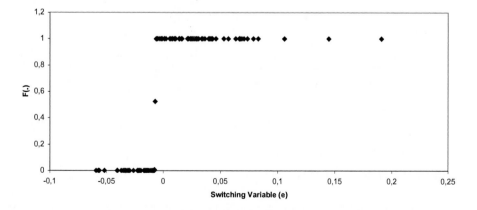

Figure 1. LSTAR Transition Functions

In terms of the ESTAR models, Brazil and Guatemala exhibit high values for γ and therefore very sharp transitions from one regime to another. The transition function for Singapore is much smoother with $\gamma = 1.817$. In this case, a one standard deviation shock to e_{t-d} leads to a new regime that is weighted [0.70, 0.30] towards regime 1. Figure 2 plots the ESTAR transition functions for Guatemala and Singapore and highlights the difference in the smoothness of transition.

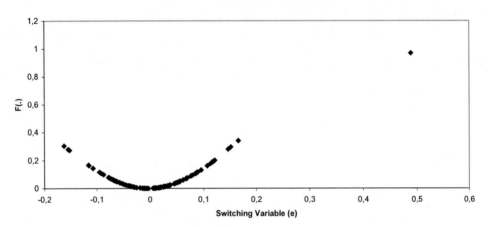

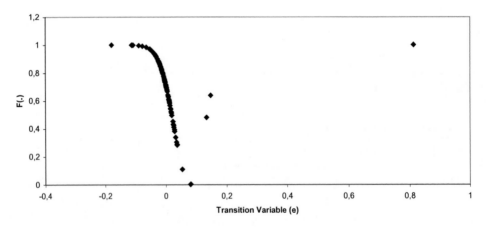

Figure 2. ESTAR Transition Functions

4   Summary and Conclusion

Given the existing literature on non-linearities in OECD real exchange rates, this is the first study that takes a more comprehensive examination of non-linearities in the case of LDCs. The application of smooth transition autoregressive modeling to thirty LDCs suggests that there is evidence of non-linear adjustment in sixteen cases. Furthermore, there is considerable variation in the smoothness of adjustment from one regime to another. Where non-linearities are confirmed, it is the LSTAR model that is most appropriate. This finding is consistent with rigidities with respect to nominal exchange rates and prices inducing asymmetries in real exchange rate adjustment. This study raises a number of avenues for future research. First, the very sharp transitions in some LDCs from one regime to another suggest that it would be interesting to also investigate non-linearities within a Markov switching or threshold model framework. Second, future research might consider whether forms of non-linearities, other than those tested for here, are appropriate. Finally, this study notes a lack of evidence that non-linear behavior of the real exchange rate is confined to high inflation LDCs. This suggests that researchers should examine the theoretical explanations for non-linearities and their relevance to LDCs more closely.

References

[1]   Bahmani-Oskooee, M. (1993), "Purchasing Power Parity Based on Effective Exchange Rate and Cointegration: 25 LDCs' Experience with its Absolute Formulation." *World Development*, **21**, 1023-31.

[2]   Banerjee, A., Dolado, J., Galbraith, J. and D. Hendry (1993), "Cointegration, Error Correction, and the Econometric Analysis of Non-stationary Data." Oxford: Oxford University Press.

[3]   Fuller, W. A. (1976), *Introduction to Time-Series Analysis*, New York: John Wiley & Sons.

[4]   Granger, C. and T. Terasvirta (1993), *Modeling Nonlinear Economic Relationships*, New York: Oxford University Press.

[5]   Hamilton, J.D. (1989), 'A New Approach to the Economic Analysis of Nonstationary Time Series and the Business Cycle', *Econometrica*, **57**, 357-384.

[6]   Holmes, M. J. (2001) "New Evidence on Real Exchange Rate Stationarity and PPP in Less Developed Countries", *Journal of Macroeconomics*, **23**, 601-15.

[7]   Iannizzotto, M. (2001), "Exchange Rate Misalignment and Nonlinear Convergence to Purchasing Power Parity in European Exchange Rate Mechanism", *Applied Financial Economics*, **11**, 511-26.

[8]   Kapetanios, G., Shin, Y. and A. Snell (2003), "Testing for a Unit Root in a Nonlinear STAR Framework", *Journal of Econometrics*, **112**, 359-79.

[9]   Leyborne S. and P. Mizen (1997), 'Disinflation and Central Bank Independence in Australia, Canada and New Zealand: Evidence from Smooth Transition Analysis', Discussion Paper 97/6, Department of Economics, University of Nottingham.

[10] Liu, P., (1992) "Purchasing Power Parity in Latin America: A Cointegration Analysis." *Weltwirtschaftliches Archiv,* **128**, 662-80.

[11] Mahdavi, S., and S. Zhou (1994), "Purchasing Power Parity in High Inflation Countries: Further Evidence." *Journal of Macroeconomics*, **16**, 403-22.

[12] McNown, R., and M. Wallace (1989), "National Price Levels, Purchasing Power Parity, and Cointegration: A Test of Four High Inflation Economies." *Journal of International Money and Finance*, **8**, 533-45.

[13] McMillan, D. and A. Speight (2001), 'Non-linearities in the Black Market Zloty-Dollar Exchange Rate: Some Further Evidence', *Scottish Journal of Political Economy*, **11**, 2, 209-20.

[14] Michael, P., Nobay, A. R. and D. Peel (1997), 'Transactions Costs and Nonlinear Adjustments in Real Exchange Rates: An Empirical Investigation', *Journal of Political Economy*, **105**, 862-79.

[15] Mills, T. (1995), 'Business Cycle Asymmetries and Non-linearities in UK Macroeconomic Time-Series', *Ricerche Economiche*, **49**, 97-24.

[16] Ocal, N. and D. Osborn (2000), 'Business Cycle Non-Linearities in UK Consumption and Production', *Journal of Applied Econometrics*, **15**, 27-43.

[17] Obstfeld, M. and A.M. Taylor (1997), "Nonlinear Aspects of Goods Market Arbitrage and Adjustment: Heckscher's Commodity Points Revisited", *Discussion Paper* No. **1672**, CEPR.

[18] Parsley, D. and H. Popper (2001), "Official exchange rate arrangements and real exchange rate behavior", *Journal of Money, Credit and Banking*, **33**, 976-93.

[19] Said, S.E., and D. A. Dickey (1984), "Testing for Unit Roots in Autoregressive Moving Average Models of Unknown Order." *Biometrica*, **71**, 599-608.

[20] Sarno, L. (2000a), 'Systematic Sampling and Real Exchange Rates', *Weltwirtschaftliches Archiv*, **136**, 1, 24-57.

[21] Sarno, L. (2000b), 'Real Exchange Rate Behavior in High Inflation Countries: Empirical Evidence from Turkey, 1980-97', *Applied Economics Letters*, **7**, 285-91.

[22] Sarantis, N. (1999), "Modeling Non-Linearities in Real Effective Exchange Rates", *Journal of International Money and Finance*, **18**, 27-45.

[23] Schwert, G.W. (1989), "Tests for unit roots: A Monte Carlo investigation", *Journal of Business and Economic Statistics*, **7**, 147-59.

[24] Sercu, P. Uppal, R. and C. van Hulle (1995), "The Exchange Rate in the Presence of Transactions Costs", *Journal of Finance*, **50**, 1309-19.

[25] Serletis, A. and P. Gogas (2000), 'Purchasing Power Parity, Non-linearity and Chaos', *Applied Financial Economics*, **10**, 6, 615-22.

[26] Taylor, M.P., Peel, D. and L. Sarno (2001), "Nonlinear Mean-reversion in Real Exchange Rates: Toward a Solution to the Purchasing Power Puzzle", *International Economic Review*, **42**, 1015-42.

[27] Terasvirta, T. (1994), 'Specification, estimation, and evaluation of smooth transition autoregressive models', *Journal of American Statistic Association*, **89**, 281-12.

[28] Terasvirta, T. and H. M. Anderson (1992), 'Characterizing Nonlinearities in Business Cycles Using Smooth Transition Autoregressive Models', *Journal of Applied Econometrics*, **7**, S119-36.

[29] Tong, H. (1983), *Threshold Models in Nonlinear Time Series Analysis*, New York: Springer-Verlag.

[30] Tong, H. (1990), *Non-linear Time Series: A Dynamical System Approach*, Oxford University Press, Oxford.

[31] Tsay, R. (1989), 'Testing and Modeling Threshold Autoregressive Processes', *Journal of the American Statistical Association*, **84**, 231-40.

In: International Macroeconomics: Recent Developments   ISBN: 1-59454-901-X
Editor: Amalia Morales Zumaquero, pp. 133-152   © 2006 Nova Science Publishers, Inc.

Chapter 8

EXCHANGE RATE FLEXIBILITY AND REAL ADJUSTMENTS IN EMERGING MARKET ECONOMIES[1]

José García Solanes[*]

Universidad de Murcia, Departamento de Fundamentos del Análisis Económico

Facultad de Economía y Empresa

Universidad de Murcia. Campus de Espinardo, 30100 Murcia

Abstract

This paper analyses the extent to which managed floating helps macroeconomic stabilisation and contributes to real adjustment, in the face of real external disturbances in emerging market economies. We find that optimal policy reactions, as opposed to "fear of floating", may explain why nominal exchange rates have exhibited lower variability than nominal interest rates in developing countries along the recent years. We show that for this to occur it is necessary that devaluation affects positively the aggregate demand. Furthermore, we demonstrate that even when the analysis is restricted to a financial context, which seems appropriate when output achieves its long run potential level, some institutional arrangements can be engineered to reduce the destabilising effects of controlled floating.

1 Introduction

Recent and very comprehensive empirical studies by Reinhart (2000) and Calvo and Reinhart (2002) document that the authorities of emerging market economies frequently intervene to dampen fluctuations in their exchange rates. Consequently, the large majority of exchange rate regimes in these countries exhibit much reduced flexibility in the form of dirty floats or soft pegs. This feature has also been outlined by McKinnon and Schnabl (2003) in the case of

---

[1] This work was presented in the III Workshop on International Economics held in Málaga, 21-22 November 2003. I wish to thank Angelos Kanas for his helpful discussion in the Workshop, and to Arielle Beyaert for her wise comments. I am also grateful to the Fundación Banco Bilbao Vizcaya Argentaria for its financial support in the frame of the "Primera convocatoria de Ayudas a la investigación en Ciencias Sociales, año 2002".

[*] E-mail address: solanes@um.es

the East Asian economies, which have pegged their currencies to the US dollar after the crisis of 1977.

According to Calvo and Reinhart (CR), the rationale behind this behaviour lies in the harmful effects that exchange rate flexibility may inflict on the economy when policy credibility is absent and the amount of dollarised debt is huge. The same authors, however, show that the dampening effects are obtained at the cost of raising the level and variability in the domestic interest rate. They remark that these results disturb investment decisions and encourage investors to borrow in foreign currencies. Nonetheless, the above-mentioned analysis is restricted to the financial side of the economy and neglects the role of the exchange rate in dealing with real problems. The most relevant ones have to do with helping adjustments in the real exchange rates in response to external real shocks, which are extremely relevant for developing countries.

Contrary to this view, which regards exchange rate management as "fear of floating", other authors argue that a managed float is a rational choice when dealing with external shocks to improve economic performance. Thus, according to the empirical evidence reported by Edwards (2002), the countries that were regarded as managed floaters during the period 1970-1998 tended to experience higher GDP per capita growth, coupled with (slightly) higher yearly rates of inflation, than other similar economies with fixed exchange rates. On the other hand, Edwards and Levy-Yeyati (2002) found that countries with flexible exchange rates are generally less affected by terms of trade shocks and tend to grow faster than countries with rigid exchange rate regimes.

Our main contention is that the extent to which an exchange rate regime contributes to real adjustment in the face of supply and demand disturbances is particularly crucial in emerging economies, where both the degree of openness to international trade and nominal flexibility are very low. For this reason, one (the main) purpose of this chapter is to provide theoretical and empirical evidence supporting the virtues of a managed floating regime for easing real adjustments. Another objective, and which is tackled first, is to demonstrate that, even in the financial environment described by CR, some institutional arrangements can be engineered to reduce the negative effects of controlled floating; that is, to curtail the increase in interest rates without affecting their variability.

Our work is organised as follows: in section 2 we analyse the financial aspects of managed floating and make some qualifications to the main conclusions of CR. In section 3 we shift to real aspects, and examine the relative advantages and shortcomings of a managed floating in stabilising the economy and adjusting the real exchange rate. In section 4 we test the Balassa-Samuelson hypothesis in a group of developing countries that have adopted some kind of managed floating in recent years. Section 5 provides some concluding remarks and policy implications. Finally, we provide two Appendixes at the end of this work. The first one builds a simple model to demonstrate the effects of monetary policy when the country risk is important; and the second one includes a description of the data sources and the method we used to elaborate some indexes applied in our empirical study.

2   Financial Implications of Exchange Rate Floating

The CR framework refers to a small open developing economy in which authorities try to do their best in an environment characterised by high capital mobility, incomplete markets, imperfect information and dollarised liabilities. Under such conditions, the monetary authorities are exceedingly fearful of exchange rate movements and react with two kinds of intervention to dampen exchange rate swings: first, intervening in the foreign exchange market, and second, setting an optimal level for the domestic interest rate. The main result is that, because of the risk premium, the nominal interest rate is pushed to a high level both in terms of absolute amount and variability.

In the CR model, workers and investors have incomplete information and make decisions at the start of the period, before shocks are realised, on the basis of their expectations concerning the interest rate. The central bank observes the shocks and responds by establishing an optimal interest rate in each period. Its objective function is:

$$W = i \frac{\left(c - \eta i^e + \varsigma\right)}{k} - \frac{b}{2}\pi^2 \tag{1}$$

where W is the nominal wealth, and i (i^e) stands for the current (expected) nominal interest rate; π is the deviation of the inflation rate from its target (taken to be zero). The parameter k and b are the monetary base multiplier and the social weight attached to inflation stabilisation, respectively. ς is a random shock with zero mean and constant variance. The terms in brackets represent the (log of) demand for money, and the first part of the right hand side is the revenue from seignorage.

Assuming purchasing power and uncovered interest-rate parity conditions and normalising the foreign interest and inflation rates to zero, the objective function is:

$$W = i \frac{\left(c - \eta i^e + \varsigma\right)}{k} - \frac{b}{2}(i - \rho)^2 \tag{1'}$$

where ρ is the risk premium, assumed to be an i.i.d. variable.

Calvo and Reinhart maximise (1') with respect to the interest rate, under the assumption that the central bank cannot commit to a state-contingent rule (Cournot solution), and obtain the following results for the expected and current interest rates:

$$i^e = \frac{c}{bk + \eta} \tag{2}$$

$$i = \rho + \frac{\varsigma}{bk} + \frac{c}{bk + \eta} \tag{3}$$

The third term of the right hand side of (3) is the inflation premium in the long run, and is due to a) the presence of seignorage in the objective function, and b) the temptation to generate surprise inflation to obtain extra seignorage. This second element makes the result a third best equilibrium, as is usual when the Cournot solution is coupled to a source of economic distortion (the seignorage revenue). The solution is represented graphically by point

A in Figure 1. The position of the indifference curve I is given by the expected interest rate in (2).

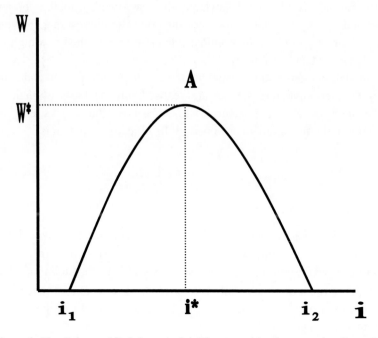

Figure 1. The Calvo and Reinhart model. The central bank acts under discretion.

Let us now see what happens in the CR model if the central bank could commit to a state-contingent rule of the interest rate. In this case, we solve the problem by maximising the expected inflation function:

$$\underset{i_t,\,i_t^e}{Max}\, E_{t-1}\left\{i_t\,\frac{c - \eta i_t^e + \varsigma}{k} - \frac{b}{2}(i_t - \rho)^2\right\} - \lambda\left(i_t^e - E_{t-1}i_t\right)$$

(4)

where λ is the Lagrange multiplier.

Taking first derivatives with respect to i and i^e, and eliminating λ, we obtain:

$$\frac{c - \eta i_t^e + \varsigma}{k} - b(i_t - \rho) + E_{t-1}\left(i_t\,\frac{-\eta}{k}\right) = 0$$

(5)

Applying expectations in (5), and solving $E_{t-1}i_t$, we get:

$$E_{t-1}i_t = i^e = \frac{c}{2\eta + bk}$$

(6)

Substitution of this value in (5) allows the current interest rate to be obtained:

$$i_t = \rho + \frac{\varsigma}{bk} + \frac{c}{2\eta + bk}$$

(7)

As can be seen, the inflation premium is lower in this case because it is devoid of the part attributed to the central bank's temptation to cheat systematically. The average interest rate, $E_{t-1}i_t$, will equal the desirable inflation rate.

Since the expected interest rate is lower in this solution, the equilibrium is found at a point on the upper solid indifference curve, as represented by point B in Figure 2. However, this solution suffers from time inconsistency as reflected by the fact that the indifference curve has a positive slope at that point. For the expected value of the interest rate attached to curve II, which is known at the beginning of the period, the optimal choice for the central bank is point C. Consequently, commitment to a state-contingent rule appears unfeasible. The literature shows suggested improvements to remove the inflation bias under discretion, and in our case we apply the solution recommended by Walsh (1995) in the context of the Barro-Gordon (1983) model.

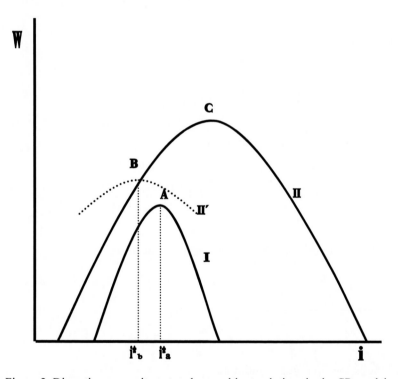

Figure 2. Discretion, commitment and second-best solutions in the CR model.

According to this solution, a simple linear inflation contract is designed in such a way that the central bank is assigned this wealth function:

$$W = \frac{c - \eta i^e - \varsigma}{k} i - \frac{b}{2}(i - \rho)^2 - di$$

(8)

where d is a positive parameter which measures the linear interest-penalty imposed to central bank.

Maximisation of this function leads to:

$$i^e = \frac{c - kd}{bk + \eta}$$

(9)

$$i = \rho + \frac{\varsigma}{bk} + \frac{c - dk}{bk + \eta}$$

(10)

The optimal value of d is that for which the new expected interest rate equals the value given by (6) in order to ensure that the optimal point belongs to the indifference curve II:

$$\frac{c - dk}{bk + \eta} = \frac{c}{2\eta + bk}$$

Resolving d gives:

$$d = \frac{c\eta}{k(bk + 2\eta)}$$

(11)

Substituting this value in the wealth function:

$$W = \frac{c - \eta i_t^e + \varsigma}{k} i - \frac{b}{2}(i - \rho)^2 - \frac{c\eta}{k(bk + 2\eta)} i$$

(12)

Deriving the first order conditions, and tacking expectations we obtain:

$$i^e = \frac{c}{2\eta + bk}$$

(13)

and, substituting in the first order condition:

$$i = \rho + \frac{\varsigma}{k} + \frac{c}{2\eta + bk}$$

(14)

This is the same value as that obtained under commitment and is consequently represented by the same point (B) in Figure 2. However, it is time consistent and corresponds to the maximum point of the indifference curve II', which is generated by the new utility function (8). In short, this point is a second best solution that allows the interest rate to be reduced compared with the solution under discretion. Furthermore, this solution does not imply higher variability in the interest rate because since ρ and ζ are assumed to be uncorrelated, for both solutions we have:

$$\sigma_i^2 = \sigma_\rho^2 + \frac{\sigma_\zeta^2}{b^2 k^2}$$

(15)

Combining (14) with the uncovered interest parity condition, we obtain the rate of exchange-rate variation:

$$\varepsilon = \frac{\zeta}{bk} + \frac{c}{bk + 2\eta}$$

(16)

This expression indicates that the linear contract solution also contributes to dampening exchange rate fluctuations.

The general conclusion of this section is that, even if we restrict our analysis to the financial factors and focus our attention on long run equilibrium, as in the CR model, there is still scope to diminish the destabilising effects of managed exchange rate intervention without increasing instability. In the next section our analysis turns to the real side of the economy and to the problems involved in shorter run adjustments.

3   Real Shocks and Exchange Rate Management

In this section we consider a small open country with three important features characteristic of an emergent market economy. First, it has important nominal rigidities, mainly in the downward; second, it is frequently hit by supply real shocks, and third, it suffers a high country risk. Taking into account these characteristics we analyse the extent to which the managed floating regime facilitates a) the stabilisation task of monetary policy, and b) the correct adjustment of the real exchange rate.

For these purposes, we will assume that the authorities adjust the aggregate demand to achieve an appropriate combination of output and inflation in response to shocks, in the same lines, for instance, as Barro and Gordon (1983) model. In that framework, the behaviour of the private sector is summarised by a short run aggregate supply, which is obtained under the assumption that wages are set in advance, based on inflation expectations. Furthermore, the government seeks to minimise a quadratic loss function, which depends on deviations of both inflation and output.

In the following lines we will analyse the way in which the central bank must use the available operating (demand) targets to stabilise the economy and to adjust correctly the real exchange rate. We will assume that a real supply disturbance hits the economy and that the central bank reacts following a two-step strategy. First, it determines the level of the aggregate demand, which enables the optimal combination of output and inflation to be achieved along the supply curve. Second, it decides the appropriate combination of the two operating targets, which are the short-term interest rate and the nominal exchange rate, to obtain the optimum aggregate demand and the new equilibrium value of the real exchange rate. Let us analyse, in turn, this procedure more formally. The results will allow us to derive the relative advantages of a managed float as compared to a strict peg.

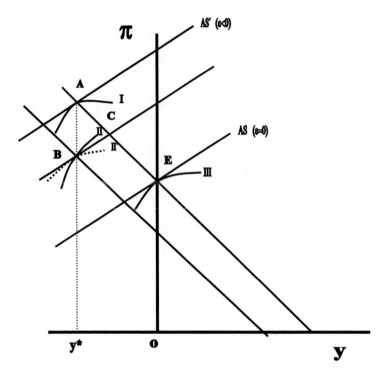

Figure 3. The Barro and Gordon's Model. Discretion, commitment and second best solutions after a negative supply shock.

Suppose that the economy is initially in a long run equilibrium situation as described by point E in Figure 3 and that a negative supply shock occurs that shifts the aggregate supply upwards to the position AS $(\varepsilon<0)$[2]. In a first reaction the central bank will decide an aggregate demand that moves the equilibrium point to C which is at the intersection of the supply curve and the locus of the tangency points (expansion line). We denote this optimal demand AD_t^o, and assume that it depends on an autonomous expenditure $\bar{d}$, which the most important component is the government deficit, the real interest rate (r) and the real exchange rate (q):

$$AD_t^o = \bar{d}_t - r_t + \gamma q_t \tag{17}$$

where γ measures the relative effect of variations in the real-exchange rate on the aggregate demand, compared to the coefficient of the real interest rate which we normalise to one. All variables are in logs except for the interest rate. The real exchange rate is defined as the

---

[2] The level of potential output is normalised to zero.

relative price of the foreign good, so that an increase in q indicates a real depreciation of the domestic currency.

Tacking into account the Fisher equation and the fact that the current real exchange rate is equal to the expected level of this variable minus its expected variation, we can write:

$$AD_t^o = \bar{d}_t - i_t + \pi_t + \gamma\left(q_{t+1}^e - \Delta q\right)$$

(18)

Denoting s the log of the nominal exchange rate, and Δs its expected change along this period, it is clear that $\Delta q = \Delta s + \pi_t^* - \pi_t$. Consequently:

$$AD_t^o = \bar{d}_t - (i_t - \pi) + \gamma\left(q_{t+1}^e - \Delta s - \pi_t^* + \pi_t\right)$$

(19)

Furthermore, uncovered interest parity establishes that:

$$\Delta s + \rho = i_t - i_t^*$$

(20)

From equations (19) and (20) we can resolve the nominal interest rate and the expected variation of the nominal exchange rate:

$$i_t = \pi_t - \frac{1}{1+\gamma}\left(AD_t^o - \bar{d}_t - \gamma\pi_t^* - \gamma\rho - \gamma q_{t+1}^e\right)$$

(21)

$$\Delta s = \pi_t - \pi_t^* - \frac{1}{1+\gamma}\left(AD_t^o - \bar{d}_t + r_t^* + \rho - \gamma q_{t+1}^e\right)$$

(22)

Equations (21) and (22) indicate how the operating targets can be set simultaneously to achieve the desired level of the (optimum) aggregate demand corresponding to point C. To obtain the current exchange rate that satisfies the targeted variation given by (22), we need an equation for the expected change in the exchange rate. If we adopt, for instance, the mechanism of Dornbusch (1976), the expected exchange-rate change will be:

$$\Delta s = \delta(\bar{s}_t - s_t)$$

(23)

were $\bar{s}_t$ is the long run equilibrium value of the nominal exchange rate, and δ is a positive parameter smaller than 1, that measures the speed to which the current exchange rate approaches its long run level. Assuming for now that $\bar{s}_t$ is given, s_t can be solved combining (22) and (23):

$$s_t = \bar{s}_t - \frac{1}{\delta}\left(\pi - \pi^*\right) + \frac{1}{\delta(1+\gamma)}\left(AD_t^o - \bar{d}_t + r_t^* + \rho - \gamma q_{t+1}^e\right)$$

(24)

Equations (21) and (24) indicate that in order to reduce the aggregate demand, as required for going from point E to point C, the central bank must increase the nominal interest rate and appreciate the domestic currency. The short run equilibrium point will change several times before reaching the long run equilibrium represented by point A (Cournot solution) in Figure 3, which output is the new potential level after the shock. If the inflation bias is removed, by signing for instance an inflation contract with the central bank, the final equilibrium point will be B.

Note that, contrary to CR, in our model variations in i_t take place simultaneously as those in s_t, in response to foreign shocks, and are not a strategy to dampen exchange rate swings.

It is worth outlining that the central bank can rely on the exchange rate as a useful lever of stabilisation policy in so far as it ensures normal or conventional effects on the aggregate demand, as we have assumed so far. However, the possibility exists that a devaluation of the domestic currency produces contractionary effects on the aggregate demand. The latter result is specific of some developing countries, which are particularly affected by capital market imperfections and strong balance sheet effects. In Appendix I we derive the necessary conditions for this abnormal result using an IS-LM model, for an open economy, that includes those crucial features of emerging countries[3]. Since the conditions for this result are extreme and not usually met, we will assume that devaluation causes expansionary effects on the aggregate demand, which amounts to saying that the parameter γ in equation (17) is positive.

The nominal exchange rate may also be managed to adjust the real exchange rate (RER) towards the equilibrium level determined by real fundamentals. Let us examine, for instance, what would happen in the case where a deterioration of the terms of trade takes place. The theory of real exchange-rate determination postulates a depreciating effect in the RER (Δq). In terms of the model explained above, this negative real shock implies an increase in both the expected RER for the next period (Δq_{t+1}^e) and the long run equilibrium level of the nominal exchange rate ($\Delta\bar{s}$). As a result, the nominal interest rate will increase (equation (21)). However, the effect on the current nominal exchange rate is undetermined unless we get more information about the parameters γ and δ and the relative adjustments in $\Delta\bar{s}$ and Δq_{t+1}^e in response to the shock. For normal situations in which the variation in $\Delta\bar{s}$ is more intense than, Δq_{t+1}^e the likely result is a current depreciation of the domestic currency (Δs_t).

In any case, if the managed exchange rate level is not in accordance with the equilibrium RER, the current account will serve as the transmission mechanism to bring the exchange rate into equilibrium. Suppose, for instance, that the exchange rate is overvalued because it has been targeted too low. This situation will cause a current account deficit and increase both foreign indebtedness and the country risk premium. From equation (24) we derive that an increase in $\Delta\rho$ leads the central bank to depreciate its currency (Δs_t)[4].

---

[3] For a more elaborated model, based on microfounded decisions, see Céspedes, Chang and Velasco (2002).

[4] In the case where the exchange rate floats freely, the current account imbalances put in motion portfolio adjustments that modify both interest rates and exchange rates. In turn, these modifications gradually bring the current account to zero, which is its long run equilibrium. Models which account for the stock-flow

The contribution of nominal exchange rate variations to adjust the RER is particularly valuable in the depreciating case, because in this situation the alternative way to bring down the RER (Δq), which is by reducing domestic prices, seems very costly or even unfeasible in developing countries.

Equations (21) and (24) provide the rationale for one of the puzzles raised by Calvo and Reinhart (2002) concerning volatilities in interest and exchange rates. These authors found that in developing countries the variability of the first variable is higher than that of the second one. In their opinion this is a striking finding in "declared" flexible exchange regimes, which can only be explained by the fact that central bank uses the interest rate to smooth exchange rate fluctuations[5]. Our model provides scope to analyse this situation distinguishing two kinds of disturbances. In the case of temporary changes in market beliefs and other financial lurches that modify the country risk premium, the flexible exchange rate should react more intensively than the interest rate provided that, as empirical evidence tends to indicate, $\delta < 1/\gamma$. The arguments of CR explaining why the facts show a different pattern for these variabilities, as a result of massive intervention in the foreign exchange market, would be acceptable in this case.

However, when external disturbances are caused by real factors (variations in AD, $\overline{d}$, r^* and q^e in formula (24)), the implied simultaneous adjustments in $\overline{s}$ provide dampening results in s_t. For instance, in the case of a positive real supply shock, the authorities react expanding the aggregate demand to obtain an optimal combination of output and inflation, and this causes a nominal depreciation (Δs_t). But, at the same time, $\overline{s}$ decreases, as a result of the shock, and reduces the net fluctuation of s_t. This cushioning effect could explain why s_t fluctuates less intensively than i_t.

Let us now examine what happens when the authorities fix firmly the exchange rate of its currency with respect to a foreign strong one. In this case, the central bank cannot modify the exchange rate, and the level of the aggregate demand (AD^f) must be derived from equation (22) by imposing $\Delta s = 0$ on it:

$$AD_t^f = (1+\gamma)\left(\pi_t - \pi_t^*\right) + \overline{d}_t - r_t^* - \rho + \gamma q_{t+1}^e \qquad (25)$$

This equation indicates that the aggregate demand depends on external factors and on the fiscal budget. The implications for policy stabilisation follows directly from this equation:

a) Domestic monetary policy expansions have contractionary effects to the extent to which an increase in the money supply causes a loss of foreign reserves, which in turn pushes up the country risk.

---

implications of the current account imbalance include, for instance, the portfolio models of Branson (1977) and Frenkel and Mussa (1988).

[5] This feature was also remarked by Lahiri and Végh (2000).

b) Domestic fiscal policy expansions have a direct positive effect on the aggregate demand, but this effect can be seriously curtailed, or even reversed, by the induced increase in the country risk premium[6].

As can be seen, the presence of the country risk term may substantially change the results of macroeconomic policies, with respect to the propositions of the standard Mundell-Fleming model in a context of fixed exchange rate and perfect capital mobility.

As far as adjustments of the RER are concerned, it seems evident that the fixed exchange rate regime makes those variations slower and/or more costly in terms of output and employment, to the extent that they are channeled through modifications in domestic prices. As explained above, difficulties and costs increase when the required adjustment of the RER implies reductions in domestic prices.

As a general conclusion of the whole section, it should be stressed that managed floating facilitates stabilisation of the economy in the short run, and paves the way for real exchange-rate adjustment, provided that variations in the exchange rate work as conventionally expected. However, if devaluation affects the aggregate demand abnormally, the country would do better by firmly pegging his currency to a strong foreign one or by joining a monetary union. The relative advantage of a managed peg increases with the frequency of negative real shocks because the downwards adjustment of prices, which are the only way to lower the real value of the domestic currency under a fixed rate system, is particularly costly and painful in developing countries.

4   Real Exchange Rates and Productivity Differentials[7]

Since the managed exchange rate regime makes adjustment easier in the real exchange rate towards its equilibrium level, one would expect the theories of real exchange-rate determination to be more easily fulfilled in economies which have adopted this exchange-rate regime[8]. For the particular case of economies that are predominantly affected by real supply disturbances, the Balassa-Samuelson hypothesis (BSH) would go a long way to explaining medium-run real exchange rate changes. To test this proposition empirically we applied the BSH to a group of Latin American countries that have adopted some kind of exchange rate flexibility in recent years[9].

---

[6] Ortiz and Rodríguez (2002) build an IS-LM model with country risk to explain the results of some fiscal measures implemented in Argentina under the currency board regime.

[7] This section has been written with the research assistance provided by Fernando E. Torrejón.

[8] Since in a regime of managed floating the exchange rate can jump quickly to restore equilibrium, it is reasonable to think that misalignments will be short lived, in contrast with the pegged exchange rate where the shadow or equilibrium exchange rate is potentially different from the actual observed exchange rate.

[9] In accordance with the exchange rate arrangements declared to the International Monetary Fund, the eleven countries which we include in the empirical analysis adopted managed flexibility, ranging from crawling pegs to independent floating, throughout most of the years of our sample. The fixed exchange rate regime was the exception, and is found in very few countries and years: Nicaragua (1991), Ecuador (1992, 2000, 2001), and Venezuela (1994, 1995). In all of these cases, the countries adopted a currency board with respect to the US Dollar.

According to the BSH, labour productivity differentials between tradable and non-tradable sectors determine the price of non-tradables relative to tradables (named the "relative price" hereafter). Under Cobb-Douglas technology in both sectors, it can easily be seen that:

$$ln\, RP_{it} = ln\left(\frac{a_i^T}{a_i^N}\right) + ln\left(\frac{\vartheta_{i,t}^T}{\vartheta_{i,t}^N}\right)$$

(26)

where RP is the relative price and a^T, a^N are the labour shares in value added in the tradable and non-tradable goods sectors, respectively. Labour productivity in tradable and non-tradable sectors is represented by ϑ^T and ϑ^N, respectively. Subscripts i and t denote country and date.

Assuming that technical parameters do not change, and grouping the terms corresponding to the relative price and the productivity of the non-tradable sector in the left-hand side for empirical purposes, we obtain this transformed expression:

$$ln\, RP_{it} + ln\,\vartheta_{i,t}^N = b_i + ln\,\vartheta_{i,t}^T$$

(27)

We interpret Eq. (27) as a restriction on the long-run trends in the relative price and the labour productivity in each sector. In the following lines we will test whether $(ln\, RP_{it} + ln\,\vartheta_{i,t}^N)$, which we call the "composite variable", and $ln\,\vartheta_{i,t}^T$ are cointegrated and whether the cointegrating slope is one. We will also explore the possibility that the cointegration relationship holds with a trend.

We use annual data from Bolivia, Chile, Colombia, Costa Rica, Ecuador, México, Nicaragua, Paraguay, Peru, Uruguay and Venezuela, and construct indexes for prices and labour productivity in each sector. In Appendix II we describe the sources and the procedure followed to calculate aggregate sector indexes from the raw data provided by individual branches of activity. The period covered is imposed by the availability of data for the whole set of countries, and corresponds to the years 1991-2001. Since the individual series are not sufficiently long for time series analysis in each country, we work with panel data and apply Pedroni (1999)'s panel method, which was expressly designed to deal with this problem.

First of all, we examined the trend in behaviour of each series in the panel by applying the method suggested by Levin and Lin (1993) to ascertain the integration order of each series. We applied the test to both filtered and not filtered series, and considered alternatively the possibility of one or two lags[10]. Since we could not reject the null hypothesis of non-stationarity, and found evidence against two-order integration, we concluded that each series has a unit root. In a second stage, we proceeded to look at cointegration relationships. We began with the hypothesis that, in the long run, the log of the composite variable and the log of the productivity in the tradable sector are cointegrated.

---

[10] A higher number of lags would not be reasonable account taken of the size of our sample.

Table 1 contains the results of Pedroni's panel test assuming that the null hypothesis is that the two variables are not cointegrated. The statistics Panel-t (PT) and Panel-t (P) reject the null hypothesis at the 5% and 1% level, respectively. Consequently, the panel test provides strong evidence that relative prices and relative productivities are, in fact, cointegrated as the Balassa-Samuelson model predicts. However, the point estimates of coefficient $\hat{a}$, presented in the bottom column of Table 1, are generally distinct from one, and even negative in four cases. For this reason, we tested the stronger prediction of the BS model that the slope in the cointegration relationship is 1.0.

Table 1 The Balassa-Samuelson model. Cointegration test with the Pedroni (1999) Method for panel data

$$\text{Regression: } (ln\, RP + ln\, \vartheta^N)_{i,t} = \gamma_i + \beta\, ln\, \vartheta^T_{i,t} + \varepsilon_{i,t}$$

11 Latin American countries 1991-2001

Pedroni (1999) test. Period 1991-2001		
Statistics		**p-value**
Panel-υ	48.52	0.17
Panel-ρ	-29.58	0.6
Panel-t (PT)	-8.84	0.05
Panel-t (P)	-128.8	0.00
Estimated value of β		
Countries		
Bolivia		0.898552
Chile		0.535975
Colombia		0.658681
Costa Rica		-0.109722
Ecuador		1.215595
Mexico		-0.126483
Nicaragua		0.038861
Paraguay		1.296599
Peru		-0.060837
Uruguay		0.790096
Venezuela		-0.220163

1. The null hypothesis is Ho: the estimated residuals of all individuals of the panel have a unit root (no cointegration). According to the statistics 1υ and 3t, Ho is rejected at 1% of significance.
2. Estimates of β were obtained with OLS with fixed effects for a balanced panel of data.
3. γ_i is the specific parameter for fixed effects.

In order to verify that the slope is equal to 1.0, we performed a unit root test for the variable $(ln\,RP + ln\,\vartheta^N - ln\,\vartheta^T)_{i,t}$, which we denote "$d_{i,t}$", applying the Levin and Lin (1993) and the Im-Pesaran and Shin (2002) tests for panel data. The null hypothesis is that $d_{i,t}$ has a unit root as opposed to being stationary. If the null is rejected we accept the stronger version of the BSH for this group of Latin American countries taken as a whole. In Table 2 we report the results for the whole set of countries.

As it is apparent from Table 2, the adjusted statistics of Levin and Lin (1993) indicate that the null hypothesis is rejected when we include both one and two lags. In the case of model 1, which has no independent term and shows no trend, the null hypothesis is rejected at 1% for one and two lags. In the case of model 2 the null hypothesis is rejected at 5% when one lag is included.

Table 2. Unit root test on stationarity of $(ln\,RP + ln\,\vartheta^N - ln\,\vartheta^T)_{i,t}$

Method of Levin and Lin (1993) to test that $\beta = 1$

11 Latin American countries 1991-2001

	Model 1		Model 2	
	One lag	Two lags	One lag	Two lags
Filtered series				
t-statistics of $\hat{\rho}$	-3.06	-3.20	-6.06	-6.13
t*-statistics of $\hat{\rho}$	-2.93	-3.07	-2.14	-1.23
p-value	0.0017**	0.0011**	0.0162*	0.1096
Non filtered series				
t-statistics of $\hat{\rho}$	-3.09	-2.74	-6.67	-4.77
t*-statistics of $\hat{\rho}$	-2.97	-2.64	-1.97	1.40
p-value	0.0015**	0.0042**	0.024*	0.92

1. The null hypothesis is Ho: each of the panel members has a unit root, as opposed to the alternative H_1: all of the individuals of the panel are stationary.
2. Model 1 does not include an independent term or any trend in the autoregressive equation. Model 2 includes an independent term.
3. (*), (**) indicate 5% and 1% significance, respectively.

Table 3 reports the results obtained with the IPS test. The null hypothesis is rejected again at 5% when the model includes a trend and a constant. These results do not change when the series is filtered. Overall, the results lend support to the strong version of BSH in the set of countries taken as a whole. The relative price and the relative productivity appear to be cointegrated, and the coefficient relating both variables is close to one. However, the results are not so clear for countries considered individually, since the Pedroni's test provides negative point estimates of coefficient β for four countries (Table 1).

Table 3 Unit root test on stationarity of $(ln\,RP + ln\,\vartheta^N - ln\,\vartheta^T)_{i,t}$

Method of Im-Pesaran and Shin (2002) to test that $\beta = 1$

11 Latin American countries 1991-2001

	Model 1	Model 2
	Without lags	Without lags
Non filtered series		
t-bar NT	-1.63	-2.80
Critical value	-1.93	-2.74*
Filtered series		
t-bar NT	-1.83	-2.92
Critical value	-1.93	-2.74*

1. The null hypothesis is Ho: each of the panel members has a unit root, as opposed to the alternative H_1: some members of the panel are stationary and some are not.
2. Model 1 includes an independent term. Model 2 includes an independent term and a trend.
3. The critical values correspond to N= 10, and T= 10.
4. (*) indicates 5% significance.

5   Concluding Remarks

The choice of an appropriate exchange rate regime for developing countries has been the object of intense scrutiny and policy debate in recent years[11]. Some authors have focused their attention on the financial aspects of the problem and found that, by intervening in the foreign exchange and domestic money markets, the authorities of these countries are pursuing a sub-optimal course of action and introducing destabilising forces in investment decisions and output variations. We demonstrate that even in the financial framework of Calvo and Reinhart (2002), which seems appropriate when output has achieved its long run level, there is scope for reducing the level of the domestic interest rate without increasing its volatility and, consequently, for dampening the destabilising effects of managed floating. A simple linear contract with the central bank concerning the level of the interest rate is a useful device for this purpose.

Paradoxically, the above authors do not include these "real" investment and output consequences in the welfare function of their models. Instead, they neglect real shocks and consider that full employment and purchasing power parity are normal assumptions for these countries. We believe that the virtues and failures of exchange rate regimes must be evaluated within the general framework of economic policy, where stabilisation and exchange rate adjustments play an important role. This is particularly relevant in countries suffering high unemployment rates and frequent and variable real disturbances. For this reason, a substantial

---

[11] See E. C. B. (2003) for a systematic overview of the different arguments and theoretical positions.

part of this paper has been devoted to showing the positive effects of exchange rate management in this field.

We find that the advantages of managed floating increase with the frequency of asymmetric real shocks and the presence of nominal rigidities. For this to occur, which is also evident in the theory of optimal currency areas, it is necessary for a devaluation to affect the aggregate demand in the normal or conventional way. Since such an effect is not evident in developing countries, we obtain the conditions under which it can be achieved. As in previous work by Céspedes, Chang and Velasco (2001), we show that debt ratios and risk premiums would have to reach unrealistically high steady levels to generate the abnormal case.

Furthermore, we show that optimal policy reactions, in the face of real external shocks, as opposed to "fear of floating", may explain why nominal exchange rates have exhibited lower variability than nominal interest rates in developing countries along the recent years.

In the empirical part of the work we obtain evidence to support the Balassa-Samuelson hypothesis in eleven Latin American countries that have adopted some kind of managed exchange-rate regime in recent years. Although this result, obtained for the period 1991-2001, cannot be taken as direct or immediate proof of the advantages of managed floating, it does constitute a good and favourable sign that this system makes adjustments in the real exchange rates quicker and less painful.

The results of this paper are in the same line as Ball (1999) and Ades (2002), who demonstrated that many countries try to stabilise their economies by following a Taylor rule for an open economy and take into consideration the real exchange rate when conducting monetary policy. If this is the case, the efforts of these economies to manage floating should be regarded as a symptom of a "fear of fixing" rather than a "fear of floating".

Appendix I

The effects of exchange rate variations on the aggregate demand

Let us consider the following IS-LM model for a small open and developing country:

$$Y = Y\left(\overset{-}{i}, \overset{+}{D}, \overset{+}{X}, \overset{+}{S} \right)$$

$$\text{(I.1)}$$

$$i = i^* + z\left(\overset{-}{S} \right) + \rho\left(\overset{+}{D}, \overset{+}{S} \right)$$

$$\text{(I.2)}$$

$$M = L\left(\overset{-}{i}, \overset{+}{Y} \right)$$

$$\text{(I.3)}$$

The signs above variables indicate the sign of the corresponding partial derivatives. Equation (I.1) is a standard IS equation indicating that the aggregate demand Y depends negatively on interest rate i, and positively on government deficit D, autonomous net exports X, and exchange rate S, defined as the price of the foreign country. Variables i and S are nominal and real since in this kind of models it is assumed that the expected rate of inflation is zero.

Equation (I.2) is the uncovered interest parity condition. In an economy with a managed exchange rate, international capital mobility implies that the domestic interest rate is equal to the sum of world interest rate i^*, the expected variation in the exchange rate z, and a risk premium ρ. We assume that, ceteris paribus, a higher S today means a lower expected depreciation[12]. The function ρ contains the main novelty of this model, which we explain in the following lines.

The extensive literature on country risk indicates that the risk premium grows with government deficit and falls with the net wealth of the residents. In turn, the net wealth decreases when the domestic currency depreciates since developing countries have huge amounts of dollarised debt. The country risk premium measures the imperfections of the international capital market; its sensitivity with respect to the exchange rate (ρ_e) reflects the importance of the "balance-sheet effect". As it will be seen, the last features are crucial for the functioning and results of the model in these countries.

Equation (I.3) is a standard LM function where demand for money depends positively on domestic output and negatively on the domestic interest rate.

Tacking derivatives and solving the model for the three endogenous variations (dY, dM, di), we obtain that an unexpected (managed) devaluation produces the following results on the aggregate demand, the money supply and the interest rate:

$$\frac{dy}{dS} = \left(z_S + \rho_S\right)Y_i + Y_S \tag{I.4}$$

$$\frac{dM}{dS} = \left(z_S + \rho_S\right)\left(L_i + L_Y Y_i\right) + Y_S L_Y \tag{I.5}$$

$$\frac{di}{dS} = \left(z_S + \rho_S\right) \tag{I.6}$$

These equations indicate that for very vulnerable economies, that is for countries with a very sensitive risk premium to exchange rate variations ($\left|\rho_S\right| > \left|z_S\right|$)- as a result of important balance-sheet effects- devaluation may produce contractionary impacts on the aggregate demand (note that the partial derivative, Y_i, has a negative sing). Furthermore, under these circumstances, devaluation also may induce an endogenous contraction in the money supply and an increase in domestic interest rate.

---

[12] This assumption is in accordance with the Dornbusch mechanism of expectations formation adopted in section 3 of this work.

For robust economies, in which $|z_S| > |\rho_S|$, devaluation has expansionary effects in both the aggregate demand and the money supply, and reduces the domestic interest rate.

Appendix II

Data sources and construction of some variables for the test of Balassa and Samuelson Hypothesis

Main sources: central banks, national institutes of statistics, CEPAL, and Labour International Organisation.

The ranking of the branches of activity was taken from the United Nations Statistical Papers, *Series M, Nr 4/Review 3.* New York, 1990.

Goods were grouped under the headlines of tradables and non-tradables according to the general criteria accepted in the literature and the extent of data availability. In the group of tradables we included manufactures, transports, storage and communications, and mining and quarrying. Within the group of non-tradables we included electricity, gas and water, construction, wholesale and retail commerce, motor repairing, home goods, hotels and restaurants, financial intermediation, estate activities, hiring, and other trade activities.

Because lack of data in important aspects such as output and/or employment, the following activities and goods were excluded: education, health and social work, other social service activities, home services, non-governmental organisations, agriculture, forestry, hunting and fishing, and public administration.

For each sector we constructed indexes for prices and average labour productivity. As far price indexes are concerned, we obtained them dividing the aggregate nominal output by the real aggregate output in the sector. Aggregate outputs were obtained as a weighted sum of outputs of individual branches.

To calculate the average labour productivity in each sector we measured previously total employment as a weighted sum of employment in individual branches. Then we divided real production by employment in each sector.

References

[1]   Ades, A. (2002), "Taylor Rules in Emerging Markets", in *Goldman Sachs Emerging Market Strategy,* **02**, 12 (July).

[2]   Ball, L. (1999), "Policy Rules for Open Economies", in J. B. Taylor (Ed) *Monetary Policy Rules,* University of Chicago Press.

[3]   Barro, R. J. and Gordon, D. B. (1983), "Rules, Discretion and Reputation in a Model of Monetary Policy", *Journal of Monetary Economics,* **17** (1): 101-122.

[4]   Branson, W. (1977), "Asset Markets and Relative Prices in Exchange Rate Determination", *Sozialwissenschaftliche Annalen,* Vol. 1: 69-89.

[5]   Calvo, G. amd C. Reinhart (2002), "Fear of Floating", *Quarterly Journal of Economics,* Vol. CXVII, (May): 379-408.

[6] Céspedes, L. F., R. Chang, and A. Velasco (2002), "IS-LM-BP in the Pampas", *Working Paper* **9337**, NBER.

[7] Dornbusch, R. (1976), "Expectations and exchange rate dynamics", *Journal of Political Economy,* **84**: 1161-1176, December.

[8] European Central Bank (2003), "Exchange rate regimes for emerging economies", *Monthly Bulletin*, February, 53-66.

[9] Edwards, S. (2002), "The great exchange rate debate after Argentina", *North American Journal of Economics and Finance,* **13**:237-252.

[10] Edwards, S. And E. Levy-Yeyati (2002), "Flexible Exchange Rates as Stock Absorbers: An Empirical Investigation", *UCLA Working Paper*.

[11] Frenkel, J. and M. Mussa (1988), "Exchange Rates and the Balance of Payments", in R. Jones and P. Kennen (eds), *Handbook of International Economics*, North Holland, Amsterdam.

[12] Im, Pesaran and Shin (2002), "Testing for Unit Roots in Heterogeneous Pannels", Mimeo.

[13] Lahiri, A., and C. A. Végh (2001), "Living with the Fear of Floating: An Optimal Policy Perspective", in *Preventing Currency Crisis in Emerging Markets*, S. Edwards and F. Frankel (eds), Chicago: University of Chicago Press for the National Bureau of Economic Research.

[14] Levin, A. and Lin, C. F. (1993), "Unit Roots Test in Panel Data: New Results", Department of Economics, University of California at San Diego, Discussion Paper.

[15] McKinnon R. and Schnabl (2003), "The East Asian Dollar Standard, Fear of Floating, and Original Sin", Stanford University Working Paper 03-001.

[16] Ortiz, J. and C. Rodríguez (2002), "Country Risk and the Mundell-Fleming Model Applied to the 1999-2000 Argentine Experience", *Journal of Applied Economics,* Vol. 2 (November): 327-348.

[17] Reinhart, C. (2000), "Mirage of Floating Exchange Rates", *American Economic Review*, Vol. 90, Iss. 2 (May): 65-70.

[18] Pedroni, P. (1999), "Critical Values for Cointegration Tests in Heterogeneous Panels with Multiple Regressors", in A. Banerjee (edt) *Special Issue of the Oxford Bulletin of Economics and Statistics*, Oxford.

[19] *Walsh, C. E. (1995), "Optimal Contracts for Central Bankers", American Economic Review*, **85** (1): 150-167.

In: International Macroeconomics: Recent Developments   ISBN 1-59454-901-X
Editor: Amalia Morales Zumaquero pp. 153-205   © 2006 Nova Science Publishers, Inc.

Chapter 9

IMPERFECT KNOWLEDGE EXPECTATIONS, UNCERTAINTY PREMIA AND EXCHANGE RATE DYNAMICS

Roman Frydman[1]* *and Michael D. Goldberg*[2]†
[1]Department of Economics, New York University 269 Mercer Street,
New York, New York 10012
[2]Whittemore School of Business and Economics, University of
New Hampshire, McConnell Hall, Durham, NH 03824

1 Introduction

The *Rational Expectations Hypothesis* (REH) has become so ubiquitous in modern economics that the economic analyst need not give a second thought as to how expectations should be modeled. The rigorous modeling of expectations delivered by the REH makes possible the formulation of models purged of "free" parameters. This produces sharp predictions and opens the way for the rigorous testing of cross-equation restrictions on the parameters of the RE-based models. In this way, the RE revolution transformed Economics into a normal science and overturned all previous conceptions of how economists should treat the expectations of the agents whose economic behavior they are trying to model.

Pre-REH conceptions of the expectations formation process attached great importance to psychological and sociological factors.[1] Knight for example, in his classic book, introduced the distinction between measurable uncertainty - which he called "risk" - and "true uncertainty"," which cannot "by any method be reduced to an objective, quantitatively determined probability (Knight [1921], p. 321)." For Knight, the uncertainty of events arises from their uniqueness. Keynes's perspective brought the problem closer to modern concerns. With his beauty contest example, Keynes underscored the role played by subjective guesses of the average opinion in the formation of individual expectations of asset

---

*E-mail address: roman.frydman@nyu.edu, (212) 998-8967
†E-mail address: michaelg@cisunix.unh.edu, (603) 862-3385
[1]The following discussion on pre-REH conceptions draws on Frydman [1982] and Frydman and Phelps [1983].

prices. Because there is only the most "flimsy" basis for estimating average opinion, it is a factor that creates uncertainty about stock prices (Keynes [1937], p. 156). In modern terms, Keynes's position was that such subjective and psychological factors influencing the average opinion would preclude the precise modeling of individual expectations by an outside investigator, including other agents and economic analysts. Hayek [1948] drew a now widely recognized distinction between individual rationality and the economic problem which society faces. He argued that this problem is not one of individual choice but "rather a problem...of the utilization of knowledge which is not given to anyone in its totality" (Hayek [1948], p. 78). In laying the foundations of modern macroeconomic theory, in terms of microfoundations and intertemporal optimization, Phelps argued that there was no presumption that an outside investigator could accurately model each individual's expectations on each island about "the world imagined"(Phelps et. al [1970], p. 22).[2]

One of the main objectives of this paper is to offer an alternative approach to modeling expectations that recognizes the importance of imperfect knowledge and yet preserves the postulate of individual rationality. Our approach, dubbed *Imperfect Knowledge Forecasting* (IKF), builds on the idea of *Theories Consistent Expectations* (TCE), proposed in Frydman and Phelps [1990] and developed in Goldberg [1991] and Goldberg and Frydman [1993,1996a] according to which the extant stock of economic models provides agents with *qualitative* knowledge that can be used in forming individual expectations. We will point out in the present paper that if the outside observer, including the economic analyst as well as any other agent, attempts to characterize fully (i.e. in terms of fixed rules or their generalizations) individual expectations and their updating *in a world of imperfect knowledge,* the resulting formulations are, in general, inconsistent with the postulate of individual rationality.[3] Consequently, our formulation of the expectation formation process involves "free" parameters arising from the subjective expectations of rational agents; and since we want to preserve, in general, the postulate of individual rationality, we do not impose precise quantitative restrictions on these "free" parameters. These free parameters can be interpreted as the subjective elements that the earlier literature argued were important for modeling the expectations formation process of individual agents. Nowadays these subjective elements are often viewed as introducing elements of irrationality into economic modeling. However, in contrast to the conventional belief that expectations based on departures from the REH can at best be considered as "boundedly rational", the imperfect knowledge expectations, as formulated in this paper, are rational in a world characterized by imperfect knowledge. Although our approach brings back the subjective elements considered so important by the pre-REH literature, it preserves the basic insight of RE that agents can use models, although only in a qualitative sense, to look forward in forming individual expectations.

Imperfect knowledge expectations can be embedded into any model of the underlying structure of the macroeconomy. In this paper we develop our approach within the context of the foreign exchange market and use a particularly simple form for the underlying structure

---

[2]For a formal analysis of inconsistency of the precise modeling of individual forecast functions with individual rationality in the context of the REH-version of Phelps's "island model", see Frydman [1983].

[3]For a formal proof for the individual forecast functions based on least-squares learning rules, see Frydman [1982]. Recently, Evans and Honkapohja [2001, p.359] have also recognized that the assumption that agents use forecast functions based on constant-gain learning algorithms may imply "regularities in forecast errors which can be exploited"

of the economy: a modified version of the overshooting model due to Dornbusch [1976] and Frankel [1979] (the DF model). This model has been criticized for its assumptions of exogenous money and income processes, and a constant equilibrium real exchange rate as well as for lacking explicit microfoundations.[4] However, this old workhorse of open-economy macroeconomics serves our purposes well in that its simplicity allows us to focus our attention on the role played by imperfect knowledge in exchange rate dynamics. More importantly, it is widely recognized that under RE, the DF model generates implications that are grossly inconsistent with the behavior of exchange rates during the floating rate period.[5]. As we shall show in this paper, once REH is replaced by IKF, the DF model offers surprising promise in explaining the hitherto anomalous aspects of the floating rate experience.

The remainder of the paper is structured as follows. In section 2 we formulate our approach to the modeling of individual expectations in a world of imperfect knowledge. In doing so we allow for the heterogeneity of individual expectations. Our framework allows for expectations based on the qualitative use of economic models, as well as on other atheoretical components of personal knowledge, including technical rules, other rules of thumb and individual guesses.

In section 3 we reconsider the notion of equilibrium in the monetary class of models, i.e., uncovered interest rate parity (UIP). As is well known, this condition is difficult to justify on empirical grounds. This problem is known as the excess returns puzzle.[6] This leads us to propose an alternative approach to modeling excess returns and equilibrium in the foreign exchange market. Our approach is based on the prospect theory proposed in Kahneman and Tversky [1979]. We follow Benartzi and Thaler [1995] and assume that individual agents are "myopically loss averse": agents are more sensitive to reductions than to increases in wealth, the effect of the level of wealth is assumed to be of second order, and that they monitor returns on their investments relatively frequently. However, we develop a dynamic version of myopic loss aversion that accounts for the evolution of agents' assessments of losses during episodes of persistent movements of the exchange rate from benchmark levels.[7] We show in the context of our model of the foreign exchange market that loss averse agents will in general require a premium to compensate them for the potential losses on holding foreign exchange, which we call an uncertainty premium. This leads us to a new specification of equilibrium in the foreign exchange market in which the aggregate expected excess return is equal to the aggregate uncertainty premium. In order to check for empirical relevance of this new equilibrium condition, which we refer to as uncertainty adjusted uncovered interest rate parity (UAUIP), we provide preliminary evidence showing that our dynamic model of the uncertainty premium and the behavior of excess returns is consistent with the data.

In section 4 we begin to examine the implications of our monetary model with IKF and UAUIP. With imperfect knowledge, agents will, in general, revise their assessments of the short-run movement of the exchange rate by incorporating new information available to

---

[4]See for example Obstfeld and Rogoff [1996], chapter 9.

[5]For survey articles see Frankel and Rose [1995] and Taylor [1995].

[6]For review articles, see Lewis [1995] and Engel [1996].

[7]Prospect theory has become quite popular in modeling the behavior of asset prices under RE. For example, see Barberis, Huang and Santos [2001], Barberis and Huang [2001] and references therein.

them as well as updating the methods, models and guesses they use. We refer to movements of expectations resulting from all forms of updating as *expectations dynamics*. Since our notion of expectations dynamics allows subjective elements, in addition to economic models and statistical procedures, the resulting solution for the time paths of the endogenous variables involve "free" parameters. We solve the model in two stages. In the first stage, the general solution of the model is derived under the assumption of imperfect knowledge expectations with virtually no restrictions imposed on the expectations dynamics. Although the general solution leads to some qualitative implications concerning steady-state values, nothing in particular can be said about the time paths of the endogenous variables implied by the model until additional assumptions are made concerning the expectations dynamics. However, instead of completely closing the model with one fixed expectational rule and generating a fully determinate solution of the model, we ask in the second stage whether there exists reasonable scenarios of expectations dynamics that produce, within the context of our model, exchange rate dynamics matching up with the important features of the data.

The second stage of our analysis is carried out in section 5, where we begin to explore the potential of our model to illuminate important features of the empirical record on exchange rates. In particular, we provide a specific example of how the general solution, together with additional qualitative assumptions on expectations dynamics, can produce persistent movements of the exchange rate away from PPP. Since in this second stage of the solution we do not assume one fixed rule governing the expectations dynamics in all subperiods, we do not derive fully determinate solutions for the time paths of the endogenous variables and therefore we do not obtain precise quantitative implications from our model. Instead, with qualitative assumptions on the expectations dynamics, our model produces only qualitative implications about the movements of the endogenous variables. The question we ask is whether there exist reasonable qualitative assumptions on expectations dynamics that lead to persistent movements of the exchange rate away over successive subperiods. To guide us in evaluating various qualitative assumptions, we make use of some of the findings from the literature on behavioral economics. We show that there are reasonable qualitative assumptions on expectations dynamics leading to persistent movements of the exchange rate away from PPP, although because of the qualitative nature of our assumptions, we cannot determine precisely the rate at which the exchange rate moves away or when this movement away might end.

We also show, contrary to conventional wisdom, that persistent movements of the exchange away from PPP over extended time periods do not require the presence of nonfundamental factors, rather such behavior is the consequence of imperfect knowledge. In this sense the IKF approach to the foreign exchange market developed in this paper is similar to the analysis of the boom and bust cycles (i.e., long-swings) in Soros [1987, 2000] which emphasizes that such asset-price dynamics cannot be understood without imperfect knowledge. Our approach is also similar to the work of Schulmeister [1983,1987], which models the long-swings behavior of exchange rates by substituting qualitative assumptions about exchange rate expectations for the REH.

We conclude the paper by discussing how our monetary model with IKF and an uncertainty premium sheds new light on the exchange-rate disconnect puzzle, which includes the Meese-Rogoff forecasting puzzle, the Baxter-Stockman neutrality-of-exchange-rate-regime puzzle, and the puzzle that empirical exchange rate models fit poorly in sample.

2   The Model

The DF model consists of equilibrium conditions for the money and foreign exchange markets, a price-adjustment equation, and the assumption that agents' expectations are formed according to the rational expectations hypothesis (REH). The model can be written as follows:

$$m_r = \gamma p_r + \phi y_r - \lambda i_r \tag{1}$$

$$E(\dot{s}) - i_r = 0 \tag{2}$$

$$\dot{p}_r = \delta \left[\alpha \left(s - p_r - q_n \right) - v \left(i_r - i_n \right) \right] + \dot{\bar{p}}_r \tag{3}$$

where s is the log level of the exchange rate (defined as the domestic currency price of foreign currency), m_r, p_r and y_r denote the log levels of relative (domestic minus foreign) money supplies, goods prices and incomes respectively, i_r is the relative level of short-run nominal interest rates, and q_n is the "natural" log level of the real exchange rate, which is assumed to be exogenous to the model and constant.[8] The variable i_n is the "natural" level of relative nominal interest rates, which is equal to the steady-state level of the expected relative rate of inflation, π_r, plus the natural level of relative real interest rates, r_n. We assume that r_n is exogenous to the model and constant, and therefore set $r_n = 0$. The symbol "−" denotes the goods-market clearing value of a variable. The DF model is closed by assuming that expectations are formed according to the REH, i.e., $E(\dot{s})$ is the conditional expectation of the solution for $\dot{s}$ implied by the model 1-3.

In this paper we follow the DF model in using equations (1) and (3) to model money market equilibrium and price adjustment, respectively. But we depart from the basic DF framework in two fundamental ways. First, we replace expectations formed according to the REH with expectation functions consistent with our assumption that agents are endowed with imperfect knowledge of how the exchange rate might be related to macroeconomic fundamentals. Second, we replace the assumption of risk-neutral agents and UIP in equation (2) with an equilibrium condition that arises from assuming imperfect knowledge and myopically loss-averse agents along the lines of Kahneman and Tversky [1979] and Benartzi and Thaler [1995]. The remainder of this section develops our IKF framework and the next section develops an alternative specification for equilibrium in the foreign exchange.

2.1   Imperfect Knowledge and the Formation of Individual Expectations

We adopt the fundamental insight of the RE approach that extant economists' models play a potentially important role in the formulation of agents expectations. However, we replace the assumption that each agent forms his expectation based on the particular model being analyzed by the economist by the assumption that individuals form their expectations based on imperfect knowledge.[9] We will refer to such expectations as *Imperfect Knowledge Expectations* (IKF) The framework of imperfect knowledge expectations used here builds on

---

[8]Both Dornbusch [1976] and Frankel [1979] set q_n to be consistent with absolute PPP, i.e., q_n=0.

[9]For early arguments that the conventional formulation of "rational expectations" may be difficult to reconcile with individual rationality in decentralized markets, see Frydman [1982, 1983], Frydman and Phelps [1983] and Phelps [1983]. Frydman and Phelps [1983] also discuss logical problems raised by the existence of a plurality of models and imperfect knowledge for the meaning and applicability of the REH.

the earlier development of *Theories Consistent Expectations* (TCE).[10] However, in addition to the qualitative use of models assumed by the TCE framework, IKF also allows for expectations formed on the basis of other atheoretical components of personal knowledge, including technical rules, other rules of thumb and individual guesses.[11] The following assumptions characterize the framework of imperfect knowledge expectations:

- *Imperfect Knowledge of Economic Models: Theories Consistent Expectations:* To the extent that agents make use of economists' models, their knowledge of those models is *imperfect* in the sense that the stock of existing models provides individual agents with only *qualitative knowledge* about how endogenous variables might be related to exogenous (predetermined) variables. Such qualitative knowledge consists of the algebraic signs (but not magnitudes) of the coefficients of important explanatory variables that might be useful in forecasting, as well as qualitative information about the long-run equilibrium levels of the endogenous variables.

- *Imperfect Knowledge:* In forming their expectations individual agents make use of knowledge available to them, including qualitative knowledge of extant models, as defined above, atheoretical forecast functions suggested by technical trading rules and other rules of thumb as well as personal guesses based on the idiosyncratic evaluation of information available to the individual agents. *We recognize that neither the economic analyst nor economic agents are able to characterize fully (i.e. in terms of fixed rules or their generalizations) these subjective and idiosyncratic elements contained in individual and aggregate forecast functions.*

We use the framework of imperfect knowledge to formulate a replacement for RE in the DF model. If the RE framework were used, along with the usual assumptions of stability and constant growth rates for relative money and income levels, then the DF model in equations (1)-(3) would imply the following familiar equation for exchange rate expectations:

$$E_{\mathrm{RE}}(\dot{s}) = \theta(\bar{s}_{\mathrm{RE}} - s) + \dot{\bar{s}}_{\mathrm{RE}} \tag{4}$$

where

$$\bar{s}_{\mathrm{RE}} = \frac{1}{\gamma}\left(m_r - \phi y_r\right) + \frac{\lambda}{\gamma}\pi_r + q_n \tag{5}$$

and π_r denotes secular levels of expected relative inflation rates, i.e., $\pi_r = \frac{1}{\gamma}(\dot{m}_r - \phi\dot{y}_r)$ and θ is the stable root of the system, redefined to be positive. The steady-state value of the exchange rate under RE, $\bar{s}_{\mathrm{RE}}$ in equation (5) is the PPP nominal exchange rate, given the full adjustment of good prices.

Although equation (4) has been shown to be useful for forecasting at long horizons, it is well known that it fails at short-term forecasting horizons.[12] Since movements of the

---

[10]The idea of TCE was first proposed in Frydman and Phelps [1990] and developed in the context of the monetary models of the exchange rate in Goldberg [1991] and Goldberg and Frydman [1993,1996a].

[11]As we shall further discuss in Section 7, the individual knowledge also involves some tacit knowlege, or personal knowledge, that is outside of existing knowledge and goes beyond what can be communicated in explicit terms. For a seminal discussion of the role of personal knowledge in market behavior, see Polanyi [1962].

[12]For evidence that equations like 4 are useful for forecasting at long-horizons see Mark [1995].

exchange rate away from PPP levels tend to be large and persistent, there are clearly extended time periods during which equation (4) would fail at short-term forecasting. Moreover, recent research surrounding the so-called PPP puzzle suggests that nominal exchange rates converge to PPP levels much more slowly than nominal prices converge towards their steady-state values.[13]. This implies that in the "medium-run", defined as the period required for convergence of prices to their steady-state values, the value of the exchange rate will, in general, be substantially different than $\bar{s}_{RE}$ and PPP.[14] Thus, if the PPP level of the exchange rate, $\bar{s}_{RE}$ in (4), is replaced by this medium-run, non-RE level of the exchange rate, then the resulting forecasting equation might be a plausible representation of agents' forecasting behavior in a world characterized by sticky prices.

The analysis in this paper develops such a representation of the individual and the market (average across agents) forecast functions under the assumption of imperfect knowledge. Denoting the medium-run value of the exchange rate under imperfect knowledge by $\bar{s}_{IK}$ yields the qualitative structure of the individual forecast functions assumed to be used by individual agents:

$$E(\dot{s}) = \theta(\bar{s}_{IK} - s) + \dot{\bar{s}}_{IK} \qquad (6)$$

We model imperfect knowledge in the following way. Each individual agent, i, is assumed to form a forecast (an assessment) of the future, medium-run level of the exchange rate ($\bar{s}_{IK}$) which we denote by $\tilde{s}_i$. In arriving at forecasts of $\bar{s}_{IK}$, agents can combine statistical estimation based on a model and data deemed relevant by the agent at a given moment of time with their subjective judgements based on the information and qualitative knowledge available to them. The framework of IKF, defined above allows for a number of assumptions on the qualitative structure of $\tilde{s}_i$, but we postpone the introduction of such assumptions until section 4, where such specificity will be required for the derivation of our results concerning the role of fundamentals in the explanation of persistent departures of the exchange rate from PPP levels.

Our objective here is to specify the general structure of our model under the assumptions that the individual agents' forecast functions have a qualitative structure given by the function in (6) and that individual agents make *their own subjective* assessments of θ, $\bar{s}_{IK}$ and $\dot{\bar{s}}_{IK}$ on the basis of the imperfect knowledge available to them. Under these assumptions, the short-run forecast of the rate of change of the exchange rate of agent i, $E_i(\dot{s})$, is given by:

$$E_i(\dot{s}) = \tilde{\theta}_i(\tilde{s}_i - s) + \dot{\tilde{s}}_i, \quad i = 1...N \qquad (7)$$

where $\tilde{\theta}_i$ and $\dot{\tilde{s}}_i$ are agent i's assessments of the speed at which s tends towards $\bar{s}_{IK}$ and the rate of change of $\bar{s}_{IK}$, $\dot{\bar{s}}_{IK}$ respectively, and N denotes an arbitrarily large number of market participants.

---

[13]Since equation 4 implicitly assumes that nominal prices and exchange rates converge at the same rate to their PPP levels, it is not surprising that it would not be useful in the short-term forecasting. For further discussion and empirical evidence on this point, see Engel and Morley [2001] and references therein.

[14]The term "medium-run" is used instead of the more common term "long-run" to describe goods-market clearing levels because with imperfect knowledge, such equilibrium levels provide only temporary anchors due to structural shifts in agents' expectations functions. We discuss this issue more fully in section 4 below.

To aggregate (7) over all agents, we use weights, w_i, $i = 1...N$, equal to the proportions of the individual agents' wealth relative to the total wealth invested in the foreign exchange market.[15] This yields the following equation for the average (market) expectation function, $E(\dot{s})$:

$$E(\dot{s}) = \tilde{\theta}(\tilde{s} - s) + \dot{\tilde{s}} \tag{8}$$

where $\tilde{\theta}$ and $\dot{\tilde{s}}$ are weighted averages of individual assessments given by:

$$\tilde{\theta} = \sum_i w_i \tilde{\theta}_i, \quad 0 < w_i < 1, \; i = 1...N \text{ and } \sum_i w_i = 1,$$

$$\dot{\tilde{s}} = \sum_i w_i \dot{\tilde{s}}_i$$

and $\tilde{s}$ is the market's assessment of $\bar{s}_{IK}$, which can also be written as a weighted average of the individual assessments, $\tilde{s}_i$:

$$\tilde{s} = \sum_i W_i \tilde{s}_i, \quad \text{where } 0 < W_i = \frac{w_i \tilde{\theta}_i}{\sum_i w_i \tilde{\theta}_i} < 1 \tag{9}$$

Thus, the forecast functions in (7) are tantamount to assuming that individual agents (and, consequently, the market), form assessments of $\bar{s}_{IK}$ and $\dot{\tilde{s}}_{IK}$ and then expect the exchange rate will tend towards their assessments with the speeds $\tilde{\theta}^i$.

Finally, we note that the replacement of the RE forecast functions in (4) with the forecast functions based on imperfect knowledge in (8) still results, as is the case under RE, in forecast functions which are model consistent, though in a qualitative rather than quantitative sense. As we shall show in section 4, if individual agents use the forecast functions in (7), then the differential equation describing the actual rate of change in the exchange rate implied by the model, is of the same qualitative form as equations (7) and (8).

3 Myopic Loss Aversion and Uncertainty Adjusted Uncovered Interest Rate Parity

One of the basic assumptions of the monetary class of models is the assumption of risk neutral agents, which together with perfect capital mobility, implies that equilibrium in the foreign exchange market is described by the uncovered interest rate parity (UIP) condition in equation (2). With UIP, the expected excess return on holding foreign bonds at each point in time is zero. As is well known, the assumption of UIP is difficult to reconcile with the empirical record: observed expected excess returns are often nonzero and large, highly volatile and experience numerous sign reversals during floating-rate regimes. The literature offers two main explanations of such behavior.[16] One explanation holds that expected

---

[15]In general, the w_i's may vary over time. However, to make the analysis tractable we assume that these weights are constants.

[16]See Lewis [1996] and Engel [1996] for surveys of this literature.

excess returns are in fact zero and that the problem lies in our inability to accurately observe expected excess returns because of small-sample bias arising from peso problems or learning or because exchange rate expectations are "irrational." The other and more dominant explanation is that agents are risk averse and require compensation (in the form of a risk premium) for holding non-diversifiable risky foreign exchange positions, i.e., it is risk-adjusted expected excess returns that are zero. It seems uncontroversial to suggest that although these explanations may eventually prove to play some role in explaining the behavior of observed expected excess returns, the greater part of the puzzle remains.

In this paper we propose an alternative approach to modeling excess returns and equilibrium in the foreign exchange market. Our approach is based on the prospect theory proposed by Kahneman and Tversky [1979]. We follow Benartzi and Thaler [1995] and assume that individual agents are "myopically loss averse": agents are more sensitive to reductions than to increases in wealth, the effect of the level of wealth is assumed to be of second order, and that they monitor returns on their investments relatively frequently. However, we develop a dynamic version of myopic loss aversion that accounts for the evolution of agents' assessments of losses during episodes of persistent movements of the exchange rate from benchmark levels.[17]

The basic idea behind our approach to modeling excess returns and equilibrium in the foreign exchange market is the following: Departures from UIP occur because although the exchange rate does move in a direction consistent with UIP whenever expectations or relative interest rates change, the exchange rate movement is short of what is required for UIP to hold. For example, suppose that the market's expectation, $E(\dot{s})$, is given by equation (8) and that agents in the aggregate revise upward their assessment of the medium-run value of the exchange rate, causing $E(\dot{s})$ to rise. This revision leads to an increase in the expected excess return on buying foreign currency, an incipient capital flow into foreign currency and an increase in s. However, we show that because of imperfect knowledge and myopic loss aversion, market agents are unwilling, in the aggregate, to bid the exchange rate far enough for UIP to hold.[18] The next two subsections develop a formalization of this approach.

3.1   Uncertainty Adjusted Uncovered Interest Rate Parity

At every point in time both domestic and foreign agents operating in the foreign exchange market face a decision on whether to buy or sell foreign exchange. This decision depends on their individual assessments of the relative returns from each decision. The excess return on buying foreign assets over the return on buying domestic assets, which we denote by R, can be approximated as follows:

$$R = \triangle s_{t+1} - i_r \qquad (10)$$

---

[17]Prospect theory has become quite popular in modeling the behavior of asset prices under RE. For example, see Barberis, Huang and Santos [1999], Barberis and Huang [2001] and references therein.

[18]An alternative approach to modeling this idea would be to drop the assumption of perfect capital mobility and assume that, because of borrowing constraints or transaction costs, the capital flows forthcoming whenever $E(\dot{s}) - i_r \neq 0$ are too small relative to the underlying flows arising from the imbalance between domestic saving and investment. We plan to explore this alternative in a followup to this paper.

where $\triangle$ denotes the first-difference operator. If individual agents are risk neutral, then their decision to buy or sell foreign exchange depends on their assessment of the expected excess return. Using (8) we can write the aggregate expected excess return, $E(R)$, as follows:

$$E(R) = \tilde{\theta}\left(\tilde{s} - s\right) + \dot{\tilde{s}} - i_r \qquad (11)$$

If borrowing constraints and transactions costs are small enough, so that the perfect capital mobility assumption applies, then equilibrium in the foreign exchange market requires the aggregate (market) expectation of the excess return, $E(R)$, to equal zero, i.e., it requires UIP. However, if individual agents are loss averse, their decision to buy or sell foreign exchange depends on their assessment of the expected utility of each decision and as we shall show shortly, the equilibrium in the foreign exchange market with loss averse agents occurs at levels of the exchange rate at which UIP *does not* hold.

To formalize loss aversion and the notion of equilibrium in the context of our model of the foreign exchange market, we assume that *at every point in time* an individual agent assigns non-zero probabilities, denoted by $\tilde{p}_{k,i}$, to a finite number, say K, of potential realizations of R from the set of all potential realizations $\mathcal{R}$.[19]. If an individual agent buys the foreign currency, then the potential losses on this speculation are all negative realizations of R. Conversely, if an individual agent sells the foreign currency, then the potential losses are all positive realizations of R. Thus, we define the set of potential losses and gains from buying or selling foreign currency as follows:

Definition 1 *Let $\mathcal{R}^-$ and $\mathcal{R}^+$ be the sets of negative and positive realizations of R, respectively, so that $\mathcal{R} = \mathcal{R}^- \cup \mathcal{R}^+$. The set of potential losses from buying (selling) the foreign currency $\mathcal{R}_i^{\mathrm{LB}}(\mathcal{R}_i^{\mathrm{LS}})$ is the subset of negative (positive) values of excess returns in $\mathcal{R}$, i.e., $\mathcal{R}_i^{\mathrm{LB}} = \mathcal{R}^-$ and $\mathcal{R}_i^{\mathrm{LS}} = \mathcal{R}^+$. The complementary sets of potential gains from buying and selling the foreign currency, $\mathcal{R}_i^{\mathrm{GB}}$ and $\mathcal{R}_i^{\mathrm{GS}}$, respectively, are defined in an analogous manner, so that $\mathcal{R}_i^{\mathrm{GB}} = \mathcal{R}^+$ and $\mathcal{R}_i^{\mathrm{GS}} = \mathcal{R}^-$.*

To specify a decision rule for buying or selling foreign currency by loss averse agents we use the following simple functional form for the individual utility, which captures the loss aversion of the individual investor:

$$v_i(R) = \begin{cases} R & \text{if } R \in \mathcal{R}_i^{\mathrm{GB}} \text{ or } \mathcal{R}_i^{\mathrm{GS}} \\ \lambda R & \text{if } R \in \mathcal{R}_i^{\mathrm{LB}} \text{ or } \mathcal{R}_i^{\mathrm{LS}} \end{cases} \quad \lambda_i > 1 \qquad (12)$$

where $v_i(R)$ is the utility function defined over potential gains and losses from the buying or selling of foreign currency as given by Definition 1 and λ_i is the coefficient of loss aversion.[20]

---

[19]The set R is the union of sets of potential realizations of excess returns taken into account by individual agents. It is implicitly assumed that if a particular realization $R_k \in R$ is not considered relevant for the individual agent i, the probability assigned by the agent to R_k is equal to zero.

[20]This utility function is a special case of the utility function originally proposed by Kahneman and Tversky [1979] and has become the standard in the literature. e.g., see Benarzi and Thaler [1995] and Barberis, Huang and Santos [1999]. The value of λ has been reported in the literature to be in excess of 2. See Benartzi and Thaler [1995] and references therein for further discussion.

Using expression (12) and Definition 1, we follow Benartzi and Thaler [1995] and define the "prospective excess return" of an individual agent facing payoffs $R_k \in \mathcal{R}$ from buying foreign currency as follows:

$$E_i^{\mathrm{B}}[v(R)] = \sum_{k \in K_i^{\mathrm{GB}}} \tilde{p}_{k,i} R_k + \lambda_i \sum_{k \in K_i^{\mathrm{LB}}} \tilde{p}_{k,i} R_k \equiv G_i^{\mathrm{B}} + \lambda_i L_i^{\mathrm{B}} \tag{13}$$

where K_i^{GB} and K_i^{LB} denote the sets of integers for realizations in the sets $\mathcal{R}_i^{\mathrm{GB}}$ and $\mathcal{R}_i^{\mathrm{LB}}$, respectively, and G_i^{B} and L_i^{B} denote the (truncated) expected gain and loss of an individual agent i who buys foreign currency.[21] Analogously, the prospective excess return from selling foreign currency is given by:

$$E_i^{\mathrm{S}}[v(R)] = \sum_{k \in K_i^{\mathrm{GS}}} \tilde{p}_{k,i} R_k + \lambda_i \sum_{k \in K_i^{\mathrm{LS}}} \tilde{p}_{k,i} R_k \equiv G_i^{\mathrm{S}} + \lambda L_i^{\mathrm{S}} \tag{14}$$

where G_i^{S} and L_i^{S} denote the (truncated) expected gain and loss of an individual agent i who sells foreign currency.

Remark 1 *We note that if the individual is loss averse, then he will attempt to buy foreign currency if $E_i^{\mathrm{B}}[v(R)] > 0$ or sell foreign currency if $E_i^{\mathrm{S}}[v(R)] < 0$. Furthermore, an individual agent will not attempt to alter his holdings of the domestic and foreign currency assets if either $E_i^{\mathrm{B}}[v(R)] \leq 0$ or $E_i^{\mathrm{S}}[v(R)] \geq 0$.*[22,23]

Definition 1 and expressions (13) and (14) readily imply that for a given set of values R_k, and the associated individual assessments of probabilities $\tilde{p}_{k,i}$, *only one* of the following four relationships can be satisfied: either $E_i^{\mathrm{B}}[v(R)] > 0$, or $E_i^{\mathrm{S}}[v(R)] < 0$, or $E_i^{\mathrm{B}}[v(R)] = 0$ or $E_i^{\mathrm{S}}[v(R)] = 0$. Thus, our decision rule based on the prospective excess return generates an unambiguous decision to sell, buy or hold an unchanged stock of foreign currency.

Denoting by I^{B} and I^{S} the groups of agents for whom $E_i^{\mathrm{B}}[v(R)] > 0$ (to be referred to as buyers) and $E_i^{\mathrm{S}}[v(R)] < 0$ (to be referred to as sellers), respectively, the aggregate (market) prospective excess return is given by:

$$E[v(R)] = \sum_{i \in I^{\mathrm{B}}} w_i E_i^{\mathrm{B}}[v(R)] + \sum_{i \in I^{\mathrm{S}}} w_i E_i^{\mathrm{S}}[v(R)] \equiv E^{\mathrm{B}}[v(R)] + E^{\mathrm{S}}[v(R)]$$

$$\equiv G^{\mathrm{B}} + \lambda^{\mathrm{B}} L^{\mathrm{B}} + G^{\mathrm{S}} + \lambda^{\mathrm{S}} L^{\mathrm{S}} \tag{15}$$

where G^{B}, L^{B}, G^{S} and L^{S} are market averages of G_i^{B}, L_i^{B}, G_i^{S} and L_i^{S}, respectively and λ is the weighted averages of λ_i in each group defined as $\lambda = \sum \lambda_i \frac{\Sigma w_i G_i}{G}$. To simplify

---

[21]In what follows we will refer to G_i^{B} and L_i^{B} as agent i's expected gain and loss, respectively, although strictly speaking G_i^{B} and L_i^{B} are the average of potential individual gains and losses based only on the truncated gain and loss parts of the set of individual probabilities, $\tilde{p}_{k,i}$, respectively.

[22]Of course, since buying (selling) foreign currency is tantamount to selling (buying) domestic currency, the decisions concerning changes in the portfolio of domestic and foreign assets could be equivalently formulated in terms of the buying and selling of domestic currency.

[23]The intuition behind this decison rule, based on the calculation of the prospective excess return by loss averse agents, is analogous to the conventional decision rule based on the expected excess return for risk neutral agents.

the presentation, we assume that the averages of the parameters of loss aversion in the two groups of agents are the same and equal to some $\lambda > 1$. [24]

Given this notation, the aggregate (market) expected excess return is given by

$$E(R) = \sum_{i \in I^{\mathrm{B}}} w_i \left(G_i^{\mathrm{B}} + L_i^{\mathrm{B}}\right) + \sum_{i \in I^{\mathrm{S}}} w_i \left(G_i^{\mathrm{S}} + L_i^{\mathrm{S}}\right) \equiv G^{\mathrm{B}} + G^{\mathrm{S}} + L^{\mathrm{B}} + L^{\mathrm{S}} \equiv G + L \quad (16)$$

We are now ready to replace the UIP equilibrium condition with the following equilibrium condition for the foreign exchange market:

$$E[v(R)] = 0 \qquad (17)$$

or equivalently, from (15) and (16)

$$E(R) = E(\dot{s}) - i_r = U \qquad (18)$$

where

$$U = E(R) - E[v(R)] = (1 - \lambda)L^{\mathrm{B}} + (1 - \lambda)L^{\mathrm{S}} \equiv (1 - \lambda)L \equiv U^{\mathrm{B}} + U^{\mathrm{S}} \qquad (19)$$

Condition (17) simply states that equilibrium in foreign exchange market requires an equality between the expected utility of buyers from buying foreign currency and the expected utility of sellers from selling foreign currency. Equivalently, condition (18) and the definition of U in (19) imply that in equilibrium the aggregate expected excess return is the (linear transformation) of expected losses aggregated across all agents. Note that the two components of U in equation (19) are opposite in sign, reflecting the fact that losses for buyers and sellers are negative and positive realizations of R, respectively. Also note that U^{B} and U^{S} denote the premia required by loss averse buyers and sellers for buying and selling foreign currency, respectively. Thus, positive values of the aggregate U can be interpreted as the excess premium required by loss averse buyers of foreign currency. As we shall show in the next subsection, the market's excess loss aversion as captured by U is related in our model to imperfect knowledge and the associated uncertainty faced by individual agents when forecasting the future excess return. Thus, we refer to U as an aggregate *uncertainty premium* and the equilibrium condition in (17) as *Uncertainty Adjusted Uncovered Interest Rate Parity (UAUIP)*.

In order for equation (17) to serve as the equilibrium condition for the foreign exchange market, we need to specify how changes in $E[v(R)]$ are connected to changes in the exchange rate, s. To this end we use the notation introduced above to write the expression for the individual expected excess return as follows:

$$E_i[R]] = G_i + L_i \qquad (20)$$

---

[24] We note that although this assumption substantially simplifies the presentation, it does not involve any loss of generality. In particular, this assumption does not constrain the average prospective utilities of buyers and sellers to be the same, since in our model the losses and gains of agents in each group will change over time. We also note that an agent will sometimes belong to a group of buyers and at other times belong to a group of sellers, and thus it seems reasonable to suppose that the average λ is very similar for both groups.

Comparing (13), (14) and (20) readily implies that since $\lambda_i > 1$, an increase (decrease) in $E_i[v(R)]$ for either buyers or sellers implies an increase (decrease) of $E_i[R]$. However, it is possible for $E_i[R]$ to increase and for $E_i^B[v(R)]$ and/or $E_i^S[v(R)]$ to turn negative at the same time. These possibilities mean that although an agent expects a positive excess return on buying foreign currency, his loss aversion parameter λ_i and/or his assessment of prospective losses is so large, that he decides nonetheless not to alter his holdings of domestic and foreign currency assets or even sell foreign currency. Analogously, for the sellers, $E_i[R]$ can increase and $E_i^S[v(R)]$ and/or $E_i^B[v(R)]$ can turn positive at the same time. We rule out such cases of extreme loss aversion and assume that:

- An upward (downward) revision of $E_i(R)$ by either a buyer or a seller necessarily implies an upward(downward) revision of the individual assessment of $E_i[v(R)]$.

The rationale for this assumption is as follows:

Remark 2 *Although the speculation of the loss averse agent might be tempered by his greater sensitivity to potential losses than if he were a risk neutral agent, a revision of his assessment $E_i(R)$ either upwards or downwards is assumed to lead to speculation in the direction consistent with the direction of change of $E_i(R)$.*

We are now ready to discuss the stability of the equilibrium condition in (17). Without a loss of generality, suppose that $E[v(R)]$ increases from a point of equilibrium. This increase implies that the weight of buyers of foreign currency, as measured by $E^B[v(R)]$ in (15), is larger than the weight of sellers of foreign currency, as measured by $E^S[v(R)]$ in(15), i.e., $E^B[v(R)] > -E^S[v(R)]$. This in turn leads to a bidding up of the price of foreign exchange, s. From (11), an increase in s leads to a decrease in $E_i(R)$ for all agents, so that the weight of buyers of foreign exchange (i.e., $E^B[v(R)]$, which is positive) necessarily falls and the weight of sellers of foreign exchange (i.e., $E^S[v(R)]$, which is negative) necessarily rises. Thus, given our assumption concerning the positive relationship between $E_i(R)$ and $E_i[v(R)]$, an increase in s, *ceteris paribus*, leads to an unambiguous fall in $E[v(R)]$. Equilibrium in the foreign exchange market is reestablished when the increase in s is large enough so that once again there is a balance between the weight of buyers and sellers, i.e., when $E[v(R)] = 0$.

3.2 Modeling the Uncertainty Premium

To make the equilibrium condition in equation (18) fully operational and examine the implications of our approach for understanding the persistence of expected excess returns, persistent movements of s away from PPP and other aspects of exchange rate behavior, we need to develop a dynamic model for equilibrium movements in the aggregate uncertainty premium, U. There are two aspects of this problem. The first concerns the behavior of U due to changes in $E(R)$ arising from changes in $\tilde{s}$, $\dot{\tilde{s}}$, i_r, and the second involves the adjustment of U back to equilibrium through changes in s. Given that changes in U depend on changes in the expected losses of buyers and sellers (i.e., L^B and L^S), we need to specify how such changes are connected to changes in $\tilde{s}$, $\dot{\tilde{s}}$, i_r and s. In the remainder of this section we reformulate the prospect theory in the context of our model of the foreign exchange market and examine the implications of the assumptions of IKF and loss aversion for the movement of U over time.

As we show below in section 5, under the assumption of imperfect knowledge, our model gives rise to the possibility of persistent movements of the exchange rate away from the purchasing power parity (PPP) level over an extended period of time. In Frydman and Goldberg [2003] we extend this analysis and show that such swings away are followed by persistent movements back to PPP, a crossing through the PPP level and a continuation of the movement away from PPP in the other direction. As is well known, the actual movement of exchange rates during floating-rate periods has indeed exhibited such long-swings behavior, with U.S. dollar rates providing the most prevalent examples.[25] Thus, although movements away from PPP have been quite large and persistent, there are market forces at work that have kept such movements bounded: large misalignments from PPP have been followed eventually by persistent countermovements back. Thus, PPP has served as a nonstandard long-run anchor for floating exchange rates.

In modeling the uncertainty premium, therefore, we assume that individual agents recognize the long-swings nature of exchange rates around PPP and take into account persistent movements away from and towards PPP in arriving at their assessments of the probabilities $\tilde{p}_{k,i}$ of the realizations of the excess return R_k. In particular, we assume individual agents view the PPP level as a "benchmark level" in that they use the gap from PPP as one of the factors in assessing the potential losses on buying or selling foreign exchange.[26]

We formalize this assumption as follows. Denote an individual assessment of the PPP level by $\tilde{s}_i^{\text{PPP}}$, where $\tilde{s}_i^{\text{PPP}}$ can be written as $\tilde{s}_i^{\text{PPP}} = p_r - \tilde{q}_{n,i}$. The gap from PPP can be thought about in two ways, the gap between $\tilde{s}_i$ and $\tilde{s}_i^{\text{PPP}}$ (i.e., $\tilde{s}_i - \tilde{s}_i^{\text{PPP}}$) and the gap between s and $\tilde{s}_i^{\text{PPP}}$ (i.e., $s - \tilde{s}_i^{\text{PPP}}$). As such, let the individual assessment of the PPP gap, $\widetilde{gap}_i^{\text{PPP}}$, be defined as follows:

$$\widetilde{gap}_i^{\text{PPP}} \equiv (1 - a)(\tilde{s}_i - \tilde{s}_i^{\text{PPP}}) + a(s - \tilde{s}_i^{\text{PPP}}) \tag{21}$$

where $0 < a < 1$. We assume that as the individual agent's assessment of the distance from the PPP level increases, he takes into account the possibility of a reversal in the direction of movement of the exchange rate by changing his assessment of the expected losses, L_i, defined in equation (20). We can formally characterize the relationship between L_i^{B}, L_i^{S}, and $\widetilde{gap}_i^{\text{PPP}}$ by the following assumption, that will be referred to as the *gap effect*:

- *Gap Effect:* As an individual buyer's (seller's) assessment of the PPP gap, $\widetilde{gap}_i^{\text{PPP}}$, increases, he revises upwards (downwards) his assessment of the absolute value of the potential losses.

---

[25]The evidence on long swings in exchange rates that revolve around PPP levels comes from many places. For evidence that nominal exchange rates move persistently away from PPP levels for extended periods see Frankel [1985] and Obstfeld [1985,1995], among many others. For evidence that these swings revolve around PPP levels see the cointegration studies of Juselius [1995], Frankel and Rose [1996] and Papell [1997]), among others, as well as studies on the long-horizon predictability of PPP and monetary fundamentals (e.g., Mark [1995] and Mark and Sul [2001]. See also Obstfeld [1995] and references therein.

[26]Of course, the issue of whether PPP holds in a long-run sense is still an open issue. See Froot and Rogoff [1995] and references therein. For our purposes, what is important is that market agents have in mind some long-run benchmark level which in some sense coordinates their views about exchange rate movements. Given the empirical record, PPP seems like a natural choice.

For example, suppose a buyer believes that the gap from PPP, as measured by $\widetilde{gap}_i^{\text{PPP}}$, is positive and revises his assessment $\tilde{s}$ upwards or s moves higher. Since this buyer is assumed to recognize the long-swings nature of exchange rates, he becomes less confident that the movement away from PPP will continue as the gap from PPP grows. He revises upwards, therefore, his assessment of the magnitude of the potential losses, i.e. $-L_i^{\text{B}}$ increases. Similarly, consider a seller who believes that $\widetilde{gap}_i^{\text{PPP}} > 0$ and revises his assessment $\tilde{s}$ upwards or s moves higher, that is $\widetilde{gap}_i^{\text{PPP}}$ increases. Since this seller bets on the movement of the exchange rate towards the PPP level and since he also recognizes the long-swings behavior of exchange rates, the increase in the PPP gap makes him more confident that his bet will lead to smaller losses.[27] Thus, the seller revises downwards his assessment of the potential losses, i.e., L_i^{S} decreases.[28]

We are now ready to examine the implications of imperfect knowledge and loss aversion for movements of U arising from movements in $\tilde{s}$, $\dot{\tilde{s}}$, i_r and s. As we show in this subsection, distinguishing between changes in $\tilde{s}$, $\dot{\tilde{s}}$ and i_r, and s is important for the modeling of the uncertainty premium. We begin by examining changes in U due to changes in $\tilde{s}$, and note that $\tilde{s}$ can increase, for example, because either the group of buyers (i.e., those for whom $E(R) > 0$) or the group of sellers (i.e., those for whom $E(R) < 0$) raise their assessments of the medium-run anchor or because market agents, who were initially sellers, raise their assessments enough so as to cause them to switch over to the buying side.

To fix ideas, suppose we start from a position of equilibrium in the foreign exchange market so that initially $E[v(R)] = 0$ and suppose that the aggregate $E(R)$ jumps due to a jump in $\tilde{s}$. Consider first the behavior of U *prior to any movement in* s. To this end, we define U_i as the difference for an individual agent i between his prospective and expected excess returns. Using the notation of the previous section, the expression for U_i is given by

$$U_i = E_i(R) - E_i[v(R)] = (1 - \lambda_i)L_i \tag{22}$$

From (21), a jump in $\tilde{s}$ leads to a revision of agents' assessment of the PPP gap, and thus to a revision of their assessment of the potential losses. In addition to this gap effect on potential losses, we suppose that there is also a *size effect* associated with a change in the absolute value of $E(R)$. Since an individual agent is assumed to understand that his expectation of the excess return is based on imperfect knowledge and he is assumed to be loss averse, it seems reasonable to assume that as an individual revises upwards (downwards) his assessment of the magnitude of the excess return, he recognizes that greater bets based on the revised $E_i(R)$ may to lead to a larger (smaller) magnitude of the potential losses. Thus, we assume the following:

- *Size Effect:* As an individual agent revises his assessment of the absolute value of $E_i(R)$ upwards (downwards), his new higher (lower) assessment of the magnitude of $E_i(R)$ is accompanied by an increase (decrease) in the absolute value of the agent's assessment of the expected loss.

---

[27]Recall that the losses of the sellers are positive changes of the exchange rate.

[28]Our assumption that the PPP level is treated by agents as a benchmark level in assessing the potential losses is reminiscent of the role of the "safe" rate of interest in Keynes' development of liquidity preference, see Keynes [1936].

Remark 3 *We note that the gap effect and the size effect on potential losses arising from changes in $\tilde{s}_i$ always work in the same direction irrespective of whether an agent is a buyer or a seller. This is because for a buyer (seller) an increase in $E_i(R)$ always implies an increase (decrease) in the absolute value of $E_i(R)$ and because an increase in $\widetilde{gap}_i^{PPP}$ always implies an increase (decrease) in the absolute value of the expected losses of buyers (sellers) irrespective of whether $\widetilde{gap}_i^{PPP}$ is positive or negative in value.*

Our assumptions about the gap and size effects, together with our assumption about the positive relationship between $E_i(R)$ and $E_i[v(R)]$ imply the following condition:

Condition 1 *If $E_i[v(R)]$ turns positive (negative) subsequent to a jump in $\tilde{s}_i$, then both $E_i(R)$ and U_i are positive (negative) and the absolute value of the change in $E_i(R)$ is greater than the absolute values of the changes in U_i and $E_i[v(R)]$.*

Remark 4 *We note that Condition 1 is consistent with the spirit of prospect theory and loss aversion in that it implies that when an agent, say a buyer, revises his assessment $\tilde{s}$ upwards, he buys foreign currency, but his speculation is tempered by his greater sensitivity to the increases in potential losses.*

Although the assumptions we have made concerning individual agents lead to unambiguous movements in U_i associated with a jump in $\tilde{s}_i$ (namely condition 1), two additional assumptions concerning distribution effects are needed to determine the movement of the aggregate U associated with a jump in $\tilde{s}$ Without a loss of generality, suppose the jump in $\tilde{s}$ involves an increase, so that $E(R)$ increases and $E[v(R)]$ becomes positive. But unlike at the individual level, U may rise or fall and be positive or negative when $E[v(R)]$ rises from a point of equilibrium.

In terms of the sign of U, if $E(R) > 0$, then the "size" of $E^B(R)$ is greater than the "size" of $E^B(R)$, and given our assumption about the size effect, it is reasonable to suppose that in this case the expected loss of buyers (which involve negative realizations of R) outweighs the expected loss of sellers (which involve positive realizations of R). This reasoning leads to the following distributional assumption:

- *Distributional Assumption 1*: If $E(R) > 0$ ($E(R) < 0$), so that the weight of buyers (sellers) dominates, then the expected losses of the buyers (sellers) are assumed to dominate in determining the sign of $L = L^B + L^S$, i.e., if $E(R) > 0$ ($E(R) < 0$), then $L < 0$ and $U > 0$ ($L > 0$ and $U < 0$).

To consider the implication of this assumption for the movement in U, suppose, without a loss of generality, that $E(R)$ and U are initially negative. If the increase in $\tilde{s}$ leads to a change in the sign of $E(R)$, then it also leads to an unambiguous increase in U. Since both $E(R)$ and $E[v(R)]$ turn positive, U also becomes positive and $\triangle E(R) > \triangle U$.

However, if the increase in $\tilde{s}$ does not lead to a sign change in $E(R)$, then the above distributional assumption does not unambiguously determine the direction of movement of the aggregate U. To show this assume that prior to the increase in $\tilde{s}$, $E(R) > 0$ and note that an increase in $E[R]$ can be associated with either: 1) an increase in both $E^B[R]$ and $E^S[R]$; 2) an increase in $E^B[R]$ and a decrease in $E^S(R)$ where $\triangle E^B(R) > -\triangle E^S(R)$; or

3) a decrease in $E^{\text{B}}(R)$ and an increase $E^{\text{S}}(R)$ where $\triangle E^{\text{S}}(R) > -\triangle E^{\text{B}}(R)$. In the first case, the size and gap effects on expected losses imply that both $(1 - \lambda) L^{\text{B}}$ and $(1 - \lambda) L^{\text{S}}$ increase, leading to increases in both U^{B} and U^{S} and an unambiguous increase in U. But, in cases two and three, the size and gap effects imply that U^{B} and U^{S} move in opposite directions so that U may either rise or fall.

To rule out this ambiguity in the direction of change in U we make an additional distribution assumption which is a "dynamic" version of our first distributional assumption. Thus, we assume that if the magnitude of the change in the assessment of R on the part of buyers is larger than the change for sellers, then the change in the expected losses of buyers will dominate the change in the aggregate L. This reasoning leads to our second distributional assumption:

- *Distributional Assumption 2:* If the buyers (sellers) side of the market dominates in terms of the *change* in $E(R)$, then buyers (sellers) also dominate the market in terms of the *change* in expected losses, e.g., if $\triangle E^{\text{B}}(R) > -\triangle E^{\text{S}}(R)$ (case 2), then $\triangle U^{\text{B}} > -\triangle U^{\text{S}}$, and if $\triangle E^{\text{S}}(R) > -\triangle E^{\text{B}}(R)$ (case 3), then $\triangle U^{\text{S}} > -\triangle U^{\text{B}}$.[29]

The foregoing argument can be summarized by the following Proposition:

Proposition 2 *If $\tilde{s}$ increases (decreases), causing $E[v(R)]$ to become positive (negative), then both $E(R)$ and U increase (decrease) and the absolute value of the change in $E(R)$ will be greater than the absolute values of the changes in U and $E[v(R)]$. Furthermore, if $E(R) > 0$ $(E(R) < 0)$, then $U > 0$ $(U < 0)$.*

Proof. Proposition 2 follows directly from Condition 1 and our two distributional assumptions. ∎

Proposition 2 implies that the increase in $\tilde{s}$ leads to increases in $E[v(R)]$, $E(R)$ and U, which could involve sign reversals in $E(R)$ and U. With $E[v(R)] > 0$, the weight of the buyers dominate and this puts upward pressure on s. Thus, a change in $\tilde{s}$ leads to a change in s in the same direction. Before we examine the implications of movements in s for movements in U, we point out that all of the foregoing individual and distributional assumptions concerning changes in $E[v(R)]$, $E(R)$ and U also apply to one-time changes in both $\tilde{s}$ and i_r. This is because the size and gap effects on expected losses always work in the same direction and although changes in $\tilde{s}$ and i_r do not involve gap effects, they do involve size effects.

As for the connection between movements of s and expected losses, it is clear from equations (11) and (21) that such movements will be associated with both a gap effect and a size effect. In addition to these effects, we assume that movements in s are also associated with what we call a *trend effect* on expected losses. In a world of imperfect knowledge and loss aversion, it is reasonable to suppose that if a particular movement of s is in the direction consistent with that expected (i.e., *an agent has predicted correctly the right side of the market in terms of expected R*), then such a movement will lead to greater confidence

---

[29]Although not needed, we assume that this assumption also applies to case 1. Note that our second distributional assumption is consistent with our first distributional assumption, the latter indicating that sign changes in $E(R)$ cause sign changes in U. With sign reversals, however, case 3 can be ruled out.

in the expected direction of movement and to a reduction in the assessment of potential losses.[30] We note that such a trend effect does not arise with changes in $\tilde{s}$, $\dot{\tilde{s}}$ or i_r. This argument motivates the following assumption:

- *Trend Effect*: If the change in s is positive (negative), then those agents who have bet on a positive change (i.e., buyers) reduce (increase) their assessment of the potential losses and those agents who have bet on a negative change (i.e. sellers) increase (reduce) their assessment of the potential losses.

Remark 5 *We note that the gap effect and the trend effect on expected losses arising from changes in s necessarily work in opposite directions for both buyers and sellers; whereas the trend effect and the size effect necessarily work in the same direction. For example, consider a buyer and suppose that $\widetilde{gap}_i^{\mathrm{PPP}} > 0$ and $E_i^{\mathrm{B}}(R) > 0$. An increase in s implies a negative gap effect (i.e., an increase in the expected loss), and since $E_i^{\mathrm{B}}(R)$ decreases and s moves in the direction of the bet by the buyer, it is also associated with positive size and trend effects (i.e., a decrease in the expected loss).*

For ease of presentation, we will refer to the combined trend and size effects as a velocity effect. Given that the velocity and gap effects on expected losses work in the opposite directions, the expected losses of buyers and sellers may rise or fall with the movements in s. However, as we shall explain next, it is reasonable to suppose that the velocity effect dominates the gap effect for both buyers and sellers. Moreover, we will also explain why the offsetting influence of the gap effect is likely to be substantial (insignificant) when s moves away from (towards) PPP.

Consider first a movement of s away from PPP. Suppose, for example, that the gap from PPP is positive (i.e., $\widetilde{gap}^{\mathrm{PPP}} > 0$) and s rises, causing the PPP gap to increase further. Buyers (sellers), who bet on a movement of s away from (back to) PPP, gain (lose) confidence in their decision to buy (sell) as the exchange rate moves their way (against them) and causes them to revise downward (upward) their assessments of the potential losses. However, buyers and sellers are always cognizant of the long-swings nature of exchange rate movements, and so the widening of the PPP gap tempers the revisions of their expected losses. For buyers, the growing gap diminishes their confidence in their bet on a further movement away from PPP and so moderates the fall in their expected losses arising from the exchange rate moving their way. By the same token, a widening gap causes sellers to become more confident in their bet on a countermovement back to PPP and so for them too, it moderates their reassessments of the potential losses, i.e., it moderates the increase in the expected losses arising from the exchange rate moving against them. This argument suggests that if the PPP gap is "large," the offsetting influence of the gap effect would be substantial and a rising s would be associated with small revisions in the expected losses of both buyers and sellers.

---

[30]We note that empirical evidence suggests, rather strongly, that $E(R)$ is overwhemingly dominated by the magnitude and the sign of $E(\dot{s})$. As we report in Frydman and Goldberg [2001b], out of 340 observations from the survey data (to be discussed below, there are only 3 observations where $E(\dot{s})$ and $E(R)$ are of opposite signs. Furthermore, daily exchange rate movements are typically on the order of betweem 0.5 to 1 percent, whereas the interest rate differential for major currency markets is typically between 0-10 percent on the annual basis. For example, at the time of writing this paper, the U.S.-German interest rate differential was 1 percent annually, which translates into a daily interest rate differential of 0.003 percent.

Now consider a movement of s back to PPP and again suppose that the $\widetilde{gap}^{\text{PPP}} > 0$, i.e., s falls. As s falls back to PPP, buyers lose confidence in their decision to buy, as the exchange rate moves against them. It is reasonable to suppose that the falling gap does very little to assuage their concern about a persistent countermovement back to PPP. By the same token, the fall in s increases the confidence of sellers in their decision to sell, and it is reasonable to suppose that the falling gap does very little to temper this increased confidence. Thus, for movements of s towards PPP, the velocity effect dominates the gap effect and the moderating influence of the gap effect is likely to be small for both buyers and sellers.

The foregoing argument motivates the following assumption:

- For both buyers and sellers, the velocity effect due to changes in s always dominates the gap effect irrespective of whether the movement of s is away from or towards PPP. [31]Furthermore, whenever s moves away from (towards) PPP the offsetting influence of the gap effect is assumed to be substantial (insignificant) relative to the magnitude of the velocity effects.

This assumption, in turn, leads to the following proposition:

Proposition 3 *If the adjustment to equilibrium involves an increase (decrease) in the exchange rate, s, then the adjustment to equilibrium will also involve a decrease (increase) in the aggregate uncertainty premium, U.*

Proof. Suppose that the adjustment to equilibrium involves an increase in s. Since the velocity effect is associated with the decrease in the aggregate expected losses, $L = L^{\text{B}} + L^{\text{S}}$, and it is assumed to dominate the gap effect, 19 implies that the aggregate uncertainty premium U increases. Analogous argument shows that if the adjustment to equilibrium involves a fall in s, the aggregate uncertainty premium decreases.[32] ∎

Remark 6 *We note that Propositions 2 and 3 imply that when $\tilde{s}$ and s move in the same direction, their impacts on the aggregate U work in opposite directions. For example, if $\tilde{s}$ rises, causing s to rise as well, then the rise in $\tilde{s}$ leads to an increase in U and the rise in s leads to a decrease in U.*

We are now ready to examine the equilibrium movement of the aggregate uncertainty premium, U, which can be thought about as involving a sequence of two steps, namely, a first step arising from the initial change in $\tilde{s}$ and a second step arising from the adjustment of s back to equilibrium, and note that for one-time jumps, the changes in $\tilde{s}$ and s are always in the same direction. Remark 6 indicates that the change in the equilibrium level of U depends on the relative magnitudes of the first-step and second-step effects, since these

---

[31]We note, assuming that the velocity effect dominates the gap effect rules out an apparent inconsistency which would be implicitly implied by the domination of the gap effect over the velocity effect. If the gap effect were dominant this would mean, for example, that if the agents increase their expectation of $E(R)$, the would actually bid down rather than up the equlibrium level of the exchange rate.

[32]We note that this proposition also requires that the assessment of $\tilde{q}_n$ (and therefore $\tilde{s}^{\text{PPP}}$) does not differ systematically between the groups of buyers and sellers.

effects always work in opposite directions. In general, then, a particular change in $\tilde{s}$ could lead to a rise or fall in the equilibrium U. However, in a world of imperfect knowledge and loss aversion it is reasonable to assume that the gap effect arising from a change in $\tilde{s}$ (as we have already argued in connection with a change in s) is also significantly larger when this change involves a movement away from PPP; and this allows us to determine the direction of movement of the equilibrium U.

Consider first movements away from PPP and suppose again that the $\widetilde{gap}^{PPP} > 0$ and $\tilde{s}$ increases. With $\tilde{s}$ rising, Proposition 2 implies that $E[v(R)]$, $E(R)$ and U increase. For ease of presentation assume that the increase in $E(R)$ is associated with increases in both $E^B(R)$ and $E^S(R)$.[33] Thus, the increase in U is associated with buyers raising and sellers lowering their assessments of the potential losses, as the size and gap effects for both buyers and sellers work in the same direction. Given that buyers and sellers both revise their assessments, $\tilde{s}$, upward away from PPP, the gap effect on the expected losses of both groups will likely be large and so the first-step increase in U will likely be large. The resulting increase in s, however, works to strengthen the confidence of buyers in their decision to buy (as s moves their way) and weaken the confidence of sellers in their decision to sell (as s moves against them), leading to a fall in U. But this fall in U will be limited because as already noted, it is reasonable to assume that the resulting increase in the PPP gap will have a significant moderating influence on the reassessments of both buyers and sellers. Given that the gap effect magnifies the impact on U arising from the change in $\tilde{s}$ and moderates the impact on U arising from the change in s, it is reasonable to assume the following:

- If the changes in $\tilde{s}$ and s involve movements away from PPP, then the impact on U due to the change in $\tilde{s}$ will dominate the impact on U due to the change in s.

This assumption leads to the following lemma describing movements in the equilibrium U:

Lemma 4 *When the movements of $\tilde{s}$ and s are away from PPP, the direction of movement of the equilibrium U will be determined by the direction of movement implied by the first-step impact arising from the change in $\tilde{s}$.*

Proof. Denote the changes in the aggregate expected losses of buyers and sellers associated with the change in $\tilde{s}$ in the first step by $\triangle^1 L^B$ and $\triangle^1 L^S$, respectively. Analogously, denote the changes in the losses associated with the adjustment of s in the second step by $\triangle^2 L^B$ and $\triangle^2 L^S$, respectively. With this notation, equation 19 readily implies that the change in the equilibrium U arising from the changes in $\tilde{s}$ and s can be written as follows:

$$\triangle U = (1 - \lambda)\left[\left(\triangle^1 L^B + \triangle^2 L^B\right) + \left(\triangle^1 L^S + \triangle^2 L^S\right)\right] \tag{23}$$

We note that the reasoning leading up to this lemma implies that the changes in L^B and L^S work in the same direction in terms of their impact on U for both the first and second steps. However, the direction of change in U will depend on whether $\tilde{s}$ (and thus

[33]The reasoning leading up to proposition 7 below also applies for the "mixed cases" where the changes in $E^B(R)$ and $E^S(R)$ are of opposite sign if distributional assumption 2 holds.

$E(R))$ increases or decreases. Consider first the case of an increase in $\tilde{s}$. Propositions 2 and 3 imply that $\triangle^1 L^B < 0$ and $\triangle^2 L^B > 0$ and our assumption that the impact on U due to the change in $\tilde{s}$ will dominate the impact on U due to the change in implies that $-\triangle^1 L^B > \triangle^2 L^B$. For the sellers, Propositions 2 and 3 imply that $\triangle^1 L^S < 0$ and $\triangle^2 L^S > 0$ and our assumption concerning the relative magnitudes of the first- and second-step changes implies that $-\triangle^1 L^S > \triangle^2 L^S$. Substituting these inequalities into equation 23 immediately implies that an increase in $\tilde{s}$ implies an increase in the equilibrium U once the adjustment of s occurs, i.e., $\triangle U > 0$.

Analogous reasoning implies that a fall in $\tilde{s}$ leads to a decrease in the equilibrium U once the adjustment of s occurs, i.e., $\triangle U < 0$. ∎

Although Lemma 4 establishes the direction of change of the equilibrium uncertainty premium when movements of $\tilde{s}$ and s are away from PPP, the change in the absolute value of the equilibrium U depends on the initial magnitude of U. Again suppose that $\tilde{s}$ increases, which according to Proposition 2 and Lemma 4, leads to an increase in the equilibrium level of U. If $E(R) = U > 0$ initially, then the resulting increase in the equilibrium U will involve an increase in its absolute value. If, however, $E(R) = U < 0$ initially, then the resulting increase in the equilibrium U will involve a fall in its absolute value. In view of the empirical evidence mentioned in footnote [?] above, these conditions on the sign of initial $E(R)$ can be interpreted in terms of the market being on the right or the wrong side in its prediction of the sign of the excess return R defined in 10.

Remark 7 *We note that since the magnitude of changes in s is typically two orders of magnitude bigger than the interest rate differential, the market's expectation of a positive (negative) $E(R)$ can be interpreted as the expectation of the increase (decrease) in s. Since the change in $\tilde{s}$ is associated with the change in s in the same direction, the positive(negative) $E(R)$ can be referred to as the market being on balance on the right (wrong) side in predicting the excess return. Analogously, if $\tilde{s}$ increases, the market will be said to be on the wrong side if $E(R) < 0$ initially.*

The foregoing argument leads to the following proposition, where we denote a movement of $\tilde{s}$ away from PPP from above (below) as one involving a positive (negative) $\widetilde{gap}^{PPP}$ and an increase (fall) in $\tilde{s}$:

Proposition 5 *If the change in $\tilde{s}$ involves a movement away from PPP, either from above or from below, and the market on balance is on the right side (wrong side), then the change in $\tilde{s}$ will lead to an increase (decrease) in the absolute value of the equilibrium uncertainty premium, U.*

Proof. Proposition 5 follows directly from Proposition 2 and Lemma 4. ∎

Remark 8 *We note that the relationship between the magnitudes of the gap and velocity effects is most likely nonlinear. For example, buyers and sellers may be concerned with the gap effect only when the PPP gap has surpassed some critical level. In this case, the moderating influence of the gap effect will be small for "small" levels of the PPP gap, so that the first-step impact on U arising from changes in s will no longer dominate. To* *simplify the presentation and make the analytical solution of the model more tractable we abstract from such nonlinear considerations in this paper.*[34]

Now consider equilibrium changes in U when changes in $\tilde{s}$ and s involve movements toward PPP. Assume that the $\widetilde{gap}^{\text{PPP}} < 0$, so that a movement towards PPP implies that $\tilde{s}$ increases. As before, the increase in $\tilde{s}$ leads to increases in $E[v(R)]$, $E(R)$ and U, which in turn leads to a rise in s. But now with a movement towards PPP, the role of the gap effect is assumed to be insignificant on both steps. This leaves, then, a size effect working to push U up on the first step against a combined size and trend effect working to push U down on the second step. Thus, without a significant gap effect to magnify and moderate the impact on U arising from the increases in $\tilde{s}$ and s, respectively, the second-step impact involving the change in s will be dominant. It is reasonable, therefore, to assume the following:

- If the change in $\tilde{s}$ and s involve movements towards PPP, then the impact on U due to the change in s will dominate the impact on U due to the change in $\tilde{s}$.

This assumption leads to the following lemma describing movements in the equilibrium U:

Lemma 6 *When the movements of $\tilde{s}$ and s are towards PPP, the direction of movement of the equilibrium U will be determined by the direction of movement implied by the second-step impact arising from the change in s.*

Proof. See the proof to Lemma 4. ∎

Thus, with Lemma 6, the increase in $\tilde{s}$ leads to a fall in the equilibrium level of U. However, as with Lemma 4, Lemma 6 establishes the direction of change of the equilibrium uncertainty premium and not whether the absolute value of the equilibrium U rises or falls. Again, the magnitude of change in the absolute value of U depends on whether the market on balance is on the right side or wrong side, i.e., whether initially $E(R) = U > 0$ or $E(R) = U < 0$, respectively. This leads to the following proposition:

Proposition 7 *If the change in $\tilde{s}$ involves a movement towards PPP, either from above or below, and the market on balance is on the right side (wrong side), then the absolute value of the equilibrium U will decrease (increase).*

Proof. *Proposition 7 follows directly from Proposition 3 and Lemma 6.* ∎

Remark 9 *We note that Propositions 5 and 7 together imply that movements of $\tilde{s}$ away from (towards) PPP, either from above or below, will lead to increases (decreases) in the absolute value of the equilibrium U when the market on balance is on the right side; whereas the converse will be true when the market on balance is on the wrong side .*

We are now ready to translate the implications of Propositions, 2, 5 and 7 into a dynamic model of the equilibrium U. Consider first one-time jumps in the equilibrium U arising from one-time jumps in $\tilde{s}$, $\dot{\tilde{s}}$ and/or i_r. Proposition 2, which applies to changes in all three

---

[34]In Frydman and Goldberg [2001b] we allow for nonlinearity in the relationship between the PPP gap and the aggregate uncertainty.

variables, implies that when there is a jump, $E(R)$ and U move in the same direction, where the change in U is smaller than the change in $E(R)$. This leads to the following equation for the first-step change in U:

$$U^- - U_0 = \eta \left[E(R^-) - E(R_0) \right]$$
$$\equiv \eta \left[\left(\tilde{\theta} \left(\tilde{s}^- - s_0 \right) + \dot{\tilde{s}}^- - i_r^- \right) - \left(\tilde{\theta} \left(\tilde{s}_0 - s_0 \right) + \dot{\tilde{s}}_0 - i_{r_0} \right) \right]$$
$$\equiv \eta \left[\tilde{\theta} \left(\tilde{s}^- - \tilde{s}_0 \right) + \left(\dot{\tilde{s}}^- - \dot{\tilde{s}}_0 \right) - \left(i_r^- - i_{r_0} \right) \right]$$

where a superscript "$-$" denotes a value *prior to* the impact effect on s, a subscript "0" denotes initial value, prior to any jump in $\tilde{s}$, $\dot{\tilde{s}}$ or i_r, and η is an adjustment parameter where $0 < \eta < 1$. Note that the magnitude of η depends on the degree of loss aversion and the magnitude by which aggregate losses change. Equation (19) reveals that a larger degree of loss aversion as measured by λ and a larger change in the expected losses in the aggregate, L, will lead to a larger change in U given a one-time change in $\tilde{s}$, $\dot{\tilde{s}}$ or i_r, and therefore to a larger η.

As for the second step involving a change in s, Propositions 5 and 7 imply that the impact on U always works to counteract the impact from the first step, although if the movement of s is away from (towards) PPP, then the second-step impact only partially (more than) counteracts the first-step impact. This leads to the following equation for the change in the equilibrium level of U:

$$U^+ - U_0 = \rho \left(U^- - U_0 \right) \tag{24}$$

where U^+ denotes the value of U subsequent to the impact effect on s and ρ is another adjustment parameter. According to Proposition 5, when the change in s involves a movement away from PPP, the equilibrium level of U, U^+, lies in between its initial value, U_0, and its first-step level, U^-, implying that for movements away, the value of ρ is between zero and one. The magnitude of ρ in this case depends on the relative magnitudes of the first-step and second-step impacts. As the magnifying and moderating roles played by the gap effect on the first and second steps, respectively, increases, so does the magnitude of ρ. For movements of s towards PPP, Proposition 7 implies that the absolute value of U^+ is smaller (larger) than the absolute value of U_0 when the market on balance is on the right (wrong) side, implying that for movements towards, $-1 < \rho < 0$. Here too, the magnitude of ρ depends on the relative magnitudes of the first and second step changes. As the magnitude of the second step increases, so too does the absolute value of ρ.

Combining equations (**??**) and (24) yields the following equation for the equilibrium aggregate uncertainty premium:

$$U^+ = U_0 + \omega \left[\tilde{\theta} \left(\tilde{s}^- - \tilde{s}_0 \right) + \left(\dot{\tilde{s}}^- - \dot{\tilde{s}}_0 \right) - \left(i_r^- - i_{r_0} \right) \right] \tag{25}$$

where $\omega = \eta \rho$. Returning to our example of an increase in $\tilde{s}$, there are two basic cases. When the increase in $\tilde{s}$ involves a movement away from PPP, the adjustment parameter is ω is between 0 and 1, and the equilibrium uncertainty premium rises, i.e., $U^+ - U_0 > 0$. Furthermore, if on balance the market is on the right (wrong) side, i.e., $U_0 > 0$ ($U_0 <$

0), then the absolute value of the equilibrium uncertainty premium increases (decreases). And when the increase in $\tilde{s}$ involves a movement toward PPP, the adjustment parameter ω is negative and between -1 and 0, and the equilibrium uncertainty premium falls, i.e., $U^+ - U_0 < 0$. If on balance the market is on the right (wrong) side, i.e., $U_0 > 0$ ($U_0 < 0$), then the absolute value of the equilibrium uncertainty premium decreases (increases).

Equation (25), which governs the jump in the equilibrium U, also governs the jump in the equilibrium s. To see this note the following:

$$U^+ = \tilde{\theta}\left(\tilde{s}^- - s^+\right) + \dot{\tilde{s}}^- - i_r^- \tag{26}$$

Plugging equation (26) into equation (25), together with the definition of U_0 leads to the following equation governing the jump in the equilibrium s:

$$s^+ = s_0 + (1 - \omega)\left[\left(\tilde{s}^- - \tilde{s}_0\right) + \frac{1}{\tilde{\theta}}\left(\dot{\tilde{s}}^- - \dot{s}_0\right) - \frac{1}{\tilde{\theta}}\left(i_r^- - i_{r0}\right)\right] \tag{27}$$

Since the adjustment parameter ω is between 0 and 1 (-1 and 0) when the change in s involves a movement away from (towards) PPP, then a given increase in $\tilde{s}$ will lead to a smaller (larger) increase in s.

We now turn to a formulation of the continuous movements of the equilibrium U over time that is consistent with Propositions 5 and 7. To this end, we write the rate of change in U as a function of the rate of change of the agents' assessment of the PPP gap, $\widetilde{gap}^{\mathrm{PPP}}$ as follows:

$$\dot{U} = f(\dot{\widetilde{gap}}^{\mathrm{PPP}}) \tag{28}$$

where $\widetilde{gap}^{\mathrm{PPP}} = (1 - a)(\tilde{s} - \tilde{s}^{\mathrm{PPP}}) + a(s - \tilde{s}^{\mathrm{PPP}})$ and $0 < a < 1$. Using the log-linear approximation of (28) and integrating it for positive and negative values of the $\widetilde{gap}^{\mathrm{PPP}}$ yields:

$$U = \sigma\left|\widetilde{gap}^{\mathrm{PPP}}\right| + d = \sigma\left|(1 - a)(\tilde{s} - \tilde{s}^{\mathrm{PPP}}) + a(s - \tilde{s}^{\mathrm{PPP}})\right| + d \tag{29}$$

where σ is a slope parameter measuring the sensitivity of the equilibrium U to continuous changes in the absolute value of the PPP gap and d is a constant scaling factor which will be determined below. It is reasonable to assume that $|\sigma| < \tilde{\theta}$, which ensures that the impact of a given movement in $\tilde{s}$ influences $E[v(R)]$ in the same direction, i.e., the movement of U due to a movement of $\tilde{s}$ is smaller in magnitude than the resulting movement in $E(\dot{s})$. We show in the next section that this assumption also ensures stability of the model. Propositions 5 and 7 imply that the algebraic sign of σ depends on two factors: the sign of U and whether on balance the market is on the right or the wrong side in predicting the sign of excess returns. If $U > 0$, then $\sigma > 0$ ($\sigma < 0$) when movements in the PPP gap are associated with the market being on the right (wrong) side, and if $U < 0$, then $\sigma < 0$ ($\sigma > 0$) when movements in the PPP gap are associated with the market being on the right (wrong) side. Thus, the algebraic signs of U and σ will match (not match) when the market on balance is on the right (wrong) side.

3.3   Some Empirical Evidence

Since the difficulty of explaining the behavior of expected excess returns has been widely acknowledged, it may seem puzzling that we suggest here that the UAUIP equilibrium condition in (18) and a simple formulation of the uncertainty premium in equations (25) and (29) might actually capture the movement of the expected excess returns over time. [35]

To provide some empirical support for equations (25) and (29), we ran a regression of expected excess returns on the absolute value of the actual PPP gap $(s - s^{PPP})$ using monthly data from DRI on the DM/\$ exchange rate and one-month Eurodollar and Euromark inter-est rates. Forecasts of the four-week ahead DM/\$ exchange rate were obtained from Money Market Services International (MMS). To obtain a PPP exchange rate series we first esti-mated the absolute PPP exchange rate using the BigMac PPP exchange rate reported by the *Economist* for April 1993 (which is a DM/\$ exchange rate of 2.02) and then used infla-tion differentials (derived from CPI series from the IFS data bank) to estimate the absolute PPP exchange rate both forwards and backwards. The data set spans the period between February 1983 and June 1995.

As we have already noted above, Propositions 5 and 7 imply that the algebraic sign of the coefficient of the absolute value of the of the gap term in 29 depends in part on the sign of $E(R)$. Thus we estimated the following specification that allows for the separate slope parameters for positive and negative expected excess returns:

$$E(R) = \beta_0 + \beta_1 |s - s^{PPP}| + \beta_2 |s - s^{PPP}| \tag{30}$$

where β_1 and β_2 denote the slope coefficient associated with positive and negative expected excess returns, respectively.[36] The results are presented in the following table:

Table 1

	Expected Excess Returns
Constant	-0.319***
	(0.122)
Absolute Value of the PPP Gap For Positive Expected Excess Returns	0.051***
	(0.006)
Absolute Value of the PPP Gap For Negative Expected Excess Returns	-0.025***
	(0.008)

Adjusted $R^2 = 59.6\%$ and , D-W Statistic=2.03.

Standard errors in parenthesis. *** denotes p-values less than or equal to 0.01.

---

[35]The evidence presented here comes from our forthcoming paper, Frydman and Goldberg [2001b]. This paper presents an extensive discussion and empirical analysis of the excess returns puzzle.

[36]We note that this empirical implementation implicitly assumes that movements in the actual PPP gap capture reasonably well movements in the average of agents' assessments of the PPP gap

The results presented in Table I provide remarkable support for our model of expected excess returns. The slope coefficients on the gap terms are highly significant and the estimated regression explains a substantial part of the variability of expected excess returns. Interestingly, β_1 and β_2 are significantly positive and negative, respectively. This result is consistent with our theory that the PPP gap serves as an important benchmark in agents' assessments of the potential losses and therefore plays an important role in understanding the behavior of excess returns in the foreign exchange market.

4   The General Solution of the Monetary Model With IKF and UAUIP

In this section we begin to explore the implications of our monetary model consisting of equations (1) and (3), imperfect-knowledge expectations as characterized in equation (8) and uncertainty adjusted uncovered interest rate parity as formalized in equations (18), (25) and (29). As already emphasized above, in a world of imperfect knowledge, agents are unable to characterize fully the subjective elements contained in the aggregate forecast function. Thus, in general, *rational* agents will revise their assessments of the short-run movement of the exchange rate by incorporating new information available to them as well as updating the methods, models and guesses they use. In this paper, we depart from the usual approach of specifying a particular set of learning rules assumed to be used by individual agents. Instead, we model "learning" in a general way, by first placing virtually no restrictions on agents' updating of their individual methods, models and guesses in deriving the general solution of the model.[37] We refer to movements of expectations resulting from all forms of updating as *expectations dynamics.*

In general, expectations dynamics can take two forms in the model: they can involve either one-time jumps in $\tilde{s}$ and/or $\dot{\tilde{s}}$ or continuous movement of $\tilde{s}$ over time (governed by the constant rate $\dot{\tilde{s}}$). We allow for both types of expectations dynamics in deriving the general solution in this section. The standard approach for dealing with such behavior is to specify one rule (or set of rules) that governs the expectations dynamics of all agents. This allows the analyst to completely close the model and derive time paths for the endogenous variables that are fully determined.

The consequence of not precisely characterizing the updating of expectations is that the solution of the model with the assumption of imperfect knowledge *necessarily entails some degree of indeterminacy* in the derived time paths of endogenous variables. A useful way to think about this implication of imperfect knowledge is to view the solution and the derivation of the implications of the model as a two-stage process. In the first stage, the general solution of the model is derived under the assumption of imperfect knowledge expectations with virtually no restrictions imposed on the expectations dynamics. Although the general solution leads to some qualitative implications concerning steady-state values,

---

[37]We say virtually no restrictions because the revision of methods and models may, in general, involve nonlinearities in the differential equations of the system. This would occur, for example, if the updating of the parameters contained in $\tilde{s}$ depended partly on one or more of the endogenous variables. Our solution below allows for such non-linear updating by assuming this behavior can be modeled as piece-wise linear functions of time. See below for more details.

nothing in particular can be said about the time paths of the endogenous variables implied by the model until additional assumptions are made concerning the expectations dynamics. However, instead of completely closing the model with one fixed expectational rule and generating a fully determinate solution of the model, we ask in the second stage whether there exists reasonable scenarios of expectations dynamics that produce, within the context of our model, exchange rate dynamics matching up with the important features of the data. It is important to emphasize that because imperfect knowledge expectations cannot be fully determined by any outside investigator, the second stage of our solution involves only *semi-closing* of the model. Although our expectational assumptions allow us to derive *specific qualitative* implications of the model, they fall short of fully determining the time paths of the endogenous variables.

In this section we derive the general solution of our monetary model and discuss its basic character and how it differs from the standard RE solution. We then show in the next section that there are reasonable scenarios of expectations dynamics that give rise to persistent movements of s away from PPP. This should be compared with the widely recognized difficulties of the monetary model with RE in explaining this kind of behavior.

To clarify what is meant by expectations dynamics in this paper, we briefly discuss an example. Suppose that the individual agents' expectations of $\bar{s}_{IK}$, defined on page **??**, lead to the following equation for the market's theories consistent expectations of the medium-run value of the exchange rate:

$$\tilde{s} = \tilde{\beta}'_f X_f + \tilde{\beta}'_n X_n \tag{31}$$

where X_f and X_n denote column vectors of the fundamental (macroeconomic) variables and non-fundamental factors agents use in forming their expectations and the row vectors $\tilde{\beta}'_f$ and $\tilde{\beta}'_n$ contain market averages of the weights agents attach to these fundamental variables and non-fundamental factors, respectively. In general, the updating of the market's assessments of $\tilde{s}$ and $\dot{\tilde{s}}$, which are formed according to (31), can be based on: 1) new information about the values of the variables and factors in X_f and X_n, given unchanged values of the parameters $\tilde{\beta}'_f$ and $\tilde{\beta}'_n$; 2) inclusions or exclusions in the set of fundamental variables and non-fundamental factors used by agents in forecasting, i.e., changes in the compositions of X_f and X_n; and 3) revisions in the weights agents attach to these variables and factors. Such changes and revisions in the models used by agents can lead to continuous changes in one or more of the parameters of equation (31), one-time changes (jumps) in the parameters of equation (31) or changes in the compositions of X_f and X_n. Thus, updating of expectations may influence the rate at which $\tilde{s}$ moves over time or lead to one-time jumps in $\tilde{s}$ and/or $\dot{\tilde{s}}$.

It is important to emphasize that the equation in (31) is used for illustrative purposes only. In general, individual expectations formation will involve hunches and guesses and other methods that are difficult to capture through equations like (31). However, the influence of such elusive factors on the market's expectation is assumed to be captured in our model through their effect on the rate of change of $\tilde{s}$ over time and through discontinuous jumps in $\tilde{s}$ and/or $\dot{\tilde{s}}$.

4.1 Solving the Model

The general solution of the model consists of equations describing the time paths of the exchange rate, relative goods prices, relative interest rates and, by implication, the real exchange rate. Since we allow for expectations dynamics of all types, these time paths involve continuous movements over time as well as discontinuous jumps at discrete points in time. Thus, the solution of the model consists of an arbitrarily large number, M, of continuous time paths defined over subperiods of time, j ($j = 1....M$). Each of the continuous time paths corresponds to a subperiod of time during which the updating of expectations leads to only continuous movements in the parameters of agents' forecasting functions, as captured in the magnitude of $\dot{\tilde{s}}$. In deriving the continuous time paths in each subperiod, we make use of the conventional assumptions of constant growth rates for money and income levels.[38] We also assume for tractability reasons that $a = 0$ in the definition of the $\widetilde{gap}^{\text{PPP}}$ in equation (29).[39]

Discontinuous movements of the endogenous variables occur as the updating of expectations leads to one-time jumps in $\tilde{s}$ and/or $\dot{\tilde{s}}$. Each time the updating of expectations causes a jump in $\tilde{s}$ and/or $\dot{\tilde{s}}$ it marks the beginning of a new subperiod of time characterized by new continuous time paths for the endogenous variables. As discussed in the previous section, the impact of one-time jumps in $\tilde{s}$ and/or $\dot{\tilde{s}}$ on the exchange rate is given by equation (27). Since goods prices are sticky, this equation also determines the impact effect on q.[40]

The solutions for the time paths for s, p_r, i_r and q can be represented by the following piece-wise continuous function:

$$z(t) = \sum_j I_j z_j(t) \tag{32}$$

where $z(t)$ is a column vector of the time paths of the endogenous variables, $z_j(t) = [s_j(t), p_{r_j}(t), i_{r_j}(t), q_j(t)]$ denotes a column vector of the continuous time paths for the endogenous variables over subperiod j, where subperiod j is defined as the time period where $t_j \leq t < t_{j+1}$ and I_j is a 4×4 diagonal matrix, where each element along the diagonal is equal to 1 for all $t_j \leq t < t_{j+1}$ and 0 otherwise.

The magnitudes of the discontinuous movements of the time paths between the separate subperiods (or pieces) in equation (32) depend on the magnitude of the change in the equilibrium uncertainty premium required by agents at time t_j. Discontinuous movements can occur because of one-time jumps in $\tilde{s}$ and/or $\dot{\tilde{s}}$ arising from expectations dynamics, the magnitudes of which are governed by equation (27), or because of a change in the sign of the absolute-value function in equation (29). The latter occurs when $\tilde{s}$ shoots through $\tilde{s}^{\text{PPP}}$. As will become clear shortly, a shooting through of PPP leads to discontinuous movements in the rates of change of the endogenous variables and not to discontinuous movements in their levels.

---

[38] We allow for one-time jumps in the policy variables in the next section.

[39] This assumption greatly simplifies the solution of the model. With this assumption we are using $\tilde{s} - \tilde{s}^{\text{PPP}}$ as a proxy in capturing the gap affect on the expected losses of buyers and sellers. Using $s - \tilde{s}^{\text{PPP}}$ leaves the main results unchanged.

[40] Note that equation (27) also applies to one-time changes in the policy variables $m_r, y_r, \dot{m}_r$ and $\dot{y}_r$. We explore the implications of such changes in the policy environment in Fydman and Goldberg [2001a].

The solutions for the continuous time paths in any subperiod j are as follows:[41]

$$s(t)_j = c_{1_j} e^{-\theta_j t} + \bar{s}_j \tag{33}$$

$$p_r(t)_j = c_{2_j} e^{-\theta_j t} + \bar{p}_{r_j} \tag{34}$$

$$i_r(t)_j = c_{3_j} e^{-\theta_j t} + \bar{i}_{r_j} \tag{35}$$

$$q(t)_j = c_{4_j} e^{-\theta_j t} + \bar{q}_j \tag{36}$$

where

$$\theta = \frac{\delta \left[\alpha\gamma + \left(\tilde{\theta} - \tilde{\sigma} \right) \alpha\lambda + \nu\gamma\tilde{\theta} \right]}{\lambda\tilde{\theta}} \tag{37}$$

$$\begin{aligned}
\bar{s}_j &= \bar{s}^* + \frac{(\nu\gamma + \alpha\lambda)\left(\tilde{\theta} - \tilde{\sigma}_j D_j\right)}{G}(\tilde{s}_j - \bar{s}^*) + \frac{\upsilon\gamma}{G}\left(\dot{\tilde{s}}_j - \tilde{\pi}_{r_j}\right) + \frac{\upsilon\gamma}{G}\left(\dot{\tilde{s}}_j - \pi_r^*\right) \\
&\quad + \frac{\tilde{\sigma}_j D_j \nu\lambda}{G}\left(\tilde{\pi}_{r_j} - \pi_r^*\right) + \frac{\tilde{\sigma}_j D_j (\nu\gamma + \alpha\lambda)}{G}(\tilde{q}_n - q_n) - \frac{\nu\gamma + \alpha\lambda}{G} d_j
\end{aligned} \tag{38}$$

$$\begin{aligned}
\bar{p}_j &= \bar{p}_r^* + \frac{\alpha\lambda\left(\tilde{\theta} - \tilde{\sigma}_j D_j\right)}{G}(\tilde{s}_j - \bar{s}^*) + \frac{\alpha\lambda}{G}\left(\dot{\tilde{s}}_j - \pi_r^*\right) + \frac{\tilde{\theta}\nu\lambda}{G}\left(\tilde{\pi}_{r_j} - \pi_r^*\right) \\
&\quad + \frac{\tilde{\sigma}_j D_j \alpha\lambda}{G}(\tilde{q}_n - q_n) - \frac{\alpha\lambda}{G} d_j
\end{aligned} \tag{39}$$

$$\begin{aligned}
\bar{i}_j &= \pi_r^* + \frac{\alpha\gamma\left(\tilde{\theta} - \tilde{\sigma}_j D_j\right)}{G}(\tilde{s}_j - \bar{s}^*) + \frac{\alpha\gamma}{G}\left(\dot{\tilde{s}}_j - \pi_r^*\right) \\
&\quad + \frac{\tilde{\theta}\nu\gamma}{G}\left(\tilde{\pi}_{r_j} - \pi_r^*\right) + \frac{\tilde{\sigma}_j D_j \alpha\gamma}{G}(\tilde{q}_n - q_n) - \frac{\alpha\gamma}{G} d_j
\end{aligned} \tag{40}$$

$$\begin{aligned}
\bar{q}_j &= \bar{s}_j - \bar{p}_j = q_n + \frac{\nu\gamma\left(\tilde{\theta} - \tilde{\sigma}_j D_j\right)}{G}(\tilde{s}_i - \bar{s}^*) + \frac{\upsilon\gamma}{G}\left(\dot{\tilde{s}}_j - \tilde{\pi}_{r_j}\right) \\
&\quad - \frac{\nu\lambda\left(\tilde{\theta} - \tilde{\sigma}_j D_j\right)}{G}\left(\tilde{\pi}_{r_i} - \pi_r^*\right) + \frac{\tilde{\sigma}\nu\gamma}{G}(\tilde{q}_{n_i} - q_n) - \frac{\nu\gamma}{G} d_j
\end{aligned} \tag{41}$$

$$G = \alpha\gamma + \alpha\lambda\left(\tilde{\theta} - \tilde{\sigma}_j D_j\right) + \tilde{\theta}\nu\gamma \tag{42}$$

---

[41]Note that we have dropped the subscript "IK" from the goods-market clearing solutions for notational convenience.

and the symbols "‾" and "*" denote respectively goods-market clearing level and the value that is obtained in the standard DF case with RE, i.e.,

$$\bar{s}^* = \frac{1}{\gamma}(m_r - \phi y_r) + \frac{\lambda}{\gamma}\pi_r + q_n, \tag{43}$$

$$\bar{p}_r^* = \frac{1}{\gamma}(m_r - \phi y_r) + \frac{\lambda}{\gamma}\pi_r \tag{44}$$

$$\pi_r^* = \frac{1}{\gamma}(\dot{m}_r - \phi \dot{y}_r) \tag{45}$$

The variable D captures our assumption that the equation for U in (29) contains an absolute-value function: D equals 1 when $\tilde{s}_j - \tilde{s}_j^{PPP} > 0$ and -1 when $\tilde{s}_j - \tilde{s}_j^{PPP} < 0$ and $-\theta_j$ is the root of the system for subperiod j. The absolute value of the slope parameter $\tilde{\sigma}$, which we have already assumed is less than $\tilde{\theta}$ for all subperiods, is also assumed to be constant. However, the sign of $\tilde{\sigma}$ changes as either the sign of U changes or the market on balance switches from being on one side to the other. Hence, the values of $\tilde{\sigma}$ and θ are period specific, giving rise to the j subscripts. The constants of integration in equations (33) through (36) in any subperiod j, are given by $c_j = [z(t_j) - \bar{z}_j(t_j)]e^{\theta_j t}$, where $z(t_j)$ is determined by money market equilibrium for $i_r(t_j)$ and by equation (27) for $s(t_j)$ and $q(t_j)$. Of course with sticky prices, $p_r(t_j)$ is given.

The continuous time paths for any subperiod j in equations (33) through (36) are standard in form, in that they depend on two terms: a short-run adjustment term and a corresponding medium-run level.[42] Given that $\tilde{\theta} > \tilde{\sigma}$ for all subperiods j (see the preceding section), the root of the system in any subperiod, $-\theta_j$, is negative, implying that the dynamics in any given time period will involve a tendency of the endogenous variables to move monotonically and continuously toward their medium-run levels. The reduced-form time path for the exchange rate in any subperiod j in equation (33) can be rewritten as follows:

$$\dot{s}_j = \theta_j(\bar{s}_j - s_j) + \dot{\bar{s}}_j \tag{46}$$

Equation (46) shows that if all agents use the functional form of the expectations function in equation (8), then it is qualitatively rational for them to do so. This leads to the following remark:

Remark 10 *Expectations functions based on equation (8) are model consistent in a qualitative sense, in that the functional form of agents' expectations functions is the same as the functional form of the differential equation describing the actual movement of the exchange rate in (46).*

The medium-run levels of the system for any subperiod j are given in equations (38) through (41). Inspection of these solutions reveals that the medium-run values towards which the system tends in any one time period depend not only on the underlying structural

---

[42] We use the term "medium-run" level instead of the more common terms "long-run" or "steady-state" level because the equilibrium levels in equations (38) through (41) change as agents revise the methods and models used in forecasting, implying that the endogenous variables never fully adjust to the medium-run levels of any one subperiod j. We discuss this implication of expectations dynamics more fully below.

parameters of the economy, but also on the beliefs of agents, as captured by $\tilde{s}$, $\dot{\tilde{s}}$, $\tilde{\pi}_r$, $\tilde{q}_n$, $\tilde{\theta}$ and $\tilde{\sigma}$. Note that this result is no different than what is obtained under the standard RE case, although with RE, the parameters of the reduced form relating endogenous and exogenous variables and the beliefs of agents about these parameters are one and the same. It should also be noted that if each individual agent was endowed with perfect quantitative knowledge of the underlying structural parameters, *and each agent believed that all other agents are also endowed with such perfect knowledge and moreover each agent believed that all other agents form their forecasts based on this knowledge and the stable arm of the DF model (i.e., if $\tilde{s} = \bar{s}^*$, $\dot{\tilde{s}} = \pi_r^* = \tilde{\pi}_r$, $\tilde{q}_n = q_n$, $\tilde{\sigma} = d = 0$), then the medium-run solutions* for subperiod j in equations (38) through (41) would collapse to the long-run solutions obtained from the standard DF model.

This result that the medium-run solutions in equations (38) through (41) depend partly on agents' beliefs leads to two immediate implications.

- *First, these medium-run values are period specific, i.e., each time expectations dynamics lead to jumps in $\tilde{s}$ and/or $\dot{\tilde{s}}$, the medium-run values towards which the tends over time (as goods prices adjust) shift to new values with possibly new rates of change. Hence, the medium-run solutions in equations (38) through (41) possess j subscripts.*

- *Second, although the medium-run levels in every subperiod act as anchors toward which the endogenous variables of the system tend as goods prices adjust, the eventual jumps in $\tilde{s}$ and/or $\dot{\tilde{s}}$ due to expectations dynamics imply that the system never fully converges to the medium-run levels of any one subperiod.*

The second implication is interesting because it implies that the equilibrium relationship between the exchange rate and fundamentals and non-fundamental factors (i.e., the medium-run relationship in equation (38)) will be structurally unstable, as the updating of expectations leads to changes in the compositions of X_f and X_n and to revisions in $\tilde{\beta}'_f$ and $\tilde{\beta}'_n$. In Frydman and Goldberg [1996b], we suggest that this result is the key to explaining the Meese and Rogoff [1983] puzzle that standard exchange rate models (with their fixed coefficients and fixed set of fundamentals) fit poorly out of sample[43].

The second implication is also interesting because it differs from what is obtained under RE, namely under RE and a given policy environment, the steady-state solutions of the model serve as long-run anchors towards which the exchange rate and prices fully converge assuming stability. Also, under RE, the long-run anchors of the monetary model necessarily imply a persistent or monotonic movement of the exchange rate back to PPP. But as we show below, with IKE, the medium-run anchors of the monetary model may imply a persistent movement of the exchange rate away from PPP.

4.2   The Basic Character of the General Solution

We are now ready to examine the basic character of the general solution of the monetary model with imperfect knowledge as given in equations (32) through (41) and further com-

---

[43] See section 6 below for more discussion on this point.

pare it to the solution obtained under RE. In contrast to the solution with RE, the goods-market clearing solutions in equations (39) and (40) are in general inconsistent with PPP. This can be seen from equation (41), which reveals that the goods-market clearing level of the real exchange rate, $\bar{q}_j$, equals its PPP level, q_n, only when agents' expectations are based on perfect knowledge of the structural parameters. Furthermore, as we show below, the medium-run anchor towards which the exchange rate tends in any one subperiod, $\bar{s}_j$, can itself move persistently either away from or towards PPP levels, and if the movement is towards PPP and subperiod j endures long enough, then this anchor will shoot through PPP and begin moving away from the other side. In the remainder of this section we establish the long-swings behavior of $\bar{s}$. We then show that such behavior in any one subperiod depends on the interplay between the expectations dynamics and the rate of change of fundamentals, which we measure by $\dot{\bar{s}}^*$. Finally, we establish the conditions under which a persistent movement of $\bar{s}$, either away from or towards PPP, in any one subperiod leads to a similar movement of the exchange rate in the same subperiod.

Consider first the long-swings behavior of $\bar{s}$, which we establish in the following proposition:

Proposition 8 *The time path of $\bar{s}_j$ over any subperiod j will involve a persistent movement either away from or towards the time path of the medium-run level of the actual PPP exchange rate, $\bar{s}_j^{PPP}$, where $\bar{s}_j^{PPP} = \bar{p}_{r_j} + q_n$, as long as $\dot{\bar{s}}_j \neq \dot{\bar{s}}^*$. If initially subperiod j involves a persistent movement of $\bar{s}_j$ away from PPP levels, then the movement away will endure for as long as subperiod j endures. If initially the time path of $\bar{s}_j$ involves a persistent movement towards PPP levels and subperiod j endures long enough, then the time path of $\bar{s}_j$ will shoot through the time path of $\bar{s}_j^{PPP}$ and begin moving away from PPP levels from the other side.*

Proof. Differentiating equations (38) and (39) with respect to time yields the following relationships:

$$\dot{\bar{s}}_j = \frac{\alpha\gamma + \tilde{\sigma}_j D_j \nu\gamma}{G}\dot{\bar{s}}^* + \frac{(\nu\gamma + \alpha\lambda)\left(\tilde{\theta} - \tilde{\sigma}_j D_j\right)}{G}\dot{\bar{s}}_j \tag{47}$$

$$\dot{\bar{s}}_j^{PPP} = \dot{\bar{p}}_{r_j} = \frac{\alpha\gamma + \tilde{\theta}\nu\gamma}{G}\dot{\bar{s}}^* + \frac{\alpha\lambda\left(\tilde{\theta} - \tilde{\sigma}_j D_j\right)}{G}\dot{\bar{s}}_j \tag{48}$$

where we have used the fact that $\dot{\bar{p}}_r^* = \dot{\bar{s}}^*$ in equation (48) and the assumptions that $\tilde{q}_n$ and q_n are constant. Since the coefficients associated with $\dot{\bar{s}}_j$ and $\dot{\bar{s}}^*$ sum to one in both equations, we can express the rate of change of the gap between $\bar{s}_j$ and $\bar{s}_j^{PPP}$ as a function of the difference, $\dot{\bar{s}}_j - \dot{\bar{s}}^*$. This is obtained by subtracting equation (48) from (47), yielding the following:

$$\dot{\bar{s}}_j - \dot{\bar{s}}_j^{PPP} = \frac{\nu\gamma\left(\tilde{\theta} - \tilde{\sigma}_j D_j\right)}{G}\left(\dot{\bar{s}}_j - \dot{\bar{s}}^*\right) \tag{49}$$

If $\dot{\bar{s}}_j \neq \dot{\bar{s}}^*$, then $\dot{\bar{s}}_j - \dot{\bar{s}}_j^{PPP} \neq 0$. Given that $\dot{\bar{s}}_j$, $\dot{\bar{s}}^*$, $\tilde{\sigma}_j$ and D_j are all constant by definition, it follows that the sign of $\dot{\bar{s}}_j - \dot{\bar{s}}_j^{PPP}$ does not change over any subperiod j, i.e., the gap between $\bar{s}_j$ and $\bar{s}_j^{PPP}$ either increases or decreases over the entire length of any subperiod j. Thus, if initially the movement of $\bar{s}_j$ is away from PPP levels, either from above or below, then this movement away will continue for as long as subperiod j endures. Also, if initially the movement of $\bar{s}_j$ is towards PPP levels and subperiod j endures long enough, then the time path of $\bar{s}_j$ will shoot through $\bar{s}_j^{\text{PPP}}$ and continue to move persistently away from PPP in the other direction. ∎

We note that the expectations dynamics inherent in $\dot{\tilde{s}}_j$ can include the updating of expectations arising not only from new information on fundamental variables and non-fundamental factors, but also revisions of the models and methods used for forecasting. Thus, $\dot{\tilde{s}}_j$ will, in general, differ from the rate of change of fundamentals, $\dot{\bar{s}}^*$. This readily leads to the following corollary to Proposition 8:

Corollary 1 *With imperfect knowledge, the medium-run anchor for the exchange rate will, in general, move persistently either away from or towards its PPP level in any subperiod j; and if the movement is towards PPP and subperiod j endures long enough, then $\bar{s}_j$ will shoot through PPP and begin moving away from the other side.*

Remark 11 *It is important to emphasize that although Proposition 8 and Corollary 1 establish that the medium-run anchor for the exchange rate will involve persistent movements either away from or towards PPP in any one subperiod, it does not determine: 1) the particular direction of movement of $\bar{s}_j$ (i.e. whether it will move away or towards); 2) the length of time that subperiod j will endure; and 3) whether subsequent subperiods will involve movements of $\bar{s}$ in the same direction as in subperiod j. These questions can be addressed only with additional assumptions concerning the particular nature of the unfolding process of expectations dynamics, which we begin to explore in the next section.*

It is clear from equation (49) that the ultimate direction of movement of the medium-run anchor, $\bar{s}_j$, depends on the relationship between the expectations dynamics in subperiod j, as captured by $\dot{\tilde{s}}_j$, and the rate of change of fundamentals, $\dot{\bar{s}}^*$. In preparation for the example to be considered in the next section it is useful to summarize the conditions on the expectations dynamics operating through $\dot{\tilde{s}}_j$ that determines the direction of movement of $\bar{s}_j$, i.e. whether the movement is away from or towards PPP levels. The following corollary to Proposition 8 states these conditions:

Corollary 2 *Persistent movements away from PPP levels require $\dot{\tilde{s}}_j - \dot{\bar{s}}^* > 0$ if they originate from above and $\dot{\tilde{s}}_j - \dot{\bar{s}}^* < 0$ if they originate from below; whereas persistent movements toward PPP levels require $\dot{\tilde{s}}_j - \dot{\bar{s}}^* < 0$ if they originate from above and $\dot{\tilde{s}}_j - \dot{\bar{s}}^* > 0$ if they originate from below. Furthermore, whenever $\dot{\tilde{s}}_j > \dot{\bar{s}}^* (\dot{\tilde{s}}_j < \dot{\bar{s}}^*)$ and thus $\bar{s}_j$ moves away from (towards) PPP levels, then the following inequalities also hold $\dot{\tilde{s}}_j > \dot{\bar{s}}_j > \dot{\bar{s}}_{ppp_j}$ ($\dot{\tilde{s}}_j < \dot{\bar{s}}_j < \dot{\bar{s}}_{ppp_j}$).*

Proof. The first part of the Corollary **??** follows directly from equation (49). The inequalities in the second part follow from equations (47) and (48) (given that $\dot{\tilde{s}}_j \neq \dot{\bar{s}}^*$) and the fact that the coefficients associated with $\dot{\bar{s}}^*$ and $\dot{\tilde{s}}_j$ sum to one in both equations. ∎

The economic intuition behind Proposition 8 and Corollary 1 is as follows. Exchange rate expectations matter for the exchange rate, through the UAUIP condition in equation

18, leading to medium-run solutions that depend on the aggregate expectation $\tilde{s}_j$ in equations (39) through (42). With imperfect knowledge, the level of this market expectation is not constrained to be consistent with PPP, as is the case with RE. In fact, as we show in the next section, $\tilde{s}_j$ can depend solely on macroeconomic fundamentals and yet imply the expectation of a further movement away from PPP. Moreover, with imperfect knowledge, the rate at which the aggregate expectation changes over time, $\dot{\tilde{s}}_j$, which depends partly on how agents update their methods and models, is not constrained to maintain a constant real exchange rate, as is the case with RE. In general, the magnitude of $\dot{\tilde{s}}_j$ will imply persistent movement in $\bar{s}_j$ either towards or away from PPP levels over subperiod j, and if the movement is towards PPP and subperiod j endures long enough, then by definition (i.e., given a constant $\dot{\bar{s}}_j - \dot{\bar{s}}_j^{\text{PPP}}$), the time path of $\bar{s}_j$ will shoot through PPP, leading to a movement of $\bar{s}_j$ away from PPP levels from the other side.

The time paths of s and p_r, of course, do not depend solely on the movements of the medium-run anchors $\bar{s}_j$ and $\bar{p}_{r_j}$, since according to equations 33 and 34 these time paths also depend on excess demand terms. Thus, whether the nominal exchange rate moves away from or towards actual PPP levels (given by s_j^{PPP}) over any subperiod j, depends partly on the magnitudes of these excess demand terms. We summarize the movement of $s_j - s_j^{\text{PPP}}$ and its connection to the movement of $\bar{s}_j - \bar{s}_j^{\text{PPP}}$ during any subperiod j in the following proposition:

Proposition 9 *For any subperiod j, if the time paths of $s_j - s_j^{\text{PPP}}$ and $\bar{s}_j - \bar{s}_j^{\text{PPP}}$ move in the same direction initially, then these time paths will both move monotonically in the same direction throughout subperiod j, i.e., a persistent movement of $\bar{s}_j$ either away from or towards $\bar{s}_j^{\text{PPP}}$ will be matched by a similar movement of s_j either away from or towards s_j^{PPP}, and if the time path of $\bar{s}_j$ shoots through its PPP level, then s too will shoot through its PPP level, assuming that subperiod j endures long enough. If during subperiod j the time paths of $s_j - s_j^{\text{PPP}}$ and $\bar{s}_j - \bar{s}_j^{\text{PPP}}$ move in opposite directions initially, then these time paths will eventually move in the same direction if subperiod j endures long enough.*

Proof. The connection between the time paths of $s_j - s_j^{\text{PPP}}$ and $\bar{s}_j - \bar{s}_j^{\text{PPP}}$ can be seen by rewriting equation (36) as follows:

$$\dot{s}_j - \dot{s}_j^{\text{PPP}} = \dot{q}_j = \theta_j \left(\bar{q}_j - q_j \right) + \left(\dot{\bar{s}}_j - \dot{\bar{s}}_j^{\text{PPP}} \right) \tag{50}$$

where we have used the fact that $\dot{\bar{q}}_j = \dot{\bar{s}}_j - \dot{\bar{s}}_j^{\text{PPP}}$. Since neither the value of the excess-demand term (i.e., $\theta_j \left(\bar{q}_j - q_j \right)$) nor the value of the secular-trend term (i.e., $\left(\dot{\bar{s}}_j - \dot{\bar{s}}_j^{\text{PPP}} \right)$) changes sign over any subperiod j, there are two possible cases, either the time paths of $s_j - s_j^{\text{PPP}}$ and $\bar{s}_j - \bar{s}_j^{\text{PPP}}$ move in the same direction initially or they move in opposite directions initially.

The first case can arise either because both the excess-demand term and the secular-trend term imply a movement of $s_j - s_j^{\text{PPP}}$ in the same direction, i.e., $sign \left(\dot{\bar{s}}_j - \dot{\bar{s}}_j^{\text{PPP}} \right) = sign \left(\theta_j \left(\bar{q}_j - q_j \right) \right)$ or because even though the excess-demand and secular-trend terms imply movements of in opposite directions, the magnitude of the secular-trend term dominates, so that $\left| \dot{\bar{s}}_j - \dot{\bar{s}}_j^{\text{PPP}} \right| > \left| \theta_j \left(\bar{q}_j - q_j \right) \right|$. Given that the absolute value of the excess demand term during any subperiod j falls monotonically and the fact that $\dot{\bar{s}}_j - \dot{\bar{s}}_j^{\text{PPP}}$ is constant (via Proposition 8), it follows that in this case, $s_j - s_j^{\text{PPP}}$ and $\bar{s}_j - \bar{s}_j^{\text{PPP}}$ move monotonically in the same direction throughout subperiod j. Thus, a persistent movement of $\bar{s}_j$ either away from or towards $\bar{s}_j^{\text{PPP}}$ will be matched by a similar movement of s_j either away from or towards s_j^{PPP}, and if $\bar{s}_j$ shoots through $\bar{s}_j^{\text{PPP}}$, then s too will shoot through s_j^{PPP} if subperiod j endures long enough.

The second case arises only because the excess-demand and secular-trend terms imply movements of $s_j - s_j^{\text{PPP}}$ in opposite directions and the excess-demand term dominates so that $\left| \dot{\bar{s}}_j - \dot{\bar{s}}_j^{\text{PPP}} \right| < |\theta_j (\bar{q}_j - q_j)|$. In this case, since the absolute value of the excess demand term falls monotonically, eventually the secular trend term will dominate if subperiod j endures long enough. From this point forward, a movement of $\bar{s}_j$ either away from or towards $\bar{s}_j^{\text{PPP}}$ will be matched by a similar movement of s_j either away from or towards s_j^{PPP}, and if $\bar{s}_j$ shoots through $\bar{s}_j^{\text{PPP}}$, then s too will shoot through s_j^{PPP} if subperiod j endures long enough. ∎

Given that $\dot{\bar{s}}_j$ differs in general from the rate of change of fundamentals, $\dot{\bar{s}}^*$, we have the following corollary to Propositions 8 and 9:

Corollary 3 *With imperfect knowledge, the exchange rate will, in general, move persistently either away from or towards its PPP level in any subperiod j; and if the movement is towards PPP and subperiod j endures long enough, then s will shoot through PPP and begin moving away from the other side.*

Proposition 9 and Corollary 3 are also illustrated in figures 1a through 1c. The first case is depicted in Figure 1a. In the figure we have $\theta_j (\bar{q}_j - q_j) = \theta_j \left[(\bar{s}_j - s_j) - \left(s_j^{\text{PPP}} - \bar{s}_j^{\text{PPP}} \right) \right] > 0$ (since $\bar{s}_j - s_j > 0$ and $\bar{s}_j - \bar{s}_j^{\text{PPP}} < 0$), so that with $s_j - s_j^{\text{PPP}} > 0$, both the excess demand and secular trend terms imply a persistent movement of s_j away from s_j^{PPP} from above. Figure 1b depicts the second case, where we have $\theta_j \left[(\bar{s}_j - s_j) - \left(s_j^{\text{PPP}} - \bar{s}_j^{\text{PPP}} \right) \right] > 0$, but with $s_j - s_j^{\text{PPP}} < 0$. Also, in the figure, the excess-demand term implies a movement of s_j towards s_j^{PPP} from below, whereas the secular-trend term implies a movement of s_j away from s_j^{PPP} from below; and the excess-demand dominates initially. However, the secular trend term eventually dominate assuming subperiod j endures long enough, implying that eventually, both s_j and $\bar{s}_j$ move monotonically away from their PPP levels from below. In figure 1c, we have $\bar{s}_j - s_j > 0$ and $\bar{s}_j - \bar{s}_j^{\text{PPP}} > 0$, so that the excess-demand term could imply either a falling or a rising time path for $s_j - s_j^{\text{PPP}}$. But since the time path for $s_j - s_j^{\text{PPP}}$ is clearly falling, figure 1c provides a depiction of the first case. And since the movements of s_j and $\bar{s}_j$ are towards their PPP levels initially and subperiod j endures long enough, both s_j and $\bar{s}_j$ shoot their PPP levels.

To complete the analysis of the general character of the solution for s and $\bar{s}$ we need to consider the case in which the time path of $\tilde{s}_j$ intersects the time path of $\tilde{s}_j^{\text{PPP}}$. If such an intersection occurs during some subperiod j, then the absolute value function in equation (29) implies that the value of D changes sign. As we now show, this discrete change in D leads to a new subperiod, $j+1$, characterized by new time paths for the medium run anchors, in which the relationship between $s - \bar{s}$ and $s^{\text{PPP}} - \bar{s}^{\text{PPP}}$ can flip in sign, i.e., a positive gap between s and $\bar{s}$, for example, which is initially associated with $s^{\text{PPP}} - \bar{s}^{\text{PPP}} > 0$, can be associated with $s^{\text{PPP}} - \bar{s}^{\text{PPP}} < 0$ once D switches sign. We also show, however, that despite this flip in sign, the basic character of the time paths of s and $\bar{s}$ are unchanged with switches in D.

We establish this result in two steps. Consider first the relationship between $s - \bar{s}$ and $s^{\text{PPP}} - \bar{s}^{\text{PPP}}$, which we summarize in the following lemma:

Lemma 10 *A positive or negative gap between s_j and $\bar{s}_j$ could be associated with either a positive or a negative gap between s_j^{PPP} and $\bar{s}_j^{\text{PPP}}$ during any subperiod j.*

Proof. Equations (1), (8), (18) and (29) lead to the following relationship:

$$s_j - \bar{s}_j = -\frac{1}{\bar{\theta}} \left(\frac{\gamma}{\lambda} - \tilde{\sigma}_j D_j \right) \left(s_j^{\text{PPP}} - \bar{s}_j^{\text{PPP}} \right) \tag{51}$$

Equation (??), which must hold at every point in time, shows that if $\frac{\gamma}{\lambda} - \tilde{\sigma}_j D_j > 0$ ($\frac{\gamma}{\lambda} - \tilde{\sigma}_j D_j < 0$), then a positive gap between s_j^{PPP} and $\bar{s}_j^{\text{PPP}}$ will be associated with $s_j - \bar{s}_j < 0$ ($s_j - \bar{s}_j > 0$). ∎

Lemma 10 was used in constructing figures 1a and through 1c and it also plays a role in the next section when we examine the possibility of countermovements back to PPP. Furthermore, this result differs from what is obtained in the standard DF model. It is useful, therefore, to explore the intuition behind this Lemma 10.

In the standard DF model $U = \bar{U} = \tilde{\sigma} = 0$, so that a disequilibrium in the goods market involving $s^{\text{PPP}} - \bar{s}^{\text{PPP}} < 0$ ($s^{\text{PPP}} - \bar{s}^{\text{PPP}} > 0$) must be matched by $s - \bar{s} > 0$ ($s - \bar{s} < 0$). The intuition here is tied to the familiar overshooting implication of the model. For example, consider a one-time increase in relative money supplies, which leads to a fall in relative interest rates (in order to preserve relative money market equilibrium) and increases in $\bar{s}$ and $\bar{p}_r$ (and $\bar{s}^{\text{PPP}}$) on impact. If we start from a position of goods market equilibrium, then these impact effects lead to $i_r - \bar{i}_r < 0$ and $s^{\text{PPP}} - \bar{s}^{\text{PPP}} < 0$. The fall in i_r, in turn, requires a fall in the expected rate of change of the exchange rate, $E(\dot{s})$, in order to preserve UIP and equilibrium in the foreign exchange market. But with $E(\dot{s}) = \theta(\bar{s} - s) + \dot{\bar{s}}$, a fall in $E(\dot{s})$ requires not only that s rises, but that this rise overshoots the rise in $\bar{s}$, i.e., $s - \bar{s} > 0$.

With an uncertainty premium that depends on the gap between $\tilde{s}$ and $\tilde{s}^{\text{PPP}}$, however, a one-time increase in relative money supplies may lead to an overshooting or an undershooting of $\bar{s}$ by s. Whether s overshoots depends on the sensitivity of U to changes in the PPP gap (i.e., the absolute value of $\tilde{\sigma}$) and whether the magnitudes of U and $\tilde{s} - \tilde{s}^{\text{PPP}}$ are of the same sign. To see this assume that the increase in m_r leaves $\tilde{s}$ and $\dot{\tilde{s}}$ unchanged (we will drop this assumption in the next subsection). From equations (38) and (39), the increase in m_r leads to increases in $\bar{s}$ and $\bar{p}_r$ (and $\bar{s}^{\text{PPP}}$), so that as with the DF model, if we begin from a position of goods market equilibrium, then both $s^{\text{PPP}} - \bar{s}^{\text{PPP}}$ and $i_r - \bar{i}_r$ become negative on impact.[44] Suppose that $U > 0$, $\tilde{\sigma} > 0$ and $\tilde{s} - \tilde{s}^{\text{PPP}} = \tilde{s} - p_r - \tilde{q}_n > 0$ (so that $D > 0$) before and after the jump in m_r. In this case, $U - \bar{U}$ becomes positive on impact since when $p_r - \bar{p}_r < 0$ and $\tilde{s} - p_r - \tilde{q}_n > 0$, $\tilde{\sigma}(\tilde{s} - p_r - \tilde{q}_n) > \tilde{\sigma}(\tilde{s} - \bar{p}_r - \tilde{q}_n)$; and the more sensitive U is to changes in $\tilde{s} - \tilde{s}^{\text{PPP}}$, the greater is the gap between U and $\bar{U}$. If on impact the magnitude of $U - \bar{U}$ dominates, so that $U - \bar{U} > |p_r - \bar{p}_r|$, which will be the case when

---

[44]Note with $\tilde{s}$ and $\dot{\tilde{s}}$ unchanged, the increase in m_r impacts $\bar{s}$ and $\bar{p}_r$ only through $\bar{s}^*$.

$\tilde{\sigma} > \frac{\gamma}{\lambda}$, then s undershoots $\bar{s}$. If instead, $U < 0$ and $\tilde{\sigma} < 0$, then we necessarily have $\tilde{\sigma} < \frac{\gamma}{\lambda}$ and on impact $U - \bar{U} < 0$ and s overshoots $\bar{s}$. The intuition behind this result follows from the role played by U in tempering agents' desire to push s in one direction or another. A larger change in U implies a smaller change in s given a change in m_r. If $U > \bar{U}$ ($U < \bar{U}$), then the change in s required to maintain UAUIP when m_r increases is smaller (larger) than the change in $\bar{s}$ required to maintain UAUIP evaluated at medium-run levels.

Equation (51) also shows that the relationship between $s - \bar{s}$ and $s^{\text{PPP}} - \bar{s}^{\text{PPP}}$ can flip in sign, the conditions for which we summarize in the following corollary to Lemma 10:

Corollary 4 *If $|\tilde{\sigma}| > \frac{\gamma}{\lambda}$, then the relationship between $s - \bar{s}$ and $s^{\text{PPP}} - \bar{s}^{\text{PPP}}$ will flip in sign whenever either $\tilde{\sigma}$ or D switches sign.*

Proof. Corollary 4 follows directly from equation (51). ∎

We are now ready to show that when a new subperiod is ushered in due to a shooting through of s^{PPP} by $\tilde{s}$, causing a switch in the sign of D, the basic character of the new subperiod, in terms of the direction of movement of $\bar{s} - \bar{s}_j^{\text{PPP}}$, is unchanged from the preceding subperiod. This result is summarized in the following proposition:

Proposition 11 *If subperiod j ends only because the time path of $\tilde{s}_j$ intersects the time path of s_j^{PPP}, causing the value of D to switch in sign, then the direction of movement of $\bar{s}_j - \bar{s}_j^{\text{PPP}}$ must be same both before and after the switch in D.*

Proof. Our assumption that $\tilde{\theta} > \tilde{\sigma}$ ensures that the coefficient on $\dot{\tilde{s}}_j - \dot{\tilde{s}}^*$ in equation (51) does not change sign when D switches. Thus, the sign of $\dot{\bar{s}} - \dot{\bar{s}}^{\text{PPP}}$ will not change when D switches, implying that the direction of movement of $\bar{s}_j - \bar{s}_j^{\text{PPP}}$ before and after a switch in D must be the same. ∎

Proposition 11 is illustrated in figure 2, which plots two successive time periods, j and $j + 1$, where the transition between subperiods occurs only because the time paths of $\tilde{s}_j$ and s_j^{PPP} intersect during subperiod j. For simplicity we have assumed in the figure that $\tilde{q}_n = q_n$, so that $\tilde{s}_j^{\text{PPP}} = s_j^{\text{PPP}}$. The time paths in the figure are drawn so that both the excess-demand and secular-trend terms imply a movement of s_j towards s_j^{PPP}. Given the way the time paths for the secular trend terms are drawn, this implies that during subperiod j, $\tilde{\sigma}_j > 0$ and $\tilde{\sigma}_j D_j > \frac{\gamma}{\lambda}$. According to Propositions 8 and 9, the movements of s_j and $\bar{s}_j$ towards PPP levels endure for as long as subperiod j endures. However, because in the figure $\left| \dot{\tilde{s}}_j - \dot{s}_j^{\text{PPP}} \right| < 0$, the time paths of $\tilde{s}_j$ and s_j^{PPP} intersect, causing a switch in D and discontinuous movements in the levels and rates of change of $\bar{s}$ and $\bar{s}^{\text{PPP}}$. This occurs at time t_{j+1} in the figure. Since D does not enter equation (27), no discontinuous movements occur in the levels of s and s^{PPP}. The discontinuous jumps in the levels of $\bar{s}$ and $\bar{s}^{\text{PPP}}$ are given in the following equations:

$$\frac{\triangle \bar{s}^{\text{PPP}}}{\triangle D} = -\frac{\tilde{\sigma} \alpha \lambda}{G^+} \left(\tilde{s} - \bar{p}_{r_0} - \tilde{q}_n \right) \tag{52}$$

$$\frac{\triangle \bar{s}}{\triangle D} = -\frac{\tilde{\sigma} \left(\upsilon \gamma + \alpha \lambda \right)}{G^+} \left(\tilde{s} - \bar{p}_{r_0} - \tilde{q}_n \right) \tag{53}$$

where $\bar{p}_{r_0}$ denotes the initial value of $\bar{p}_r$ at the point at which D changes in sign and $G^+ = \alpha\gamma + \alpha\lambda\left(\tilde{\theta} - \tilde{\sigma}D^+\right) + \tilde{\theta}\nu\gamma$, where D^+ denotes the value of D subsequent to its switch in value. Note, that the impact effects on $\bar{s}$ and $\bar{s}^{\text{PPP}}$ are discrete because the change in D is discrete. Thus we use the finite-change symbol $\triangle$. Also note that the impact effects on $\bar{s}$ and $\bar{s}^{\text{PPP}}$ implied by equations (52) and (53) are such that the relationship between $s_j - \bar{s}_j$ and $s_j^{\text{PPP}} - \bar{s}_j^{\text{PPP}}$ flips. Although the switch in D preserves the sign of $\dot{\bar{s}} - \dot{\bar{s}}^{\text{PPP}}$, it is possible for the movement of s and s^{PPP} in subperiod $j + 1$ to involve a widening gap initially, if on impact the sign of the excess-demand term were to change and dominate the secular-trend term. However, according to Proposition 9, the persistent movement of s towards PPP levels that occurs during subperiod j must eventually continue during subperiod $j + 1$, with the implication that s will shoot through s^{PPP}, if subperiod $j + 1$ endures long enough.[45]

It is important to note that, as with time path for $\bar{s}_j$, the foregoing analysis establishes that the exchange rate, s, will involve persistent movements either away from or towards PPP in any one subperiod. It does not determine, however, 1) the particular direction of movement of s_j (i.e. whether it will move away or towards); 2) the length of time that subperiod j will endure; and 3) whether subsequent subperiods will involve movements of s in the same direction as in subperiod j. These questions can be addressed only with additional assumptions concerning the particular nature of the unfolding process of expectations dynamics. This is the topic to which we now turn.

5   Expectations Dynamics and Persistent Movements Away From PPP

In this section we begin to explore the potential of our model to illuminate important features of the empirical record on exchange rates. In particular, we provide a specific example of how the general solution, together with additional qualitative assumptions on expectations dynamics, can produce persistent movements of the exchange rate away from PPP both within a given subperiod and along the time -path consisting of more than one subperiod, each beginning with a jump in $\tilde{s}$ and/or $\dot{\tilde{s}}$. A complete analysis of this problem would entail a general analysis of long swings and as such, would require deriving general conditions on expectations dynamics that give rise to persistent movements of the exchange rate away from PPP, together with the conditions leading to a countermovement and a shooting through of PPP levels.[46] Although such an analysis is beyond the scope of this paper, the example analyzed here illustrates the potential of our approach for explaining the long-swings tendency of exchange rate movements.

Since in this second stage of the solution we do not assume one fixed rule governing the expectations dynamics in all subperiods, we do not derive fully determinate solutions for the time paths of the endogenous variables and therefore we do not obtain precise quantitative implications from our model. Instead, with qualitative assumptions on the exchange rate dynamics, our model produces only qualitative implications about the movements of

---

[45]We note that that the possibility that the relationship between $s - \bar{s}$ and $s^{\text{PPP}} - \bar{s}^{\text{PPP}}$ can flip in sign implies that an appreciating exchange rate may be associated with either rising or falling interest rate differential as goods prices adjust to their equilibrium levels.

[46]For such an analysis, see Frydman and Goldberg [2001a].

the endogenous variables. The question we ask is whether there exist reasonable qualitative assumptions on expectations dynamics that lead to persistent movements of the exchange rate away over successive subperiods. To guide us in evaluating various qualitative assumptions, we make use of some findings from the literature on behavioral economics. We show below that there are reasonable qualitative assumptions on expectations dynamics leading to persistent movements of the exchange rate away from PPP, although because of the qualitative nature of our assumptions, we cannot determine precisely the rate at which the exchange rate moves away or when this movement away might end. We also show, contrary to conventional wisdom, that persistent movements of the exchange away from PPP over successive subperiods do not require the presence of non-fundamental factors.

5.1   A Persistent Movement Away From PPP

We have already established in Propositions 8 and 9 that s and $\bar{s}$ either move away from or towards PPP in any subperiod j. Without the loss of generality, consider some subperiod j during which both s_j and $\bar{s}_j$ move away from their PPP levels from above. According to Corollary 2, then, $\dot{\bar{s}}_j > \dot{\bar{s}}^*$ and $\dot{\bar{s}}_j > \dot{\bar{s}}_j > \dot{\bar{s}}_j^{\text{PPP}}$.[47] In general, the expectations dynamics operating through $\dot{\bar{s}}_j$ could arise because agents obtain new information about potentially relevant fundamental variables and non-fundamental factors, or because they update their methods, models and guesses continuously over time. However, since it is commonly believed that the presence of non-fundamental factors is required for persistent movements of s away from PPP, it is important to highlight that with IKE, such movements can arise solely due to agents' attempts at interpreting movements in macroeconomic fundamental variables. We establish this result in the following proposition:

Proposition 12 *A persistent movement of s_j away from its PPP level can arise in any subperiod j even if the exchange rate forecasts of all agents are based solely on macroeconomic fundamental variables.*

   Proof. Without the loss of generality, suppose during some subperiod j, $s_j > s_j^{\text{PPP}}$. Assume that each agent's assessment, $\tilde{s}_i$, during subperiod j depends solely on macroeconomic fundamentals, i.e., $\tilde{s}_i = \tilde{\beta}'_{f_i} X_f$, where we omit the subscript j for ease of presentation. In the aggregate, then, the market's assessment, $\tilde{s}$, will depend solely on macroeconomic fundamentals, i.e., $\tilde{s} = \tilde{\beta}'_f X_f$. This implies that the rate of change of the market's assessment, $\dot{\tilde{s}}$, is given as follows:

$$\dot{\tilde{s}} = \tilde{\beta}'_f \dot{X}_f + \dot{\tilde{\beta}}'_f X_f \tag{54}$$

In general, with IKE, $\dot{\tilde{s}} \neq \dot{\tilde{s}}^*$.[48] If $\dot{\tilde{s}} > \dot{\tilde{s}}^*$, then $\dot{\tilde{s}} - \dot{\tilde{s}}^{\text{PPP}} > 0$ according to Corollary **??** of the preceding section. Proposition 9 then implies that s moves persistently away from

---

[47]Note that since we analyze a case in which $\bar{s}_j > \bar{s}_j > \bar{s}_j^{\text{PPP}}$, subperiod j is similar to the one depicted in Figure 1a.

[48]Note that the updating of the weights attached to fundamentals, $\dot{\tilde{\beta}}'_f$, can, in general, involve non-fundamental factors (e.g., market psychology and technical factors). For the purposes of this proof, we assume such factors are not present.

s_j^{PPP} from above either throughout subperiod j or at some point during subperiod j if the subperiod endures long enough. ∎

Our earlier work on Theories Consistent Expectations (TCE) provides a particular example of IKF in which market agents make use of economists' models when interpreting movements in macroeconomic fundamentals. With TCE, however, agents' (and the analyst's) knowledge of these models is *imperfect* in the sense that the stock of existing models provides only *qualitative knowledge* about how endogenous variables might be related to exogenous (predetermined) variables. Agents' theories are assumed to inform them in three qualitative ways: 1) they indicate the important macroeconomic variables that should be included in forecasting functions; 2) they indicate the algebraic signs of the weights that should be attached to these fundamental variables; and 3) they provide qualitative information about the long-run equilibrium levels of the endogenous variables. Expectations functions possessing explanatory variables matching those implied by agents' theories and where the weights attached to these explanatory variables are consistent in sign with one or more of these theories are said to be theories consistent.

With TCE, the market's assessment, $\tilde{s}$, can be written as follows:

$$\tilde{s} = \tilde{\beta}'_p X_f^p + \tilde{\beta}'_n X_f^n \tag{55}$$

where X_f^p and X_f^n, which we refer to as *positive* and *negative* fundamentals, respectively, are defined as fundamentals that, based on agents' theories, lead to the prediction of an increase in the exchange rate whenever their values increase and decrease, respectively, i.e., $\tilde{\beta}'_p > 0$ and $\tilde{\beta}'_n < 0$. For example, if agents' theories consisted only of the monetary models, then $X_f^p = [m_r \quad \dot{m}_r \quad \tilde{q}_n]$ and $X_f^n = [y_r \quad \dot{y}_r]$.

Assuming TCE leads to a further clarification of the meaning of Proposition 12. In using their theories to look forward, agents place theories consistent weights on a set of fundamentals. These weights and the values of the fundamentals gives rise to a market forecast concerning the future, medium-run level of the exchange rate, $\tilde{s}$, during some subperiod, j. However, with imperfect knowledge, $\tilde{s} \neq \bar{s}^{\text{PPP}}$ and $\dot{\tilde{s}} \neq \dot{\bar{s}}^*$. Without the loss of generality, suppose that the weights agents attach to the positive fundamentals relative to the negative fundamentals implies $\dot{\tilde{s}} > \dot{\bar{s}}^*$, i.e., agents place greater (smaller) weights on X_f^p (X_f^n) than what is implied by the unobservable $\bar{s}^*$. Thus, if $s_j > s_j^{\text{PPP}}$, then as the fundamental variables move over subperiod j, agents will interpret these movements as reasons to bid up the exchange rate relative to PPP.[49] Hence, non-fundamental factors are not necessary for producing reasonable accounts of a persistent movement of s away from PPP.

5.2 Persistent Movements Away Over Successive Subperiods

The length of time that subperiod j will endure and whether successive subperiods also involve a rising s away from PPP depends on the character of the expectations dynamics in terms of frequency and magnitude of the discontinuous jumps in $\tilde{s}$ and $\dot{\tilde{s}}$. In what follows we make use of two simplifying assumptions on the expectations dynamics in order provide

---

[49]In Goldberg and Frydman [1996a,b,2001] we find that exchange rate expectations over monthly horizons do depend on macroeconomic fundamentals and that the weights agents attach to fundamentals are theories consistent.

a particular example of how our model can produce persistent movements of s away from PPP over successive subperiods. In general, discontinuous movements of $\tilde{s}$ and $\dot{\tilde{s}}$, if they are large enough, can cause the equilibrium value of U to change sign, causing the sign of $\tilde{\sigma}$ to change as well. Also, in general, a movement away from PPP from above can be associated with a positive or negative $E(R)$. Since the purpose of this section is to provide a simple example rather than a complete analysis of long swings, we make use of the following assumptions: 1) subperiod j is assumed to involve an $E(R) > 0$ (i.e., we assume the market on balance is on the right side); and 2) expectations dynamics are such that discontinuous movements of $\tilde{s}$ and $\dot{\tilde{s}}$ do not lead to switches in the sign of $\tilde{\sigma}$.

We begin with the following definition of reinforcing changes in $\tilde{s}$ and $\dot{\tilde{s}}$:

Definition 2 *Given that subperiod j involves a movement of s away from PPP from above, then increases (decreases) in $\tilde{s}$ and $\dot{\tilde{s}}$, which lead to increases (decreases) in $E(\dot{s})$, will be referred to as reinforcing (non-reinforcing).*

One of the common ways of explaining a persistent movement of s away from PPP is to rely on bandwagon effects, i.e., increases in $\tilde{s}$ and $\dot{\tilde{s}}$ generate increases in s and $\dot{s}$, leading to further increases in $\tilde{s}$ and $\dot{\tilde{s}}$, and so on (e.g., the rational-bubble model of Blanchard and Watson [1982] and Meese [1986]). One of the interesting implications of our model is that although one-time increases in $\tilde{s}$ and $\dot{\tilde{s}}$ unambiguously lead to a rise in q, implying a further movement away from PPP, these increases do not necessarily lead to an increase in $\dot{q}$, i.e., increases in $\tilde{s}$ and $\dot{\tilde{s}}$ can actually lead to a slowing down of the movement of s away from PPP in the subsequent subperiod.

Remark 12 *We note that although the value of $\dot{q}$ may fall from one subperiod to the next as $\tilde{s}$ and $\dot{\tilde{s}}$ both rise, as long as $\dot{q} > 0$, the movement away from PPP will continue over time during each subperiod. This should be contrasted with the bandwagon behavior behind the RE bubble story, which requires exponential growth in the payoff relevant variables in order for the bubble to continue.*

The following two lemmas establish this aspect of the model. Consider first a one-time change in $\dot{\tilde{s}}$.

Lemma 13 *Although a one-time increase (decrease) in $\dot{\tilde{s}}$ necessarily leads to an increase in q on impact, producing a new subperiod, $j+1$, it does not necessarily lead to an increase (decrease) in $\dot{q}$ on impact. However, if subperiod $j+1$ endures long enough, then eventually the value of $\dot{q}_{j+1}$ will be higher than its prior value during subperiod j, $\dot{q}_j$.*

Proof. Since a discontinuous change in $\dot{\tilde{s}}$ leads to a jump in s in the same direction according to equation (27) of section [] and good prices are sticky, a one-time increase in $\dot{\tilde{s}}$ unambiguously leads to a one-time increase in q and a further movement of s away from PPP on impact. Thus, a change in $\dot{\tilde{s}}$ that reinforces the original expectation of a movement away leads to a reinforcing change in the levels of s and q.

As for the effect on $\dot{q}$, equation (36) implies that a one-time change in $\dot{\tilde{s}}$ works through two channels. To see this, differentiate equation (36) with respect to time, yielding the following:

$$\dot{q} = \dot{s} - \dot{s}^{PPP} = \theta \left(\bar{q} - q \right) + \left(\dot{\bar{s}} - \dot{\bar{s}}^{PPP} \right) \tag{56}$$

Plugging in the solutions for $\bar{q}$ in equation (41) and $\dot{\bar{s}} - \dot{\bar{s}}^{PPP}$ in equation (49) and then differencing with respect to $\dot{\bar{s}}$ yields the following two effects:[50]

$$\frac{\triangle \theta \left(\bar{q} - q \right)}{\triangle \dot{\bar{s}}} = - \frac{(1-\omega)\,\theta \left[\alpha \gamma + \left(\tilde{\theta} - \tilde{\sigma}_j D_j \right) \alpha \lambda \right]}{G \tilde{\theta}} = A_1 < 0 \tag{57}$$

$$\frac{\triangle \left(\dot{\bar{s}}_j - \dot{\bar{s}}_j^{PPP} \right)}{\triangle \dot{\bar{s}}} = \frac{\nu \gamma \tilde{\theta} \left(\tilde{\theta} - \tilde{\sigma}_j D_j \right)}{G \tilde{\theta}} = A_2 > 0 \tag{58}$$

where we continue to use the finite-change symbol $\triangle$.

Equations (57) and (58) show that a one-time increase in $\dot{\bar{s}}$ has two offsetting effects on $\dot{q}$, a negative effect through the excess-demand term and a positive effect through the secular-trend term. Thus, a one-time increase in $\dot{\bar{s}}$, which reinforces $E(\dot{s})$, may not reinforce the rate at which s moves away from PPP on impact in the new subperiod, $j+1$. However, because the magnitude of the excess-demand term in equation (56) declines monotonically over time during the new subperiod, whereas the secular-trend term remains constant, eventually a point is reached at which the higher secular-trend term dominates if subperiod $j+1$ endures long enough. Thus, although the increase in $\dot{\bar{s}}$ may lead to a fall in $\dot{q}$ on impact, eventually the increase in $\dot{\bar{s}}$ will reinforce the rate at which s moves away from PPP. ∎

Equations (57) and (58) lead to the following condition for one-time changes in $\dot{\bar{s}}$ to be reinforcing in terms of both $E(\dot{s})$ and q on impact:

$$\alpha \left(1 - \omega \right) < \frac{\nu \gamma \tilde{\theta} \left(\tilde{\theta} - \tilde{\sigma}_j D_j \right)}{\theta \left[\gamma + \left(\tilde{\theta} - \tilde{\sigma}_j D_j \right) \lambda \right]} > 0 \tag{59}$$

The condition in equation (59) reveals that the ability of the secular-trend effect to dominate on impact when changes in $\dot{\bar{s}}$ occur, depends on the parameters α and ω. The parameter α measures the sensitivity of price-adjustment to changes in the real exchange rate in equation (3), i.e. it provides a measure of the degree of exchange-rate pass-through. The parameter ω measures the degree to which the gap effect on potential losses offsets the velocity effect due to changes in s. At one extreme, agents' assessments of the potential losses depend on the gap from PPP to such a degree that it completely offsets the velocity effect, in which case $\omega = 1$. At the other extreme, agents view this gap effect as unimportant, in which case no offsetting takes place and $\omega = 0$. This analysis leads to the following conclusion:

Conclusion 14 *The likelihood that reinforcing changes in $\dot{\bar{s}}$ will reinforce in terms of $\dot{q}$ on impact rises as the degree of exchange-rate pass-through falls and the importance of the PPP gap for agents' assessments of the potential losses increases.*

---

[50] In deriving equation (57), it is necessary to solve out for d_j using equation (29).

If the condition in (59) holds, then the increase in $\tilde{s}$ leads to increases in both q and $\dot{q}$ on impact, and as such, reinforces the movement away from PPP throughout the length of subperiod $j + 1$. We note that the evidence on the low degree of exchange-rate pass-through (e.g., see Engel [2000]) and the evidence reported in table 1 on the importance of the PPP gap in explaining excess returns is suggestive that the condition in (59) might be consistent with empirical evidence. It is also important to note that even if this condition does not hold, the increase in $\tilde{s}$ may still preserve the sign on $\dot{q}$ and therefore, preserve the movement of s away from PPP throughout subperiod j. Furthermore, even if $\dot{q}$ does turn negative on impact during subperiod $j + 1$, according to Lemma 13, eventually a point is reached when $\dot{q}$ turns positive and the movement away over time during subperiod $j + 1$ resumes.

The fact that $\dot{q}$ will eventually positive may have little importance for the exchange rate, since the new subperiod, $j+1$ may not last long enough, i.e., $\tilde{s}$ may jump again prior to $\dot{q}_{j+1}$ becoming positive. Furthermore, it is reasonable to suppose that $\tilde{s}$ rises when $\dot{\tilde{s}}$ rises. And again, although the increase in $\tilde{s}$ reinforces the movement of s away from PPP in levels, it may not reinforce the rate at which s moves away in the new subperiod. The following lemma establishes this implication of one-time changes in $\tilde{s}$:

Lemma 15 *Although a one-time increase (decrease) in $\tilde{s}$ necessarily leads to an increase in q on impact, producing a new subperiod, $j+1$, it does not necessarily lead to an increase (decrease) in $\dot{q}$ on impact. Furthermore, if the sign of $\dot{q}$ changes on impact, then eventually the sign of $\dot{q}_{j+1}$ will be the same as the sign $\dot{q}_j$ if subperiod j endures long enough.*

Proof. Since a discontinuous change in $\tilde{s}$ leads to a jump in s in the same direction according to equation (27) of section [] and good prices are sticky, a one-time increase in $\tilde{s}$ unambiguously leads to a one-time increase in q and a further movement of s away from PPP on impact. Thus, a change in $\tilde{s}$ that reinforces the original expectation of a movement away leads to a reinforcing change in the levels of s and q.

As for the effect on $\dot{q}$, equation (49) shows that a one-time change in $\tilde{s}$ has no effect on the secular trend term in equation (56). Thus, a change in $\tilde{s}$ influences $\dot{q}$ solely through an excess-demand effect. Differentiating equation (56) with respect to $\tilde{s}$ yields the following:

$$\frac{\triangle\theta\,(\bar{q} - q)}{\triangle\tilde{s}} = -\frac{\left[\lambda\left(\tilde{\theta} + \tilde{\sigma}_j D_j\right) - \gamma\right]\alpha\lambda\theta\,(1 - \omega)}{G\lambda} = B \qquad (60)$$

which may be positive or negative. If positive, then the one-time increase in $\tilde{s}$ will lead to an increase in $\dot{q}$, and therefore reinforce the movement away from PPP on impact, and if negative, then the one-time increase in $\tilde{s}$ will lead to a decrease in $\dot{q}$, and therefore will not reinforce the movement away from PPP. If the jump in $\tilde{s}$ does lead to a fall in $\dot{q}$ on impact so that $\dot{q}$ becomes negative, then eventually $\dot{q}$ will become positive if subperiod $j + 1$ endures long enough. This follows because the magnitude of the excess-demand term in equation (56) declines monotonically over time during the new subperiod, whereas the secular-trend term remains constant. ■

Lemmas 13 and 15 imply that one-time increases in $\tilde{s}$ and $\dot{\tilde{s}}$ necessarily reinforce the movement of s away from PPP on impact in levels, but not necessarily it terms of $\dot{q}$, which may actually fall on impact with reinforcing changes in $\tilde{s}$ and $\dot{\tilde{s}}$. And of course, $\tilde{s}$ and $\dot{\tilde{s}}$

may not increase, but rather decrease. The following three lemmas establish conditions under which one-time changes in $\tilde{s}$ and $\dot{\tilde{s}}$ preserve the movement of s away from PPP over successive subperiods.

Consider first the issue of whether reinforcing changes in $\tilde{s}$ and $\dot{\tilde{s}}$ are in fact reinforcing on impact in terms of $\dot{q}$. This leads to the following lemma:

Lemma 16 *There is some nonzero degree of exchange-rate pass through, as measured by α, and some nonzero degree to which the PPP gap matters for agents' assessments of the potential losses, as measured by ω, that ensures reinforcing increases in $\tilde{s}$ and $\dot{\tilde{s}}$ together are reinforcing in terms of $\dot{q}$ on impact.*

Proof. Without the loss of generality, let $\Delta\dot{\tilde{s}} = c\Delta\tilde{s}$, where reinforcing changes in both $\tilde{s}$ and $\dot{\tilde{s}}$ imply that the parameter c, which could move over time, is positive. Equations (57), (58) and (60) reveal that if $A_1c + B > 0$, then the combined increases in $\tilde{s}$ and $\dot{\tilde{s}}$ together necessarily imply that $\dot{q}$ rises on impact irrespective of the magnitudes of α and ω. In the case where $A_1c + B < 0$, the following condition must be met for one-time increases in $\tilde{s}$ and $\dot{\tilde{s}}$ to be reinforcing in terms of $\dot{q}$ on impact:

$$(1 - \omega)\alpha < \frac{A_2}{-(A_1c + B)} \tag{61}$$

Thus, there are nonzero values of α and ω such that reinforcing changes in $\tilde{s}$ and $\dot{\tilde{s}}$ together are reinforcing in terms of $\dot{q}$ on impact. ∎

As with the condition in equation (59), the condition in equation (61) is not required for a continuation of the movement away from PPP during the beginning of subperiod $j + 1$, given increases in $\tilde{s}$ and $\dot{\tilde{s}}$. As before, all that is required is for the sign of $\dot{q}$ to be preserved in the new subperiod. If the condition in equation (61) does not hold, then equations (57), (58) and (60) imply the following condition on the magnitude of the change in $\tilde{s}$ (and therefore $\dot{\tilde{s}}$) for preserving the sign of $\dot{q}$:

$$0 < \Delta\tilde{s} < \frac{\dot{q}_0}{-[(1 - \omega)\alpha(A_1c + B) + A_2c]} \tag{62}$$

Equation (62) says that if the reinforcing changes in $\tilde{s}$ and $\dot{\tilde{s}}$ do not reinforce $\dot{q}$ on impact, then as long as they are not too "large," in the sense of equation (62), the movement of s away from PPP will be preserved in the new subperiod, $j + 1$.

Consider now the possibility that the expectations dynamics leading to subperiod $j + 1$ involve one-time decreases in $\tilde{s}$ and $\dot{\tilde{s}}$. As before, q moves in the same direction as the direction of movement of $\tilde{s}$ and $\dot{\tilde{s}}$, implying that on impact, the movement of s is back to PPP. The fall in $\tilde{s}$ and $\dot{\tilde{s}}$ can also lead to a fall in $\dot{q}$ on impact. If $A_1c + B > 0$, then equations (57), (58) and (60) imply the following condition on the magnitude of the fall in $\tilde{s}$ (and therefore $\dot{\tilde{s}}$) required for preserving the sign of $\dot{q}$ not only on impact, but throughout subperiod $j + 1$:[51]

$$0 > \Delta \tilde{s} > \frac{-\dot{q}_0}{[(1 - \omega)\,\alpha\,(A_1 c + B) + A_2 c]} \tag{63}$$

Thus, if the non-reinforcing changes in $\tilde{s}$ and $\dot{\tilde{s}}$ are not too "large," in the sense of equation (63), then the movement of s away from PPP will be preserved on impact in the new subperiod, $j + 1$.

We note that equations (62) and (63) readily reveal the range of changes in $\tilde{s}$ and $\dot{\tilde{s}}$ that preserve the sign of $\dot{q}$ depend on the parameters ω and α. This leads to the following proposition:

Proposition 17 *The range of changes in $\tilde{s}$ and $\dot{\tilde{s}}$ that preserve the movement of s away from PPP in successive subperiods, both reinforcing and non-reinforcing, increases as the degree of exchange-rate pass through decreases and the degree to which the PPP gap matters for agents' assessments of the potential losses increases.*

Proof. Proposition 17 follows directly from equations (62) and (63). ∎

We are now ready to establish the qualitative assumptions on the expectations dynamics leading from one subperiod to the next that maintain the movement of s away from PPP over successive subperiods. This is done in the following proposition:

Proposition 18 *If the changes in $\tilde{s}$ and $\dot{\tilde{s}}$ that occur from one subperiod to the next are not too large, as defined in equations (62) and (63), or if such changes are reinforcing and equation (61) holds, then the expectations dynamics leading to successive subperiods will involve persistent movements of s away from PPP levels.*

Proof. Proposition 18 follows directly from equations (61), (62) and (63). ∎

Proposition 18 provides the conditions on expectations dynamics that if satisfied, will lead to a continuation of the movement of s away from PPP over successive subperiods. This naturally leads to the question of whether these conditions make sense from an empirical and behavioral standpoint. It is important to re-emphasize that all subperiods involve a persistent movement of s either away from or towards PPP. If s is above PPP during some subperiod j and during this subperiod agents either place greater weight on the positive fundamental variables in $\dot{\tilde{s}}$ than the corresponding weights in $\dot{\tilde{s}}^*$ or use non-zero weights on non-fundamental factors in $\dot{\tilde{s}}$, then s will move away from PPP over time during subperiod j. This then raises the question of whether the expectations dynamics leading from one subperiod to the next does or does not reinforce the movement of s away from PPP, and if not, then are the changes in $\tilde{s}$ and $\dot{\tilde{s}}$ large enough to counteract the underlying dynamic working to push the exchange rate away.

The answer here depends on how buyers and sellers revise their methods and models over time. As we have argued in section [], it is reasonable to suppose in a world of imperfect knowledge and loss aversion that the trend in the exchange rate plays an important role

---

[51]Note if $A_1 c + B < 0$, then $(1 - \omega)\,\alpha\,(A_1 c + B) + A_2 c$ could still be positive, implying that a second condition on the size of $\Delta \dot{\tilde{s}}$ must be met in order for the sign of $\dot{q}$ to be preserved throughout subperiod $j + 1$, i.e., $0 > \Delta \tilde{s} > \frac{-\dot{q}_0}{A_2 c}$

for agents' assessments of the potential gains and losses. Thus, if the trend in the exchange rate involves a movement away from PPP from above and the policy environment is unchanged (i.e., barring surprises in the way the fundamental variables move over time), then there is an inherent bias for expectations dynamics to involve reinforcing changes in $\tilde{s}$ and $\dot{\tilde{s}}$, as the trend effect leads to greater confidence on the part of buyers and less confidence on the part of sellers. Such changes in $\tilde{s}$ and $\dot{\tilde{s}}$, in turn, lead to a jump in s further away from PPP on impact, and whether they are also reinforcing in terms of $\dot{q}$ depends on the condition in equation (61). But even if this condition is not met, the movement of s away from PPP during successive subperiods will be preserved as long as the changes in $\tilde{s}$ and $\dot{\tilde{s}}$ are not too large, in the sense of equation (62).

Interestingly, the literature on behavioral economics lends some plausibility to the argument that expectations dynamics tend to involve revisions that are not too large in magnitude. For example, one of the cornerstones of the behavioral model of investor sentiment of Shleifer (2000) is a phenomenon well documented by psychologists called conservatism. Psychologists have found that individuals are slow to change their beliefs in the face of new evidence. It is useful to quote directly from Shleifer (2000, p.127):

> Edwards [1968] benchmarks a subject's reaction to new evidence against that of an idealized rational Bayesian in which the true normative value of a piece of evidence is well defined. In his experiments individuals update their posteriors in the right direction, but by too little relative to the rational Bayesian benchmark....A conventional first approximation to the data would say that it takes anywhere from two to five observations to do one observation's worth of work in inducing the subject to change his opinions.[52]

Even though the trend during subperiod j involves a movement of s away and from above, it is certainly possible for the expectations dynamics to involve decreases in $\tilde{s}$ and $\dot{\tilde{s}}$. Such non-reinforcing changes lead to a jump in the exchange rate back to PPP and possibly to a fall in $\dot{q}$. However, if $\dot{q}$ does fall and the decreases in $\tilde{s}$ and $\dot{\tilde{s}}$ are not too large, in the sense of equation (63), then the movement of s away from PPP will be preserved in subsequent subperiods. Again, the phenomenon of conservatism lends plausibility to the argument that expectations will tend to involve revisions that are not too large in magnitude. But now, with non-reinforcing changes in $\tilde{s}$ and $\dot{\tilde{s}}$, the trend in s away from PPP that was established in subperiod j will have a tempering effect on the magnitudes of the changes in $\tilde{s}$ and $\dot{\tilde{s}}$. This then provides added plausibility to the argument that if changes in $\tilde{s}$ and $\dot{\tilde{s}}$ are not reinforcing, and the policy environment remains unchanged, then such changes will tend to preserve the underlying dynamic working to push the exchange rate away from PPP.

Of course at any point of time, expectations dynamics could involve "large" non-reinforcing changes in $\tilde{s}$ and $\dot{\tilde{s}}$ that cause not only a fall in both q and $\dot{q}$, but also causes $\dot{q}$ to become negative, i.e., a countermovement could set in at any point in time. Such an event could be tied to an abrupt change in the policy environment (i.e., a decline in $\dot{\tilde{s}}^*$) or an abrupt change in the way market agents interpret the movements of fundamental variables

---

[52]We note, that because of imperfect knowledge "the true normative value of a piece of evidence" is *not* not so "well defined" in the context of our model. As such, the magnitude of the updating found by Edwards most likely overstates the magnitude of the updating that would occur with IKE.

and/or non-fundamental factors. Both possibilities could be triggered for any number of reasons. But our assumption that the PPP gap serves as a benchmark for agents in their assessments of the potential gains and losses implies that there exists some level of the gap from PPP beyond which expectations dynamics will tend to involve non-reinforcing changes in $\tilde{s}$ and $\overset{*}{s}$ that lead to a countermovement back to PPP over successive subperiods. When precisely such a countermovement will occur is ultimately unforecastable. This assumption that the gap from PPP serves as a benchmark level is reminiscent of Keynes's story behind the relationship between the rate of interest and the speculative motive for holding money: "What matters is not the *absolute* level of r but the degree of its divergence from what is considered a fairly *safe* level of r, having regard to those calculations of probability which are being relied on (Keynes [1936], p. 201, italics original)."

The foregoing discussion on the plausibility of the assumptions on the expectations dynamics that lead to movements of s away from PPP over successive subperiods leads to the following conclusion:

Conclusion 19 *The qualitative implications of our monetary model with IKF and uncertainty premia are consistent with the recurring episodes of persistent movements of the exchange rate away from PPP that have characterized the modern period of floating rates.*

It is important to emphasize that in saying this, we are suggesting neither that long-swings will necessarily occur during any time period, nor that one can predict such movements in the exchange rate. The ultimate movement of the exchange rate over any time period depends on the particular expectations dynamics prevailing at the time and it is our position that such dynamics is largely unpredictable. However, our theoretical model suggests that if the expectations dynamics leading to successive subperiods tends to be consistent with the conditions in Proposition (18), then one should expect episodes, that might last extended periods of time, during which exchange rates s moves persistently away from PPP.

The fact that exchange rates do tend to move persistently away from PPP levels, followed by persistent movements back, raises the question of why speculators do not speculate so as to cut short any movement away before it goes too far. The answer to this question appears to be twofold. First, in our model with heterogenous agents there are both buyers and sellers, and if the movement of s is away from above, then the sellers are in fact the market agents who do take contrarian positions and whose speculation works to cut short the movement away. Second, myopic loss aversion works to limit the number of market agents who either increase their contrarian position or switch to the contrarian position from initially being long (a buyer). This is because the evaluation period of most loss averse agents may be too short for them to be willing to incur the risk of exploiting their knowledge that eventually the exchange rate will revert back to its benchmark level of PPP. This is because no agent knows precisely when the exchange rate will cease moving away and begin moving back and such a countermovement may be a long time coming.

For example, consider late 1983 and the beginning of 1984, when $/DM exchange rate was overvalued relative to PPP by 40 percent on some accounts, and yet the dollar continued to appreciate for an additional year before eventually turning around in early 1985. Thus, loss averse agents who contemplate taking contrarian positions must contemplate the possibility of waiting longer than their evaluation period. If several evaluation periods elapse without the exchange rate turning around, then although the contrarian position will eventually turn out to be correct, market agents who take such positions long before the countermovement and who must account for near-term losses will not be around to enjoy their "superior" forecasts.

Why should evaluation periods be relatively short? Thaler and Benartzi [1995], who examine the relative return on stocks and bonds, suggest that the answer is due to corporate governance, i.e., portfolio managers are routinely evaluated on a quarterly basis, making it very difficult for portfolio managers to pursue contrarian strategies longer than two or three quarters. In the foreign exchange market, institutional arrangements impose extremely short evaluation periods. For example, it is well known that in order to manage exchange rate risk, commercial banks place strict position limits on the size of the open positions that their traders can carry overnight. Most junior traders are obliged to close all open positions and tally up before retiring for the day.[53] With such short evaluation periods, the knowledge that eventually the exchange rate will move back to PPP will have little significance. As such, the speculative capital forthcoming in such a world will sometimes tend to be insufficient to counteract the underlying dynamics that works to push the exchange rate away from PPP for extended periods of time. [54]

6   IKF and the Exchange Rate Disconnect Puzzle

This paper has developed a new framework for modeling exchange rate expectations, one that recognizes that agents must cope with imperfect knowledge and yet is consistent with the postulate of individuality rationality. We showed how this new framework, when embedded into a modified monetary model, leads to an explanation of swings in exchange rates away from PPP levels. We also found that such swings may occur even though all agents may rely exclusively on macroeconomic fundamentals when forming exchange rate expectations.

In this concluding section, we discuss how our approach sheds new light on another puzzle in the international finance literature, the exchange-rate disconnect puzzle. The exchange rate disconnect puzzle arrises because researchers have had great difficulty in empirically establishing a connection between exchange rate movements and macroeconomic fundamentals. The evidence comes from a number of sources, including the inability of empirical exchange rate models to fit well when based on in-sample regression analysis (e.g., Frankel [1983,1984]) or when based on out-of-sample fit (e.g., Meese and Rogoff [1983]) and the empirical regularity that although exchange rates are much more volatile during flexible-rate regimes, this higher volatility is not accompanied by a matching differential in the volatility of macroeconomic fundamentals.[55] Dornbusch and Frankel conclude that

---

[53]See for example Kubarych [1983] and Grabbe [2000], among others.

[54]In Frydman, Goldberg, Kocher and Frisch [2001] we explore the possibilty of the connection between exploitable profit opportunities at long horizons and corporate governance mechanisms of the trading institutions.

[55]We note that recent cointegration studies on the monetary model produce have produced some positive results. See for example, MacDonald and Taylor [1994], Cushman, Lee and Thorgeirsson [1996], Diamandis, Geogoutsos and Kouretas [1996] and Papell [1997]).

"exchange rates are moved largely by factors other than the obvious, observable, macroeconomic fundamentals. Econometrically, most of the "action" is in the error term (Dornbusch and Frankel [1988])."

Again, our monetary model with IKF and uncertainty premia provides a simple explanation of this puzzle. With IKF and expectations dynamics, the parameters of the aggregate forecasting function will be unstable, implying that the parameters of the reduced form relating the exchange rate to a set of macroeconomic fundamentals will be unstable. Thus, with IKF, *no one exchange rate model with fixed coefficients would be expected to fit well over the entire modern period of floating rates.* Meese remarks that "the most menacing empirical regularity that confronts exchange rate modelers is the failure of the current generation of empirical exchange rate models to provide stable results across subperiods of the modern floating rate period (Meese [1986], p.365)."[56] And yet virtually all of the empirical evidence used to illustrate the disconnection between exchange rates and fundamentals is based on studies that fit one exchange rate model with fixed coefficients over the entire sample period. We show in Goldberg and Frydman [1996a,b] that when one allows for episodic changes in the parameters of reduced-form exchange rate models as a way to grossly approximate the structural change arising from expectations dynamics, the exchange rate models perform remarkably well. For example, we find that when episodic structural change is incorporated into the analysis, monetary models outperform the random walk model in out-of-sample fit at the shorter forecasting horizons by margins as large as 70 percent in root mean square error.

As for the neutrality of exchange rate regime puzzle, it is clear that the expectational problem differs sharply over fixed and floating exchange rate regimes. The idea here is that with IKF, expectations dynamics will be more volatile during flexible-rate regimes than fixed-rate regimes. This implies that the place to look for the unexplained volatility during flexible-rate periods may not be in greater volatility of macroeconomic fundamentals, but rather in the greater volatility of agents' expectations functions. We pursue this line of research in a forthcoming paper.

References

[1] Barberis, N., Huang, M. and T. Santos (2001), "Prospect Theory and Asset Prices," *Quarterly Journal of Economics,* **116**, pp. 1-53.

[2] Barberis, N., Huang, M. (2001), "Mental Accounting, Loss Aversion, and Individual Stock Returns," National Bureau of Economic Research, *Working Paper* **8190**.

[3] Benartzi, S. and R.H. Thaler (1995), "Myopic Loss Aversion and the Equity Premium Puzzle," *Quarterly Journal of Economics,* **110,** pp. 73-92.

---

[56]The evidence that empirical exchange rate models are temporally unstable is overwhelming. See for example Boughton [1987], Meese and Rogoff [1988] and our earlier work, which shows that empirical exchange rate models are not only unstable, but that this instability takes on a particularly striking form: different sets of macroeconomic fundamentals are found to be significant during different subperiods of floating (see Goldberg and Frydman [1996a,b, 2001a]).

[4] Blanchard, O. and M. Watson (1982), *"Bubbles, Rational Expectations and Financial Markets,"* in P. Wachtel (ed.), *Crises in the Economic and Financial Structure*, Lexington, MA: Lexington Books.

[5] Boughton, J. M. (1987), "Tests of the Performance of Reduced-Form Exchange Rate Models," *Journal of International Economics*, **23**, pp. 41-56.

[6] Cushman, D., S. S. Lee, T. Thorgeirsson (1996), "Maximum Likelihood Estimation of Cointegration in Exchange Rate Models for Seven Inflationary OECD Countries," *Journal of International Money and Finance*, Vol. 15, No. 3, pp. 337-368.

[7] Diamandis, P. F., D. A. Georgoutsos and G. P. Kouretas (2000), "The Monetary Model in the Presence of I(2) Components: Long-Run Relationships, Short-Run Dynamics and Forecasting of the Greek Drachma, *Journal of International Money and Finance*, **19**, pp. 917-941.

[8] Dornbusch, R. (1976), "Expectations and Exchange Rate Dynamics," *Journal of Political Economy*, December, pp. 11161-1174.

[9] Dornbusch, R. and J.A. Frankel (1988), "The Flexible Exchange Rate System: Experience and Alternatives," in S. Borner (ed.), *International Finance and Trade*, London: Macmillan.

[10] Engel, C.A. (2000), "Local-Currency Pricing and the Choice of Exchange Rate Regime," *European Economic Review*, **44**, pp. 1449-1472.

[11] Engel, C.A. (1996), "The Forward Discount Anomaly and the Risk Premium: A Survey of Recent Evidence," *Journal of Empirical Finance*, **3**, pp. 123-191.

[12] Engel, C. And J. Hamilton (1990), "Long Swings in the Exchange Rate: Are They in the Data and Do Markets Know It?," *American Economic Review*, September, pp. 689-713.

[13] Engel, C.A. and J.C. Morley (2001), *"The Adjustment of Prices and the Adjustment of the Exchange Rate,"* mimeo. April.

[14] Evans, G. W. and S. Honkapohja (2001), *Learning and Expectations in Macroeconomics,* Princeton: Princeton University Press.

[15] Frankel, J. A. (1985), "The Dazzling Dollar," *Brookings Papers on Economic Activity*, **1**, pp. 199-217.

[16] Frankel, J. A. (1984), "Tests of Monetary and Portfolio Balance Models of Exchange Rate Determination," in J. Bilson and R. Marston (eds.), *Exchange Rate Theory and Practice*, Chicago: University Chicago Press.

[17] Frankel, J. A. (1983), "Monetary and Portfolio Balance Models of Exchange Rate Determination," in J. Bhandari and B. Putnam (eds.), *Economic Interdependence and Flexible Exchange Rates*, Cambridge: MIT press.

[18] Frankel, J.A. (1979), "On the Mark: A Theory of Floating Exchange Rate Based On Real Interest Differentials," *American Economic Review*, September, pp. 610-622.

[19] Frankel, J.A. and A.K. Rose (1995), "Empirical Research on Nominal Exchange Rates," in G. Grossman and K. Rogoff (eds.), *Handbook of International Economics, Vol. III*, Amsterdam: North-Holland, pp. 1689-1729.

[20] Froot, K.A. and K. Rogoff (1995), "Perspectives on PPP and Long-Run Real Exchange Rates," in G. Grossman and K. Rogoff (eds.), *Handbook of International Economics, Vol. III*, Amsterdam: North-Holland, pp. 1647-1688.

[21] Frydman, R. (1982), "Towards an Understanding of Market Processes: Individual Expectations, Learning and Convergence To Rational Expectations Equilibrium," *American Economic Review,* **72**, pp. 652-668.

[22] Frydman, R. (1983), "Individual Rationality, Decentralization, and the Rational Expectations Hypothesis," in Frydman, R. and E.S. Phelps (1983), *Individual Forecasting and Aggregate Outcomes: "Rational Expectations" Examined,* New York: Cambridge University Press.\

[23] Frydman, R. and M. Goldberg (2003), "Imperfect Knowledge Expectations and Long-Swings in the Foreign Exchange Market," forthcoming C.V. Starr Center for *Applied Economics Working Paper.*

[24] Frydman, R. and E.S. Phelps (1983), "Introduction" in R. Frydman and E.S. Phelps (1983), *Individual Forecasting and Aggregate Outcomes: "Rational Expectations" Examined,* New York: Cambridge University Press.

[25] Frydman, R. and E. S. Phelps (1990), "Pluralism of Theories Problems in Post-Rational-Expectations Modeling," paper presented at the *1990 Siena Summer Workshop on "Expectations and Learning"*, June 20-30.

[26] Goldberg, M. D. (2000), "On Empirical Exchange Rate Models: What Does a Rejection of the Symmetry Restriction on Short-Run Interest Rates Mean?," *Journal of International Money and Finance*, October, pp. 673-688.

[27] Goldberg, M. D. (1995), "Symmetry Restrictions and the Semblance of Neutrality in Exchange Rate Models," *Journal of Macroeconomics*, Vol. 17, No. 4, Fall, pp. 579-599.

[28] Goldberg, M. D. (1991), "Reconsidering the Basic Relationships Between Exchange Rates, Exchange Rate Expectations and Macroeconomic Fundamentals," Ph.D. Dissertation, New York University, October.

[29] Goldberg, M. D. and R. Frydman (2001), "Macroeconomic Fundamentals and the DM/$ Exchange Rate: Temporal Instability and the Monetary Model," forthcoming in the *International Journal of Finance and Economics*.

[30] Goldberg, M. D. and R. Frydman (1996a),"Imperfect Knowledge and Behavior in the Foreign Exchange Market," *Economic Journal*, July, pp.869-893.

[31] Goldberg, M. D. and R. Frydman (1996b), "Empirical Exchange Rate Models and Shifts in the Co-Integrating Vector", *Journal of Structural Change and Economic Dynamics*, **7**, pp. 55-78.

[32] Goldberg, M. D. and R. Frydman (1993), "Theories Consistent Expectations and Exchange Rate Dynamics," in Frisch, H. and A. Wörgöter (eds.), *Open-Economy Macroeconomics*, London: MacMillan Publishing, chapter 23.

[33] Hayek, F.A. (1948), *Individualism and Economic Order,* Chicago: University of Chicago Press.

[34] Juselius, K. (1995), "Do Purchasing Power Parity and Uncovered Interest Rate Parity Hold in the Long-Run?: An Example of Likelihood Inference in a Multivariate Time Series Model," *Journal of Econometrics*, **69**, pp. 211-240

[35] Kahneman, D. and A. Tversky (1979), "Prospect Theory: An Analysis of Decision Under Risk," *Econometrica, 47*, pp. 263-291.

[36] Keynes, J.M. (1936), *The General Theory of Employment, Interest and Money,* New York: Harcourt, Brace and World.

[37] Keynes, J.M. (1937), "The General Theory of Employment,"*Quarterly Journal of Economics,* **51***,* pp. 209-223.

[38] Knight, F.H. (1921), *Risk, Uncertainty and Profit,* Boston:Houghton Mifflin.

[39] Lewis, K. (1995), "Puzzles in International Financial Markets," in G. Grossman and K. Rogoff (eds.), *Handbook of International Economics, Vol. III*, Amsterdam: North-Holland, pp. 1913-1917.

[40] MacDonald, R. and M. P. Taylor (1994), "The Monetary Model of the Exchange Rate: Long-run Relationships, Short-Run Dynamics and How to Beat a Random Walk," *Journal of International Money and Finance*, **13** (3), pp. 276-290.

[41] Mark, N. (1995), "Exchange Rates and Fundamentals: Evidence on Long-Horizon Predictability," *American Economic Review*, **85**, pp. 201-218.

[42] Mark, N. and D. Sul (2001), "Nominal Exchange Rates and Monetary Fundamentals: Evidence from a Small Post-Bretton Woods Panel," *Journal of International Economics*, **53**, pp. 29-52.

[43] Meese, R. (1986), "Testing for Bubbles in Exchange Markets: A Case of Sparkling Rates?," *Journal of Political Economy*, **94**, No. 2, pp. 345-373.

[44] Meese, R. and K. Rogoff (1988), "Was it Real? The Exchange Rate-Interest Differential Relation Over the Modern Floating-Rate Period," *Journal of Finance*, September, pp. 993-948.

[45] Meese, R. and K. Rogoff (1983), "Empirical Exchange Rate Models of the Seventies: Do They Fit Out of Sample?," *Journal of International Economics*, February, pp. 3-24.

[46] Obstfeld, M. (1995), "International Currency Experience: New Lessons and Lessons Relearned," *Brookings Papers on Economic Activity*, **1**

[47] Obstfeld, M. and K. Rogoff (1999), *Foundations of International Finance,* (Cambridge, US: The MIT Press).

[48] Papell, D. H. (1997), "Cointegration and Exchange Rate Dynamics," *Journal of International Money and Finance*, Vol. 16, No. 3, pp. 445-460.

[49] Phelps, E.S. (1983), "The Trouble with "Rational Expectations" and the Problem of Inflation Stabilization," in R. Frydman and E.S. Phelps (1983), *Individual Forecasting and Aggregate Outcomes: "Rational Expectations" Examined,* New York: Cambridge University Press.

[50] Phelps, E.S. *et al.* (1970), *Microeconomic Foundations of Employment and Inflation,* New York: Norton.

[51] Polanyi, M. (1962), *Personal Knowledge,* Chicago: University of Chicago Press.

[52] Schulmeister, S. (1983), "Exchange Rates, Prices and Interest Rates: Reconsidering the Basic Relationships of Exchange Rate Determination," C.V. Starr Center For Applied Economics *Working Paper* No. **83**-13, July.

[53] Schulmeister, S. (1987), "Currency Speculation and Dollar Fluctuations," *Banca Nazionale del Lavoro Quarterly Review*, No. **167**, December, pp. 343-365.

[54] Shleifer, A. (2000), *Inefficient Markets: An Introduction To Behavioral Finance,* Oxford, UK: Oxford University Press.

[55] Soros, G. (1987), *The Alchemy of Finance*, New York: Simon and Schuster.

[56] Soros, G. (2000), *Open Society: Reforming Global Capitalism*, New York: Public Affairs.

[57] Taylor, M. (1995), "The Economics of Exchange Rates," *Journal of Economic Literature*, Vol. 33, March, pp. 13-47.

In: International Macroeconomics: Recent Developments   ISBN: 1-59454-901-X
Editor: Amalia Morales Zumaquero, pp. 207-225   © 2006 Nova Science Publishers, Inc.

Chapter 10

FINANCIAL GLOBALIZATION, CRISES, AND CONTAGION[*]

Sergio L. Schmukler[1], Pablo Zoido[2] and Marina Halac[1]
[1]World Bank
[2]Stanford University

Abstract

Different forces and potential benefits are pushing towards increasing financial globalization. However, globalization can carry important risks. This paper reviews the literature on crises and contagion in the context of financial globalization. Countries with weak fundamentals become more prone to crises when they liberalize their financial sectors. Globalization can also lead to crises in countries with sound fundamentals, due to imperfections in financial markets or external factors. Moreover, open economies are exposed to contagion via different channels such as real links, financial links, and herding behavior. Still, in the long run, the net effects of financial globalization are likely to be positive. The main challenge for policymakers is thus to manage the process as to take advantage of the opportunities, while minimizing the risks.

I   Introduction

Financial globalization is not a new phenomenon, but today's depth and breath are unprecedented.[1] Capital flows have existed for a long time. In fact, according to some

---

[*] This paper is a product of the background work for the Globalization World Bank Policy Research Report. We thank the participants of the Globalization Policy Research Report and seminar participants at a workshop organized by the World Bank Managing Volatility Thematic Group for very helpful discussions. We also thank Amar Bhattacharya, David Dollar, Patrick Honohan, Chang-Tai Hsieh, and Rick Mishkin, who gave us several specific comments and suggestions. The findings, interpretations, and conclusions expressed in this paper are entirely those of the authors. They do not necessarily represent the views of the World Bank, its Executive Directors, or the countries they represent. E-mail addresses: pzoido@stanford.edu, sschmukler@worldbank.org, and mhalac@worldbank.org.

[1] We define financial globalization as the integration of a country's local financial system with international financial markets and institutions. This integration typically requires that governments liberalize the domestic financial sector and the capital account.

measures, the extent of capital mobility and capital flows a hundred years ago is comparable to today's.[2] At that time, however, only few countries and sectors participated in financial globalization, and capital flows tended to follow migration and were generally directed towards supporting trade flows. It was not until the 1970s that the world witnessed the beginning of a new wave of financial integration. Decreasing capital controls and increasing capital mobility with a growing participation of a wide range of developing countries in the global financial system characterized the post-Bretton Woods era, leading to a more integrated world economy towards the 1990s.

There are different forces that are pushing towards an increasing financial globalization. These forces are governments, borrowers, investors, and financial institutions. Governments allow globalization by liberalizing restrictions on the domestic financial sector and the capital account of the balance of payments. As shown in Kaminsky and Schmukler (2003), there has been a gradual lifting of restrictions in developed and emerging countries during the last 30 years.[3] Firms and even households have been increasingly participating of financial globalization by borrowing abroad and thus relaxing their financial constrains and smoothing consumption and investment. International investors have taken advantage of financial globalization to achieve cross-country risk diversification. As a consequence of the liberalization of financial markets, both institutions and individuals in developed countries can now easily invest in emerging markets through different instruments. Financial institutions have also played an important role in globalization. The gains in information technology have diminished the importance of geography, allowing international corporations to service several markets from one location. Moreover, the increased competition in developed countries has led banks and other non-bank financial firms to look for expanding their market shares into new businesses and markets, and the liberalization of the regulatory systems in developing countries has opened the door for international firms to participate in local markets.

The forces that are pushing towards globalization are driven by the benefits that this process can yield. The main potential benefit of financial globalization for developing countries is the development of their financial system; that is, more complete, deeper, more stable, and better-regulated financial markets.[4] There are two main channels through which financial globalization promotes financial development. First, financial globalization implies that new sources of capital and more capital become available allowing countries to better smooth consumption, deepening financial markets, and increasing the degree of market discipline. Second, financial globalization leads to a better financial infrastructure, which can mitigate information asymmetries and thus reduce problems of adverse selection and moral hazard. A large literature provides evidence on the positive effect of financial globalization on the development of the financial sector. For example, several papers show that the

---

[2] Several authors analyze different measures of financial globalization, arguing that there were periods of high financial globalization in the past. See Bordo, Eichengreen, and Irwin (1999), Obstfeld and Taylor (1998), Quinn (2003), and Taylor (1996).

[3] There were also periods of reversals, in which restrictions were re-imposed. The most substantial reversals took place in the aftermath of the 1982 debt crisis and in the middle 1990s in Latin America, and in the aftermath of the Asian crisis in Asia.

[4] As widely discussed in the literature, a better functioning financial system with more credit fosters economic growth. See, among others, Atje and Jovanovic (1993), Beck and Levine (2002), King and Levine (1993), Levine (2000), Levine, Loayza, and Beck (2000), and Levine and Zervos (1998). Also, for a microeconomic perspective, see Demirguc-Kunt and Maksimovic (1998) and Rajan and Zingales (1998).

liberalization of the stock market increases equity prices and investment.[5] Other works using firm-level evidence find that firms that participate in international capital markets, mainly through cross listing, benefit from abnormal returns and lower cost of capital, as well as increased liquidity and lower volatility.[6,7] Studies on foreign bank entry show that the competitive pressure created by foreign banks lead to improvements in banking system efficiency.[8]

Despite the driving forces and potential benefits, financial globalization also carries some risks, especially for developing countries.[9] This paper reviews the literature on crisis and contagion in the context of financial globalization. Financial globalization can lead to crises in countries with weak fundamentals as the economies become subject to the reaction of domestic and foreign investors. Globalization can also lead to crises in countries with sound fundamentals. Imperfections in international financial markets and external factors that determine capital flows make open economies more prone to crises. Furthermore, countries that integrate into world financial markets become exposed to contagion. Crises can spillover to other countries through real links, financial links, or capital market imperfections such as herding behavior or panics.

Even with the larger exposure to crises and contagion, the evidence suggests that the net effects of financial globalization are still positive, at least in the long run. The main challenge for policy makers is therefore to manage the integration process as to take full advantage of the opportunities, while minimizing its risks. This task is not easy, particularly because financial globalization influences the instruments available to policymakers. In a more integrated world, governments are left with fewer policy tools and thus international financial coordination becomes more important.

The organization of this paper is as follows. Section II and III study how globalization can lead to financial crises and contagion. Section IV presents evidence on the net effects of globalization. Section V discusses the policy options and section VI concludes.

II Financial Globalization and Crises

There are different channels through which financial globalization can be related to crises. When a country liberalizes its financial system, it becomes subject to market discipline exercised by both foreign and domestic investors. When a country is closed, only domestic investors monitor the economy. In an open economy, foreign capital effectively enforces market discipline. Foreign capital is particularly effective in imposing this kind of discipline given its footloose nature; foreign capital can more easily shift investment across countries.

---

[5] See Bekaert and Harvey (2000), Henry (2000), and Kim and Singal (2000).

[6] See Errunza and Miller (2000), Foerster and Karolyi (1999), and Miller (1999).

[7] Note, however, that the migration by firms to developed country securities markets can adversely affect the emerging securities markets that they leave behind. Levine and Schmukler (2003), for example, show that the internationalization of firms reduces the liquidity of the remaining firms in the domestic markets. Other papers on this topic are Alexander, Eun, and Janakiramanan (1987), Domowitz, Glen, and Madhavan (1998 and 2001), Hargis (1997 and 2000), Hargis and Ramanlal (1998), Karolyi (1996 and 2002), Moel (2001), Schmukler and Vesperoni (2003), and Smith and Sofianos (1997).

[8] See Claessens, Demirgüç-Kunt, and Huizinga (1998), Demingüç-Kunt, Levine, and Min (1998), and Martinez Peria, Powell, and Vladkova (2002).

[9] De la Torre, Levy Yeyati, and Schmukler (2002) explain the differences between developed and developing countries that make it so difficult for the latter to successfully integrate into international financial markets.

Domestic capital tends to have more restrictions to invest internationally. In the long run, the joint force of domestic and foreign investors might prompt open economies to improve their fundamentals. But in the short run, the stringent market discipline enforced by foreign investors means more reaction to unsound fundamentals. If countries have weak fundamentals, their vulnerability increases when they liberalize their financial sectors. The larger and rapid response by foreign investors makes economies more fragile and prone to crises. If there is a region of fundamentals where crises can occur, the probability that a crisis happen is higher when the country becomes integrated with world financial markets.

Globalization can also lead to crises if there are imperfections in international financial markets. As a consequence, open countries are more prone to crises regardless of their fundamentals. The imperfections in financial markets can generate bubbles, irrational behavior, herding behavior, speculative attacks, and crashes among other things. Imperfections in international capital markets can lead to crises in countries with sound fundamentals. For example, if investors believe that the exchange rate is unsustainable they might speculate against the currency, what can lead to a self-fulfilling balance of payments crisis regardless of market fundamentals. This is largely illustrated in the literature following Obstfeld (1986).[10] Imperfections can as well deteriorate fundamentals. For example, moral hazard can lead to overborrowing syndromes when economies are liberalized and there are implicit government guarantees, increasing the likelihood of crises, as argued in Corsetti, Presenti, and Roubini (1999) and McKinnon and Pill (1997).[11]

Even in countries with sound fundamentals and in the absence of imperfections in international capital markets, globalization can lead to crises due to the importance of external factors. If a country becomes dependent on foreign capital, sudden shifts in foreign capital flows can create financing difficulties and economic downturns. These shifts do not necessarily depend on country fundamentals. Calvo, Leiderman, and Reinhart (1996) argue that external factors are important determinants of capital flows to developing countries. In particular, they find that world interest rates were a significant determinant of capital inflows into Asia and Latin America during the 1990s. Economic cyclical movements in developed countries, a global drive towards diversification of investments in major financial centers, and regional effects tend to be other important global factors. Frankel and Rose (1996) highlight the role that foreign interest rates play in determining the likelihood of financial crises in developing countries.

The nature of capital flows is also key to understand the risks that foreign capital entails. Several papers stress that sudden reversals are more abrupt when capital inflows are in the form of portfolio flows or short-term capital movements rather than direct foreign investment. When countries rely excessively on short-term capital inflows relative to their ability to generate cash on short notice, they become vulnerable to sudden reversals of capital flows

---

[10] Note that self-fulfilling crises can also take place in a closed domestic banking sector as shown in the literature following Diamond and Dybvig (1983).

[11] The arguments that claim that market imperfections are the cause of crises when countries integrate with financial markets imply that imperfections are more prevalent in international markets than in domestic markets. Imperfections in financial markets can exist even in closed countries. If imperfections are more important in domestic markets than in the foreign markets, as one could expect given their degree of development, financial globalization does not necessarily lead to crises through this channel.

and, consequently, to liquidity crises.[12] The liberalization of capital account transactions, by allowing this type of short-term capital flows, may increase the likelihood of crises.

Evidence on Crises

While crises can be associated with financial liberalization, the evidence suggests that crises are complex; they are not just the consequence of globalization. The data indicate that crises have been a recurrent feature of financial markets for a long time, both in periods of economic integration and in periods of economic disintegration. There are several causes of financial crises, some related to financial globalization while others to domestic factors.

The particular relation between globalization and crises has inspired many studies that compare today's wave of globalization and the frequency of crises with that of a hundred years ago. For example, Bordo, Eichengreen, and Irwin (1999) conclude that given the level of integration prevalent in the global economy today, it is surprising that financial instability is not worse. They claim that this pattern can be attributed to the development of institutional innovations both at a global level, like the International Monetary Fund (IMF) or the Bank of International Settlements (BIS), and at a local level, such as better accounting standards and contract enforcement. Bordo et al. (2001) study the frequency, duration, and output impact of crises during the last 120 years. They compare the crises of the 1980s and 1990s with three distinct historical periods: the gold standard era (1880-1913), the inter-war years (1919-1939), and the Bretton Woods period (1945-1971). They conclude that crises are more frequent today than during the Bretton Woods and the gold standard periods. Today's frequency of crisis is comparable to the inter-war years. There is little evidence that crises have grown longer or output losses have become larger. Bordo et al. conclude that, even if more frequent, crises have not become more severe.

Several studies find that financial liberalization increases the probability of financial crises. Demirgüç-Kunt and Detragiache (1999) study the relation between financial liberalization and banking crises in 53 countries during 1980-1995. They find that banking crises are more likely to occur in liberalized financial systems, though the impact of liberalization on the fragility of banks is weaker when the institutional environment is strong. Glick and Hutchison (1999), investigating a sample of 90 banking crises, 202 currency crises, and 37 twin crises, find that twin crises are mainly concentrated in financially liberalized emerging economies.

The crisis literature suggests that financial liberalization leads to crises by triggering excessive booms and busts in financial markets. Tornell and Westerman (2002) show that many countries that liberalized their financial markets witnessed the development of lending booms, which sometimes ended in twin crises. Kaminsky and Reinhart (1999) show that in both banking and balance of payment crises, a shock to financial institutions such as financial liberalization or increased access to international capital markets fuels the boom phase of the cycle by providing access to financing. The financial vulnerability of the economy increases as the unbacked liabilities of the banking system mount. Kaminsky and Schmukler (2003) also find that financial liberalization causes larger cycles in the short run, though this is only supported by evidence from emerging markets and not from mature markets.

---

[12] Why countries borrow short term despite its associated risks is a question that has received much attention. See

Though globalization can lead to crises, the literature also stresses the importance of domestic factors as key determinants of crises. Kaminsky and Reinhart (1999) highlight that crises, while occurring mostly in the post-liberalization period, are also typically preceded by a multitude of weak and deteriorating economic fundamentals. Frankel and Rose (1996) argue that domestic factors such as slow growth and a boom in domestic credit increase a country's likelihood of experiencing a financial crisis. Caprio and Klingebiel (1997) emphasize the importance of both macroeconomic and microeconomic factors in determining banking crises. Burnside, Eichenbaum, and Rebelo (2001) argue that not only typical macroeconomic indicators such as actual deficits but also other factors like large prospective deficits (associated with implicit bailout guarantees to failing banks) can determine crises. They claim that this was the case of the Asian crisis, where governments were actually running small deficits or surpluses.

Other papers show that both domestic and foreign investors can trigger crises, emphasizing that it is not possible to conclude from the evidence that foreign investors are the main destabilizing group. Frankel and Schmukler (2000) argue that domestic investors seem to be the ones that run first when problems arise, as if they had more information. Foreign investors tend to follow domestic investors. Furthermore, other papers fail to find that foreign investors add to volatility. For example, Choe, Kho, and Stulz (1999) find no evidence that foreign investors had a destabilizing effect on Korea's stock market between 1996 and 1997. On the other hand, Kim and Wei (1999) find that in Korea foreign investors were more prone to herding behavior than local ones.

III Financial Globalization and Contagion

Besides the crises generated in one country, financial globalization can also lead to financial crises through contagion.[13] Indeed, a main characteristic of the crises that erupted since the mid 1990s in emerging economies is that they engulfed a number of countries. For example, the crisis originated in Thailand was rapidly transmitted to Indonesia, Malaysia, Korea, and the rest of East Asia. A similar, but less strong financial shock had occurred after the Mexican devaluation of 1994. Moreover, the 1998 crisis in Russia had much larger contagious effects, being felt not only in other emerging markets but also in developed countries.

Though there is no generally accepted definition, broadly speaking, contagion can be understood as the cross-country spillover effects, namely a crisis in one country is transmitted to other countries. As in the case of domestic crises, this transmission of crises across countries can be due to economic fundamentals (economic links between countries) or to capital market imperfections. In a more restrictive sense, others would argue that contagion is the spillover effects (or the cross-country co-movement) not related to economic fundamentals (Masson 1999).[14,15]

Broner, Lorenzoni, and Schmukler (2003) and references therein for an analysis.

[13] Dornbusch, Park, and Claessens (2000) survey the literature on contagion. Further references can be found at www.worlbank.org/contagion.

[14] These two definitions of contagion rule out the occurrence of crises in different countries that are due to common shocks. For example, a drop in oil prices might generate crises in oil producing countries, no matter which country is hit first. The studies of contagion try to isolate these effects and understand, on the other hand, how domestic crises generate crises somewhere else.

Three broad channels of contagion have been identified in the literature: real links, financial links, and herding behavior. "Real links" can explain easily spillover effects across countries. These real links have generally been associated with trade and/or FDI. When two countries trade with each other or when they compete in third foreign markets in similar products, a devaluation of one country's exchange rate reduces the international price competitiveness of the other country. To the extent that the two countries are competing for FDI inflows from the industrial nations to maintain an industrial edge, the impact of one country's currency devaluation on the other is even larger. Consequently, if one country devalues the currency, then pressure will mount in other closely "linked" countries to also devalue their currencies to re-balance their external sectors (see Gerlach and Smets 1996). Real links are probably adding some regional features to financial crises.

The recent crises, however, have had such widespread effects across countries and regions that some found it hard to demonstrate that real links explain the transmission of shocks. Moreover, the magnitude of recent swings in asset prices is not closely related to any real link among economies. Financial markets have reacted so strongly that economists have argued in favor of spillover effects, not explained by real channels.

In the absence of real links among economies, there might exist "financial links," which still connect countries. This linkage is created when international investors engage in global diversification of financial portfolios and connect different economies financially. Countries with internationally traded financial assets and liquid markets tend to be subject to contagion. Banks and institutional investors can spread a crisis from one country to another. For example, when international investors decide to shift their portfolios following the outbreak of a crisis in one country, they need to sell assets from third countries to hedge their positions as discussed in Kodres and Pritsker (2002). This mechanism puts downward pressure in asset values from these countries, thus propagating the initial shock. Another example of financial links is when leveraged institutions face "margin calls" (Calvo 1998). When the value of their collateral falls, due to a negative shock in one country, banks and mutual funds need to raise liquidity to meet future redemptions and to increase their reserves. Therefore, they sell part of their portfolio on the countries that are still unaffected by the initial shock. This mechanism propagates the shock to other economies.

Even when there are no real or financial links, both domestic and international financial markets might transmit shocks across countries due to herding behavior or panics. At the root of this herding behavior is asymmetric information. Information is costly so investors remain uniformed. Therefore, investors try to infer future price changes based on how other markets are reacting. Additionally, in the context of asymmetric information, what the other market participants are doing might convey information that each uniformed investor does not have (Calvo and Mendoza 2000).[16] This type of reaction leads to herding behavior and panics.

The issue of herding behavior is one of multiple equilibria. If markets regard a country's state to be good, then large capital inflows can take place. If markets judge the country as being in a bad state, then rapid capital outflows and a crisis can take place. In a world of "multiple" equilibria, external shocks can quickly force the economy to shift from a "good" to

---

[15] It is useful to clarify that though contagion has been mostly studied in the context of crises, contagion can also take place during "good" times. For example, some associate the high capital flows to developing countries (which led to overborrowing) and the financing of the technological firms (which led to a generalized asset bubble) to some type of "irrational exuberance" or contagion phenomena that occurred during the late 1990s.

[16] In Rigobon (1998) investors also face a signal extraction problem when making their investment decisions.

a "bad" equilibrium. When investors suddenly become concerned about emerging markets for any reason, Wall Street reacts and European markets follow. When investors observe a crisis in Thailand, they react to it thinking about a potential crisis in Indonesia and Malaysia, and a crisis indeed takes place. Both developed and developing countries markets are subject to these panics. Because investors know little about developing countries, they are probably more prone to herding behavior in these markets. Uninformed investors are the ones that find market changes more informative.

Evidence on Contagion

There are different approaches to test for the presence of contagion. Most though not all of the tests can be classified into four categories: (i) unexplained correlations, (ii) contagious news, (iii) increasing probabilities, (iv) clustering of extreme returns. The studies that try to understand contagion through changes in correlations see whether the return correlations across countries increase during crisis times, as if investors sell assets across countries regardless of the fundamentals. The discussion among these papers is how to measure correlations properly at a time that shocks are very large (see Corsetti, Pericoli, and Sbracia 2002 and Forbes and Rigobon 2002). The studies that analyze news try to determine what types of news impact markets, whether these impacts occur beyond the presence of significant news, and whether news from one country are transmitted across borders (see Baig and Goldfajn 1999 and Kaminsky and Schmukler 1999). The papers that look at probabilities ask whether the probability of having a crisis increases with the occurrence of crises somewhere else and how these probabilities are affected by real and financial links (see Eichengreen, Rose, and Wyplosz 1996). The studies that analyze the clustering of extreme events try to determine whether the very large negative or positive asset returns across countries occur around the same time (see Bae, Karolyi, and Stulz 2003).

As in the case of crises, contagion effects have motivated studies that compare the degree of globalization and contagion today with that of the past. Bordo and Murshid (2002), for example, contrast the pattern of transmission of shocks under the pre-World War I classical gold standard (1880-1914), with that in the post-Bretton Woods era (1975-2000). They conclude that financial market shocks were more globalized before 1914 compared to the present. They claim that this difference in systemic stability between the two eras of globalization reflects factors such as strong cross-country interdependence fostered through links to gold in the past, the growing financial maturity of advanced countries, and the widening of the center to include a more diverse group of countries spanning several regions. On the other hand, Neal and Weidenmier (2001) argue that apparent contagion during the gold standard period can more readily be interpreted as responses to common shocks.

Regarding the different channels of contagion, the evidence suggests that all of them have played important roles in the transmission of crises. Several papers highlight the importance of trade links. Eichengreen, Rose, and Wyplosz (1996) offer a number of examples of trade links leading to contagion in the European context. They argue that the attacks on the United Kingdom in September 1992 and the depreciation of the sterling might have damaged Ireland's international competitiveness. This is also the case for Spain and Portugal or Finland and Sweden. In all these cases the depreciation of a country's currency lead to the debilitation of its most important trade partner or competitor. They also argue, however, that trade links are not the only channel of contagion. The Mexican crisis of 1994-95 affected not only Mexican trading partners but also countries like Hong Kong, Malaysia, and Thailand with little trade links with Mexico. Glick and Rose (1999) show more generally, and especially for emerging economies, that currency crises affect clusters of countries tied together by international trade, after accounting for macroeconomic and financial factors. Forbes (2003) uses firm-level information to test what types of firms were most affected by the East Asian and Russian crises. Results show that a product-competitiveness and income effect were both important transmission mechanisms, suggesting that trade links are main channels of contagion.

Financial links are also very important to understand contagion. The evidence suggests that institutional investors have withdrawn funds from different countries when a crisis hit one of the countries in which they had invested.[17] As a consequence, the fact that some countries are connected through international financial intermediaries make them sensitive to foreign crises. The evidence suggests that contagion during the crises of Mexico in 1994 and Thailand in 1997-98 are best explained by financial sector linkages among these countries.

Financial contagion has been studied through different mechanisms. For example, Camarazza, Ricci, and Salgado (2000), Kaminsky and Reinhart (2000), and Van Rijckeghem and Weder (2003) show the importance of banking spillovers or the "common creditor argument." According to these papers, a strong financial link to the major bank lender to a crisis country (in terms of being highly indebted to that lender or highly represented in its portfolio) increases the country's financial vulnerability. Van Rijckeghem and Weder find that bank exposures to a crisis country help predict bank flows in third countries after the Mexican and Asian crisis, though not after the Russian crisis (where there is evidence of a generalized outflow from emerging markets). Other works, including Frankel and Schmukler (1998) and Kaminsky, Lyons, and Schmukler (2000 and 2001), highlight the role of mutual funds in spreading crises. Mutual funds sell assets from one country when prices fall in another, thus transmitting the shock. Kaminsky, Lyons, and Schmukler (2001) find that in the aftermath of the Thai crisis, the largest mutual fund withdrawals affected Hong Kong and Singapore, which have the most liquid financial markets. Kaminsky, Lyons, and Schmukler (2000) show that the 1994 Mexican crisis spread so rapidly to Argentina and Brazil via the massive withdrawals by mutual funds (specialized in Latin America) from those two countries.

The evidence is also consistent with contagion unrelated to fundamentals, either financial or trade related. Kaminsky and Schmukler (1999) and Favero and Giavazzi (2000) suggest that herding behavior is present and can be a major driving force of contagion. Kaminsky and Schmukler study what types of news triggered the large daily changes in stock prices in Asia in 1997-98. They find that some of those large changes cannot be explained by any apparent substantial news, but seem to be driven by herd instincts of the market itself. Favero and Giavazzi test for the presence of contagion across the money markets of ERM member countries in 1988-1992. They find that contagion within the ERM was a general phenomenon, not limited to a subset of weaker countries, and suggest that multiple equilibria due to expectation shifts, herding behavior, or other mechanisms might have been at play.

Besides studying the different channels of contagion, the literature also provides some evidence on the geographical extent of spillovers. Kaminsky and Reinhart (2003) differentiate

---

[17] For a theoretical model of financial links see Allen and Gale (1999).

two types of contagion, namely contagion from one periphery country to another periphery country and contagion from one periphery country to another via a center country. By analyzing crises in the late 1990s (Brazil, Russia, and Thailand), they find that financial turbulence only spreads globally when it affects asset markets in one or more of the world's financial centers; otherwise, spillovers are confined to countries in the same region. Frankel and Schmukler (1998) find that the 1994 Mexican crisis spread to Asia passing through the New York investor fund community, while it hit Latin America stock markets more directly.

In sum, the evidence suggests that crises can spillover to other countries through different channels. While the relative importance of each link is hard to determine, it is clear that all these channels require that economies are open and integrated with the rest of the world. A country that does not trade internationally or that does not have assets being held by foreign investors has less transmission channels and is therefore less exposed to contagion effects. Also, most economists would agree that a country needs to have a certain degree of vulnerability to suffer from contagion. If the economic fundamentals are very solid, the probability of being hit by an external shock diminishes substantially.

IV Net Effects of Globalization

The previous sections argued that globalization can be associated with financial crises and contagion. In this section we try to understand which are the net effects of financial globalization. Is the link between globalization, crises, and contagion important enough to outweigh the potential benefits of globalization? The evidence is still very scarce, though there are some findings that can help answer this question. On the one hand, it is far from clear that open countries are more volatile and suffer more from crises. On the other hand, the evidence suggests that liberalization spurs output growth and reduces output and consumption growth volatility. While volatility increases in the short run after liberalization and integration with world markets, it tends to decrease in the long run. The evidence holds even when including crisis episodes, suggesting that the net effects of financial globalization are positive.

Bekaert, Harvey, and Lundblad (2003) estimate that equity market liberalization leads to an approximate one percent increase in annual real per capita GDP growth over a five-year period. They show that these effects are significant even after controlling for macro and institutional reforms and financial development.[18] Tornell, Westermann, and Martinez (2003) show that financial liberalization leads to higher average long-run growth even though it also leads to occasional crises, and that this gain in growth is over and above the gain derived from trade liberalization. Edwards (2001) finds that countries with a more open capital account have outperformed countries that have restricted capital mobility, though this effect occurs only after a country has achieved a certain degree of economic development. Regarding volatility, Bekaert, Harvey, and Lundblad (2002) show that equity market liberalizations decrease output and consumption growth volatility, confirming the expected benefits to international risk sharing. These results are not fully accounted for by macro reforms or financial development, and are particularly strong when excluding the 1997-2000 years, dominated by consequences of East Asia crisis.

---

[18] Conversely, Edison et al. (2002) do not find that international financial integration per se accelerates economic growth when controlling for particular economic, financial, institutional, and policy characteristics.

The growth-enhancing financial deepening that follows liberalization is not a smooth process but takes place through boom-bust cycles. When countries first liberalize their financial sector, volatility and crises might arise, particularly in countries with vulnerable fundamentals. Kaminsky and Schmukler (2003) examine the short- and long-run effects of liberalization on capital markets and find that financial liberalization is followed by more pronounced boom-bust cycles in the short run in emerging markets.[19] However, financial liberalization leads to more stable markets in the long run, as the quality of institutions improve. While the cycles in the stock market are intensified in the aftermath of liberalization, three years after liberalization they become less pronounced.

V Policy Options

There are different views on how governments can maximize the benefits of globalization and minimize its risks. The recent experience with crises and contagion has generated large disagreements on policy recommendations.

On one side, some argue that government intervention is at the root of recent crises, and thus favor no policy action. In this view, international capital markets are efficient and developed (or at least international financial markets are more efficient than financial markets in developing countries). Therefore, countries with underdeveloped financial markets would benefit from full financial liberalization, with minimal government intervention. Certain types of government intervention create distortions that can lead to moral hazard and crises. Akerlof and Romer (1993) show that government guarantees can induce firms to go broke at society's expense (looting). They claim that once looting becomes established in one sector, it can distort production in other sectors.

On the other side, some claim that existing distortions may warrant policy actions. According to this view, inefficient international financial markets debilitate the argument for unregulated financial integration. Moreover, as crises are so costly for emerging markets, governments should adopt policy measures aimed at preventing them. Among the policy options available to policymakers, those that have received much attention are related to capital controls and risk management.

One of the main consequences of globalization for policymaking is that the number of instruments at the country level diminishes. When the domestic financial system integrates with the rest of the world, it is more difficult for countries to monitor and regulate the transactions outside its borders. For example, local authorities are able to regulate the activities of the local subsidiary of an international bank, but it is more difficult to regulate the parent company and subsidiaries in other countries, which can be linked to the local bank. Also, the ability of capital to move freely in and out of the country makes government intervention less effective. Below we discuss how financial globalization influences the policies available to policymakers.

---

[19] In contrast, the evidence from mature markets shows larger bull markets but less pronounced bear markets in the aftermath of deregulation, supporting the view that liberalization is beneficial even in the short run.

Capital Controls

The proposals on capital controls suggest that international capital flows should be restricted to reduce the probability or mitigate the effects of sudden shifts in foreign capital.[20] Anomalies such as asymmetric information, moral hazard, asset bubbles, speculative attacks, herding behavior, and contagion are present in international financial markets. So economies open to capital flows suffer the consequences of these imperfections. The recent crises showed that international financial markets punished similarly countries with different fundamentals and policies. In this context, Krugman (1998), Stiglitz (2000), and Tobin (2000) argue that government intervention to restrict cross-country capital movements can be socially beneficial. Governments can mitigate the cost of volatile capital flows, reducing excessive risk taking and making markets less vulnerable to external shocks, and still pursue integration with international financial markets.

There is a large literature on the effects of capital controls, consisting primarily of case studies and with little systematic cross-country evidence.[21] On the whole the literature is inconclusive about the effects of capital controls. While capital controls appear to have no effect on the total volume of flows, some papers suggest that they do change the maturity composition of flows. Controls can alter the composition of capital flows in the direction usually intended by these measures, reducing the share of short-term and portfolio flows while increasing that of FDI. However, the evidence suggests that when controls work, they do so only on a temporary basis (see Kaminsky and Schmukler 2001). As time passes, controls become ineffective; market participants find ways to circumvent the controls. Also, as discriminating between domestic and foreign capital becomes more difficult when economies are integrated with the rest of the world, capital controls are unlikely to work in globalized countries.

Risk Management

Risk management policies focus on strengthening the domestic financial sector and sequencing financial liberalization. This view argues that opening a weak domestic financial sector to large capital movements is potentially risky.[22] If the domestic financial sector does not manage risk properly, does not have sufficient reserves and capital, or does not have the right incentives, large capital inflows and outflows can create severe problems in the domestic financial sector. Foreign competition can also debilitate local financial intermediaries.

---

[20] Following the classification in Frankel (1999), the main proposals can be divided in different categories: (1) controls on outflows, which restrict investors to move capital outside the country; (2) controls on aggregate inflows, which are intended to keep capital from flowing into the country rather than restricting the exit of capital once it is in the country; (3) controls on short-term inflows, a-la Chile, to avoid the build up of short-term debt; and (4) controls on foreign exchange transactions, or "Tobin tax," aimed at imposing a small uniform tax on all foreign exchange transactions, regardless of their nature.

[21] For studies on Latin America, see De Gregorio, Edwards, and Valdes (1998), Edwards (1999), Gallego, Hernandez, and Schmidt-Hebbel (1999), and Soto (1997) for Chile, Edwards and Khan (1985) for Colombia, and Cardoso and Goldfajn (1998) for Brazil. For studies on Asia, see Kaplan and Rodrik (2001) and Reisen and Yeches (1993). Some cross-country studies are Montiel and Reinhart (1999) and Kaminsky and Schmukler (2001b).

[22] Arteta, Eichengreen, and Wyplosz (2001) and Edwards (2001) provide evidence supporting the need of an adequate sequencing for capital account liberalization.

Governments might thus want to regulate and supervise financial systems. A proper risk management helps to avoid and manage crises. First, as a preventive measure, countries with solid financial sectors will probably suffer fewer crises and less pronounced recessions. Second, countries with sound financial sectors will have more flexibility to cope with external shocks and to take corrective measures during a crisis. The policies towards the financial sector should also be accompanied by the right incentives for sound corporate finance. Claessens, Djankov, and Nenova (2000) argue that the institutional structures that influence corporate behavior help explain financial crises, especially through the link between the corporate sector and weakened financial institutions. Kawai, Newfarmer, and Schmukler (2001) argue that one of the most important lessons of the East Asian crisis is that highly leveraged and vulnerable corporate sectors were a key determinant of the depth of the crisis.[23]

While most economists may agree that having a robust financial sector is key for a successful integration with international financial markets, the issue of the sequencing of financial liberalization is much more arguable. The standard recommendation on sequencing is to first clean up domestic financial institutions and change government institutions, and then deregulate the industry and open up the capital account. But can countries implement institutional reforms before liberalization? Kaminsky and Schmukler (2003) compare the timing of financial liberalization and institutional reforms for a sample of 28 countries and find that reforms to institutions occur mostly after liberalization. These results cast doubts on the notion that governments should introduce institutional reforms before they start deregulating the financial sector. On the contrary, the evidence suggests that liberalization fuels institutional reforms. While the country remains closed it is difficult to achieve a very robust financial system. The liberalization and the gradual integration of the financial system with international financial markets and institutions tend to speed up the reform process to achieve a resilient financial system.

There are several reasons that can explain why financial liberalization might prompt institutional reforms. First, as discussed in Rajan and Zingales (2001), well-established firms often oppose reforms that promote financial development because it breeds competition. However, opposition by incumbents may be weaker in the presence of worldwide abundance of trade and cross-border flows. Second, the liberalization and the gradual integration with international financial markets by itself may help to fortify the domestic financial sector. Foreign investors have overall better skills and information and can thus monitor management in ways that local investors cannot. Liberalization, moreover, allows firms to access mature capital markets. Firms listing on foreign stock markets are in the jurisdiction of a superior legal system and have higher disclosure standards.

VI Conclusions

In the last decades, countries around the world have become more financially integrated, driven by the potential benefits of financial globalization. However, financial globalization can carry important risks. The crises of the 1990s, after many countries liberalized their

---

[23] Krugman (1999) argues that company balance sheet problems may have a role in causing financial crises. Currency crises lead to an increase in foreign denominated debt, which combined with declining sales and higher interest rates, weaken the corporate sector and in turn the financial system. Johnson et al. (2000) show how weak corporate governance might hamper the economy and lead to currency depreciations and recessions.

financial system, have questioned in part the gains of globalization. Countries with weak fundamentals are more prone to crises as they become subject to the reaction of domestic and international markets. Imperfections in international financial markets as well as external factors that determine capital flows make countries more vulnerable to crises regardless of their fundamentals. Moreover, the cross-country transmission of crises is characteristic of open economies. Completely closed economies should be isolated from foreign shocks. But when a country integrates with the global economy, it becomes exposed to contagion through different channels.

The evidence suggests that the net effects of financial globalization are still positive, with risks being more prevalent right after countries liberalize. Crises and contagion seem to be the price that some countries have to pay to integrate with the international financial system. The challenge for policymakers is to manage the process as to take full advantage of the opportunities, while minimizing the risks. Though not all conditions are to be met before governments liberalize the financial sector, countries should ensure that the financial system is prepared to cope with foreign capital flows and external shocks. More comprehensive policies for risk management are needed to build solid economies, in particular in terms of regulation and supervision of the financial system. As countries become more integrated, governments have less policy instruments, so there is also an increasing need for international financial policy coordination.

References

[1]   Akerlof G. A. and Romer, P. M., 1993, "Looting: The Economic Underworld of Bankruptcy for Profit." *Brookings Papers on Economic Activity*, **2,** pp. 1-73.

[2]   Alexander, G., Eun, C., and Janakiramanan, S., 1987, "Asset Pricing and Dual Listing on Foreign Capital Markets: A Note." *Journal of Finance*, **42**, pp. 151-158.

[3]   Allen, F., and Gale, D., 2000, "Financial Contagion." *Journal of Political Economy*, **108**, pp. 1-33.

[4]   Arteta, C., Eichengreen, B., and Wyplosz, C., 2001, "When Does Capital Account Liberalization Help More than It Hurts?" *IMF Seminar Series*, 2001:71, pp. 1-39.

[5]   Atje, R., and Jovanovic, B., 1993, "Stock Markets and Development." *European Economic Review*, **37**:2-3, pp. 632-640.

[6]   Bae, K, Karolyi, A., and Stulz, R., 2003, "A New Approach to Measuring Financial Contagion." *Review of Financial Studies*, **16**:3, pp. 717-763.

[7]   Baig, T., and Goldfajn, I., 1999, "Financial Market Contagion in the Asian Crisis." *IMF Staff Papers*, **46**:2, pp. 167-195.

[8]   Beck, T., and Levine, R., 2002, "Stock Markets, Banks, and Growth: Panel Evidence." *NBER Working Paper* **9082**, July. Forthcoming in *Journal of Banking and Finance*.

[9]   Bekaert, G., Harvey C., 2000, "Foreign Speculators and Emerging Equity Markets." *Journal of Finance*, **55**, pp. 562-613. January.

[10]   Bekaert, G., Harvey, C., and Lundblad, C., 2003, "Does Financial Globalization Spur Growth?" Mimeo.

[11]   Bekaert, G., Harvey, C., and Lundblad, C., 2002, "Growth Volatility and Equity Market Liberalization." Mimeo

[12]   Bordo, M. D., Eichengreen, B., and Irwin, D. A., 1999, "Is Globalization Today Really Different than Globalization a Hundred Years Ago?" in S. Collins and R. Lawrence (eds.) Brookings Trade Forum 1999, Brookings Institution, Washington, D.C.

[13]   Bordo, M, Eichengreen, B., Klingebiel, D., and Martinez-Peria, M. S., 2001, "Financial Crises: Lessons from the Last 120 Years." *Economic Policy*, April.

[14]   Bordo, M., and Murshid, A. P., 2002, "Globalization and Changing Patterns in the International Transmission of Shocks in Financial Markets." *NBER Working Paper* **9019**, June.

[15]   Broner, F., Lorenzoni, G., and Schmukler, S., 2003, "Why Do Emerging Markets Borrow Short Term?" Mimeo University of Maryland, Princeton University, and World Bank.

[16]   Burnside, C., Eichenbaum, M., and Rebelo S., 2001, "Prospective Deficits and the Asian Currency Crises" *Journal of Political Economy*, **109**:6, pp. 1155-1197.

[17]   Calvo, G., 1998, "Capital Flows and Capital-Market Crises: The Simple Economics of Sudden Stops." *Journal of Applied Economics*, **1**:1, pp. 35-54.

[18]   Calvo, S., Leiderman, L., and Reinhart, C., 1996, "Inflows of Capital to Developing Countries in the 1990s." *Journal of Economic Perspectives*, **10**:2, pp 123-139.

[19]   Calvo, G. and E. Mendoza, 2000, "Rational Contagion and the Globalization of Securities Markets." *Journal of International Economics*, **51**:1, pp. 79-113.

[20]   Caramazza, F., Ricci, A., and Salgado, R., 2000, "Trade and Financial Contagion in Currency Crises." *IMF Working Paper* **00/55**, March.

[21]   Caprio, G., and Klingebiel, D., 1997, "Bank Insolvency: Bad Luck, Bad Policy, or Bad Banking?" Annual Bank Conference on Development Economics 1996, *World Bank Economic Review*, January.

[22]   Cardoso, E., and Goldfajn, I., 1998, "Capital Flows to Brazil: The Endogeneity of Capital Controls." *IMF Staff Papers*, **45**, pp. 161-202.

[23]   Choe, H., Kho, B., and Stulz, R., 1999, "Do Foreign Investors Destabilize Stock Markets? The Korean Experience in 1997." *Journal of Financial Economics*, **54**:2, pp. 227-64.

[24]   Claessens, S., Demirgüç-Kunt, A., and Huizinga H., 1998, "How Does Foreign Entry Affect the Domestic Banking Market?" *World Bank Policy Research Working Paper* **1918**.

[25]   Claessens, S., Djankov, S., and Nenova, T., 2000, "Corporate Risk around the World." *World Bank Policy Research Working Paper* **2271**.

[26]   Corsetti, G., Presenti, P., and Roubini, N., 1999, "What Caused the Asian Currency and Financial Crisis?" *Japan and the World Economy*, **11**:3, pp. 305-373.

[27]   Corsetti, G., Pericoli, M., and Sbracia, M., 2002, "Some Contagion, Some Interdependence: More Pitfalls in Testing for Contagion." IMF Seminar Series, 2003:74, pp. 1-28.

[28]   De Gregorio, J., Edwards, S., and Valdes, R., 1998, "Capital Controls in Chile: An Assessment." Central Bank of Chile, *Working Paper* **59**.

[29]   De la Torre, A., Levy Yeyati, E., and Schmukler, S., 2002, "Financial Globalization: Unequal Blessings." *International Finance* **5**:3, pp. 335-357.

[30]   Demirguc-Kunt, A., and Detragiache, E., 1999,"Financial Liberalization and Financial Fragility." In Pleskovic B. and J. Stiglitz (eds.), Proceedings of the World Bank Annual Conference on Development Economics, May 1999.

[31]   Demirguc-Kunt, A., Levine, R., and Min, H., 1998, "Opening to Foreign Banks: Issues of Efficiency, Fragility, and Growth." In Proceedings of the Bank of Korea Conference on The Implications of Globalization of World Financial Markets, December.

[32]   Diamond, D., and Dybvig, P., 1983, "Bank Runs, Deposit Insurance, and Liquidity." *Journal of Political Economy*, **91**, pp. 401-419.

[33]   Domowitz, I., Glen, J., and Madhavan, A. 1998, "International Cross-Listing and Order Flow Migration: Evidence from an Emerging Market." *Journal of Finance*, **53**:6, pp. 2001-2027.

[34]   Domowitz, I., Glen, J., and Madhavan, A., 2001, "Liquidity, Volatility and Equity Trading Costs Across Countries and Over Time." *International Finance*, **4**:2, pp. 221-255.

[35]   Dornbusch, R., Park, Y., and Claessens, S., 2000, "Contagion: Understanding How it Spreads." *World Bank Research Observer*, **15**:2, pp. 177-97.

[36]   Edison, H., Levine, R., Ricci, L, and Slok, T, "International Financial Integration and Economic Growth." Journal International Money and Finance, **21**:6, pp. 749-776.

[37]   Edwards, S. and Khan, M., 1985, "Interest Rate Determination in Developing Countries: A Conceptual Framework." *IMF Staff Papers*, **32**, pp. 377-403.

[38]   Edwards, S., 1999, "How Effective are Capital Controls?" *Journal of Economic Perspectives*, **4,** pp. 65-84.

[39]   Edwards, S., 2001, "Capital Mobility and Economic Performance: Are Emerging Economies Different?" *NBER Working Paper* **8076**, January.

[40]   Eichengreen, B., Rose, A., and Wyplosz C., 1996, "Contagious Currency Crises," *Scandinavian Journal of Economics,* **98**:4, pp. 463-484.

[41]   Errunza, V., and Miller, D., 2000, "Market Segmentation and the Cost of Capital in International Equity Markets." *Journal of Financial and Quantitative Analysis*, **35**:4, pp. 577-600.

[42]   Favero, C. A., Giavazzi F., 2000, "Looking for Contagion: Evidence from the ERM." *CEPR Discussion Paper Series* **2591**.

[43]   Foerster, S., and Karolyi, A., 1999, "The Effects of Market Segmentation and Investor Recognition on Asset Prices: Evidence from Foreign Stocks Listing in the United States." *Journal of Finance*; **54**, pp. 981-1013.

[44]   Forbes, K., 2003, "The Asian Flu and Russian Virus: The International Transmission of Crises in Firm-Level Data." *Journal of International Economics*, forthcoming.

[45]   Forbes, K., and Rigobon, R., 2002, "No Contagion, Only Interdependence: Measuring Stock Market Co-movements." *Journal of Finance*, **57**:5, pp. 2223-2261.

[46]   Frankel, J., 1999, "Proposals Regarding Restrictions on Capital Flows," *African Finance Journal*, **1**:1, pp. 92-104.

[47]   Frankel, J., Rose, A., 1996, "Currency Crashes in Emerging Markets: An Empirical Treatment." *Journal of International Economics*, **41**:3-4, pp. 351-366.

[48]   Frankel, J. and Schmukler, S., 1998, "Crisis, Contagion, and Country Funds." in R. Glick (ed.), Managing Capital Flows and Exchange Rates, Cambridge University Press.

[49]   Frankel, J. and Schmukler, S., 2000, "Country Funds and Asymmetric Information." *International Journal of Finance and Economics*, **5**, pp. 177-195.

[50]   Gallego, F., Hernández, L., and Schmidt-Hebbel, K., 1999, "Capital Controls in Chile: Effective? Efficient? Endurable?" Mimeo, Central Bank of Chile.

[51]   Gerlach, S., and Smets, F., 1995, "Contagious Speculative Attacks." *European Journal of Political Economy*, **11**, pp. 45-63.

[52]   Glick R., and Hutchison, M., 1999 "Banking and Currency Crises: How Common Are Twins?" In R. Glick, R. Moreno, and M. Spiegel (eds.), Financial Crises in Emerging Markets, Cambridge University Press.

[53]   Glick, R., and Rose, A., 1999, "Contagion and Trade: Why Are Currency Crises Regional?" *Journal of International Money and Finance*, **18**:4, pp. 603-617.

[54]   Hargis, K., 1997, "When Does Multimarket Trading Improve the Quality of the Primary Market? Evidence from International Cross-Listings." Goldman, Sachs and Co. Working Paper.

[55]   Hargis, K., 2000, "International Cross-Listing and Stock Market Development in Emerging Economies." *International Review of Economics and Finance*, **9**:2, pp. 101-122.

[56]   Hargis, K., and Ramanlal P., 1998, "When Does Internationalization Enhance the Development of Domestic Stock Markets?" *Journal of Financial Intermediation*, **7**, pp. 263-292.

[57]   Henry, P., 2000, "Stock Market Liberalization, Economic Reform, and Emerging Market Equity Prices." *Journal of Finance*, **55**, pp. 529-564.

[58]   Johnson, S., Boone, P., Breach, A., and Friedman, E., 2000, "Corporate Governance in the Asian Financial Crisis." *Journal of Financial Economics*, **58**:1-2, pp. 141-186.

[59]   Kaminsky, G., and Reinhart, C., 2003, "The Center and the Periphery: The Globalization of Financial Turmoil." *NBER Working Paper* **9479**, February.

[60]   Kaminsky, G. and C. Reinhart, 1999, "The Twin Crises: Causes of Banking and Balance of Payments Problems." *American Economic Review*, 89, pp. 473-500.

[61]   Kaminsky, G., and Reinhart, C., 2000, "On Crises, Contagion, and Confusion," *Journal of International Economics*, **51**:1, pp. 145-168.

[62]   Kaminsky, G., Schmukler, S., 2003, "Short-Run Pain, Long-Run Gain: The Effects of Financial Liberalization," *NBER Working Paper* **9787**, June.

[63]   Kaminsky, G., Schmukler, S., 2001, "Short- and Long-Run Integration: Do Capital Controls Matter?" in S. Collins and D. Rodrik (eds.), Brookings Trade Forum 2000, Brookings Institution, Washington, D.C.

[64]   Kaminsky, G., Lyons, R. and Schmukler, S., 2000, "Managers, Investors, and Crisis: Mutual Fund Strategies in Emerging Markets." *NBER Working Paper* **7855**. Forthcoming in *Journal of International Economics*.

[65]   Kaminsky, G., Lyons, R., and Schmukler, S., 2001, "Economic Fragility, Liquidity, and Risk: The Behavior of Mutual Funds During Crises," Mimeo, World Bank.

[66]   Kaplan, E., Rodrik, D., 2001, "Did the Malaysian Capital Controls Work?" *CEPR Discussion Paper Series* **2754**.

[67]   Karolyi, A., 1996, "What Happens to Stock that List Shares Abroad?" Mimeo, University of Western Ontario.

[68]   Karolyi, A., 2002, "The Role of ADRs in the Development and Integration of Emerging Equity Markets." Mimeo.

[69]   Kawai, M., Newfarmer, R., and Schmukler, S., 2001, "Crisis and contagion in East Asia: Nine Lessons," *World Bank Policy Research Working Paper* **2610**. Forthcoming in *Eastern Economic Journal*.

[70] Kim, E., Singal, V., 2000. "Stock Market Openings: Experience of Emerging Economies." *Journal of Business*, **73**, 1, pp. 25-66.

[71] King, R., and Levine, R., 1993, "Finance and Growth: Schumpeter Might Be Right." *Quarterly Journal of Economics*, **108**:3, 717-37.

[72] Kodres, L., and Pritsker, M., 2002, "A Rational Expectations Model of Financial Contagion." *Journal of Finance*, **57**, pp. 769-799.

[73] Krugman, P., 1998, "Saving Asia: It's Time to Get Radical." Fortune, September 67, 1998, pp. 74-80.

[74] Krugman, P., 1999. "Balance Sheets, the Transfer Problem, and Financial Crises." Manuscript. Massachusetts Institute of Technology.

[75] Levine, R., 2000, "International Financial Liberalization and Economic Growth." *Review of International Economics*, **9**:4, pp. 688-702.

[76] Levine, R., Loayza, N., and Beck, T., 2000, "Financial Intermediation and Growth: Causality and Causes." *Journal of Monetary Economics*, **46**:1, pp. 31-77.

[77] Levine, R., and Schmukler, S., 2003, "Migration, Spillovers, and Trade Diversion: The Impact of Internationalization on Stock Market Liquidity." *NBER Working Paper* **9614**.

[78] Levine, R., and Zervos, S., 1998, "Stock Markets, Banks, and Economic Growth." *American Economic Review*, **88**:3, pp. 537-558.

[79] Masson, P., 1999, "Contagion: Monsoonal Effects, Spillovers, and Jumps Between Multiple Equilibria." in P. R. Agenor, M. Miller, D. Vines, and A. Weber (eds), The Asian Financial Crisis: Causes, Contagion and Consequences. Cambridge University Press, Cambridge, UK.

[80] Martinez Peria, S., Powell, A., and Vladkova, I., 2002, "Banking on Foreigners: The Behavior of International Bank Lending to Latin America, 1985-2000.*" World Bank Policy Research Working Paper* **2893**.

[81] McKinnon, R., and Pill, H., 1997, "Credible Economic Liberalizations and Overborrowing." *American Economic Review*, **87**, 2, pp. 189-93.

[82] Miller, D., 1999, "The Market Reaction to International Cross-Listings: Evidence from Depositary Receipts." *Journal of Financial Economics*, **51**, pp. 103-23.

[83] Moel, A., 2001, "The Role of American Depositary Receipts in the Development of Emerging Markets." *Economia*, **2**:1, pp. 209-273.

[84] Montiel, P., and C. Reinhart, 1999, "Do Capital Controls Influence the Volume and Composition of Capital Flows? Evidence from the 1990s." *Journal of International Money and Finance*, **18**, 4, pp. 619-635.

[85] Neal, L., and Weidenmier, M., 2001, "Crises in the Global Economy from Tulips to Today: Contagion and Consequences," *NBER Working Paper* **9147**, September.

[86] Obstfeld, M., 1986, "Rational and Self-fulfilling Balance of Payments Crises." *American Economic Review*, **76**:1, pp. 72-81.

[87] Obstfeld, M., and Taylor, A., 1998, "The Great Depression as a Watershed: International Capital Mobility over the Long Run." In Bordo, M. D., Goldin, C., and N. White, E. N. (eds.), The Defining Moment: The Great Depression and the American Economy in the Twentieth Century, Chicago: University of Chicago Press.

[88] Quinn, D., 2003, "Capital Account Liberalization and Financial Globalization, 1890-1999: A Synoptic View." *International Journal of Finance and Economics*, **8**:3, pp. 189-204.

[89] Rajan, R., and Zingales, L., 1998, "Financial Dependence and Growth." *American Economic Review*, **88**:3, pp. 559-586.

[90] Reisen, H., and Yeches, H., 1993,"Time-Varying Estimates on the Openness of the Capital Account in Korea and Taiwan." *Journal of Development Economics*, **41**, pp. 285-305.

[91] Rigobon, R., 1998, "Informational Speculative Attacks: Good News Is No News." Mimeo, Massachusetts Institute of Technology, January.

[92] Schmukler, S. and Vesperoni, E., 2003, "Financial Globalization and Debt Maturity in Emerging Economies." *IMF Working Paper* **01/95**.

[93] Smith, K., and Sofianos, G., 1997, "The Impact of a NYSE Listing on the Global Trading of Non-US Stocks." *NYSE Working Paper* **97**-02.

[94] Soto, C., 1997, "Controles a los Movimientos de Capitales: Evaluación Empírica del Caso Chileno." Banco Central de Chile.

[95] Stiglitz, J. E., 2000, "Capital Market Liberalization, Economic Growth, and Instability." *World Development*, **28** :6, pp. 1075-1086.

[96] Taylor, A., 1996, "International Capital Mobility in History: The Saving-Investment Relationship." *NBER Working Paper* **5743**.

[97] Tobin, J., 2000, "Financial Globalization." World Development, 28:6, pp. 1101-1104.

[98] Tornell, A., and Westerman, F., 2002, "Boom-Bust Cycles in Middle Income Countries: Facts and Explanation." *NBER Working Paper* **9219**, September.

[99] Tornell, A., Westermann, F., and Martinez, L., 2003, "Liberalization, Growth, and Financial Crises: Lessons from Mexico and the Developing World." Mimeo.

[100] Van Rijckeghem, C., and Weder, B., 2003, "Spillovers Through Banking Centers: A Panel Data Analysis of Bank Flows." *Journal of International Money and Finance*, **22**:4, pp. 483-509.

In: International Macroeconomics: Recent Developments   ISBN 1-59454-901-X
Editor: Amalia Morales Zumaquero pp. 227-255   © 2006 Nova Science Publishers, Inc.

Chapter 11

NEW EMPIRICAL METHODS IN CONTAGION: WHICH ONES WORK, WHICH ONES DON'T?[*]

Roberto Rigobon
MIT, Sloan School of Management, and NBER

1 Introduction

What is contagion? when it takes place? what are the theories behind it? indeed, what are the "relevant" theories behind it? how can we measure them? how can we test them? These are some of the questions that initiated what is today an extremely large literature in international macroeconomics: the contagion literature. Even though we have learned a substantial amount in the last couple of decades, in my view, unfortunately, we still have no satisfactory answers to many of the questions.

In this paper, I analyze the new empirical methods that has been used to measure the channels of contagion. This is a reduced set of the questions addressed in the contagion literature, but certainly, one of the most important ones. Recently, there has been a renew emphasis on studying what drives the shocks from one country to the other using firm level data, using information on hedge funds and mutual funds positions, and using geography and financial variables. I concentrate on these three relatively new strands of the literature. The previous methodologies have already been discussed extensively elsewhere.[1] In the end, the objective is to evaluate the theories that are consistent with the observed pattern of co-movement across international markets. In particular, the idea is to determine which theories explain a sizeable proportion of contagion. Knowing which theories are the most relevant ones will provide clear policy implications to the design of international institutions, as well as to the design of domestic policies to reduce the extent in which shocks are propagated internationally.

The paper is organized as follows: In section 2, I review the three new strands on the literature by summarizing their objectives, their approaches, their procedures, and their

---

[*]I thank Antonio Agresta, Adrienne Manns and Mannig Simidian for superb assistance. All remaining errors are mine. Comments are welcome to Roberto Rigobon, Sloan School of Management, MIT, room E52-431, Cambridge, MA 02142-1347 or to rigobon@mit.edu.
[1]See (265) and (80) for good reviews on the earlier empirical methods.

problems. Section 3 summarizes new evidence that suggests that trade is not the main transmission mechanism of contagion. Finally, in section 4 I conclude and offer avenues of research.

2   Old Questions, but New Approaches

In this section, I discuss three of the newest approaches used in the literature of contagion. These procedures mainly concentrate in answering the question of which channels find support in the data. The literature on contagion started by trying to understand when contagion had taken place; what were the characteristics of the transmission mechanism? its stability? its overall measurement? etc. Today the existence of contagion is not an issue. We know which crises were contagious and which ones don't. However, we just do not know why. The new empirical literature reflects this implicit accord and aims to offer an answer.

The three approaches either use firm level data to study the channels of contagion, estimate the contagion using spatial models, or concentrate on the importance of financial linkages by analyzing hedge/mutual funds positions. This section summarizes each of them.

2.1   Firm Level Data and the Channels of Contagion

The literature using firm level data is concerned with the question on how much can trade explain of the observed pattern of contagion / co-movement. Prominent examples in the literature studying the role of trade and financial linkages on the transmission mechanism are (38), (93), (98), and (184). Most of these papers study the impact of a crisis in one country on firm's stock prices on other countries. In general, these papers test the presence of trade channels — or what is also known as real linkages. The usual setup is that the return of firm i in country j at time t is given by

$$\Delta s_{i,j,t} = \alpha_i + (\beta_0 + \beta_1 * Trade_{i,j,c}) * \Delta s_{c,t} + \varepsilon_{i,j,t} \qquad (1)$$

where $\Delta s_{i,j,t}$ is the change in stock prices in the country of analysis, for the particular firm under study, $\Delta s_{c,t}$ is the change in the stock market index in the country under crisis, $Trade_{i,j,c}$ is the trade relationship between the firm i in country j with country c.

There are a variety of specifications for trade relationships. The variable $Trade_{i,j,c}$ can be bilateral trade in the same industrial sector across the two countries, it can be a dummy which takes value of one if the firm belong to the major exporting industries of country c, it can be total bilateral trade or total trade with major developed markets, etc. Indeed, the idea is use the firm variation to test for the different trade channels.

One advantage of this model is that it is possible to control for country and time specific transmission effects. For example, assume that instead of equation (1) the true model is the following

$$\Delta s_{i,j,t} = \alpha_i + (\beta_0 + \beta_1 * Trade_{i,j,c} + \beta_2 * D_{j,c,t}) * \Delta s_{c,t} + \varepsilon_{i,j,t} \qquad (2)$$

where $D_{j,c,t}$ is an unobservable variable. The intuition is that there could be an aggregate channel of transmission across the two countries that is common to all stocks. For example, a common shock to all firms stock prices which is indistinguishable of trade relationships at the aggregate level. Indeed, in the aggregate specification it is possible that $D_{j,c,t}$ is correlated with $Trade_{j,c}$ which is given

$$Trade_{j,c} = \sum_i Trade_{i,j,c}.$$

In this set up the aggregate regression

$$\Delta s_{j,t} = \alpha + (\beta_0 + \beta_1 * Trade_{j,c} + \beta_2 * D_{j,c,t}) * \Delta s_{c,t} + \varepsilon_{j,t} \qquad (3)$$

produces biased and inconsistent estimates because of the omitted variable bias.

In this setup, compute the abnormal return for each firm by subtracting the aggregate return equation (2) from the firm level return equation (3). This is equivalent to computing the abnormal returns per firm or industry and running the same specification. Because the common transmission mechanism works as a fixed effects, the in-between specification is

$$\Delta s_{i,j,t} - \Delta s_{j,t} = (\alpha_i - a) + (\beta_1 * (Trade_{i,j,c} - Trade_{j,c})) * \Delta s_{c,t} + \varepsilon_{i,j,t} - \varepsilon_{j,tf} \quad (4)$$

where β_1 can be consistently estimated.[2]

The main advantage of the methodology is that it can estimate consistently the trade channel by looking at the firm variation. However, the main disadvantage is that it is under-estimating the overall transmission mechanism by exactly eliminating the common aspect. For instance, the R^2 of equation (4) is not how much trade explains of the contagion, but how much it explains the firm level variation. This might be an important question but not the relevant one when we are aiming to understand why contagion is taking place. In other words, the significance of β_1 indicates how good is trade in explaining the cross-sectional variation, not how much trade explains of the transmission of shocks. In fact, β_1 captures the importance of the trade channel only if $D_{j,c,t}$ is uncorrelated with $Trade_{j,c}-$ But if this is the case, there is no need to use firm level data in the first place. On the other hand, it is likely that $D_{j,c,t}$ is correlated with $Trade_{j,c}$ then the interpretation of the coefficients in equation (4) have to be taken cautiously.

As I discuss further in Section 3, I believe that trade contributes little to the overall contagion, but have explanatory power on the cross-section. For example, it could be the case that trade explains less than 2 percent of the aggregate contagion, but 98 percent of the firm differences. But the puzzle in contagion is not why one stock price falls by a larger percent more than other, the question is why some countries, at some times suffer an overall drop that is several times their usual standard deviation.

There is another disadvantage that is important to remember − if this avenue of research is to be pursued. The firm level data, in most cases, is yearly and contagion is a high frequency event. The time aggregation bias is likely to produce spurious regressions. This is particularly important in emerging markets, where policy actions are extremely likely to exist in this time frame. Hence, in the end, what we could be assigning or measuring as the contagion effects at firm levels could be the result of the differential effect that policies have.

---

[2]It is important to notice that the residuals now have cross-firm correlations and therefore it is crucial to run FGLS to correct for it.

In conclusion, this methodology always biases downward the importance of any aggregate contagion channel. I believe that around crises the common component of individual shocks is large, especially during contagious. For example, theories that explain contagion based on financial linkages or changes in risk premium are going to be obviated by the methodology. Therefore, if contagion occurs as an aggregate event, then moving to firm level data actually obscures the question of what are the relevant transmission mechanisms.

2.2 Spatial Models of Contagion

Spatial models are becoming popular because of their simplicity and because they are able to capture one of the most prominent characteristics of contagion – its regional features. Since the seminal contribution by (87) regional effects have been found over and over again in the contagion literature. Regardless of the methodologies of the procedures to measure the transmission mechanism, it is a fact that contagion has a strong regional and neighbor effect. See (70), (83), (82), (148), (25), (24), (86), (115), (138), (262), (265)and (211) for more examples.

Spatial models take this aspect to the core of the estimation and evaluate the importance of these channels at the aggregate level. This is an infant literature, however, and only very few paper have attempted to estimate contagion – see (149) and (187). The general idea of Spatial models is to estimate aggregate regressions explaining the propagation of shocks across countries where the channel of transmission is related to neighbor, regional, and distance variables.[3] The idea is to estimate for each country

$$\Delta s_{j,t} = \alpha + (\beta_0 + \beta_1 * Spatial_{j,c}) * \Delta s_{c,t} + \varepsilon_{j,t}$$

where $Spatial_{j,c}$ include variables that are related to distance, sharing border, regional dummies, or network matrices describing the propagation.

For example, a typical specification is the following

$$
\begin{bmatrix} \Delta s_{1,t} \\ \Delta s_{2,t} \\ \vdots \\ \Delta s_{N,t} \end{bmatrix} = \alpha + \left(\beta_0 + \beta_1 * \begin{bmatrix} 0 & d_{1,2} & \cdots & d_{1,N} \\ d_{2,1} & 0 & \cdots & d_{2,N} \\ \vdots & \vdots & \ddots & \vdots \\ d_{N,1} & d_{N,2} & \cdots & 0 \end{bmatrix} \right) * \begin{bmatrix} \Delta s_{1,t} \\ \Delta s_{2,t} \\ \vdots \\ \Delta s_{N,t} \end{bmatrix} + \begin{bmatrix} \varepsilon_{1,t} \\ \varepsilon_{2,t} \\ \vdots \\ \varepsilon_{N,t} \end{bmatrix}
$$

$$(5)$$

where the residuals are assumed to be uncorrelated across countries, and $d_{i,j}$ is either the distance between country i and country j, or a dummy indicating they share border, or a distance variable adjusted by relative GDP's ($d_{i,j} = dist_{i,j} * GDP_j / GDP_i$) which captures the fact that shocks generated in larger countries should have lager effects.

The network spatial model assumes that contagion is transmitted to the closest neighbors of each country, and from there to other countries. So, for example, during the crisis in Mexico, the contagion from Mexico to Argentina requires that the shock is transmitted to Honduras and Guatemala, and from there to Panama, and from there to Colombia, etc. until we reach Argentina. Hence, closer countries receive a contagion of β_1, countries that

---

[3]These papers use measures of distance to investigate the extent of contagion; and therefore, they are in the spirit of (70) which also find that regional variables are significant explaining contagion.

need two branches to be reached suffer β_1^2 contagion, and countries that require N branches suffer only β_1^N.

In the end, several of these matrices can be constructed using different criteria or theories, and their relative importance can be easily assess.

The main advantage of this procedure is that the identification problem is easily solved, and the issues of endogeneity (so important in the contagion literature)[4] can be dealt specifically. The reason is the following, define

$$\Phi\left(\alpha, \beta_0, \beta_1\right) = \left(1 - \beta_0 - \beta_1 \begin{bmatrix} 0 & d_{1,2} & \cdots & d_{1,N} \\ d_{2,1} & 0 & \cdots & d_{2,N} \\ \vdots & \vdots & \ddots & \vdots \\ d_{N,1} & d_{N,2} & \cdots & 0 \end{bmatrix}\right) \begin{bmatrix} \Delta s_{1,t} \\ \Delta s_{2,t} \\ \vdots \\ \Delta s_{N,t} \end{bmatrix} - \alpha.$$

The coefficients α, β_0, β_1 from equation (5) can be estimated by GMM by imposing that the off-diagonal elements of the covariance matrix of Φ are zero. This will estimate the coefficients and the country structural variances. Notice that even though by construction all countries are simultaneously determined the parameters of interest are estimated consistently.

The main problem is the interpretation of the results. Unfortunately spatial variables lack of economic meaning from the propagation point of view. For example, it is the case that countries in the same region have similar policies, similar ratings, they have stronger trade relationships, and more importantly, they are usually part of the same asset class. So, imagine that the true model of contagion is one in which the transmission takes place entirely through financial linkages that are organized around a geographical criteria, then spatial models might be capturing financial channels only. What makes the problem even harder is that there is strong multicollinearity between spatial, trade, and financial variables.

2.3   Financial Linkages and Hedge/Mutual Funds Positions

Financial linkages has received considerable attention by the empirical literature. There are two strands of the literature. One that estimates the effect directly. Most of these papers try to find the aggregate contagion effect through the different financial intermediaries – banks, hedge funds, mutual funds, etc. And a second one that measures indirectly the relevance on the financial linkages.

2.3.1   Direct Evidence

The literature started by testing the role of bank relationships in the transmission of contagion. (141) find support for the common lender hypothesis in bank lending for the Asian

---

[4]In the contagion literature see (46), (47), (79), (80), (150), and (267) for papers dealing with the endogeneity. All these papers use heteroscedasticity to solve the problem of identification. The first reference to identification using shifts in second moments was introduced by (253). More recently, this identification approach has been extended and further developed. (267) has extended the method when the variance can be described by regimes. for a detailed description of the methods used here. (245) study the case in which the residuals have an ARCH or GARCH structure. (248) and (249) analyze the non-linear case. For other applications to time series see (272), (273), (?), (?). For applications in cross-sectional data see (?).

case. (223) and (224) study the transmission that takes place through the banking sector in European countries, and also find that it plays an important role in the propagation of shocks.

The banking sector is a small part of the international financial system. Recent papers have used newer data sets providing information about the positions and decisions of the other financial institutions. Kenneth Froot, together with a series of coauthors, have studied the properties of international equity flows to a broad class of international investors (actually, almost the universe of them). See (107), (108), and (106). In these paper, he does not discuss the problem of contagion specifically, but his evidence suggests that there is important momentum trading and strong correlations on portfolio reallocations among investors – both should drive contagion.

Using mutual fund data, (110) study the behavior of mutual funds around crises, and find results indicating that the financial linkages are an important determinant of the transmission mechanism. Similarly, (144) find that holdings of mutual funds exhibit important contagion. See also (81), (147), (212), and (210) for further studies on investors portfolio holdings and contagion.

It is important to notice that these papers have not compared the different channels – i.e. how much is explained by trade versus how much by financial linkages. The only papers that have done so have used firm level data, and as was argued above, this results will tend to underestimate the importance of the financial linkages (or any other aggregate channel).

2.3.2   Indirect Evidence

The strongest evidence on the relative importance of financial linkages over other channels of contagion comes from high frequency data and using changes in credit ratings to evaluate the change in the co-movement. (146) show that credit rating downgrades affect both the level and the degree of contagion in the short run. clearly, a change in the credit rating should have no implications on trade patterns in the short run, but they have a strong impact on the conditional correlation. Additionally, (86) show that the access to financial markets of several countries is heavily affected by countries suffering crises elsewhere. Both papers indicate the importance of financial linkages on the access to external funds and the price of the stock market.

In the same line of argument, (262) finds that the degree of contagion, or co-movement, between Mexico and other major Latin American countries shifted significantly when Mexico was upgraded to investment grade. In fact, the propagation of shocks measured as the point estimates correlations reduced by more than a half (from about 70 percent to less than 27). I argue that this is evidence that financial linkages are the main transmission mechanism explaining co-movement across countries – in the four months period where the analysis is performed trade patterns did not change at all and still the co-movement shifted dramatically.

3   The Need of a New Approach

In my view, the empirical literature on contagion has evolved along two stages or genera-tions. The first stage dealt with the question of existence. The literature started from the simple question of whether contagion exists and when. I believe that now we do have good methods to detect contagion and the empirical literature has dealt with most of the prob-lems present in the data. The second stage (or generation) concentrated on the evidence of the different theories. The new question, in principle was why contagion existed. The purpose was to evaluate and text each of the theories, and most of the empirical evidence has devoted to study each channel separately: bilateral trade, trade of similar goods in the same world market, monetary policy coordination, political and policy contagion, common lenders, common financial markets, common asset classes, etc. In general, the message from this literature is that everything matters depending on the time, crises, and countries chosen. Even though this process has been useful to understand what are the main trans-mission mechanisms, I believe it is time that the literature starts comparing the different theories.

Recent papers had raised the same challenge (See (?), (261), (145)) and in this section I would like to summarize their findings. These papers are mainly distinguishing between the two most frequently studied channels in the literature: trade versus financial linkages. These paper describe two approaches that will be useful in future research to disentangle the importance of each channel. I name the approaches by looking at the economic problem they intend to solve.

3.1   Sample Selection

Most of the literature studies the propagation of shocks across emerging markets. I find interesting that in most of these papers, the countries included in the analysis are Argentina, Brazil, Chile, Colombia, Mexico, Peru, and Venezuela in Latin America, and China, Hong Kong, Korea, Indonesia, Malaysia, Philippines, Singapore, Thailand, and Taiwan in South East Asia. These are what I call the "Sweet 16".[5] It is interesting that this list of countries coincides exactly with the countries that are important for international financial markets.

For example, Honduras, Guatemala, El Salvador, Nicaragua, Belize, Ecuador, Panama, Costa Rica, Bolivia, Paraguay, Uruguay, not a single island in the Caribbean, nor a single island in the Pacific, nor Vietnam, and several other smaller countries in these two conti-nents are not in this list (what about Africa where usually the only country considered is South Africa). The countries excluded are both small countries in terms of GDP, but they are even smaller in terms of their relative importance in international markets.

One very interesting aspect is that this smaller countries did not suffer from contagion during the Mexican 94, Asian 97 and Russian 98 crises − the most violent ones. Why these countries did not suffer from contagion? because they do not trade in goods? Absolutely not! Indeed, the trade share and the measures of openness of these smaller countries is much larger than the Sweet 16.

---

[5]"Sweet 16" is in regards to the NCAA College Basketball playoffs. If you do not know what this is, next March you should.

The fact that we consistently include only the Sweet 16 countries in the contagion analysis implies that the estimates on trade could be capturing financial linkages, and the results could be spurious. Let me propose a model that will clarify this point. Assume the return of stock markets is given by

$$AX_t = \varepsilon_t$$

where the matrix A describes the contemporaneous relationships across stock markets where the diagonal is equal to one, and the off-diagonal elements are $-\alpha_{ij}$. Assume that ε_t are the structural shocks which we assume to be uncorrelated across countries. If we look at the structural equation of country i it looks as follows

$$x_{i,t} = \underbrace{\alpha_{i1}x_{1,t} + \alpha_{i2}x_{2,t} + \cdots + \alpha_{iN}x_{N,t}}_{\text{does not include } i} + \varepsilon_{i,t}.$$

Assume that each element α_{ij} is equal to the following model

$$\alpha_{ij} = \alpha_0 + \alpha_1 Trade_{ij} + \alpha_2 Financial_{ij}$$

where α_0 is the average world linkage, $Trade_{ij}$ are the variables related to trade relationships (either bilateral or with a third market) and $Financial_{ij}$ are the variables related to financial linkages (same asset class, common lender, etc.).

In the typical empirical implementation when financial variables are unobservable, the following regression is estimated for each country

$$x_{i,t} = \sum \left(a_0 + a_1 Trade_{ij} \right) x_{j,t} + \nu_{i,t}.$$

In this model, we have omitted variable bias if $Trade_{ij}$ and $Financial_{ij}$ are correlated. In fact, if $Trade_{ij}$ and $Financial_{ij}$ are positively correlated the estimates of a_1 are upward biased. Because the countries that are always included in the contagion literature have strong financial linkages (all the Sweet 16 are important for international financial markets) we should expect that $Trade_{ij}$ and $Financial_{ij}$ are highly correlated. For example, the Latin American asset class is mostly described by the 7 countries listed above, and similar for the South East Asian class. So, it is possible that all the trade results are driven by this spurious regression.

The simplest test is to include variables that have strong trade linkages but that DO NOT have strong financial linkages. In other words, introduce the small countries in the analysis. In this case, because a large set of countries has zero (or almost zero) in the financial linkages variable the bias on a_1 should decrease.

It should be obvious what the result of this exercise provides — trade is not important for the transmission mechanism. And the reason is that contagion to the small countries is zero not because they do not trade goods, it is because they do not trade financial assets.

For instance, assume that we want to explain the contagion from Russia to the rest of the world and we only analyze the "Sweet 16". The trade relationship between Russia and Brazil is small. Obviously they trade some similar goods with the U.S., but in general the variable $Trade$ for those two countries is small. So, because the contagion from Russia to Brazil (and for that matter to all the big seven countries in Latin America) was substantial, the only possibility is to estimate a large a_1. In other words, given that a large shock in

Russia (big negative $x_{russia,t}$) caused a big drop in the stock markets in Latin America (relatively big negative $x_{i,t}$) we need a large a_1 that multiplied by a small $Trade_{russia,i}$ produces a sizeable elasticity. However, if this elasticity where to be correct, then if we were to predict the impact of Russia on other countries in eastern Europe (which had stronger trade relationships with Russia than Latin America) and other countries in Asia and Africa (such as Egypt, Israel, Pakistan, Syria, etc. which also have stronger trade relationships with Russia than Latin America) we should have expected much bigger drops in stock markets than the ones we actually observed. In fact, if we choose the closest trade partners of Russia the effect through trade is tiny (Finland, Norway, Ukraine, U.S., and Check Republic).

In the end, doing the exercise should indicate that trade relationships have little to do with the contagion observed in emerging markets. It is important to highlight that this does not mean that trade is irrelevant. Still it is the case that trade will explain the differences across firms and sectors. But the average effect (which is what we should be aiming to explain) cannot be rationalized by trade.

Finally, I believe that trade is important in developed economies. In fact, the theories of contagion based on financial linkages require that financial markets are not well functioning, and therefore, I would expect trade to be the most important mechanism in developed markets. Hence, not everything is lost in this respect.[6]

3.2 Anticipated versus Unanticipated

The second aspect that casts doubts on all real linkages as the transmission mechanism of contagion is the fact that the contagious crises have been roughly unanticipated, while the not contagious ones have occurred in smaller countries, not belonging to the "watch list" of financial markets, or more importantly, anticipated.

In the world there have been several events that have caused contagion: The Bretton Woods collapse in the early 70's; the Debt Crises at the beginning of the 80's; the U.S. stock market collapse in 1987; the ERM abandonment in early 90's; the Mexican crisis in 94; the Asian crises in 1997; the Russian collapse in 1998; the high-tech crisis in the U.S. in 2000; September 11; and the Enron − accounting scandals in the U.S. All these events occurred in relatively big financial markets are transmitted around the world either among developed economies, or at least, among developing markets.

Paradoxically, during the same periods, we have had at least other 53 crisis that have not being contagious.[7] In this list (which is not exhaustive whatsoever) there are countries that belong to the list of contagious crises indicated above, but that in these collapses they did not cause contagion. Granted, in the list of 53 crises several come from small markets, however, not all of them. Excluding some of the OECD countries, there are four crises that deserve our attention − the most recent ones: Brazil 99, Ecuador 00, Turkey 01, Argentina 02. These countries are relevant for financial markets, and still these massive collapses had almost no international implications. Brazilians depreciation has some effects in Argentina

---

[6]Actually, I have written papers in this regard where the impact of trade relationship is studied. See (260).

[7]The crises are: four recent ones that will be discussed in detail: Brazil 99, Ecuador 00, Turkey 01, Argentina 02 and then the rest: Argentina 70-75-81-86-89-90, Bolivia 85, Brazil 86-89-90-91, Chile 71-72-73-74-76, Colombia 85, Denmark 79, Ecuador 99, Finland 82, Indonesia 78-86, Israel 74-77- 83-84, Malaysia 75, Mexico 76, Norway 86, Peru 76-87, Philippines 70, Spain 76-77-82, Sweden 77-81-82, Thailand 78-84, Turkey 70-80-94, Uruguay 71, Venezuela 84-86-89-94-95.

– but here the trade channel might explain the propagation given that the countries share at least 30 percent of their international trade. Argentina's collapse created a crisis in Uruguay – again an extremely large trade relationship – but it had almost no effect in Chile and Brazil. If trade were so powerful that countries with tiny trade relationships like Russia and Brazil had a strong transmission mechanism, how it is possible that Brazil has zero effect in Russia, and Argentina zero in Mexico?

In fact, if we concentrate on Mexico 94, Asia 97, Russia 98, Brazil 99, Turkey, 01, and Argentina 02, all six crises are of the same order of magnitude (regarding the size of the collapse in asset prices), from countries that are relatively the same in size, the same in international markets, and still the first three were contagious and the last three were not.

The main difference is their degree of anticipation. The first three crises were not anticipated in the same degree as the second set of three crises. This point has been raised by (145), (?), and (261). (145) measure the degree of anticipation by the spread on sovereign debt. They find that the spread increased in Brazil, Turkey and Argentina well before the crisis took place (at least 6 months in each of them), while the spreads in Mexico, Asia, and Russia barely moved before the exchange rate collapses.

Obviously there is an important problem of using interest rates, given that interest rates are the symptom of a crisis and not a measure of their anticipation. This problem has been solved by (261) where they measure the degree of anticipation by looking at the number of news in international news papers to evaluate the degree of anticipation – where the news are collected from LexisNexis. They find the exact same pattern.

Figures ?? to ?? plot the news for each country together with the exchange rate. The daily news variable is measured on the left hand side axis, and the spot exchange rate is measured on the right hand side axis.

There are two clear patterns in these figures: anticipated and unanticipated crises. The best example of the unanticipated crisis is Thailand. In this case the number of news increase only after the exchange rate devaluation has taken place. In fact, the number of news the month before the crisis is about the same as the one that exists in any given month before the crisis. The Russian case looks similar, although, there is some anticipation. Notice that the concentration of news increases slightly when the economy is approaching the crisis. Almost the same pattern can be seem in Mexico. On the other hand, observe that the Argentinean, Brazilian and Turkish experiences are very different. In these cases, the number of news increased significantly at least six months before the crisis took place. Indeed, the collapses of the exchange rates only increased the average number of news slightly the week after. In the Turkish and Argentinean cases the number of news actually goes down the two weeks after the depreciation of the exchange rate (in comparison to the two weeks before). In both cases, the news picked up again when market participants realized that (i) the political crisis deepened and (ii) international lending institutions considered that the first adjustment of the exchange rate was insufficient. (261) show formally these results.

This is evidence that financial linkages is the only channel consistent with these findings. A simple example might reinforce the intuition. Assume that the channel of contagion is trade and assume that an unanticipated devaluation of ten percent in one country requires a devaluation of three percent on another one. The drop of three percent in the second country is the fall in the dollar wage needed to achieve external and internal balance. In other words, this is the change in relative prices that returns the economy to equilibrium. If the crisis is perfectly anticipated, investors devalue at the time the information is provided and the overall effect is the exact same three percent − some taking place when the possibility of the crisis is realized, and some taking place when the actual collapse occurs. In the end, both reach the same steady state because it is only that shift in relative prices the one that moves the economy to the equilibrium. These are the implications that arise from general equilibrium models with non-tradable sector, such as the seminal contributions by (3), (4) and (2) in the Dependent Economy, or in models with only tradable goods such as in (1) in the context of a Ricardian economy.

On the other hand, financial linkages imply that the overall contagion effect might be different depending on the degree of anticipation. To clarify the intuition assume that contagion takes place because investors are subject to margin calls, à la Calvo.[8] In this model, a fall in one asset price leads to a decrease in value of the investors' portfolio. If this drop is large enough, so the value of the portfolio is below some threshold, then international investors are required to set aside some cash (to cover for the losses). If investors sell off some of the other assets in the portfolio to cover the margin calls, and this selling puts price pressures in other asset prices, then contagion is generated. In this simple framework, if the crisis is unanticipated, the effect on the portfolio takes the full impact of the price drop, and the margin call is maximized. If the crisis is anticipated, international investors take actions that shall reduce (or minimize) the price impact.

4   Final Thoughts

The theoretical literature on contagion has offerred several theories to explain the co-movement that takes place across countries' stock markets during crises, and among emerging and developed markets. The empirical literature, on the other hand, initially devoted its attention to the existence of contagion, and only after it was confirmed, it evaluated the significance of each of the theories. In the end, most of the theories find some support in the data.

Even though I agree on the theoretical soundness of most of the theories, it is hard for me to believe that all of them are equally relevant in explaining the propagation of shocks across emerging markets. I believe that now it is time to test the relevance of each one. This paper offers avenues to achieve this objective. There are important issues of sample selection and the release of information that have to be taken care to compare the different theories of contagion.

My preliminary reading of these new literature is that trade explains a small proportion of the observed co-movement. Trade is only able to explain the differential impact on firms, but not the aggregate behavior. In other words, if we take two firms affected by the Russian crisis trade explains the difference in the reactions between the two. This is important, however, it is small part of the international co-movement. It is crucial to remember that this is not a statement about the soundness of trade or other real linkages theories − not at all. This is a claim about the variance decomposition if we were able to compute it. The aim should be, therefore, to understand which theories have practical bearing, and to lead research toward that goal.

---

[8] See (40).

References

[1] Rudiger Dornbusch and Stanley Fischer and Paul Samuelson, 1977, Comparative Advantage, Trade, and Payments in a Ricardian Model with a Continuum of Goods, *American Economic Review,* vol. 67, No. 4, pp. 823-839.

[2] Rudiger Dornbusch, 1980, *Open Economy Macroeconomics*, Basic Books, New York.

[3] W. Salter, 1959, Internal and External Balance: The Role of Price and Expenditure Effects, *The Economic Record*, pp. 226-38.

[4] Trevor W. Swan, 1960, Economic Control in a Dependent Economy, Economic Record, vol. 36, pp. 51-66.

[5] Tim Bollerslev and Roberto F. Engle and Jeffrey M. Wooldridge, 1988, A Capital Asset Pricing Model with Time Varying Covariance, *Journal of Political Economy*, vol. 96, pp. 116-31

[6] Tim Bollerslev, 1990, Modelling the Coherence in Short-Run Nominal Exchange Rates: A Multivariate Generalized ARCH Model, *Review of Economics and Statistics*, vol. 72, pp. 498-505

[7] Francis X. Diebold and Mark Nerlove, 1989, The Dynamics of Exchange Rate Volatility: A Multivariate Latent Factor ARCH Model, *Journal of Applied Econometrics*, vol. 4, pp. 1-21

[8] Darrell Duffie and Kenneth Singleton, 1993, Simulated Moments Estimator of Markov Models of Asset Prices, *Econometrica*, vol. 61, pp. 929-52

[9] Robert F. Engle and Victor K. Ng and Michael Rothschild, 1990, Asset Pricing with a Factor-ARCH Covariance Structure: Empirical Estimates for Treasury Bills, *Journal of Econometrics*, vol. 45, pp. 213-37

[10] Robert F. Engle and Kenneth F. Kroner, 1993, Multivariate Simultaneous Generalized ARCH, University of California at San Diego, vol. Mimeo

[11] A. R. Gallant and G. Tauchen, 1996, Which Moments to Match?, *Econometric Theory,* vol. 12, No. 4, pp. 657-81

[12] C. Gourieroux and A. Monfort and E. Renault, 1993, Indirect Inference, *Journal of Applied Econometrics,* vol. 8, pp. S85-118

[13] Graciela Kaminsky and Sergio Schmukler, February, 2001, Emerging Markets Instability: Do Sovereign Ratings Affect Country Risk and Stock Returns?, George Washington University Mimeo

[14] William P. Killeen and Richard K. Lyons and Michael J. Moore, 2001, *Fixed Vs. Floating: Lessons from EMS Order Flow,* University of California at Berkeley, vol. Mimeo

[15] D. Abreu and D. Pearce and E. Stacchetti, 1990, Toward a Theory of Discounted Repeated Games with Imperfect Monitoring, *Econometrica*, vol. 58, No. 5, pp. 1041-1063

[16] Alberto Ades, 1997, *The Economics of Balance of Payments Crises and Contagion*, In Goldman Sachs, The Foreign Exchange Market

[17] Alberto Ades, 1997, *The Economics of Balance of Payments Crises and Contagion*, In Goldman Sachs, The Foreign Exchange Market

[18] Pierre-Richard Agénor and Joshua Aizenman, 1997, Contagion and Volatility with Imperfect Credit Markets, *IMF Working Paper* **WP/97/127**

[19] Pierre-Richard Agénor and Joshua Aizenman, 1997, Contagion and Volatility with Imperfect Credit Markets, *IMF Working Paper* **WP/97/127**

[20] D. W. K. Andrews and E. Zivot, 1992, Further Evidence on the Great Crash, the Oil Price Shock, and the Unit Root Hypothesis, *Journal of Business anmd Economic Statistics,* vol. 10, pp. 251-70

[21] Eduardo Fernandez Arias and Ricardo Hausmann and Roberto Rigobon, 1998, Contagion in Bond Markets, *IDB Working Paper*

[22] Jushan Bai, 1997, Estimation of a Change Point in Multiple Regression Models, *The Review of Economics and Statistics,* pp. 551-563

[23] Hushan Bai and Robin L. Lumsdaine and James H. Stock, 1998, Testing for and Dating Common Breaks in Multivariate Time Series, *Review of Economic Studies,* vol. 65, pp. 395-432

[24] Taimur Baig and Ilan Goldfajn, February, 2000, *The Russian Default and the Contagion to Brazil,* Universidade Catolica, Mimeo

[25] Taimur Baig and Ilan Goldfajn, 1998, *Financial Markets Contagion in the Asian Crises,* IMF Mimeo

[26] A. Banerjee and R. L. Lumsdaine and J. H. Stock, 1992, Recursive and Sequential Tests of the Unit Root and Trend Break Hypotheses: Theory and International Evidence, *Journal of Business and Economic Statistics,* vol. 10, pp. 271-88

[27] Abhijit Banerjee, August, 1992, A Simple Model of Herd Behavior, *Quarterly Journal of Economics,* vol. 107, No. 3, pp. 797-817

[28] A. P. Barten and Lise Salvas Bronsard, November, 1970, Two-Stage Least Squares Estimation with Shift in the Structural Form, *Econometrica*, vol. 38, No. 6, pp. 938-941

[29] Ritu Basu, 2002, Financial Contagion and Investor Learning: An Empirical Investigation, *IMF Working Paper:* **02-218**

[30] Ritu Basu, 1998, Contagion Crises: The Investor's Logic, University of California, Los Angeles, mimeo

[31] Santiago Bazdresch and Alejandro Werner, February, 2000, *Contagion of International Financial Crises: The Case of Mexico,* Banco de Mexico, Mimeo

[32] Roberto Benelli, January, 1999, *Testing for Contagion with Markov Switching Vector Autoregressions*, MIT Mimeo

[33] Roberto Benelli, January, 1999, *Testing for Contagion with Markov Switching Vector Autoregressions,* MIT Mimeo

[34] Elisabetta Bertero and Colin Mayer, 1990, Structure and Performance: Global Interdependence of Stock Markets Around the Crash of October 1987, *European Economic Review,* vol. 34, pp. 1155-1180

[35] Elisabetta Bertero and Colin Mayer, 1990, Structure and Performance: Global Interdependence of Stock Markets Around the Crash of October 1987, *European Economic Review,* vol. 34, pp. 1155-1180

[36] B.H. Boyer and M.S. Gibson and M. Loretan, 1999, Pitfalls in Tests for Changes in Correlations, Federal Reserve Board, *International Finance Discussion Paper,* vol. 597R

[37] Brian H. Boyer and Michael S. Gibson and Mico Loretan, March, 1999, Pitfalls in Tests for Changes in Correlations, Federal Reserve Board, *IFS Discussion Paper* No. **597R**

[38] Robin J. Brooks and Marco Del Negro, January, 2003, Firm-Level Evidence on Global Integration, *IMF Working Paper*

[39] Guillermo Calvo and Enrique Mendoza, December, 1998, Rational Contagion and the Globalization of Security Markets, University of Maryland, vol. Mimeo

[40] Guillermo Calvo, February, 1999, Contagion in Emerging Markets: When Wall Street is a Carrier, University of Maryland, vol. Mimeo

[41] Guillermo Calvo and Enrique Mendoza, December, 1998, Rational Contagion and the Globalization of Security Markets, University of Maryland, vol. Mimeo

[42] Guillermo Calvo, February, 1999, Contagion in Emerging Markets: When Wall Street is a Carrier, University of Maryland, vol. Mimeo

[43] Guillermo Calvo and Enrique Mendoza, 2000, Rational Contagion and the Globalization of Security Markets, *Journal of International Economics*, vol. 51, pp. 79-113

[44] Andrew Caplin and John Leahy, June, 1994, Business as Usual, Market Crashes, and Wisdom After the Fact, American Economic Review, vol. 84, No. 3, pp. 548-565

[45] Andrew Caplin and John Leahy, June, 1994, Business as Usual, Market Crashes, and Wisdom After the Fact, American Economic Review, vol. 84, No. 3, pp. 548-565

[46] Guglielmo Maria Caporale and Andrea Cipollini and Nicola Spagnolo, February, 2002, *Testing for Contagion: A Conditional Correlation Analysis.*, CEMFE Mimeo

[47] Guglielmo Maria Caporale and Andrea Cipollini and Panicos Demetriades, October, 2002, Monetary Policy and the Exchange Rate During the Asian Crisis: Identification Through Heteroskedasticity, CEMFE Mimeo

[48] Paul Cashin and Manmohan Kumar and C. John McDermott, 1995, International Integration of Equity Markets and Contagion Effects, *IMF Working Paper* **WP/95/110**

[49] Paul Cashin and Manmohan Kumar and C. John McDermott, 1995, International Integration of Equity Markets and Contagion Effects, *IMF Working Paper* **WP/95/110**

[50] V.V. Chari and Patrick Kehoe, March, 1999, Herds of Hot Money, Federal Reserve Bank of Minneapolis Research Department, vol. Mimeo

[51] V.V. Chari and Patrick Kehoe, March, 1999, Herds of Hot Money, *Federal Reserve Bank of Minneapolis Research Department,* vol. Mimeo

[229] Songnian Chen and Shakeeb Khan, December, 1999, $\sqrt{n}$-Consistent Estimation of Heteroskedastic Sample Selection Models, University of Rochester, Mimeo

[53] Terence Tai-Leung Chong, October, 1995, Partial Parameter Consistency in a Misspecified Structural Change Model, *Economics Letters,* vol. 49, No. 4, pp. 351-57

[54] Terence Tai-Leung Chong, 1999, Asymptotic Distribution of the Sup-Wald Statistic under Specification Errors, *Structural Change and Economic Dynamics,* vol. 10, pp. 421-30

[55] Ray Chou and Victor Ng and Lynn Pi, 1994, Cointegration of International Stock Market Indices, *IMF Working Paper* **WP/94/94**

[56] Ray Chou and Victor Ng and Lynn Pi, 1994, Cointegration of International Stock Market Indices, *IMF Working Paper* **WP/94/94**

[57] G. C. Chow, 1960, Test of Equality Between Sets of Coefficients in Two Linear Regressions., *Econometrica*, vol. 28, pp. 591-605

[58] Stijn Claessens and Rudiger Dornbusch and Yung Chul Park, 2000, Contagion: How It Spreads and How It Can Be Stopped?, Mimeo. Paper prepared for World Bank/IMF conference: "Financial Contagion: How it Spreads and How it Can Be Stopped?"

[59] Stijn Claessens and Rudiger Dornbusch and Yung Chul Park, 2000, Contagion: How It Spreads and How It Can Be Stopped?, Mimeo. Paper prepared for World Bank/IMF conference: "Financial Contagion: How it Spreads and How it Can Be Stopped?"

[60] Stijn Claessens, 1995, The Emergence of Equity Investment in Developing Countries: Overview, *The World Bank Economic Review,* vol. 9 (1), pp. 1-17

[61] Stijn Claessens, 1995, The Emergence of Equity Investment in Developing Countries: Overview, *The World Bank Economic Review,* vol. 9 (1), pp. 1-17

[62] H. Cole and Timothy Kehoe, 1996, *A Self-Fulfilling Model of Mexico's 1994-95 Debt Crisis*, Federal reserve bank of Minneapolis, vol. mimeo

[63] H. Cole and Timothy Kehoe, 1996, A Self-Fulfilling Model of Mexico's 1994-95 Debt Crisis, Federal reserve bank of Minneapolis, vol. mimeo

[64] Robert A. Connolly and F. Albert Wang, June, 2000, On Stock Market Return Co-Movements: Macroeconomic News, Dispersion of Beliefs, and Contagion., University of North Carolina, Mimeo

[65] Robert A. Connolly and F. Albert Wang, 1998, International Equity Market Co-Movement: Economic Fundamentals or Contagion?, University of North Carolina, Mimeo

[66] Giancarlo Corsetti and Paolo Pesenti and Nouriel Roubini and Cedric Tille, December, 1998, Competitive Devaluations: A Welfare-Based Approach, NY University, mimeo

[67] Giancarlo Corsetti and Paolo Pesenti and Nouriel Roubini and Cedric Tille, December, 2000, Competitive Devaluations: Toward A Welfare-Based Approach, *Journal of International Economics,* vol. 51, pp. 217-241

[68] Giancarlo Corsetti and Marcello Pericoli and Massimo Stracia, February, 2003, 'Some Contagion, some Interdependence' More Pitfalls in Tests of Financial Contagion, Corsetti's web page: http://www.econ.yale.edu/ corsetti/

[69] Jose DeGregorio and Rodrigo Valdes, January, 2000, Crisis Transmission: Evidence from the Debt, Tequila, and Asian Flue Crises, Universidad Catolica, Chile, Mimeo

[70] Jose De Gregorio and Rodrigo Valdes, Editor Stijn Claessens and Kristin Forbes, 2001, Crisis Transmission: Evidence from the Debt, Tequila and Asian Flu Crises, book International Financial Contagion, Mimeo, pp. 97-126, Kluwer Academic Publishers, Boston, MA

[71] Morris DeGroot, 1989, Probability and Statistics, Addison-Wesley, Massachusetts

[72] Morris DeGroot, 1989, Probability and Statistics, Addison-Wesley, Massachusetts

[73] W.J. Dixon and F.J. Massey, 1983, Introduction to Statistical Analysis, Ed.4th, McGraw-Hill, New York

[74] W.J. Dixon and F.J. Massey, 1983, Introduction to Statistical Analysis, Ed.4th, McGraw-Hill, New York

[75] Allan Drazen, March, 1998, Political Contagion in Currency Crisis, University of Maryland Mimeo

[76] Allan Drazen, March, 1998, Political Contagion in Currency Crisis, University of Maryland Mimeo

[77] Jean-Marie Dufour, 1982, Generalized Chow Tests for Structural Change: A Coordinate-Free Approach, *International Economic Review,* vol. 23, pp. 565-575

[78] Jean-Marie Dufour and Eric Ghysels and Alastair Hall, February, 1994, Generalized Predictive Tests and Structural Change Analysis in Econometrics, *International Economic Review,* vol. 35, No. 1, pp. 199-227

[79] Mardi Dungey and Vance L. Martin, February, 2001, Contagion Across Financial Markets: An Empirical Assessment, Australian National University Mimeo

[80] Mardi Dungey and Renee Fry and Brenda Gonzalez-Hermosillo and Vance Martin, February, 2003, Empirical Modelling of Contagion: A Review of Methodologies, Mardi's web page: http://rspas.anu.edu.au/economics/staff/dungey.

[81] Hali Edison and Frank Warnock, January, 2003, The Determinants of U.S. Investor's Holdings of Emerging Market Equities, *IMF Working Paper*

[82] Sebastian Edwards and Raul Susmel, April, 2000, Interest Rate Volatility and Contagion in Emerging Markets: Evidence from the 1990's, UCLA, Mimeo

[83] Sebastian Edwards, October, 1998, Interest Rate Volatility, Capital Controls, and Contagion, *NBER Working Paper* **6756**

[84] Sebastian Edwards, October, 1998, Interest Rate Volatility, Capital Controls, and Contagion, *NBER Working Paper* **6756**

[85] Sebastian Edwards, 1998, Interest Rate Volatility, Capital Controls, and Contagion, *NBER Working Paper* **6756**

[86] Barry Eichengreen and Ashoka Mody, February, 2000, Contagion from the Russian Crisis: Who Was Infected and Why?, UC Berkeley, Mimeo

[87] Barry Eichengreen and Andrew Rose and Charles Wyplosz, 1996, Contagious Currency Crises, *NBER Working Paper* **5681**

[88] Barry Eichengreen and Andrew Rose and Charles Wyplosz, 1996, Contagious Currency Crises, *NBER Working Paper* **5681**

[89] H. Erlat, 1983, A Note on Testing Structural Change in a Single Equation Belonging to a Simultaneous System, *Economic Letters,* vol. 13, pp. 185-89

[90] Stefano Fachini, Sept.-Oct., 1989, A Montecarlo Experiment on the Power of Variable Addition Tests for Parameter Stability, *Giornale Degli Economisti e Annali di Economia,* vol. 48, No. 9-10, pp. 497-506

[230] Franklin M. Fisher, 1976, *The Identification Problem in Econometrics*, Ed.Second, Robert E. Krieger Publishing Co., New York

[92] Franklin M. Fisher, 1976, *The Identification Problem in Econometrics,* Ed.Second, Robert E. Krieger Publishing Co., New York

[93] Kristin Forbes, 2000, The Asian Flu and Russian Virus: Firm-Level Evidence on How Crises Are Transmitted Internationally, *NBER Working Paper* **7807**

[94] Kristin Forbes and Roberto Rigobon, 1999, Measuring Contagion: Conceptual and Empirical Issues, MIT Mimeo. Paper prepared for World Bank/IMF conference: "Financial Contagion: How it Spreads and How it Can Be Stopped?"

[95] , Kristin Forbes, 1999, How Are Shocks Propagated Internationally? Firm-Level Evidence from the Russian and Asian Crises, MIT Mimeo., note = MIT Mimeo

[96] Kristin Forbes, 1999, How Are Shocks Propagated Internationally? Firm-Level Evidence from the Russian and Asian Crises, MIT Mimeo., note = MIT Mimeo

[97] Kristin Forbes and Roberto Rigobon, 1999, Measuring Contagion: Conceptual and Empirical Issues, MIT Mimeo. Paper prepared for World Bank/IMF conference: "Financial Contagion: How it Spreads and How it Can Be Stopped?"

[98] Menzie D. Chinn and Kristin J. Forbes, March, 2003, A Decomposition of Global Linkages in Financial Markets Over Time, *NBER wp* **9555**

[99] Kristin Forbes and Roberto Rigobon, July, 1999, No Contagion, Only Interdependence: Measuring Stock Market Co-Movements., Journal of Finance, Forthcoming

[100] Kristin Forbes and Roberto Rigobon, September, 2000, Measuring Contagion: Conceptual and Empirical Issues, MIT mimeo

[255] Kristin Forbes and Roberto Rigobon, August, 2000, Contagion in Latin America: Definitions, Measurement, and Policy Implications, MIT mimeo

[102] Kristin Forbes, 2000, How Important is Trade in the International Spread of Crises?, *Paper prepared for NBER Conference on Currency Crises Prevention.*

[103] Kenneth Froot and Paul O'Connell and Mark Seasholes, February, 2000, *The Portfolio Flows of International Investors,* Harvard University, Mimeo

[104] K. Froot and P O'Connell and M Seasholes, 1998, *The Portfolio Flows of International Investors,,* Harvard Business School, mimeo

[105] K. Froot and P O'Connell and M Seasholes, 1998, *The Portfolio Flows of International Investors,,* Harvard Business School, mimeo

[106] Jessica Tjornhom Donohue and Kenneth A. Froot, September, 2002, *The Presistence of Emerging Market Equity Flows*, *NBER wp* **9241**

[107] Kenneth A. Froot and Paul G. J. O'Connell and Mark S. Seasholes, August, 1998, The Portfolio Flows of International Investors,, *NBER wp* **6687**

[108] Kenneth A. Froot and Tarun Ramadorai, August, 2002, Currency Returns, Institutional Investor Flows, and Exchange Rate Fundamentals, *NBER wp* **9101**

[109] Gaston Gelos and Ratna Sahay, February, 2000, Financial Markets Spillovers in Transition Economies, IMF, Mimeo

[110] R. Gaston Gelos and Shang-Jin Wei, October, 2002, Transparency and International Investor Behavior, *NBER wp* **9260**

[111] Stefan Gerlach and Frank Smets, 1995, Contagious Speculative Attacks, *European Journal of Political Economy,* vol. 11, pp. 45-63

[112] Stefan Gerlach and Frank Smets, 1995, Contagious Speculative Attacks, *European Journal of Political Economy,* vol. 11, pp. 45-63

[113] Carlo Favero and Francesco Giavazzi, February, 2000, Looking for Contagion: Evidence from the 1992 ERM Crisis, Bocconi University, Mimeo

[114] Reuven Glick and Andrew Rose, August, 1998, Contagion and Trade: Why are Currency Crises Regional?, Mimeo

[115] Reuven Glick and Andrew Rose, August, 1999, Contagion and Trade: Why are Currency Crises Regional?, *Journal of International Money and Finance,* vol. 18, pp. 603-617

[116] Taimur Baig and Ilan Goldfajn, 1998, *Financial Markets Contagion in the Asian Crises,* IMF Mimeo

[117] Morris Goldstein and Graciela Kaminsky and Carmen Reinhart, June, 2000, Assessing Financial Vulnerability : An Early Warning System for Emerging Markets, Institute for International Economics

[118] José De Gregorio and Rodrigo Valdés, February, 2000, Crisis Transmission: Evidence from the Debt, Tequila and Asian Flu Crises, Universidad Catolica de Chile, Mimeo

[119] Denis Gromb and Dimitri Vayanos, 2002, Equilibrium and Welfare in Markets with Financially Constrained Arbitrageurs, *Journal of Financial Economics,* vol. 66, pp. 361-407

[231] Trygve Haavelmo, March, 1947, Methods of Measuring the Marginal Propensity to Consume, *Journal of the American Statistical Association,* vol. 42, pp. 105-122

[121] Trygve Haavelmo, March, 1947, Methods of Measuring the Marginal Propensity to Consume, *Journal of the American Statistical Association,* vol. 42, pp. 105-122

[122] P. Hackl and A.H. Westlund, Editor Walter Kramer, 1989, Statistical Analysis of "Structural Change": An Annotated Bibliography., book Econometrics of Structural Change, Physica-Verlag Heidelberg, Germany

[123] Yasushi Hamao and Ronald Masulis and Victor Ng, 1990, Correlations in Price Changes and Volatility Across International Stock Markets, *The Review of Financial Studies,* vol. 3, No. 2, pp. 281-307

[124] Yasushi Hamao and Ronald Masulis and Victor Ng, 1990, Correlations in Price Changes and Volatility Across International Stock Markets, *The Review of Financial Studies,* vol. 3, No. 2, pp. 281-307

[232] James D. Hamilton, 1990, Analysis of Time Series Subject to Changes in Regime, *Journal of Econometrics,* vol. 45, pp. 39-70

[233] James D. Hamilton, 1994, Time Series Analysis, Princeton University Press, Princeton, New Jersey

[127] James D. Hamilton, 1994, Time Series Analysis, Princeton University Press, Princeton, New Jersey

[234] Jerry A. Hausman, 1978, Specification Tests in Econometrics, Econometrica, vol. 46, pp. 1251-72

[129] Sushil Bikhchandani and David Hirshleifer and Ivo Welch, October, 1992, A Theory of Fads, Fashion, Custom, and Cultural Change as Information Cascades, *Journal of Political Economy,* vol. 100, No. 5, pp. 992-1026

[130] Jiro Hodoshima, 1988, Estimation of a Single Structural Equation with Structural Change, *Econometric Theory,* vol. 4, pp. 86-96

[131] Jiro Hodoshima, 1992, Finite-Sample Properties of Single-Equation Estimators under Structural Change, *Journal of Econometrics,* vol. 53, pp. 189-209

[235] Bo E. Honore, March, 1992, Simple Estimation of a Duration Model with Unobserved Heterogeneity, *Econometrica*, vol. 58, No. 2, pp. 453-73

[236] Bo E. Honore and Ekaterini Kyriazidou and Christopher Udry, Jan.-Feb., 1997., Estimation of Type 3 Tobit Models Using Symmetric Trimming and Pairwise Comparisons., *Journal of Econometrics,* vol. 76, No. 1-2, pp. 107-28

[237] Joel Horowitz, 1992, A Smoothed Maximum Score Estimator for the Binary Response Model, *Econometrica*, vol. 60, pp. 505-531

[238] Joel Horowitz, 1993, Semiparametric Estimation of a Work-Trip Mode Choice Model, *Journal of Econometrics,* vol. 58, pp. 49-70

[136] Joel Horowitz, 1992, A Smoothed Maximum Score Estimator for the Binary Response Model, *Econometrica*, vol. 60, pp. 505-531

[137] Joel Horowitz, 1993, Semiparametric Estimation of a Work-Trip Mode Choice Model, *Journal of Econometrics,* vol. 58, pp. 49-70

[138] Takatoshi Ito and Yuko Hashimoto, December, 2002, High Frequency **Contagion** of Currency Crises in Asia, *NBER wp* 9376

[139] Philippe Jorion, Editor Robert Aliber, 1989, The Linkages Between National Stock Markets, book The Handbook of International Financial Management, vol. The Handbook of International Financial Management., publisher Dow-Jones Irwin., Illinois

[140] Philippe Jorion, Editor Robert Aliber, 1989, The Linkages Between National Stock Markets, book The Handbook of International Financial Management, vol. The Handbook of International Financial Management., Dow-Jones Irwin., Illinois

[141] Garciela Kaminsky and Carmen Reinhart, February, 2000, The Center and the Periphery: Tales of Financial Turmoil, GWU, Mimeo

[142] Graciela Kaminsky and Carmen Reinhart, November, 1998, *On Crises, Contagion, and Confusion*, University of Maryland mimeo

[143] Graciela Kaminsky and Carmen Reinhart, November, 1998, *On Crises, Contagion, and Confusion*, University of Maryland mimeo

[144] Graciela Kaminsky and Richard Lyons and Sergio Schmukler, February, 2000, Economic Fragility, Liquidity and Risk: The Behavior of Mutual Funds During Crises, and Managers, Investors, and Crises: Mutual Fund Strategies in Emerging Markets, Mimeo

[145] Gracieal L. Kaminsky and Carmen Reinhart and Carlos A. Vegh, January, 2003, The Unholy Trinity of Financial Contagion, University of Maryland, mimeo

[146] Graciela Kaminsky and Sergio Schmukler, September, 2002, Emerging Market Instability: Do Sovereign Ratings Affect Country Risk and Stock Returns?, *World Bank Economic Review*

[147] Andrew Karolyi, 2003, The Role of ADRs in the Development and Integration of Emerging Equity Markets, Ohio State mimeo

[148] Kee-Hong Bae and G. Andrew Karolyi and Rene M. Stulz, September, 2000, A New Approach to Measuring Financial Contagion, *NBER Mimeo* **7913**

[149] Kelejian and Tavlas and Hondroyiannis, 2003, A Spatial Modeling Approach to Contagion, mimeo

[150] Mervyn King and Enrique Sentana and Sushil Wadhwani, 1994, Volatility and Links Between National Stock Markets, Econometrica, vol. 62, pp. 901-33

[151] Mervyn King and Sushil Wadhwani, 1990, Transmission of Volatility Between Stock Markets, *Review of Financial Studies*, vol. 3, No. 1, pp. 5-33

[152] Laura Kodres and Matthew Pritsker, 1999, A Rational Expectations Model of Financial Contagion, Mimeo. Board of Governors of the Federal Reserve System

[153] Laura Kodres and Matthew Pritsker, 1999, A Rational Expectations Model of Financial Contagion, Mimeo. Board of Governors of the Federal Reserve System

[239] T.C. Koopmans and H. Rubin and R.B. Leipnik, Editor Tjalling C. Koopmans, 1950, Measuring the Equation Systems of Dynamic Economics, series = Cowles Commission for Research in Economics, vol. Statistical Inference in Dynamic Economic Models, chapter = II, pp. 53-237, John Wiley and Sons, New York

[155] T.C. Koopmans and H. Rubin and R.B. Leipnik, Editor Tjalling C. Koopmans, 1950, Measuring the Equation Systems of Dynamic Economics, series = Cowles Commission for Research in Economics, vol. Statistical Inference in Dynamic Economic Models, chapter = II, pp. 53-237, John Wiley and Sons, New York

[156] Mark Kritzman and K Lowry and A-S Vanroyen, Spring, 2001, Risk, Regimes, and Overconfidence, *The Journal of Derivatives*, pp. 33-42

[157] Paul Krugman, 1998, *What Happened to Asia?*, MIT mimeo

[158] A Kyle, 1989, Informed Speculation with Imperfect Competition, *Review of Economic Studies,* vol. 56, No. 3, pp. 317-355

[159] Albert S. Kyle and Wei Xiong, August, 2001, Contagion as a Wealth Effect, *Journal of Finance,* vol. 56, No. 4, pp. 1401-1440

[160] Sang Bin Lee and Kwang Jung Kim., 1993, Does the October 1987 Crash Strengthen the Co-Movements Among National Stock Markets?, *Review of Financial Economics,* vol. 3, No. 1, pp. 89-102

[161] Sang Bin Lee and Kwang Jung Kim., 1993, Does the October 1987 Crash Strengthen the Co-Movements Among National Stock Markets?, *Review of Financial Economics,* vol. 3, No. 1, pp. 89-102

[162] R.S. Lipster and A.N. Shiryayev, 1978, *Statistics of Random Processes II: Applications,* Springer-Verlag, New York

[163] Robert S. Liptser and Albert N. Shiryayev, 1978, *Statistics of Random Processes II: Applications,* Springer-Verlag, New York

[164] Robert S. Liptser and Albert N. Shiryayev, 1978, *Statistics of Random Processes II: Applications,* Springer-Verlag, New York

[165] Andrew W. Lo and Whitney K. Newey, 1985, A Large-Sample Chow Test for the Linear Simultaneous Equation, *Economic Letters,* vol. 18, pp. 351-53

[166] Alexandra Lomakin and Salvador Paiz, May, 1999, Measuring Contagion in the Face of Fluctuating Volatility, *MIT Sloan project,* **15.036**

[167] Alexandra Lomakin and Salvador Paiz, May, 1999, Measuring Contagion in the Face of Fluctuating Volatility, *MIT Sloan project,* **15.036**

[168] François Longuin and Bruno Slonik, 1995, Is the Correlation in International Equity Returns Constant: 1960-1990, *Journal of International Money and Finance*, vol. 14, No. 1, pp. 3-26

[169] François Longuin and Bruno Slonik, 1995, Is the Correlation in International Equity Returns Constant: 1960-1990, *Journal of International Money and Finance,* vol. 14, No. 1, pp. 3-26

[170] M. Loretan and W.B. English, 2000, Evaluating 'Correlation Breakdowns' During Periods of Market Volatility, book International Financial Markets and the Implications for Monetary and Financial Stability, pp. 214-231, Bank for International Settlements, Basel, Switzerland

[171] Mico Loretan and William B. English, February, 2000, Evaluation "Correlation Breakdowns" During Periods of Market Volatility, Federal Reserve Board, Mimeo

[172] Robin L. Lumsdaine and Serena Ng, 1999, Testing for ARCH in the Presence of a Possible Misspecified Conditional Mean, *Journal of Econometrics,* vol. 93, pp. 257-79

[173] J.G. MacKinnon, Editor Walter Kramer, 1989, Heteroskedasticity Robust Tests for Structural Change, book Econometrics of Structural Change, Physica-Verlag Heidelberg, Germany

[241] Charles Manski, 1975, Maximum Score Estimation of the Stochastic Utility Model of Choice, *Journal of Econometrics,* vol. 3, pp. 205-228

[242] Charles Manski, 1985, Semiparametric Analysis of Discrete Response: Asymptotic Properties of the Maximum Score Estimator, Journal of Econometrics, vol. 27, pp. 313-334

[176] Charles Manski, 1975, Maximum Score Estimation of the Stochastic Utility Model of Choice, *Journal of Econometrics,* vol. 3, pp. 205-228

[177] Charles Manski, 1985, Semiparametric Analysis of Discrete Response: Asymptotic Properties of the Maximum Score Estimator, Journal of Econometrics, vol. 27, pp. 313-334

[178] Paul Masson, 1997, Monsoonal Effects, Spillovers, and Contagion, IMF Mimeo

[179] Paul Masson, 1998, Contagion: Monsoonal Effects, Spillovers, and Jumps Between Multiple Equilibria, *IMF Working Paper* **98/142**

[180] Ronald I. McKinnon and Huw Pill, Editor T. Ito and A.O. Krueger, 1996, Credible Liberalizations and International Capital Flows: The Overborriwing Syndrome., book Financial Deregulation and Integration in East Asia, Chicago University Press, Chicago

[181] Ronald I. McKinnon and Huw Pill, 1998, The Overborriwing Syndrome: Are East Asian Economies Different?, book Managing Capital Flows and Exchange Rates: Perspectives from the Pacific Basin, pp. 322-55, Cambridge, University Press, Cambridge, New York, and Melbourne

[182] Enrique G. Mendoza and Katherine A. Smith, October, 2002, Margin Calls, Trading Costs, and Asset Prices in Emerging Markets: The Financial Mechanics of the 'Sudden Stop' Phenomenon, NBER wp 9286

[183] Marcus Miller and Kannika Thampanishvong and Lei Zong, January, 2003, Learning to Forget? Contagion and Political Risk in Brazil, University of Warwick, mimeo

[184] Randall Morck and Fan Yang and Bernard Yeung, January, 2003, *The Changing Degree of Comovement in Emerging Economy Stock Returns,* University of Alberta, mimeo

[185] Sendhil Mullainathan, 1998, *A Memory Based Model of Bounded Rationality,* MIT Mimeo

[186] Sendhil Mullainathan, 1998, *A Memory Based Model of Bounded Rationality,* MIT Mimeo

[187] Alvaro Novo, 2002, *Contagious Currency Crises: A Patial Probit Approach,* mimeo

[188] Maurice Obstfeld, 1986, Rational and Self-Fulfilling Balance of Payments Crises, *American Economic Review,* vol. 76, pp. 72-81

[189] Maurice Obstfeld, 1986, Rational and Self-Fulfilling Balance of Payments Crises, *American Economic Review,* vol. 76, pp. 72-81

[190] Yung Chul Park and Chi-Young Song, February, 2000, Financial Contagion in the East Asian Crisis - with Special Reference to the Republic of Korea, Korea University, Mimeo

[191] P. Perron, 1989, The Great Crash, the Oil Price Shock and the Unit Root Hypothesis, *Econometrica*, vol. 57, pp. 1361-1401

[192] Robert Pindyck and Julio Rotemberg, December, 1990, The Excess Co-Movement of Commodity Prices, *The Economic Journal,* vol. 100, No. 403, pp. 1173-1189

[193] Robert Pindyck and Julio Rotemberg, November, 1993, The Comovement of Stock Prices, The Quarterly Journal of Economics, vol. 108, No. 4, pp. 1073-1104

[194] Robert Pindyck and Julio Rotemberg, December, 1990, The Excess Co-Movement of Commodity Prices, *The Economic Journal,* vol. 100, No. 403, pp. 1173-1189

[195] Robert Pindyck and Julio Rotemberg, November, 1993, The Comovement of Stock Prices, *The Quarterly Journal of Economics,* vol. 108, No. 4, pp. 1073-1104

[243] J. L. Powell, 1986, Symmetrically Trimmed Least Squares Estimation for Tobit Models, *Econometrica*, vol. 54, pp. 1435-60

[197] Steven Radelet and Jeffrey Sachs, April, 1998, *The East Asian Financial Crisis: Diagnosis, Remedies, Prospects.*, Harvard Institute for International Development, Mimeo

[198] Steven Radelet and Jeffrey Sachs, April, 1998, The Onset of the East Asian Financial Crisis., Harvard Institute for International Development, Mimeo

[199] Steven Radelet and Jeffrey Sachs, April, 1998, *The East Asian Financial Crisis: Diagnosis, Remedies, Prospects.,* Harvard Institute for International Development, Mimeo

[200] Steven Radelet and Jeffrey Sachs, April, 1998, *The Onset of the East Asian Financial Crisis.,* Harvard Institute for International Development, Mimeo

[201] Lucrezia Reichlin, December, 1989, *Structural Change and Unit Root Econometrics, Economics Letters,* vol. 31, No. 3, pp. 231-33

[202] Sara Calvo and Carmen Reinhart, 1995, Capital Inflows to Latin America: Is There Evidence of Contagion Effects, Mimeo. World Bank and International Monetary Fund

[203] Sara Calvo and Carmen Reinhart, 1995, Capital Inflows to Latin America: Is There Evidence of Contagion Effects, Mimeo. World Bank and International Monetary Fund

[204] Ehud Ronn, 1998, The Impact of Large Changes in Asset Prices on Intra-Market Correlations in the Stock and Bond Markets, Mimeo

[205] Ehud Ronn, 1998, The Impact of Large Changes in Asset Prices on Intra-Market Correlations in the Stock and Bond Markets, Mimeo

[206] Jeffrey Sachs and Aaron Tornell and Andres Velasco, May, 1996, Financial Crises in Emerging Markets: The Lessons from 1995, *NBER Discussion Paper*, vol. No. 5576

[207] Jeffrey Sachs and Aaron Tornell and Andres Velasco, May, 1996, Financial Crises in Emerging Markets: The Lessons from 1995, *NBER Discussion Paper*, vol. No. 5576

[208] Sergio Schmukler and Luis Serven, 2002, Pricing Currency Risk under Currency Boards, *Journal of Development Economics,* vol. 69, No. 2, pp. 367-391

[247] Enrique Sentana and Gabriele Fiorentini, June, 1999, Identification, Estimation and Testing of Conditional Heteroskedastic Factor Models, CEMFI mimeo

[210] Rene M. Stulz, January, 2003, *What Explains Daily Equity Flows to Emerging Markets,* Ohio State University, mimeo

[211] G. Andrew Karolyi and Rene M. Stulz, July, 1996, Why Do Markets Move Together? An Investigation of U.S. - Japan Stock Return Comovements, *The Journal of Finance,* vol. 51, No. 3, pp. 951:986

[212] Rene Stulz, March, 1999, International Portfolio Flows and Security Markets, The Charles A. Dice Center for Reseach in Financial Economics, vol. WP 99-3

[213] G. Andrew Karolyi and Rene M. Stulz, July, 1996, Why Do Markets Move Together? An Investigation of U.S. - Japan Stock Return Comovements, *The Journal of Finance,* vol. 51, No. 3, pp. 951:986

[214] Rene Stulz, March, 1999, International Portfolio Flows and Security Markets, The Charles A. Dice Center for Reseach in Financial Economics, vol. WP 99-3

[215] H. Theil, 1971, Principles of Econometrics, New York, Wiley

[216] Panayiotis Theodossiou and Emel Kahya and Gregory Koutmos and Andreas Christofi, 1997, Volatility Reversion and Correlation Structure of Returns in Major International Stock Markets, *The Financial Review,* vol. 32, No. 2, pp. 205-224

[217] Panayiotis Theodossiou and Emel Kahya and Gregory Koutmos and Andreas Christofi, 1997, Volatility Reversion and Correlation Structure of Returns in Major International Stock Markets, *The Financial Review*, vol. 32, No. 2, pp. 205-224

[218] Rodrigo Valdés, 1996, Emerging Market Contagion: Evidence and Theory, MIT Mimeo

[219] Rodrigo Valdés, 1996, *Emerging Market Contagion: Evidence and Theory,* MIT Mimeo

[248] Roger Klein and Francis Vella, March, 2000, Employing Heteroskedasticity to Identify and Estimate Triangular Semiparametric Models, Rutgers mimeo

[249] Roger Klein and Francis Vella, March, 2000, Identification and Estimation of the Binary Treatment Model Under Heteroskedasticity, Rutgers mimeo

[250] Matthew D. Shapiro and Mark W. Watson, Editor Stanley Fischer, 1988, Sources of Business Cycle Fluctuations, *NBER Macroeconomics Annual 1988,* MIT Press, Cambridge, Mass.

[223] Caroline Van Rijckeghem and Beatrice Weder, forthcoming, 2003, Financial Contagion: Spillover Effects Through Banking Centers, *Journal of International Money and Finance*

[224] Caroline Van Rijckeghem and Beatrice Weder, August, 2001, Sources of Contagion: Is It Finance or Trade?, *Journal of International Economics*, vol. 54, No. 2, pp. 293-308

[225] Kathy Yuan, 2000, Asymmetric Price Movements and the Borrowing Constraint: A REE Model of Crises, Contagion and Confusion, MIT mimeo

[226] Kathy Yuan, January, 2000, Asymmetric Price Movements and Borrowing Constraints: A REE Model of Crisis, Contagion, and Confusion., MIT Mimeo

[227] Olivier J. Blanchard and Peter Diamond, 1989, The Beveridge Curve, *Brookings Papers in Economic Activity*, vol. 1, pp. 1-76

[228] Olivier Blanchard and Danny Quah, 1989, The Dynamic Effects of Aggregate Demand and Aggregate Supply Disturbances, *American Economic Review,* vol. 79, pp. 655-73

[229] Songnian Chen and Shakeeb Khan, December, 1999, $\sqrt{n}$-Consistent Estimation of Heteroskedastic Sample Selection Models, University of Rochester, Mimeo

[230] Franklin M. Fisher, 1976, The Identification Problem in Econometrics, Ed.Second, Robert E. Krieger Publishing Co., New York

[231] Trygve Haavelmo, March, 1947, Methods of Measuring the Marginal Propensity to Consume, *Journal of the American Statistical Association,* vol. 42, pp. 105-122

[232] James D. Hamilton, 1990, Analysis of Time Series Subject to Changes in Regime, *Journal of Econometrics,* vol. 45, pp. 39-70

[233] James D. Hamilton, 1994, Time Series Analysis, Princeton University Press, Princeton, New Jersey

[234] Jerry A. Hausman, 1978, Specification Tests in Econometrics, *Econometrica*, vol. 46, pp. 1251-72

[235] Bo E. Honore, March, 1992, Simple Estimation of a Duration Model with Unobserved Heterogeneity, *Econometrica*, vol. 58, No. 2, pp. 453-73

[236] Bo E. Honore and Ekaterini Kyriazidou and Christopher Udry, Jan.-Feb., 1997., Estimation of Type 3 Tobit Models Using Symmetric Trimming and Pairwise Comparisons., *Journal of Econometrics,* vol. 76, No. 1-2, pp. 107-28

[237] Joel Horowitz, 1992, A Smoothed Maximum Score Estimator for the Binary Response Model, *Econometrica*, vol. 60, pp. 505-531

[238] Joel Horowitz, 1993, Semiparametric Estimation of a Work-Trip Mode Choice Model, *Journal of Econometrics,* vol. 58, pp. 49-70

[239] T.C. Koopmans and H. Rubin and R.B. Leipnik, Editor Tjalling C. Koopmans, 1950, Measuring the Equation Systems of Dynamic Economics, series = Cowles Commission for Research in Economics, vol. Statistical Inference in Dynamic Economic Models, chapter = II, pp. 53-237, John Wiley and Sons, New York

[240]

[241] Charles Manski, 1975, Maximum Score Estimation of the Stochastic Utility Model of Choice, *Journal of Econometrics,* vol. 3, pp. 205-228

[242] Charles Manski, 1985, Semiparametric Analysis of Discrete Response: Asymptotic Properties of the Maximum Score Estimator, *Journal of Econometrics,* vol. 27, pp. 313-334

[243] J. L. Powell, 1986, Symmetrically Trimmed Least Squares Estimation for Tobit Models, *Econometrica*, vol. 54, pp. 1435-60

[244] Thomas J. Rothenberg and Paul A. Ruud, April-May, 1990, Simultaneous Equations with Covariance Retrictions, *Journal of Econometrics,* vol. 44, No. 1-2, pp. 25-39

[245] Enrique Sentana and Gabriele Fiorentini, June, 2001, Identification, Estimation and Testing of Conditional Heteroskedastic Factor Models, *Journal of Econometrics,* vol. 102, No. 2, pp. 143-164

[246] Enrique Sentana, 1992, Identification of Multivariate Conditionally Heteroskedastic Factor Models, LSE, FMG Discussion Paper, vol. 139

[247] Enrique Sentana and Gabriele Fiorentini, June, 1999, Identification, Estimation and Testing of Conditional Heteroskedastic Factor Models, CEMFI mimeo

[248] Roger Klein and Francis Vella, March, 2000, Employing Heteroskedasticity to Identify and Estimate Triangular Semiparametric Models, Rutgers mimeo

[249] Roger Klein and Francis Vella, March, 2000, Identification and Estimation of the
Binary Treatment Model Under Heteroskedasticity, Rutgers mimeo

[250] Matthew D. Shapiro and Mark W. Watson, Editor Stanley Fischer, 1988, Sources
of Business Cycle Fluctuations, *NBER Macroeconomics Annual* 1988, MIT Press,
Cambridge, Mass.

[251] Sewall Wright, January, 1921, Correlation and Causation, *Journal of Agricultural
Research*

[252] Sewall Wright, May, 1923, *The Theory of Path Coefficients*, Genetics

[253] Philip G. Wright, 1928, The Tariff on Animal and Vegetable Oils, series = The Institute of Economics, The Macmillan Conpany, New York

[254] Kristin Forbes and Roberto Rigobon, October, 2002, No Contagion, Only Interdependence: Measuring Stock Market Co-Movements., *Journal of Finance*, vol. 57, No.
5, pp. 2223-2261

[255] Kristin Forbes and Roberto Rigobon, 2001, Contagion in Latin America: Definitions,
Measurement, and Policy Implications, Economia, vol. 1, No. 2, pp. 1-46

[256] Kristin Forbes and Roberto Rigobon, Editor Stijn Claessens and Kristin Forbes,
2001, Measuring Contagion: Conceptual and Empirical Issues, book International
Financial Contagion, Kluwer Academic Publishers

[257] Ricardo Hausmann and Roberto Rigobon, Editor J.M. Davis, R. Ossowski, and
A. Fedelino, 2003, An Alternative Interpretation of the 'Resource Curse': Theory
and Policy Implications, book Fiscal Policy Formulation and Implementation in Oil-
Producing Countries, chapter = 2, pp. 13-44, International Monetary Fund, Washington D.C.

[258] Osmel Manzano and Roberto Rigobon, Editor Daniel Lederman and William F. Mal-
oney, 2003, Resource Curse or Debt Overhang?, book Natural Resources and Development: Are They a Curse? Are They Destiny?, Stanford Univesity Press

[259] Stavros Panageas and Roberto Rigobon, June, 2002, Contagious Effects of Portfolio
Insurance, MIT mimeo

[260] Anna Pavlova and Roberto Rigobon, July, 2003, Asset Prices and Exchange Rates,
NBER wp 9834

[261] Roberto Rigobon and Shang-Jin Wei, 2003, Testing for the Channels of Contagion:
Financial versus Real Linkages, MIT mimeo

[262] Roberto Rigobon, December, 2002, The Curse of Non-Investment Grade Countries,
Journal of Development Economics, vol. 69, No. 2, pp. 423-449

[263] Roberto Rigobon, June, 1999, Does Contagion Exists?, The Investment Strategy Pack, Banking Department of the BIS

[264] Robrto Rigobon, December, 2002, Disinflation and Fiscal Reform: A Neoclassical Perspective., *Journal of International Economics,* vol. 58, No. 2, pp. 265-97

[265] Roberto Rigobon, Editor Sebastian Edwards and Jeffrey Frankel, 2002, Contagion: How to Measure It?, book Preventing Currency Crises in Emerging Markets, MIT Mimeo: http://web.mit.edu/rigobon/www/., pp. 269-334, University of Chicago Press

[266] Roberto Rigobon, June, 2001, Identification Through Conditional Heteroskedasticity, MIT Mimeo

[267] Roberto Rigobon, November, 2003, Identification Through Heteroskedasticity., Review of Economics and Statistics, vol. 85, No. 4

[268] Roberto Rigobon, Jan, 1998, Informational Speculative Attacks: Good News is No News, mimeo, MIT

[269] Roberto Rigobon, November, 1998, On the Measurement of Interdependence: Trade or Macroeconomic Similarities, MIT Mimeo

[270] Roberto Rigobon, September, 2002, On the Measurement of the International Propagation of Shocks: Is the Transmission Stable?, *Journal of International Economics,* vol. Forthcoming

[271] Roberto Rigobon, September, 2000, A Simple Test for the Stability of Linear Models under Heteroskedasticity, Omitted Variable, and Endogneous Variable Problems., MIT Mimeo: http://web.mit.edu/rigobon/www/.

[272] Roberto Rigobon and Brian Sack, February, 2002, The Impact of Monetary Policy on Asset Prices, NBER Working Paper 8794

[273] Roberto Rigobon and Brian Sack, forthcoming, 2003, Measuring the Reaction of Monetary Policy to the Stock Market, Quarterly Journal of Economics, vol. 118, pp. 639-669

In: International Macroeconomics: Recent Developments
ISBN: 1-59454-901-X
Editor: Amalia Morales Zumaquero, pp. 257-284
© 2006 Nova Science Publishers, Inc.

Chapter 12

CREDIBILITY AND DURATION IN TARGET ZONES: EVIDENCE FROM THE EMS

Simón Sosvilla-Rivero[1] and Francisco Pérez-Bermejo[2]

[1]Univ. Complutense de Madrid and Foundation for Applied Economic Research, FEDEA
[2]Foundation for Applied Economic Research, FEDEA

Abstract

This paper is devoted to the past, present, and future of the European Monetary System (EMS). After examining its background, the paper reviews the structure and operation of the EMS, as well as the theoretical framework used to explain exchange-rate movements inside official fluctuation bands. Moreover, we offer some comments and assessment on the EMS in the light of empirical papers examining the EMS from both the credibility and currency crisis approaches, with special emphasis on the survival of the central parities. Finally, drawing on the EMS experience, we make some remarks on new EMS, linking the currencies of non-euro area Member States to the euro, both current European Union Member States and future candidates.

1 Introduction

The European Monetary System (EMS) constituted an important intermediary step to European Monetary Union (EMU), which is now regarded as a very efficient monetary arrangement for most countries of the European Union (UE). Indeed, the EMS is considered to be the most ambitious experiment since the Bretton-Woods system.

The aim of this paper is to provide an assessment on the past, present, and future of the EMS. To that end, Section 2 examines its background and reviews its structure and operation features, as well as offering a brief account of its historical evolution. In Section 3 we review the theoretical framework used to explain exchange-rate movements inside official fluctuation bands and comment some empirical evidence examining the credibility of the EMS. Section 4 is devoted to the theoretical models designed to examine the currency crises, and we review some empirical evidence on the relevance of this literature in the case of the EMS, with special emphasis on the survival of the central parities. Finally, Section 5 offers some concluding remarks drawing on the EMS experience, as well as some considerations on the new EMS, linking the currencies of non-euro area Member States to the euro, both current European Union Member States and future candidates.

2   The European Monetary System

The EMS was created on account of a Resolution of the European Council on the 5th December 1978. It entered into force on the 13th March 1979, according to an agreement celebrated the same day between the central banks of the countries that formed part of the now UE. The EMS was launched as an attempt to foster economic integration and the co-ordination of economic policies in the EU. In particular, the EMS was established to achieve "a greater measure of monetary stability" among the members of the EU (Commission of the European Communities, 1979, p. 94) in a moment characterised by the excessive exchange rate volatility, that could have adversely affected the European integration process.

The EMS gave birth to a new symbolic currency, the European Currency Unit (ECU), predecessor of the euro. The ECU was a composed currency (or currency basket), formed by given percentages of each one of the participating currencies, established in function to the contribution of the respective countries to the GDP of the EU and to the intra-European trade. These weights were initially chosen so that ECU 1 be worth US\$ 1. The composition of the ECU was subject to periodic reviews every five years. Table 1 shows the composition of the ECU set at each quinquennial reviews, together with the weight of each currency in the ECU. From this table we can see that the ECU consisted literally of so many Deutchemarks, so many French francs, etc. However, the actual weight of each currency in the basket changed because of exchange-rate movements, so the weights shown in the table are those prevailing in different dates. The composition of and the last weights are shown in Table 1. When the euro was introduced in 4 January 1999, it replaced the ECU at par (that is, at a 1:1 ratio), ceasing the ECU to exist. Although it was originally an accounting unit for all EU transactions and the community's internal budget, the latter was used in travellers' cheques and bank deposits, though it was never issued as a note or coin.

Table 1. Composition and weighting of the ECU

	Amount in one ECU			Weights (%)		
	13 Mar. 1979 through 14 Sep. 1984	17 Sep. 1984 though 21 Sep. 1989	21 Sep. 1989 through 31 Dec. 1998	13 Mar. 1979	17 Sep. 1984	31 Dec. 1998
Belgian franc	3.800	3.850	3.431	9.64	8.57	8.52
Danish krone	0.217	0.219	0.1976	3.06	2.69	2.65
Deutschemark	0.828	0.719	0.6242	32.98	32.08	31.94
Dutch guilder	0.286	0.256	0.2198	10.51	19.06	9.88
French franc	1.150	1.310	1.332	19.83	10.13	20.33
Greek drachma	n.a.	1.15	1.44	n.a.	1.31	0.44
Irish punt	0.00759	0.00871	0.008552	1.15	1.20	1.09
Italian lira	109.0	140.0	151.8	9.49	9.98	7.85
Portuguese escudo	n.a	n.a.	1.393	n.a.	n.a.	0.70
Spanish peseta	n.a	n.a.	6.885	n.a.	n.a.	4.14
UK pound sterling	0.0885	0.0878	0.08784	13.34	14.98	12.46

Note: n.a.= not applicable

The centrepiece of the EMS was the European Regimen Mechanism (ERM), an adjustable peg system in which each currency had a central rate expressed in terms of ECU. These central rates determined a grid of bilateral central rates *vis-à-vis* all other participating currencies, and defined a band around these central rates within the exchange rates could fluctuate freely. Therefore, the arrangement was designed to be both fully European (with no reference to the US Dollar or to the gold) and symmetric (no currency played any special role, in contrast to the US Dollar in the Bretton Woods system). The size of this band was initially set at ±2.25 per cent, so that the exchange rate between any two currencies could move by (at most) 4.5 per cent. For some countries (Italy until 1990, Portugal, Spain and the UK) the band fluctuation band was set at ±6 per cent, allowing a maximal range of fluctuation of 12 per cent. After almost a year of unprecedented turmoil in the history of the EMS, the fluctuation bands of the ERM were broadened in August 1993 to $\pm$ 15% except for Dutch guilder and Deutschemark, which remained with the narrow bands of $\pm$ 2.25 per cent.

In order to keep these bilateral rates within the margins, the participating countries were obliged to intervene in the foreign exchange market if a currency approached the limits of its band. Therefore, the responsibility for maintaining each bilateral exchange rate within its margin was explicitly shared by both countries. In return, there was a strong collective commitment to provide mutual support through bilateral, automatic and unlimited interventions. Indeed, a central bank could not stop intervening as long as its parity *vis-à-vis* any other member currency was pressed against the limit. For this purpose, special credit facilities were established. The European Monetary Co-operation Fund (EMCF) provided short- and medium-term credit facilities to its members. The most important of these instruments was the Very Short Term Financing (VSTF) facility, which provided finance for intervention in the foreign-exchange markets.

The EMS was a system of pegged, but adjustable, exchange rates in which the central parity grid could be altered to take into account changing economic conditions and relative performance of the participant economies. If they decided by mutual agreement that a particular parity could not be defended, realignments of the central rates were permitted. This consensus rule implied that, in effect, each country gave up exclusive control of its own exchange rate. Table 2 shows the main realignments and changes in the EMS during the 1979-1998 period. As can be seen, there were nineteen realignments in the EMS history, twelve of them being prior to the currency turmoil of the subperiod 1992-1993. On the other hand, many changes affected more than one currency, such as the band increase. In general, high-inflation countries needed to periodically devaluate their currencies with respect to the ECU in order to maintain competitiveness in relation to a low-inflation country such as Germany. In this respect, early proponents of the EMS stressed the point that the frequency of realignments should not be regarded as a criterion of success or failure of the system (Commission of the European Communities, 1979, p. 78).

Table 2. Main realignments and changes in the ERM (1979-1998)

13.03.1979	ERM starts to operate with the BFR, DKR, DM, FF, IRL, LIT and HFL. They are in the narrow band ($\pm$ 2.25% fluctuation), except the LIT in the wide band ($\pm$ 6% fluctuation).
24.09.1979	Realignment (DKR –3%, DM +2%)
30.11.1979	Realignment (DKR –5%)
23.03.1981	Realignment (LIT –6%)
5.10.1981	Realignment (DM +5.5%, FF –3%, HFL +5.5%, LIT –3%)
22.02.1982	Realignment (BFR –8.5%, DKR -3%)
14.06.1982	Realignment (DM +4.25%, FF –5.75%, HFL +4.25%, LIT –2.75%)
22.03.1983	Realignment (BFR +1.5%, DKR +2.5%, DM +5.5%, FF –2.5%, IRL –3.5%, HFL +3.5%, LIT –2.5%)
22.07.1985	Realignment (BFR +2%, DKR +2%, DM +2%, FF +2%, IRL +2%, HFL +2%, LIT –6%)
7.04.1986	Realignment (BFR +1%, DKR +1%, DM +3%, FF –3%, HFL +3%)
4.08.1986	Realignment (IRL –8%)
12.01.1987	Realignment (BFR +2%, DM +3%, HFL +3%)
19.06.1989	The PTA joins the ERM with the wide band ($\pm$ 6%)
8.01.1990	The LIT joins the narrow band ($\pm$ 2.25%). Realignment (LIT –3.6774%)
8.10.1990	The UKL joins the ERM with the wide band ($\pm$ 6%)
6.04.1992	The ESC joins the ERM with the wide band ($\pm$ 6%)
14.09.1992	Realignment (BFR +3.5%, DKR +3.5%, DM +3.5%, ESC +3.5%, FF +3.5%, IRL +3.5%, HFL +3.5%, LIT –3.5%, PTA +3.5%, UKL +3.5%)
17.09.1992	The UKL and the LIT suspend their participation in the ERM. Realignment (PTA –5%)
23.11.1992	Realignment (ESC -6%, PTA –6%)
1.02.1993	Realignment (IRL -10%)
14.05.1993	Realignment (ESC –6.5%, PTA –8%)
2.08.1993	The ERM fluctuation bands are widened to $\pm$ 15%, except for the DM and the HFL
9.01.1995	The ATS joins the ERM with the new wide band ($\pm$ 15%)
6.03.1995	Realignment (ESC –3.5%, PTA –7%)
14.10.1996	The FIM joins the ERM with the new wide band ($\pm$ 15%)
25.11.1996	The LIT re-joins the ERM with the new wide band ($\pm$ 15%)
16.03.1998	Realignment (IRL +3%). The DR joins the ERM with the new wide band ($\pm$ 15%)

Note: ATS, BFR, DKR, DM, DR, ESC, FF, FIM, HFL, IRL, LIT, PTA and UKL denote, respectively, the Austrian schilling, the Belgian franc, the Danish krone, the Deustchemark, the Greek drachma, the Portuguese escudo, the French franc, the Finnish markka, the Dutch guilder, the Irish pound, the Italian lira, the Spanish peseta and the Pound sterling.

Figures 1a to 1h show the evolution of the exchange rates during the ERM history [1]. Following De Grauwe (2000), we can distinguish four different subperiods in the experience of the ERM. The first subperiod extended from the ERM inception, in March 1979, to January 1987. During this subperiod, the relatively large band fluctuations in the EMS (compared to those in the Bretton Woods system), together with relatively small and frequent realignments, helped to reduce the size of speculative capital movements and stabilised the system. The second subperiod, the so-called "New ERM", lasted from 1987 to the end of

---

[1] The fluctuation bands were built following Honohan (1979). We took into account the lack of symmetry between the two intervention limits due to the requirement that the upper intervention limit for currency X with respect to currency Y equals the lower intervention limit for currency Y with respect to currency X.

1991, coinciding with increasing confidence in the ERM, the removal of capital controls, and a greater convergence in the economic fundamentals. During these years there was not any realignment[2] The third subperiod covered successive crises of September 1992 and August 1993, where the evolution of the EMS into a truly fixed exchange rate system with almost perfect capital mobility led to credibility losses in a context of policy conflict among EMS countries about how to face the severe recession experienced in 1992-93. Finally, a fourth subperiod initiated after the crisis of 1993, when the EMS changed its nature in drastic ways: the EMS gained credibility with the enlargement of the fluctuation bands to ±15% (reducing the scope for large speculative gains) and with the fixed exchange rate commitment among potential EMU member countries. As a result, speculation became a stabilising factor and the market rates converged closer and closer to the fixed conversion rates, although the world was hit by a major crisis during the second half of 1998 (De Grauwe et al., 1999).

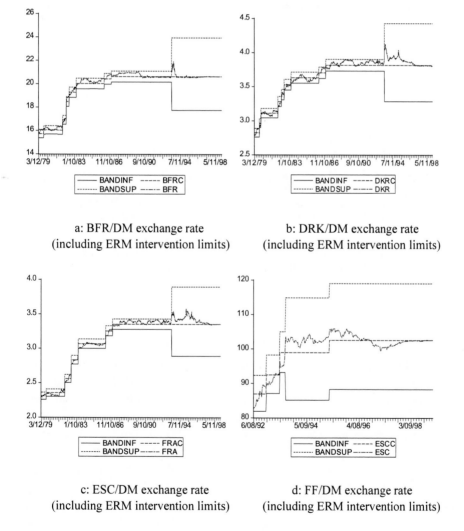

a: BFR/DM exchange rate
(including ERM intervention limits)

b: DRK/DM exchange rate
(including ERM intervention limits)

c: ESC/DM exchange rate
(including ERM intervention limits)

d: FF/DM exchange rate
(including ERM intervention limits)

---

[2] The 1990 technical realignment was due to the switching of the Italian lira to the narrow ±2.25 per cent band, bringing its central parity closer to its weak margin.

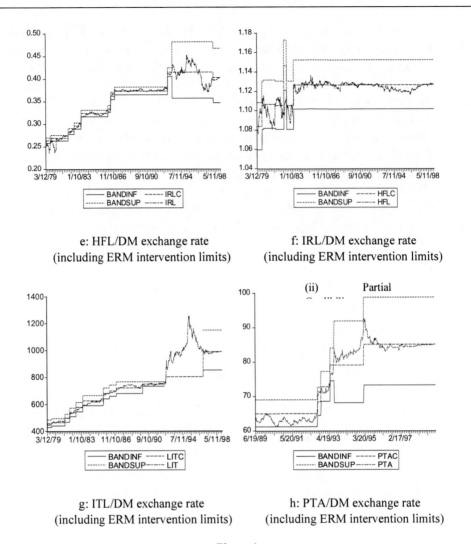

e: HFL/DM exchange rate
(including ERM intervention limits)

f: IRL/DM exchange rate
(including ERM intervention limits)

g: ITL/DM exchange rate
(including ERM intervention limits)

h: PTA/DM exchange rate
(including ERM intervention limits)

Figure 1

As mentioned above, although initially designed as a symmetric system around the ECU, a general consensus emerged that the EMS worked in an asymmetric way, with Germany assuming the leading role and the remaining countries passively adjusting to German monetary policy actions. In their turn, the follower countries found beneficial to behave in such a way, since they could take advantage of the firmly established anti-inflation credibility of the German Bundesbank (see, e.g., Giavazzi and Pagano, 1988, or Mélitz, 1988). On the other hand, these countries would have retained for some time a degree of monetary autonomy by resorting to capital controls, which would have allowed them to dissociate the evolution of domestic (i.e., onshore) interest rates from those prevailing in the Euromarket (i.e., offshore) (see Rogoff, 1985, or Giavazzi and Giovannini, 1989).

A common result to most of the empirical papers in this area is the finding that, both in terms of size and persistence, the effect is stronger from German variables to the other EMS countries' variables, rather than the other way round. In other words, whereas monetary policy in the other EMS countries would have being affected not only by German actions but by the other EMS partners also, German monetary policy would have operated rather independently.

This would point to a special role of Germany within the EMS, even though the hypothesis of German leadership or dominance might appear too strong. In von Hagen and Fratianni's words: "(I)n the short run, the EMS is best portrayed as an interactive web of monetary policies, where Germany is an important player, but not the dominant one (...) (I)t is tempting to conclude that many observers have mistaken German dominance with the relative strength of Germany and the relative weakness of France in the EMS" (von Hagen and Fratianni,1990, p. 373). Indeed, results in Bajo-Rubio et al. (2001) suggest that, for the whole period of analysis, there is two-way causality between, on the one hand, interest rates in Belgium, Denmark and the Netherlands, and, on the other hand, those in Germany. However, for the cases of France, Ireland, Italy, Portugal, Spain and the UK, causality is only found running from Germany to those countries. Overall, these results could be taken as a first indication of the special role played by Germany within the EMS, even though we cannot talk of "dominance" in a strict sense.

With the beginning of EMU, the former EMS ceased to have effect. It was replaced by the new modified exchange rate mechanism (the so-called ERM-II), which connected the currencies of the Member States outside the euro area to the euro (see Deutsche Bundesbank, 1998). This was important to ensure that excessive exchange-rate fluctuations do not cause problems in the internal market. Initially, only Denmark and Greece participated in ERM-II: a fluctuation margin of ±2.25% was set for the DKR (being 1 euro= 7.46038 DKR the central rate) and a standard margin of ±15% was agreed for the Greek dracma (GRD) (setting the central rate at 1 euro=340.750 GRD). Greece adopted the euro on 1 January 2001, leaving the ERM-II. On 27 June 2004, the Estonian kroon (being the central rate 1 euro=15.6466 kroon), the Lithuanian lita (with a central rate of 1 euro=3.45280 litas) and the Slovenian tolar (setting the central rate at 1 euro=239.640 tolar) joined ERM-II. On 2 May 2005 three other Member States joined ERM-II: Cyprus (beign the central rate 1 euro=0.585274 pound), Latvia (with a central rate of 1 euro=0.702804 lats) and Malta (setting the central rate at 1 euro=0.429300 liras). Slovakia followed suit on 25 November 2005 (being the central rate 1 euro=38.4550 koruna). For all these new members a standard margin of ±15% was stablished.

3   Credibility

3.1   Theoretical Framework

In the standard target zone model, inspired by Krugman (1991) the (log of the) exchange rate, x_t, depends both on a scalar measure of exchange rate fundamentals, f_t, and on its own expected rate of expected change, $E_t(dx / df)$, with the parameter γ indexing the importance of the latter effects:

$$x_t = f_t + \gamma E_t(dx_t / df)$$

(1)

where $E_t(\bullet)$ denotes an expectation taken conditionally on the information available at time t.

Equation (1) is a stochastic first-order differential equation. By ruling out speculative bubbles, the forward expectations solution can be derived (Bertola, 1994) where the saddle path exchange rate is equal to the discounted value of the future expected fundamentals:

$$x_t = \frac{1}{\gamma} \int_t^{\infty} E_t(f_\tau) e^{-(\tau-t)/\gamma} d\tau \tag{2}$$

In order to obtain a relationship between the contemporaneous exchange rate and the fundamentals:

$$x_t = x(f_t) \tag{3}$$

additional assumptions on the stochastic process of the fundamentals are needed.

3.1.1   The Free-Float Case

In the absence of intervention, f_t, is assumed to follow a Brownian motion process with drift μ and rate of variance σ^2:

$$df_t = \mu dt + \sigma dW_t \tag{4}$$

where dw_t is a standard Weiner process. Then, integrating (2) yields:

$$x_t = f_t + \gamma\mu \tag{5}$$

Therefore, in a free-float exchange rate regime characterized by no interventions, there would be a linear relationship between the contemporaneous exchange rate and the fundamentals. In the simplest case when the drift μ is zero, such relationship could be represented as the 45 degree line (see Figure 2). Therefore, the freely floating exchange rate must not deviate excessively from the fundamentals when the latter takes arbitrary large (positive or negative) values.

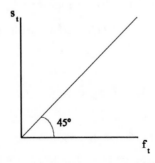

Figure 2: The exchange rate-fundamental relationship under the free-float case

3.1.2   A target Zone with Perfectly Credible Bands

In Krugman's (1991) basic target zone model, it is assumed that monetary authorities intervene in order to keep the exchange rate within a specific band around a central parity:

$$\underline{x} \le x_t \le \overline{x} \tag{6}$$

where $\underline{x}$ and $\overline{x}$ are the lower and upper edges of the exchange rate bands. From (6), the fundamental indicator is restricted to a band that corresponds to the exchange rate band:

$$\underline{f} \le f_t \le \overline{f} \tag{7}$$

where the lower and upper edges of the fundamental band satisfy $\underline{x} = x(\underline{f})$ and $\overline{x} = x(\overline{f})$.

In order to derive the exchange rate function (3) for the target zone case, and assuming that interventions in the exchange rate market are marginal, the expected exchange rate depreciation term in (1) can be derived using Ito's lemma. This results in a second-order differential equation for the exchange rate as a function of the fundamentals, with general solution as follows:

$$x_t = \gamma\mu + f_t + A_1 e^{\lambda_1 f_t} + A_2 e^{\lambda_2 f_t} \tag{8}$$

where $\lambda_1 > 0$ and $\lambda_2 < 0$ are the solutions of the characteristic equation

$$\lambda^2 \alpha \sigma^2 / 2 + \lambda \alpha\mu - 1 = 0 \tag{9}$$

and the constants of integration constants A_1 and A_2 being determined by the conditions that the exchange rate function $x(f)$ is flat at the edges of the fundamental band.

These boundary conditions are generally called "smooth pasting", which require that the path of x_t be tangent to the band, removing the possibility of one-way bets on the exchange rate at it approaches the boundaries. This smooth pasting property is one of the two main results of Krugman's model and implies that the exchange rate should be a non-linear function of the underlying fundamentals. The second main result is that the exchange rate function $x(f)$ looks life the S-curve in Figure 3 (again drawn for the simplest case when the drift μ is zero). Note that the exchange rate lies below the 45 degree line in the upper half of the figure and above it in the lower half. This is the so-called "honeymoon" effect: in a perfectly credible target zone, the expectations of future interventions to stabilize the exchange rates drag it towards the middle of the band, making it more stable than the underlying fundamental. Algebraically, this "bias due to the band" is represented by the exponential term in (8).

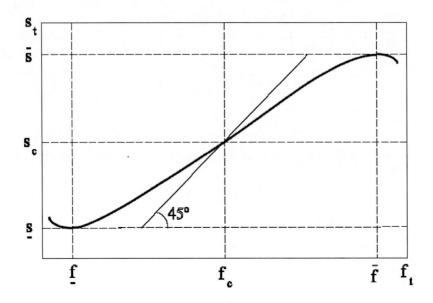

Figure 3: The exchange rate-fundamental relationship under a perfectly credible target zone

3.1.3   A Target Zone with Credibility Problems

Unlike Krugman's model, exchange rate realignments do occur fairly frequently, as seen in Section 2. Bertola and Caballero (1992) present a simple model of discrete exchange-rate intervention that allows for stochastic realignments. In addition to the fundamentals, the (log of the) central parity c_t, which is also a stochastic variable, is included in the determination of the exchange rate. For convenience, define:

$$x_t' \equiv x_t - c_t \tag{10}$$

$$f_t' \equiv f_t - c_t \tag{11}$$

so that x' and f' represents, respectively, the log deviation of the exchange rate and the fundamental from central parity. Using these identities, equation (1) can be re-written as:

$$x_t' = f_t' + \gamma E[(dx_t + dc_t)/dt] \tag{12}$$

Bertola and Caballero (1992) consider it possible for the official authorities to change the central parity only when the exchange rate reaches the bands. As a consequence, the term:

$$\frac{1}{dt} E[dc_t]$$

in (12) is zero inside the band, and therefore the solution is:

$$x_t^* = \gamma\mu + f_t^* + Ae^{\lambda_1 f_t^*} + Ae^{\lambda_2 f_t^*} \tag{13}$$

where λ_1 and λ_2 depend again on the parameters α, μ and σ, and only one constant, A, is to be determined since we are assuming a symmetric band.

Using identities (10) and (11), equation (13) can also be expressed in terms of the fundamentals and the central parity:

$$x_t = \alpha\mu + f_t + Ae^{\lambda_1(f_t-c_t)} - Ae^{\lambda_2(f_t-c_t)} \tag{14}$$

When f reaches either of the boundaries, the authorities may either intervene to bring the exchange rate back to the initial central parity (c_t) (i.e., defend the current parity) or declare a new fluctuation band $c_{t+1} = c_t \pm (\overline{x} - \underline{x})$ and unchanged width (i.e., realign the central parity). Probabilities $(1-p)$ and p are assigned respectively to these two options. As a result, depending on the value of p, the relationship between the contemporaneous exchange rate and the fundamental $[x_t = c(f_t)]$ assumes different shapes. When $0 < p < \frac{1}{2}$, the perfect credible target zone model is obtained, producing the S-shaped relationship. When $p = \frac{1}{2}$, the market evaluates as equally probable both an intervention and a realignment, the solution then coinciding with the free-floating 45 degree line. Finally, when $p > \frac{1}{2}$ expectations of future changes in the exchange rate are triggered even before the exchange rate reaches the boundaries, the $x(f)$ function being everywhere steeper than it could be under free float. Therefore, the solution locus becomes an inverted S, now the band for fundamentals being smaller than the exchange rate band (see Figure 4, drawn for the simplest case when the drift μ is zero).

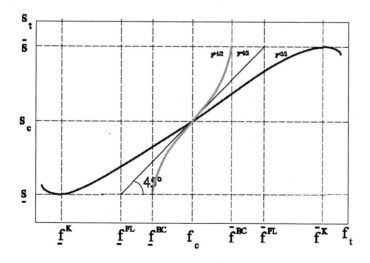

Figure 4; The exchange rate-fundamental relationship under an imperfectly credible target zone

3.2   The Credibility Issue

Credibility can be defined as the degree of confidence that economic agents assign to the announcements made by policymakers. In a context of an exchange rate target zone, like the EMS, credibility refers to the perception of economic agents with respect to the commitment to maintain the exchange rate around a central parity. Therefore, the possibility that the official authorities change the central parity could be anticipated by the economic agents, triggering expectations of future changes in the exchange rate that could act as a destabilising element of the system.

In this section we present four credibility measures developed in the literature. Some of them have been widely employed in empirical works, while others, like the marginal credibility indicator, have received much less attention.

3.2.1   Svensson's Simple Test

Svensson (1991) presented a simple test to study the credibility of a target zone exchange rate regime with fluctuation bands. There are two traditional versions of this test. In the first one, it is assumed that there is no arbitrage, while in the second version uncovered interest parity (UIP) is assumed to hold. In order to compare this indicator with the one based on the drift-adjustment method, a more recent variant of the former is usually estimated.

To that end, we can calculate a 100% confidence interval for the expected rate of realignment of the exchange rate under study *vis-à-vis* the German mark, using the three-month interbank rate. Taking into account the UIP hypothesis, the expected rate of realignment is bounded according to:

$$i_t - i_t^* - (\overline{x}_t - x_t) / \tau \le E_t \left[\Delta c_{t+\tau} \right] / \tau \le i_t - i_t^* - (\underline{x}_t - x_t) / \tau \tag{15}$$

where x_t is the deviation of the log exchange rate s_t from the log central parity c_t, $\underline{x}_t$ and $\overline{x}_t$ are the lower and upper bounds of the exchange rate bands, τ is the maturity (valued at 3/12 for a 3-month maturity), $i - i^*$ is the interest rate differential, and $E[\bullet]$ is the expectation operator.

3.2.2   The Drift-Adjustment Method

This method, originally proposed by Bertola and Svensson (1993), computes an econometric estimate of the expectations of economic agents regarding the realignment in the ERM. These realignment expectations constitute an inverse measure of credibility. The drift-adjustment method also assumes UIP to hold.

In this method, the expected rate of devaluation g_t^τ is obtained from:

$$g_t^\tau = i_t - i_t^* - E_t \left[\Delta x_{t+\tau} \middle| nr \right] / \tau \tag{16}$$

This procedure implies estimating the expected rate of depreciation within the band in absence of realignment (*nr*) [the last term on the right-hand side of equation (16)], and then computing the expected rate of devaluation g_t^τ. Once g_t^τ has been estimated, the corresponding 90 percent confidence intervals can be calculated. These intervals can be directly compared with those of the more recent version of Svensson's simple test.

The expected rate of depreciation within the band can be estimated using a linear regression model where the exchange rate and the domestic and foreign interest rates are taken as explanatory variables:

$$\frac{x_{t+\tau} - x_t}{\tau} = \sum_j \alpha_j d_j + \beta_1 x_t + \beta_2 i_t^* + \beta_3 i_t + \varepsilon_{t+\tau}$$

(17)

where $x_{t+\tau}$ and x_t are the exchange rate (log) deviation from the central parity in period $t+\tau$ and t, respectively, and where i_t and i_t^* are the national and German three-month interest rates, respectively. The variables d_j denote the dummies for the subperiods between the realignments and the widening of the bands.

3.2.3   Models of Discrete Choice

This kind of models aims to estimate the probability of realignment by means of econometric techniques. To that end, explanatory variables are used to compute that probability, assuming normal or logistic distributions. Among the explanatory variables, it is usual to include the interest rate differential, the inflation differential, the current account balance, and the unemployment rate, leading to estimates using monthly or quarterly data.

A logit model based on the following equation could be estimated:

$$P_t = P(y_t = 1) = \Phi(z', \delta) = \frac{e^{z_t'\delta}}{1 + e^{z_t'\delta}}; \qquad z_t'\delta = \delta_1 + \delta_2 z_{1t}$$

(18)

where $\Phi(\bullet)$ is the logistic distribution function ($\Phi(\lambda)$ is the probability that a normally distributed random variable with zero mean and unit variance does not exceed λ), z_{1t} denotes an explanatory variable, and $P(y_t = 0) = 1 - P_t$. The parameters in equation (18) are estimated by maximizing the logarithm of the likelihood function with respect to individual observations:

$$LogL = \sum_{t=1}^{T} y_t \log \Phi(z'_t, \delta) + \sum_{t=1}^{T} (1 - y_t) \log\left[1 - \Phi(z'_t, \delta)\right]$$

(19)

The drift-adjustment method estimates the 90% confidence interval. If both limits of the interval were simultaneously greater than, or less than, zero, the agents would have expected realignments with 90% confidence. Assuming that when $y_t=0$ there is no credibility and that when $y_t=1$ there is credibility, we use the drift-adjustment method to design the logit model. In other words, when $y_t=0$ the limits of the confidence interval for the expected rate of realignment are both simultaneously greater than or less than zero. When $y_t=1$ this does not occur. This strategy allows us to obtain the probability that agents assign to the credibility of the exchange rate regime at each moment of time.

3.2.4   Marginal Credibility

This credibility measure proposed by Weber (1991) focuses on the ability of policy announcements to influence the public's expectations. It measures the impact of official announcements on exchange rates and may be thought of as the weight placed on the announcement when the public forms their expectations. This credibility measure is equal to one if the policy-maker always makes fully credible announcements, and tends to zero as the announcements become non-credible. Marginal credibility (α_t) is defined as:

$$s_t - E_{t-1}\left[s_t\right] = \gamma + \alpha_t \left[c_t - E_{t-1}\left[s_t\right]\right] + u_t \tag{20}$$

where the expectation operator is conditional on the information available in *t-1*, and u_t is a random disturbance.

Ledesma et al. (2005) applied these credibility indicators to weekly exchange and interest rate data from eight ERM countries (Belgium, Denmark, France, Ireland, Italy, the Netherlands, Portugal and Spain) covering the complete EMS history. Their empirical application differs from previous studies in the literature in three main respects. First, their main contribution is the use of several credibility indicators, some of which have never been applied before to all of the currencies under study. This allows them to strengthen the results obtained in this paper. Second, they analyse a longer period than that of previous studies, covering the complete EMS history. Third, they have carried out a comparison of the prediction qualities of the different indicators, in order to explore their ability to capture the main ERM events (realignments, changes in the fluctuation bands and speculative pressures).

The country-by-country analysis made by Ledesma et al. (2005) led them to the following main conclusions:

(i)   before the currency crisis in late 1992 and for most of the countries, the exchange rate policy was credible, except for the Italian case (a similar conclusion is derived in Weber, 1991).

(ii)   the 1992 currency turbulence was accompanied, in the first instance, by credibility losses in all countries, except Belgium and the Netherlands. This is consistent with the fact that the Dutch guilder and the Belgian franc, along with the Deutschmark, were the only currencies that were not affected by speculative attacks during the fall of 1992

(iii)   after the widening of the fluctuation bands there was a gain in credibility for the currencies participating in the ERM, with the exception of the Belgian franc and the Irish pound. This is consistent with, and tends to confirm, the claims by both Ayuso et al. (1994) and Sosvilla-Rivero et al. (1999) that the broadening of the bands led to a decrease in volatility to levels comparable to those prevailing before the crisis.

4 Currency Crises

In the last decade, some experiences as the turbulence of the European ERM in 1992-93, the Turkish lira crises in 1994 and 2001, the collapse of the Mexican peso in 1994, the East Asian turmoil during 1997-98, the Russian currency disturbances in 1998, or the crisis of the Brazilian real in 1999, have renewed the interest in the analysis of the potential causes of currency crises. Accordingly, extensive literature has sprung up in recent times in order to explore the underlying factors behind such phenomena. Specifically, two are the main strands of research, the so-called First and Second-Generation currency crises models.

In this section, we briefly review this literature, at both the theoretical and empirical level. In addition, we present the main results of our recent empirical investigation about the potential causes behind the subsequent devaluation episodes within the EMS, a work that can be considered as a first attempt to reconcile the implications of these two predominant theories, often viewed as mutually excluded.

4.1 Theoretical Framework

4.1.1 First Generation Models of Currency Crises

First generation literature is built on Krugman's (1979) seminal paper, whose partial-equilibrium scenario points out the incompatibility of overly expansionary policies and the indefinite maintenance of a fixed exchange rate regime. Such policies arise as a result of weak economic fundamentals and are materialised in an excess of internal credit relative to money demand growth. Then, sustaining the exchange rate parity requires the gradual reduction of foreign reserves that, following a simple arbitrage argument, leads to a speculative attack against the currency. This attack forces authorities to abandon the fixed regime, switching to a flexible exchange rate one.

Let's highlight the basic lines of the model. Consider a simple monetary economy in which the (real) demand for domestic money depends negatively on the domestic nominal interest rate (i_t):

$$\frac{M_t}{P_t} = \alpha_0 - \alpha_1 i_t \ , \quad \alpha_1 > 0$$

$$(21)$$

where M_t is the nominal money demand and P_t is the domestic price level. Under capital mobility, perfect asset substitution and perfect foresight, the domestic nominal interest rate is linked to the foreign rate (i^*) - which is fixed since our focus is on a small open economy - by the interest parity condition:

$$i_t = i^* + \frac{\dot{E}_t}{E_t}$$

$$(22)$$

where E_t is the exchange rate, expressed as units of foreign currency per domestic currency,

and $\dfrac{\dot{E_t}}{E_t}$ represents the expected (and actual, given the perfect foresight assumption) rate of

change in the exchange rate. Domestic and foreign prices are related through Purchasing-Power Parity condition:

$$P_t = P^* E_t \tag{23}$$

in which the foreign price level (P^*) is assumed constant as long as the small open economy hypothesis holds.

Finally, the money supply is determined by two components: the domestic credit, or the stock of domestic assets owned by the central bank, and the foreign reserves:

$$M_t = C_t + \bar{E} f_t \tag{24}$$

where C_t is the domestic credit, $\bar{E}$ the fixed exchange rate and f_t represents the stock of international reserves expressed in foreign currency units.

Since the exchange rate is fixed, the central bank must intervene in the money market to make domestic monetary conditions consistent with the fixed rate. To get this goal, authorities have two instruments at their disposal: variations in C_t and/or in f_t. However models *à la* Krugman establish a restrictive premise about the evolution of the domestic credit, that is assumed to grow at an exogenous (positive) constant rate γ :

$$\frac{\dot{C_t}}{C_t} = \gamma \,,\, \gamma > 0 \tag{25}$$

Under this strong assumption, the sole instrument available to defend the exchange rate is the persistent exhaustion of the foreign reserves stock at the same rate as the domestic credit grows, given that the fixed rate implies a constant money demand:

$$\frac{\dot{f_t}}{f_t} = -\gamma \tag{26}$$

Rational investors, who hold assets in domestic currency and know the finite stock of reserves committed to defend the currency, realise that in absence of a speculative attack they will incur a capital loss, given that reserves will continue declining through time while authorities keep their promise to convert national into foreign currency at a fixed price. Then investors launch an attack that anticipates the date at which authorities would have run out of reserves and forces them to abandon the fixed rate switching to a float one. This is the basic framework of first generation models, also named *exogenous policy* models, in which rational financial markets respond to expansionary monetary policies that, in the long run, are inconsistent with the maintenance of a fixed exchange regime.

Several papers have extended Krugman's model in several directions. Flood and Garber (1984) introduce the notion of shadow exchange rate, named the floating rate that clears the foreign exchange market in the precise time when collapse takes place. Other papers consider imperfections in the markets for goods (i.e., sticky prices) and assets (i.e., imperfect capital mobility) [see, e.g., Calvo (1987) and William (1988)], introduce uncertainty about the threshold of foreign reserves committed to defend the currency [see Otani (1989) and William (1989), among others] or regarding the domestic credit expansion [see Blanco and Garber (1986) and Dornbusch (1987)]. Finally, other contributions propose some policy prescriptions to preserve a fixed rate regime; among others the introduction of controls on short-term capital movements (see Eichengreen et al., 1995) or the introduction of an international lender-of-last resort to provide cash on demand under certain circumstances (see Kindleberger, 1996).

Empirically, first generation models have been extensively applied to the analyses of currency crises in developing economies, especially Latin-American countries. Blanco and Garber (1986) estimate the one-step-ahead probability of devaluation for the Mexican peso from 1973 to 1982 using quarterly data; their results show how the estimated probabilities of devaluation jumped to peak values of 20 percent in the preceding moments of the two most important peso devaluations occurred in 1976 and 1982, respectively. The growth of the domestic credit played a central role in explaining these devaluations.

Cumby and Van Wijnbergen (1989) find similar results in their case-study of Argentina. Using monthly data from 1979 to 1981, they focus on the one-step-ahead probability of collapse; their results highlight the incompatibility between the domestic credit policy followed by the authorities and the maintenance of the crawling peg system as the major source of the peso collapse at the beginning of 1981.

The rationale of first generation models have also been used to explain some episodes in target zones. In their study of 16 devaluations occurred in Denmark, Finland and Sweden between 1979 and 1989, Edin and Vredin (1993) estimate the one-step-ahead probability of devaluation, and its expected size (measured as the change in the central parity of the target zone) conditional on a devaluation taking place. Their empirical model included a broad set of fundamentals: money supply, output, foreign interest rates, foreign price levels, international reserves and real exchange rates. Among them, the indicators with a higher explanatory power were money supply, output and the stock of reserves; the remaining variables were statistically insignificant in explaining the probability and the expected size of devaluations.

Ötker and Pazarbaşioğlu (1997) evaluates the role of macroeconomic fundamentals in generating episodes of speculative pressures on six currencies (e.g., Belgium, Denmark, France, Ireland, Italy and Spain) participating in the ERM, between 1979 and 1993. The observed regime changes are first estimated using a set of speculative pressures that includes short-term interest rate deviations from the anchor country (Germany), the deviation of the spot rate from the central parity and the change in official foreign reserves. The contribution of a group of variables representing the state of the economy (i.e., central banks' domestic credit, output, the short-term interest rate and price level of the anchor country and the real exchange rate) is then evaluated. The results show how episodes of speculative pressures were generally preceded of a deterioration in economic fundamentals, particularly in France, Denmark, Ireland and Spain.

A common criticism to first generation models is the overly simplistic scenario that they set out. The passive behavior of the monetary and fiscal authorities compared to the "rational" disposition of private agents is quite far from reality (Saquib (2002)). Moreover, at the empirical level, these models failed in providing an adequate explanation of the ERM crisis during 1992-93 or the Mexican collapse in 1994. These and other shortcomings moved the literature towards a new line of research.

4.1.2   Second Generation Models of Currency Crises

In a sound contribution to this emerging literature, Obstfeld (1986) showed how speculative attacks could arise even when the stance of monetary and fiscal policies was consistent, at least in the short-run, with the exchange regime. This was the pioneer work for a new generation of models that emphasized the key role played by self-fulfilling expectations in explaining currency crises.

A crucial assumption in this setting is that authorities do not fix their policy stance in a mechanical way as first generation models suggested. Instead of this, authorities adopt an optimizing behavior that takes into account agents' expectations. At the same time, agents form such expectations using conjectures about authorities' responses. This circularity opens the door to the appearance of multiple equilibria and self-fulfilling speculative attacks, even in circumstances where the economic conditions are consistent with the maintenance of a fixed rate.

As a conclusion we might say that while in first generation models rational financial markets anticipate the crises, in the second generation framework crises are provoked by markets themselves. We present a simple model by Sachs et al. (1996) that highlights the main implications of these also called *endogenous-policy* models.

Let's consider a small open economy with a policymaker and a private sector composed of many (atomistic) agents. As typically in this framework, the policymaker wants to minimize a quadratic loss function subject to his budget constraint:

$$\begin{cases} \underset{\{x_t,\pi_t\}}{\text{Min}} \ L = \frac{1}{2}\left(\alpha\pi_t^2 + x_t^2\right), \ \alpha > 0 \\ \\ \text{s.t. } Rb_t = x_t + \theta\left(\pi_t - \pi_t^e\right), \theta > 0 \end{cases} \tag{27}$$

Assuming purchasing power parity and interest parity hold, π_t represent the actual rate of inflation that will coincide with the expected rate of devaluation (easily derived from equation (23) in the Krugman's setting), and x_t is the (policy determined) tax revenue; the rationale for this loss function is that policymakers dislike inflation (or devaluation) and taxes (interpreting the preferences of the private sector).

In the resources constraint, b_t represents the real stock of net commitments of the policymaker, R the real interest rate (that should equal the world interest rate, given the small open economy assumption) and π_t^e is the given expected rate of inflation (devaluation).

Solving the problem expressed in equation (27) we obtain:

$$x_t = \frac{\lambda}{1-\lambda}\theta\pi_t, \quad \text{and} \quad \pi_t = \frac{1}{\theta}(1-\lambda)\left(Rb_t + \theta\pi_t^e\right), \quad \text{where} \quad \lambda \equiv \frac{\alpha}{\alpha+\theta^2} < 1 \tag{28}$$

Substituting into the loss function yields:

$$L^d(b_t) = \frac{1}{2}\lambda\left(Rb_t + \theta\pi_t^e\right)^2 \tag{29}$$

where the superscript d stands for "devaluing".

We now turn to analyze the case when the policymaker has the pre-commitment to maintain a fixed exchange rate, what means $\pi = 0$ (i.e., actual devaluation rate equals zero).

Rewriting the original problem under this assumption yields:

$$\begin{cases} \underset{\{x_t\}}{\text{Min}} \ L = \frac{1}{2}x_t^2 \\ \\ \text{s.t. } Rb_t + \theta\pi_t^e = x_t \end{cases} \tag{30}$$

where the corresponding loss function is given by:

$$L_t^f(b_t) = \frac{1}{2}\left(Rb_t + \theta\pi_t^e\right)^2 \tag{31}$$

where the superscript f stands for "fixing". But in this simple setting we are not taking into account some other non-economic costs associated with the decision of devaluing. We are referring to political costs (i.e., loss of pride, voter disapproval, maybe even removal from office) that the empirical evidence have shown not negligible. For simplicity we will model such costs using an exogenous (fixed) amount $c > 0$.

The policymaker will find optimal to devalue if $L^d(b_t, \pi_t^e) + c < L^f(b_t, \pi_t^e)$, using equations (29) and (31) becomes:

$$Rb_t + \theta\pi_t^e > k, \quad \text{where} \quad k \equiv (1-\lambda)^{-1/2}(2c)^{1/2} > 0 \tag{32}$$

This is the central equation in the Sachs' model; it summarizes the possible set of equilibria that may arise from the interaction between the policymaker's actions and the agents' expectations. According to this condition a devaluation will take place whenever the stock of debt or expectations of devaluation are too high. But a natural question is how these expectations are formed given the temptation to devalue summarized in equation (32), or posed in a similar way, what set of values for π_t^e constitute a rational expectation equilibrium given the policymaker actions. Several outcomes are possible; let's analyze the two extreme cases:

i) First assume that agents set $\pi_t^e = 0$. This will be a rational expectations equilibrium only if the policymaker opt to maintain the pre-committed fixed rate, what considering the condition stated by equation (32) means:

$$Rb_t \leq k \tag{33}$$

ii) Now assume perfect foresight holds (i.e., the size of expected and actual devaluation concur), then from equation (28) we obtain: $\theta\pi_t = \theta\pi_t^e = \dfrac{1-\lambda}{\lambda}Rb_t$. Substituting this expression into (32) yields:

$$Rb_t > \lambda k \tag{34}$$

These two conditions, depicted in Figure 5, are very useful to determine the set of plausible equilibria. As can be seen, the different levels of debt give rise to the partition of the state space in three different regions:

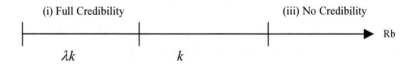

Figure 5: Debt levels and multiple equilibria

Full Credibility: For low levels of debt (smaller than λk) the full credible region operates, in which the only rational expectations equilibrium is not devaluing and setting expectations to zero; in fact, in this region the policymaker will opt for maintaining the fixed rate regardless of devaluation expectations.

No Credibility: For high levels of debt (larger than k) the policymaker will inevitably devalue, independently of the agents' expectations; thus the only equilibrium arise from devaluing and setting positive devaluation expectations. This is the region where the pre-committed fixed rate is not credible.

Partial Credibility: For intermediate levels of debt (larger than λk but smaller than k) two rational equilibria arise. This is the partial credibility zone where the fixed regime may survive or not depending on the probability assigned by the private sector. If agents expect a devaluation of the precise size $\pi_t^e = \frac{1}{\theta}\left[(1-\lambda)/\lambda\right]Rb_t$, then such expectations will be validated by the policymaker since defending the pre-committed rate will not be optimal (i.e., $L^d > L^f$); on the contrary, if agents expect no devaluation, no devaluation will take place since it will be optimal (i.e., $L^d < L^f$) for the policymaker to keep the fixed regime.

Summarizing these results, this model offers a very simple setting to demonstrate how self-fulfilling speculative attacks can cause the collapse of the fixed regime. It is important to note the two main implications of this model: a) Self-fulfilling episodes do not occur at any level of economic fundamentals, represented in this setting by the the real stock of debt. Only for intermediate levels of debt, in the range of the partial credibility zone, multiple equilibria may arise; b) Devaluation expectations are self-fulfilling because they tend to validate themselves since they make it more costly for the policymaker to maintain the pre-committed fixed regime. This cannot be the case if the level of debt is too high (low), then devaluation expectations become irrelevant since the unique optimal option for the policymaker would be to maintain (renege) the fixed rate.

Second generation models offer an appealing scenario to explain some currency crises occurred in the mid-90s, especially the 1992-93 EMS turmoil and the crisis of the Mexican peso in 1994. Eichengreen and Wyplosz (1993) analyze the realignments within the EMS during the two-year period 1992-93. They find that the origin of the speculative pressures suffered by the participating currencies was a sudden change in the agents' expectations, prompted by the strict requirements established in the Maastricht Treaty (1992) and the gradual removal of capital controls.

Jeanne (1997) compares the role of fundamentals and speculative pressures in the case of the French franc 1992-93 crisis. He concludes that self-fulfilling speculation was at work although weak fundamentals might have prepared ground for speculation.

Agénor and Masson (1999) analyze the collapse of the Mexican peso trying to identify the factors underlying such crisis. They propose a model in which interest rate differentials and real exchange rate appreciation are used to evaluate the credibility of the policymaker in maintaining the pegged rate; estimation results indicate that prior to the peso collapse there was no significant increase in devaluation fears and no perceived shift in the authorities' policy preferences, but the increase in the interest rate differential that occurred after the devaluation may have resulted from such a shift.

On the contrary, second generation models fail to provide an adequate conceptual framework when applied to more recent episodes, mainly the East Asian 1997-98 crisis. This prompted the arising of a new generation of models that stress the relation between financial and currency crises, treating them as "twin" phenomena. These constitute the so-called Third-Generation currency models, whose scope goes beyond our focus. For interested readers some customary references are Chang and Velasco (1998), Corsetti et al. (1999) and Krugman (1999).

Other promising lines of research that concentrates an increasing proportion of present literature are the analysis of contagion effects, deeply treated in Schmukler and Zoido (2003) and Rigobon (2003), and the application of the tools of microstructure finance. The latter approach permits to take into account not only relevant economic fundamentals but also market participants sentiments by incorporating both macro (interest rates, money supply, foreign reserves, etc.) and micro variables (order flow, inventory, etc.) [see Frankel et al. (1996), Evans and Lyons (1999) and Lyons (2001)].

4.2   Empirical Evidence for the EMS

Maroto-Illera et al. (2002) depart from the previous papers by using duration analysis to examine the survival of the central parities in the ERM. They applied this approach to eight currencies participating in the ERM, using quarterly data of exchange rates *vis-á-vis* the Deustchemark for the first quarter 1979 to the fourth quarter 1998 period, covering the complete history of the EMS.

These authors make use of the two main theoretical frameworks (first- and second-generation models of currency crisis), as well as considering an eclectic model that combines features of both models. Following the empirical applications of the first generation models, they start by estimating the probability of a regimen change as a function of economic fundamentals. As domestic factors, the money supply, the current account balance, the unemployment rate, the price level, the production level, the central parity, the level of international reserves and the real exchange rate are included. As for the foreign factors, they consider the money supply, the current account balance, the price level and the production level of the anchor country. In contrast with the first generation models of currency crisis, second generation models emphasise the role of speculative proxies as potential causes of such crises. Following the empirical literature in this area, they examine the role of the following variables in explaining the probability of a regimen change: the level of international reserves, the interest rate differential with respect to Germany, a credibility measure, the share price index and the central parity deviation. Finally, in an attempt to improve the explanatory power of these two approaches, the eclectic model combines the explanatory variables suggested by both models. Given that they examine the entire ERM history (from 1979 to 1998), combining features of both approaches could be a sensible option in order to take into account the possibility of different types of crises during the eighties (perhaps more related with weak county fundamentals) and the nineties (when the beliefs of foreign exchange market participants and the policy makers' reputational capital seemed to play a major role).

In the context of a target zone, like the ERM, the analysis of the duration of the central parities is a very interesting question given the central role played by credibility, as we have seen in previous sections. If the dependence on duration is found to be positive (i.e., as time passes the probability of a change in the regime takes place increases) then economic fundamentals would have played a key role in the establishment of the exchange regimes. This view could be supported by the strict requirements imposed in the Maastricht Treaty (1992) to the potential candidates to join the Economic and Monetary Union (EMU). On the contrary, if the dependence on duration is found to be negative (i.e., as time passes the probability of a regime change decreases), then credibility would have been the relevant question considered by the authorities in determining their exchange policies.

Maroto-Illera et al. (2002) conclude that the probability of maintaining the current regime decreases very rapidly for the short durations (less than 4 quarters), to register then smoother variations as time increases. Therefore, for those regimes with high durations, the ERM would have been relatively stable, while for the (more common) regimes associated with short durations would have been more unstable. The probability of maintaining a certain regime is estimated to be 0.56.

Furthermore, these authors, after undertaking an exhaustive analysis to compare and validate alternative models, find that the eclectic specification would be the most appropriate to fit their data set. Their results suggest that the real exchange rate, the interest differentials and the central parity deviation would have negatively affected the duration of a given central parity, while credibility, the level of international reserves and the price level in the anchor country would have positively influenced such duration. Therefore, the empirical evidence presented in Maroto-Illera et al. (2002), suggesting that the sustainability of a given exchange rate regime in the ERM was affected both by fundamental variables and by investors' expectations on government behaviour, might indicate that to prevent currency crises it is not sufficient to pursue sound economic policies, but policymakers must enhance their reputational capital with respect to their commitment to maintain the exchange rate around a central parity.

5   Concluding Remarks

This paper has been devoted to the past, present, and future of the EMS. As we have seen, the EMS was launched as an attempt to foster economic integration and the co-ordination of economic policies in the EU, giving birth to a new symbolic currency (the ECU, predecessor of the euro). The centrepiece of the EMS was the ERM, an adjustable peg system with a number of interesting features. First, it was fully European (with no reference to the US Dollar or to the gold). Second, it was initially designed to be symmetric (no currency played any special role, in contrast to the US Dollar in the Bretton Woods system). Third, the responsibility for maintaining each bilateral exchange rate within its margin was explicitly shared by both countries, establishing a strong collective commitment to provide mutual support through bilateral, automatic and unlimited interventions.

We have distinguished four different subperiods in the experience of the ERM. In the first subperiod (March 1979-January 1987), the relatively large fluctuation bands in the EMS coupled with relatively small and frequent realignments, helped to reduce the size of speculative capital movements and stabilised the system. The second subperiod (January 1987-December 1991), coincided with increasing confidence in the ERM, the removal of capital controls and a greater convergence in the economic fundamentals, not registering any realignment. The third subperiod (September 1992-August 1993) was characterised by successive crises due to credibility losses in a context of policy conflict among EMS countries about how to face the severe recession experienced in 1992-93. The fourth subperiod (August 1993-December 1998) witnessed credibility gains with the enlargement of the fluctuation bands to ±15% and with the fixed exchange rate commitment among potential EMU member countries.

Following Krugman (1991), growing theoretical literature has attempted to explain exchange rate movements inside official fluctuation bands such as those of the EMS with the help of target zone models. The basic idea is that the bands, as long as they are credible, have stabilising effects on market expectations of the future behaviour of the underlying exchange rate. Therefore, credibility becomes a key issue in examining the behaviour of the EMS, since the possibility that the official authorities change the central parity could be anticipated by the economic agents, triggering expectations of future changes in the exchange rate that could act as a destabilising element of the system.

Therefore, after revising the theoretical behaviour of an exchange rate in both a target zone with perfectly credible bands and a target zone with credibility problems, we have reviewed some empirical evidence dedicated to the analysis of the ERM credibility. Some conclusions can be drawn on this analysis of the evolution of the perception of economic agents with respect to the commitment to maintain the exchange rate around a central parity. First, before the currency crisis in late 1992 and for most of the countries, the exchange rate policy was credible, except for the Italian case. Second, the 1992 currency turbulence was accompanied, in the first instance, by credibility losses in all countries, except Belgium and the Netherlands. Finally, after the widening of the fluctuation bands there was a gain in credibility for the currencies participating in the ERM, with the exception of the Belgian franc and the Irish pound.

On the one hand, the ERM turmoil in 1992-93 renewed the interest in the analysis of the potential causes of currency crises. An extensive theoretical and empirical literature has sprung up in recent times in order to explore the underlying factors behind such phenomena. We have briefly reviewed this literature, where two are the main strands of research, the so-called first- and second-generation currency crises models. The first generation models stress the role of weak economic fundamentals, such as monetary and/or fiscal imbalances, in explaining currency crises, while the second-generation models point out that crises may arise without any noticeable change in economic fundamentals. Two crucial assumptions in these models are the introduction of nonlinearities and the reaction of government policies to changes in private behaviour. The empirical evidence examined in this paper suggest that an eclectic model that combines the explanatory variables suggested by both first- and second-generation models would be the most appropriate to fit ERM data. In particular, the real exchange rate, the interest differentials and the central parity deviation would have negatively affected the duration of a given central parity in the ERM, while credibility, the level of international reserves and the price level in the anchor country would have positively influenced such duration.

One can learn some important lessons from the experience of the EMS. First, that a regional exchange rate system constitutes a good compromise between free floating and international exchange system which is not very realistic at the moment, Second, that stable exchange rate are not sufficient to obtain better growth prospects, being the latter influenced by a host of factors (see, e. g., Blanchard *et al,.*1985) . Third, domestic monetary policy independence must be abandoned if the exchange rate is rigidly fixed. Finally, a fixing exchange rate can only work as a transitory device towards full monetary policy (see De Grauwe, 2000).

Regarding the future of the EMS, we have to remember that in 2004 ten new countries (i.e., Czech Republic, Estonia, Cyprus, Latvia, Lithuania, Hungary, Malta, Poland, Slovenia and Slovakia) will become EU members states, although this will not imply immediate membership in EMU. After a two-year derogation period, their convergence will be evaluated on the basis of the Maastricht Treaty. But, in contrast to the past experiences of United Kingdom and Denmark, these Accession Countries (AC) will not be granted with opt-out clauses in joining the EMU. In other words, the way toward the adoption of the euro is a non-return one.

Among the four convergence criteria (i.e., price stability, sustainable fiscal position, exchange rate stability and low interest rates) that will be used in evaluating the catching-up process of these economies, the exchange rate stability[3] is perhaps the most striking one, given the crucial role that exchange regime plays in determining macroeconomic stability and investment climate.

Since the assessment of exchange rate stability includes as a mandatory the participation in the Exchange Rate Mechanism II (ERM-II) for at least two years, most of the AC are expected to join it. In fact, over the past years the euro has increasingly gained importance as the main reference currency in both the pegged and managed regimes prevailing in the AC countries: Estonia and Lithuania have a currency board pegged to the euro, while Cyprus and Hungary unilaterally shadow ERM-II (with an official announced central rate and fluctuation bands of ± 15%).

The ERM-II is a pegged but adjustable system in which central parities are defined against the euro and not between all other participating currencies. Hence, this bilateral nature, in contrast to the multilateral one of its predecessor the ERM, is expected to reduce the frequency and the scope of interventions. Central rates and fluctuation bands are set by common agreement involving the ministers of the euro zone, the European Central Bank (ECB) and National Central Bank (NCB) governors of the AC.

The standard fluctuation band is ± 15%, while not excluding the possibility of setting a narrower band. Intervention support of the ECB to the National Central Banks (NCB) is automatic at the margins of the band (marginal interventions), any interventions within the band (intra-marginal interventions) need not be (but may be) supported by the ECB. Finally, realignments of central parity are made by the common procedure, which both the ECB and the member states have the right to initiate.

As any other fixed regime the ERM-II is expected to be "leading", strictly meaning that the design of economic policies must take into account the maintenance of the pre-committed rate. Hence, participation in the system is expected to play a stabilizing role in AC's economies.

First of all, ERM-II will contribute to get exchange rate steadiness. "Its stabilizing role should derive from the announcement of the central parity, which should provide the markets with a lead and thereby reduce exchange rate fluctuations" (Czech National Bank, 2003, p. 5). This role must be enhanced by the ECB's intervention assistance, though in principle such support is only planned at the margins.

Moreover, arguments in favor of the ERM-II highlight its function in disciplining national authorities to pursue consistent macroeconomic policies. In particular, past experiences show the importance of price stability and sustainable public finances for maintaining a credible fixed regime.

However a carefully revision of recent episodes should warn us about some potential problems associated with the participation in a system like the ERM-II. With limited exchange rate flexibility and an environment of increasing capital mobility, the large capital inflows that will be directed towards these economies (mainly in the form of foreign direct

---

[3] The EU in its documents on the fulfillment of the exchange-rate convergence criterion clearly states: "the observance of the normal fluctuations margins provided for the exchange-rate mechanism of the European Monetary System, for at least two years, without devaluing against the currency of any other Member State", *Treaty on European Union, Article 121 (1)*.

investment) are expected to exert appreciating pressures on domestic currencies. Alarmingly, large capital inflows figured in virtually every financial crisis of the 1990s.

Other features that characterized recent crises, and that are still present in accession economies, are the basic development of their financial systems, limiting to a great extent the managing of interest rates as a defensive device, and the higher levels of inflation, pushing up real exchange rates and increasing the probability of future realignments be needed.

Finally some credibility problems may arise from the fact that central parities are subject to realignment: In the case of such transition economies involved in a catching-up process the credibility of the central rate may be eroded over time.

These and other potential shortcomings have not gone unnoticed for some of the AC. For example in the Czech Republic (one of the most likely members to join the ERM-II in the next two years), its National Bank in a brief report that analyses the exchange rate convergence criterion states: "The ERM-II has certain stabilizing potential. This potential, however, is dependent on the level of transformation of the economy, the degree of alignment of economic cycle, and on economic policy consistency. For transition economies or for countries with insufficiently consolidated structural or fiscal policies, the balance of the costs and benefits of joining the ERM-II is not necessarily clear-cut" (Czech National Bank, 2003, p. 6). Furthermore, it is stated that "[s]taying in the ERM-II for longer than the minimum required period is not deemed desirable or beneficial to macroeconomic stability" (Czech National Bank, 2003, p. 10).

A deep look into the evolution of the ERM indicates that to prevent a currency crisis is not sufficient to pursue sound economic policies, but policymakers must enhance their reputational capital with respect to their commitment to maintain the exchange rate around the central parity. This is a very valuable lesson that AC's authorities must not forget in their way toward formal entry into the EMU.

References

[1] Agénor, P.-R. and Masson, P. (1999): "Credibility, reputation, and the Mexican peso crisis". *Journal of Money, Credit and Banking*, Vol. 31, pp.71-84.

[2] Ayuso, J., Pérez-Jurado, M. and Restoy, F. (1994): "Is exchange rate risk higher in the ERM after the widening of fluctuation bands?". Working Paper 9419, Banco de España.

[3] Bajo-Rubio, O., Sosvilla-Rivero, S. and Férnandez-Rodríguez, F.(2001): "Asymmetry in the EMS: New evidence based on non-linear forecasts". *European Economic Review*, Vol. 45, pp. 451-473.

[4] Bertola, G. and Caballero, R. J. (1992): "Target zones and realignments". *American Economic Review*, Vol. 82, pp. 520-536.

[5] Bertola, G. and Svensson, L.E.O. (1993): "Stochastic devaluation risk and the empirical fit of target zone models". *Review of Economic Studies*, Vol. 60, pp. 689-712.

[6] Blanco, H. and Garber, P. (1986): "Recurrent devaluation and speculative attacks on the Mexican peso". *Journal of Political Economy*, Vol. 94, pp. 148-166.

[7] Calvo, G. A. (1987): "Balance of payments crises in a cash-in-advance economy". *Journal of Money, Credit and Banking*, Vol. 19, pp. 19-32.

[8] Chang, R. and Velasco, A. (1998): " Financial crises in emerging markets: A canonical model". *Working Paper* **6606**, National Bureau of Economic Research (NBER) .

[9]   Czech National Bank (2003): "ERM II and the Exchange-rate Convergence Criterion". Information material for the Czech Government . Available at http://www.cnb.cz/en/pdf/ERM_II_vlada_15_07_03_en.pdf

[10] Commission of the European Communities (1979): "The European Monetary System". *European Economy*, July.

[11] Corsetti, G., Pesenti, P. and Roubini, N. (1999): "Paper tigers? A model of the Asian crisis?". *European Economic Review*, Vol. 43, pp. 1211-1236.

[12] Cumby, R.E. and Van Wijnbergen (1989): "Financial policy and speculative runs in a crawling peg: Argentina, 1979-1981". *Journal of International Economics*, Vol. 27, pp. 111-127.

[13] De Grauwe, P. (2000): Economics of monetary union, Fourth edition (Oxford: Oxford University Press).

[14] De Grauwe, P., Dewachter, H. and Veestraeten, D. (1999): "Explaining recent European exchange-rate stability". *International Finance*, Vol. 2, pp.1-31.

[15] Deutsche Bundesbank (1998): "Operational features of the new European exchange-rate mechanism", Monthly Report, October, pp. 17-23.

[16] Dornsbusch R. (1987): "Collapsing exchange rate regimes". *Journal of Development Economics,* Vol. 27, pp. 71-83.

[17] Edin, P. A. and Vredin, A. (1993): "Devaluation risk in target zones: Evidence from the Nordic countries". *Economic Journal*, Vol. 103, pp. 161-175.

[18] Eichengreen, B. and Wyplosz, C. (1993): "The unstable EMS". *Brooking Papers on Economic Activity*, Vol. 1, pp. 51-143.

[19] Eichengreen, B., Tobin, J. and Wyplosz, C. (1995): "Two cases for sand in the wheels of international finance". *Economic Journal*, Vol. 105, pp. 162-172.

[20] Evans, M. and Lyons, R. (1999): "Order flow and exchange rate dynamics". Working Paper 7317, *National Bureau of Economic Research (NBER)*.

[21] Flood, R. P. and Garber, P. M. (1984): "Collapsing exchange-rate regimes: Some linear examples". Journal of International Economics, Vol. 17, pp. 1-13.

[22] Frankel, J., Galli, G. and Giovannini, A. (1996): The Microstructure of Foreign Exchange Markets (Chicago: University of Chicago Press).

[23] Giavazzi, F. and Pagano, M. (1988): "The advantage of tying one's hands. EMS discipline and Central Bank credibility". *European Economic Review*, Vol. 32, pp.1055-1075.

[24] Honohan, P. (1979): "A guide to the arithmetic of the EMS exchange-rate mechanism". Central Bank of Ireland Quarterly Bulletin, Autumn.

[25] Jeanne, O. (1997): "Are currency crises self-fulfilling? A test". *Journal of International Economics,* Vol. 43, pp. 263-286.

[26] Kindleberger, C. (1996): Manias, Panics, Crashes: A History of Financial Crises. Third Edition (Chichester: John Willey & Sons).

[27] Krugman, P. (1979) : "A model of balance-of-payments crises". *Journal of Money, Credit and Banking*, Vol. 11, pp. 311-325.

[28] Krugman, P. (1991): "Target zones and exchange rate dynamics". Quarterly Journal of Economics. Vol. 106, pp. 669-682.

[29] Krugman, P. (1999): "Balance sheets, the transfer problem, and financial crises". Available at http://www.mit.edu/people/krugman/index.html – hard.

[30] Ledesma-Rodríguez, F., Navarro-Ibañez, M., Pérez-Rodríguez, J. and Sosvilla-Rivero, S. (2005): "Assesing the credibility of a target zone: Evidence from the EMS". *Applied Economics*, Vol. 37, pp. 2265-2287.

[31] Lyons, R. (2001): The Microstructure Approach to Exchange Rates (Cambridge, MA: The MIT Press).

[32] Maroto-Illera, R., Pérez-Bermejo, F. and Sosvilla-Rivero, S. (2002): "An eclectic approach to currency crises: Drawing lessons from the EMS experience". *Working Paper* 2002-22, FEDEA. Available at ftp://ftp.fedea.es/pub/Papers/2002/dt2002-22.pdf.

[33] Mélitz, J. (1988): "Monetary discipline and cooperation in the European Monetary System: A synthesis", in: F. Giavazzi, S. Micossi and M. Miller (eds.) The European Monetary System (Cambridge: Cambridge University Press), pp. 51-79.

[34] Obstfield, M. (1986): "Rational and self-fulfilling balance-of-payments crisis". *American Economic Review*, Vol. 76, pp. 71-81.

[35] Obstfeld, M. (1994): "The logic of currency crises". Working Paper 4640, *National Bureau of Economic Research (NBER)*.

[36] Otani, K. (1989): "The collapse of a fixed exchange rate with a discrete realignment of the exchange rate". *Journal of Japanese and International Economics*, Vol. 17, pp. 250-269.

[37] Ötker, I. and Pazarbaşioğlu, C. (1997): "Speculative attacks and macroeconomic fundamentals: Evidence from some European countries". *European Economic Review*, Vol. 41, pp. 847-860.

[38] Rigobon, R. (2003): "Empirical methods in contagion: Which ones work, whoch ones don't?". In A. Morales-Zumaquero (ed.), Progress in Economics Research, Special Issue on International Macroeconomics. New York: Nova Science Publishers.

[39] Rogoff, K. (1985): "Can exchange rate predictability be achieved without monetary convergence? Evidence from the EMS". *European Economic Review*, Vol.28, pp, 93-115.

[40] Sachs, J.; Tornell, A. and Velasco, A. (1996): "The Mexican peso crisis: Sudden death or death foretold?". *Journal of International Economics*, Vol. 41, pp. 265-283.

[41] Saquib, O. (2002): "Interpreting currency crises a review of theory, evidence and issues". *Working Paper* **303**, German Institute for Economic Research (DIW).

[42] Schmukler, S. and Zoido, P. (2003): "Financial globalization, crises, and contagon". In A. Morales-Zumaquero (ed.), Progress in Economics Research, Special Issue on International Macroeconomics. New York: Nova Science Publishers.

[43] Sosvilla-Rivero, S., Fernández-Rodríguez, F. and Bajo-Rubio, O. (1999): "Exchange rate volatility in the EMS before and after the fall". *Applied Economics Letters*, Vol. 6, pp. 717-722.

[44] Svensson, L.E.O. (1991): "The simplest test of target zone credibility". *IMF Staff Papers*, Vol. 38, pp. 655-665.

[45] von Hagen, J. and Fratianni, M. (1990): "German dominance in the EMS: Evidence from interest rates". *Journal of International Money and Finance*, Vol. 9, pp. 358-375.

[46] Weber, A. (1991): "EMS credibility". *Economic Policy*, Vol. 12, pp. 58-102.

[47] William, A. (1988): "The collapse of a fixed exchange regime with sticky prices and imperfect substitutability between domestic and foreign bonds". *European Economic Review*, Vol. 32, pp. 1817-1838.

[48] William, A. (1989): "Devaluation expectations and speculative attacks on the currency". *Scandinavian Journal of Economics*, Vol. 91, pp. 97-116.

In: International Macroeconomics: Recent Developments   ISBN: 1-59454-901-X
Editor: Amalia Morales Zumaquero, pp. 285-308   © 2006 Nova Science Publishers, Inc.

Chapter 13

BEHAVIOR OF NOMINAL AND REAL EXCHANGE RATES IN TRANSITION ECONOMIES

Fabrizio Coricelli[1], Boštjan Jazbec[2] and Igor Masten[3]
[1]University of Siena, Central European University, Budapest and CEPR
[2]University of Ljubljana, Slovenia
[3]European Institute University, Florence, and University of Ljubljana, Slovenia

I   Introduction

Transition to a full-fledged market economy entailed major structural and institutional changes. Opening up of the economies has implied pressure for large changes in relative prices, including the real exchange rate. The opening up of the capital account has increased the exposure of transition countries to shocks originating in international financial markets. This paper analyzes the behavior of exchange rates, both nominal and real, since the start of transition. It emphasizes three main factors affecting such behavior. First, the role of the exchange rate during the stabilization phase following the launch of liberalization and reform policies; second, the effects of structural change and productivity dynamics on the real exchange rate and finally, the role of different policy rules in affecting the relationship between exchange rates and inflation.

The paper then discusses the choice of the exchange rate regime, which is crucial for accompanying the process of integration, both "real" and financial, in the world economy, and especially with the European Union.

Countries that are candidate for entry in the European Union (CEECs) are following a highly heterogeneous path, despite the common goal of accession to the European Union, and thus eventually to the Eurozone. A few countries have adopted a currency board system, while others have opted for floating exchange rates with inflation targets. In between these two extremes there are countries that manage the exchange rate. In this paper we first attempt to evaluate whether such heterogeneity in exchange rate regimes is justified on structural heterogeneity of the different countries and by different policy goals. We then analyze the workings of different policy rules, highlighting the fact that for small open economies, as most CEECs are, the contrast between exchange rate and inflation targets is largely artificial.

For small open emerging market economies, the possibility of running an effective and independent monetary policy is limited. Therefore, even if desirable from a theoretical point of view, floating rates and independent monetary policy geared towards achievement of inflation targets are hardly feasible in practice for small open emerging economies. In the paper we emphasize the reasons for such difficulties and identify the main channels through which the exchange rate affects the economy. An essential component of this analysis is the relationship between exchange rates and inflation, the so-called pass-through issue. We provide a review of the empirical literature on pass-through in transition countries and conclude that pass-through depends on structural characteristics of the countries and on the specific policy rules adopted. The paper concludes by arguing that in transition countries pass-through tends to be high and thus nominal exchange rate behavior plays a key role in affecting inflation rather than the real exchange rate.

II Macroeconomic Reforms and Inflation Stabilization

In spite of the common objective of creating a market economy, transition countries are a highly heterogeneous group. Aslund, Boone and Johnson (1996) look at the correlation between political regime and economic policies - aimed especially at macroeconomic stabilization - and conclude that in these terms, transition economies can be divided into five groups. The first group of countries like Poland (1990)[1], former Czechoslovakia (1991), Estonia (1992), Latvia (1992), and Albania (1992), was initially ruled by liberal governments which enforced radical reforms in order to stabilize and liberalize the economies. Inflation usually soared in the beginning of the reform, but was then brought rapidly down to less than 50 percent. A second group of countries has proceeded with less radical reforms enforced, however, also by non-socialist governments: Hungary, Lithuania, Bulgaria, Russia, and the Kyrgyzstan. With the exception of Hungary, all these countries had higher inflation after two years of reform than the countries from the first group, and none had inflation of less than 50 percent by 1994. In the third group there are countries where the former communists stayed in power and delayed the reform. This was the case of Romania, Moldova, Belarus, Ukraine, Kazakhstan, Uzbekistan, and Turkmenistan. Significant cuts in inflation rates were gained only in years of 1994 and 1995. However, in some countries from this group (Belarus and Romania) the macro projections of increasing inflation have indeed materialized in recent years. The fourth group consists of war-torn countries of the former Soviet Union: Georgia, Armenia, Azerbaijan, and Tajikistan which entered the transition with high inflation and remained there until 1995 when even in these countries were able to cut down the inflation from over 1000 percent at the beginning of transition in 1991. The last group represents countries of former Yugoslavia which began the macroeconomic stabilization already at the end of the 80s and entered the transition with relatively low rates of inflation in comparison with other transition economies. Data on inflation in respected groups of countries are presented in Table 1. Aslund, Boone and Johnson (1996) define the degree of reform on two criteria: how rapidly inflation was brought under control, and the change in the level of the liberalization index as measured by de Melo, Gelb and Denizer's index (1996)[2].

---

[1] The take-off of the reform as determined by Aslund, Boone, and Johnson (1996).
[2] For the purpose of the paper focus is only on the inflation rates.

Although some countries have tried to undertake early and radical stabilization and liberalization and others have chosen to delay the implementation of these policies, the central problem in many transition economies is still the one of controlling inflation. Despite significant differences in economic structure and institutional frameworks, the inflation and stabilization experiences of transition and market economies are similar in many respects. Monetary accommodation and lack of financial discipline are crucial in sustaining inflation. However, the transition economies have started the process of disinflation with inherited instabilities in the system. Price liberalization and privatization fueled the inflationary spiral and almost endangered economic and political reformation of previously centrally planned economies. The evidence on transition economies confirms the overdetermination of prices and wages in these economies (Sahay and Vegh, 1995). The source of inflation inertia has been usually linked to the traditional factors of excessive money and wage growth, but also to an underlying natural pressure for real exchange rate appreciation and relative price adjustments (Coricelli and Jazbec, 2003). Additional characteristics of the transition economies have been increasing capital inflows to the region. Although these inflows could be the sign of a growing confidence in transition countries, they could also bring their own problems, which have already been demonstrated particularly in the Czech Republic, Russia, and Hungary in recent years.

An attempt to stabilize the inflationary economy requires the choice of nominal anchors. The history of the inflation stabilization tells us that either the nominal exchange rate or the money supplies are among the most effective nominal anchors to be used in inflation stabilization throughout the world. The relevant additional anchors generally fall under money or credit constraints, nominal interest rates, price and wage controls. Fisher, Sahay and Vegh (1996) emphasize the need for action in transition economies in six areas: macroeconomic stabilization; price liberalization; trade liberalization and current account convertibility; enterprise reform (especially privatization); the creation of a safety net; and the development of the institutional and legal framework for a market economy (including the creation of a market-based financial system). One cannot separate one area of action from the others. However, the sound macroeconomic stabilization is necessary for the success of all other reforms since it forces some state enterprises to contract as a consequence of the implementation of hard-budget constraints and pushes people into a new private sector.

Table 1: Inflation rates in percents (end-year) and classification of reforms in transition economies

	1991	1992	1993	1994	1995	1996	1997	1998	1999	2000	2001
Radical reform											
Poland	60,4	44,3	37,6	29,4	21,6	18,5	13,2	8,6	9,8	8,5	3,6
Czech Republic	52,0	12,7	18,2	9,7	7,9	8,6	10,0	6,8	2,5	4,0	4,1
Slovak Republic	58,3	9,1	25,1	11,7	7,2	5,4	6,4	5,6	14,2	8,4	6,5
Estonia	303,8	953,5	35,6	41,7	28,9	14,8	12,5	4,2	3,8	5,0	4,2
Latvia	262,4	959,0	35,0	26,3	23,1	13,1	7,0	2,8	3,2	1,8	3,2
Albania	104,1	236,6	30,9	15,8	6,0	17,4	42,1	8,7	-1,0	4,2	3,5

	1991	1992	1993	1994	1995	1996	1997	1998	1999	2000	2001
Gradual Reform											
Hungary	32,2	21,6	21,1	21,2	28,3	19,8	18,4	10,3	11,2	10,1	6,8
Bulgaria	338,9	79,4	63,8	121,9	32,9	310,8	578,6	0,9	6,2	11,4	4,8
Lithuania	345,0	1161,0	188,8	45,0	35,7	13,1	8,4	2,4	0,3	1,4	2,0
Russia	161,0	2506,1	840,0	204,4	128,6	21,8	10,9	84,5	36,8	20,1	18,8
Kyrgyzstan	170,0	1259,0	1363,0	95,7	32,3	34,9	14,7	18,4	39,9	9,5	3,8
Ex-communist											
Romania	222,8	199,2	295,5	61,7	27,8	56,9	151,4	40,6	54,8	40,7	30,2
Moldova	151,0	2198,0	837,0	116,1	23,8	15,1	11,1	18,2	43,8	18,5	6,4
Belarus	93,0	1559,0	1996,0	1959,9	244,2	39,3	63,4	181,7	251,3	107,5	46,3
Ukraine	161,0	2730,0	10155,0	401,0	181,7	39,7	10,1	20,0	19,2	25,8	6,1
Kazakhstan	137,0	2984,0	2169,0	1158,3	60,4	28,6	11,2	1,9	17,8	9,6	6,4
Uzbekistan	169,0	910,0	885,0	1281,4	116,9	64,3	27,6	26,1	25,2	28,0	24,2
Turkmenistan	155,0	644,0	9750,0	1327,9	1261,5	445,8	21,5	19,8	21,2	7,4	11,7
War-torn											
Georgia	131,0	1177,0	7488,0	6473,9	57,4	13,7	7,3	7,2	10,9	4,6	3,4
Armenia	25,0	1341,0	10896,0	1761,0	32,2	5,8	21,8	-1,3	2,1	0,4	3,0
Azerbaijan	126,0	1395,0	1294,0	1788,0	85,0	6,5	0,4	-7,6	-0,5	2,2	1,5
Tajikistan	204,0	1364,0	7344,0	1,1	2133,3	40,5	163,6	2,7	30,1	60,8	12,5
Former Yugoslavia											
FYR Macedonia	229,7	1935,0	241,8	55,0	9,0	-0,6	2,6	0,8	2,3	6,0	3,7
Croatia	250,0	938,0	1149,0	-3,0	3,8	3,4	3,8	5,4	4,4	7,4	2,6
Slovenia	247,1	92,9	22,8	19,5	9,0	9,0	8,8	6,5	8,0	8,9	7,0

Source: EBRD Transition Report 1999 and 2002, Aslund, Boone and Johnson (1996).

While inflation dynamics in transition economies can be described by the same basic factors that are used in market economies, there are critical institutional and historical legacies from the centrally planned era, which have affected the transition process. Calvo and Kumar (1994) summarize four striking features of former centrally planned economies in the transition to a market-based system. First, output in all transition economies has dramatically declined. Some estimates range between 20 to 40 percent (EBRD Transition Reports). The decline in output has been accompanied by sharp increases in unemployment. In some countries, the unemployment rate came to about 15 percent of the work force. Second, in the period after price liberalization, inflation sharply increased. It should be noted that some countries entered the transition with very high inflation rates (e.g. Yugoslavia and consequently all former Yugoslav republics). Third, in most countries, large fiscal deficits have emerged as a result of the dramatic decline in tax revenues, largely because of the steep drop in output. This fall in government revenue has not been matched by an equal reduction in public spending. Governments in many countries have continued subsidizing state-owned firms to prevent further output decline and rise in unemployment. And fourth, there has been a huge initial deterioration of the external current account and depreciation of the real exchange rate. Nonetheless, the real exchange rate of most transition countries has appreciated significantly since the onset of the reforms, adversely affecting the competitiveness of the exporting sectors (Krajnyak and Zettelmeyer, 1998).

Macroeconomic policies in transition economies have primarily focused on containing the inflationary consequences of price liberalization and what was considered to be a significant monetary overhang. Supply shortages and deteriorating real monetary balance have accelerated the inflation rates across the region. To cut down the inflationary expectations immediately, most transition economies have introduced exchange-rate-based stabilization programs. In so doing, the credibility of the stabilization programs across the region was at least temporarily established. People were able to daily check the progress of the stabilization by looking at current exchange rates. This effect was reflected in a relatively successful stabilization of the velocity of money and stable money demand in a very short period of time.

The main driving force behind the initial output decline and its later recovery were structural reforms implemented during the transition process. It is argued that in spite of different initial conditions and approaches to macroeconomic stabilization across transition economies, once the structural reforms had begun, most economies have experienced similar paths of output development and macroeconomic performance. Following the same line of argument, one could argue that the relative price development should exhibit similar, if not the same, pattern in transition economies. The evidence on almost all transition economies indeed reflects a continuous appreciation of the real exchange rate after initial devaluation of domestic currencies initiated by price liberalization. Since the real exchange rate is a function of a number of fundamental real variables, which change over time, the most intriguing question is to determine which actual exchange rates are in line with their fundamentals. In an attempt to provide an answer to this question, two main approaches to the real exchange rate modeling can be widely recognized (Clark, 1996). The first one characterizes the equilibrium exchange rate as a desirable real exchange rate consistent with an ideal macroeconomic performance establishing internal and external balance. The internal balance is defined as the level of economic activity that keeps the inflation rate constant, while the external position is balanced if the external current account can be regarded not only as sustainable, but also as appropriate based on desired levels of savings and investment. In this sense, *desirable real exchange rate* is a normative measure. On the other hand, *natural real exchange rate* is a positive concept, which involves the specification and estimation of an equation that explains the actual movements of the real exchange rate in terms of changes in economic fundamentals. A distinctive characteristic of both definitions is characterization of the fundamentals that are believed to determine the real exchange rate. While the first concept attempts to find desirable and potential economic variables, the second concept simply concentrates on the actual movements of the determinants of the real exchange rate. The concept of an equilibrium real exchange rate is especially delicate in transition economies. As these economies were going through massive structural changes whose dynamics directly affect the determination of the fundamentals and consequently, the real exchange rate, it would be too ambitious to define the equilibrium real exchange rate for the transition economies in early stages of transition (Coricelli and Jazbec, 2001). For that reason, the notion of the actual real exchange rate is used in what follows, although some reflection is also cast on equilibrium real exchange models.

III How to Measure Real Exchange Rate?

Problems encountered in the measurement of both concepts of the real exchange rate are usually associated with the multiplicity of theories underlying the real exchange rate definition and with difficulties involved in the use of alternative price or cost indices. Any survey on the modeling and estimating the real exchange rate, therefore, necessarily offers a biased view on the subject. Any view may easily be questioned on the grounds of different approaches to a growing literature on real exchange rate economics. To reduce the subjectivity of the approach, only the basic concepts within both approaches to the real exchange rate modeling are presented in what follows. In so doing, the clarity of the real exchange rate definitions is hopefully established.

III.1 Real Exchange Rate as the Relative Price of Tradable to Non-Tradable Goods

If E is the nominal exchange rate defined as units of domestic currency per unit of foreign currency, P_T^f is the world price of tradables in terms of foreign currency, and P_N is the price of non-tradable goods, the real exchange rate, e, can be identified as:

$$e = \frac{E P_T^f}{P_N}.$$

(1)

Assuming that the Law of One Price holds, $P_T = E P_T^f$, expression (1) is written as:

$$e = \frac{P_T}{P_N}.$$

(2)

The Law of One Price defines tradable goods as those goods whose prices are determined entirely by prices abroad and the nominal exchange rate. In this formulation, all other goods are implicitly non-traded in the sense that their prices are determined by other factors besides international prices. Expression (2) summarizes incentives that guide resource allocation across the tradable goods and non-tradable goods sectors. An increase of e defined as (2) represents depreciation. An increase in the real exchange rate makes the production of traded goods relatively more profitable, inducing resources to move out of the non-tradable to tradable sector. Additionally, the real exchange rate as defined in (2) provides an approximation of the degree of competitiveness of the country's tradable sector and measures the cost of domestic production of the tradables. A decline in the real exchange rate reflects the fact that there has been a decrease in the domestic cost of producing tradable goods. If there are no changes in the world price of tradables, this decline in the real exchange rate represents an improvement of the country's degree of international competitiveness. Finally, the above expression might reflect the composition of the non-tradable goods' consumption in the total consumption. Given both the tradable goods price and the supply of non-tradables, a decline of the real exchange rate reflects the fact that there is an increase in consumption of non-tradable goods and vice versa.

The above definition, however, generally suffers from three problems (De Grauwe, 1996). First, it ignores the impact of the changes in the nominal exchange rate. Second, it is not clear whether the price of tradables, P_T, should include the issue of exchange rate controls on international trade. The presence of such exchange rate controls raises the question of whether to define a real exchange rate inclusive or exclusive of them (Edwards, 1994). And third, it is empirically questionable whether the Law of One Price for tradables holds continuously. Apart from the absence of transportation costs, the validity of the Law of One Price demands perfect markets, perfect competition and free entry. This is manifestly not the case in practice, even if there are always market forces working in that direction. Empirical research indicates that prices of similar goods in various countries tend to move in the same direction, but are not identical (Obstfeld, 1985; Micossi and Milesi-Ferretti, 1994; De Gregorio, Giovannini, and Wolf, 1994). Even if theoretical concepts of the real exchange rate measured as the relative price of tradables in terms of non-tradable goods are reasonably straightforward, their empirical measurement raises difficult practical problems particularly in finding operational counterparts for the required price indices of tradable and non-tradable goods (De Gregorio, Giovannini, and Krueger, 1993; Hinkle and Nsengiyumva, 1999). In constructing the price indices required for calculating the real exchange rate, one major conceptual issue is how to actually classify goods as tradable and non-tradable. In principle, tradable goods consist of all goods that enter international trade as exports or imports. Tradables do not actually have to be traded but only be capable of being exported or imported. Tradability of a certain good is usually established by the ratio of exports or imports - or even the sum of exports and imports - over the total production of that good. De Gregorio, Giovannini, and Wolf (1994) take any good whose ratio of exports to its total volume of production is greater than 10 percent as a tradable good. On this criterion, the agriculture, mining, manufacturing, and transportation sectors are classified as tradable and all other sectors as non-tradable (Chinn, 1997). On the other hand, however, only a few goods and services are totally non-tradable with respect to the real exchange rate index. Additionally, even if the tradability of a good is established, the data required for calculating the real exchange rate are often not available. At most, national income statistics provide value-added GDP data measured by sectors, which classify as data for the purpose of calculating the implicit price deflators for different sectors of the economy. This method of calculating the real exchange rate has, however, two major shortcomings (Hinkle and Nsengiyumva, 1999). The first results from the conceptual difficulties of classifying the different sectors of production as tradable and non-tradable sectors. This is particularly difficult in many transition economies, which lack tracking of long time series and were exposed to structural changes that transformed previously non-traded sectors to the traded sectors. The second shortcoming stems from the high level of aggregation of the data on GDP by sector of origin. This problem is widely associated with services, which mainly include public administration and government, whose prices could not be taken as market determined. Generally, however, there is no consensus on which appropriate qualitative dividing line to use in classifying sectors as tradable and non-tradable. Mostly, it is the matter of a qualitative judgment about which production sectors should be classified as tradables based on the extent of actual or potential participation in foreign trade. The various criteria used in the empirical literature still remain arbitrary and are not necessarily appropriate for all countries.

III.2 Real Exchange Rate as Deviation from Purchasing Power Parity (PPP)

A more traditional concept of the real exchange rate relies on the Purchasing Power Parity (PPP) doctrine. The PPP doctrine is basically a notion that the exchange rate between the currencies of any pair of countries should equilibrate to a ratio of aggregate price indices for the two countries multiplied by an appropriate constant scale factor, or that the percentage change in the exchange rate should equal the difference between the percentage rates of inflation in the two countries. As a parity or arbitrage condition that characterizes the equilibrium relationship between an exchange rate and a ratio of price indices, PPP does not necessarily imply that causation simply runs in one direction, although in using the PPP assumption as a building block for the exchange rate determination models, it has in general been assumed that causation runs from changes in exogenous variables through changes in the ratio of price indices to changes in the exchange rate (Isard, 1987).

Accordingly, the bilateral real exchange rate, e, is equal to the bilateral nominal exchange rate, E, multiplied by the ratio between the foreign price level, P^f, and the domestic price level, P. Denoting the deviation from PPP by e_{PPP}, we have:

$$e_{PPP} = \frac{EP^f}{P}.$$

(3)

Expression (3) defines the deviation from the PPP view of the real exchange rate for a particular country. The bilateral real exchange rate is the simplest and easiest to calculate of all other measures of the real exchange rate indices. The term appreciation is used to refer to an increase in the value of the home relative to foreign currency. Graphically, an appreciation corresponds to a decrease in the real exchange rate index, e, defined in (3). Although this definition of the real exchange rate has been widely used in literature, it suffers from two major measurement problems. First, proxies for the ratio between foreign and domestic price levels have to be chosen. Should the Wholesale Price Index (WPI), which contains mainly tradable goods prices in the two countries, be used? Or, should the Consumer Price Index (CPI), which contains a large share of non-tradable goods prices in the two countries, be used? Second, it is unclear which nominal exchange rate, E, is the most appropriate. Should a nominal bilateral exchange rate with respect to the foreign currency be used? Or should one use a nominal multilateral rate that considers the variability of the exchange rates of a large number of foreign trade partners? In that case, which country's weights and averaging method for computing the multilateral real exchange rate should be used?

The multilateral or real effective exchange rate is used when multiple trading partners are considered. Sometimes, the term 'effective' is used to describe the exchange rate index, which includes the effects of tariffs, subsidies, and other charges on the domestic costs of imports and domestic prices of exports (Hinkle and Nsengiyumva, 1999). The multilateral real exchange rate index is defined as a weighted version of equation (3) where appropriate weights, g_i, for each foreign countries, i = 1,...,N, are used. The sum of weights must equal one. The multilateral real exchange rate can be calculated either as a geometric or arithmetic average. Although the arithmetic average is easier to calculate, the geometric averaging technique is usually used because it has certain properties of symmetry and consistency that an arithmetic index does not. The geometric multilateral real exchange rate, e_{PPP}^m, is defined as the following:

$$e_{PPP}{}^m = \prod_{i=1}^{N}(E_i P_i^f)^{gi}(\frac{1}{P}).$$

(4)

Practical calculations of the multilateral real exchange rate involve many techniques, which in general provide mathematically equivalent results; however, in general, they use different statistical information as by-products. These methods decompose the components of the multilateral real exchange rate index differently and proved supplementary empirical information useful in analyzing the evolution of the exchange rate indices (Brodsky, 1982). In addition to problems related to calculations of the bilateral real exchange rate, the multilateral exchange rate involves problems of the choice of an appropriate weighting scheme and possible adjustments for shares of trade represented in calculations (Hinkle and Nsengiyumva, 1999). It is again the extent of qualitative judgments that matters in determining which approach one should take in calculating the multilateral real exchange rate.

If the Law of One Price holds for traded goods, it is possible to calculate any of the various concepts of the real exchange rate indices from given values of the others. However, empirically, the Law of One Price holds at best only loosely for traded goods, and measurement errors affect the accuracy of all the empirical real exchange rate measures. Edwards (1989) provides an interesting point discussing the problems related to the definitions of the real exchange rates as expressed in equations (2) and (3). Assume that the price indices, P^f and P, for foreign and home country, respectively, are geometric weighted averages of tradable and non-tradable prices:

$$P^f = P_N^{f\,\alpha} P_T^{f\,1-\alpha} \quad \text{for foreign country}$$

(5)

$$P^f = P_N{}^\beta P_T{}^{1-\beta} \quad \text{for home country}$$

(6)

Assume further that the country in question is a small country and that the Law of One Price holds for tradable goods. Log-differentiating equations (2), (3), (5), and (6), and combining them gives the relation between percentage changes in the real exchange rate, e, and the PPP real exchange rate, e_{PPP}, as follows[3]:

$$\dot{e} = \frac{1}{\beta}\dot{e}_{PPP} + \frac{\alpha}{\beta}(\dot{P}_T^f - \dot{P}_N^f).$$

(7)

---

[3] Dot over a variable represents the percentage change of the variable.

Expression (7) shows that, in general, changes in the two definitions of the real exchange rate will differ. Moreover, changes in the two definitions of the real exchange rate can even go in the opposite direction, depending on the behavior of foreign relative prices $(\dot{P}_T^f - \dot{P}_N^f)$. Relative prices in the domestic economy may move differently from those abroad due to various shocks. Generally, two main sources of shock are considered: productivity growth in the traded goods sector and changes in the terms of trade. However, even if the foreign relative price of tradables in terms of non-tradable goods does not change, the change in domestic relative price of tradables will be proportional to the change in the *external* exchange rate, e$_{PPP}$. Since β, the share of the non-tradable sector in the home economy, is positive but less than one, the change in the domestic relative price of tradables in terms of non-tradables, e, will be larger than the change in its *external* real exchange rate. If, for example, e$_{PPP}$ depreciates because of foreign inflation or a devaluation, the relative price of tradables will depreciate by more through the effect of the Law of One Price on the prices of traded goods, which changes by the full amount on the devaluation or foreign price increase. The opposite holds for an appreciation of the *external* real exchange rate. Also, one can show that a depreciation of the foreign relative price of a tradable good can cause an appreciation of the *external* domestic real exchange rate even though its domestic relative price of tradables in terms of non-tradables has depreciated. To see this effect, equation (7) is solved for the *external* real exchange rate index, e$_{PPP}$, as the following:

$$\dot{e}_{PPP} = \beta\dot{e} - \alpha(\dot{P}_T^f - \dot{P}_N^f). \tag{8}$$

It is even possible in some circumstances for the domestic *external*, e$_{PPP}$, and *internal*, e, real exchange rate to move in opposite directions. Such a situation will occur if the change in the foreign relative price of tradable goods is greater than the change in domestic *internal* real exchange rate. Furthermore, the larger is the share of non-tradables abroad relative to a share in the home country, and the greater is the change in the foreign relative price of tradable goods, the likelihood of such contrary movements in a country's *external* and *internal* real exchange rates will be greater. Moreover, taxes and administered price effects may create a further divergence between the *external* and *internal* domestic real exchange rates. These findings are especially important when the determination and development of the real exchange rate in transition economies are analyzed.

Identification of such economic fundamentals is central to the proper interpretation of movements in the real exchange rates and, therefore, the efficacy of any attempt by policy-makers to effect changes in them. Since inconsistencies in the data may pose serious analytical problems in some cases, the best practice would typically involve constructing and analyzing several measures of the real exchange rate indices. All *external* indices of real exchange rate measures contain the nominal exchange rate. Movements in nominal exchange rates tend to be much larger than those in the various measures of the relative domestic and foreign prices because nominal exchange rates respond quickly to monetary as well as real shocks to the economy. It is true, however, that over the longer term, changes in fundamental determinants, especially productivities in different sectors and terms of trade, cause the different measures of the real exchange rates to diverge significantly. On the other hand, exchange rate regimes seemed not to play any direct role in explaining output performance and real exchange rate behavior in transition economies. The fixed exchange rate regime was used mainly to better contain the inflationary pressure, and as such, it affected the real output growth only indirectly through better inflation performance (Fisher and Sahay, 2000).

IV Evolution of the Exchange Rate Regimes

All transition economies have undergone major reforms, all of which have had appreciable consequences for their real exchange rate values. Changes in production and productivity, trade liberalization and removal of state subsidies, restrictive monetary policy accompanied by tax reform, underlying process of financial innovations and bank restructuring, are among the factors that played an important role in determining the key relative price in transition economies. Moreover, these economies had to choose an exchange rate regime that was appropriate for facilitating the reorientation of their trade toward world market and that was primarily used as a nominal anchor in an attempt to stabilize the economy. Government budget deficits spilled over into current account deficits, which were primarily financed by foreign capital inflows. To these inflows, that exceeded the surge in imports, central banks responded with sterilized intervention and active exchange rate policies.

The evolution of exchange rate regimes has mainly been affected by the liberalization of capital controls (Corker et al., 2000). Most advanced transition economies liberalized long-term capital flows. Additionally to the differences in exchange rate regimes and liberalization of capital flows, transition countries employed different monetary policies. Different patterns of inflation dynamics in transition economies seem to be associated to different exchange rate regimes (Table 2). Table 2 presents the exchange rate regimes in selected transition economies with shifts in regimes from less flexible - or fixed - to more flexible as they occurred during transition. Dates presented in bold stands for current exchange rate regime.

Table 2: Exchange rate regimes in acceding countries, 1990-2003

	1990	1991	1992	1993	1994	1995	1996	1997	1998	1999	2000	2001	2002	2003
Estonia	...a	...a	0	0	0	0	0	0	0	0	0	0	0	0
Latvia	...a	...a	0	0	0	0	0	0	0	0	0	0	0	0
Lithuania	...a	...a	1	1		0	0	0	0	0	0	0	0	0
Slovenia	...a	3	3	3	3	3	3	3	3	3	3	3	3	3
Hungary	1	1	1	1	1	1-2	2	2	2	2	2	2-4-5	5	5
Poland	1	1	2	2	2	4	4	4	4	4	4-7	7	7	7
Slovakia	1	1	1	1	1	1	5	5	5-6	6	6	6	6	6
Czech Rep.	1	1	1	1	1	1	5	5-6	6	6	6	6	6	6

(a) no home currency in circulation
0: formal or de facto currency board
1: peg to a currency or to a basket with fluctuation margins less than or equal to ±2,25%
2: crawling peg with fluctuation margins of less than or equal to ±2,25%
3: float with active management by monetary authorities (implicit crawling peg)
4: crawling peg with fluctuation margins of more than ±2,25%
5: peg to a currency or a basket with fluctuation margins of more than ±2,25%
6: float with heavy regular interventions
7: free float punctual interventions

Regime shift

Source: Égert and Kierzenkowski (2003)

The switch of exchange rate regimes broadly corresponds to the fading of structural reform effects, surge of capital inflows, and further price liberalization. It is believed that more active exchange rate policy could on one hand circumvent the pressing problem of real exchange rate appreciation, and on the other act as a shock absorber against asymmetric real shocks. Table 3 presents the evolution of the EBRD transition indicators on foreign exchange and trade liberalization. Shaded areas correspond to acceding transition economies entering the EU in 2004. Not surprisingly, index of foreign exchange and trade liberalization improved around 1996 and 1997. As shown in Coricelli and Jazbec (2001), this improvement corresponds to a diminishing effect of structural reforms on the real exchange rate determination in transition economies. In the middle of the 90s, advanced transition economies were on average in the fifth or sixth year of the transition process when with respect to the behavior of real exchange rate productivity and demand factors began to affect the real exchange rate more than structural reforms. In the same period, exchange rate regimes switched from less to more flexible framework with respect to the regimes employed at the beginning of 90s.

Table 3: EBRD Transition Indicators - Index of Foreign Exchange and Trade Liberalization

	1992	1993	1994	1995	1996	1997	1998	1999	2000	2001
Albania	4,0	4,0	4,0	4,0	4,0	4,0	4,0	4,0	4,3	4,3
Armenia	2,0	2,0	2,0	3,0	4,0	4,0	4,0	4,0	4,0	4,0
Azerbaijan	1,0	1,0	1,0	2,0	2,0	2,3	3,0	3,3	3,3	3,3
Belarus	1,0	1,0	1,0	2,0	2,0	1,0	1,0	1,0	1,7	2,0
Bulgaria	3,0	3,0	4,0	4,0	4,0	4,0	4,0	4,3	4,3	4,3
Croatia	3,0	3,0	4,0	4,0	4,0	4,0	4,0	4,0	4,3	4,3
Czech Republic	4,0	4,0	4,0	4,0	4,3	4,3	4,3	4,3	4,3	4,3
Estonia	3,0	3,0	4,0	4,0	4,0	4,0	4,0	4,0	4,3	4,3
FYR Macedonia	3,0	3,0	4,0	4,0	4,0	4,0	4,0	4,0	4,0	4,0
Georgia	1,0	1,0	1,0	2,0	3,0	4,0	4,0	4,0	4,3	4,3
Hungary	4,0	4,0	4,3	4,3	4,3	4,3	4,3	4,3	4,3	4,3
Kazakhstan	1,0	2,0	2,0	3,0	4,0	4,0	4,0	3,0	3,3	3,3
Kyrgyzstan	2,0	2,0	3,0	4,0	4,0	4,0	4,0	4,0	4,0	4,0
Latvia	2,0	3,0	4,0	4,0	4,0	4,0	4,0	4,3	4,3	4,3
Lithuania	2,0	3,0	4,0	4,0	4,0	4,0	4,0	4,0	4,0	4,3
Moldova	2,0	2,0	2,0	4,0	4,0	4,0	4,0	4,0	4,0	4,3
Poland	2,0	4,0	4,0	4,0	4,3	4,3	4,3	4,3	4,3	4,3
Romania	3,0	3,0	4,0	4,0	4,0	4,0	4,0	4,0	4,0	4,0
Russia	3,0	3,0	3,0	3,0	4,0	4,0	2,3	2,3	2,3	2,7
Slovak Republic	4,0	4,0	4,0	4,0	4,3	4,0	4,3	4,3	4,3	4,3
Slovenia	3,0	4,0	4,0	4,0	4,3	4,3	4,3	4,3	4,3	4,3
Tajikistan	1,0	1,0	1,0	2,0	2,0	2,0	2,7	2,7	3,0	3,3
Turkmenistan	1,0	1,0	1,0	1,0	1,0	1,0	1,0	1,0	1,0	1,0
Ukraine	1,0	1,0	1,0	3,0	3,0	3,0	2,7	3,0	3,0	3,0
Uzbekistan	1,0	1,0	2,0	2,0	2,0	1,7	1,7	1,0	1,0	1,7

Source: EBRD Transition Report 2001 and 2002.

The transition indicators score from 1 to 4 with 0.3 decimal points added or subtracted for improvements or declines in ratings. While CEE4 countries liberalized their trade and foreign exchange system to the standards and performance norms of advanced industrial economies, they still lag behind reforms in prices liberalization, especially in the public sector and non-market prices. The shift in exchange rate regimes in Czech Republic and Hungary broadly corresponds to the liberalization of trade and current account convertibility, while in Poland shift toward free floating happened only in 2001. Although Slovenia officially targeted M3 throughout the last decade, tightly managed exchange rate regime was substantially supported by capital controls on short-term capital flows and extensive sterilization policy. Despite the variety of approaches to the exchange rate policy, the acceding countries have all made substantial progress in reducing inflation, which has been on average below 10 percent since 1998. This points to the fact that it is the consistency of a country's entire package of economic policy that matters for the macroeconomic performance rather than the exchange rate regime per se. Although the anti-inflationary programs in advanced transition economies have been successful in bringing down inflation from almost hyperinflationary levels at the beginning of transition, the inflation rates are still above the rates required to enter the EU, and consequently EMU. As already mentioned, part of the reasons for higher inflation rates could be founded in the working of Balassa-Samuelson effect and the remaining convergence of relative prices (on the latter see Čihak and Holub (2002)). However, it is suspected that the combination of exchange rate regime and monetary policy could substantially contribute to the differences in inflation rates in CEE4 as the Czech Republic and Poland, on average produced lower inflation rates than Hungary and Slovenia in the last three years. As Czech Republic and Poland maintains relatively less managed exchange rate regimes than Hungary and Slovenia, and additionally employ inflation targets, it is believed that the combination of relatively greater flexibility of exchange rate regime and inflation target produces lower inflation.

V   Macroeconomic Stabilization and Capital Inflows

As already mentioned, one reason to switch the exchange rate regimes was the surge in capital inflows to transition countries. Net capital flows already started during the 1980s. They were largely in the form of commercial bank loans and trade finance to the state-owned banks and companies. At the outset of transition in the beginning of the 1990s, there was a large rise in the official lending, while private flows were still waiting for the signs of recovery and macroeconomic stabilization in the region. After almost a decade of transition, the magnitude of these inflows to the transition economies is still small compared to other regions - especially South Asia. Also, their composition has changed dramatically since the time of central planning. Nowadays, most of those inflows consist of foreign direct investments and equity portfolio investment. Moreover, the capital inflows tend to be distributed extremely unevenly across the receiving countries. Figure 1 presents the cumulative capital inflows and foreign direct investments (FDI) in transition economies during 1991 - 1997. If the movement of total capital inflows is difficult to explain, because they consist of private and official foreign lending together and some countries in the region had different agreements with international financial institutions (e.g., debt forgiveness in Poland in 1995), it is the FDI which reflects the progress in transition and macroeconomic stability. It is widely accepted, that portfolio investment and commercial bank lending usually follow the FDI flows in developing and emerging markets. This conclusion is firmly drawn from the fact that FDI is strongly based on human capital and natural resources endowments together with the advantages of a geographical position of a certain country. However, since FDI primarily represents long-term investment it must be the case that the long-term investors generate their investment decisions on the grounds of sound macroeconomic and political environment.

The correlation between the intensity of reforms and macroeconomic performance in the transition economies was already formally and empirically established (Aslund, Boone and Johnson (1996); Fisher, Sahay and Vegh (1996)). In the countries which implemented and conducted radical reforms, output growth was back on positive track and inflation was cut down to the levels around 10 percent. Not surprisingly, those countries are also the main recipients of FDI. Moreover, direct comparison between the strength of reforms and the volume of FDI also shows one important similarity. All radical-reformed economies with high FDI per capita have introduced the exchange rate-based stabilization programs (see Table 2). The only exceptions are Hungary and Slovenia. Aslund, Boone and Johnson (1996) classify Hungary as a gradual-reformed economy. However, some authors (Siklos (1996); Halpern and Wyplosz (1996)) claim that Hungary has indeed implemented the radical reform in order to stabilize the economy. The confusion, therefore, originates in different definitions of reform. The case of Slovenia - on the other hand - is different in the sense that Slovenian stabilization program is a school example of a money-based stabilization. The choice for the money-based stabilization in 1992 was determined by the fact that Slovenia did not have enough foreign currency reserves to support the fixed exchange rate regime. Additionally, Slovenia already performed some macroeconomic and political reforms before the 'official transition' had started.

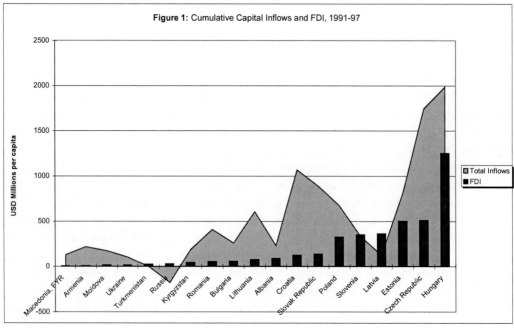

Figure 1: Cumulative Capital Inflows and FDI, 1991-97

Source: EBRD Transition Report.

VI Balassa-Samuelson Effect and Labor Market Dynamics

Studies on real exchange rate behavior in transition economies support the argument to use the productivity approach to explain the trend appreciation of the real exchange rate in transition economies (Coricelli and Jazbec, 2001; Egert 2002; Halpern and Wyplosz, 1996). There is vast potential for gains in productivity in transition economies both through more efficient use of existing resources and technologies and through upgrading technology. However, this approach should also take into account the initial conditions in transition economies at the beginning of reforms, as they significantly determined the macroeconomic policies and structural changes implied by the overall stance of the economies in those times. Decades of central planning have resulted in distorted structures of these economies. Industries had become overwhelmed in the composition of output due to the emphasis of central planners on material production, while services were largely neglected. The structure of the economy was reflected in distorted price levels as empirical studies on price development in transition economies indicate. Transition and the introduction of market-determined prices along the other market-enhanced reforms have brought about massive changes in output, employment and, last but not least, in relative prices.

In all transition economies, relative wages in the non-tradable sector increased in a first few years of the transition process corresponding to a different start of transition. After that, relative wage in non-tradable sector declined probably as a result of further labor reallocation or/and productivity increase in the tradable sector. Although similar patterns of the relative wage of non-tradables in terms of tradables are observed in transition economies, it is instructive to look at the labor market developments during transition process in order to disentangle the working of the Balassa-Samuelson effect. Figure 2 displays labor reallocation together with productivity differential between industry and services in selected transition economies[4]. The criterion for the period of observation was the year after which the relative price of tradables in terms of non-tradables has started to decline monotonically, and the longitude of time series, which ends in 1998[5].

---

[4] Detailed description of data is presented in Coricelli and Jazbec (2001).

[5] Exceptions are Romania where the relative price of tradables has indeed increased, and Estonia where the relative price of tradables started to decline already in 1990.

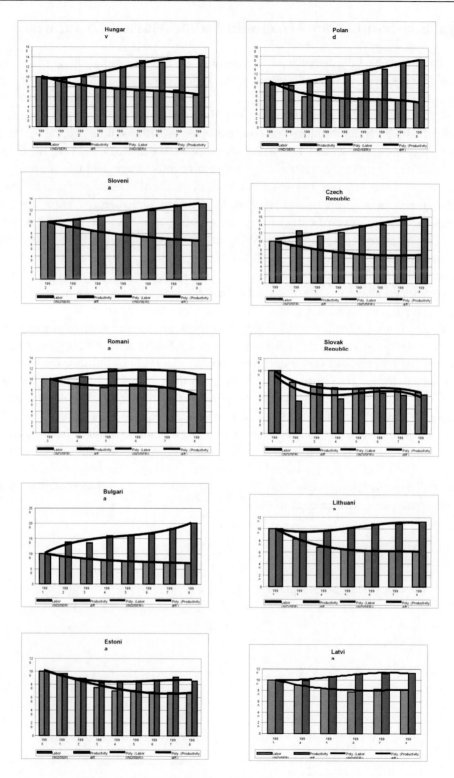

Figure 2: Labor Reallocation and Productivity Differential

Source: Coricelli and Jazbec (2001).

The labor reallocation in Figure 2 is represented by the ratio between labor employed in industry and services, which encompass both market and public services, respectively. Both measures, labor ratio and productivity differential, are indexed to the base year which corresponds to the start of the transition process. Although statistical properties of the corresponding time series are not thoroughly examined due to the short time interval, the polynomial trend of order 3 is added to Figure 2 to ease the explanation. In all cases, labor reallocation took place at the beginning of the transition process. Except in Romania, labor reallocation process stabilized into the fifth or sixth year of the transition. One would expect that productivity differential between labor productivity in industry and services would begin to increase. However, in the case of Estonia and Slovak Republic, the productivity differential even declined in the first few years, while in Lithuania, Latvia, and Romania increased only by a modest amount. Moreover, one can see from Figure 2 that only more advanced transition economies experienced the productivity differential increase once the labor reallocation ended. Surprisingly, Bulgaria experienced the most dramatic increase in productivity differential prior to 1998. For that reason, we can distinguish cases where the Balassa-Samuelson effect has indeed taken place after the initial period of labor reallocation (Poland, Czech Republic, Hungary, and Slovenia) and cases where the increase in productivity differential was mainly due to labor reallocation.

VI Exchange Rate as Shock Absorber

In this section we address the issue of desirability of the move to more flexible exchange rate arrangements by looking at the potential of exchange rate to respond to macroeconomic imbalances. Exchange rate flexibility is theoretically desirable as a tool of macroeconomic adjustment in open economies with significant nominal rigidities that impede economies to attain the flex-price equilibrium quickly after a shock. This shock-absorbing capacity is also one of the key arguments for flexibility found in the OCA theory. The theory postulates that exchange rate flexibility potentially enables a country to neutralize the adverse effects of asymmetric real shocks, that is, it can use the exchange rate to absorb asymmetric shocks. A country faced with an asymmetric real shock relative to its trading partners can use the nominal exchange rate to induce a desirable change in the real exchange rate, i.e., it exploits the expenditure switching effect. However, it is very challenging to find a solid empirical confirmation of these theoretical predictions.

The empirical analysis of the shock-absorbing role of the real exchange rate for transition economies is scarce. An exception is the study by Masten (2002), which covers three Acceding Countries: the Czech Republic, Poland and Slovenia. In order to link the empirical results to theoretical predictions correctly it is crucial to determine the nature of shocks as precisely as possible. In particular, a clear distinction has to be made along three criteria: symmetry/asymmetry of shocks, persistence of shocks (transitory or permanent) and economic origin (real or nominal). With respect to the shock-absorbing capacity of the real exchange rate, asymmetric real shocks are of primary interest, because asymmetric nominal shocks are effectively removed in a fixed exchange rate regime or in a monetary union. In this reasoning, however, lies an important caveat. Among the asymmetric real shocks we need to distinguish between permanent and transitory shocks. The former are a sign of divergent economic developments (caused by structural changes and catching-up process), and the stochastic trend they induce into the real exchange rate can be seen as an equilibrium driving process. Moreover, this trend cannot be overturned by monetary policy, which, being constrained by real interest rate parity, would indulge into an over-inflationary policy if trying to target the real exchange rate. If a country is subject to permanent asymmetric real shocks, then a monetary union will impose real costs not due to the loss of an important stabilizing tool, but because it will exhibit divergent economic developments relative to other members of the union. The critical point here is that centrally managed monetary policy in such cases amplifies the divergences. The ECB, targeting Euro-area wide aggregates, may in such circumstances act procyclically on the economy of the divergent country. However, this is no longer an issue of the effectiveness of the real exchange rate as a shock absorber but an issue of optimal monetary policy in a monetary union with heterogeneous member states. The shock-absorbing role of the real exchange rate should therefore be considered for the case of transitory real asymmetric shocks only.

From this discussion it follows that an empirical analysis of the shock-absorbing role of the real exchange rate should be based on permanent-transitory decomposition of the data. The shock-absorbing role of the real exchange rate is typically analyzed within a structural VAR framework using first-differenced data to achieve stationarity of the system (see references below). An important drawback of this approach is that it neglects the possibility of cointegration and thus is unable to distinguish permanent from transitory shocks. Masten (2002) makes a step further in this direction and estimates the common trends model (proposed by King et al. (1991)) in order to discriminate between permanent and transitory shocks. Using the stricter definition for shock-absorption (i.e., addressing it only for asymmetric real and transitory shocks) he finds no shock-absorbing role of the real exchange rate in the Czech Republic, Hungary, Slovenia, Denmark and the United Kingdom. This is the first study of the shock-absorbing role in the real exchange rate that considers also some of the Accession Countries, but its findings are in line with the findings of other authors for different sets of European countries. Very limited shock-absorbing role of the real exchange rate is, for example, found by Canzoneri, Valles, and Vinals (1996) for Austria, the Netherlands, France, Italy, Spain and the UK; and then by Thomas (1997) and Funke (2000) for the UK and Sweden respectively. The analysis by Artis and Ehrman (2000) that distinguishes between symmetric and asymmetric shocks also comes to a similar conclusion for Denmark, Sweden, Canada and the UK.

The lack of shock-absorbing capacity implies that the economic focus in the choice of exchange rate regimes should not bear heavily on potential benefits countries might have from flexible exchange rate, as they might be rather limited. An important empirical finding in Masten (2002) is that significant divergent economic movements in the Accession Countries are likely to persist in the future because they can be attributed to permanent real stochastic trends reflecting the industrial productivity improvements and permanent demand shifts due to ongoing structural reforms. This finding complements the findings of Coricelli and Jazbec (2001) using a different methodology. It is true from the theoretical point of view that also in such case exchange rate flexibility might be desirable when a country is faced with important nominal rigidities. However, as these can be considered as equilibrium driving processes the welfare loss from exchange rate stability can be rather limited. In addition, these costs should be compared to the costs of higher inflation (in presence of high exchange rate pass-trough effect as documented in Coricelli, Jazbec and Masten, 2003) and other potential benefits from exchange rate stability.

VII Exchange Rate Pass-Through

The effectiveness of flexible exchange rate regimes for macroeconomic stabilization is closely related to the exchange rate pass-through to different price indexes. In particular, the expenditure switching effect following depreciation is larger when the pass-through to import prices is larger and pass-through to consumer prices is lower (Obstfeld, 2002). Thus, the justification for the move from fixed to more flexible exchange rate regimes has to be analyzed also with relation to the empirical estimates of pass-through to consumer prices.

Heuristically it is argued that CEE countries moved from fixed to more flexible exchange rate regimes during transition for two reasons. The first was to increase the ability of curbing inflation rates toward required levels, although the main reason for the move was believed to be from pressure caused by a surge in foreign capital inflows (Corker et al., 2000). In so doing, CEE countries added a potential new source to higher inflation rates in addition to the working of the Balassa-Samuelson effect and other structural changes (adjustment of regulated prices). Namely, the move from a fixed to a more flexible exchange rate regime could backfire attempts to lower inflation as the exchange rate pass-through could add to inflationary pressure instead of suppressing it, when countries indulged into keeping depreciation rates at positive levels. The evidence on selected transition economies could partially support this kind of argument although the extent of the pass-through cannot be firmly established (Darvas, 2001; Campa and Goldberg, 2002). Taking into account caution in explaining econometric results due to short time series, Darvas (2001) finds overall low (below 40% in the long run) estimates of pass-through of nominal exchange rate to fundamental prices (food, energy, and administered prices were excluded from CPI).[6] However, in recent years he finds a higher pass-through in Hungary and Slovenia than in Poland and the Czech Republic. He tentatively concludes that part of the difference in the pass-through estimates could be attributed to the exchange rate regime, as Hungary and Slovenia had a managed exchange rate regime opposed to Poland and the Czech Republic, which had a floating regime in 2000. Although Darvas (2001) takes into account the change of the exchange rate regime in Hungary, the Czech Republic, and Poland during the transition process, the main concern explaining results for pass-through in transition economies is still the shortness of time series. This can be pernicious if one seriously considers the importance of the initial period of the labor reallocation process as explained above.

Coricelli, Jazbec and Masten (2003) estimate the pass-through effect for a subset of CEE countries using a different methodology. The authors identify the pass-through effect within a cointegration framework.[7] Cointegration analysis yields the estimate of long-run (or equilibrium) pass-through effect, however, due to a number of technical reasons we argue that, compared to single-equation estimation and structural VAR analysis, this is the most reliable approach to empirical analysis that can also lead to meaningful policy implications. Single equation analysis is due to an endogeneity problem inferior to an analysis based on VAR estimation. It can be also argued that structural VAR analysis that has been extensively

---

[6] Mihaljek and Klau (2001) find similar results for Poland, Hungary and the Czech Republic. Their analysis is based on single equation estimation and suffers from consistency problems due to endogenous determination of exchange rates and prices.

[7] Kim (1998) also uses cointegration analysis for estimation of pass-through in the US. In his analysis, however, the pass-through effect is not identified. This means that it cannot be interpreted as long-run elasticity of prices to exchange rate in the sense of Johansen (2002) and as discussed in Masten (2003).

used for estimation of pass-through (see MaCarthy, 2000 as a notable example) cannot reliably measure the pass-through effect unless one is interested in pass-through only indirectly.[8] As described in Corsetti and Dedola (2003) the correct notion of pass-through can be theoretically described as a conditional elasticity of selected prices to the nominal exchange rate. This implies that in a complex dynamic setting there are as many estimates of short-run and medium-run pass-through effect as there are shocks (equal to the dimension of the VAR). An empirical investigation of pass-through effect cannot be used for policy evaluation unless it systematically checks for all of them.

For policy issues related to the choice of exchange rate regimes in CEE countries it is important to identify what are the inflationary consequences of permanent changes in the exchange rate or (as is more commonly observed for countries with flexible rates) in the depreciation rates. One can argue that the pass-through effect following permanent changes will have a much stronger influence on prices as changes that are perceived to be only transitory. Turning back to the issue of estimation, we argue that it is crucial to empirically distinguish between permanent and transitory changes of exchange rate changes. Permanent changes can be effectively captured by cointegration analysis. Any SVAR analysis should therefore show a number of different pass-through estimates following transitory shocks (that eventually disappear) and *only one* long-run pass-through effect after any permanent shocks. This follows from the fact that any long-run co-movement between inflation and depreciation rate is constrained by the measure of pass-through obtained with cointegration analysis. Studies using SVAR approach do not check for these properties. It is for this technical reason that we believe that a properly estimated and identified measure of equilibrium pass-through effect into domestic prices should be central for policy implications with respect to exchange rate regimes.[9] The reason for this is very basic: any central bank with the objective to stabilize the inflation rate in the medium and long term should take seriously into account the equilibrium consequences of their policy action. The same holds for the choice of exchange rate regime.

Taking all these considerations into account, Coricelli, Jazbec and Masten (2003) come to the following results. A higher growth rate of nominal exchange rate results in equally higher difference between domestic and foreign inflation in Slovenia and Hungary. This evidence of perfect equilibrium pass-through to CPI inflation can be associated with more accommodative exchange rate policy. Moreover, innovations to the exchange rate in Slovenia transfer most strongly to domestic inflation. In Hungary, on the other hand, exchange rate innovations have comparatively smaller effect. The point estimate of pass-through effect for Poland shows is smaller than one (point estimate of 0.8), but not significantly different. Nevertheless, the result offers a tentative conclusion that the effect of the exchange rate growth on inflation is smaller than in Slovenia and Hungary. The country with the lowest effect of exchange rate on prices is the Czech Republic, with the estimate of pass-through of roughly 0.5.

---

[8] The most comprehensive study in terms of the number of CEE countries included in the analysis has been performed by Bitans (2003), who employs a structural VAR analysis, but looks only at impulse responses of prices to an exchange rate shock and hence does not directly measure the pass-through effect.

[9] The study of Coricelli, Jazbec and Masten (2003) also discusses the issue of identification of pass-through effect in cointegration analysis. Identification is not automatically obtained, as showed by Johansen (2002). Other studies, estimating pass-through with cointegration analysis, do not deal with this issue. In addition, by performing the I(2) cointegration analysis Coricelli et al. (2003) treat prices and nominal exchange rates as processes integrated of order two, which is recently a common finding in the literature. Other studies on pass-through do not check for this possibility.

Even though these results are obtained only for a subset of CEE countries they nevertheless enable some policy implications to be drawn, especially for the countries about to join the EMU in the following years. The most important conclusion is that in any policy design the important effect of the nominal exchange rate on prices should not be underestimated. The path of nominal exchange rate within a more general exchange rate regime arrangement during disinflation should be given a priority role. In the period after 2000, inflation rates have been lower in the Czech Republic and Poland than in Hungary and Slovenia. As the Czech Republic and Poland maintain relatively less managed exchange rate regimes than Hungary and Slovenia, and additionally employ inflation targets, it is believed that such a combination produces lower inflation. However, in the case of Poland the costs in terms of output and unemployment appear very large. In the case of the Czech Republic it appears that the exchange rate features as a main intermediate target to achieve the final target on inflation, as is natural in a small open economy. Before adopting the euro, all candidate countries will have to enter the ERM2 system with an agreed central parity and a ±15 % band. It is argued in the paper that the pre-adoption period could generate persistent inflationary pressure if candidate countries will attempt to maintain external competitiveness and use exchange rate as a shock absorber. The case of Greece in this process, which has been forced twice to revalue its parity to cope with inflationary pressures in the ERM mechanism, is a notable example. One can thus expect rising interest rates and output volatility in ERM2 prior to actual adoption of the euro. Such volatility will be affected by the regime of full capital mobility that the countries have to adopt upon entry in the European Union. Results in the paper suggest that the best policy would be the adoption of the euro as early as possible. Before actual adoption, a pre-announced path of moderate depreciation within inflation targeting regime might be the second-best option for exchange rate policy.

VIII   Concluding Remarks

The paper reviewed the behavior of exchange rates, nominal and real, since the start of transition. An important stylized fact is that real exchange rates appreciated in all countries, irrespective of their exchange rate regime. Disentangling the different forces affecting the behavior of exchange rates in different phases of transition is of paramount importance. Indeed, there is a risk of identifying as a "natural" or equilibrium phenomenon the entire magnitude of appreciation of the real exchange rate, in all countries. In fact, the appreciation reflected the extent of initial distortions, the workings of the Balassa-Samuelson effect and, more recently, the opening up of the capital account coupled with fluctuations in economic policy regimes. Focusing on CEECs, the paper concludes that these are very small and very open economies. Specifically, they have achieved an extremely high degree of integration, both real and financial, with the European Union. For these countries adopting the euro is the step that ratifies the completion of such a process of integration. It is rather ironic that European institutions, such as the European Central Bank and the European Commission, together with several government representatives of CEECs, are suggesting to delay the adoption of the euro into a distant future, assuming against theoretical and especially empirical evidence that the exchange rate represents an important shock absorber and an instrument to ensure higher growth and lower unemployment in CEECs.

References

[1]   Arratibel, O., Rodriguez-Palenzuela, D. and Thimann, C. (2002), "Inflation Dynamics and Dual Inflation in Accession Countries: A "New Keynesian" Perspective", *ECB Working Paper Series*, No. **132**.

[2]   Aslund, A, Boone, P., and Johnson, S. (1996), "How to Stabilize: Lessons from Post-communist Countries", *Brookings Papers on Economic Activity*, No. **1**, Washington.

[3]   Artis, M.J., and Ehrmann, M. (2000), "The Exchange Rate - A Shock-absorber or a Source of Shocks? A Study of Four Open Economies", *CEPR Discussion Paper*, No. **2550**.

[4]   Bitans, M (2003),"Pass-through of Exchange Rates to Domestic Prices in Eastern European Countries: Do Regime Changes Matter?", *mimeo,* Bank of Latvia.

[5]   Brodsky, A. D. (1982), "Arithmetic Versus Geometric Effective Exchange Rates", *Weltwirtschaftsliches Archiv*, Vol. 116, No. 3, 546-562.

[6]   Calvo, G. A., and Kumar, M. S. (1994), "Money Demand, Bank Credit, and Economic Performance in Former Socialist Countries", *IMF Staff Papers*, Vol. 41, No. 2, June.

[7]   Campa, M. J. and Goldberg, L.S. (2002), "Exchange Rate Pass-Through into Import Prices: A Macro or Micro Phenomenon?", *NBER Working Paper Series,* No. **8934**.

[8]   Canzoneri, M., Valles, J., and Vinals, J. (1996), "Do Exchange Rates Move to Address International Macroeconomic Imbalances?", *CEPR Discussion Papers,* No. **1498**.

[9]   Chinn, M. D. (1997), "Sectoral Productivity, Government Spending and Real Exchange Rates: Empirical Evidence for OECD Countries", *NBER Working Paper*, No. **6017**, April.

[10] Choudhri, E. U., Faruqee, H. and Hakura, D. S. (2002), "Explaining the Exchange Rate Pass-Through in Different Prices", *IMF Working Paper*, No. **224**.

[11] Clark, B. P. (1996), "Concepts of Equilibrium Exchange Rates", *Journal of International and Comparative Economics*, **20**, 133-140.

[12] Coricelli, F. and Jazbec, B. (2001), "Real Exchange Rate Dynamics in Transition Economies", *CEPR Discussion Paper*, No. 2869.

[13] Coricelli, F. and Jazbec B. (2002), "Accession to the European Union: Real Exchange Rate Dynamics for Candidate Countries", *Rivista di Politica Economica*, Vol. XCII, No. 1-2, pp. 109-138.

[14] Coricelli, F. and Jazbec B. (2003), "Exchange Rate Arrangements in the Accession to the EMU", *Comparative Economic Systems*, forthcoming.

[15] Coricelli, F., Jazbec B. and Masten, I. (2003),"Exchange Rate Pass-Through in Candidate Countries", *CEPR Discussion Paper* No. **3894**

[16] Corker, R., Beaumont C., van Elkan, R. and Iakova, D. (2000), "Exchange Rate Regimes in Selected Advanced Transition Economies: Coping with Transition, Capital Inflows, and EU Accession", *IMF Policy Discussion Paper*, No. 3.

[17] Corsetti, G. and Dedola, L. (2003),"Macroeconomics of International Price Discrimination", *mimeo*, Yale University.

[18] Čihak, M. and Holub, T. (2001), "Convergence of Relative Prices and Inflation in Central and Eastern Europe", *IMF Working Paper,* No. 124.

[19] Darvas, Z. (2001), "Exchange Rate Pass-Through and Real Exchange Rate in EU Candidate Countries", *Deutsche Bundesbank Discussion Paper* No. **10**.

[20] De Grauwe, P. (1996), *International Money*, Oxford University Press.

[21] De Gregorio, J., Giovannini, A., and Krueger, T. H. (1993), "The Behavior of Nontradable Goods Prices in Europe: Evidence and Interpretation", *IMF Working Paper*, No. **45**, May.

[22] De Gregorio, J., Giovannini, A., and Wolf, H. C. (1994), "International Evidence on Tradables and Nontradables Inflation", *IMF Working Paper*, No. **33**, March.

[23] De Melo, M., Gelb, A., and Denizer, C. (1996), "From Plan to Market: Patterns of Transition", *Policy Research Working Paper* **1564**, World Bank.

[24] Edwards, S. (1989), "Real Exchange Rates in the Developing Countries: Concepts and Measurement", *NBER Working Paper*, No. **2950**.

[25] Edwards, S. (1994), "Real and Monetary Determinants of Real Exchange Rate Behavior: Theory and Evidence from Developing Countries", in Williamson, J. ed., *Estimating Equilibrium Exchange Rates*, Washington, D.C., Institute for International Economics.

[26] Egert, B. (2002), "Investigating the Balassa-Samuelson Hypothesis in the Transition: Do We Understand What We See? A Panel Study", *Economics of Transition,* Vol. 10, No. 2, July, 273-309.

[27] Egert, B., Kierzenkowski, R. (2003), "Asymmetric Fluctuation Bands in ERM and ERMII: Lessons from the Past and Future Challenges for EU Acceding Countries", *William Davidson Working Paper*, No. **597**.

[28] Fisher, S., and Sahay, R. (2000), "The Transition Economies After Ten Years", *IMF Working Paper*, No. 30.

[29] Fisher, S., Sahay, R., and Vegh, C. A. (1996), "Stabilization and Growth in Transition Economies: The Early Experience", *Journal of Economic Perspectives*, Vol. 10, No. 2, Spring, 45-66.

[30] Funke, M., "Macroeconomic Shocks in Euroland vs the UK: Supply, Demand or Nominal?", *mimeo*, University of Hamburg, 2000.

[31] Garcia, C. J. and Restrepo, J. E. (2001), "Price Inflation and Exchange Rate Pass-Through in Chile", *Working Paper* N° **128**, Central Bank of Chile.

[32] Goldfajn, I. and da Costa Werlang, S. R. (2000), "The Pass-Through from Depreciation to Inflation: A Panel Study", *Banko Central do Brazil Working Paper*, No. **5**.

[33] Isard, P. (1987), "Lessons from Empirical Models of Exchange Rates", *IMF Staff Papers*.

[34] Habib, M. M. (2002), "Financial Contagion, Interest Rates and the Role of the Exchange Rate as Shock Absorber in Central and Eastern Europe", *BOFIT Discussion Papers,* No.7.

[35] Halpern, L., and Wyplosz, C. (1996), "Equilibrium Exchange Rates in Transition Economies", *IMF Working Paper,* No. **125**.

[36] Hinkle, E. L., and Nsengiyumva, F. (1999), "External Real Exchange Rates: Purchasing Power Parity, the Mundell-Fleming Model, and Competitiveness in Traded Goods", in Hinkle, E. L., and Montiel, P. J. (eds.), *Exchange Rate Misalignment: Concepts and Measurement for Developing Countries*, Oxford University Press.

[37] Johansen, Soren (2002), "The Interpretation of Cointegration Coefficients in the Cointegrated Vector Autoregressive Model", *Preprint No. 14*, Department of Theoretical Statistics, University of Copenhagen.

[38] Kim, K-H. (1998), "US Inflation and the Dollar Exchange Rate: A Vector Error-correction Model", *Applied Economics*, **30**, 613-619.

[39] Krajnayak, K., and Zettelmeyer, J. (1998), "Competitiveness in Transition Economies: What Scope for Real Appreciation?", *IMF Staff Papers*, Vol. 45, No. 2, June.

[40] Masten, I. (2002), "How Important is the Shock-Absorbing Role of the Real Exchange Rate?", *EUI Working Paper,* 2002/6.

[41] Masten, I. (2003), "Cointegration Approach to Estimating Exchange Rate Pass-Through: The Role of Exchange Rate Regimes in Inflationary Performance in Acceding Countries", *mimeo,* European University Institute.

[42] McCarthy, J. (2000), "Pass-Through of Exchange Rates and Import Prices to Domestic Inflation in Some Industrialized Economies", *Federal Reserve Bank of New York Staff Report* No. **3** (September).

[43] Micossi, S., and Milesi-Ferretti, G. M. (1994)"Real Exchange Rates and the Prices of Non-Tradable Goods", *IMF Working Paper*, 19, February.

[44] Mihaljek, D. and Klau M. (2001),"A Note on the Pass-Through from Exchange Rate and Foreign Price Changes to Inflation in Selected Emerging market Economies", *BIS Papers* No.**8.**

[45] Obstfeld, M. (2002),"Exchange Rates and Adjustment: Perspective from the New Open-Economy Macroeconomics", Monetary and Economic Studies, Special Edition.

[46] Obstfeld, M. (1985), "Floating Exchange Rates: Experience and Prospects", *Brookings Papers on Economic Activity*, **2**, 369-464.

[47] Sahay, R., and Vegh, C. A. (1995), "Inflation and Stabilization in Transition Economies: A Comparison with Market Economies", *IMF Working Paper*, No. **8**.

[48] Siklos, L. P. (1996), "Capital Flows in a Transitional Economy and the Sterilization Dilemma: The Hungarian Case", *IMF Working Paper,* No. **86**.

In: International Macroeconomics: Recent Developments   ISBN: 1-59454-901-X
Editor: Amalia Morales Zumaquero, pp. 309-333   © 2006 Nova Science Publishers, Inc.

Chapter 14

REAL EXCHANGE RATES IN TRANSITION ECONOMIES: THE ROLE OF FOREIGN CAPITAL, LABOUR PRODUCTIVITY AND REGULATED PRICES[1]

Balázs Égert[*] and Kirsten Lommatzsch[**]
[1]Economist, Oesterreichische Nationalbank, Foreign Research Division, and Research
fellow at MODEM, University of Paris X-Nanterre and at the William Davidson Institute
[2]Economist, DIW-Berlin

Abstract

In this paper, different sources of the appreciation of the real exchange rate in transition economies are investigated. Besides the traditional B-S effect that works through productivity-induced market-based service inflation, the role of regulated prices, the non-tradable component of tradable goods is analysed and, most importantly, it is argued that the main source of real appreciation in the transition countries is the change in supply capacities, which consists not only of a higher quality of produced goods, but also a shift in the composition of output towards goods of higher quality that leads to an increase in the price of tradable goods. Based on a variety of time series and panel cointegration techniques, it is shown that changes in labour productivity are not only strongly connected to the CPI-based real exchange rate but also to the PPI-deflated real exchange rate. This finding is very robust against different econometric techniques and thus lends strong empirical support in favour of the tradable price channel. However, because the estimated coefficient of labour productivity is usually lower when the PPI-based real exchange rate is used, the B-S effect and regulated prices may also determine long-term real exchange rate movements, although to a much lesser extent that assumed in the literature.

---

[1] The opinions expressed in the paper are those of the authors and do not necessarily correspond to the official
   views of the Oesterreichische Nationalbank.
[*] E-mail address: balazs.egert@oenb.co.at and begert@u-paris10.fr
[**] E-mail address: klommatzsch@diw.de

I Introduction

From the outset of the transition process from central planning towards market economy the real exchange rate has been on an appreciating path in a number of transition countries of Central and Eastern Europe. Rosati (1996), Halpern and Wyplosz (1997) and Krajnyák and Zettelmeyer (1998) were among the first to document this phenomenon for a large number of countries. The appetite of empirical researchers for investigating features of the long-term real exchange rate continued to grow since then, chiefly because the run-up to the EU and the subsequent euro adoption put the issue on top of policy-makers agenda[2].

Although the real appreciation of the currencies, measured in effective terms, is far from being negligible, what really catches one's eyes is the extent of the appreciation real exchange rates vis-à-vis the German mark and the euro witnessed since the early 1990s. As shown in Table 1, annual average appreciation of the real exchange rate based on the consumer price index (CPI) was close to or even higher than 3 per cent from 1993 to 2002 in the Czech Republic, Hungary, Poland and Slovakia whereas it reached roughly 2 per cent p.a. in Slovenia[3]. The most popular explanation for this phenomenon is the Balassa-Samuelson effect (B-S effect hereafter), usually linked to a fast catch-up process. High structural inflation rates and the resulting real appreciation of the domestic currency stem from fast growth based on productivity increases in the sector exposed to international competition. If productivity gains in the open sector exceed those witnessed in the closed sector, market-based service prices in the latter will increase faster provided wages tend to equalise across sectors. This, all things being equal, results in higher overall inflation. Going one step further, if the rate of growth in the productivity differential is higher in the home country compared with that in the foreign country, the CPI-deflated real exchange rate will appreciate because of the positive inflation differential triggered by productivity-led service price inflation.

However, Table 1 also reveals that the producer price index-based (PPI) real exchange rate vis-à-vis the German mark/Euro appreciated nearly as much as the CPI-deflated real exchange rate over the period from 1993 to 2002. It turns out that in all countries except for Slovenia the appreciation of the PPI-based real exchange rate amounted to roughly 70% of the CPI-based real appreciation. Taking PPI as a proxy for prices of tradable goods, this provides evidence for the fact that the B-S effect might explain only part of the appreciation of the CPI-based real exchange rate.

Table 1. The CPI and PPI-based real exchange rate vis-à-vis the German mark/Euro, 1993-2002

in %		RER-CPI	RER-PPI
Czech Republic	1993-2002	-42.4	-32.4
	1995-2002	-36.8	-29.0
Hungary	1993-2002	-26.9	-15.7
	1995-2002	-32.3	-24.7

---

[2] See e.g. Coricelli and Jazbec (2001), De Broeck and Sloek (2001), Fischer (2002), Kim and Korhonen (2002), Lommatzsch and Tober (2002), MacDonald and Wojcik (2002), Smidkova et al. (2002), Égert and Lahrèche (2003) and Rahn (2003).

[3] The exchange rate is expressed as units of the domestic currency over one unit of foreign currency. Hence, a decrease/increase in the exchange rates corresponds to an appreciation/depreciation of the currency.

in %		RER-CPI	RER-PPI
Poland	1993-2002	-37.4	-26.1
	1995-2002	-34.0	-23.8
Slovakia	1993-2002	-34.2	-24.3
	1995-2002	-29.6	-20.8
Slovenia	1993-2002	-18.2	-9.7
	1995-2002	-11.1	-3.5

Source: Authors' own calculations
Note: Negative/positive figures denote an appreciation/depreciation of the real exchange rate

According to professional wisdom, the appreciation of the real exchange rate deflated using tradable prices indicates loss of competitiveness. In the case of the transition economies, part of this appreciation could, however, be related to a successful economic transformation and catch-up process.

Moreover, a score of service items as well as energy are still regulated or fall into administered or regulated prices[4]. Their share in the CPI basket of the acceding countries can be as high as 25% (Poland 2002). And more importantly, in some of the countries, increases in prices of regulated services systematically exceeded those of market services over the period under study. Further to this, the difference in regulated prices has been positive relative to the reference country, i.e., Germany, where these prices also represent some 20% of CPI. Hence, even the real appreciation based on service prices might not be fully explained by productivity increases spilling over into higher market service prices.

In this article, an attempt is made to disentangle factors leading to the real appreciation of the currencies. The rest of the paper is structured as follows: Section II provides a more detailed look at factors that lead to the trend-appreciation of the real exchange rate during the transition and catch-up period. Section III describes the data and time-series and panel estimation techniques employed in the paper. Subsequently, Section IV presents and comments on the results. Finally, Section V draws some concluding remarks.

II Appreciation of the Real Exchange Rate in Transition Economies

The appreciation of the real exchange rate in the acceding countries can stem from different sources. Different channels through which the appreciation of the real exchange rate can occur in the long-run and possible interconnections are depicted in a graphical manner in Figure 1. The most conventional one is the "traditional" B-S effect, i.e., the productivity-driven market service inflation. Notwithstanding the fact that this B-S model is found recently to explain only a small part of the real appreciation of the currencies (see e.g., Burgess et al. (2003), Égert (2002), Égert et al. (2003), Flek et al. (2002) and Kovács et al. (2002)), productivity advances in the open sector can also impact on tradable prices in two different ways. First, productivity gains may feed into tradable prices through their non-tradable component. Second, and more importantly, productivity gains can also lead to increases in tradable prices because of quality improvements and better pricing possibilities. Changes in regulated prices are also likely to contribute to positive inflation differentials and thus to the

---

[4] Administered and regulated prices will be used interchangeably in the remainder of the paper.

real appreciation either directly or spilling onto market non-tradable prices and the non-tradable component of tradable prices. The last channel operates through expectations related to future productivity gains that leads to an appreciation of the nominal exchange rate. It should be noted that some of the aforesaid channels may be specific to or can be accentuated in transition countries. This section is devoted to the presentation of each of these channels, and special attention is paid to how changes in productivity can affect prices of tradable goods.

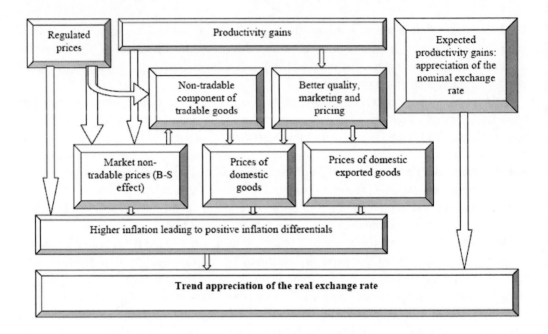

Figure 1. Long-Run Appreciation of the Real Exchange Rate in Transition Economies

II.1   Market-Based Non-tradables and the B-S Effect

The B-S effect is the most common explanation of a rising price level and a real appreciation during the process of fast economic growth. It rests on the observation that price levels of countries at different stages of economic development usually differ, and that poorer countries may witness the appreciation of their real exchange rates during the catch-up process.

The theoretical backdrop of this trend appreciation is elaborated in the B-S model (Balassa (1964) and Samuelson (1964)) (B-S henceforth). The model rests on an economy split into two sectors, producing respectively tradable and non-tradable goods. It is assumed that market forces are at work in both sectors. This has an important implication because in the public sector and those falling under regulation, wages and prices will not behave such as described hereafter. First, PPP is assumed to be verified for the tradable sector. Hence, prices in this sector are given exogenously. Second, wages are linked to the level of productivity in the open sector. Third, wages tend to equalise across sectors so that the wage level in the closed sector is comparable to that in the open sector. Finally, prices in the sheltered sector depend on wages, i.e., unit labour costs rather than on the level of productivity in this sector.

Let us now assume that the home country is the developing country with low productivity levels while the foreign country is the developed country with high productivity levels in the open sector. Prices for tradable goods are given by PPP in both countries. In the home country, low productivity in the open sector implies low wages in the same sector, which in turn means low wages and low prices in the market-based closed sector. By contrast, high productivity in the open sector implies high wages[5] in the same sector, which is reflected in high wages and high prices in the market-based closed sector. So, the true key to differing market-driven non-tradable prices and thus overall price levels ought to be sought in differing productivity levels.

If the home (developing) country is able to catch-up systematically with the foreign (developed) country in economic terms, productivity is expected to rise correspondingly in the open sector. When productivity improves faster in the open sector than in the market-based sheltered sector, market-determined non-tradable prices are expected to rise because of the wage spill-over from tradables to non-tradables. And this gives rise to an increase of the overall price level. If the home country's productivity differential between the open and the market-based sheltered sector exceeds that in the foreign country, the price level will rise faster in the former, implying a positive inflation differential. This in turn will be reflected in the appreciation of home country's real exchange rate.

It is worth pausing to summarise the propositions of the B-S model:

1.) Different productivity levels imply, via differences in market-based non-tradable prices, different price levels expressed in the same currency.
2.) The real and nominal exchange rates of low productivity (typically developing) countries seem undervalued in PPP terms.
3.) If productivity growth is higher in the open sector than in the sheltered sector, non-tradable prices and thus the overall price level will rise (also referred to as structural inflation).
4.) Higher growth in the productivity differential in the home country than in the foreign country is reflected in faster increases of the price level, leading to the real appreciation of the home currency (convergence towards PPP).

However, these propositions hinge on the following assumptions:

1.) wages are linked to productivity in the open sector
2.) wages tend to equalise across sectors
3.) PPP holds for the open sector.

The last assumption has an important implication: The whole appreciation of the CPI-based real exchange rate comes from increases in non-tradable prices, and this can be fully ascribed to the B-S effect (the appreciation of the CPI-based real exchange rate). By contrast,

---

[5] Higher productivity means that more goods can be produced using the same amount of inputs, i.e. labour and capital, so that the inputs' remuneration can be increased (i.e. higher wages) without putting competitiveness at risk (as prices are determined by PPP).

in the event that PPP is not verified for the open sector and, say, the PPI-based real exchange rate also appreciates, the B-S effect cannot explain but the difference in the CPI and the PPI-deflated real exchange rate.

Empirical research carried out for the case of the transition countries of Central and Eastern Europe provides ample evidence in favour of the fact that the higher productivity growth in the open sector leads to an increase in the relative price of non-tradable goods (cf. Égert(2002), Égert et al. (2003)). Nonetheless, the impact of the productivity-fuelled non-tradable inflation on overall inflation and thus on the real appreciation of the currencies remains rather limited mainly due to the low share of services in the CPI baskets of the transition economies as reported in Table 2 hereafter.

Table 2. The share of services in the consumer price baskets (in %)

	Food	Durable goods	Services	Year	Source
Germany	13.1	41.7	45.2	2002	Federal Statistical Office
Croatia	19.5	56.8	21.4	2001	National Bank of Croatia
Czech Republic	19.7	35.2[a]	45.1	2002	Czech National Bank
Estonia	33.8	25.7	22.7	1998-2000	Statistical Office of Estonia
Hungary	24.4	47.5	28.0	2002	Central Statistical Office, Hungary
Lithuania	40.8	40.6	18.7.	2002	Statistical Office of Lithuania
Poland	30.5	37.6	31.9	2000	National Bank of Poland
Slovakia	27.6	32.4	39.7	2002	Statistical Office of the Slovak Republic
Slovenia	22.0	49.0	29.0	2001	National Bank of Slovenia

Source: Égert et al. (2002)

Notes: The category "food" does not contain the item "tobacco and alcoholic beverages" in most of the countries. Industrial goods include energy in most cases. In all countries except the Czech Republic, all categories comprise regulated prices. The classification into food, industrial goods and services was made by the indicated source.

[a] Non-food tradables. The classification into tradables and non-tradables is taken from the Quarterly Reports on Inflation of the Czech National Bank (2002a,b).

II.2   The Role of Regulated Prices

There are two main reasons why the traditional B-S effect is only part of the story of the higher structural inflation and the appreciation of the real exchange rate in transition economies. First, a rather substantial share of services in the consumer basket still has prices regulated, and second, PPP does not hold in the open sector. As was shown in Table 1, the PPI deflated real exchange rates have also substantially appreciated. These two factors are dealt with in what follows.

The trend appreciation of the real exchange rate such as described in the B-S model and changes in tradable prices are based on sectors and prices governed by market forces. Nevertheless, adjustments in administered and regulated prices that concern mainly services, have been at the root of a large chunk of overall inflation measured by the consumer price index, especially after inflation was brought down to single-digit rates.

Increases in these prices are usually the highest and are not related to productivity growth. Regulated prices affect the price level directly and indirectly. First, an increase in regulated prices will imply an increase in the CPI by means of the items itself. Second, if they are inputs for other goods, their adjustment will increase costs and may therefore lead to a price increase also of other goods and services. Although increases in regulated prices are a principal source of higher inflation also in more developed economies, the size of adjustments is still higher in the accession countries. Some prices were left administered at the outset of the transition period when other prices were set free, because the required adjustment was considered too large, creating politically unacceptable social costs. Still ongoing considerable adjustments in regulated prices may reflect late catch-up with other prices, mainly market services. Furthermore, the current prices of regulated services still do not allow cost recovery.

It should be emphasised that most of the regulated prices need not affect the international competitiveness of products of the home country, as they refer to non-tradable goods such as rents. However, there are items, such as energy, which will affect production costs in the entire economy. On the other hand, the inclusion of energy into the producer price index already implies increases due to regulated prices also in this price measure. Figures 2 and 3 below depict the regulated price component of CPI and overall CPI, and energy prices in the domestic producer prices and the PPI for the Czech Republic, Hungary and Poland. However, increases in regulated prices cannot explain the entirety of the trend increase in the producer price index.

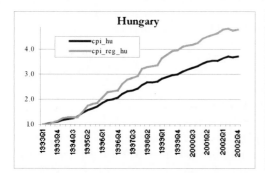

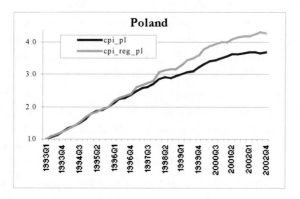

Figure 2. Consumer price index and its regulated price component

 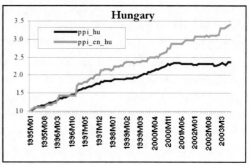

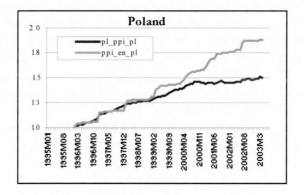

Figure 3. Producer price index and its regulated price component

Note: ppi_en= PPI of energy and water supply

II.3   The Role of Tradable Prices and Foreign Capital

The trend increase in the relative price of tradable goods towards the reference country during
the transition and catch-up process is less straightforward than that of services prices.
Furthermore, not all countries have recorded sizeable real appreciation of the producer price
index-deflated real exchange rate (Slovenia), or only at a later stage of the transition period
(Hungary). According to most models of open economies, an appreciation of the tradable
price-deflated real exchange rate indicates a loss of competitiveness and entails a worsening
of the trade balance and thus the current account. The aforementioned increase in energy
prices (regulated prices) implies a loss of competitiveness (the same goods are sold at higher
prices), so long as the quality of the products manufactured in the domestic economy does not
change. Note also that the same should apply to an increase in the market non-tradable
component of tradable prices, induced by the B-S effect. In the event that they are inputs to
the manufacturing industry, prices of tradable goods rise, leading to a worsening of the
external position.

Although most of the transition countries have been running large current account
deficits, there have been episodes of improvements in the trade balance and the current
account in spite of the real appreciation of the exchange rate. Export revenues measured in
foreign currency have indeed experienced tremendous growth and have grown nearly as much
as imports. Therefore, the trend appreciation of the PPI-deflated real exchange rate, as a

proxy for the real exchange rate of tradable goods, may also be related to the transition and catch-up process. And this should be investigated in more depth.

At the beginning of the transition process, the countries produced goods of lower quality and lower technological content, in particular when compared with more developed countries. The liberalisation of foreign trade necessitated a substantial nominal and real devaluation of the currencies, because exports broke down after the dissolution of the Council of Mutual Economic Assistance (CMEA/COMECON) and imports surged due to pent-up demand for foreign goods. Uncertainties surrounding demand for foreign currency coupled with fast trade liberalisation led policy makers to prefer larger devaluation than what the external imbalances would have required as argued by Rosati (1996). For instance, the devaluation of the Polish zloty against the US dollar in early 1990 resulted in an exchange rate that was roughly 20 per cent weaker than the then prevailing black market rate (Rosati (1994)).

These devaluations may have led to or may have amplified initial undervaluation, also detected in Halpern and Wyplosz (1997) and Krajnyák and Zettelmeyer (1998) by means of panel estimations. It could therefore be argued that part of the real appreciation over the last 10 years or so reflects adjustment towards equilibrium. However, this explanation appears insufficient. If the initial devaluation were too large, the correction towards the pre-transition levels should have occurred within the next few years. Instead, real appreciation in both CPI and PPI terms proved to be a rather steady process. Figure 4 shows the development of the real exchange rate towards Germany since 1985. Notwithstanding the fact that prices and exchange rates in the 1980s basically reflected intentions of the planning authorities, important insights can be gained regarding the process of real appreciation since the start of the transition.

Real devaluation was the sharpest in the Czech Republic (Czechoslovakia prior to 1993), where market based information or world market relative prices played a rather limited role in determining the planned price and exchange rate system, and where the uncertainties as regards market assessment of competitiveness were the highest. Note that the devaluation was the lowest in Hungary, where some market orientated reforms were introduced since the late 1960s. Furthermore, because price liberalisation for items included in the CPI basket started in the mid-1980s, the CPI-deflated real exchange rate started appreciating earlier than the real exchange rate based on PPI. However, in all three countries the devaluation proved to be rather lasting possibly because the currencies were strongly overvalued when entering transition from plan to market and thus facing the challenge of market forces.

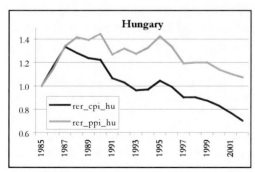
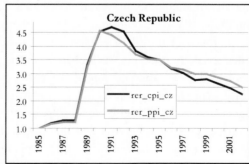

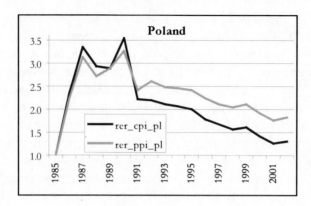

Figure 4. Real exchange rates vis-à-vis the DEM since the late-1980s

Source: OECD Main Economic Indicators and Czech National Bank.
Note: Prior to 1993, the nominal exchange rate used for the Czech Republic is the one that prevailed for Czechoslovakia.

Therefore, the huge initial devaluation may have been necessary because domestic supply lacked competitiveness in domestic and foreign markets. But the real exchange rate may appreciate if domestic supply capacities and product quality increase, i.e., during the transition and catch-up process. The transition from plan to market entails a change in incentive structures and a reallocation of existing resources. And this already improves supply. However, a sustained catch-up process requires investments into human as well as fixed capital and quality improvements are needed in capital stock, technology, managerial and organisational skills and in infrastructure.

Foreign capital and in particular foreign direct investment (FDI) can play a very beneficial role in this regard. In the transition countries, FDI gave rise to very rapid changes in the composition of GDP and especially in that of manufactured goods. A marked shift occurred from predominantly low quality, low value added, and labour and raw material intensive goods towards products of increasingly higher quality and higher value-added that triggered increased foreign demand for these products. This may have at the same time supported simultaneous economy-wide quality improvement of goods and services, even if changes in the domestically orientated goods and services may have occurred more slowly. Hence, both exported goods and those sold primarily in domestic markets have changed markedly. It should be, however, underlined that exported goods can differ to a large extent from those sold in the domestic market, with regard to both quality and technological content.

Improved quality then leveled prices since goods of higher quality are associated with higher prices. In principle, such changes in the price level should not be reflected in inflation rates and the real appreciation of the currency. Nevertheless, adjusting inappropriately for quality improvements may result in higher inflation of tradable goods and the subsequent appreciation of the PPI-based real exchange rate.

Prices may also increase and thus the real exchange rate may appreciate when quality improvements go in tandem with better reputation. The outset of transition was characterised by a strong bias towards imported foreign goods. With ameliorating quality and better marketing of domestically manufactured goods and with a higher capacity of the countries to produce goods of the more preferred foreign brands, the bias towards imported goods may become weaker. In other words, domestic and foreign demand for goods produced domestically increase.

While exported goods enter the trade balance directly and increase export revenues, higher quality of domestic goods sold in domestic markets reduces import elasticities and thus impacts on the trade balance indirectly. In this context, higher prices are an accompanying phenomenon of the growth in non-price competitiveness. Changes in non-price competitiveness of goods produced in the home country and improving supply capacities could indeed reverse the strong initial devaluation and lead to a steady appreciation of the real exchange rate measured in PPI and CPI terms.

Hence, in addition to productivity-induced service price inflation along the lines of the B-S model, successful catch-up may also entail real appreciation based on improvement in supply capacities and quality of tradable goods.

Figure 5 below shows that the five selected transition countries have witnessed, over the period from 1995 to 2002, a strong increase in export revenues expressed in German mark at current prices. More specifically, Hungary and Poland can sport the highest increases, whereas export growth proved the slowest in Slovenia[6]. Another general observation is that in countries with better export performance the real exchange rate appreciated more (Hungary, Poland) than in countries with lower export growth (Slovenia).

Export performance in transition countries seems to be indeed closely related to privatisation strategies and to attitudes towards foreign direct investment inflows. Foreign direct investment has had particularly beneficial effects on exports, which became the engine of economic growth.[7] FDI helped economic restructuring by means of financing fixed capital investment and implementing state-of-the-art technology and Western-style organisational structures and schemes. But most importantly, FDI often aimed at export sectors and hence created export capacities. Foreign involvement made access to foreign markets easier. However, because countries adopted different strategies towards privatisation and capital inflows, the extent to which they benefited from FDI differs largely. Whereas privatisation in Hungary relied heavily on sales to foreign investors, in the Czech Republic foreign capital started to pour in on a wider scale only after reforms accelerated in 1997. Political instability in Slovakia prevented direct investments from flowing in until 1998 and Slovenia has been hesitating to open up its economy to foreign investments until quite recently. It turns out that export revenues have grown most in countries with large foreign investments.

---

[6] Growth in export revenue is also pronounced in 1993 and 1994. However, real appreciation is less marked.
[7] See e.g. Darvas and Sass (2001), Sgard (2001), Campos and Coricelli (2002) and Benacek et al. (2003)

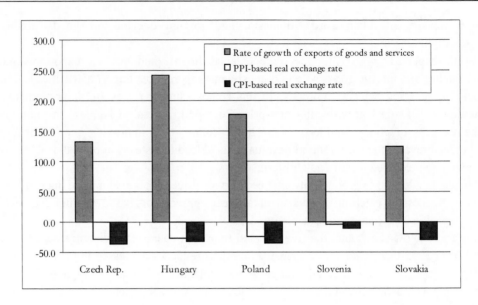

Figure 5. Real Exchange Rates and Export Revenues, Changes from 1995 to 2002

The above-described increase in the price of tradable goods can also be shown in a more formal way. Let us consider a two-country, two-good framework where the external equilibrium is defined as a balanced trade balance with abstracting from capital flows. The supply side of the home and foreign economies are given by the following functions:

$$Y = f(A, t, K, L) \tag{1}$$
$$Y^* = f(A^*, t^*, K^*, L^*) \tag{2}$$

where * denotes the foreign economy and t stands for technology. Technology and capital stock is initially higher in the foreign country compared with those in the domestic one and this implies higher foreign GDP. Each country produces one good and consumes both. Goods are at least imperfect substitutes, so that PPP does not hold. Let us now assume that t*>t and Δt*< Δt. Hence, GDP growth is higher in the domestic economy due to technological catch-up.

The demand side of the two economies are described with utility functions in which both goods enter in both economies. The utility of consuming the domestic good is a positive function of technology: The higher the technological content, the higher the utility. Demand for the domestic good therefore depends on technology. With increasing technological content, demand for the domestic good increases both in the domestic and the foreign economy. In addition, it is assumed that in the home country, demand for the foreign good is negatively linked to the technological content of the domestic good but it does not affect the demand for the foreign good in the foreign economy.

The demand functions of the domestic and foreign economies can be described as follows:

$$D = C(\overset{+}{Y}, \overset{+}{t}, \overset{-}{P/P^*}) + C^*(\overset{+}{Y}, \overset{-}{t}, \overset{+}{P/P^*}) \tag{3}$$

$$D^* = C(\overset{+}{Y}^*, \overset{+}{t}, \overset{-}{P/P^*}) + C^*(\overset{+}{Y}^*, \overset{+}{P/P^*}) \tag{4}$$

where D, C, Y, A and P stand for demand, consumption, GDP, technology and prices, respectively. Equilibrium is determined when the current account is balanced. Note that because of the assumption of no capital flows, the current account (CA) equals the trade balance. Hence:

$$CA = 0 \tag{5}$$

$$P \cdot Q = P^* Q^* \tag{6}$$

with Q denoting the quantity of exported goods. Exports of the domestic good are given by the demand for the domestic good in the foreign economy, whilst imports of the foreign good are determined by domestic demand for the foreign good. The equilibrium condition can be derived by substituting the foreign demand for domestic good (exports) and the domestic demand for foreign good (imports) into Eq. (6):

$$CA = 0 = P/P^* \cdot C(\overset{+}{Y}^*, \overset{+}{t}, \overset{-}{P/P^*}) - C^*(\overset{+}{Y}, \overset{-}{t}, \overset{+}{P/P^*}) \tag{7}$$

A change of the relative price due to the growth of technology in the domestic economy can be shown from the total differential of this equilibrium condition. Normalising P* to 1 (P denotes the relative price henceforth), the total differential becomes:

$$dCA = P \cdot \left[\frac{\partial C}{\partial Y^*} dY^* + \frac{\partial C}{\partial t} dt + \frac{\partial C}{\partial P} dP \right] - \left[\frac{\partial C^*}{\partial Y} \frac{\partial Y}{\partial t} dt + \frac{\partial C^*}{\partial t} dt + \frac{\partial C^*}{\partial P} dP \right] \tag{8}$$

Setting the rate of growth of foreign GDP to 0, i.e. $dY^* = 0$, and re-arranging terms as in Eq. (9) – (11), the total differential becomes:

$$P \cdot \frac{\partial C}{\partial t} dt - \frac{\partial C^*}{\partial Y} \frac{\partial Y}{\partial t} dt - \frac{\partial C^*}{\partial t} dt = \frac{\partial C^*}{\partial P} dP - P \cdot \frac{\partial C}{\partial P} dP \tag{9}$$

$$\left[P \cdot \frac{\partial C}{\partial t} - \frac{\partial C^*}{\partial Y} \frac{\partial Y}{\partial t} - \frac{\partial C^*}{\partial t} \right] \cdot dt = \left[\frac{\partial C^*}{\partial P} - P \cdot \frac{\partial C}{\partial P} \right] \cdot dP \tag{10}$$

$$\frac{dP}{dt} = \frac{P \cdot \dfrac{\partial C}{\partial t} - \dfrac{\partial C^*}{\partial Y} \dfrac{\partial Y}{\partial t} - \dfrac{\partial C^*}{\partial t}}{\dfrac{\partial C^*}{\partial P} - P \cdot \dfrac{\partial C}{\partial P}} \tag{11}$$

The expression in the denominator is positive because import of the foreign good increases with the real appreciation ($\partial C^*/\partial P \succ 0\,\delta$) and export of the domestic good are a decreasing function of the relative price ($\partial C/\partial P \prec 0\,\delta$). The overall effect of the change in technology on the relative price depends on the expression in the nominator. Export, positively related to technology ($\partial C/\partial t \succ 0$), is multiplied by the relative price. The second term represents imports connected to income and works towards real depreciation if real income increases. The third term is negative ($\partial C^*/\partial t \prec 0$), i.e., higher supply capacities result in declining imports because domestic goods of higher quality are consumed instead. Therefore, the overall effect depends on whether or not the increase in exports and the decrease in imports, a result of the higher technological content of domestic products exceed the increase in imports linked to higher income. Thus, for the overall effect to be positive, increases in imports related to higher income should be lower than the growth of exports and the decline in imports due to technological change:

$$P \cdot \frac{\partial C}{\partial t} - \frac{\partial C^*}{\partial t} > \frac{\partial C^*}{\partial Y}\frac{\partial Y}{\partial t} \tag{12}$$

As discussed earlier, price increases leading to real appreciation based on this mechanism may have two sources. On the one hand, if quality changes are not appropriately dealt with, they are passed through onto prices. On the other hand, goods of better reputation can be priced differently, which is impossible to correct for when calculating inflation.

Indeed, productivity advances in the tradable sector are the source of such price increases similarly to the case of the B-S model. This implies that productivity gains could not only operate through non-tradable prices but also via the tradable price channel[8].

It should be, however, noted that real appreciation can be also a result of the appreciation of the nominal exchange rate due to capital inflows. This appreciation will be sustainable only if capital inflows are related to productive foreign investment that trigger future productivity gains and an increase in future export revenues that could counterbalance the deterioration of the current account. In addition, not only the current account deficit has to be reduced by future export revenues, but the higher foreign debt has to be serviced and repaid.

III Reduced Form Equation and Data Definitions

The above developed theoretical framework connects the real exchange rate to labour productivity in industry (PROD) and to regulated prices (REG). However, other exchange rate determination models also include foreign debt, the real interest differential, and the openness ratio. Accordingly, the reduced form of the real exchange rate looks as follows:

$$RER = RER(\overset{-}{PROD}, \overset{-}{REG}, \overset{+}{FDEBT}, \overset{-}{RIR}, \overset{+/-}{OPEN}) \tag{13}$$

---

[8] This could indeed explain why earlier research showed the traditional B-S effect to be very important, despite the small share of market services in the consumer basket, as regards the appreciation of the real exchange rate.

Labour productivity in industry (PROD) is expected to be negatively related to the real exchange rate, i.e., an increase/decrease in productivity should lead to an appreciation/depreciation of the real exchange rate. Productivity primarily stands for higher supply capacities that can lead to an appreciation through the channel of changes in preferences in line with increasing technological content of and thus demand for the domestic good in the domestic and foreign economies. The sector that is likely to benefit the most from technological catch-up and produces most of exported goods is industry. However, labour productivity in industry also captures the traditional (market non-tradable prices) and the indirect (non-tradable component of tradable goods) B-S effect that operates through service prices. But, as mentioned earlier, this effect is rather limited due to the small share of non-tradables in CPI of transition countries.

Labour productivity is computed as average labour productivity in the home country relative to labour productivity in Germany. Two measures are used. PROD1 is calculated using industrial production over industrial employment obtained from the Main Economic Indicators of the OECD, the International Financial Statistics of the IMF or the WIIW. PROD2 is obtained as value added over sectoral employment in industry obtained from national accounts. Value added in industry and industrial production based measures can exhibit significantly different developments, which may depend on cost and productivity developments in services as well as the extent to which manufacturing relies on inputs from other sectors.

Labour productivity is completed with *regulated prices (REG)* which rose the fastest among the components of the CPI over the last 10 years or so. Regulated prices constitute a cost-push factor on one hand, which may erode competitiveness if it raises the price of tradable goods. On the other hand, however, only part of the regulated prices directly affects costs of tradable goods. So, a correction of the exchange rate may not be needed for maintaining external balance. Furthermore, a rise in regulated prices lowers disposable income. In sum, an increase/decline in regulated prices is expected to bring about an appreciation/depreciation of the real exchange rate. As noted earlier, regulated prices do not only concern CPI but also PPI. Regulated prices in PPI, mainly energy prices, have been increased regularly and have exceeded rises in the overall price index.

The regulated price differential in the home country and those in Germany are mainly based on regulated prices provided by national sources. Thus, series come from the respective national banks for the Czech Republic, Hungary, Poland and Slovenia. Regulated prices for Germany are obtained from the Federal Statistical Office of Germany. Series for Estonia corresponds to that used in Égert (2003). For the cases of Latvia and Lithuania, regulated prices are proxied by rents.

Foreign debt as percentage of GDP (FDEBT) is expected to lead to a depreciation of the real exchange rate due to the higher interest payments to the rest of the world.

The real interest rate differential (RIR) reflects imbalances between investment and savings, i.e., stands for capital flows that accompany these imbalances. It is expected to be negatively connected to the real exchange rate implying that an increase leads to the real appreciation of the currency. *Real interest differential* towards Germany is computed as the one-year treasury bill yield in period t are divided by CPI or PPI in period t. Thus, the real interest differential is determined *ex post*.

Openness (OPEN), computed as exports and imports of goods and services over GDP, can stand for higher exports resulting from increasing supply capacities and is thus negatively connected with the real exchange rate. However, *openness (OPEN)* is traditionally viewed as an indicator of trade liberalisation. Increasing openness indicates a higher degree of trade liberalisation. Because it comes through the abolishment of trade barriers and thus allowing foreign products to enter more freely the country, an increase in openness is to worsen the trade balance. Hence, a rise in openness is expected to yield a depreciation of the real exchange rate. The expected sign is therefore ambiguous. *Openness* is computed as nominal exports and imports of goods and services expressed in nominal GDP.

The real exchange rate is calculated using average quarterly nominal exchange rates vis-à-vis the German mark, expressed as units of domestic currency over one unit of foreign currency, deflated by the consumer and the producer price indices.

The reduced form equation is tested using a dataset that consists of quarterly time series for the Czech Republic, Hungary and Poland. The period spans from 1994:Q1 to 2002:Q4 for the Czech Republic and Hungary and from 1993:Q1 to 2002:Q4 for Poland.

Tests are also carried out for a panel composed of quarterly data for 8 transition countries (including in addition Estonia, Latvia, Lithuania, Slovakia and Slovenia) and spanning from 1995 to 2002. The data used in the paper are drawn from the following sources: Main Economic Indicators/OECD, International Financial Statistics/IMF, WIIW Monthly Database, NewCronos/Eurostat, Datastream and different national sources (statistical offices and national banks).

The series are transformed into a natural logarithm with the exception of the interest rate series. They are also seasonally adjusted either by the national statistical offices or by means of the X-12 ARIMA procedure. Exceptions are regulated prices and interest rates series. All series, except interest rates are computed with a basis of 100 in 1992 and 1993.

IV Econometric Techniques and Testing Strategy

It is professional wisdom that a large number of macroeconomic time series are integrated of order 1. This is tested for employing conventional ADF and PP tests. If series turn out to be I(1) processes, the appropriate estimation technique to use is the cointegration approach. In this paper, we use four different types of cointegration techniques: the Engle and Granger (EG) technique, the Dynamic OLS (DOLS) popularised by Stock and Watson (1993), the Autoregressive Distributed Lag (ARDL) approach of Pesaran et al. (2001) and the Maximum Likelihood estimator of Johansen. The EG approach to cointegration is based on the following static equation such as:

$$Y_t = \beta_0 + \sum_{i=1}^{n} \beta_i X_{i,t} + \varepsilon_t$$

$$(16)$$

Eq. (1) does not account for endogeneity of the regressors and serial correlation in the residuals. This is corrected for using DOLS that includes leads and lags of the regressors in first differences:

$$Y_t = \beta_0 + \sum_{i=1}^{n} \beta_n X_{i,t} + \sum_{i=1}^{n} \sum_{j=-k_1}^{k_2} \gamma_{i,j} \Delta X_{i,t-j} + \varepsilon_t$$

$$(17)$$

with k1 and k2 denoting respectively leads and lags. The error correction form of the ARDL model is given in Eq. (18) where the dependent variable in first differences is regressed on the lagged values of the dependent and independent variables in levels and first differences:

$$\Delta Y_t = \beta_0 + \rho(Y_{t-1} + \sum_{i=1}^{n} \beta_n X_{i,t-1}) + \sum_{j=1}^{l_1} \eta_j \Delta Y_{t-j} + \sum_{i=1}^{n} \sum_{j=0}^{l_2} \gamma_{i,j} \Delta X_{i,t-j} + \varepsilon_t$$

(18)

where l1 and l2 are the maximum lags. In the EG, FMOLS and DOLS approaches, whether or not Y and X are cointegrated is examined by testing for unit root in the residuals and applying critical values tabulated in MacKinnon (1996). In contrast to this, Pesaran et al. (2001) employ a bounds testing approach. Using conventional F-tests, the null of $H_0 : \rho = \beta_1 = ... = \beta_n$ is tested against the alternative hypothesis of $H_1 : \rho \neq 0, \beta_1 \neq 0, ..., \beta_n \neq 0$. Pesaran et al. (2001) tabulate two sets of critical values, one for the case when all variables are I(1), i.e., upper bound critical values and another one when all variables are I(0), i.e., lower bound critical values. Critical values are provided for 5 different models of which model (3) with unrestricted intercept and no trend will be used in this paper. If the test statistics are higher than the upper bound critical value, the null of no cointegration is rejected in favour of the presence of cointegration. On the other hand, an F-statistics lower than the lower bound critical value implies the absence of cointegration. In the event that the calculated F-stat lies between the two critical values, there is no clear indication regarding the absence or existence of a cointegrating relationship.

Nonetheless, in the presence of more than one cointegration relationship the aforesaid single-equation approaches cannot be used. Therefore, the Johansen cointegration technique is used for testing for the number of cointegrating vectors in a VAR framework. In the event that only one long-term relationship is found using the trace statistics, the Maximum Likelihood estimates are used as a robustness check in the following form:

$$Y_t = (m_0 + m_1 t + (1 + \alpha \beta')Y_{t-1}) - \sum_{i=1}^{p-1} \Phi_i \Delta Y_{t-i} + \varepsilon_t$$

(20)

where Y represents the vector including the dependent and the independent variables.

We first conduct a general-to-specific model selection strategy that involves top-down and bottom-up F pre-search coupled with sample split analysis so as to identify blocks of statistically significant variables. Departing with 4 different sets of variables described in Section IV, the general-to-specific approach to model selection is performed using the OLS estimation technique. The residuals of the models chosen are subsequently checked for stationarity à la Engle and Granger and the selected models are taken as an input for the estimation of the DOLS and ARDL. Leads and lags are determined based on the usual information criteria: (Schwarz, Akaike and Hannan-Quinn).

Next, the VAR-based Johansen approach is used to verify the number of cointegration relationships that might link the variables. The detection of a single long-term relationships that turns out to be stable over time then validates results of the single-equation methods. The Johansen technique involves the roots of the VAR model to be verified (to ensure stationarity of the AR processes), tests for normality and serial correlation. Furthermore, both the rank of cointegration and parameter constancy are analysed. How a model is finally selected depends largely on whether there is consensus among the four different tests on cointegration and whether or not all the variables included into the model are found statistically significant and sign according to our expectations described in Section VI.

Besides time series techniques, panel techniques are also applied to the panel composed of 8 countries. Analogously to the time series analysis, stationarity is tested for by means of the panel unit root test proposed by Im et al. (2003) (IPS henceforth). The t-bar statistic is constructed as a means of individual ADF statistics to test the null hypothesis of a unit root. The IPS uses country-specific autoregressive coefficients from the ADF equation that secures a high degree of heterogeneity across members of the panel. Both model including trend and intercept and model comprising only intercept will be employed.

Subsequently, panel cointegration tests are employed to detect long-term relationships and in estimating the corresponding coefficients. For this purpose, the residual-based tests of the type Engle and Granger developed in Pedroni (1999) are used. Pedroni(1999) develops seven tests of which the first four statistics are based on pooling along within-dimension whereas the last three tests rest on pooling along between-dimension. Only the last three tests (group rho-statistic, group pp-statistic, group ADF-statistic) will be employed because they allow for heterogeneity in the autoregressive term. According to Pedroni (1999), of the seven tests, the group ADF-stat is the most powerful for samples of small size. Coefficients of the cointegrating vector are then determined using FMOLS and DOLS estimators. Kao and Chiang (2000) show that both the OLS and FMOLS estimators exhibit small-sample bias and that the DOLS estimator appears to outperform both estimators.

V   Estimation Results

Because conventional unit root tests, i.e., ADF and PP indicate that most of the series are not stationary in levels but turn out to be stationary in first differences, the cointegration techniques developed appear the most appropriate approach to test for long-term relationships connecting the real exchange rate to the underlying fundamentals.

We set out to test two sets of equations. First, the CPI-based real exchange is regressed on the gamut of variables described earlier. In this case, the productivity variable is likely to impact on the real exchange rate through three different channels: (a) the traditional BS effect, (b) the indirect BS effect through an increase in the service prices as inputs, and (c) tradable prices because of improved quality and reputation. Second, the PPI-deflated real exchange rate is regressed on the same set of variables to test the importance of the traditional BS effect for the real exchange rate determination. If labour productivity proves to be important in both relationships, the indirect BS effect, and most importantly, the increase in tradable prices brought about by productivity changes make the real exchange rate appreciate systematically. The theoretical framework developed earlier is supported if the two sets of equations yield similar results.

Employing the EG, DOLS, ARDL and Johansen cointegration techniques, estimations are performed for the period 1994-2002 for the Czech Republic and Hungary and for 1993-2002 for the case of Poland.

Results obtained for time series are reported in Tables 3 to 5. With regard to the Czech Republic, the specification including the difference in labour productivity, the regulated price differential and foreign debt is retained as the most reliable and economically the most compelling. This specification appears remarkably robust given that all methods detect the presence of a cointegrating vector linking the aforementioned variables. Moreover, all the variables are found statistically significant, have the expected sing and the size of the estimated coefficients based on different techniques is fairly comparable. These observations apply not only to the equations including the CPI-based real exchange rate but also to those in which the PPI-deflated real exchange rate is used.

The fact that the estimated coefficients for the difference in productivity is very similar for the CPI and PPI-based real exchange rate equations provides strong empirical support to the theoretical framework according to which real appreciation comes mainly through tradable prices. Nevertheless, coefficients tend to be slightly lower especially when the EG and ARDL techniques are employed indicating that the CPI-based real exchange rate is likely to appreciate, although to a much lesser extent, because of changes in the relative price of market non-tradable items.

The regulated price differential enters both the CPI and PPI-based specifications and an increase in the differential results in an appreciation of the real exchange rates. Nonetheless, the estimated coefficients are roughly twice as high as in the case when the CPI-based real exchange rate is used. This may indicate that the difference between the CPI and PPI-based real exchange rates may be partly explained by the regulated price differential.

As regards to foreign debt, a rise/fall induces a depreciation/appreciation of the real exchange rate and the estimated coefficients are rather similar for the CPI and the PPI-based equations.

Table 3a. Cointegration tests for the CPI-based real exchange rate, Czech Republic, 1994-2002

	EG		DOLS SIC,HQ (0,1)		AIC(1,1)		ARDL(1,1) SIC,AIC, HQ		JOH. M3,k=3		
SIC	1	-5.199**	3		-5.528**	3	-5.339**	6.84**	R=0	73.04***	RS ok
AIC	1	-5.199**	3		-5.528**	3	-5.339**		R=1	32.23***	AC ok
HQ	1	-5.199**	3		-5.528**	3	-5.339**		R=2	8.99	JB 0..016
									R=3	0.01	ST 1
	Coeff	t-stat	Coeff	t-stat	coeff	t-stat	Coeff	t-stat	coeff	t-stat	
PROD2	-0.701	-5.51	-0.948	-7.198	-1.021	-6.568	-0.793	-4.108	-0.649	-16.641	
REGD	-0.362	-6.713	-0.361	-3.674	-0.379	-2.667	-0.471	-3.066	-0.457	-32.643	
FDEBT	0.190	4.089	0.292	4.043	0.308	3.063	0.326	3.514	0.278	18.533	

Note: *,** and *** denote respectively the presence of cointegration at the 10%, 5% and 1% levels, respectively. EG represent the Engle and Granger residual based tests. SIC, AIC and HQ in the first column of the Table stand for the Schwarz, Akaike and the Hannan-Quinn information cirteria based on which the lag length is selected for the ADF tests. Below DOLS and ARDL are shown the information criteria and, in parentheses, the chosen leads and lags (DOLS) and lags for dY and dX (ARDL). The test statistics shown below ARDL is the F-stat as in Pesaran et al. (2001). JOH represents the Johansen cointegration technique. k stands for the lag length chosen for the VAR. The trace-test statistics are given below. In the last column, RS and AC are roots of the model and autocorrelation. "ok" indicates that the inverse roots of the model are lower than 1 and the absence of serial correlation in the residuals. JB stands for the Jarque-Bera multivariate normality tests. A figure higher than 0.05 indicates that normality is accepted. Finally, ST indicates the number of cointegration relationship(s) that turn out to be stable over time.

Table 3b. Cointegration tests for the PPI-based real exchange rate, Czech Republic,1994-2002

	EG		DOLS(1,1) SIC,AIC,HQ		ARDL(1,1) SIC,AIC,HQ		JOH. M3,k=3		
SIC	1	-5.122**	4	-5.604**	6.163**		R=0	84.06***	RS ok
AIC	1	-5.122**	4	-5.604**			R=1	39.56***	AC ok
HQ	1	-5.122**	4	-5.604**			R=2	9.23	JB 0..012
							R=3	0.06	ST 1
	Coeff	t-stat	coeff	t-stat	coeff	t-stat	coeff	t-stat	
PROD2	-0.632	-5.155	-0.974	-6.791	-0.716	-3.927	-0.699	-19.971	
REGD	-0.220	-4.227	-0.210	-1.596	-0.317	-2.334	-0.359	-25.643	
FDEBT	0.189	4.236	0.259	2.793	0.293	3.145	0.278	19.857	

Note: As for Table 3a.

Results for Hungary are reported in Tables 4a and 4b, which are less robust when compared with the case of the Czech Republic in that cointegration tests reach no clear consensus on whether or not the variables are linked through a long-term cointegration relationship. In particular, the EG and on some occasions the ARDL technique could not detect the presence of cointegration. However, the DOLS, the Johansen and in some cases the ARDL techniques reveal that both the CPI and the PPI-deflated real exchange rates are connected to the difference in labour productivity, foreign debt and openness. The coefficients are statistically significant and are correctly signed. Thus, an increase/decrease in labour productivity leads to an appreciation/depreciation of both the CPI and the PPI-based real exchange rate. This indeed confirms our conjecture stipulating the role of tradable prices in the appreciation of the real exchange rate. However, the estimated coefficients for the CPI-based specification are larger than those found for the PPI-deflated real exchange rate. This shows that the higher appreciation of the CPI-deflated real exchange rates may be a result of a rise in the price of market non-tradables, i.e., the B-S effect. The regulated price differential does not enter the equation. Because of possible multi-collinearity between labour productivity and the regulated price differential, the higher coefficient may also capture the impact of regulated prices on the CPI-based real exchange rate.

Foreign debt and the openness ratio are positively related to both the CPI and PPI-based real exchange rates. Hence, an increase in these variables yields a depreciation of the real exchange rate.

Table 4a. Cointegration test for the CPI-based real exchange rate in Hungary, 1994-2002

	EG		DOLS SIC(1,3)		AIC,HQ (2,3)		ARDL (1,2) ARDL_ SIC		JOH M3,k=3		
SIC	0	-2.136	1	-4.848**	1	-6.825**	3.466^a		R=0	74.14***	RS no
AIC	0	-2.136	4	-4.834**	4	-4.69**			R=1	20.46	AC ok
HQ	0	-2.136	4	-4.834**	4	-4.69**			R=2	7.77	JB 0.002
									R=3	1.18	ST 1
	coeff	t-stat	Coeff	t-stat	coeff	t-stat	Coeff	t-stat	coeff	t-stat	
PROD2			-2.344	-12.02	-2.489	-7.493	-2.099	-3.164	-2.099	-22.570	
FDEBT			0.811	9.482	0.908	6.795	0.622	2.551	0.730	19.211	
OPEN			0.590	6.855	0.633	4.052	0.434	2.346	0.511	13.447	

Note: As for Table 3a., (a) means that the ARDL test statistics cannot decide whether there is cointegration at the 10% significance level

Table 4b. Cointegration test for the PPI-based real exchange rate in Hungary, 1994-2002

	EG		DOLS SIC,HQ (2,3)		AIC(3,3)		ARDL SIC(1,0)	AIC,HQ (1,1)		JOH M3,k=3		
SIC	0	-2.747	1	-5.936**	1	-8.101**	2.109	4.032*		R=0	45.09*	RS no
AIC	0	-2.747	1	-5.936**	3	-5.068**				R=1	20.24	AC ok
HQ	0	-2.747	1	-5.936**	3	-5.068**				R=2	8.16	JB
												0.110
										R=3	3.58	ST 1?
	coeff	t-stat	Coeff	t-stat	Coeff	t-stat		coeff	t-stat	coeff	t-stat	
PROD2			-1.967	-5.821	-2.951	-2.735		-0.902	-2.077	-1.098	-7.572	
FDEBT			0.958	7.041	1.319	3.636		0.401	1.677	0.549	9.305	
OPEN			0.486	3.059	0.927	1.916		0.004	0.029	0.056	1.000	

Note: As for Table 3a.

As far as Poland is concerned, our preferred relationship is the one including labour productivity and the real interest differential. Although cointegration is found only using DOLS and ARDL when the CPI-based real exchange rate is considered, all techniques are able to detect cointegration for the PPI-based equations. Generally, both productivity and the real interest differential turn out to be highly significant and bear the expected sign. Productivity is found to impact on both the CPI and PPI-based real exchange rates, thus supporting our conjecture. The reason for the large differences in the size of the estimated coefficients in the case of the CPI and the PPI-based equations are likely to be very similar to what we observed for Hungary. The negative sign of the real interest differential shows that a rise/fall in this variable results in the appreciation/depreciation of the real exchange rate. This finding is in sharp contrast with the cases of the Czech Republic and Hungary where the real interest differential is not found entering significantly the long-term relationship. This could be explained by the inefficiency of the Czech financial markets and the long-lasting crawling peg system in Hungary that impaired interaction between the real interest differential and the real exchange rate.

Table 5a. Cointegration tests for the CPI-based real exchange rate in Poland, 1993-2002

	EG		DOLS SIC(2,0)		AIC,HQ (3,3)		ARDL SIC(1,0)		AIC,HQ (3,0)		JOH M3,k=2	
SIC	0	-3.552	0	-4.134**	0	-6.486**	3.552[a]		5.533**		R=0	21.69
AIC	0	-3.552	0	-4.134**	0	-6.486**					R=1	5.04
HQ	0	-3.552	0	-4.134**	0	-6.486**					R=2	1.19
	Coeff	t-stat	Coeff	t-stat	coeff	t-stat	Coeff	t-stat	Coeff	t-stat		
PROD1			-0.893	-14.277	-1.056	-14.051	-0.83	-2.878	-0.808	-3.46		
INTCPI			-0.009	-4.501	-0.007	-3.049	-0.008	-2.059	-0.008	-2.398		

Note: As for Table 3a.

Table 5b. Cointegration tests for the PPI-based real exchange rate in Poland, 1993-2002

	EG		DOLS				ARDL (1,0)		JOH		
			SIC,H Q(0,0)		AIC(2,3)		SIC,AIC, HQ		M3, k=1		
SIC	0	-5.608**	0	-6.229**	0	-7.657**	13.601**		R=0	41.05***	RS ok
AIC	0	-5.608**	0	-6.229**	2	-2.647			R=1	4.06	AC ok
HQ	0	-5.608**	0	-6.229**	2	-2.647			R=2	0.19	JB 0.685

	Coeff	t-stat	Coeff	t-stat	Coeff	t-stat	Coeff	t-stat	t-stat	coeff	ST 1
PROD1	-0.483	-12.305	-0.458	-12.873	-0.634	-10.78	-0.453	-4.83	-0.453	-13.324	
INTPPI	-0.006	-5.746	-0.007	-7.536	-0.005	-3.666	-0.007	-5.386	-0.007	-7.778	

Note: As for Table 3a.

Using the panel including eight transition economies, both the CPI and the PPI-deflated real exchange rates are regressed on labour productivity, foreign debt and the openness ratio. As shown in Table 6, all the cointegration tests reject the null hypothesis of no cointegration and thus suggest that the aforesaid variables are linked via a long-term cointegrating vector. Furthermore, figures reported in Table 7 reveal that the estimated coefficient for labour productivity is statistically significant and has the expected sign, irrespective of whether the FMOLS or DOLS technique and whether the CPI or the PPI-based real exchange rate is employed. This strongly supports the view that the appreciation of the real exchange rate is to a large extent due to changes in tradable prices induced by productivity increases. The size of the coefficient seems to be systematically higher for the CPI-based real exchange rate when compared with that obtained for the PPI-based real exchange rate. Thus, productivity-induced service price inflation also contributes to real appreciation.

Foreign debt is highly significant but enters the relationship with the wrong sign, i.e., an increase in the debt leads to an appreciation of the real exchange rate. This is in contrast with what is found earlier for the cases of the Czech Republic and Hungary. A possible explanation for this may be that most of the countries included into the panel attracted foreign investments on a wide scale only after the risk associated with an unstable political and legal environment was reduced and reforms were put in place. In addition, the inherited foreign debt was low. On average, foreign debt may reflect therefore capital inflows instead of increasing interest payments related to the foreign debt. Burgess et al. (2003) also find the wrong sign between net foreign assets and the real exchange rate for the three Baltic countries, and this may dominate in our panel as well.

Openness bears a positive sign to the real exchange rate. Hence, an increase in openness leads to the depreciation of the real exchange rate. Therefore, a rise in the openness ratio may signal increased trade liberalisation that in turn necessitates depreciation.

Table 6. Panel cointegration tests, 1995-2002

		RER_CPI		RER_PPI	
		FMOLS	DOLS	FMOLS	DOLS
		p-values			
P5	None	0.001	0.001	0.001	0.001
	Const	0.000	0.000	0.000	0.000
	Const+trend	0.000	0.000	0.000	0.000
P6	None	0.003	0.002	0.001	0.001
	Const	0.000	0.000	0.000	0.000
	Const+trend	0.000	0.000	0.000	0.000
P7	None	0.003	0.002	0.001	0.002
	Const	0.000	0.000	0.000	0.000
	Const+trend	0.000	0.000	0.000	0.000

Note: P5, P6 and P7 are respectively the Pedroni group rho-statistic, group pp-statistic, group ADF-statistic

Table 7. Coefficient estimates, 1995-2002

		RER_CPI		RER_PPI	
FMOLS		Coeff	t-stat	Coeff	t-stat
	PROD1	-0.968	-9.989	-0.763	-7.307
	FDEBT	-0.382	-11.768	-0.265	-7.581
	OPEN	0.266	2.859	0.284	2.841
DOLS		Coeff	t-stat	Coeff	t-stat
	PROD1	-0.829	-7.998	-0.668	-5.990
	FDEBT	-0.320	-9.221	-0.221	-5.912
	OPEN	0.386	3.891	0.376	3.518

VI Concluding Remarks

In this paper, sources of the appreciation of the real exchange rate in transition economies were investigated. Besides the traditional B-S effect that work through productivity-induced market-based service inflation, the role of regulated prices, the non-tradable components of tradable goods were analysed. Most importantly, it is argued that the main source of real appreciation in transition economies is the change in supply capacities, which is reflected not only in a higher quality of goods produced domestically, but also a shift in the composition of output towards goods of higher quality that leads to an increase in the price of tradable goods. To support our intuition, a theoretical model is developed that formally shows the link between the price of tradable goods and their technological content.

Based on a variety of time series and panel cointegration techniques, it is shown that changes in labour productivity are not only strongly connected to the appreciation of the CPI-based real exchange rate but also to that of the PPI-deflated real exchange rate. This finding is very robust against different econometric techniques and thus lends strong empirical support in favour of our proposition according to which the appreciation of the real exchange rate mainly took place through the tradable price channel. However, because the estimated coefficient of labour productivity is usually lower when the PPI-based real exchange rate is used, we argue that the B-S effect and regulated prices may also determine long-term real exchange rate movements, although to a much lesser extent than assumed in the literature.

It is also noteworthy that fundamental factors that shape long-term real exchange rate movements appear to differ strongly across the three countries under study and the panel of eight countries. Whereas in Poland, the real interest differential is found, besides productivity, to determine the real exchange rate in the long run, foreign debt and openness play a role in addition to productivity in Hungary. In the Czech Republic, regulated prices seem to directly impact on the real exchange rate. Furthermore, whilst an increase in foreign debt leads to a depreciation of the real exchange rate both in the Czech Republic and Hungary, the opposite effect is found when performing the panel estimations. All in all, it is fair to say that although the impact of productivity increases on the real exchange rate appears to be strong in every country, how other variables affect the real exchange rate in the long run may be influenced by initial conditions and country-specific factors such as monetary policy, the choice of the exchange rate regime and the speed with which capital controls were abolished.

References

[1] Balassa, B. 1964. The purchasing-power parity doctrine: a reappraisal. *Journal of Political Economy* **72**(6). 584-596.

[2] Benacek, V., Prokop, L. and Visek, J.A. 2003. Determining factors of the Czech foreign trade balance: Structural issues in trade creation. *Czech National Bank Working Paper* No. **3**.

[3] Burgess, R., Fabrizio, S. and Y. Xiao. 2003. Competitiveness in the Baltics in the Run-Up to EU Accession. *IMF Country Report* No. **114**. April.

[4] Campos. N. and Coricelli, F. 2002. Growth in Transition: What we know, what we don't and what we should. *Journal of Economic Literature*. **40**(3). 793-836.

[5] Coricelli, F. and B. Jazbec. 2001. Real Exchange Rate Dynamics in Transition Economies, *CEPR Discussion Papers Series* No. **2869**. July.

[6] Coudert, V. and C. Couharde. 2002. Exchange Rate Regimes and Sustainable Parities for CEECs in the Run-up to EMU Membership. *CEPII Working Paper* No.**15**.

[7] Darvas, Zs. and Sass, M. 2002. Changes in Hungarian Foreign Trade and Trade Balance with the European Union In Pavlos Karadeloglou (ed.) *Enlarging the EU: The Trade Balance Effect.* **51**-88. Hampshire. England: Palgrave Macmillan Publisher.

[8] De Broeck, M. and T. Sløk. 2001. Interpreting Real Exchange Rate Movements in Transition Countries. *IMF Working Paper* No. **56**. May. Washington D.C.

[9] Égert, B. 2002. Investigating the Balassa-Samuelson Hypothesis in the Transition: Do We Understand What We See? A Panel Study. *Economics of Transition* **10**(2). 273-309.

[10] Égert, B. 2003. Nominal and real convergence in Estonia: The Balassa-Samuelson (dis)connection – Tradable goods, regulated prices and other culprits. Bank of Estonia *Working Paper* No **4**.

[11] Égert, B. and A. Lahrèche-Révil. 2003. Estimating the Fundamental Equilibrium Exchange Rate of Central and Eastern European Countries: The Challenge of EMU Enlargement. *CEPII Working Paper* No. **5**. and Weltwirtschaftliches Archiv (forthcoming).

[12] Égert, B., Drine, I., Lommatzsch, K. and Rault, Ch. 2002. The Balassa-Samuelson effect in Central and Eastern Europe: Myth or Reality? *William Davidson Institute Working Paper* No. **483**. July.

[13] Égert, B., Drine, I., Lommatzsch, K. and Rault, Ch. 2003. The Balassa-Samuelson effect in Central and Eastern Europe: Myth or Reality? *Journal of Comparative Economics*. **31**(3). 552-572.

[14] Fischer, Ch. 2002. Real Currency Appreciation in Accession Countries: Balassa-Samuelson and Investment Demand. Bank of Finland BOFIT Discussion Paper No. 8.

[15] Flek, V., L. Marková and J. Podpiera. 2002. Sectoral Productivity and Real Exchange Rate Appreciation: Much Ado About Nothing? *Czech National Bank Working Paper Series* No **4**.

[16] Halpern, L. and Ch. Wyplosz. 1997. Equilibrium Exchange Rates in Transition Countries. *IMF Staff Papers* **44**(4). 430-461.

[17] Im, K. S., Pesaran, M. H. and Shin, Y. 2003. Testing for unit roots in heterogeneous panels. *Journal of Econometrics*. **115**(1). 53-74.

[18] Kao, Chihwa and Chiang, Min-Hsien, 2000, On the estimation and inference of a cointegrated regression in panel data, Advances in Econometrics, 15: Nonstationary panels, panel cointegration and dynamic panels, pp. 179-222.

[19] Kim, B-Y. and I. Korhonen. 2002. Equilibrium Exchange Rates in Transition Countries: Evidence from Dynamic Heterogeneous Panel Models. *BOFIT Discussion Papers* No. **15**.

[20] Kovács, M.A. (ed.). 2002. On the Estimated Size of the Balassa-Samuelson Effect in Five Central and Eastern European Countries. *National Bank of Hungary Working Paper* No. **5**.

[21] Krajnyák, K. and J. Zettelmeyer. 1998. Competitiveness in Transition Economies: What Scope for Real Appreciation? *IMF Staff Papers* No. **45**(2). 309-62.

[22] Lommatzsch, K. and S. Tober. 2002b. What is Behind the Real Appreciation of the Accession Countries' Currencies? An investigation of the PPI-based Real Exchange Rate. presented at "Exchange rate strategies during the EU Enlargement". Budapest. 27-30 November.

[23] MacDonald, R. and C. Wójcik. 2002. Catching-Up: The Role of Demand and Supply Side Effects on the Real Exchange Rate of Accession Countries. *Focus on Transition* No. **2**. 38-57.

[24] MacKinnon, J. G. 1996. Numerical Distribution Functions for Unit Root and Cointegration Tests. *Journal of Applied Econometrics.* **11**(6). 601-618.

[25] Pedroni, P. 1999. Critical Values for Cointegration Tests in Heterogeneous Panels with Multiple Regressors. *Oxford Bulletin of Economics and Statistics.* **61**. Supplement 1. 653-670.

[26] Pesaran, M. H., Shin, Y. and Smith, R. J. 2001. Bounds testing approaches to the analysis of level relationships. *Journal of Applied Econometrics.* **16**(3). 289-326.

[27] Rahn, J. 2003. Bilateral Equilibrium Exchange Rates of the EU Accession Countries Against the Euro. *BOFIT Discussion Papers* No. **11**.

[28] Rosati, D. 1994. Outpit decline during transition. *Economics of Transition.* **2**(4). 419-441.

[29] Rosati, D. 1996. Exchange rate policies during transition from plan to market. *Economics of Transition.* **4**(1). 159-186.

[30] Samuelson, P. A. 1964. Theoretical notes on trade problems. *Review of Economics and Statistics* **46**(2). 145-154.

[31] Sgard, J. 2001. Direct foreign investments and productivity growth in Hungarian firms, 1992-1999. *CEPII Working Paper* No. **19**. December.

[32] Šmídková, K., R. Barrell and D. Holland. 2002. Estimates of Fundamental Real Exchange Rates for the Five EU Pre-Accession Countries. *Czech National Bank Working Paper Series* No. **3**.

[33] Stock, J. and Watson, M. W. 1993. A simple estimator of cointegrating vectors in higher order integrated systems. *Econometrica.* **61**(4). 783-820.

In: International Macroeconomics: Recent Developments   ISBN: 1-59454-901-X
Editor: Amalia Morales Zumaquero, pp. 335-350   © 2006 Nova Science Publishers, Inc.

Chapter 15

THE REAL EXCHANGE RATE BEHAVIOR IN TRANSITION ECONOMIES: THE CASE OF SERBIA

Zorica Mladenovic

University of Belgrade, Faculty of Economics
Kamenicka 6, 11000 Belgrade, Serbia and Montenegro

1   Introduction

The real exchange rate behavior in transition economies is one of the key issues currently discussed by applied economists and policy makers. This comes from the significant role the real exchange rate plays in establishing the degree of competitiveness of an economy and in reflecting the performance of all reshaping markets. Furthermore, the movements of the real exchange rate in transition economies may influence inflation and output as well as determine short-term portfolio inflows.

Available econometric results suggest that some of the main features of the real exchange rate in transition economies are: a downward trend (i.e., the real exchange rate appreciation), significant role of permanent component (i.e., the real exchange rate has a unit root) and sometimes peculiar (i.e., non-linear) accommodation to fundamentals.[1] However, as transition economies have followed different fiscal and monetary polices, the path of the real exchange rate dynamics may be explained by different factors.

There are a number of factors that might be associated with the long-run real exchange rate in transition economies (Montiel, 1999). First, domestic supply-side factors should be

---

[1] Halpern and Wyplosz (1997), Corriceli and Jazbec (2001), Jazbec (2001), Grafe and Wyplosz (1999), Peel and Speight (1996), Taylor and Sarno (2001), Dibooglu and Kutan (2001), Kim and Korhonen (2002), Mastnek (2002).

considered, especially variables related to the Balassa-Samuelson effect.[2] Second, demand-side factors may be important, such as fiscal policy measures that induce changes in the composition of government spending between traded goods and non-traded goods.[3] Other proposed factors include changes in the international economic environment (e.g., terms of trade), net foreign assets and trade openness.[4]

The purpose of this paper is to contribute to the discussion of the real exchange rate in transition economies, by taking into account monthly macroeconomic variables in Serbia during period of 1995 – 2002. In this interval Serbian economy went through cycles of short-lived macroeconomic stability, after the hyperinflation episode of 1992-1993, and high inflation with the actual transition process started in 2000 upon political changes which took place. The unstable economic environment caused the presence of several structural breaks in the movement of the key economic variables, which is an econometric issue important *per se*.

Two main issues will be discussed in this paper. First, the relative importance of nominal and real shocks in movements in the Serbian real exchange rate will be assessed by employing the structural VAR methodology, as suggested by Dibooglu and Kutan (2001). The structural VAR decomposition is based on the Blanchard-Quah (1989) approach implying the long-run neutrality of nominal shocks. Using the variance decomposition and the impulse response calculations we determined how the impact of monetary and productivity shocks evolve throughout time. As pointed in Dibooglu and Kutan (2001), this type of decomposition is useful in making distinction between temporary and permanent components of the real exchange rate, which may help in assessing effectiveness of monetary and exchange rate policies.

Second, the main determinants of the Serbian real exchange rate in the long run will be identified within the Johansen (1995) multivariate cointegration framework. The short-run dynamics of the real exchange rate will also be considered by using the equilibrium correction model.

The paper is structured as follows. In Section 2 we give an overview of the economic policy in Serbia. Section 3 provides information about data properties and methodology followed in order to assess relative importance of monetary and nominal shocks in the real exchange rate variability. Section 4 discusses cointegration results achieved to determine the long-run behaviour of the real exchange rate as well as to describe its short-run dynamics. Concluding remarks are given in Section 5.

---

[2] The Balassa-Samuelson theorem assumes that purchasing power parity holds for the market of traded goods, but that ratio of prices of traded and non-traded goods may evolve differently in one country than in another, as productivity in poorer countries grows faster in the traded-goods sector than in the non-traded goods sector. The potential for productivity growth in the traded goods sector of poorer countries is higher than in richer countries. It is further presumed that productivity in the non-traded sector rises more slowly, while wages remain the same in both sectors. In such case, the real exchange rate appreciates in the country with higher growth. (Recent empirical evidence on the Balassa-Samuelson effect may be found in MacDonald and Ricci, 2001, 2002).

[3] If the income elasticity of non-traded goods is larger than unity, than their relative price will move along with living standards which will cause appreciation of the real exchange rate. Further, if government expenditure is biased toward traded goods and the share of government expenditure in GDP increases over time, the real exchange rate will depreciate.

[4] For example, if trade regime is more open, it is likely to expect the real exchange rate depreciation. Trade restrictions may increase domestic prices of traded goods, which further leads to raise of composite price index and the real exchange rate appreciation.

2   Economic Policy in Serbia[5]

After Yugoslavia disintegrated in 1991, Serbian economy was characterized by severe hyperinflation that was extreme by all international standards (Petrovic, Bogetic and Vujoševic, 1999). As all classical hyperinflation, this one was also driven by monetization of the large fiscal deficit that was partly due to political factors connected to the disintegration of the country. The hyperinflation was halted in January 1994 and the economy went to the process of sharp remonetization through June 1994.

From mid 1994 to mid 1998 the fragile macroeconomic stability was obtained with high inflation of about 50% per annum. In fall 1998 the Kosovo conflict exploded. The political situation further detoriated by NATO bombing in spring of 1999. As a consequence, the economic situation worsened: the output dropped sharply and domestic currency strongly depreciated causing significant demonetization. For example, domestic currency depreciated 80% while real GDP decreased 23% in 1999. However, the official inflation rates remained relatively low, as the price control was widely practiced.

Upon democratic changes in October 2000, the Serbian economy was facing large macroeconomic imbalances. Apart from the structural imbalances, the main problem was extensive price control and repressed inflation, sharp demonetization of the economy and extreme real depreciation of the domestic currency. Hence, the first goal of the new government was to achieve price and monetary stability that would prevent deficits and their monetization.

The exchange rate was fixed in October 2000 at its parallel market value which was five times greater than the official one. This was just a recognition of the actual situation since almost all transactions had been done at the black market rate. At the same time, internal convertibility was introduced and exchange rate unified. Two months later, managed float was introduced.

As domestic currency exhibited large real depreciation at the parallel market in 1999 and through September 2000, the space was left for real appreciation in the period of initial stabilization. This did happen. Hence, the exchange rate was used as a nominal anchor since it hardly changed during the first year of stabilization. This policy helped stabilize inflation after it surged 27% and 19%, respectively in October and November 2000 upon price control was lifted and upon administrative price adjustments and tax reform in subsequent years. The annual inflation rate (end of period) was 39% in 2001 and 14% in 2002. At the same time, the annual real exchange rate appreciation (on average) was 41% in 2001 and 15% in 2002.

During the first two years of stabilization and reforms, real GDP increased by 5.5% in 2001 and by 4% in 2002. Nevertheless, the overall industry is of main interest since its share in total output is around one third. Its growth rates were 0% in 2001 and 1.9% in 2002.

On the other side, the current account deficit widened in the last years. In 2002 export remained at extremely low levels reflecting, in part, economic restructuring and limited access to networks abroad.[6]   Imports grew at a much faster rate, which can be partly explained by rising demand for imported goods after many years of isolation. Thus, the question has been open whether the appreciation of the real exchange rate became too costly in terms of a loss of competitiveness. However, there are opinions that the real exchange rate

---

[5] For detailed explanation see Arsic, Mladenovic and Petrovic (2001).
[6] IMF Staff Report (2003).

appreciation does not necessary imply exchange rate misalignment and loss of competitiveness, unless equilibrium long-run real exchange rate has a downward trend.[7] Anyhow, achieving higher rates of growth in export and industrial production while keeping inflation rates low remains the main task of political authorities in Serbia.

3   Econometric Results of Assessing Relative Importance of Nominal and Real Shocks

The empirical analysis reported in this section is based on the following two monthly macroeconomic time series: prices (p_t), and the real exchange rate (e_t). The original data were converted into logarithms prior to modeling. Prices are measured by the consumer price index. The real exchange rate is constructed as the ratio of nominal exchange rate and consumer price index corrected by German inflation. The sample covers the period: January 1995 – February 2003.[8]

A   Time Series Properties

Time series considered exhibit different trend behavior. While prices show a strong upward trend, the real exchange rate followed a path of changing trend, that was rising intensively from mid 1997 until October 2000 and falling afterwards. (See Fig. 1).

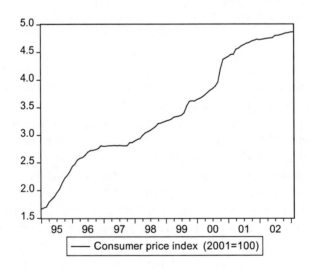

---

[7] Jazbec (2001).

[8] The sources for the data are as follows. The price index is taken from various issues of the Yugoslav and the Serbian Statistical Office publications. When official exchange rates coincides with the market ones, they are taken from the National Bank of Serbia publication; otherwise, the black market exchange rate are used. The black market exchange rate was widely known and followed.

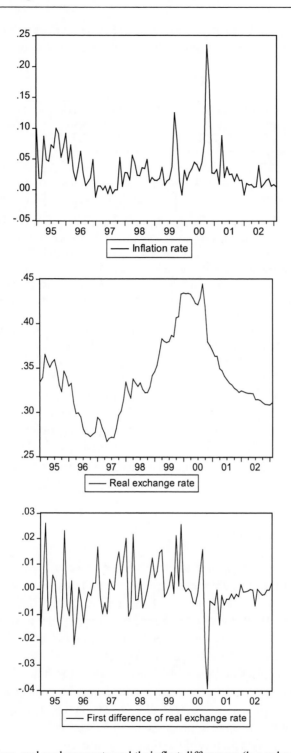

Fig. 1 Prices, real exchange rate and their first differences (log values in levels)

In order to find out whether this trend is deterministic or stochastic, we employ three unit-root tests: the augmented Dickey-Fuller test (Fuller, 1976), the Elliot-Rothenberg-Stock test (Elliot, Rothenberg and Stock, 1996) and the Kwiatkowski-Phillips-Schmidt-Shin test (Kwiatkowski, Phillips, Schmidt and Shin, 1992). The results are reported in Table 1.

Table 1. Unit-Root Tests

	Augmented Dickey-Fuller test (ADF)		Elliot-Rothenberg-Stock test (ERS)		Kwiatkowski-Phillips-Schmidt- Shin test (KPSS)	
	p_t	e_t	p_t	e_t	p_t	e_t
Unit root in the level	-2.07	-1.57	-1.67	-1.67	0.30	0.32
Unit root in the first difference	-4.91	-4.70	-5.39	-2.37	0.27	0.20

Note: The number of lags in ADF test is chosen using general-to-specific approach starting with the maximum lag equal to 11 (the integer part of $12(98/100)^{0.25}$). The number of lags for the ERS and the KPSS test is chosen using the modified SC criteria (Ng and Perron, 2001). All criteria applied suggest that the number of correction is equal to 1 for prices and 3 for real exchange rate. The discrimination between I(1) and I(0) is based on the model with constant and trend with the 5% critical value for ADF test –3.46 (MacKinnon, 1991) and –3.04 for ERS test (Elliot, Rothenberg and Stock, 1996). The discrimination between I(2) and I(1) is based on the model without trend, such that the 5% critical values are respectively –2.89 and –1.94 for ADF and ERS tests. The 5% critical values for KPSS test, that makes discrimination between I(0) and I(1) are 0.15 for model with constant and trend and 0.46 for model with constant (Kwiatkowski, Phillips, Schmidt and Shin, 1992).

The results clearly indicate that prices and the real exchange rate are integrated of order one, i.e., their first differences are stationary. Having obtained that series analyzed are integrated of order one, we can now proceed to the full cointegration analysis. However, the application of several cointegration tests show that these two series are not cointegrated, implying that their system analysis should be based on their first differences (i.e., Δp_t and Δe_t).

B Methodological Issues

The baseline model used to determine the relative importance of nominal and real shocks in the variability of the real exchange rate is the vector autoregressive model. In our analysis we consider VAR model of first differences of the real exchange rate and prices. As these variables are stationary, VAR model of finite order can always be rewritten as the system of two equations in which each variable is given as a function of current and lagged shocks of infinite order (i.e., vector moving average model). Let us denote by $\square_{pt}$ and $\square_{et}$ respectively shocks in movement of prices and the real exchange rate. From the economic point of view, shocks in prices can be considered as nominal shocks that reflect changes in money supply or exchange rate devaluation. On the other side, shocks in the real exchange rate can be interpreted as shocks due to change of productivity or technology.

Moving average representation is of the following form:

$$\begin{bmatrix} \Delta p_t \\ \Delta e_t \end{bmatrix} = \begin{bmatrix} A(L) & B(L) \\ C(L) & D(L) \end{bmatrix} \begin{bmatrix} \varepsilon_{pt} \\ \varepsilon_{et} \end{bmatrix}$$

where $A(L)$, $B(L)$, $C(L)$ and $D(L)$ are polynomials of infinite order in the lag operator L.

In order to assess the impact of shocks on the dynamics of both variables as well as their relative importance in the variability of the variables, it is necessary to make assumptions about the relationships between these shocks. The standard way to proceed is to apply Blanchard-Quah (1989) decomposition which assumes that shocks of one variable have no long-run influence on the other variable. Namely, we accept the restriction that shocks in prices, i.e., nominal shocks, have no impact on the real exchange rate in the long run. This can be represented as follows:

$$c_1 + c_2 + c_3 + \ldots = 0$$

where c_1, c_2, c_3, ...are parameters in the polynomial $C(L) = 1 + c_1 L + c_2 L^2 + c_3 L^3 + \ldots$

C   VAR Specification

The VAR of order 6 is estimated with a constant term and a few intervention dummies. The lag order is chosen using general to specific approach starting with a maximum lag of order 12. Three dummy variables (D1, D2 and D3) are included in the model in order to take care of the intervention shocks. Dummy variable D1 is associated with the sudden rise of prices in September 1999 due to the economic instability invoked by NATO bombing. It is designed in the following way: 1 for t=1999:9 and 0 otherwise. The second regime change occurred in October 2000, after significant political changes took place. They are incorporated in the model by dummy variables D2 designed in the following way: 1 for 2000:10 and 2000:11 and 0 otherwise. Model contains dummy variable D3 that is included in order to take care of several outliers in the behaviour of the real exchange rate. It is constructed in the following way: 1 for 1995:11, 1998:1, 1999:10, 1999:12, 2000:8, 2000:9, -1 for 1998:2 and 0 otherwise.

A variety of multivariate and univariate misspecification test statistics are calculated and reported in Tables 2a and 2b. The model seems well specified. There is no evidence of autocorrelation, heteroscedasticity and non-normality. The R^2 values show that a large part of the variation of the system variables is explained with the information set.

Table 2a. Misspecification Tests: Multivariate tests

Residual autocorrelation: LM_1	$\chi^2(4) = 9.19$ p-value=0.06
Residual autocorrelation: LM_6	$\chi^2(4) = 5.44$ p-value=0.24
Skewness	$\chi^2(2) = 4.27$ p-value=0.12
Kurtosis	$\chi^2(2) = 1.09$ p-value=0.58
Normality	$\chi^2(4) = 5.37$ p-value=0.27

Note: LM_m is a Lagrange multiplier test of residual autocorrelation of order m that is asymptotically distributed as $\chi^2(4)$. Normality is tested by the Jarque-Bera test that is based on the third and the fourth moments around the mean, i.e., it tests jointly for skewness and excess kurtosis of the residuals. While Jarque Bera test is asymptotically distributed as $\chi^2(4)$, the separate tests for skewness and kurtosis have $\chi^2(2)$ distribution.

Table 2b. Misspecification Tests: Univariate tests

Equation	ARCH(16)	Q(16)	Normality	R^2
Δp	14.48(0.56)	8.12(0.62)	1.57(0.46)	0.73
Δe	20.13(0.21)	15.29(0.12)	5.54(0.06)	0.66

Note: ARCH(16) is a test of autoregressive residual heteroscedasticity of order 16 distributed as $\chi^2(16)$. Q(16) is the Ljung-Box residual autocorrelation test of order 16 distributed as $\chi^2(16)$. Normality denotes the Jarque-Bera test of residual normality distributed as $\chi^2(2)$. p-values are in parentheses.

D   Variance Decomposition and the Impulse Response Analysis

The results of the variance decomposition calculation are reported in Table 3. As explained earlier, these results are derived from the Blanchard-Quah structural decomposition assuming that shocks in the price equation have no long-run effect on the real exchange rate.

Table 3. Variance Decomposition of Prices and Real Exchange rates (%)
(January 1995 – February 2003)

Month	Prices		Real exchange rate	
	Shock in Prices	Shock in real exchange rate	Shock in Prices	Shock in real exchange rate
1	29.8	70.2	20.6	79.4
3	36.3	63.7	21.6	78.4
6	36.5	63.5	21.8	78.2
9	41.3	58.7	23.4	76.6
12	41.4	58.6	23.6	76.4
18	41.6	56.4	23.8	76.2

The results indicate that nominal shocks explain about 21% of the real exchange rate variability. This portion remains relatively stable even after one year. Clearly, the real exchange rate variability is dominated by real shocks. On the other side, the variability of prices can mainly be explained by real shocks within the first 6 months. While real shocks account for 70% of variability in the first month, their influence slowly declines reaching 63% in 6 months. After that, the ratio of nominal and real shocks remains relative stable with portion of 42% to nominal shocks and 58% to real shocks.

As policy regime significantly changed in October 2000, one may argue that the whole period analyzed is not homogenous and cannot provide reliable evidence of the transition process that was triggered at the end of 2000. This is the reason we performed the same calculation on the sample that starts at September 1999. In this way we focused on the period which is not characterized by many regime policy changes. The VAR model of order 3 is now estimated with dummy variable D2. The variance decomposition results are given in Table 4.

Table 4. Variance decomposition of Prices and Real Exchange rates (%)
(September 1999 – February 2003)

Month	Prices		Real exchange rate	
	Shock in Prices	Shock in real exchange rate	Shock in Prices	Shock in real exchange rate
1	79.1	20.9	21.8	78.2
3	60.0	40.0	14.7	85.3
6	59.8	40.2	12.4	87.4
9	59.5	40.5	12.1	87.9
12	59.4	40.6	12.1	87.9

Real shocks account for a substantial fraction of variation in the real exchange rate. While nominal shocks explain only 22% of variability of the real exchange rate in the first month, its influence decrease to 12 % of variation after 6 months. Variability of prices is now dominated by variability of nominal shocks which contribute on average with 60%, while the portion of real shocks is about 40%. Hence, analysis of the shorter period did not change the conclusion about the nature of the real exchange rate variability. However, the main source of price variability differs, which can be explained by the impact of significant price liberalization.

The dynamic behaviour of the real exchange rate responses to nominal and real shocks can be observed by computing impulse response functions. The responses are obtained using the same decomposition as above. The results are depicted in Fig. 2.

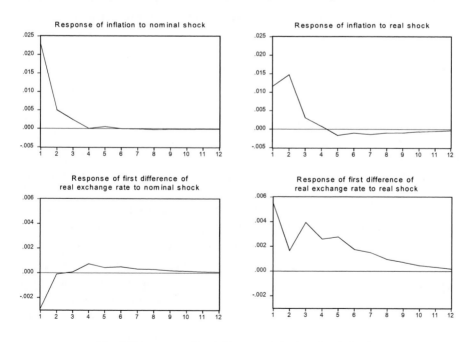

Fig. 2 Responses of variables to nominal and real shocks

The effect of the nominal shock to the real exchange rate is positive, but short-lived, implying that shock to prices leads to exchange rate depreciation. Namely, nominal shocks induce nominal depreciation of domestic currency that is higher than the price increase, which ultimately causes depreciation. A similar pattern has been detected for Poland and Hungary (Dibooglu and Kutan, 2001). On the other side, there is a substantial long-lasting positive response of the real exchange rate to real shocks.

4 Econometric Results of Determining Real Exchange Rate in the Long Run

Having obtained that most of the variability of the real exchange rate can be attributed to real shocks which have significant impact on its dynamics, our next goal is to find out whether the real exchange rate can be explained by real factors in the long run. This is the reason we are looking for the cointegration between the real exchange rate and real GDP. This variable is commonly used as a proxy for productivity and also as a proxy for the term of trades effects.[9]

Time Series Properties

Reliable monthly productivity data are not available for the Serbian economy. That can be explained by two reasons: 1. official statistical service does not cover employment of the private sector on monthly level and 2. monthly data of employment in public sector are missing for several months of 1999 and 2000. However, this variable can be approximated by monthly real GDP data. These data are also not directly available from the Statistical office. We derived them from yearly real GDP data (which cover both private and public sector) and monthly data on industrial production.[10] As the last yearly data of real GDP is available for 2002, our empirical analysis ends at December of 2002.

Construction of monthly data is based on the interpolation methodology suggested in Ginsburgh (1973) and Boot, Feibes and Lisman (1967). Data are derived from the following steps:

First approximation of monthly GDP data are obtained from yearly data by using standard interpolation technique assuming that it follows a random walk.[11] Let as denote derived values as MGDP. Applying the same approach we interpolated monthly data of industrial production and denote them MQ. Original monthly data on industrial production do exist (Q).

The linear relationship between real GDP and industrial production on a yearly level is estimated by ordinary least squares. The obtained slope estimator is denoted by b.

Final interpolated monthly real GDP data are derived as follows: MGDP+b(Q-MQ).

Constructed monthly real GDP data are approximated by monthly dynamics of industrial production. These data are not completely accurate given that agricultural production, which represents a significant part of Serbian GDP, is not included in this procedure. However, the

---

[9] Our empirical analysis is constrained by two factors. First, due to undeveloped and inconsistent time series base only real GDP variable is analyzed. Second, even this variable had to be derived as explained further.

[10] Time series data on industrial production are seasonally adjusted within X-12 ARIMA package, after obtaining that monthly industrial production can well be described by the model ARIMA(2,0,0)X(1,0,0)$_{12}$.

[11] Procedure implemented in RATS5.0 package is used (Doan, 2000).

variable derived captures variations in real GDP that can be described by variations in monthly industrial production. This variable will be denoted gdp_t in the proceeding analysis.

Monthly real GDP data represent non-stationary variables as confirmed by the application of the standard unit root tests (Table 5).[12] The logarithm values are depicted in Fig. 3.

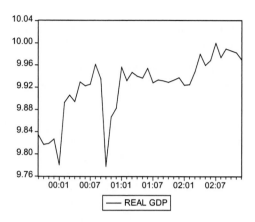

Fig. 3 Real GDP (log values)

Table 5. Unit Roots Tests (Sample: September, 1999 – December, 2002)

	Augmented Dickey-Fuller test (ADF)	Eliot-Rothenberg-Stock test (ERS)	Kwiatkowski-Phillips-Schmidt-Shin test (KPSS)
Unit root in the level	-2.36	-1.98	0.17
Unit root in the first difference	-9.89	-4.81	0.09

Note: The number of lags in ADF test is chosen using general-to-specific approach starting with the maximum lag equal to 9 (the integer part of $12(40/100)^{0.25}$). The number of lags for the ERS and the KPSS test is chosen using the modified SC criteria. The number of correction is equal to 1 for ADF test and 2 for other two unit root tests. The discrimination between I(1) and I(0) is based on the model with constant and trend with the 5% critical value for ADF test –3.53 (MacKinnon, 1991) and –3.19 for ERS test (Elliot, Rothenberg and Stock, 1996). The discrimination between I(2) and I(1) is based on the model without trend, such that the 5% critical values are respectively –2.94 and –1.95 for ADF and DF-GLS tests. The 5% critical values for KPSS test, that makes discrimination between I(0) and I(1) are 0.15 for model with constant and trend and 0.46 for model with constant (Kwiatkowski, Phillips, Schmidt and Shin, 1992).

Testing for Cointegration

The presence of cointegration between real exchange rate and real GDP is tested by the Johansen likelihood-ratio test (Johansen, 1995). The results obtained suggest that these two variables form a long-run relation for the shorter period September 1999 – December 2002.

---

[12] This application is based on the variable from which the effect of the outlier in October 2000 is eliminated. One time break can lead to inconsistent results suggesting spurious stationarity as explained in Franses and Haldrup (1994).

The baseline model is VAR of order p that can be represented in the form of the vector equilibrium correction model when variables considered are cointegrated:

$$\Delta X_t = \mu + \sum_{i=1}^{p-1} \Gamma_i \Delta X_{t-1} + \Gamma X_{t-1} + \xi_t$$

$X_t=[e,\ gdp]'_t$, μ is 2x1vector of drift, $\Gamma,\ \Gamma_1,\ \Gamma_2,...,\ \Gamma_{p-1}$ are 2x2 matrices of parameters and ξ_t is a 2x1 white noise vector, t=1999:9, …, 2002:12.

While matrices $\Gamma_1,\ \Gamma_2,...,\ \Gamma_{p-1}$ measure short-term effects, the matrix Γ captures long-run effects and can be decomposed as $\Gamma = \alpha\beta'$, where β is 2x1 cointegrating vector and α is 2x1 vector of adjustment coefficients.

The Johansen trace test statistic of the null hypothesis that there are at most r cointegrating vectors is as follows:

$$trace = -T \sum_{i=r+1}^{n} \ln(1-\lambda_i)$$

where $\lambda_{r+1},\ ...,\ \lambda_n$ are n-r smallest squared canonical correlations of X_{t-1} and ΔX_t corrected for lagged differences $\Delta X_{t-1}\tilde{\ }\Delta X_{t-p+1}$, n is the number of variables and T is the sample size. The test results are reliable only if the baseline model is well specified in terms of no residual autocorrelation and residual non-normality.[13]

The choice of the lag length was based on the values of several information criteria. One dummy variable (DEX) is included in the model in order to make distinction between two periods of different regime policies. It takes non-zero values 1 for period 1999:9 - 2000:10. The VAR model of order 1 with a constant seemed to approximately describe the variation in the data. The statistical performances are reported in Table 6.

Table 6. Misspecification Tests: Multivariate tests

Residual autocorrelation: LM_1	$\chi^2(4)$= 7.66 p-value=0.11
Residual autocorrelation: LM_4	$\chi^2(4)$ =3.88 p-value=0.42
Skewness	$\chi^2(2)$=0.43 p-value=0.81
Kurtosis	$\chi^2(2)$=1.10 p-value=0.58
Normality	$\chi^2(4)$=1.52 p-value=0.82

See note to Table 2a.

The application of the Johansen procedure is based on the assumption that the policy regime change in October 2000 influenced the long-run relation between the real exchange rate and real GDP. Hence, we restricted dummy variable DEX to enter cointegration space. The results strongly suggest that the real exchange rate cointegrates with monthly GDP (Table 7). The estimated parameter on GDP (-0.45) has correct size. The estimated parameter on dummy variable DEX (0.09) implies that mean value of the real exchange rate is 9% lower

---

[13] Cointegration results are moderately robust against excess kurtosis and ARCH effects, but not against skewness (Juselius, 2001, Rahbek, Hansen and Dennis, 2002).

in the second period. All three variables cannot be excluded from the cointegrating space, as supported by the appropriate $\chi^2(1)$ test, which confirms chosen specification.

Estimated cointegrated vector lagged one period is a statistically significant variable only in the equation for the first difference of the real exchange rate. Hence, the dynamics of the real exchange rate is adjusting to the long-run path determined by real GDP, which is a weakly exogenous variable in respect to parameters of cointegration space.

Table 7. Cointegration Test and Estimation of Cointegrating Vectors

Rank	Eigenvalue	Trace test	Cointegrating vector			Adjustment coefficients in the equation for	
			e_t	gdp_t	dex	e_t	gdp_t
R=0	0.44	26.94	1	0.43	-0.09	-0.18	-0.28
R≤1	0.11	4.58				(-4.70)	(-1.67)

Note: The standard 5% critical values for the trace test are: 19.99 for r=0 and 9.13 for r≤1 (Hansen and Juselius, 1995). However, the presence of dummy variable in cointegration space requires different critical values that are derived for partial systems, i.e., systems with exogenous variables in cointegration vectors (Harbo, Johansen, Nielsen and Rahbek, 1998). The appropriate 5% critical values for the trace test are: 25.50 for r=0 and 12.3 for r≤1 (Table 3 in Harbo, Johansen, Nielsen and Rahbek,1998). In   parentheses below the adjustment coefficients appropriate t-values are given. Δ denotes first difference.

Modeling Short-Run Dynamics

As well as examining the long-run behaviour of the real exchange rate, we wanted to explore short-term dynamics within the equilibrium correction framework. Using the long-run estimates derived in the previous step, we estimated the model, presented in Table 8:

Table 8. Equlibrium correction model

Variable	Coefficient	Standard error	t-value
$(e+0.43gdp-0.09dex)_{t-1}$	-0.178	0.038	-4.68
$\Delta gdp*(1-dex)$	-0.061	0.027	-2.26
Constant	0.058	0.013	4.46
D	0.026	0.0035	7.42

R^2=0.75, s=0.005, AR(4)=9.59(0.14), JB=5.20(0.07),
ARCH(4)=3.97(0.68), RESET=0.35(0.55)

Note: s stands for the regression standard error. The following test-statistics are reported: JB is the Jarque-Bera test statistic for normality of the residuals that under the null of normality has $\chi^2(2)$ distribution; AR(4) is the Lagrange multiplier test-statistic for fourth-order serial correlation in the residuals that under the null of no serial correlation has $\chi^2(4)$ distribution, ARCH(4) is the Lagrange multiplier statistic for testing fourth-order autocorrelated squared residuals, that under the null of no autoregressive conditional heteroskedasticity has $\chi^2(4)$ distribution. RESET is the regression specification test that tests the null of correct specification against the alternative that residuals are correlated with squared fitted values of the regressand with $\chi^2(1)$ null distribution. When appropriate, the p-value is reported in (.) after a statistic.

The presence of step dummy DEX in cointegration space required the inclusion of the corresponding impulse dummy in the equilibrium correction model. This variable, D, is designed as follows: 1 for 2000:9, -1 for 2000:10; 2000:11 and 0 otherwise. It took care of the outlier in the first difference of the real exchange rate.

The estimated equation does not display any sign of misspecification, as suggested by the reported test-statistics. The estimated adjustment coefficients (-0.18) is almost the same as one provided by the Johansen approach. This equation shows that real exchange rate dynamics is strongly adjusting to the long-run relation with real GDP, such that 18 percent of disequilibrium is corrected in each period. The short-run structure needed no modeling, which was probably due to decline of expectations in the period considered. There is also a significant negative effect from the first difference of real GDP which appeared upon policy regime change.

5   Conclusion

In this paper we have examined the behaviour of the real exchange rate in Serbia during period 1995 – 2002. We particulary focused on the recent period (1999 – 2002) of overall economic reforms.

We found that real shocks had a larger influence than nominal shocks in the variability of the real exchange rate. This result holds for both samples considered. While effects of nominal shocks on the dynamics of the real exchange rate diminish quickly, the effects of real shocks have significant long lasting effect. This indicates that the main role in determining the real exchange rate and hence in maintaining international competitiveness in Serbia should be given to the real side of economy. According to the econometric results reached, the effects of policy based on monetary and nominal exchange rate managing would only be short-lived.

The real exchange rate in Serbia in the period 1999 – 2002 is cointegrated with real GDP. This long-run relation is characterized by the presence of step dummy that makes distinction between pre and post stabilization periods. The real GDP variable has been found to be weakly exogenous to the cointegration parameters. Hence, real exchange rate is determined in the long run by real GDP. A mean shift in this linear combination suggests significant change in the real exchange rate behaviour in post stabilization period.

Based on these results, the dynamics of real exchange rate has been explained within the equilibrium correction model framework. A significant part of the dynamics in the real exchange rate is corrected each month towards equilibrium terms. There is also a significant current effect from the first difference of real GDP to the first difference of real exchange rate.

This analysis of the Serbian real exchange rate cannot be taken as full study due to incomplete information sets and short time series. However, it is, to our knowledge, the first paper to consider econometrically the real exchange rate dynamics in Serbia in recent years. It may be of help in discussing the way the exchange rate should be managed in the future Serbian transition process.

References

[1] Arsic, M., Z. Mladenovic and P. Petrovic (2001), *Macroeconomic Stabilization in the FRY, WIIW*, The Vienna Institute for International Economic Studies, Project: Global Development Network for Southeast Europe, http:/wiiw.ac.at/balkan/longterm.html.

[2] Blanchard, O. and D. Quah (1989), The Dynamic Effects of Aggregate Demand and Supply Disturbances, *American Economic Review*, **79**, 655 – 673.

[3] Boot, J.C., G.W. Feibes and J.H.C. Lisman (1967), Further Methods of Derivation of Quarterly Figures from Annual Data, *Applied Statistics*, **16**, 65 – 75.

[4] Brada, J.C. (1998), Introduction: Exchange Rates, Capital Flows, and Commercial Polices in Transition Economies, *Journal of Comparative Economics*, **26**, 613-620.

[5] Corriceli, F. and B. Jazbec (2001), Real Exchange Rate Dynamics in Transition Economies, *CEPR Discussion paper*, No. **2869**.

[6] Doan, T. (2000), *RATS, Version 5*, ESTIMA, IL.

[7] Dibooglu, S. and A. Kutan (2001), Sources of Real Exchange Rate Fluctuations in Transition Economies: The Case of Poland and Hungry, *Journal of Comparative Economics*, **29**, 257 – 275.

[8] Elliott, G., T.J. Rothenberg and J.H. Stock (1996), Efficient Tests for an Autoregressive Unit Root, *Econometrica*, **64**, 813 – 836.

[9] Franses, P.H. and N. Haldrup (1994), The Effects of Additive Outliers and Tests for Unit Root and Cointegration, *Journal of Econometrics*, **63**, 153 – 181.

[10] Fuller, W. (1976). *Introduction to Statistical Time Series*, Wiley, New York.

[11] Ginsburgh, V. (1973), A Further Note on the Derivation of Quarterly Figures Consistent with Annual Data, *Applied Statistics*, **22**, 368 – 374.

[12] Grafe, C. and C. Wyplosz (1999), A Model of the Real Exchange Rate Determination in Transition Economies, in *Balance of Payments, Exchange Rate, and Competitiveness in Transition Economies*, pp. 159-184, edited by M. Blejer and M. Skreb, Boston, Kluwer Academic.

[13] Halpern, L. and C. Wyplosz (1997), Equilibrium Exchange Rates in Transition Economies, *IMF Working Paper* **96/125** (Washington: International Monetary Fund).

[14] Harbo, I., S. Johansen, B. Nielsen and A. Rahbek (1998), Asymptotic Inference on Cointegrating Rank in Partial System, *Journal of Business and Economic Statistics*, **16**, 388 – 399.

[15] Hansen, H. and K. Juselius (1995), *CATS in RATS*, Evanston, IL: Estima, 1995.

[16] International Monetary Fund, Staff Report, Serbia and Montenegro, *First Review Under Extended Arrangement*, April 2003, (Washington: International Monetary Fund).

[17] Jazbec, B. (2001), Model of Real Exchange Rate Determination in Transition Economies, Faculty of Economics, *WP* **118**, University of Ljubljana.

[18] Juselius, K. (2001), Big Shocks, Outliers and Interventions. A Cointegration and Common Trends Analysis of Daily Bond Rates, *mimeo*, European University Institute, Florence.

[19] Kim, B.Y. and I. Korhonen (2002), Equilibrium Exchange Rates in Transition Countries: Evidence from Dynamic Heterogenous Panel Models, *BOFIT Discussion Papers* **15**/2002.

[20] Kwiatkowski, D., P.C.B. Phillips, P. Schmidt and Y. Shin (1992), Testing the Null Hypothesis of Stationarity against the Alternative of a Unit Root: How Sure are we that Economic Time Series Have a Unit Root ?, *Journal of Econometrics* **54**, 159 – 178.

[21] Masten, I. (2002), How Important Is the Shock-Absorbing Role of the Real Exchange Rate?, *Working paper*, European Univesity Institute, Florence.

[22] MacDonald, R. and L. Ricci (2001), PPP and the Balassa Samuelson Effect: The Role of the Distribution Sector, *IMF Working Paper* **01/38** (Washington: International Monetary Fund).

[23] MacDonald, R. and L. Ricci (2002), Purchasing Power Parity and New Trade Theory, *IMF Working Paper* 02/32 (Washington: International Monetary Fund).

[24] Montiel, P. (1999), Determinants of the Long-run Equilibrium Exchange Rate: An Analytical model in *Exchange Rate Misalignment: Concepts and Measurement for Developing Countries* edited by H. Lawrence and P. Montiel, World Bank, Oxford, Oxford University Press..

[25] MacKinnon, J.G. (1991) Critical Values for Cointegration Tests, in *Long-Run Economic Relationships: Readings in Cointegration,* pp. 267-276, edited by R. F. Engle and C. W.J. Granger, Oxford, Oxford University Press, 1991.

[26] Ng, S. and P. Perron (1991), Lag Length Selection and the Construction of Unit Root Test with Good Size and Power, *Econometrica*, **69**, 1519 – 1554.

[27] Peel, D.A. and E.H. Speight (1996), Non-linearities in East European Black-market Exchange Rates, *International Journal of Finance and Economics*, **2**, 39-57.

[28] Petrovic, P., Z. Bogetic and Z. Vujoševic (Mladenovic) (1999), The Yugoslav Hyperinflation of 1992-1994: Causes, Dynamics and Money Supply Process, *Journal of Comparative Economics* **27** (June 1999), 335-353.

[29] Rahbek A., E. Hansen and J. Dennis (2002), ARCH Innovation and Their Impact on Cointegration Rank Testing, *WP* **22**, Department of Theoretical Statistics and Centre for Analytical Finance, University of Copenhagen.

[30] Taylor, M.P. and L. Sarno (2001), Real Exchange Rate Dynamics in Transition Economies: A Nonlinear Analysis, *Studies in Nonlinear Dynamics and Econometrics*, October 2001, **5**, 153-177.

In: International Macroeconomics: Recent Developments   ISBN: 1-59454-901-X
Editor: Amalia Morales Zumaquero, pp. 351-370   © 2006 Nova Science Publishers, Inc.

Chapter 16

IS MODERATE INFLATION
OVER IN TRANSITION ECONOMIES?[*]

Josef C. Brada[1] and Ali M. Kutan[2]

[1]Arizona State University and The William Davidson Institute, University of Michigan
[2]Southern Illinois University, Edwardsville
and
Center for European Integration Studies (ZEI), University of Bonn

Abstract

This paper examines the moderation of inflation in three transition economies, the Czech Republic, Hungary and Poland at the end of the 1990s. We argue that the institutions for the conduct of monetary policy in these countries were relatively weak and that monetary policy was unsupported by fiscal policy and hampered by multiple objectives. Using a VAR model of inflation, we show that, under a variety of assumptions, foreign prices and the persistence of inflation were the key determinants of inflation in these countries. From this finding we conclude that the moderation of inflation in the Czech Republic, Hungary and Poland was due largely to the decline in import prices from 1997 on, and thus it is likely be a temporary phenomenon.

I   Introduction

A number of transition economies, the Czech Republic, Hungary and Poland among them, have seemingly stabilized their economies, built up the institutions required for the functioning of a modern market economy, privatized the greater part of their productive assets, restructured their industries and integrated themselves into the global economy. Perhaps most remarkably, after being stuck at double-digit levels of inflation of a "moderate"

---

[*] This research began while Kutan was a visiting scholar at the Federal Reserve Bank of St. Louis, which also provided suport during the writing of this paper We are grateful to the National Council for Eurasian and East European Research for support of the research underlying this paper

level (see, *e.g.,* Medgyessy, 1998; Dornbusch and Fischer, 1993, Ball, 1994: Burton and Fischer, 1998), at the end of 1998 or the beginning of 1999 the inflation rates of these countries, as measured by the consumer price index (CPI), fell to single digit levels, as shown in Figure 1. Indeed, on a month-on-month basis, these countries were experiencing no inflation or even deflation at the end of 1998 and the beginning of 1999.

Some observers have interpreted this outcome, which few would have predicted at the beginning of 1998, as a lesson on how to end persistent moderate inflation in other transition economies. Moreover, this seeming success in disinflating has raised expectations that these countries can easily achieve the kind of price stability that will enable them to peg to the Euro soon after their accession to European Union membership and thereafter to become part of the Euro zone. Before we accept the policy choices made by these three countries as a guide for ending moderate inflation in other transition economies, it behooves us to examine more closely whether, indeed, the results now before us can be the direct outcome of the policies followed or whether a more cautious interpretation of these results is warranted. This reexamination is all the more important as Figure 1 indicates that inflation in thee countries has begun to rebound after 1999 as oil prices have risen.

During the early stages of transition, the Czech Republic, Hungary and Poland implemented stabilization programs based on nominal anchors, primarily the exchange rate but also at times the wage rate, and they relied largely on direct controls and quantitative restrictions to implement monetary policy. Subsequently, as stabilization took hold and as their financial institutions and markets matured, all of them abandoned the pegging of their nominal exchange rates and adopted indirect methods of monetary control and, ultimately, inflation targeting.[1] In this paper, we examine whether a disinflation that reduced inflation to single digit levels, even to *low* single digit levels, could have been the outcome of the monetary policies and the institutional environment of these countries. We consider the instruments of monetary policy and argue that the process of transition and the building up of market economy institutions probably had not progressed sufficiently in the course of the 1990s to allow indirect instruments of monetary policy to bring inflation to the levels of 1998 and 1999 and to keep it at those levels or to continue such a disinflation in a less benign international environment. We are also not sanguine about the ability of monetary instruments to root out moderate inflation because, as we argue below, monetary policy is overburdened by having to pursue multiple objectives and because it is inadequately supported by fiscal policy.

---

[1] For the Czech Republic, see Begg, 1998; for Hungary, see Szapary and Jakab, 1998 and, for Poland, Wellisz, 1997. Gottschalk and Moore (2001) and Orlowski (2001) study the viability of inflation targeting as a monetary policy in these countries.

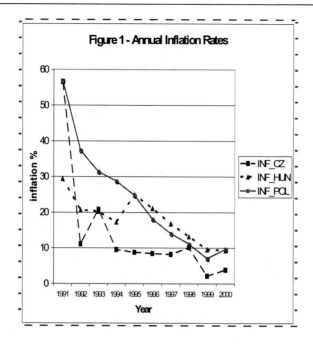

We also examine whether approaches such as inflation targeting can be used effectively by transition economies. Much of our argument rests on an analysis of the root causes of inflation in these economies. This analysis concludes that the principal causes of inflation are either exogenous or beyond the direct control of the monetary authorities. Therefore, we should be cautious in accepting recent inflation results as a signal that moderate inflation in these transition economies has been conquered by past monetary policies.

Table 1: Causality Test Results: F-Statistics – The Czech Republic

Stationary Assumption	Dependent Variable	Independent Variables			
		Money	Wages	Import Prices	Own Lags
DS	Inflation rate	**2.82** (0.05)	1.37 (0.26)	**11.64** (0.00)	**2.10** (0.10)
TS	Price level (CPI)	1.87 (0.15)	**2.36** (0.08)	**8.92** (0.00)	**8.36** (0.00)

Notes:
1. DS denotes the difference-stationary assumption while TS denotes the trend-stationary assumption. The optimal lag length in estimated VARs is chosen based on the minimizing the Akaike's information criterion and it is 3 and 4 for the TS and DS specifications, respectively.
2. All VAR estimations included three (0,1) dummy shift variables to capture the May 1997 currency crisis, the administrative price hikes for fuel and electricity, and VAT and excise taxes. The results (not reported) showed that all the dummy variables were significant at the 10 percent significance level or better.
3. Since no monthly data are available for import prices, following other studies (e.g., Laursen, 1998), this series was constructed using the exchange rate adjusted foreign wholesale price index. Specifically, the German wholesale price index adjusted for changes in the koruna/DM rate was used as a proxy for import prices in all the estimations here and that follow. The koruna/DM exchange rate is obtained using the $/koruna and DM/koruna rates assuming arbitrage.
4. The values in parentheses are the p-values for the statistical significance of the variables. Coefficients significant at the 10% level or better are in bold face.

II   The Framework for Monetary Policy

A   The Institutional Basis for Monetary Policy

While we accept the notion that the long-run effect of monetary policy is to be found in the movements of prices and not of real output, there are important short-term links between the real and monetary spheres in transition economies. On the one hand, the rate of inflation does influence the decisions of firms and consumers about the level of saving and investment as well as about the specific form that these will take. At the same time, the effectiveness of monetary policy depends to a large extent on the behavior of the real sector. The effectiveness of indirect methods of monetary control now employed in the three countries under consideration also depends on the effectiveness of monetary institutions, including capital markets and the banking system.

Although there has been some tightening of the budget constraint for firms in all three countries, it is not at all evident that this emerging financial discipline has been sufficient to drive loss-making firms into bankruptcy rather than leaving them in a limbo of growing indebtedness and payments arrears. Firms continue to run losses that are sometimes covered by government subsidies, sometimes by loans from banks and sometimes by other enterprises.[2] In such circumstances, firms may continue to lack the necessary incentives to restructure and thus to respond appropriately to changes in interest rates. Indeed, they may behave perversely, engaging in increased borrowing and in more risky investments, including leveraged takeovers of rivals, as the interest rate increases. Privatization has also reduced the effectiveness of monetary policy by placing many firms in the hands of foreign MNCs, thus enabling them to evade home-country monetary policies through their access to parent-company funds (Hawkins and Macaluso, 1977; Estrin *et al.*, 2000). There is also evidence that the real sector, meaning non-financial firms, is to a large extent self-financed, as the net flow of funds has been largely from the non-financial sector to banks rather than the other way (Dittus, 1994). Moreover, there is compelling evidence that it is the less efficient and unprofitable firms that receive a disproportionate share of the loans that are made to businesses (see, *e.g.*, Bonin and Schaffer, 1994; Coricelli, 1998, Ch. 2).

The distortions evident in the real sector also have their counterparts in the monetary sector. Commercial banks in the three countries face a number of problems. Relative to their bad loans, they appear to be under-capitalized. In Hungary and the Czech Republic, they have had to have some of their bad loans written off, while in Poland they have been encouraged to attempt to work out problem loans.[3] Neither approach has entirely resolved the problems of commercial banks, and much new lending in all three countries continues to go to firms that are likely to become problem borrowers in the future. In part, this is due to the fact that the banks are captives of enterprises to whom they have lent in the past and whose outstanding

---

[2] While explicit subsidies have been reduced, there are implicit subsidies in the form of tax-payment arrears, guarantees of loans using government-owned stock, etc., Brixi (2000), Drabek and Schneider (2000). The lack of effective bankruptcy procedures and so-called creditor passivity continue to play an important part in all three economies.

[3] For bank reforms and behavior, see Mochrie et al. (1998), van Vijnbergen (1995) and the special issue of the *Journal of Comparative Economics* (1996) dealing with commercial banking in transition economies. It is noteworthy that in 1998 Hungary had to undertake a major rescue of its two largest commercial banks while some of the largest commercial banks in the Czech Republic, although recently privatized, were arguably in worse condition at the end of the 1990s than they were at the beginning of the transition.

loans they continue to roll over through new financing rather than writing them off. In part, it is due to the fact that the commercial banks simply lack the personnel needed to make better lending decisions. Finally, the pattern of privatization in the transition economies also plays a role in the lending policies of commercial banks. Especially in the Czech Republic, the banks, although "privatized", have had the state as their largest shareholder, and thus the state's preferences regarding lending decisions may have played a decisive role. Czech commercial banks not only lend to firms, but in many cases they are also the largest share holders of these firms, creating further incentives to continue lending to problem firms.

The existence of large problem loans has led monetary authorities to maintain high spreads between lending and borrowing rates so as to boost banks' profits and thus their ability to build up their reserves. However, in addition to discouraging savers from placing funds with the banking system and firms from borrowing from it, both of which reduce the effectiveness of monetary policy, the creation of these artificial profits in the banking sector has had three other negative consequences for the effectiveness of monetary policy. One is the emergence of small under-capitalized banks that lack the skills and perhaps even the desire to make prudent loans; many of these banks have gone under or have had to be absorbed by larger banks. However, their presence in the financial system has undermined the efficiency with which credit is allocated to non-financial firms and impeded the functioning of the inter-bank credit market. A second consequence has been the entry of foreign banks, which have been alleged to engage in "cherry picking" or selecting only the most credit worthy of the local firms for clients and leaving the less attractive borrowers for the local banks. The third consequence has been that local firms have tended to borrow abroad, thus bypassing local banks and, therefore, also, domestic monetary policy.

Exacerbating the manifest weaknesses of the credit markets is the fact that stock markets in the three countries do not provide a viable substitute. They are thin and subject to extreme swings in prices, often as the result of inflows and outflows of foreign capital. Moreover, these stock markets have not been effective in raising funds through IPOs.[4] In part this is due to the rather disappointing returns that these stock markets have generated.

The foregoing discussion suggests that, to the extent that monetary policy needs to influence the behavior of banks and non-bank actors in the economy to be effective, there is reason to doubt that there has been enough progress to date to ensure that such influence will be sufficiently predictable and strong to guarantee that indirect tools of monetary policy can effectively master inflation. Moreover, the fact that monetary policy is to some extent dictated by the need to encourage the restructuring of firms, to recapitalize the banking system and to enable the government to finance its deficits suggests that the monetary authorities in these countries are likely to face severe conflicts in the formulation of monetary policy.

B   Coordination of Fiscal and Monetary Policy

A dispassionate view of economic policy in the three countries suggests that monetary policy has had to bear the brunt of the stabilization effort while governments have been relatively unwilling to make unpopular decisions to reduce fiscal deficits. In the case of Poland, Wellisz (1997) notes that, during the 1991-93 period, "[i]t is clear…that the monetization of the fiscal deficit acted as the 'motor of inflation'" (p. 165) while subsequently the government borrowed from commercial banks, driving up interest rates so that "fiscal policy…. is at the root of the credit tightness decried by borrowers" (p. 169). Of course, this same credit crunch constrains the monetary policies of the National Bank of Poland (NBP). While the government's deficit is not especially high, it is expanding as a share of GDP and thus can hardly be viewed as contributing to the fight against inflation (Kemme and Rapacki, 2000).

Much the same can be said about the contribution of fiscal policy to stabilization in Hungary, where the general government deficit reached 8.4% of GDP in 1994 (Haggard *et al.*, 1998). It was only an impending economic crisis that led to the Bokros package of reforms that, according to Kornai (1997), "…brought to an end the habitual conduct of decades – the policy of 'muddling through'" (p.125). Nevertheless, despite Kornai's optimistic assessment, the Hungarian deficit has grown again, thus leaving the battle against inflation largely to monetary policy.

In the Czech Republic, officially reported fiscal deficits have been small but increasing. During the period leading up to the speculative attack on the koruna in May 1997, the government proved unable to act to tighten fiscal policy, and it was only in the aftermath of the attack on the koruna that measures were taken to reduce the deficit (Brada and Kutan, 1999). Despite this harsh lesson, the coalition government that took over in the wake of the crisis has enacted much more expansionary budgets (Drabek and Schneider, 2000) while trying to limit the autonomy of the central bank.

In sum, while monetary policy, at least as measured by real interest rates, has been tight in all three countries, the same cannot be said for the trend in fiscal policy. Although such a policy mix may provide central bankers in the region an opportunity to create some credibility for their institutions, it also reflects a propensity on the part of politicians to evade difficult choices and to rely on monetary policy to make up for their unwillingness to restrict government spending or to increase taxes.

C   Exchange Rate Policy

The conduct of monetary policy has also been complicated by exchange rate policy and by the opening up of these countries' rather fragile financial systems to international capital flows. High interest rates and either fixed exchange rates or pre-announced crawling pegs have led to significant inflows of short-term capital. In order to avoid inflationary pressures from the inflows of foreign capital, central banks have engaged in sometimes massive sterilization.[5] Not only has this sterilization been costly for the central banks, but it also has not been entirely successful, so that targets for monetary growth have often been exceeded, even though interest rates have remained high in order to prevent sudden outflows of foreign capital. Of course, such high interest rates tend to increase costs of production, thus reducing exports and making these countries' currencies more vulnerable to speculative attack.

In sum, monetary policy in the three countries considered in this paper as yet rests on relatively weak financial markets and institutions, and it operates in an environment where the

---

[4] For example, the Czech Republic, with the highest stock market capitalization to GDP ratio in the region, has not had a single IPO.

[5] For the Czech case, see Begg (1998), for Hungary, Szapary and Jakab (1998), and Wellisz (1997) for the Polish case.

agents it seeks to influence may react to monetary policy in undesirable ways or not at all. Moreover, monetary policy is unsupported by fiscal policy and has to promote a multitude of often-conflicting objectives. IN light of these considerations it is worthwhile to ask how much of the good inflation performance of these economies at the end of the 1990s was the fortuitous result of deflation in Western Europe and of falling oil prices and how much reflected the effectiveness of domestic policies.

Table 2: Causality Test Results: F-Statistics – Hungary

Stationary Assumption	Dependent Variable	Independent Variables			
		Money	**Wages**	**Import Prices**	**Own Lags**
DS	Inflation rate	0.79 (0.58)	1.62 (0.16)	**2.92** (0.01)	**2.33** (0.04)
TS	Price level (CPI)	0.55 (0.76)	1.50 (0.19)	**2.78** (0.02)	**25.28** (0.00)

Notes
1.   See Table1.
2.   Lag length for both specifications was six based on the Akaike's criterion.
The sample period for Hungary starts in December 1990 because there were no monthly data available prior to this date. The National Bank of Hungary has also stopped publishing figures for M2 at the end of 1997. The figures for 1998 were compiled using the individual components of M2 published by the Bank.

III   Causes of Inflation and Policies for Disinflation

A   Causes of Inflation

In order to understand the role that monetary policy can play in reducing the rate of inflation, it is worthwhile to seek out the root causes of inflation in transition economies. As the discussion below shows, there are some causes that are specific to the transition economies and that do not appear to be easily combated by means of indirect monetary tools. Most important, it does not appear that the growth of the money stock is the main source of inflationary pressures in the short run.

1.   *Undervaluation of the Exchange Rate.*
     Some observers, such as Desai (1998) and Richards and Tersmann (1996), argue that inflation in transition economies is largely the result of the initial over-depreciation of their currencies. This inflation is not the outcome of the usual wage-price spiral induced by devaluation, but, rather, it is the result of the workings of the law of one price, or commodity arbitrage, which creates domestic inflation so as to reestablish purchasing power parity. Wellisz (1997) describes the process in the case of the Polish crawling peg thus: "As long as the rate of slide is set so as to result in the continuing real overvaluation (*sic!* – although the subsequent sentence indicates that this should be *undervaluation*) of the zloty, international prices exercise an upward pull on domestic prices" (p. 168).
2.   *Large Relative Price Changes.*

A characteristic of transition economies is that their relative prices were badly distorted. Given the downward stickiness of prices, the bulk of price readjustment in the course of transition thus occurs as some prices increase by large amounts and others either remain constant or increase by relatively small amounts. These large price changes, usually price increases due to the downward inflexibility of prices, have a disproportionate effect on the price index.

Pujol and Griffiths (1998) find that sectoral price changes in Poland during 1989-1995 were, indeed, quite skewed, suggesting that, in this period, some sectors were experiencing relatively large price changes while the price changes of other sectors were closely bunched. Moreover, the standard deviation of sectoral price changes around the mean was quite large, and this high standard deviation did not decline much over their sample period. Coorey *et al.* (1998) also find that the variance of relative prices does have a significant impact on the rate of inflation in 21 transition economies.

3. *The Freeling of Controlled Prices.*

A variety of prices, mostly having to do with government and municipal services, utilities and rents, and energy were not fully freed during the initial price liberalizations. Instead, governments either froze these prices or adopted a program of phased liberalization. In some cases, controlled prices were to be increased in an *ad hoc* manner until they reached equilibrium, and then decontrolled. In other cases, increases were based on a formula whereby prices would increase by a factor equal to the previous years' inflation plus some pre-specified percentage, so that they would outpace inflation, but only by a limited amount, and thus move toward equilibrium at a controlled pace. Often, rents and municipal services were priced on a cost-plus basis (see Czech National Bank, 1998, Table 3b).

Such a price setting pattern leads to the persistence of inflation because a part of the consumer price index (CPI) market basket consists of goods whose prices by definition must grow at rates that exceed the past inflation rate. Consequently, changes in the prices of regulated goods are both inimical to reductions in the rate of inflation and exogenous as far as monetary policy and its impact on inflation are concerned. The existence of these goods makes it extremely difficult to reduce inflation quickly because the burden of slowing price growth below the rates of past inflation falls on those goods in the consumer price index whose prices are not set in this way. Moreover, as prices of controlled goods are freed up, large one-time increases move the CPI upward in a way that disguises the broader tendencies in prices.

4. *Wage-Pull Inflation:*

Nominal wages in the three countries have grown more rapidly than has the CPI, so that real wages have grown steadily since the early transition. Productivity gains have been alleged to be lower than the gains in real wages. Some observers (Begg, 1998; Drabek, 1999) argue that real wage growth is the result of poor corporate governance, which leaves managers with few incentives to resist workers' demands for wage increases. Excessive backward-looking indexing of wages is often institutionalized. In the Czech Republic, tripartite negotiations between the government, labor unions and representatives have set real wage floors. In Hungary, in similar negotiations, the unions have regularly and successfully rejected government inflation forecasts in favor of projections based on past inflation. Moreover, in some countries, the Czech Republic in particular, it is the government sector that has set the pace for large wage increases.

B   What Kind of Monetary Policy for Disinflation?

Whatever institutional and environmental obstacles the monetary authorities face in their efforts to reduce inflation to single-digit levels, they also have to decide what kind of monetary policy to implement. In the early transition period, monetary policy was implemented within the context of a heterodox stabilization program utilizing multiple nominal anchors. However, the purported use of nominal anchors, especially of the nominal exchange rate, was discarded fairly early in Poland, later in Hungry and only on 1997 in the Czech Republic.[6] The abandonment of the nominal exchange anchor left central banks with the need to determine some other target for monetary policy. The money stock was regarded as an unsatisfactory target because velocity was perceived as being too variable. Interest rates, too, were problematic, in part because of the tenuous links between interest rates and the behavior of economic agents and the constraints on interest rates, both of which we have discussed above.

Consequently, an approach that was adopted by the Czech National Bank (CNB) at the end of 1997, sometime later by the Polish monetary authorities and most recently by Hungary, is inflation targeting. The concept of net inflation, which excludes from the computation of the rate of inflation the increases in the prices of price-regulated and of seasonally volatile goods, is sometimes used as a target. The Czech National Bank set two targets, a "control" target of 5.5-6.5% net inflation at the end of 1998 and a three–year target of 3.5-5.5% net inflation by the end of 2000 (Czech National Bank, 1998) .

In Poland, the Monetary Policy Council set a target of 8-8.5% growth of the CPI in 1999 and 4% for 2003. Both central banks have stressed the advantages of inflation targeting over more traditional approaches to monetary policy. One such advantage is the greater transparency of inflation targeting relative to policies that target either monetary aggregates or the exchange rate. In their adoption of inflation targeting, the CNB and the NBP and more recently the National Bank of Hungary are joining a number of central banks in developed market economies such as Canada, the United Kingdom, Germany and New Zealand all of which use inflation targeting (Mishkin and Posen, 1997).

The essence of monetary policy in countries following inflation targeting is to set inflation targets and then to pursue them without regard to output or employment objectives targets (McDonough, 1997). This requires that the central bank must have considerable independence in conducting its monetary policy, including the absence of what Masson et al. (1997) call fiscal dominance, the reliance of the state on either central or commercial bank financing. The central bank must also forego any nominal targets other than the price level. Moreover, the central bank must be able to calibrate the functional relationship between its policy instruments and future inflation.

In order to evaluate the feasibility of using inflation targeting, or even of more traditional and backward-looking approaches to monetary policy, in these transition economies, we estimate a vector autoregressive (VAR) model of the price level for each country. This model shows which causal factors are the most important sources of continuing inflation these countries and thus the feasibility of reducing inflation by means of monetary policy.

---

[6] Indeed, although the use of the exchange rate as a nominal anchor was seen as a key element of credibility for the transition economies' stabilization programs, in practice the exchange rate never served that role. For the Czech case, see Janackova (1996). Wellisz (1997) aptly sums up the Polish experience.

IV Methodological Issues

A key issue in economic modeling is whether the time series under investigation are nonstationary or stationary around a deterministic trend. Recent work using the VAR specification imposes the assumption that the series under consideration are difference-stationary (DS) (e.g., Feldstein and Stock (1994)), that is, that the original series are nonstationary. Several studies, however, question this assumption due to the low power of stationarity tests (Dejong, *et al.* (1992), Dejong (1992), Dejong and Whiteman (1991 a, b), and Rudebusch (1993)). These studies suggest that it is difficult to distinguish between DS as the null and trend-stationary (TS) as the alternative hypothesis. In a more recent paper, Canova (1998) studies the business cycle properties of a small set of real macroeconomic time series for period 1955-1986. He finds that using different detrending techniques, including a linear time trend and first-order differences, produces different – both quantitatively and qualitatively – "stylized facts" of business cycles.

This distinction is important in understanding whether shocks to inflation have permanent or transitory effects. For example, if variables are nonstationary, and consequently best represented by the DS model, then shocks to explanatory variables produce permanent shifts in inflation. This is because such shocks affect the stochastic trend component of the price level and thus cause a permanent change in the inflation rate by affecting it for all future horizons. On the other hand, if a TS model best represents the time series, then fluctuations around a trend level of these series are stationary or mean reverting. In such a model, shocks to explanatory variables have only a transitory impact on inflation as the price level returns to its trend level and the long-term inflation rate remains unchanged.

Note that under either specification there may be some persistence in the inflation rate. For a DS model, this persistence would be permanent whereas it would be only transitory under a TS model. Dornbusch and Fischer (1993) provide some indirect evidence on the appropriate specification from 12 moderate-inflation countries, including Hungary. They find that inflation persisted at moderate levels for more than a decade, thus providing support for the appropriateness of a DS specification for countries experiencing moderate inflation. Nevertheless, given the uncertainty about the existence of a unit root in economic time series and the sensitivity of the results to the different specifications used (Canova (1998); Hafer and Kutan (1997, 2001)), we model the relationship between inflation and its potential determinants using both the TS and the DS specification. To do so, we estimate two VAR systems. One system uses the log-levels of the variables along with a deterministic time trend. The other uses the log-difference of the series and excludes the trend term. The first system represents the TS specification, and the second one represents the DS specification.

V Data and Causality Tests Results

A   Data

A data set consisting of monthly observations for M2, the broad nominal money supply, the consumer price index (CPI), nominal average wages, and import prices is used in the analysis. Because no monthly data are available for import prices, following previous studies, (Laursen (1998)), this series was constructed using the exchange-rate-adjusted foreign wholesale price index. Specifically, the German wholesale price index, adjusted for changes in the domestic currency (forint, koruna, zloty)/DM rate, was used as a proxy for import prices in all the estimations. The domestic currency/DM exchange rate is obtained using the $/domestic currency and DM/domestic currency rates assuming arbitrage. The sample period runs from 1990 to the end of 1998 for Hungary and Poland, and 1993 to the end of 1998 for the Czech Republic. The sample period ends in 1998 because we wanted to use parameters in the VAR model and decomposition exercises that reflected the period leading up to and including the fall in import prices but not the period covering the subsequent increase in import prices.

All data are taken from the Harver data set, which is based on OECD data, of the Federal Reserve Bank of St. Louis, except wages, which were compiled from various issues of *PlanEcon Reports*. The data were seasonally adjusted using the multiplicative (ratio-to-moving average) seasonal adjustment technique. All estimations were carried out using the E-Views 3.1 software package.

B   Causality Test Results

Given the ongoing methodological debate discussed in the preceding section, two VAR systems were estimated. One system used all variables in log-levels and included a time trend. This system represents the trend-stationary (TS) specification. Under this specification, the dependent variable is the price level (CPI). This and other series are assumed stationary around a trend, so the shocks to the instruments of monetary policy have only transitory impact on the price level and thus on inflation. The other system uses first-differences of the data but excludes the time trend. This system represents the difference-stationary (DS) specification. Under this specification, the data series possess stochastic trends in the sense that the shocks to the system are not mean reverting over time. Series need to be first-differenced to make them stationary, so that the statistical inferences made under OLS would be valid. Each specification, TS or DS, includes a constant term.

It is important to note that the standard causality tests based on the level, *i.e.,* TS, specification are valid only if the series are trend-stationary, or if they are difference stationary and cointegrated. In other words, if the series are nonstationary but they are not cointegrated, then standard F-statistics are not valid for the level specification because they do not have the correct distribution (Sims, Stock and Watson (1990)). Because the VAR results are sensitive to the lag length, we use Akaike's information criterion to select the optimal number of lags in the estimated VARs and the number of lags used for each model are reported in the corresponding Tables 1-3 for each country. All VAR specifications also include two (0,1) dummy shift variables to capture administrative price increases for fuel and electricity as well as the introduction of, or rate changes in, VAT and excise taxes for all three countries. In addition, a dummy variable is used to account for the May 1997 currency crisis in the Czech Republic. Anticipating the discussion of our results, note that all the dummy variables were significant at the 10 percent level or better. By accounting for the impact of administrative price changes at the outset and thus netting them out of observed inflation, we are more likely to capture the impact of monetary policy instruments on inflation. In this sense, our dependent variable corresponds to the so-called "core-inflation" used in earlier studies of inflation in transition economies (Laursen, 1998).

Tables 1 through 3 report the causality test results for the Czech Republic, Hungary, and Poland, respectively.   Because our focus is on the relationship between the instruments of monetary policy and inflation, the tables report only results for the inflation rate. According to the results in Table 1, both import prices and own past lags are significant determinants of Czech inflation at the 10 percent level or better, regardless of the TS or DS specification employed. The outcome on the significance of money and wages depends on the stationarity assumption used, however. Only when the difference-stationary assumption is imposed on the data does money become a statistically significant cause of inflation at the 5 percent level. On the other hand, wages are statistically significant at the 10 percent level only if one assumes trend stationarity.

The causality results that are reported in Table 2 for Hungary paint somewhat a different picture. Both import prices and own lags significantly affect inflation behavior in Hungary at the 5 percent level of better regardless of the specification used. On the other hand, movements in wages and in broad money do not Granger-cause price movements for either specification.

The test results reported in Table 3 for Poland again indicate that both import prices and past inflation, but not wages, are significant determinants of inflation in Poland, a finding that holds for both specifications. The significance of money is sensitive to the stationarity assumption is used, however. Only under the DS specification do money supply movements Granger cause inflation at the 5 percent level. This means that the M2 growth rate has a permanent impact on inflation, but only if one believes that the series are best represented by the DS model.

Table 3: Causality Test Results: F-Statistics – Poland

Stationary Assumption	Dependent Variable	Independent Variables			
		Money	Wages	Import Prices	Own Lags
DS	Inflation rate	2.29 (0.04)	1.05 (0.40)	6.86 (0.00)	37.1 (0.00)
TS	Price level (CPI)	1.68 (0.13)	0.37 (0.89)	2.13 (0.06)	82.58 (0.00)

Notes:
1.   See Table1.
2.   Lag length for both specifications was six using the Akaike's criterion.

Overall, the causality tests results show that both import price changes and past inflation have significantly influenced the consumer price level and inflation over time in all these three countries. With respect to import prices, whose movements are dominated by exchange rate changes over the early part of the sample and then by the fall of import prices due to oil price decreases and West European deflation in the latter part of the sample, the results suggest that the foreign sector has been a major factor affecting inflation rate in the region. To the extent that inflationary expectations are assumed to be adaptive, the significance of own past price lags in our estimates implies that inflationary expectations have been very persistent and that t they have also played an important role in inflation behavior.

Although the statistical significance of import prices and past inflation is robust across countries and for both specifications, this is not the case for wages and the money supply. The results indicate that wage movements have played no statistically significant role in either Polish or Hungarian inflation, regardless of whether we use the TS or DS model. The significance of wages in the Czech Republic is sensitive to the specification used. Only under the TS model do wages have a statistically significant impact on inflation at the 10 percent significance level. This finding means that wage changes have only a temporary impact on inflation in the Czech Republic during our sample period. Thus, we can conclude that changes in nominal wages did not have a significant permanent impact on inflation in any of the countries in our sample.

Changes in broad money supply, M2, are significant for both the Czech Republic and Poland but only using the DS model. This is consistent with the expectation that, in the long run, inflation is, indeed, a monetary phenomenon. Assuming that the DS model better captures the true underlying data generating process for inflation and the other variables in our system, we find that the M2 growth rate had a permanent effect on inflation in both countries during the 1990-98 period. In terms of statistical significance, then, monetary policy can be seen as having an impact on the rate of inflation in these countries. When evaluating the effectiveness of monetary policy, however, the key question is not merely the significance of coefficients but, more important, whether the magnitude of the effect of changes in M2 on inflation is large relative to the effects of other significant factors.

VI Variance Decompositions

The foregoing regression results determined whether import prices, wages, broad money (M2), and past inflation are statistically significant in explaining the behavior of current level of inflation. The F- tests results reported earlier may be viewed as "within-sample" tests, because they do not provide an indication of the dynamic characteristics of variables in the system and their usefulness is limited to the sample period used. As a result, we next report results based on variance decompositions, which may be considered as out-of-sample tests (Masih and Masih, 2001).

To address whether a change in the money stock or in import prices generate a relatively large change in inflation, variance decompositions from the different VAR models are calculated, using the Cholesky decomposition procedure. Two orderings are used. One ordering is prices (CPI), wages, import prices and money (M2). As a check on the results, an alternative ordering of money, import prices, wages and prices also is used.

Tables 4 through 6 report the variance decompositions, using up to twelve-month horizon. Results are reported for up to four horizons, for each of the two possible orderings, and for the TS and DS specifications. Looking first at the results for the Czech Republic in Table 4, the variance decompositions generated by the first ordering, CPI, wages, import prices, M2, are reported in the upper part of the Table in panel A. These results indicate that shocks to M2 account for about 10.7 and 7.7 percent of the variation in inflation over a 12-month horizon under the DS and TS assumptions, respectively. The wage shocks play a larger role in inflation variation under the TS specification, 14.8 percent versus 7.8 percent for the DS specification. This is consistent with the evidence from the causality test results in Table 1. The limited impact of money stock and wage shocks on the rate of inflation in Table 3 stand in stark contrast to the strong impact from shocks to import prices. Over a time horizon of one year, a shock to the import price variable accounts for 29.9 and 23.3 percent of the variation in inflation under the DS and TS models, respectively. Finally, the own past shocks, representing persistence in inflation over time, account for 51.6 and 54.2 percent of variation in inflation at the end of 12-month horizon under the DS and TS models, respectively. Changing the ordering of the variables, as shown in the lower part of Table 4 in panel B, does not materially change the results.

Table 4: Variance Decompositions for Inflation: The Czech Republic

Panel A: Ordering- CPI, Wage, Import Price, Money
% of inflation explained by innovations in:

Horizon	Money		Wages		Import Prices		CPI	
	DS	TS	DS	TS	DS	TS	DS	TS
3	11.8	1.7	0.8	3.7	18.9	9.6	68.3	85.0
6	11.5	3.6	7.4	8.7	26.3	24.2	54.7	63.4
9	10.9	6.7	7.3	13.3	29.7	23.3	52.1	56.7
12	10.7	7.7	7.8	14.8	29.9	23.3	51.6	54.2

Panel B: Ordering – Money, Import Price, Wages, CPI
% of inflation explained by innovations in:

Horizon	Money		Wages		Import Prices		CPI	
	DS	TS	DS	TS	DS	TS	DS	TS
3	10.3	2.1	0.7	15.8	22.8	10.8	66.2	66.2
6	10.7	4.0	4.5	20.8	30.2	21.3	54.5	54.5
9	10.0	7.0	4.9	18.2	32.3	28.9	52.6	52.6
12	9.9	6.9	5.2	18.0	32.7	31.8	52.1	52.1

Comparing our decomposition results with those of the causality test results, we conclude that nominal wage and money supply changes have not had a significant role in explaining the behavior of inflation in the Czech Republic. At best, changes in wages and M2 can explain 18.0 (under the TS model) and 10.7 percent (under the DS model) of the total variation in inflation rate during the entire sample period. On the other hand, past inflation, which serves as a proxy for the persistence of inflationary expectations, and growth of import prices have been the main causes of inflation in the Czech Republic, jointly explaining about 75 percent of inflation variation during the 1993-98 period.

The decomposition results for Hungary are reported in Table 5. When the panel A ordering is used, M2 shocks account for 5.6 and 4.3 percent of the variation in inflation over the 12-month horizon, depending on whether the difference-stationary or trend-stationary assumption is used. The effect of wages is relatively weak, accounting for 9.4 and 18.5 of the variation in inflation under the DS and TS models, respectively. Over the 12-month horizon, import price shocks account for 7.4 and 51.6 percent of inflation variation depending whether the DS or TS assumption is used, while own past innovations account 77.6 and 25.6 percent of the variation in inflation under the DS and TS specifications respectively. The results are robust to re-ordering. Switching to the alternative ordering in panel B does not qualitatively change the results.

Note that the effects of changing the stationarity assumption are more marked for Hungary than for the Czech Republic. If one assumes trend-stationarity, shocks to import prices have a very small impact on inflation in panel A, about 7 percent. When one imposes difference stationarity on the data, however, the impact of shocks to import prices is increased to about 57 percent. These results are again robust to the re-ordering in panel B. This finding suggests that the impact of import price shocks on inflation can be best described as transitory. Similar results hold for past innovations in the rate of inflation. Under the TS specification, the past own shocks account for about 25 percent of total variation in inflation; but this effect jumps up to about 77 percent under the DS specification, suggesting that the impact of past inflation shocks on current inflation are permanent and much larger under the DS model than for the TS model.

Table 5: Variance Decompositions for Inflation: Hungary

Panel A: Ordering- CPI, Wage, Import Price, Money
% of inflation explained by innovations in:

Horizon	Money		Wages		Import Prices		CPI	
	DS	TS	DS	TS	DS	TS	DS	TS
3	2.3	0.3	6.2	1.4	1.7	1.4	89.8	96.9
6	3.3	10.2	8.6	5.9	4.4	19.5	83.6	64.3
9	4.6	6.1	9.0	16.3	6.5	43.2	79.8	34.4
12	5.6	4.3	9.4	18.5	7.4	51.6	77.6	25.6

Panel B: Ordering – Money, Import Price, Wages, CPI
% of inflation explained by innovations in:

Horizon	Money		Wages		Import Prices		CPI	
	DS	TS	DS	TS	DS	TS	DS	TS
3	6.4	7.8	7.8	1.3	3.6	8.8	82.1	82.1
6	7.4	10.6	9.4	6.3	5.2	30.8	78.0	52.2
9	7.7	6.9	9.6	18.8	7.3	41.2	75.3	33.1
12	9.1	6.6	10.0	21.6	7.7	45.2	73.1	26.5

Finally, Table 6 presents the variance decompositions for Poland. Using the panel A ordering, the effect of an M2 shock on inflation is about 11 and 2 percent under the DS and TS assumptions, respectively. Wage shocks have a very limited role in explaining inflation variation regardless of the specification used. Again, import prices and own price shocks have the strongest impact on inflation variation in Poland. The results for the import price shocks are also sensitive to the stationarity assumption employed, however. The effect of an import price shock falls from 35.0 percent to 22.6 percent when we impose the difference-stationary assumption. Using the alternative ordering produces qualitatively similar results.

Overall, the variance decomposition results indicate that import price shocks and own past innovations, meaning the persistence of expectations regarding the rate of inflation, have played the most important role in the dynamics of inflation in all the countries in our sample. The relative effects of the explanatory variables on inflation also are affected significantly by the stationarity assumption employed, but re-ordering of the variables in the estimated VAR systems did not change the results qualitatively.   For example, if one assumes trend stationarity, shocks to import prices have a much larger impact on inflation than do shocks under difference stationarity, and this result is quite robust with respect to the ordering of the variables. The result that import prices have a larger role under the TS specification in explaining inflation variation, in particular for Poland and Hungary, means that the import price changes have had a significant but transitory impact on inflation.

Table 6: Variance Decompositions for Inflation: Poland

Panel A: Ordering- CPI, Wage, Import Price, Money
% of inflation explained by innovations in:

Horizon	Money		Wages		Import Prices		CPI	
	DS	TS	DS	TS	DS	TS	DS	TS
3	11.5	3.2	0.3	1.0	14.6	14.7	73.7	81.0
6	11.3	2.2	2.9	0.8	20.9	27.2	64.8	69.0
9	11.3	2.2	4.3	1.0	21.7	33.7	62.7	63.1
12	11.1	1.9	5.5	1.7	22.6	35.0	60.7	61.5

Panel B: Ordering – Money, Import Price, Wages, CPI
% of inflation explained by innovations in:

Horizon	Money		Wages		Import Prices		CPI	
	DS	TS	DS	TS	DS	TS	DS	TS
3	16.4	3.0	0.5	0.5	13.0	13.1	70.0	83.5
6	16.5	2.5	3.2	0.4	18.5	25.0	61.7	72.1
9	17.4	2.4	4.3	0.6	19.3	31.5	59.1	65.5
12	17.5	2.5	5.3	1.4	20.0	32.7	57.2	63.3

VII Policy Implications

In the three countries we examine, nominal wage growth and the money supply are quantitatively unimportant contributors to the inflationary process in the short run. Because these two factors, which are relatively easy for monetary authorities to influence, have so little short-term impact on inflation, the decline in inflation in these countries at the end of the 1990s may not be a good indicator of the effectiveness of monetary policy and of the future ability of monetary authorities in these countries to reduce inflation to, or to contain it at, the levels seen in the late 1990s or required after accession to the European Union.

In the TS specification, the dominance of import prices suggests that changes in import prices may be the principal source of transitory shocks to inflation. This may explain why the Czech Republic, which maintained a nominal peg the longest and which, by virtue of the peg's design, actually experienced significant periods of appreciation *versus* the DM, had the lowest inflation rate of the three countries.[7] Our findings regarding the role of foreign prices in determining inflation also explain the sharp decline in inflation in the three countries at the

---

[7] The Czech Koruna was pegged to a basket consisting of the US$ and the DM. Due to fluctuations in the $/DM exchange rate, the koruna fluctuated significantly versus the DM.

end of the 1990s. Import prices measured on a month-on-month basis had fallen by as much as 10 percent by year end 1998. Tradables account for about 70 percent of the CPI in these three countries. Thus, the importance of foreign prices in propagating or, in this case, ameliorating inflation implied by our econometric results well explains the precipitous decline in the rate of inflation in these countries. It also serves to explain the increase in the rate of inflation seen in Figure 1 for 2001 and evident from monthly data for 2002.

The important role of the foreign sector in influencing inflation in our VAR specification might suggest that nominal appreciation or at least a fixing of the nominal exchange rate as a desirable policy for deflation in these countries. There are two problems with this approach. First, such a policy stance would hardly differentiate a forward-looking inflation targeting policy from the old one of a nominal exchange rate anchor. Second, it implies a real appreciation of the transition economies' currencies, an appreciation that seems incompatible with current account equilibrium, with promoting export-led growth and with preventing massive capital flows. Most critically, any peg on the eve of accession to European Union membership would have to be a credible on for the long run.

The longer-term implications seem to be equally problematic for monetary policy advocates. The other main determinant of current inflation is its past path, which can be interpreted to represent the inflationary expectations of the population. Masson *et al.* (1997) offer some insights on why inflationary expectations may persist. Among the causes of the persistence of inflationary expectations they cite are:

-symptoms of fiscal dominance, meaning the government's use of the central bank or of commercial banks to finance its deficit (p.8);
-poor starting conditions, especially levels of inflation in excess of 10% (p. 20);
-a failure to eradicate the fiscal roots of inflation (p.22).

These factors can be found to a greater or lesser extent in each of the three countries we have examined. Moreover, the monetary authorities can resolve none of them. Indeed, with the exception of the second factor, the responsibility for creating the appropriate conditions rests squarely with the governments of these countries. The importance of foreign prices and their decline at the end of the 1990s created a window of opportunity during which lower current inflation brought about by falling import prices also lowered inflationary expectations. Such a lowering of expectations could have set off a virtuous cycle of falling inflation due to the importance of the persistence of inflation for its future course. The post -2000 data on inflation provide little evidence that the governments of these three countries were able to seize this opportunity as inflation has started to rise again, even if moderated somewhat by the expectations effect.

Our results show that the decline in inflation to historically low levels experienced by the three countries at the end of the 1990s (Figure 1) is the result of external deflation that stems from exogenous declines in global commodity and energy prices and from a general global deflation. In 1998, this trend of global deflation was augmented by relatively favorable exchange rate movements between these three countries' currencies and those of their major trading partners. Thus, the sharp decline in inflation observed at the end of the 1990s in the three countries should be seen as an exogenously caused event rather than the outcome of monetary policy.[8] These exogenous factors have already begun to reverse themselves, especially in terms of energy prices. Thus, inflation remains a threat to these countries and the successes of the late 1990s may not be an accurate indicator of how well the monetary authorities in these countries can control inflation under new international circumstances.

References

[1]   Ball, Laurence, "Credible Disinflation with Staggered Price Setting". *American Economic Review,* Vol. 84, No. 1 (March, 1994), pp.282-289.

[2]   Begg, David, "Pegging Out: Lessons from the Czech Foreign Exchange Crisis". *Journal of Comparative Economics,* Vol. 26, No. 4, December, 1998, pp. 652-670.

[3]   Bonin, John and Schaffer, Mark, "Banks, Firms, Bad Debts and Bankruptcy in Hungary: 1991-1994". World Bank Working Paper, 1994.

[4]   Brada, Josef C. and Kutan, Ali M., "The Persistence of Moderate Inflation in the Czech Republic". *Post-Soviet Geography and Economics*, Vol. 40, No. 2, March-April 1999, pp. 121-134.

[5]   Brixi, Hana Polackova, "Contingent Government Liabilities: Fiscal Threat tot the Czech Republic". *Post-Soviet Geography and Economics*, Vol. 41., No. 1, January-February, 2000, pp. 63-76.

[6]   Burton, David and Fischer, Stanley, "Ending Moderate Inflations" . In Carlo Cottarelli and Gyorgy Szapary (eds.) *Moderate Inflation: The Experience of Transition Economies.* Washington: IMF and National Bank of Hungary, 1998.

[7]   Canova, Fabio. "Detrending and Business Cycle Facts." *Journal of Monetary Economics*, Vol. 41, 1998, pp. 475-512.

[8]   Christofferson, Peter, and Doyle, Peter, "From Inflation to Growth: Eight Years of Transition". International Monetary Fund Working Paper WP/98/100. July, 1998

[9]   Coorey, Sharmi, Mecagni, Mauro, and Offerdal, Erik, "Disinflation in Transition Economies: The Role of relative Price Adjustment". In Carlo Cottarelli and Gyorgy Szapary, eds., *Moderate Inflation: The Experience of Transition Economies.* Washington, D.C.: International Monetary Fund and National Bank of Hungary, 1998.

[10] Coricelli, Fabrizio, *Macroeconomic Policies and the Development of Markets in Transition Economies.* Budapest: C.E.U. Press, 1998.

[11] Czech National Bank, *Inflation Report,* April, 1998

[12] DeJong, David N., "Co-integration and Trend-Stationarity in Macroeconomic Time Series: Evidence from the Likelihood Function." *Journal of Econometrics,* Vol. 52, No. 3, June 1992, pp. 347-70.

[13] DeJong, David N., Nankervis, John C., Savin, N.E., and Whiteman, Charles H., "The Power Problems of Unit Root Tests in Time Series with Autoregressive Errors." *Journal of Econometrics,* Vol. 28, No. 2, July-September 1992, pp. 323-43.

[14] DeJong, David N. and Whiteman, Charles H., "Reconsidering Trends and Random Walks in Macroeconomic Time Series'." *Journal of Monetary Economics*, Vol. 28, No. 2, October 1991a, pp. 221-54.

---

[8] There is, of course, nothing wrong with taking advantage of such fortuitous exogenous shocks. As Burton and Fischer (1998) note in their survey of countries that have successfully ended moderate inflation, "... it is important to capitalize on favorable exogenous shocks...." (p. 34).

[15] DeJong, David N. and Whiteman, Charles H., "The Case for Trend-stationarity Is Stronger than We Thought." *Journal of Applied Econometrics*, Vol. 6, No. 4, October-December 1991b, pp. 413-21.

[16] Desai, Padma, "Macroeconomic Fragility and Exchange Rate Vulnerability: A Cautionary Record of Transition Economies". *Journal of Comparative Economics,* Vol. 26, No. 4, December 1998, pp. 605-616.

[17] Dittus, Peter, "Bank Reform and Behavior in Central Europe." *Journal of Comparative Economics*, Vol. 19, No.3, December, 1994, pp. 335-61.

[18] Dornbusch, Rudiger and Fischer, Stanley, "Moderate Inflation". *The World Bank Economic Review*, Vol. 7, No. 1, 1993, pp.1-44.

[19] Drabek, Zdenek, "A Comment on Inflation in the Czech Republic". *Post-Soviet Geography and Economics*, Vol. 40, No. 2, March-April, 1999, pp. 139-141.

[20] Drabek, Zdenek and Schneider, Ondrej, "Size of the Public Sector, Contingent Liabilities and Structural and Cyclical Deficits in the Czech Republic, 1993-1999." *Post-Soviet Geography and Economics*, Vol. 41, No. 5, July-August, 2000, pp. 311-340.

[21] Estrin, Saul, Xavier Richet and Josef C. Brada, (eds.), *Foreign Direct Investment in Central Eastern Europe.* Armonk and London: M. E. Sharpe, 2000.

[22] Feldstein, Martin J. and James Stock. " The Use of a Monetary Aggregate to Target Nominal GDP.," In N. Gregory Mankiw, ed., *Monetary Policy.* Chicago: University of Chicago Press for the NBER, 1994.

[23] Gottschalk, Jan and Moore, David., "Implementing Inflation Targeting Regimes: The Case of Poland." *Journal of Comparative Economics*, Vol. 29, No. 1, March, 2001, pp. 24-39.

[24] Hafer, R.W. and Kutan, Ali M., "More Evidence on the Money-Output Relationship." *Economic Inquiry,* Vol. 35, No. 1, January 1997, pp. 48-58.

[25] Hafer, R.W. and Kutan, Ali M., "De-Trending and the Money-Output Link: International Evidence." Working Paper, Center for European Integration Studies, Bonn, 2001. Forthcoming: *Southern Economic Journal.*

[26] Haggard, Stephan, Kaufman, Robert and Shugard, Matthew, *Hungarian Fiscal Policy Making in Comparative Perspective.* Collegium Budapest, Discussion Paper 151, 1998.

[27] Hawkins, Robert G. and Macaluso, Donald, "The Avoidance of Restrictive Monetary Policies in Host Countries by Multinational Firms." *Journal of Money, Credit and Banking*, Vol. 9, No.4, November 1977, pp. 562-71.

[28] International Monetary Fund, *Czech Republic: Selected Issues. IMF Staff Country Report No. 98/36.* Washington D.C.: International Monetary Fund, April 1998.

[29] Janackova, Stanislava, "Menova politika - uspechy i hledani novych cest." *Czech National Bank*, Working paper No. 40, 1995.

[30] Kemme, David, and Rapacki, Ryszard, "Fiscal Reform, Policy, and Constraints during Transition in Poland." *Post-Soviet Geography and Economics*, Vol. 41, No. 8, December, 2000, pp. 581-598.

[31] Kornai, Janos, "Adjustment without Recession: A Case Study of Hungarian Stabilization". In Salvatore Zecchini, ed., *Lessons from the Economic Transition.* Dordrecht: Kluwer, 1997.

[32] Laursen, T. (1998), "Inflation and its Determinants in the Czech Republic: Selected Issues". IMF, April 1998.

[33] Masih, Rumi and Sbul M. M. Masih. "Long and Short Term Dynamic Casual Transmission amongst International Stock Markets." *Journal of International Money and Finance*, Vol. 20, 2001, pp.563-587.

[34] Masson, Paul R., Savastano, Miguel, and Sharma, Sunil, "The Scope for Inflation Targeting in Developing Countries". IMF Working Paper WP/97/130. Washington, October, 1997.

[35] McDonough, William R., "A Framework for the Pursuit of Price Stability". *Federal Reserve Bank of New York Policy Review*, Vol. 3, No. 3, August, 1997, pp. 1-8.

[36] Medgyessy, Peter, "Opening Address". In Carlo Cottarelli and Gyorgy Szapary (eds.) *Moderate Inflation: The Experience of Transition Economies*. Washington: IMF and National Bank of Hungary, 1998.

[37] Mishkin, Frederic S., and Posen, A. S., "Inflation Targeting: Lessons from Four Countries". *Federal Reserve Bank of New York Policy Review*, Vol. 3, No. 3, August, 1997, pp. 9-110.

[38] Mochrie, Robert I., Schaffer, Mark E., and Bevan, Alan A., "Enterprise and Bank Restructuring in the Transition economies". *United Nations Economic   Commission for Europe*, Economic Survey of Europe 1998, No. 2. Geneva and New York: United Nations, 1998.

[39] Orlowski, Lucjan T., "Monetary Convergence of the EU Candidates to the Euro: A Theoretical Framework and Policy Implications." Working Paper, Center For European Integration Studies, Bonn, 2001.

[40] Pujol, Thierry, and Griffiths, Mark, "Moderate Inflation in Poland: A Real Story". In Carlo Cottarelli and Gyorgy Szapary, eds., *Moderate Inflation: The Experience of Transition Economies*. Washington, D.C.: International Monetary Fund and National Bank of Hungary, 1998.

[41] Richards, Anthony J. and Tersman, Gunnar H. R., "Growth, Nontradables, and Price Convergence in the Baltics". *Journal of Comparative Economics*, Vol. 23, No. 2, October, 1996, pp. 121-145.

[42] Rudebusch, Glenn D. "The Uncertain Unit Root in Real GNP." *American Economic Review,* March 1993, 264-72.

[43] Sims, Christopher, Stock, James H. and Watson, Mark W., "Inference in Linear Time Series Models with Some Unit Roots." *Econometrica*, January, 1990, pp. 113-44.

[44] Szapáry, György and Jakab, Zoltán M., "Exchange Rate Policy in Transition Economies: The Case of Hungary." *Journal of Comparative Economics*, Vol. 26, No. 4, December, 1998, pp. 691-717.

[45] van Wijnbergen, Sweder, "On the Role of Banks in Enterprise Restructuring: The Polish Example." *Journal of Comparative Economics*, Vol. 24, No.1, February, 1997, pp. 44-64.

[46] Wellisz, Stanislaw, "Inflation and Stabilization in Poland, 1990-95". In Mario I. Blejer and Marko ®kreb (eds.) *Macroeconomic Stabilization in Transition Economies*. Cambridge: Cambridge University Press, 1997.

In: International Macroeconomics: Recent Developments
Editor: Amalia Morales Zumaquero, pp. 371-392

ISBN: 1-59454-901-X
© 2006 Nova Science Publishers, Inc.

Chapter 17

OUTPUT CONVERGENCE: THE CASE OF CURRENT AND FORTHCOMING MEMBERS OF THE EUROPEAN UNION

Arielle Beyaert[1]

Departamento de Métodos Cuantitativos para la Economía
Universidad de Murcia - Spain

1 Introduction

The construction of the European Union is based on the idea that its existence is a guarantee for increased growth and welfare for the member countries taken as a whole. However, it is not clear that the geographical distribution of these beneficial effects is necessarily fair. In fact, there exists two opposite strands of thought, based on very different growth models and international trade theories.

According to some authors, economic integration increases regional and in general geographical disparities, because the production factors will be concentrated in the more developed regions as a result of increasing returns to scale and externalities. This is the postulate of the agglomeration theory of Krugman (1990) and of the endogenous growth models of Romer (1986 and 1990). On the other hand, under free factor mobility and international diffusion of technological knowledge, the more traditional international trade and growth models - based on comparative advantage and Solow framework (Solow, 1956 and subsequent literature) -, predict that economic integration will automatically promote economic convergence.

---

[1] This research was partly supported by grants form the Fundación Seneca, Project PL/8/FS/00 and from Fundación BBVA (Primera Convocatoria de Ayudas a la Investigacion en Ciencias Sociales,2002). I am grateful to my colleagues of the University of Murcia, participants in these projects, as well as to the participants in the II Workshop on International Economics, Málaga, November 2002, for their comments on earlier work. All the computer programmes have been written in Ox and have used the Bootstrap package of James Davidson (see http://hicks.nuff.ox.ac.uk/Users/Doornik/ for Ox http://www.cf.ac.uk/carbs/econ/davidsonje/software.html for the bootstrap package).

If economic convergence is automatic and takes place fast enough, free market forces would promptly erode regional inequalities and there would be no need for transferring funds from the richer to the poorer members of an economic union. On the contrary, if this convergence does not take place or is not sufficiently rapid, an explicit regional policy in favour of the less developed regions is fully justified, as long as its implementation effectively contributes to reduce the inequalities.

As far as the European economic union is concerned, three relatively poorer countries joined the EEC in the eighties: Greece entered in 1981, Spain and Portugal in 1986. In September of 2002, the European authorities agreed upon the enlargement of the Union with the entrance of ten new countries in 2004. Eight of these ten countries belonged to the former communist block and are the following: Estonia, Latvia, Lithuania, Hungary, Poland, Czech Republic, Slovak Republic and Slovenia. Two more countries will also join the EU: Cyprus and Malta. The common characteristic of these ten countries is that their per capita income is far below the present EU average.

With the incorporation of Greece, Spain and Portugal in the eighties, the regional inequalities within the frontiers of the European economic union became more evident. Partly in response to that, the Single Act, signed in 1987, established the principle of Economic and Social Cohesion, and explicitly declared that the European Community will make special efforts in reducing regional differences. The authorities took for granted that the market forces alone would not solve the regional inequalities and the decision was taken at a European level to help the less developed regions in their efforts[2]. A new design of the European Regional Policy resulted from it, and the first big reform in the distribution of the European Structural Funds was implemented. Four countries - the so-called "cohesion countries" - were the major recipients of these funds: Greece, Spain, Portugal and Ireland. Two more reforms took place in the nineties, aimed at improving the efficiency of these funds.

Nowadays, the entrance of the ten new members from Eastern Europe will thoroughly modify the economic ranking of the European regions and the distribution of the Structural Funds: these new members will stand in 2004 in a similar or worse position than the "cohesion countries" at the time of their own entrance in the EU more than a decade ago.

In such a context, it is useful to determine the extent to which the European Union constitutes a zone of automatic economic convergence or not. In particular, it is of interest to analyse first if belonging to the EU and being recipients of Structural Funds significantly helped the "cohesion countries" to converge towards the richer economies; second, it is interesting to examine to what extent the coming members share similar convergence characteristics and could benefit from the European Regional Policy.

For that purpose, in this chapter, econometric "convergence tests" are applied on the data of per-capita outputs of both existing and future member countries of the EU, splitting the sample in the late eighties when appropriate. From the results, some conclusions may be drawn about the possible benefits for the incoming countries of being a member of the European Union and a recipient of Cohesion Funds.

---

[2] In fact, the European regional policy gained renewed impetus each time an enlargement took place and new geographical economic inequalities appeared. Correspondingly, the amount of funds devoted to regional policy also increased.

Given the time span and the frequency of the available data for all these countries, it is important to use a testing procedure which takes full profit of all the sample information. This is the reason why we opt for multivariate tests which make use of the sample information from both the time-series and the cross-section dimensions. These multivariate tests are derived from unit root tests developed in the econometric and statistical literature (often called "panel unit-root tests").

However, some caution is required when specifying the null and the alternative hypothesis in the testing procedure. This aspect, which is often overlooked in the convergence empirical literature, is discussed in details in this chapter. On the other hand, most panel unit root tests are theoretically justified under the assumption of no contemporaneous correlation between the cross-section units. In convergence studies, this assumption is hardly defensible when the number of countries is low and when they moreover belong to the same geographical and/or economic area. In such a case, the practical implementation of the test has to account for this cross-section correlation. This is carried out in this chapter by means of bootstrap techniques which are also described and justified.

The rest of the chapter is structured as follows. Section 2 focuses on the econometric methodology. It contains a discussion on the specification of the hypotheses to be tested and on how panel-unit root tests, as well as the convergence tests derived from them can be improved with bootstrap critical values. Section 3 is devoted to the empirical results. The first part of Section 3 analyses the convergence process of the present members of the EU with a special emphasis on the possible effects of the intensification of the European regional policies from 1987 onwards. The second part centres on the convergence characteristics of some of the future members of the EU, taking into account the thorough institutional change that these countries experienced in the late eighties and early nineties, when they switched from a planned to a more liberal economy. Section 4 offers our conclusions.

2   Econometric Aspects of Testing Output Convergence

2.1   About the Null and the Alternative Hypotheses of Interest

Let Y_{nt}, $n = 1, \cdots, N$, $t = 1, \cdots, T$ be the log real GDP per capita in country i at time t. If the long-run growth path of country n is a_{nt}, it must be that $(Y_{nt} - a_{nt})$ contains only non-permanent shocks, because this implies that the deviations of Y_{nt} around a_{nt} will vanish in the long-run. The simplest case of non-persistence of shocks consists of $(Y_{nt} - a_{nt})$ being an I(0) variable. At the other extreme, if $(Y_{nt} - a_{nt})$ contains persistent shocks, which would be the case if it is an I(1) variable, a_{nt} cannot constitute a relevant steady state path for country n. It is however impossible to directly test whether $(Y_{nt} - a_{nt})$ is I(0) or not, because the steady state path a_{nt} is not observable.

Often, the objective is to test whether a group of N countries or regions converge towards the same steady state path. This analysis is sometimes called "across-convergence", to distinguish it from the "within-convergence" which refers to the convergence of a given country towards some long-run path[3]. For *absolute* (across-)convergence, all the N countries must share an <u>identical</u> long-run path: $a_{nt} = a_t \ \forall n$. In this case, $(Y_{nt} - a_t)$ must be I(0) around a zero mean, $\forall n$. For *conditional* (across-)convergence, the N countries share <u>parallel</u> steady state paths: $a_{nt} = a_t + c, \forall n$. The deviation $(Y_{nt} - a_t)$ is then I(0) around a mean that is not necessarily zero. This mean would basically reflect that worse initial conditions would prevent an economy from reaching the same *level* of GDP per capita as a better-endowed country, although he would share the same growth *rate*.

The path a_t however is not observed. So it is also impossible to directly test whether $(Y_{nt} - a_t)$ is I(0) or not. Note however that it can easily be cancelled out. There are in fact two basic ways of cancelling it out: working with country deviations around the cross-section mean and working with bilateral differentials. These two approaches are not completely equivalent, as we will see.

1) *Bilateral differentials*

Let us consider the differential $d_{nm,t} = Y_{nt} - Y_{mt}$ for countries n and m. If both countries converge to each other, they share the same (or parallel) steady state path a_t, so that $d_{nm,t}$ is also the differential of the deviations form their steady state path: $d_{nm,t} = (Y_{nt} - a_t) - (Y_{mt} - a_t)$. This differential must therefore be I(0) under convergence. An I(1) differential is symptom of divergence. Working on the differentials is related to the definitions of convergence of Bernard and Durlauf (1995); they call "convergence in multivariate output" the case in which the following condition is fulfilled:

$$\lim_{k \to \infty} E(y_{n,t+k} - y_{m,t+k} \mid I_t) = 0 \ \forall n \neq m$$

If the differentials are I(0) around zero, this condition is fulfilled; on the other hand, I(1) differentials violate it.

When the study on convergence is carried out on the differentials, a reference country is usually chosen as country m, and the differentials of all the other countries with respect to country m are analysed. One of the drawbacks of this approach stands in the need of choosing a reference country. In most cases, the richer or more developed country of the group is chosen, mainly because it is somehow perceived as the model to be reached by the other countries.

Note that global convergence among all countries takes place only if all the differentials with respect to the reference country are I(0). When only part of the countries converge to the reference one, some differentials will be I(0) while the others will be I(1). Let us call this situation "partial convergence". At the other extreme, when all countries diverge from the reference one, all differentials will be I(1).

Therefore, if we are interested in detecting whether a given group of countries constitutes a convergence group or not, the natural null hypothesis is:

$$H_0 : d_{nm,t} \sim I(0) \text{ for } \textbf{all } I$$

---

[3] See for instance Islam(2003) for a recent survey.

whereas the alternative of interest is

$$H_0 : d_{nm,t} \sim I(1) \text{ for some or all } i$$

These are the null and alternative addressed in multivariate *stationarity* tests. Tests of this type have been developed recently, for instance by Hadri (2000) and Hadri & Larson (2002) and are based on a multivariate extension of the stationarity KPSS test (Kwiatkowsky et al., 1992). They have not been used frequently so far. Moreover, the experience with these tests reported in the literature (see a.o. Chang, 2003) as well as the results of some simulations that we have run indicate that they are not very powerful in detecting diverging units in moderate-size panels, as is typical of convergence studies. More research is in fact required to improve their importance in small-sample conditions. In practice, as far as multivariate tests are concerned, what has been used most are panel *unit-root* tests. In these tests, the null hypothesis typically is:

$$H_0 : x_{n,t} \sim I(1) \text{ for all } n.$$

where $x_{n,t}$ is the series to be analysed that corresponds to the cross-section n. The alternative differs from one test to another. Two of the tests that have been extensively used are those due to Levine and Lin (1992, 1993) and to Im, Pesaran and Shin (1995, 2003). In what follows, we will refer to them as the LL and the IPS tests, respectively.

In the LL test, the null and the alternative are:

$$H_0 : x_{n,t} \sim I(1) \text{ for all } n \text{ against } H_A : x_{n,t} \sim I(0) \text{ for all } n$$

and it is tested on the basis of the t-ratio associated with an estimated value of ρ in the following equation:

$$\Delta x_{n,t} = c + \rho x_{n,t-1} + \sum_{i=1}^{P_i} \varphi_{n,i} \Delta x_{n,t-i} \quad n = 1, \cdots, N$$

When $x_{n,t}$ is the differential variable $d_{nm,t}$, this test is then adequate for testing global convergence. It is, however, criticized for imposing the same value of ρ for all cross-section units, which comes to assuming that all the series of the panel exhibit the same first-order autocorrelation (see for instance Maddala and Wu, 1999). This criticism, however, loses intensity in view of the simulation results of a bootstrapped version of this test obtained in Chang (2003) to which we will refer below.

The IPS test allows first-order heterogeneity among the series by estimating a distinct ρ coefficient for each unit. For this reason it has been preferred to LL in recent studies. The counterpart of this heterogeneity is the form of the alternative:

$$H_A : x_{n,t} \sim I(0) \text{ for some } n$$

This test is therefore not apt for testing global convergence, but is better designed for discarding global divergence or detecting partial convergence.

This discussion stresses the importance of choosing the testing procedure which specifies the null and the alternative in full agreement with the precise objectives of the analysis. The importance of a correct choice is even greater when the study is carried out on the deviations from a cross-section mean.

2) deviations from the cross-section mean

As an alternative to the use of the differentials, another possibility of cancelling out the unobservable steady state path consists of working in deviation from the cross-section mean.

Let $\bar{Y}_t = \frac{1}{N}\sum_{n=1}^{N} Y_{nt}$ be the cross-section mean of the log real GDP per capita of the N countries at time t. Note that under convergence of the N countries, $\bar{Y}_t - a_t = \frac{1}{N}\sum_{n=1}^{N}(Y_{nt} - a_t)$ is necessarily I(0). But then the deviation $(Y_{nt} - \bar{Y}_t) = (y_{nt} - a_t) - (\bar{Y}_t - a_t)$ is a sum of two I(0) variables and is therefore I(0) for all n. On the contrary, if $(Y_{nt} - \bar{Y}_t)$ is I(1), it is impossible that country n be converging with the other (N-1) economies towards the same steady state (or even towards parallel paths).

Evans and Karras (1996a) show that the process $\lambda_n(L)(Y_{nt} - \bar{Y}_t) = \delta_n + \varepsilon_{nt}$ will indeed have a unit root under divergence and will exhibit no unit root if the economies converge. So testing convergence comes to testing whether the series $(Y_{nt} - \bar{Y}_t)$ for the N countries exhibit or not a unit root. In this case too, the null and the alternative hypotheses have to be stated with caution and this aspect has been often overlooked in the literature.

To see this, let us first consider the case of only 2 countries: N=2. Their differential $d_{1,2,t} = Y_{1t} - Y_{2t}$ is I(0) if they converge. The deviation around the cross-section mean is $Y_{it} - \frac{1}{2}(Y_{1t} + Y_{2t})$. It is equal to $\frac{1}{2}(Y_{1t} - Y_{2t})$ for n=1 and $\frac{1}{2}(Y_{2t} - Y_{1t})$ for n=2. Under convergence both must be I(0) and if one of them is I(1) the other is automatically I(1) too. So the relevant null and alternative hypothesis are:

$$H_0 : (Y_{nt} - \bar{Y}_t) \text{ is I(0) } n = 1,2 \qquad H_1 : (Y_{nt} - \bar{Y}_t) \text{ is I(1), } n = 1,2$$

If N=3, the deviations from the cross-section mean are now:

$$(Y_{it} - \bar{Y}_t) = Y_{it} - \frac{1}{3}(Y_{1t} + Y_{2t} + Y_{3t}) = (1 - \frac{1}{3})Y_{nt} - \frac{1}{3}(\sum_{m=1,m\neq n}^{3} Y_{mt}) \text{ for } n = 1,2,3$$

If all three countries converge, all these deviations are I(0). On the contrary, if only one of them diverge from the other two (who might converge to each other), all the three deviations will be I(1). To see this, let us suppose that country 1 and 3 converge to each other but country 3 does not. Then:

$(Y_{1t} - Y_{3t})$ is I(0) but $(Y_{1t} - Y_{2t})$ and $(Y_{3t} - Y_{2t})$ are I(1).

Therefore , $Y_{1t} - \overline{Y}_t = \frac{2}{3} Y_{1t} - \frac{1}{3} Y_{2t} - \frac{1}{3} Y_{3t} = \frac{1}{3}(Y_{1t} - Y_{2t}) + \frac{1}{3}(Y_{1t} - Y_{3t})$ is the sum of an I(0) and an I(1) variable and as such is necessarily I(1). The same holds for the deviation $(Y_{3t} - \overline{Y}_t)$. At the same time, $Y_{2t} - \overline{Y}_t = \frac{1}{3}(Y_{2t} - Y_{1t}) + \frac{1}{3}(Y_{2t} - Y_{3t})$ is necessarily I(1) because it is the sum of two I(1) non-cointegrated variables. They are not cointegrated because the only cointegration relation that links Y_{1t}, Y_{2t} and Y_{3t} corresponds to a cointegration vector proportional to $(1,0,-1)$.

As a result, the relevant hypothesis to be tested are:

$$H_0 : (Y_{nt} - \overline{Y}_t) \text{ is I}(1) \text{, for all n} \quad H_A : (Y_{nt} - \overline{Y}_t) \text{ is I}(0) \text{ for all n}$$

This reasoning can easily be extended to any value of N, as well as to the case where the N countries are grouped in "convergence clubs". To see this, take N=4 and assume that countries 1 and 2 on the one hand, and countries 3 and 4 on the other constitute two different convergence clubs, so that countries 1 and 2 do not converge with countries 3 and 4. This implies that $(Y_{nt} - Y_{mt})$ is I(0) for n,m=1,2 and for n,m=3,4 but is I(1) for the other combinations of n and m. Consider then the deviation $(Y_{1t} - \overline{Y}_t)$. We have $Y_{1t} - \overline{Y}_t = \frac{1}{4}(Y_{1t} - Y_{2t}) + \frac{1}{4}(Y_{1t} - Y_{3t}) + \frac{1}{4}(Y_{1t} - Y_{4t})$, which is the sum of an I(0) $[\frac{1}{4}(Y_{1t} - Y_{2t})]$ and of two I(1) $[\frac{1}{4}(Y_{1t} - Y_{3t}) + \frac{1}{4}(Y_{1t} - Y_{4t})]$. Can this last sum be I(0)? The answer is no: the cointegration vector linking the variables Y_{1t}, Y_{3t} and Y_{4t} is $(0,1,-1)$ whereas the coefficient vector in this last sum is proportional to $(2,-1,-1)$.

In summary, the preceding arguments indicate the following: in a given group of countries, the divergence of any member of the group implies that the deviations from the cross-section mean of all the countries will be I(1).

This has several practical implications on how to test convergence with a panel of data in terms of the deviation from the panel mean, and on how to interpret the results.

The first implication concerns the type of test to be used. Any panel unit-root or stationarity test that permits some units to be I(0)n while others are I(1), either under the null of the alternative, is not valid to test convergence on deviations series.

Second, if the panel unit root test concludes that the deviations are I(1), the following step might consist of repeating the test on a new panel with a *new* cross-section mean, obtained after eliminating the country which exhibits most signs of divergence (these signs may be based on graphical inspection or on economic characteristics).

Third, it is often the case that univariate unit root or stationarity tests are applied on the difference between the GDP per capita of a given economic area "n" and the GDP of a larger economic area to which the first one belongs. For instance, it is the case when the difference of the per-capita income of a US region with respect the aggregate per capita US income is analyzed; it is also the case when the per capita output of a given European region or country is analyzed in difference from the average per capita output of the whole European Union. If the test concludes that this difference is I(1), the preceding discussion indicates that this should not be interpreted as an indication that this particular area "n" is responsible for the divergence; it merely indicates that *some* of the small areas fail to converge to the long-run path of the other areas.

Fourth, remember that an I(1) country *differential* between the GDP per capita of two economies does indicate that these two specific countries do not converge to each other. Therefore, if univariate unit-root or stationarity tests are used, the differential series are more informative that the deviations series.

2.2   Choosing a Testing Procedure

The convergence analysis of this work has to be carried out on a panel of countries of moderate size: the number of countries N as well as time span T are not very high (the maximum value for T is 60 and for N is 15). It is therefore important to take profit of all the relevant sample information, without sacrificing any dimension of the sample. It seems then reasonable to apply multivariate (panel data) convergence tests, rather than applying exclusively time-series univariate techniques. The analysis is carried out in terms of deviations from the cross-section mean, so that no reference country has to be chosen.

As explained in Section 2.1, when working with deviations, the units composing the panel are either all I(0) or all I(1). This precludes from using unit root tests such as the "t-bar" unit-root test of Im, Pesaran and Shin (1997,2003), the stationarity tests of Hadri(2000,2002) or the general F-type panel unit-root tests for dependent panels recently proposed by Chang (2003), since all these tests are considered under the alternative that some of the units may be I(1) while others are I(0). In other words, they do not test overall stationarity versus overall non-stationarity.

The test proposed by Evans and Karras (1996a), which is a modification of the LL test, does consider the null hypothesis that the deviations from the cross-section mean are all I(1) against the alternative that they are all I(0). We will first summarize Evans-Karras procedure and then consider its possible limitations and examine how to circumvent them.

2.2.1   The "EK" Procedure: what it Tests and How it Can Be Improved under Cross-Section Dependency

2.2.1.1   The Procedure as Proposed by Evans and Karras(1996a)

Consider the univariate process for the deviation of country n

$$\lambda_n(L)(y_{n,t} - \bar{y}_t) = \delta_n + u_{n,t} \tag{1}$$

where the lag polynomial $\lambda_n(L)$ may be of infinite order, with coefficients that may differ across economies. This polynomial can be written as $\lambda_n(L) = \pi_n(L)D(L)$ where $\pi_n(L)$ has all its roots outside the unit circle with $D(L) = 1$ if the economies converge and $D(L) = (1-L)$ if some of them diverge. Equation (1) then becomes

$$\pi_n(L)D(L)(y_{n,t} - \bar{y}_t) = \delta_n + u_{n,t} \tag{1'}$$

Approximating $\pi_n(L)$ by a q-degree polynomial, with q finite, equation (1') can be rewritten as

$$\Delta(y_{n,t} - \bar{y}_t) = \delta_n + \rho_n(y_{n,t-1} - \bar{y}_{t-1}) + \sum_{i=1}^{p} \varphi_{n,i}\Delta(y_{n,t-i} - \bar{y}_{t-i}) + u_{n,t}$$

(2)

In this equation, $\rho_n = 0$, $\varphi_{n,i} = \pi_{n,i}$, $p = q$ if $D(L) = 1 - L$, that is, if the economies diverge. However, $\rho_n = (\sum_{i=1}^{p+1} \pi_{n,i} - 1)$ and negative, $\varphi_{n,i} = -\sum_{j=i+1}^{p+1} \pi_{n,j}$, $p = q - 1$ if D(L)=1, that is, if the economies converge.

The proposed testing procedure is as follows:

[1] apply OLS to (2) to obtain an estimate $\hat{\sigma}_n$ of $\sigma_n^2 = V(u_{n,t})$ and use it to transform the data to $\hat{z}_{n,t} = (y_{n,t} - \bar{y}_t)/\hat{\sigma}_n$

[2] obtain the OLS estimate of ρ and its t-ratio $\tau(\hat{\rho})$ applying OLS to

$$\Delta\hat{z}_{n,t} = \delta_n + \rho\hat{z}_{n,t-1} + \sum_{i=1}^{p} \varphi_{n,i}\Delta\hat{z}_{n,t-i} + \hat{u}_{n,t}$$

(3)

[3] If the t-ratio of step [2] is sufficiently negative, reject $H_0 : \rho_n = 0 \ \forall n$ in favour of $H_1 : \rho_n < 0 \ \forall n$. If H_0 is rejected, the economies converge.

[4] If H_0 is rejected, test $H_0' : \delta_n = 0 \ \forall n$ against $H_1' : \delta_n \neq 0$ for some n in equation (2); for that purpose, estimate this equation for n=1,...N; compute then $\Phi(\hat{\delta}) = \frac{1}{N-1}\sum_{n=1}^{N} [\tau(\hat{\delta}_n)]^2$ and reject H_0' if $\Phi(\hat{\delta})$ is too large, in which case convergence would be conditional. Otherwise, convergence is absolute.

Note that steps [1] to [3] come to testing for the presence of a unit root on the basis of a Weighted Least Squares estimation. It estimates a single ρ coefficient for all the units of the panel. This single estimation of ρ guarantees that the alternative is $H_A : \rho_n < 0$ for **all** n and not $H_A : \rho_n < 0$ for **some** n. In other words, this procedure assumes the same first order autocorrelation for all the deviations from the cross-section mean. Obviously, if all the economies converge but they exhibit very heterogeneous dynamics, this procedure may lack power in detecting convergence. However, if the degree of heterogeneity is reasonable, this procedure is preferable to others procedures which allow ρ to vary: if a different ρ is estimated for each cross-section, the alternative cannot be $H_A : \rho_n < 0$ for **all** n. Moreover, the simulations carried out by Chang (2003), commented in more detail below, show that a single estimation of ρ used in combination with an appropriate critical value provides a reliable test result even under heterogeneity of the cross-section units.

Evans and Karras (1996a) demonstrate that, when N and T tend to ∞, $\tau(\hat{\rho})$ and $\Phi(\hat{\delta})$ are asymptotically N(0,1) and F, respectively. This result holds under the assumption that the errors in (2) are contemporaneously uncorrelated. The authors suggest improvements on these asymptotic values by obtaining critical values by simulations from normal independent distributions. When the number of economies is low or moderate and they moreover belong to the same geographical or economic area, the assumption of independence required for the asymptotic distribution and used in Evans-Karras simulations is difficult to sustain.

2.2.1.2 The Effect of Cross-Section Dependency

Maddala and Wu (1999) showed with simulations that the LL test -from which the EK procedure is derived and is an extension- as well as the IPS test have substantial size distortions in the presence of cross-section correlation. The reason is that the asymptotic distributions obtained under the assumption of no cross-section correlation are not valid. They suggest bootstrapping the tests in order to obtain better approximations of the critical values.

Chang (2003) develops on this idea and obtains results that can be exploited in order to improve the EK procedure. She considers several unit-root tests for heterogeneous and dependent panels. She presents new F-type test statistics corresponding to the estimation of a different ρ_n for each cross-section unit. More concretely, she considers estimating $\rho_n, n = 1, \cdots, N$ by Feasible Generalized Least Squares (FGLS) and by Ordinary Least Squares (OLS) from the following system of N equations:

$$\Delta x_{n,t} = \rho_n x_{n,t-1} + \sum_{i=1}^{p_n} \varphi_{n,i} \Delta x_{n,t-i} + \varepsilon_{n,t} \qquad n = 1, \cdots, N$$

where $x_{n,t}$ is a demeaned variable. She then constructs traditional F-type tests associated with these estimations aimed at testing:

$$H_0 : \rho_n = 0 , n = 1, \cdots, N \quad \text{against} \quad H_1 : \rho_n \neq 0 \text{ for at least 1 } n$$

Since we are normally interested in a left-tailed alternative ($\rho_n < 0$), she also builds modifications of this statistic to transform them in left-tailed statistics. At the same time, she considers the one-tailed t-statistics corresponding to FGLS and OLS estimation of a single ρ for all units, as specified in the following system:

$$\Delta x_{n,t} = \rho \, x_{n,t-1} + \sum_{i=1}^{p_n} \varphi_{n,i} \Delta x_{n,t-i} + \varepsilon_{n,t} \qquad n = 1, \cdots, N$$

in order to test:

$$H_0 : \rho_n = 0 , n = 1, \cdots, N \quad \text{against} \quad H_1 : \rho_n < 0 \text{ for all } n$$

She obtains the asymptotic distribution of these tests under cross-section correlation; these distributions are non-standard and depend heavily on nuisance parameters that define the cross-sectional dependency and the heterogeneous serial dependence.

She then proposes a bootstrap version of the different test statistics. The bootstrap samples are constructed from the residuals obtained with the unit root restriction $\rho_n = 0 \ \forall n$ imposed. The resampling is carried out so as to preserve the cross-correlation structure of the original data: the bootstrapped residuals are obtained from resampling the full *N-dimensional vectors* of OLS re-centred residuals for all the N units at a time, instead of resampling the residuals of each cross-section unit separately. More precisely, estimating the model under the null provides T' scalar residuals for each economy n; these residuals are then re-centred so that their sample mean is zero; after that, one way of resampling would consist of resampling them independently from the vector of T' residuals of economy n' (where T' is the effective number of residuals to be resampled, and n,n'=1,2,...N, with n≠n'); but this would destroy the cross-section structure of the data. In order to preserve it, instead of resampling T' scalar residuals N times, T' N-dimensional vectors of residuals are resampled once. In other words, if the recentred residuals are put in a T'xN matrix, this matrix is resampled by row, instead of element by element in each column[4]. These bootstrapped residuals are then used to build new $\{x_{n,t}, n = 1, \cdots, N, t = 1, \cdots T\}$ data that satisfy the null hypothesis (the so-called "bootstrapped" data $\{x_{n,t}^*\}$). The bootstrap critical values are obtained in the usual way: a large number of bootstrapped-data samples are generated; on each sample, the value of the test-statistics is computed. These values are then sorted so as to obtain an "empirical distribution" of the values of the test-statistic under the null. This empirical distribution serves as an approximation of the true (asymptotic) distribution of the statistic and provides therefore an approximation of the critical value that we need to conclude the test.

Chang (2003) demonstrates the asymptotic validity of the bootstrapped tests that she proposes. In other words, she proves that the bootstrapped critical value is a valid approximation of the asymptotic critical value.

In order to evaluate the performance of these tests in finite samples, she also runs simulations for N= 5 ,10 and T=100. These simulations shed light on the relative qualities of the different tests. As far as the t-type tests are concerned, which are those of major interest for our purpose, her results indicate that these bootstrapped tests have the correct size and that they perform well in terms of power, unless the cross-sections exhibit substantial heterogeneity. These results also indicate that there is not much difference between the OLS-based and the FGLS-based statistics. The OLS-based statistics is even more powerful than the FGLS for larger values of N, that is when the dimension of the cross-section correlation matrix is large.

At this point, it is convenient to remember that the method proposed by Evans and Karras (1996a) in their procedure for the estimation of ρ is a Weighted Least Squares method, which is intermediate between the OLS and the FGLS: it does not estimate the full cross-section correlation matrix, which seems to be the cause of relative lower power of FGLS when N=10 in Chang's simulations, although it does take into account that the variances may vary from one cross-section to another.

2.2.2   A Bootstrapped Version of EK Procedure under Cross-Section Dependency
The results of Chang (2003) suggest a possible way of completing the EK procedure for testing convergence in moderate-size panels in which the cross-section units cannot be

---

[4] Note that this procedure was already advocated by Maddala and Wu (1999) .

considered as independent. It would consist of bootstrapping the critical value of the test statistics by a resampling method that would preserve the cross-section dependency of the original sample of data.

It consists of the following steps for each statistic:

1) estimate the testing equation under the null, obtain the residuals and resample them preserving the cross-section dependency of the original data, proceeding as in Chang (2003)

2) generate the bootstrap samples by entering these resampled residuals in the testing equation in which the null is imposed and in which the remaining coefficients take the value that has been estimated under the null in step 1). Since the testing equation is dynamic, initial values for the data are required. These values are determined randomly while preserving the cross-section correlation [5].

3) Step 2) is repeated many times, giving rise to a large number of bootstrap samples. The test statistic is then computed on each sample. The proportion of bootstrap statistics falling to the left[6] of the value of $\tau(\hat{\rho})$ obtained in the original sample provides the probability value of the "divergence versus convergence" test. Similarly, the proportion of bootstrap statistics falling to the right[7] of $\Phi(\hat{\delta})$ calculated in the original sample approximates the probability value of the test of "absolute versus conditional" convergence.

3   Empirical Results

3.1   The Data

We have applied the bootstrapped EK procedure described in sections 2.2.1 and 2.2.2 on the log of GDP per capita of two panels of countries. The GDP per capita are expressed in constant and international (PPP) prices.

The first panel is made of semester data for 14 out of the 15 members of the current EU-15 zone[8]: Austria, Belgium, Denmark, Finland, France, Germany, Greece, Ireland, Italy, the Netherlands, Portugal, Spain, Sweden and the United Kingdom. GDP in PPP and population data come from the OECD STATISTICAL COMPENDIUM ed. 2002-2. GDP is available on a semester basis. Population data are annual. However, the population series are very smooth; as a consequence, semester frequency has been reached by linear interpolation[9]. The sample

---

[5] There are several ways of obtaining random initial values. Here we first generate initial values for the errors imposing on them a structure of cross-section correlation as estimated on the residuals from the estimations under the null on the observed data; we then use these initial errors to build up the initial observations data from the estimated moving average representation truncating the infinite MA polynomial after 30 terms (see Rayner, 1990, Berkowitz, Killian, 2000, section 2.1 and Maddala and Wu, 1999 for more details on this method).

[6] Given the alternative hypothesis, the test based on $\tau(\hat{\rho})$ is left-tailed

[7] Given the formula that defines $\Phi(\hat{\delta})$, this test is right-tailed.

[8] Data on Luxemburg are not available

[9] For Germany, the data correspond to West Germany till 1990.2 and to the re-unification from 1991.1. Therefore, the population by semester has been obtained by linear interpolation till 1990.2. After that, a cubic polynomial

extends from the first semester of 1970 to the last semester of 2000. Over this period, various countries joined the Union. The United Kingdom, Ireland and Denmark entered in 1973. Greece joined in 1981, Spain and Portugal in 1986. Finally, Austria, Finland and Sweden in 1995.

The second panel refers to annual data of GDP per capita for the following countries: the Czech Republic, Hungary, Poland together with the EU-15 countries excluding the main recipients of Structural Funds and Luxemburg (i.e., Austria, Belgium, Denmark, Finland, France, Germany, Italy, the Netherlands, Sweden and the United Kingdom). The data are expressed in 1990 constant and international Dollars and cover the period 1950-2002. They have been derived from the database of the University of Groningen (University of Groningen and the Conference Board, GGDC Total Economy Database, July 2003).

The data of the log of GDP per capita are represented in Graph 1 for the first panel and in Graph 2 for the second panel.

In Graph 1, some interesting features are readily observable: the series are upward-trending and non stationary; some sort of common trend seems present; however, Greece, Spain and Portugal seem to constitute a separate group from the richer countries which are more clustered together all over the sample period. Ireland is the only case where a country stands among the poorest countries in 1970 and ends up above any other EU-member by the end of 2000.

As far as Graph 2 is concerned, the possibility of two distinct groups is even more obvious. On the one hand, the richer countries stand together in the upper part of the graph and seem to converge, whereas Poland, Hungary and the Czech Republic which seem to be diverging from the EU-countries at least till the early nineties.

EU-15 except Luxemburg

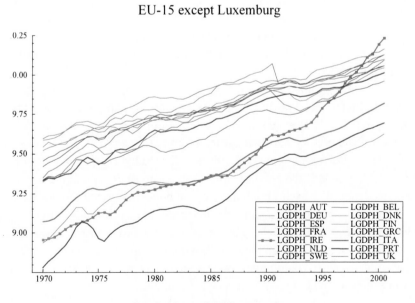

Graph 1 Log of GDP per capita

was fitted to the annual end-of-year data and the corresponding equation was used to "backcast" the value of the first semester of 1991.

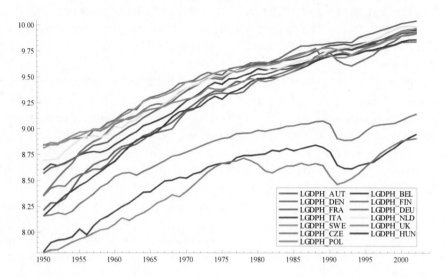

Graph 2 Log of GDP per capita of historically richer EU countries(except Luxemburg), Poland, Czech Republic and Hungary

3.2   The Convergence Tests

3.2.1   The Case of the Current Members of the EU-15

Given the interest in checking a possible influence of the reforms in the European Structural Funds and of the Single Act on convergence, the sample has been split in 1987.[10]   As a consequence the convergence tests have been applied to two sample periods: 1970.1-1986.2, 1987.1-2000.2.

In applying the tests, a choice must be made as to the value of p in equations (2) and (3). The estimation has been ran for p=0 to 7 and Portmanteau tests of no-autocorrelation of the residuals have been applied.

The results of applying the tests on the group of the ten historically richer EU countries are reproduced in Table 1. The results are presented from p=1 to p=7. Those values of p for which no autocorrelation is accepted at 5% for all countries are marked with a bold frame. When this condition is met by a vast majority of countries and some countries rejects no-autocorrelation at 5% but accept it at 2.5%, this is indicated by a discontinuous bold frame. In none of the estimated models the residuals are whitened for p=0, so that the results for this p are not reproduced here. For each sample period, the bootstrap probability values for the null H_0: $\rho_n = 0$ 8n of no convergence against the alternative H_a: $\rho_n < 0$ 8n of convergence are given in the upper row of the Table. For an easier and faster interpretation, the p-value favourable to convergence is marked in bold. When convergence is accepted, the p-value for the test of absolute against conditional convergence is provided in the second row. Here again, this value appears in bold if convergence is absolute.

---

[10] This year is chosen because it is the year of the Single Act, which established the principle of Economic and Social Cohesion and from which the new design of the European Regional Policy emerged

Table 1: Convergence tests for the initially richer countries: the whole group without Greece, Spain, Portugal and Ireland OECD semester data. Probability values in %

	Number of lags:	p=1	P=2	P=3	p=4	P=5	p=6	p=7	Conclusión
1970-1986	H_0: $\rho = 0$ $\Rightarrow$ no cvgce Ha: $\rho < 0$ $\Rightarrow$ cvgce	4.2	6.2	4.4	10.5	4.1	1.8	15.6	Signs Of ABSOLUTE CONVERGENCE
	If $\rho < 0$, H_0: $\delta_n = 0$ $\forall n$ $\Rightarrow$ absolute H_0: some $\delta_n \neq 0$ $\Rightarrow$ condit.	52.6	-	42.8	-	32.4	15.6	.	
1987-2000	H_0: $\rho = 0$ $\Rightarrow$ no cvgce Ha: $\rho < 0$ $\Rightarrow$ cvgce	10.4	1.5	2.5	2.5	0.8	0.3	0.01	ABSOLUTE CONVERGENCE
	If $\rho < 0$, H_0: $\delta_n = 0$ $\forall n$ $\Rightarrow$ absolute H_0: some $\delta_n \neq 0$ $\Rightarrow$ condit.	-	17.4	9.1	10.3	6.9	4.4	1.6	

The bold frames indicate a value of p for which the residuals for each country pass a no-autocorrelation Portmanteau test at 5%.

According to the results of this table, the 10 richer countries of the EU-15 considered here did constitute a convergent group during the last three decades. This is particularly true for the 1987-2000 period; for the first period extending from 1970 to 1986, convergence is also the dominant result. If these results are maintained when the historically poorer countries are added to the sample, it would mean that there was no need for an external intervention in favour of the poorer countries.

To check this, Table 2 contains the results of the convergence tests applied to the previous panel of 10 countries extended with the data on Spain, Portugal, Greece and Ireland. This table shows that between 1970 and 1987, the 14 countries were in a situation of convergence, although this convergence was only conditional: these countries shared parallel but not identical steady state paths. In the subsample that covers the period 1987-2000, quite a different result emerges: the statistics unambiguously take value that are typical of divergence. This is at first sight somewhat surprising since the European authorities had adopted a cohesion policy aimed at helping the poorer regions and countries to improve their relative economic position

However, Graph 1 shows that the evolution of Ireland in the last decade might explain this unexpected result: since the late eighties, this country has experienced a unique and sustained growth, to the point of reaching the highest level of GDP per capita in the year 2000. One possible explanation is that the exceptional growth in Ireland in the last fifteen years has been fostered not only by European structural funds, but also by a very efficient national economic development strategy. Furthermore, the Irish economy has proven especially attractive, as an export base for the EU market to Foreign Direct Investment projects of US companies (for a policy evaluation of the economic success of Ireland in the last decades, see Braunerhjelm et al., 2000, chapter 5).

If we then exclude the special case of Ireland from the panel and repeat the analysis, the results are those reproduced in Table 3. It shows that convergence was conditional till 1986 and became absolute from 1987 onwards. Joining all of these results, the message seems clear: at the time of their entrance in the EU, Greece, Portugal and Spain did not share the same steady state as their EU partners, but belonging to the EU and benefiting from its regional policy contributed to change this feature.

There is therefore no evidence against the usefulness of the Structural Funds for a better cohesion within the EU: the countries which constitute the EU today were initially in a situation of conditional convergence, so that the public intervention in the form of explicit policies in favour of reducing regional disparities were justified, and the statistical evidence favours the hypothesis that these policies have been effective in narrowing the country differences.

Table 2: Convergence tests for the whole group of countries EU15 except Luxemburg - OECD semester data. Probability values in %

Number of lags:		p=1	p=2	P=3	p=4	P=5	P=6	P=7	Conclusion
1970-1986	H_0: $\rho = 0 \Rightarrow$no cvgce H_a: $\rho < 0 \Rightarrow$ cvgce	0.9	8.7	3.3	1319	2.0	0.9	7.62	Signs of CONDITIONAL CONVERGENCE
	If $\rho < 0$, H_0: $\delta_n = 0$ $\forall n$ $\Rightarrow$absolute H_0: some $\delta_n \neq 0$ $\Rightarrow$condit.	0.4	-	3.7	-	1.1	0.50	-	
1987-2000	H_0: $\rho = 0 \Rightarrow$no cvgce H_a: $\rho < 0 \Rightarrow$ cvgce	29.7	45.4	17.8	18.6	6.5	2.1	21.9	DIVERGENCE
	If $\rho < 0$, H_0: $\delta_n = 0$ $\forall n$ $\Rightarrow$absolute H_0: some $\delta_n \neq 0$ $\Rightarrow$condit.					-	5.2		

The bold frames indicate a value of p for which the residuals for each country pass a no-Autocorrelation Portmanteau test at 5%. A discontinuous bold frame indicates that most countries pass the no-autocorrelation test at 5% and a few of them at 2.5%.

Table 3 : Convergence tests for richer countries plus Spain, Greece and Portugal OECD semester data. Probability values in %

Number of lags:		P=1	p=2	p=3	p=4	p=5	p=6	p=7	Conclusion
1970-1986	H_0: $\rho = 0$ no cvgce Ha: $\rho < 0$ cvgce	0.9	4.7	4.0	7.3	1.25	0.84	14.8	
	If $\rho < 0$, H_0: $\delta_n= 0$ $\forall n$ ⇒absolute H_0: some $\delta_n\neq 0$ ⇒condit.	0.2	11.7	5.2	-	1.6	1.5	-	Signs of CONDITIONAL CONVERGENCE
1987-2000	H_0: $\rho = 0$ no cvgce Ha: $\rho < 0$ cvgce	0.10	1.5	2.5	2.5	0,8	0.04	0.0	
	If $\rho < 0$, H_0: $\delta_n= 0$ $\forall n$ ⇒absolute H_0: some $\delta_n\neq 0$ ⇒condit.	50.7	17.4	9.1 =	10.3 =	6.9 =	4.4	1.6	ABSOLUTE CONVERGENCE

The bold frames indicate a value of p for which the residuals for each country pass a no -autocorrelation Portmanteau test at 5%. A discontinuous bold frame indicates that most countries pass the no-autocorrelation test at 5% and a few of them at 2.5%.

3.2.2   The Case of Some Future EU-members from Eastern Europe

Let us now analyse the relative position of the Eastern European countries in comparison with the ten initially richer EU-members. The data are annual and cover the period 1950-2002. These Eastern countries experienced profound structural and institutional changes at the end of the eighties: at that time they switched to a free-market economy and a more democratic political system. The impact of these changes on the output per capita is very apparent on graph 2. Ideally, we should then carry out a separate analysis on the data up to 1990 and on the data from that year onwards. Unfortunately, given the annual frequency of the sample, such a procedure is impossible since this would leave too little time-series information in the second subsample to estimate the testing equation. We have therefore proceeded as follows: we have tested convergence on the full sample 1950-2002 and on a shorter sample that stops in 1990. The difference in the results indicates whether the convergence capacity and characteristic of these countries might have changed in the last decade, after the institutional changes that they have carried out.

In order to avoid doubts about which countries might be held responsible for a divergence result, we first check whether the EU-10 countries constitute a convergence group or not. The results in Table 4 show that these countries exhibit strong signs of absolute convergence both over the full 1950-2002 and over the shorter 1950-1990 time periods.

Table 4: Convergence tests for the initially richer EU-countries

Annual data - 1950-2002. (University of Groningen and The Conference Board GGDC, Total Economy Database, July 2003). Probability values in %

Number of lags:		p=1	p=2	p=3	p=4	P=5	P=6	p=7	Conclusion
1950-1990	H_0: $\rho = 0$ no cvgce Ha: $\rho < 0$ cvgce	0.2	0.0	0.2	1.5	9.5	12.0	10.6	ABSOLUTE CONVERGENCE
	If $\rho < 0$, H_0: $\delta_n= 0$ $\forall n$ $\Rightarrow$absolute H_0: some $\delta_n \neq 0$ $\Rightarrow$condit.	39.6	82.3	65.4	81.1	-	-		
1950-2002	H_0: $\rho = 0$ no cvgce Ha: $\rho < 0$ cvgce	0.0	0.0	0.0	0.0	0.0	2.6	2.5	ABSOLUTE CONVERGENCE
	If $\rho < 0$, H_0: $\delta_n= 0$ $\forall n$ $\Rightarrow$absolute Ha: some $\delta_n \neq 0$ $\Rightarrow$condit.		71.3	41.1	62.2	77.6	75.9	83.6	

The bold frames indicate a value of p for which the residuals for each country pass a no-Autocorrelation Portmanteau test at 5%. A discontinuous bold frame indicates that most countries pass the no-autocorrelation test at 5% and a few of them at 2.5%.

Let us now examine the situation of Poland, Hungary and the Czech Republic. In Table 5, the results show that until 1990 these countries were diverging. However, if we add the data since 1990, the results in the lower part of Table 5 show that these countries now exhibit rather strong signs of conditional convergence. It is as if the switch to a free-market economic system has enlivened the convergence forces of their economies.

Table 5: Convergence tests Poland, Hungary and Czech Republic Annual data - 1950-2002

University of Groningen and The Conference Board GGDC Total Economy Database
Probability values in %

Number of lags:		p=1	p=2	p=3	p=4	P=5	P=6	p=7	Conclusion
1950-1990	H_0: $\rho = 0$ no cvgce Ha: $\rho < 0$ cvgce	43.1	23.6	22.8	16.6	33.3	8.9	35.8	DIVERGENCE
	If $\rho < 0$, H_0: $\delta_n= 0$ $\forall n$ $\Rightarrow$absolute H_0: some $\delta_n \neq 0$ $\Rightarrow$condit.	-	-	-	-	-	-		

Number of lags:		p=1	p=2	p=3	p=4	P=5	P=6	p=7	Conclusion
1950-2002	H_0: $\rho = 0$ no cvgce / Ha: $\rho < 0$ cvgce	22.6	5.9	3.4	1.8	3.2	0.3	2.2	Signs of CONDITIONAL CONVERGENCE
	If $\rho < 0$, H_0: $\delta_n = 0$ $\forall n$ ⇒absolute Ha: some $\delta_n \neq 0$ ⇒condit.	-		6.5	2.8	4.7	0.2	1.2	

The bold frames indicate a value of p for which the residuals for each country pass a no-Autocorrelation Portmanteau test at 5%. A discontinuous bold frame indicates that most countries pass the no-autocorrelation test at 5% and a few of them at 2.5%.

In Table 6, the analysis of table 4 and 5 is repeated on the joint panel of rich EU-countries and Eastern European future members. From the results obtained in the previous two tables, what is expected is divergence until 1990, and at most conditional convergence when data to 2002 are added. This is exactly what comes out. We may therefore conclude that these three countries stand at the moment in a situation similar to that of the recipients of structural funds around 1987. With an efficient use of these funds and of the opportunities the EU market offer to these economies, they should obtain great benefits from entering the EU that should reflect in closer GDP paths within a few years.

Table 6: Convergence tests for Poland, Hungary and Czech Republic with the historically richer EU-15 countries - Annual data - 1950-2002.

University of Groningen and The Conference Board GGDC Total Economy Database.
Probability values in %

Number of lags:		p=1	P=2	p=3	p=4	P=5	P=6	p=7	Conclusion
1950-1990	H_0: $\rho = 0$ no cvgce / Ha: $\rho < 0$ cvgce	8.5	13.5	13.0	26.0	36.0	18.8	33.7	DIVERGENCE
	If $\rho < 0$, H_0: $\delta_n = 0$ $\forall n$ ⇒absolute H_0: some $\delta_n \neq 0$ ⇒condit.	-	-	-	-	-	-		
1950-2002	H_0: $\rho = 0$ no cvgce / Ha: $\rho < 0$ cvgce	1.2	1.7	1.6	5.3	13.8	13.9	11.4	More signs of CONDITIONAL CONVERGENCE
	If $\rho < 0$, H_0: $\delta_n = 0$ $\forall n$ ⇒absolute Ha: some $\delta_n \neq 0$ ⇒condit.	3.2	4.1	2.3	7.5	-	-	-	

The bold frames indicate a value of p for which the residuals for each country pass a no-Autocorrelation Portmanteau test at 5%. A discontinuous bold frame indicates that most countries pass the no-autocorrelation test at 5% and a few of them at 2.5%.

4   Summary and Conclusion

In this chapter, we have discussed possible ways of determining whether various countries or regions are converging to each other or not by the use of multivariate unit root or stationarity tests. We have insisted on the differences between testing international output convergence by analysing the countries bilateral output-per-capita differentials and testing it on the basis of the deviations of each country per-capita output from the overall cross-section mean. In particular, we have shown the importance of specifying correctly the null and the alternative hypothesis. More specifically, we have shown that when deviations from an overall mean is used, these deviations are either all I(0) or all I(1), even when some countries of the panel converge to each other while others diverge; for the testing procedure to be valid, its null and alternative hypotheses must necessarily reflect this characteristic. On the other hand, working with bilateral differentials permits testing whether there is global convergence (in which all the countries converge to each other) as well as testing what we might call partial convergence (when at least some countries, but not necessarily all them, converge).

On the other hand, we have also stressed the importance of accounting for the contemporaneous correlation that characterizes the output series of countries that belong to the same geographical and/or economic area. It is difficult to believe that the shocks that affect the output per capita of, say, France is not related to the shock that might affect the German output per capita in the same year. The panel unit root tests used to test convergence are however built on this premise: the critical values are obtained under the assumption that the shocks are contemporaneously uncorrelated. In order to circumvent this limitation, we propose here a bootstrapped version of the convergence testing procedure proposed by Evans and Karras (1996a). The bootstrapping is carried out so that it provides critical values that take into account the specific correlation structure of the data on which the tests are applied.

This bootstrapped procedure is applied in the second part of the paper on semester data of the current members of the EU-15. The results indicate that the richer countries of the European Union have been in absolute convergence since 1970. The poorer countries who entered the Union in the eighties - Greece, Portugal and Spain - were only conditionally converging to their European partners at the time of their entrance: That is, their steady state path was parallel but not as high as those of the richer members. Since 1987, the situation has evolved so that the convergence tests applied on the data between 1987 and 2000 reveal signs of absolute convergence. This evolution points out that the Structural Funds that these countries have mostly received since 1987 may have been helpful. The case of Ireland is different, because this country experienced a very intensive growth process which may have resulted not only from an efficient use of the structural funds but also from the Foreign Direct Investment policy of the United States which have been using this country as an export base for their products towards the European countries. Ireland constitutes a case of such a fast catching-up process that it seems to have even "overshot" its goal of convergence, since it stands nowadays above the per capita output of any other EU member.

As far as the Eastern European countries are concerned, the analysis centres here on the case of Poland, Hungary and the Czech Republic, for which the available series of per-capita output cover a longer period than for any other forthcoming member. The tests indicate that these countries were diverging until 1990. However, since then, they have moved to a more liberal economic system, which has been accompanied by a different evolution of their per-capita output. The statistical tests indicate that they are now in a situation of conditional convergence with respect to each other, as well as with respect to the EU members. This is similar to the situation of Greece, Portugal an Spain at the moment they joined the EU. So it is to be hoped that these future members will be able to take full profit of their belonging to the EU.

References

[1] Barro, R.J., Sala-i-Martín, X. 1992, Convergence. *Journal of Political Economy*, **100**, April, 223-251

[2] Berkowitz, J., Kilian, L., 2000, Recent developments in bootstrapping time series. *Econometric Reviews*, **19**,1, 1-48.

[3] Bernard, A. Durlauf, S.N., 1995, Convergence in International Output. *Jounral of Applied Econometrics*, **10**, 97-108.

[4] Braunerhjelm, P. Faini, R., Norman, V., Ruane, F., Seabright, P., 2000, Integration and the Regions of Europe: how the right policies can prevent polarization. *Monitoring European Integration*, **10**, CEPR, London

[5] Chang, Y., 2003, Bootstrap unit root tests in panels with cross-sectional dependency. *Jouranl of Econometrics*, article in press.

[6] Davison, A.C., Hinkley, D.V., 1997, *Bootstrap methods and their application.* Cambridge University Press

[7] Evans, P., 1996, Using cross-country variances to evaluate growth theories. *Journal of Economic Dynamics and Control*, **20**, 1027-1049.

[8] Evans, P., 1997, How fast do economies converge? *Review of Economics and Statistics*, vol.79, May, 2, 219-225.

[9] Evans, P., 1998, Using panel data to evaluate growth theories. *International Economic Review*, vol.39, n°2, May, 295-306

[10] Evans, P., Karras, G., 1996a, Convergence revisited. *Journal of Monetary Economics*, **37**, 249-265.

[11] Evans, P., Karras, G., 1996b, Do economies converge? Evidence from a panel of U.S. States. *Review of Economics and Statistics*, vol.78, August, 3, 384-388.

[12] Hadri, K., 2000, Testing stationarity in heterogeneous panel data. *Econometrics Journal*, vol.3, 148-161.

[13] Hadri, K. and Larsson, R., 2002, Testing stationarity in heterogeneous panel data where the times dimension is finite. University of Liverpool, *Department of Economics*

[14] Horowitz, J., 2001, The bootstrap, *in* J.J.Heckman and E.Leamer, eds., *Handbook of Econometrics*, vol.5. North-Holland Publishing Co.

[15] Im, K.S., Pesaran, M.H., Shin,Y., 1995, Testing unit root in heterogeneous panels. Working paper, May 1995. Revised March 2002, downloadable from http://www.econ.cam.ac.uk/faculty/pesaran. Published with the same title in *Journal-of-Econometrics*, July 2003; 115(1): 53-74.

[16] Islam, N., 2003, What have we learnt from the convergence debate? *Journal of Economic Surveys*, **17**, 3, 309-362.

[17] Kwiatkowski, D., Phillips, P.C.B., Schmidt, P., Shin, Y., 1992, Testing the null hypothesis of stationarity against the alternative of a unit root. *Journal of Econometrics*, **54**, 91-115.

[18] Krugman, P., 1990, *Rethinking International Trade*, Cambridge, MIT Press.

[19] Levin, A., Lin, C.-F., 1992, Unit Root Tests in Panel Data: Asymptotic and Finite-Sample Properties. *Discussion Paper* **92**-93, Department of Economics, University of California San Diego. Published as Levin, A., Lin, C.F., Chu, C., 2002, *Journal of Econometrics*, **108**(1), 1-24.

[20] Levin, A., Lin, C.-F., 1993, Unit Root Tests in Panel Data: New results. Discussion Paper 93-56, *Department of Economics*, University of California San Diego.

[21] Maddala,G.S., Wu, S., 1999, A comparative of unit root tests with panel data and a new simple test. Oxford Bulletin of Economics and Statistics, *Special Issue*, **631**-652.

[22] Rayner, R.K., 1990, Bootstrapping p-values and power in the first-order autoregression: a Monte Carlo Investigation. *Journal of Business and Economic Statistics*, **8**, 251-263.

[23] Romer, P., 1986, Increasing returns and long-run growth. *Journal of Political Economy*, **94**, 500-521.

[24] Romer, P., 1990, Endogenous technological change. *Journal of Political Economy*, **98**, S71-S102.

[25] Solow, R.M., 1956, A contribution to the theory of economic growth. *Quarterly Journal of Economics*, **70**, 65-94.

INDEX

D

F

J

K

L

M

Y